ACTS
A Commentary in the Wesleyan Tradition

*New Beacon Bible Commentary

ACTS

A Commentary in the Wesleyan Tradition

Richard P. Thompson

BEACON HILL PRESS
OF KANSAS CITY

Unless otherwise indicated all Scripture quotations are from the *Holy Bible, New International Version*®
(NIV®). Copyright © 1973, 1978, 1984, 2011 by Biblica, Inc.™ Used by permission. All rights reserved
worldwide.

The King James Version of the Bible (KJV).

The following copyrighted versions of the Bible are used by permission:

The *Common English Bible* (CEB), copyright 2011. All rights reserved.

The *New American Standard Bible*® (NASB®), © copyright The Lockman Foundation 1960, 1962, 1963,
1968, 1971, 1972, 1973, 1975, 1977, 1995.

The *New English Bible* (NEB), © the Delegates of the Oxford University Press and the Syndics of the
Cambridge University Press 1961, 1970.

The *New Revised Standard Version* (NRSV) of the Bible, copyright 1989 by the Division of Christian
Education of the National Council of the Churches of Christ in the USA. All rights reserved.

Library of Congress Cataloging-in-Publication Data

Thompson, Richard P.
    Acts : a commentary in the Wesleyan tradition / Richard P. Thompson.
        pages cm. — (New Beacon Bible commentary)
    Includes bibliographical references.
    ISBN 978-0-8341-3239-9 (pbk. : alk. paper)
    1. Bible. Acts—Commentaries. I. Title.
    BS2625.53.T57 2015
    226.6'077—dc23

                                                                    2015029926

10 9 8 7 6 5 4 3 2 1

DEDICATION

To Annette

COMMENTARY EDITORS

General Editors

Alex Varughese
  Ph.D., Drew University
  Professor of Biblical Literature
  Mount Vernon Nazarene University
  Mount Vernon, Ohio

Roger Hahn
  Ph.D., Duke University
  Dean of the Faculty
  Professor of New Testament
  Nazarene Theological Seminary
  Kansas City, Missouri

George Lyons
  Ph.D., Emory University
  Professor of New Testament
  Northwest Nazarene University
  Nampa, Idaho

Section Editors

Joseph Coleson
  Ph.D., Brandeis University
  Professor of Old Testament
  Nazarene Theological Seminary
  Kansas City, Missouri

Robert Branson
  Ph.D., Boston University
  Professor of Biblical Literature
    Emeritus
  Olivet Nazarene University
  Bourbonnais, Illinois

Alex Varughese
  Ph.D., Drew University
  Professor of Biblical Literature
  Mount Vernon Nazarene University
  Mount Vernon, Ohio

Jim Edlin
  Ph.D., Southern Baptist Theological
    Seminary
  Professor of Biblical Literature and
    Languages
  Chair, Division of Religion and
    Philosophy
  MidAmerica Nazarene University
  Olathe, Kansas

Kent Brower
  Ph.D., The University of Manchester
  Vice Principal
  Senior Lecturer in Biblical Studies
  Nazarene Theological College
  Manchester, England

George Lyons
  Ph.D., Emory University
  Professor of New Testament
  Northwest Nazarene University
  Nampa, Idaho

CONTENTS

GENERAL EDITORS' PREFACE

The purpose of the New Beacon Bible Commentary is to make available to pastors and students in the twenty-first century a biblical commentary that reflects the best scholarship in the Wesleyan theological tradition. The commentary project aims to make this scholarship accessible to a wider audience to assist them in their understanding and proclamation of Scripture as God's Word.

Writers of the volumes in this series not only are scholars within the Wesleyan theological tradition and experts in their field but also have special interest in the books assigned to them. Their task is to communicate clearly the critical consensus and the full range of other credible voices who have commented on the Scriptures. Though scholarship and scholarly contribution to the understanding of the Scriptures are key concerns of this series, it is not intended as an academic dialogue within the scholarly community. Commentators of this series constantly aim to demonstrate in their work the significance of the Bible as the church's book and the contemporary relevance and application of the biblical message. The project's overall goal is to make available to the church and for her service the fruits of the labors of scholars who are committed to their Christian faith.

The *New International Version* (NIV) is the reference version of the Bible used in this series; however, the focus of exegetical study and comments is the biblical text in its original language. When the commentary uses the NIV, it is printed in bold. The text printed in bold italics is the translation of the author. Commentators also refer to other translations where the text may be difficult or ambiguous.

The structure and organization of the commentaries in this series seeks to facilitate the study of the biblical text in a systematic and methodical way. Study of each biblical book begins with an *Introduction* section that gives an overview of authorship, date, provenance, audience, occasion, purpose, sociological/cultural issues, textual history, literary features, hermeneutical issues, and theological themes necessary to understand the book. This section also includes a brief outline of the book and a list of general works and standard commentaries.

The commentary section for each biblical book follows the outline of the book presented in the introduction. In some volumes, readers will find section *overviews* of large portions of scripture with general comments on their overall literary structure and other literary features. A consistent feature of the commentary is the paragraph-by-paragraph study of biblical texts. This section has three parts: *Behind the Text*, *In the Text*, and *From the Text*.

The goal of the *Behind the Text* section is to provide the reader with all the relevant information necessary to understand the text. This includes specific historical situations reflected in the text, the literary context of the text, sociological and cultural issues, and literary features of the text.

In the Text explores what the text says, following its verse-by-verse structure. This section includes a discussion of grammatical details, word studies, and the connectedness of the text to other biblical books/passages or other parts of the book being studied (the canonical relationship). This section provides transliterations of key words in Hebrew and Greek and their literal meanings. The goal here is to explain what the author would have meant and/or what the audience would have understood as the meaning of the text. This is the largest section of the commentary.

The *From the Text* section examines the text in relation to the following areas: theological significance, intertextuality, the history of interpretation, use of the Old Testament scriptures in the New Testament, interpretation in later church history, actualization, and application.

The commentary provides *sidebars* on topics of interest that are important but not necessarily part of an explanation of the biblical text. These topics are informational items and may cover archaeological, historical, literary, cultural, and theological matters that have relevance to the biblical text. Occasionally, longer detailed discussions of special topics are included as *excurses.*

We offer this series with our hope and prayer that readers will find it a valuable resource for their understanding of God's Word and an indispensable tool for their critical engagement with the biblical texts.

Roger Hahn, Centennial Initiative General Editor
Alex Varughese, General Editor (Old Testament)
George Lyons, General Editor (New Testament)

AUTHOR'S PREFACE

Journeys. Readers of Acts and Luke's Gospel know these books tell about a lot of journeys. That may be where the idea of the Christian life as a journey comes from, because early believers were known as people on the "Way" or "journey." These prefatory words come near this book's beginning, but I offer them at the end of my own journey with Acts. Forty years ago, I first studied Acts as a high school student in my church's Bible quizzing program. Little did I know that was the beginning of an unimaginable journey that would include this remarkable book as the major focus of my scholarly work.

Journeys have a different perspective when others travel with you. They grace your life along the way. This entire project was undertaken while serving as professor of New Testament and chair of the Department of Religion in the School of Theology and Christian Ministries at Northwest Nazarene University. I could not ask for a better group of colleagues who support and encourage one another as friends and scholars than those who serve on the faculty and staff of our school. The context they create has helped nurture my thought and progress in incalculable ways. I am also most grateful for the university's support through a recent sabbatical, which provided dedicated time for a major project like this. Special thanks are extended to Mark Maddix (dean, School of Theology and Christian Ministries) and Burton Webb (vice president for Academic Affairs) for supporting that leave.

Having taught in small Christian university settings for over twenty years (Olivet Nazarene University, Spring Arbor University, and Northwest Nazarene University), I have been blessed to journey with some incredible students. These students have been in all sorts of courses: general education, Greek, exegesis, and Luke-Acts (certainly!). Their insights have helped me see things I may not have seen myself. Their lives have touched mine. And this project is what it is because they have been part of my journey.

Still others have walked alongside me more recently in this project. I am thankful for the insight of pastors like Erik Gernand, Daryl Johnson, and Jonathan Privett at various stages of the work. Special thanks are extended to Kent Brower (vice principal, senior research fellow and senior lecturer in Biblical Studies at Nazarene Theological College, Manchester, United Kingdom) who, as my section editor, worked closest with me. His editorial skill and scholarly expertise made the final project better. I also offer my deepest gratitude to George Lyons, my former professor and retired colleague who, as New Testament editor of this commentary series, gives extraordinary leadership and editorial oversight to this larger project, as well as lending a steady editor's hand as needed.

But one has been with me for most of this journey. My wife, Annette, has listened to (or put up with!) more sermons or thoughts about something in Acts than any person should have to endure. She first suggested that Acts should be the general area for my dissertation work. Little did she know that suggestion would someday cause her to spend many evenings and Saturdays alone during the last six years because commentary work put her husband behind closed doors and behind a desk with mounds of books and journal articles. So I am most thankful, Annette, for your patience, support, and encouragement. You have made the completion of this project possible.

Dick Thompson
February 2014

ABBREVIATIONS

With a few exceptions, these abbreviations follow those in *The SBL Handbook of Style* (Alexander 1999).

General

→	see the commentary at
AD	anno Domini (precedes date) (equivalent to CE)
BC	before Christ (follows date) (equivalent to BCE)
BCE	before the Common Era
CE	Common Era
ca.	circa, approximate time
ch(s)	chapter(s)
e.g.	*exempli gratia*, for example
esp.	especially
et al.	*et alii*, and others
etc.	*et cetera*, and the rest
f(f).	and the following one(s)
i.e.	*id est*, that is
km	kilometers
ktl.	*kai ta loipa* (Greek: etc.)
lit.	literally
LXX	Septuagint (Greek translation of the OT)
m	meters
MS	manuscript
MSS	manuscripts
MT	Masoretic Text (of the OT)
n(n).	note(s)
NT	New Testament
OT	Old Testament
v(v)	verse(s)
vs.	versus

Modern English Versions

CEB	Common English Bible
KJV	King James Version
NASB	New American Standard Bible
NEB	New English Bible
NIV84	New International Version (1984 edition)
NIV	New International Version (2011 edition)
NRSV	New Revised Standard Version

Print Conventions for Translations

Bold font	NIV (bold without quotation marks in the text under study; elsewhere in the regular font, with quotation marks and no further identification)
Bold italic font	Author's translation (without quotation marks)

Behind the Text:	Literary or historical background information average readers might not know from reading the biblical text alone
In the Text:	Comments on the biblical text, words, phrases, grammar, and so forth
From the Text:	The use of the text by later interpreters, contemporary relevance, theological and ethical implications of the text, with particular emphasis on Wesleyan concerns

Old Testament

Gen	Genesis	Dan	Daniel		
Exod	Exodus	Hos	Hosea		
Lev	Leviticus	Joel	Joel		
Num	Numbers	Amos	Amos		
Deut	Deuteronomy	Obad	Obadiah		
Josh	Joshua	Jonah	Jonah		
Judg	Judges	Mic	Micah		
Ruth	Ruth	Nah	Nahum		
1—2 Sam	1—2 Samuel	Hab	Habakkuk		
1—2 Kgs	1—2 Kings	Zeph	Zephaniah		
1—2 Chr	1—2 Chronicles	Hag	Haggai		
Ezra	Ezra	Zech	Zechariah		
Neh	Nehemiah	Mal	Malachi		
Esth	Esther				
Job	Job				
Ps/Pss	Psalm/Psalms				
Prov	Proverbs				
Eccl	Ecclesiastes				
Song	Song of Songs/				
	Song of Solomon				
Isa	Isaiah				
Jer	Jeremiah				
Lam	Lamentations				
Ezek	Ezekiel				

(Note: Chapter and verse numbering in the MT and LXX often differ compared to those in English Bibles. To avoid confusion, all biblical references follow the chapter and verse numbering in English translations, even when the text in the MT and LXX is under discussion.)

New Testament

Matt	Matthew
Mark	Mark
Luke	Luke
John	John
Acts	Acts
Rom	Romans
1—2 Cor	1—2 Corinthians
Gal	Galatians
Eph	Ephesians
Phil	Philippians
Col	Colossians
1—2 Thess	1—2 Thessalonians
1—2 Tim	1—2 Timothy
Titus	Titus
Phlm	Philemon
Heb	Hebrews
Jas	James
1—2 Pet	1—2 Peter
1—2—3 John	1—2—3 John
Jude	Jude
Rev	Revelation

Apocrypha

Bar	Baruch
Bel	Bel and the Dragon
1-2 Esd	1-2 Esdras
Ep Jer	Epistle of Jeremiah
Jdt	Judith
1—2 Macc	1—2 Maccabees
3—4 Macc	3—4 Maccabees
Sir	Sirach/Ecclesiasticus
Tob	Tobit
Wis	Wisdom of Solomon

OT Pseudepigrapha

2 Bar.	2 Baruch (Syriac Apocalypse)
3 Bar.	3 Baruch (Greek Apocalypse)
1 En.	1 Enoch (Ethiopic Apocalypse)
4 Ezra	4 Ezra
Jos. Asen.	Joseph and Aseneth
Jub.	Jubilees
Odes Sol.	Odes of Solomon
Pss. Sol.	Psalms of Solomon
Sib. Or.	Sibylline Oracles
T. Jac.	Testament of Jacob
T. Jud.	Testament of Judah

Dead Sea Scrolls

1QS	Serek Hayaḥad or Rule of the Community
4Q175	Testimonia
11QT	Temple Scroll

Josephus

Ag. Ap.	Against Apion
Ant.	Jewish Antiquities
J.W.	Jewish War
Life	The Life

Philo

Alleg. Interp.	*Allegorical Interpretation*
Contempl.	*On the Contemplative Life*
Creation	*On the Creation of the World*
Decal.	*On the Decalogue*
Dreams	*On Dreams*
Embassy	*On the Embassy to Gaius*
Flaccus	*Against Flaccus*
Hypoth.	*Hypothetica*
Joseph	*On the Life of Joseph*
Migration	*On the Migration of Abraham*
Moses	*On the Life of Moses*
QG	*Questions and Answers on Genesis*
Spec. Laws	*On the Special Laws*
Virtues	*On the Virtues*

Rabbinic Literature

'Abot	*Avot*
b.	Babylonian Talmud
B. Bat.	*Bava Batra*
Ber.	*Berakhot*
Ketub.	*Ketubbot*
m.	Mishnah
Mak.	*Makkot*
Naz.	*Nazir*
Qidd.	*Qiddushin*
Sanh.	*Sanhedrin*

New Testament Apocrypha and Pseudepigrapha

Acts Paul	*Acts of Paul*
Gos. Pet.	*Gospel of Peter*

Apostolic Fathers

Barn.	*Barnabas*
1—2 Clem.	*1—2 Clement*
Did.	*Didache*
Ign. *Eph.*	Ignatius, *To the Ephesians*
Ign. *Phld.*	Ignatius, *To the Philadelphians*

Other Church Fathers

Chrysostom, John
Hom. Act.	*Homilies in the Acts of the Apostles*
Hom. 2 Tim.	*Homilies in the Epistle of 2 Timothy*

Cyril of Jerusalem
Cat. Lect.	*Catechetical Lectures*

Eusebius
Hist. eccl.	*Ecclesiastical History*

Hippolytus
Haer.	*Refutation of All Heresies*

Irenaeus
Haer.	*Against Heresies*

Justin Martyr
1 Apol.	*First Apology*
2 Apol.	*Second Apology*
Dial.	*Dialogue with Trypho*

Origen
Cels.	*Against Celsus*

Tertullian
Marc.	*Against Marcion*

Other Greek and Latin Works

Achilles Tatius
Leuc. Clit.	*The Adventures of Leucippe and Cleitophon*

Aeschylus

Ag.	*Agamemnon*
Eum.	*Eumenides*
Apollonius of Rhodes	
Argon.	*Argonautica*
Appian	
Bell. civ.	*Civil Wars*
Apuleius	
Metam.	*Metamorphoses (The Golden Ass)*
Aratus	
Phaen.	*Phaenomena*
Aristophanes	
Pax	*Peace*
Aristotle	
Eth. eud.	*Eudemian Ethics*
Eth. nic.	*Nichomachean Ethics*
Poet.	*Poetics*
Pol.	*Politics*
Chariton	
Chaer.	*Chaereas and Callirhoe*
Chion of Heraclea	
Ep.	*Epistles*
Cicero	
Caecin.	*Pro Caecina*
Flac.	*Pro Flacco*
Inv.	*De inventione rhetorica*
Nat. d.	*De natura deorum*
De or.	*De oratore*
Phil.	*Orationes philippicae*
Verr.	*In Verrem*
Demosthenes	
1 Aristog.	*1 Against Aristogeiton*
1 Philip.	*1 Philippic*
Dio Cassius	
Hist.	*Roman History*
Dio Chrysostom	
Alex.	*To the People of Alexandria*
Dei cogn.	*Man's First Conception of God (Olympic Discourse)*
Rhod.	*To the People of Rhodes*
Socr.	*Socrates*
2 Tars.	*Second Tarsic Discourse*
Diogenes Laertius	
Vit. phil.	*Vitae Philosophorum*
Dionysius of Halicarnassus	
Ant. rom.	*Roman Antiquities*
Pomp.	*Epistula ad Pompeium Geminum*
Epictetus	
Diatr.	*Diatribai (Dissertationes)*
Euripides	
Bacch.	*Bacchanals*
Herc. fur.	*Madness of Hercules*
Iph. taur.	*Iphigeneia at Tauris*
Herodotus	
Hist.	*Histories*
Homer	
Il.	*Iliad*
Od.	*Odyssey*
Iamblichus	
Pythag.	*Life of Pythagoras*
Juvenal	
Sat.	*Satirae*
Livy	
Hist.	*History of Rome*

18

Lucian
    Alex.   *Alexander the False Prophet*
    Eunuch.   *The Eunuch*
    Hist.   *How to Write History*
    Nav.   *Navigium (The Ship)*
    Peregr.   *De morte Peregrini*
    Tox.   *Toxaris*
Ovid
    Metam.   *Metamorphoses*
Pausanias
    Descr.   *Description of Greece*
Petronius
    Satyr.   *Satyricon*
Philostratus
    Vit. Apoll.   *Vita Apollonii*
Pindar
    Pyth.   *Pythian Odes*
Plato
    Alc.   *Alcibiades*
    Apol.   *Apology of Socrates*
    Euthyphr.   *Euthyphro*
    Gorg.   *Gorgias*
    Laws   *Laws*
    Phaed.   *Phaedo*
    Resp.   *Republic*
    Soph.   *Sophist*
    Tim.   *Timaeus*
Pliny the Elder
    Nat.   *Natural History*
Plutarch
    Curios.   *De curiositate*
    Def. orac.   *De defectu oraculorum*
    Frat. amor.   *De fraterno amore*
    Is. Os.   *De Iside et Osiride*
    Max. princ.   *Maxime cum principibus philosophiam esse disserendum*
    Quaest. conv.   *Quaestionum convivialum libri IX*
    Quaest. nat.   *Quaestiones naturales (Aetia physica)*
    Reg. imp. apophth. *Regum et imperatorum apophthegmata*
    Sept. sap. conv. *Septem sapientium convivium*
    Stoic. rep.   *De Stoicorum repugnantiis*
    Superst.   *De superstitione*
Polemo
    Physiogn.   *Physiognomonica*
Polybius
    Hist.   *Histories*
Quintilian
    Inst.   *Institutio oratoria*
Rhet. Her.   *Rhetorica ad Herennium*
Seneca
    Ep.   *Moral Essays*
    Nat.   *Naturales quaestiones*
Sophocles
    Oed. col.   *Oedipus at Coloneus*
Strabo
    Geogr.   *Geography*
Suetonius
    Aug.   *The Life of Augustus*
    Claud.   *The Life of Claudius*
    Tit.   *The Life of Titus*
    Vesp.   *Vespasian*
Tacitus
    Ann.   *Annals*

Hist.	*History*
Thucydides	
War	*History of the Peloponnesian War*
Virgil	
Aen.	*Aeneid*
Xenophon	
Cyr.	*Cyropaedia*
Eph.	*Ephesians*
Hell.	*Hellenica*
Mem.	*Memorabilia*

Secondary Sources: Journals, Reference Works, and Series

AB	Anchor Bible
ABD	*Anchor Bible Dictionary*—see Freedman (1992)
ACCS	Ancient Christian Commentary on Scripture
ACNT	Augsburg Commentary on the New Testament
ANTC	Abingdon New Testament Commentaries
ASNU	Acta seminarii neotestamentici upsaliensis
BAFCS	*The Book of Acts in Its First Century Setting*
BBR	*Bulletin for Biblical Research*
BBB	Bonner biblische Beiträge
BDAG	*A Greek-English Lexicon of the New Testament and Other Early Christian Literature* (3rd ed.)—see Bauer et al. (2000)
BDF	*Greek Grammar of the New Testament and Other Early Christian Literature*—see Blass and Debrunner (1961)
BECNT	*Baker Exegetical Commentary on the New Testament*
BETL	Bibliotheca ephemeridum theologicarum lovaniensium
Bib	*Biblica*
BR	*Biblical Research*
BT	*The Bible Translator*
BTB	*Biblical Theology Bulletin*
BWA(N)T	Beiträge zur Wissenschaft vom Alten (und Neuen) Testament
BZ	*Biblische Zeitschrift*
CBQ	*Catholic Biblical Quarterly*
EBib	Etudes bibliques
EgT	*Église et théologie*
EKKNT	Evangelisch-katholischer Kommentar zum Neuen Testament
ESEC	Emory Studies in Early Christianity
ETL	*Ephemerides theologicae lovanienses*
ETR	*Etudes théologiques et religieuses*
FRLANT	Forschungen zur Religion und Literatur des Alten und Neuen Testaments
HTKNT	Herders theologischer Kommentar zum Neuen Testament
HTR	*Harvard Theological Review*
ICC	International Critical Commentary
Int	*Interpretation*
IVPNTC	InterVarsity Press New Testament Commentary
JAAR	*Journal of the American Academy of Religion*
JAC	Jahrbuch für Antike und Christentum
JBL	*Journal of Biblical Literature*
JETS	*Journal of the Evangelical Theological Society*
JRS	*Journal of Roman Studies*
JSNT	*Journal for the Study of the New Testament*
JSNTSup	Journal for the Study of the New Testament: Supplement Series
JTS	*Journal of Theological Studies*
KEK	Kritisch-exegetischer Kommentar über das Neue Testament
LCBI	Literary Currents in Biblical Interpretation
LD	Lectio divina
LEC	Library of Early Christianity
LNTS	Library of New Testament Studies
LPS	Library of Pauline Studies
LSJ	*A Greek-English Lexicon* (9th ed.)—see Liddell and Scott (1996)
MNTC	Moffatt New Testament Commentary

NAC	New American Commentary
NCB	New Century Bible
NIBC	New International Bible Commentary
NICNT	New International Commentary on the New Testament
NIDB	*New Interpreter's Dictionary of the Bible*—see Sakenfeld et al. (2006-9)
NovT	*Novum Testamentum*
NTD	Das Neue Testament Deutsch
NTS	*New Testament Studies*
OBO	Orbis biblicus et orientalis
OBT	Overtures to Biblical Theology
OTNT	Ökumenischer Taschenbuchkommentar zum Neuen Testament
PCNT	Paideia Commentaries on the New Testament
PerRS	*Perspectives in Religious Studies*
PiNTC	Pillar New Testament Commentary
PrTMS	Princeton Theological Monograph Series
R&T	*Religion and Theology*
RSR	*Recherches de science religieuse*
SANT	Studien zum Alten und Neuen Testament
SBLDS	Society of Biblical Literature Dissertation Series
SBLMS	Society of Biblical Literature Monograph Series
SBLSP	Society of Biblical Literature Seminar Papers
SBLSymS	Society of Biblical Literature Symposium Series
SNTSMS	Society for New Testament Studies Monograph Series
SP	Sacra Pagina
StBL	Studies in Biblical Literature
SUNT	Studien zur Umwelt des Neuen Testaments
SwJT	*Southwestern Journal of Theology*
TDNT	*Theological Dictionary of the New Testament*—see Kittel and Friedrich (1964-76)
THKNT	Theologischer Handkommentar zum Neuen Testament
TLZ	*Theologische Literaturzeitung*
TNTC	Tyndale New Testament Commentaries
TynBul	*Tyndale Bulletin*
TZ	*Theologische Zeitschrift*
WUNT	Wissenschaftliche Untersuchungen zum Neuen Testament
WW	*Word and World*
ZBK	Zürcher Bibelkommentare
ZECNT	Zondervan Exegetical Commentary on the New Testament
ZNW	*Zeitschrift für die neutestamentliche Wissenschaft und die Kunde der älteren Kirche*

Greek Transliteration

Greek	Letter	English
α	alpha	a
β	bēta	b
γ	gamma	g
γ	gamma nasal	n (before γ, κ, ξ, χ)
δ	delta	d
ε	epsilon	e
ζ	zēta	z
η	ēta	ē
θ	thēta	th
ι	iōta	i
κ	kappa	k
λ	lambda	l
μ	mu	m
ν	nu	n
ξ	xi	x
ο	omicron	o
π	pi	p
ρ	rhō	r
ρ	initial rhō	rh
σ/ς	sigma	s
τ	tau	t
υ	upsilon	y
υ	upsilon	u (in diphthongs: au, eu, ēu, ou, ui)
φ	phi	ph
χ	chi	ch
ψ	psi	ps
ω	ōmega	ō
ʼ	rough breathing	h (before initial vowels or diphthongs)

Hebrew Consonant Transliteration

Hebrew/ Aramaic	Letter	English
א	alef	ʼ
ב	bet	b
ג	gimel	g
ד	dalet	d
ה	he	h
ו	vav	v or w
ז	zayin	z
ח	khet	ḥ
ט	tet	ṭ
י	yod	y
כ/ך	kaf	k
ל	lamed	l
מ/ם	mem	m
נ/ן	nun	n
ס	samek	s̜
ע	ayin	ʻ
פ/ף	pe	p; f (spirant)
צ/ץ	tsade	ṣ
ק	qof	q
ר	resh	r
שׂ	sin	ś
שׁ	shin	š
ת	tav	t; th (spirant)

BIBLIOGRAPHY

Achtemeier, Paul J. 1986. An Elusive Unity: Paul, Acts, and the Early Church. *CBQ* 48:1-26.
———. 1987. *The Quest for Unity in the New Testament Church: A Study in Paul and Acts*. Philadelphia: Fortress.
Adam, A. K. M. 2006. Poaching on Zion: Biblical Theology as Signifying Practice. Pages 17-34 in *Reading Scripture with the Church: Toward a Hermeneutic for Theological Interpretation*. Grand Rapids: Baker Academic.
Alexander, Loveday C. A. 1993. *The Preface to Luke's Gospel: Literary Convention and Social Context in Luke 1.1-4 and Acts 1.1*. SNTSMS 78. Cambridge: Cambridge University Press.
———. 1999. Formal Elements and Genre: Which Greco-Roman Prologues Most Closely Parallel the Lukan Prologues? Pages 9-26 in *Jesus and the Heritage of Israel*. Edited by David P. Moessner. Harrisburg, PA: Trinity Press International.
———. 2005. *Acts in Its Ancient Literary Context: A Classicist Looks at the Acts of the Apostles*. LNTS 298. New York: T&T Clark.
Allen, O. Wesley, Jr. 1997. *The Death of Herod: The Narrative and Theological Function of Retribution in Luke-Acts*. SBLDS 158. Atlanta: Scholars Press.
Andersen, T. David. 1988. The Meaning of *ECHONTES CHARIN PROS* in Acts 2.47. *NTS* 34:604-10.
Anderson, Janice Capel. 2004. Reading Tabitha: A Feminist Reception History. Pages 22-48 in *A Feminist Companion to the Acts of the Apostles*. Edited by Amy-Jill Levine. Cleveland, OH: Pilgrim Press.
Arrington, French L. 1988. *The Acts of the Apostles: An Introduction and Commentary*. Peabody, MA: Hendrickson.
Arterbury, Andrew E. 2009. The Downfall of Eutychus: How Ancient Understandings of Sleep Illuminate Acts 20:7-12. Pages 201-21 in *Contemporary Studies in Acts*. Edited by Thomas E. Phillips. Macon, GA: Mercer University Press.
Aune, David E. 1987. *The New Testament in Its Literary Environment*. LEC 8. Philadelphia: Westminster Press.
Bachmann, Michael. 1980. *Jerusalem und der Tempel: Die geographisch-theologischen Elemente in der lukanischen Sicht des jüdischen Kultzentrums*. BWA(N)T. Stuttgart: Verlag W. Kohlhammer.
Balch, David L. 1985. Acts as Hellenistic Historiography. Pages 429-32 in *SBLSP* (1985). Edited by Kent Harold Richards. Atlanta: Scholars Press.
———. 1989. Comments on the Genre and a Political Theme of Luke-Acts: A Preliminary Comparison of Two Hellenistic Historians. Pages 343-61 in *SBLSP* (1989). Edited by David Lull. Atlanta: Scholars Press, 1989.
———. 1990a. The Areopagus Speech: An Appeal to the Stoic Historian Posidonius against Later Stoics and the Epicureans. Pages 52-79 in *Greeks, Romans, and Christians: Essays in Honor of Abraham J. Malherbe*. Edited by David L. Balch, Everett Ferguson, and Wayne A. Meeks. Minneapolis: Fortress.
———. 1990b. The Genre of Luke-Acts: Individual Biography, Adventure Novel, or Political History? *SwJT* 33 (Fall):5-19.
Balch, David L., Everett Ferguson, and Wayne Meeks, eds. 1990. *Greeks, Romans, and Christians: Essays in Honor of Abraham J. Malherbe*. Minneapolis: Fortress.
Barnes, Timothy David. 1969. Apostle of Trial. *JTS* 20:407-19.
Barrett, C. K. 1994. *A Critical and Exegetical Commentary on the Acts of the Apostles 1-14*. ICC. Edinburgh: T&T Clark.
———. 1998. *A Critical and Exegetical Commentary on the Acts of the Apostles 15-28*. ICC. Edinburgh: T&T Clark.
Bartchy, S. Scott. 1991. Community of Goods in Acts: Idealization or Social Reality? Pages 309-18 in *The Future of Early Christianity: Essays in Honor of Helmut Koester*. Edited by Birger A. Pearson. Minneapolis: Fortress.
Barthes, Roland. 1970. L'analyse structurale du récit: A propos d'Actes X-XI. *RSR* 58:17-37.
Bassler, Jouette M. 1985. Luke and Paul on Impartiality. *Bib* 66:546-52.
Bauckham, Richard, ed. 1995a. *The Book of Acts in Its Palestinian Setting*. BAFCS 4. Grand Rapids: Eerdmans.

———. 1995b. James and the Jerusalem Church. Pages 415-80 in *The Book of Acts in Its Palestinian Setting*. Edited by Richard Bauckham. BAFCS 4. Grand Rapids: Eerdmans.

———. 1996. James and the Gentiles (Acts 15.13-21). Pages 154-84 in *History, Literature, and Society in the Book of Acts*. Edited by Ben Witherington III. Cambridge: Cambridge University Press.

———. 2008. *Jesus and the God of Israel: God Crucified and Other Studies on the New Testament's Christology of Divine Identity*. Grand Rapids: Eerdmans.

Bauer, Walter. 2000. *A Greek-English Lexicon of the New Testament and Other Early Christian Literature*. 3rd ed. Translated and edited by William F. Arndt, F. Wilbur Gingrich, and Frederick W. Danker. Chicago: University of Chicago Press.

Baur, Ferdinand Christian. 1876. *Paul, the Apostle of Jesus Christ, His Life and Work, His Epistles and His Doctrine: A Contribution to a Critical History of Primitive Christianity*. 2 vols. Translated by Eduard Zeller. Edited by Allan Menzies. London: Williams & Norgate.

Béchard, Dean P. 2001. Paul among the Rustics: The Lystran Episode (Acts 14:8-20) and Lucan Apologetic. *CBQ* 63:84-101.

———. 2003. The Disputed Case against Paul: A Redaction-Critical Analysis of Acts 21:27—22:29. *CBQ* 65:232-50.

Benoit, Pierre. 1950. Remarques sur les 'sommaires' de Actes 2. 42 à 5. Pages 1-10 in *Aux sources de la tradition chrétienne: Mélanges offerts à M. Maurice Goguel*. Bibliothèque théologique. Paris: Delachaux et Niestlé.

Beyer, Hermann Wolfgang. *therapeuō ktl.* Pages 128-32 in vol. 3 of *TDNT*.

Binder, Donald D. 1999. *Into the Temple Courts: The Place of the Synagogues in the Second Temple Period*. SBLDS 169. Atlanta: Scholars Press.

Black, C. Clifton. 1998. John Mark in the Acts of the Apostles. Pages 101-20 in *Literary Studies in Luke-Acts: Essays in Honor of Joseph B. Tyson*. Edited by Richard P. Thompson and Thomas E. Phillips. Macon, GA: Mercer University Press.

Blass, Friedrich, and A. Debrunner. 1961. *A Greek Grammar of the New Testament and Other Early Christian Literature*. Translated and edited by Robert W. Funk. Chicago: University of Chicago Press.

Blomberg, Craig L. 1984. The Law in Luke-Acts. *JSNT* 22:53-80.

Blue, Bradley. 1994. Acts and the House Church. Pages 119-22 in *The Book of Acts in Its Graeco-Roman Setting*. Edited by David W. J. Gill and Conrad Gempf. BAFCS 2. Grand Rapids: Eerdmans.

Bock, Darrell L. 2007. *Acts*. BECNT. Grand Rapids: Baker Academic.

———. 2012. *A Theology of Luke and Acts: God's Promised Program, Realized for All Nations*. Biblical Theology of the New Testament. Grand Rapids: Zondervan.

Boismard, Marie-Émile. 1988. Le 'concile' de Jérusalem (Act 15,1-33). *ETL* 64:433-40.

Boismard, Marie-Émile, and Arnaud Lamouille. 1984. *Le texte occidental des Actes des Apôtres: Reconstitution et réhabilitation*. 2 vols. Paris: Éditions Recherche sur les Civilisations.

———. 1990. *Les Actes des deux Apôtres*. 3 vols. EBib. Paris: J. Gabalda.

Borgen, Peder. 1969. From Paul to Luke: Observation toward Clarification of the Theology of Luke-Acts. *CBQ* 31:168-82.

———. 1982. Catalogues of Vices, the Apostolic Decree, and the Jerusalem Meeting. Pages 126-41 in *The Social World of Formative Christianity and Judaism*. Edited by Ernest S. Frerichs, Jacob Neusner, Peder Borgen, and Richard Horsley. Philadelphia: Fortress.

Borse, Udo. 1980. Kompositionsgeschichtliche Beobachtungen zum Apostelkonzil. Pages 195-211 in *Begegnung mit dem Wort: Festschrift für Heinrich Zimmermann*. Edited by Josef Zmijewski. BBB 53. Bonn: Peter Hanstein.

Bovon, François. 1970. Tradition et rédaction en Actes 10,1-11,18. *TZ* 26:22-45.

———. 1983. Israel, die Kirche und die Völker im lukanischen Doppelwerk. *TLZ* 108:403-14.

———. 1987. *Luke the Theologian: Thirty-Three Years of Research (1950-1983)*. PrTMS 12. Allison Park, PA: Pickwick.

Brawley, Robert L. 1987. *Luke-Acts and the Jews: Conflict, Apology, and Conciliation*. SBLMS 33. Atlanta: Scholars Press.

———. 1990. *Centering on God: Method and Message in Luke-Acts*. LCBI. Louisville, KY: Westminster/John Knox Press.

———. 1998. The God of Promises and the Jews in Luke-Acts. Pages 279-96 in *Literary Studies in Luke-Acts: Essays in Honor of Joseph B. Tyson*. Edited by Richard P. Thompson and Thomas E. Phillips. Macon, GA: Mercer University Press.

Brehm, H. Alan. 1990. The Significance of the Summaries for Interpreting Acts. *SwJT* 33 (Fall):29-40.

Brodie, Thomas L. 1990. Luke-Acts as an Imitation and Emulation of the Elijah-Elisha Narrative. Pages 78-85 in *New Views on Luke and Acts*. Edited by Earl Richard. Collegeville, MN: Liturgical Press.

Brower, Kent E., and Andy Johnson, eds. 2007. *Holiness and Ecclesiology in the New Testament*. Grand Rapids: Eerdmans.

Brown, H. Stephen. 1996. Paul's Hearing at Caesarea: A Preliminary Comparison with Legal Literature of the Roman Period. Pages 319-32 in *SBLSP* (1996). Edited by Eugene H. Lovering Jr. Atlanta: Scholars Press.

Bruce, F. F. 1973. The Holy Spirit in the Acts of the Apostles. *Int* 27:166-83.

———. 1979. *Men and Movements in the Primitive Church: Studies in Early Non-Pauline Christianity*. Exeter: Paternoster.

———. 1984. *The Acts of the Apostles: The Greek Text with Introduction and Commentary*. 2nd ed. Grand Rapids: Eerdmans.

———. 1986. The Apostolic Decree of Acts 15. Pages 115-24 in *Studien zum Text und zur Ethik des Neuen Testaments: Festschrift zum 80. Geburtstag von Heinrich Greeven*. Edited by Wolfgang Schrage. Berlin: Walter de Gruyter.

———. 1988. *The Book of the Acts*. Revised ed. NICNT. Grand Rapids: Eerdmans.

———. 1990. The Significance of the Speeches for Interpreting Acts. *SwJT* 33 (Fall): 21-28.

Bryan, Christopher. 1988. A Further Look at Acts 16:1-3. *JBL* 107:292-94.

Büchsel, Friedrich. *krinō ktl*. Pages 933-54 in vol. 3 of *TDNT*.

Bulley, Alan D. 1994. Hanging in the Balance: A Semiotic Study of Acts 20:7-12. *EgT* 25, no. 2:171-88.

Bultmann, Rudolf. *peitharcheō*. Pages 9-10 in vol. 6 of *TDNT*.

———. *pisteuō ktl*. Pages 174-228 in vol. 6 of *TDNT*.

Burridge, Richard A. 1992. *What Are the Gospels? A Comparison with Graeco-Roman Biography*. SNTSMS 70. Cambridge: Cambridge University Press (2nd ed., Grand Rapids: Eerdmans, 2004).

Byrskog, Samuel. 2003. History or Story in Acts—A Middle Way? The "We" Passages, Historical Intertexture, and Oral History. Pages 257-83 in *Contextualizing Acts: Lukan Narrative and Greco-Roman Discourse*. Edited by Todd Penner and Caroline Vander Stichele. Atlanta: Society of Biblical Literature.

Cadbury, Henry J. 1920. *The Style and Method of St. Luke*. Cambridge, MA: Harvard University Press.

———. 1927. *The Making of Luke-Acts*. New York: Macmillan (2nd ed., 1958; reprint, Peabody, MA: Hendrickson, 1999).

———. 1933a. Dust and Garments. Pages 269-77 in *Additional Notes to the Commentary on Acts*. Edited by Kirsopp Lake and Henry J. Cadbury. The Beginnings of Christianity 5. London: Macmillan.

———. 1933b. Roman Law and the Trial of Paul. Pages 297-338 in *Additional Notes to the Commentary on Acts*. Edited by Kirsopp Lake and Henry J. Cadbury. The Beginnings of Christianity 5. New York: Macmillan.

———. 1933c. *Hypozōmata*. Pages 345-54 in *Additional Notes to the Commentary on Acts*. Edited by Kirsopp Lake and Henry J. Cadbury. The Beginnings of Christianity 5. London: Macmillan.

———. 1933d. The Speeches in Acts. Pages 402-27 in *Additional Notes to the Commentary on Acts*. Edited by Kirsopp Lake and Henry J. Cadbury. The Beginnings of Christianity 5. London: Macmillan.

Callan, Terrance. 1985. The Preface of Luke-Acts and Historiography. *NTS* 31:576-81.

———. 1993. The Background of the Apostolic Decree (Acts 15:20, 29; 21:25). *CBQ* 55:284-97.

Callen, Barry L., and Richard P. Thompson, eds. 2004. *Reading the Bible in Wesleyan Ways: Some Constructive Proposals*. Kansas City: Beacon Hill Press of Kansas City.

Campbell, William Sanger. 2007. *The "We" Passages in the Acts of the Apostles: The Narrator as Narrative Character*. Studies in Biblical Literature. StBL 14. Atlanta: Society of Biblical Literature.

Cancik, Hubert. 1997. The History of Culture, Religion, and Institutions in Ancient Historiography: Philological Observations Concerning Luke's History. *JBL* 116:673-95.

Capper, Brian. 1995. The Palestinian Cultural Context of Earliest Christian Community of Goods. Pages 323-56 in *The Book of Acts in Its Palestinian Setting*. Edited by Richard Bauckham. BAFCS 4. Grand Rapids: Eerdmans.

———. 1998. Reciprocity and the Ethic of Acts. Pages 499-518 in *Witness to the Gospel: The Theology of Acts*. Edited by I. Howard Marshall and David Peterson. Grand Rapids: Eerdmans.

Carroll, John T. 1988. Luke's Portrayal of the Pharisees. *CBQ* 50:604-21.

Carter, Charles W., and Ralph Earle. 1959. *The Acts of the Apostles*. Evangelical Commentary of the Bible. Grand Rapids: Zondervan.

Cassidy, Richard J. 1987. *Society and Politics in the Acts of the Apostles*. Maryknoll, NY: Orbis.

Cassidy, Richard J., and Philip J. Scharper, eds. 1983. *Political Issues in Luke-Acts*. Maryknoll, NY: Orbis.

Chambers, Kathy. 2004. "Knock, Knock—Who's There?" Acts 12:6-17 as a Comedy of Errors. Pages 89-97 in *A Feminist Companion to the Acts of the Apostles*. Edited by Amy-Jill Levine. Cleveland, OH: Pilgrim Press.

Chance, J. Bradley. 1988. *Jerusalem, the Temple, and the New Age in Luke-Acts*. Macon, GA: Mercer University Press.

Chapman, Stephen B. 2008. Saul/Paul: Onomastics, Typology, and Christian Scripture. Pages 214-43 in *The Word Leaps the Gap: Essays on Scripture and Theology in Honor of Richard B. Hays*. Edited by J. Ross Wagner, C. Kavin Rowe, and A. Katherine Grieb. Grand Rapids: Eerdmans.

Ciampa, Roy E. 2011. "Examining the Scriptures"? The Meaning of *anakrinontes tas graphas* in Acts 17:11. *JBL* 130:527-41.

Clabeaux, John J. 2005. The Story of the Maltese Viper and Luke's Apology for Paul. *CBQ* 67:604-10.

Clark, Andrew C. 1998. The Role of the Apostles. Pages 169-80 in *Witness to the Gospel: The Theology of Acts*. Edited by I. Howard Marshall and David Peterson. Grand Rapids: Eerdmans.

Clarke, Andrew D. 1994. Rome and Italy. Pages 455-81 in *The Book of Acts in Its Graeco-Roman Setting*. Edited by David W. J. Gill and Conrad Gempf. BAFCS 2. Grand Rapids: Eerdmans.

Co, Maria Anicia. 1992. The Major Summaries in Acts: Acts 2,42-47; 4,32-35; 5,12-16 Linguistic and Literary Relationship. *ETL* 68:49-85.

Cohen, Shaye J. D. 1986. Was Timothy Jewish (Acts 16:1-3)? Patristic Exegesis, Rabbinic Law, and Matrilineal Descent. *JBL* 105:251-68.

———. 1987. *From the Maccabees to the Mishnah*. LEC 7. Philadelphia: Westminster Press.

———. 1989. Crossing the Boundary and Becoming a Jew. *HTR* 82:13-33.

Combet-Galland, Corina. 1977. Actes 4/32-5/11. *ETR* 52:548-53.

Conzelmann, Hans. 1961. *The Theology of St. Luke*. Translated by Geoffrey Buswell. Philadelphia: Fortress.

———. 1987. *Acts of the Apostles*. Translated by James Lumburg, A. Thomas Kraabel, and Donald H. Juel. Hermeneia. Philadelphia: Fortress.

Cook, Michael J. 1988. The Mission to the Jews in Acts: Unraveling Luke's "Myth of the 'Myriads.'" Pages 102-23 in *Luke-Acts and the Jewish People: Eight Critical Perspectives*. Edited by Joseph B. Tyson. Minneapolis: Augsburg.

Croy, N. Clayton. 1997. Hellenistic Philosophies and the Preaching of the Resurrection (Acts 17:18, 32). *NovT* 39:21-39.

Culy, Martin M., and Mikeal C. Parsons. 2003. *Acts: A Handbook on the Greek Text*. Waco, TX: Baylor University Press.

Dahl, Nils A. 1957-58. "A People for His Name" (Acts Xv.14). *NTS* 4:319-27.

Danker, Frederick W. 1983. Reciprocity in the Ancient World and in Acts 15:23-29. Pages 49-58 in *Political Issues in Luke-Acts*. Edited by Richard J. Cassidy and Philip J. Scharper. New York: Orbis.

Darr, John A. 1992. *On Character Building: The Reader and the Rhetoric of Characterization in Luke-Acts*. LCBI. Louisville, KY: Westminster/John Knox Press.

———. 1998. Irenic or Ironic? Another Look at Gamaliel before the Sanhedrin (Acts 5:33-42). Pages 121-40 in *Literary Studies in Luke-Acts: Essays in Honor of Joseph B. Tyson*. Edited by Richard P. Thompson and Thomas E. Phillips. Macon, GA: Mercer University Press.

Daube, David. 1990. On Acts 23: Sadducees and Angels. *JBL* 109: 493-97.

Delling, Gerhard. *statis*. Pages 568-71 in vol. 10 of *TDNT*.

Dibelius, Martin. 1956. *Studies in the Acts of the Apostles*. Translated by Mary Ling. London: SCM Press.

Downing, F. Gerald. 1986. Freedom from the Law in Luke-Acts. *JSNT* 26:49-52.

———. 1988. Law and Custom: Luke-Acts and Late Hellenism. Pages 148-58 in *Law and Religion: Essays on the Place of the Law in Israel and Early Christianity*. Edited by Barnabas Lindars. Cambridge, UK: James Clarke.

Dunn, James D. G. 1991. *The Partings of the Ways: Between Christianity and Judaism and Their Significance for the Character of Christianity*. Philadelphia: Trinity Press International.

———. 1996. *The Acts of the Apostles*. Narrative Commentaries. Valley Forge, PA: Trinity Press International.

———. 2006. *Unity and Diversity in the New Testament: An Inquiry into the Character of Earliest Christianity*. Revised ed. London: SCM Press.

———. 2009. *Beginning from Jerusalem*. Christianity in the Making. Grand Rapids: Eerdmans.

Dupont, Jacques. 1964. *The Sources of the Acts*. Translated by Kathleen Pond. New York: Herder and Herder.

———. 1979. *The Salvation of the Gentiles: Essays on the Acts of the Apostles*. Translated by John R. Keating. New York: Paulist Press.

———. 1984. *Nouvelles études sur les Actes des Apôtres*. LD 118. Paris: Éditions du Cerf.

———. 1985a. Un peuple d'entre les nations (Actes 15.14). *NTS* 31:321-35.

———. 1985b. Je rebâtirai la cabane de David qui est tombée (Ac 15,16=Am 9,11). Pages 19-32 in *Glaube und Eschatologie: Festscrift für Werner Georg Kümmel*. Edited by Erick Grässer and Otto Merk. Tübingen: J. C. B. Mohr.

du Toit, Andrie B. 2000. A Tale of Two Cities: "Tarsus or Jerusalem" Revisited. *NTS* 46:375-402.

Earle, Ralph. 1965. The Acts of the Apostles. Pages 247-598 of vol. 7 in *Beacon Bible Commentary*. 10 vols. Edited by A. F. Harper et al. Kansas City: Beacon Hill Press of Kansas City.

Esler, Philip Francis. 1987. *Community and Gospel in Luke-Acts: The Social and Political Motivations of Lucan Theology*. SNTSMS 57. Cambridge: Cambridge University Press.

Evans, Craig A., and James A. Sanders. 1993. *Luke and Scripture: The Function of Sacred Tradition in Luke-Acts*. Minneapolis: Fortress.

Fiensy, David A. 1995. The Composition of the Jerusalem Church. Pages 213-36 in *The Book of Acts in Its Palestinian Setting*. Edited by Richard Bauckham. BAFCS 4. Grand Rapids: Eerdmans.

Finger, Reta Halteman. 2007. *Of Widows and Meals: Communal Meals in the Book of Acts*. Grand Rapids: Eerdmans.

Fitzmyer, Joseph A. 1980. Jewish Christianity in Acts in Light of the Qumran Scrolls. Pages 233-57 in *Studies in Luke-Acts*. Edited by Leander E. Keck and J. Louis Martyn. Philadelphia: Fortress.

———. 1989. *Luke the Theologian: Aspects of His Teaching*. New York: Paulist Press.

———. 1998. *The Acts of the Apostles: A New Translation with Introduction and Commentary*. AB 31. New York: Doubleday.

Flemming, Dean. 2002. Contextualizing the Gospel in Athens: Paul's Areopagus Address as a Paradigm for Missionary Communication. *Missiology* 30:199-214.

Foakes-Jackson, F. J. 1931. *The Acts of the Apostles*. MNTC. New York: Harper & Brothers.

Foakes-Jackson, F. J., and Kirsopp Lake, eds. 1920–33. *Beginnings of Christianity*. 5 vols. London: Macmillan.

Foerster, Werner. *sōzō ktl*. Pages 965-1024 in vol. 7 of *TDNT*.

Fowl, Stephen E., and L. Gregory Jones. 1991. *Reading in Communion: Scripture and Ethics in Christian Life*. Grand Rapids: Eerdmans.

Freedman, David Noel, et al., eds. 1992. *Anchor Bible Dictionary*. 6 vols. New York: Doubleday.

Gager, John G. 1986. Jews, Gentiles, and Synagogues in the Book of Acts. Pages 91-99 in *Christians among Jews and Gentiles: Essays in Honor of Krister Stendahl on His Sixty-fifth Birthday*. Edited by George W. E. Nickelsburg with George W. MacRae. Philadelphia: Fortress.

Garnsey, Peter. 1966. The *Lex Julia* and Appeal under the Empire. *JRS* 58:167-89.

Garrett, Susan R. 1989. *The Demise of the Devil: Magic and the Demonic in Luke's Writings*. Minneapolis: Fortress.

———. 1990. Exodus from Bondage: Luke 9:31 and Acts 12:1-24. *CBQ* 52:656-80.

Gärtner, Bertil. 1955. *The Areopagus Speech and Natural Revelation*. ASNU. Uppsala, Sweden: Gleerup.

Gasque, W. W. 1989. *A History of the Interpretation of the Acts of the Apostles*. Peabody, MA: Hendrickson.

Gaston, Lloyd. 1986. Anti-Judaism and the Passion Narrative in Luke and Acts. Pages 127-53 in *Paul and the Gospels*. Vol. 1 of *Anti-Judaism in Early Christianity*. Edited by Peter Richardson with David Granskou. Studies in Christianity and Judaism 2. Waterloo, ON: Wilfrid Laurier University Press.

Gaventa, Beverly Roberts. 1986. *From Darkness to Light: Aspects of Conversion in the New Testament*. OBT 20. Philadelphia: Fortress.

———. 1988. Toward a Theology of Acts: Reading and Rereading. *Int* 42:146-57.

———. 2003. *The Acts of the Apostles*. ANTC. Nashville: Abingdon.

————. 2004. What Ever Happened to Those Prophesying Daughters? Pages 49-60 in *A Feminist Companion to the Acts of the Apostles*. Edited by Amy-Jill Levine. Cleveland, OH: Pilgrim Press.

Gilchrist, J. M. 1996. The Historicity of Paul's Shipwreck. *JSNT* 61:29-51.

Gill, David W. J. 1994a. Achaia. Pages 433-53 in *The Book of Acts in Its Graeco-Roman Setting*. Edited by David W. J. Gill and Conrad Gempf. BAFCS 2. Grand Rapids: Eerdmans.

————. 1994b. Acts and the Urban Élites. Pages 105-18 in *The Book of Acts in Its Graeco-Roman Setting*. Edited by David W. J. Gill and Conrad Gempf. BAFCS 2. Grand Rapids: Eerdmans.

————. 1995. Paul's Travels through Cyprus (Acts 13:4-12). *TynBul* 46/2:219-28.

Gill, David W. J., and Conrad Gempf, eds. 1994. *The Book of Acts in Its Graeco-Roman Setting*. BAFCS 2. Grand Rapids: Eerdmans.

Gill, David W. J., and Bruce W. Winter. 1994. Acts and Roman Religion. Pages 79-103 in *The Book of Acts in Its Graeco-Roman Setting*. Edited by David W. J. Gill and Conrad Gempf. BAFCS 2. Grand Rapids: Eerdmans.

Gooch, Paul W. Conscience. Pages 719-26 in vol. 1 of *NIDB*.

Goodenough, Erwin R. 1980. The Perspective of Acts. Pages 51-59 in *Studies in Luke-Acts*. Edited by Leander E. Keck and J. Louis Martyn. Philadelphia: Fortress.

Gowler, David B. 1991. *Host, Guest, Enemy and Friend: Portraits of the Pharisees in Luke and Acts*. ESEC 2. New York: Peter Lang.

Green, Joel B. Festus. 1992. Pages 794-95 in vol. 2 of *ABD*.

————. 1998. Salvation to the End of the Earth: God as the Saviour in the Acts of the Apostles. Pages 83-106 in *Witness to the Gospel: The Theology of Acts*. Edited by I. Howard Marshall and David Peterson. Grand Rapids: Eerdmans.

————. 2004. Is There a Contemporary Wesleyan Hermeneutic? Pages 123-34 in *Reading the Bible in Wesleyan Ways: Some Constructive Proposals*. Edited by Barry L. Callen and Richard P. Thompson. Kansas City: Beacon Hill Press of Kansas City.

————. 2008. "In Our Own Languages": Pentecost, Babel, and the Shaping of Christian Community in Acts 2:1-13. Pages 198-213 in *The Word Leaps the Gap: Essays on Scripture and Theology in Honor of Richard B. Hays*. Edited by J. Ross Wagner, C. Kavin Rowe, and A. Katherine Grieb. Grand Rapids: Eerdmans.

Gregory, Andrew F. 2003. *The Reception of Luke and Acts in the Period before Irenaeus: Looking for Luke in the Second Century*. WUNT 2, 169. Tübingen: Mohr Siebeck.

————. 2010. The Reception of Luke and Acts and the Unity of Luke-Acts. Pages 82-93 in *Rethinking the Unity and Reception of Luke and Acts*. Edited by Andrew F. Gregory and C. Kavin Rowe. Columbia, SC: University of South Carolina Press.

Grundmann, Walter. *tharreō*. Pages 25-27 in vol. 3 of *TDNT*.

————. *tapeinos ktl*. Pages 1-26 in vol. 8 of *TDNT*.

Haacker, Klaus. 1985. Das Bekenntnis des Paulus zur Hoffnung Israels nach der Apostelgeschichte des Lukas. *NTS* 31:437-51.

Haenchen, Ernst. 1971. *The Acts of the Apostles: A Commentary*. Translated by Bernard Noble and Gerald Shinn. Philadelphia: Westminster Press.

————. 1980. The Book of Acts as Source Material for the History of Early Christianity. Pages 258-78 in *Studies in Luke-Acts*. Edited by Leander E. Keck and J. Louis Martyn. Philadelphia: Fortress.

Hamm, Dennis. 1986. Acts 3:1-10: The Healing of the Temple Beggar as Lucan Theology. *Bib* 67:305-19.

————. 1990. Paul's Blindness and Its Healing: Clues to Symbolic Intent (Acts 9; 22 and 26). *Bib* 71:3-72.

Harnack, Adolf. 1909. *The Acts of the Apostles*. Crown Theological Library. New York: G. P. Putnam's Sons.

Harrill, J. Albert. 2000. The Dramatic Function of the Running Slave Rhoda (Acts 12:13-16): A Piece of Greco-Roman Comedy. *NTS* 46:150-57.

————. 2011. Divine Judgment against Ananias and Sapphira (Acts 5:1-11): A Stock Scene of Perjury and Death. *JBL* 130:351-69.

Havelaar, Henriette. 1997. Hellenistic Parallels to Acts 5.1-11 and the Problem of Conflicting Interpretations. *JSNT* 67:63-82.

Hays, Richard B. 1996. *The Moral Vision of the New Testament: A Contemporary Introduction to New Testament Ethics*. San Francisco: HarperSanFrancisco.

Head, Peter. 1993. Acts and the Problem of Its Texts. Pages 415-44 in *The Book of Acts in Its Ancient Literary Setting*. Edited by Bruce W. Winter and Andrew D. Clarke. BAFCS 1. Grand Rapids: Eerdmans.

Hedlun, Randall J. 2010. A New Reading of Acts 18:24—19:7: Understanding the Ephesian Disciples Encounter as Social Conflict. *R&T* 17:40-60.

Hedrick, Charles W. 1981. Paul's Conversion/Call: A Comparative Analysis of the Three Reports in Acts. *JBL* 100:415-32.

Heil, John Paul. 1999. *The Meal Scenes in Luke-Acts: An Audience-Oriented Approach.* SBLMS 52. Atlanta: Scholars Press.

Hemer, Colin J. 1990. *The Book of Acts in the Setting of Hellenistic History.* Winona Lake, IN: Eisenbrauns.

Hengel, Martin. 1979. *Acts and the History of Earliest Christianity.* Translated by John Bowden. Philadelphia: Fortress.

Hermann, Johannes, and Werner Foerster. *klēros ktl.* Pages 758-85 in vol. 3 of *TDNT.*

Hill, Craig C. 1992. *Hellenists and Hebrews: Reappraising Division within the Earliest Church.* Minneapolis: Fortress.

Hillard, T. W., Alanna Nobbs, and Bruce W. Winter. 1993. Acts and the Pauline Corpus I: Ancient Literary Parallels. Pages 183-214 in *The Book of Acts in Its Ancient Literary Setting.* Edited by Bruce W. Winter and Andrew D. Clarke. BAFCS 1. Grand Rapids: Eerdmans.

Holladay, Carl R. 1999. Acts and Fragments of Hellenistic Jewish Historians. Pages 171-98 in *Jesus and the Heritage of Israel.* Edited by David P. Moessner. Harrisburg, PA: Trinity Press International.

Horsley, G. H. R. 1986. Speeches and Dialogue in Acts. *NTS* 32:609-14.

Hubbard, Moyer V. 2005. Urban Uprisings in the Roman World: The Social Setting of the Mobbing of Sosthenes. *NTS* 51:416-28.

Humphrey, Edith M. 1995. Collision of Modes?—Vision and Determining Argument in Acts 10:1—11:18. *Semeia* 71:65-84.

Jervell, Jacob. 1972. *Luke and the People of God: A New Look at Luke-Acts.* Minneapolis: Augsburg.

———. 1984. *The Unknown Paul: Essays on Luke-Acts and Early Christian History.* Minneapolis: Augsburg.

———. 1988. The Church of Jews and Godfearers. Pages 11-20 in *Luke-Acts and the Jewish People: Eight Critical Perspectives.* Edited by Joseph B. Tyson. Minneapolis: Augsburg.

———. 1996. *The Theology of the Acts of the Apostles.* Cambridge: Cambridge University Press.

———. 1998. *Die Apostelgeschichte: Übersetzt und erklärt.* KEK. Göttingen: Vandenhoeck & Ruprecht.

Johnson, Luke T. 1977. *The Literary Function of Possessions in Luke-Acts.* SBLDS 39. Missoula, MT: Scholars Press.

———. 1981. *Sharing Possessions: Mandate and Symbol of Faith.* OBT 9. Philadelphia: Fortress.

———. 1992. *The Acts of the Apostles.* SP 5. Collegeville, MN: Liturgical Press.

Jones, Scott J. 1995. *John Wesley's Conception and Use of Scripture.* Nashville: Kingswood Books.

Juel, Donald. 1983. *Luke-Acts: The Promise of History.* Atlanta: John Knox Press.

———. 1992. Hearing Peter's Speech in Acts 3: Meaning and Truth in Interpretation. *WW* 12:43-50.

Kearsley, R. A. 1994. The Asiarchs. Pages 363-76 in *The Book of Acts in Its Graeco-Roman Setting.* Edited by David W. J. Gill and Conrad Gempf. BAFCS 2. Grand Rapids: Eerdmans.

Keck, Leander E., and J. Louis Martyn, eds. 1980. *Studies in Luke-Acts.* Philadelphia: Fortress.

Keener, Craig S. 1993. *The IVP Bible Background Commentary: New Testament.* Downers Grove, IL: InterVarsity Press.

Kennedy, George A. 1980. *Classical Rhetoric and Its Christian and Secular Tradition from Ancient to Modern Times.* Chapel Hill, NC: University of North Carolina Press.

Kilgallen, John J. 1990. Did Peter Actually Fail to Get a Word In? *Bib* 71:405-10.

Kittel, Gerhard, and Gerhard Friedrich, eds. 1964-76. *Theological Dictionary of the New Testament.* 10 vols. Translated by Geoffrey W. Bromiley. Grand Rapids: Eerdmans.

Klauck, Hans-Josef. 2003. *Magic and Paganism in Early Christianity: The World of the Acts of the Apostles.* Translated by Brian McNeil. Minneapolis: Fortress.

Klinghardt, Matthias. 1988. *Gesetz und Volk Gottes: Das lukanische Verständnis des Gesetzes nach Herkunft, Funktion und seinem Ort in der Geschichte des Urchristentums.* WUNT 2, 32. Tübingen: J. C. B. Mohr.

Knox, John. 1942. *Marcion and the New Testament: An Essay in the Early History of the Canon.* Chicago: University of Chicago Press.

———. 1987. *Chapters in a Life of Paul.* Rev. ed. Macon, GA: Mercer University Press.

Kremer, Jacob, ed. 1979. *Les Actes des Apôtres: Traditions, rédaction, théologie.* BETL 48. Leuven: Leuven University Press.

Krodel, Gerhard. 1986. *Acts.* ACNT. Minneapolis: Augsburg.

ACTS

Kurz, William S. 1990. Narrative Models for Imitation in Luke-Acts. Pages 171-89 in *Greeks, Romans, and Christians: Essays in Honor of Abraham J. Malherbe*. Edited by David L. Balch, Everett Ferguson, and Wayne Meeks. Minneapolis: Fortress.

————. 1993. *Reading Luke-Acts: Dynamics of Biblical Narrative*. Louisville, KY: Westminster/John Knox Press.

Lake, Kirsopp. 1933a. The Apostolic Council of Jerusalem. Pages 195-212 in *Additional Notes to the Commentary on Acts*. Edited by Kirsopp Lake and Henry J. Cadbury. The Beginnings of Christianity 5. New York: Macmillan.

————. 1933b. The Communism of Acts II. and IV.-V. and the Appointment of the Seven. Pages 140-51 in *Additional Notes to the Commentary on Acts*. Edited by Kirsopp Lake and Henry J. Cadbury. The Beginnings of Christianity 5. New York: Macmillan.

Lake, Kirsopp, and Henry J. Cadbury, eds. 1933a. *The Acts of the Apostles: English Translation and Commentary*. The Beginnings of Christianity 4. New York: Macmillan.

————. 1933b. The Winds. Pages 338-44 in *Additional Notes to the Commentary on Acts*. Edited by Kirsopp Lake and Henry J. Cadbury. The Beginnings of Christianity 5. New York: Macmillan.

Larkin, William J., Jr. 1995. *Acts*. IVPNTC. Downers Grove, IL: InterVarsity Press.

Leary, T. J. 1992. Paul's Improper Name. *NTS* 38:467-69.

Lentz, John Clayton, Jr. 1993. *Luke's Portrait of Paul*. SNTSMS 77. Cambridge: Cambridge University Press.

Levine, Amy-Jill, ed. 2004. *A Feminist Companion to the Acts of the Apostles*. Cleveland, OH: Pilgrim Press.

Levinskaya, Irina. 1996. *The Book of Acts in Its Diaspora Setting*. BAFCS 5. Grand Rapids: Eerdmans.

Levinsohn, Stephen H. 1987. *Textual Connections in Acts*. SBLMS 31. Atlanta: Scholars Press.

Levison, John R. 2009. *Filled with the Spirit*. Grand Rapids: Eerdmans.

Liddell, Henry George, and Robert Scott. 1996. *A Greek-English Lexicon*. 9th ed. (with revised supplement). Revised by Henry Stuart Jones. Oxford: Clarendon.

Litwak, Kenneth D. 2005. *Echoes of Scripture in Luke-Acts: Telling the History of God's People Intertextually*. JSNTSup 282. New York: T&T Clark.

Lohfink, Gerhard. 1975. *Die Sammlung Israels: Eine Untersuchung zur lukanischen Ekklesiologie*. SANT. Munich: Kösel.

Lohse, Eduard. *prosōpon ktl*. Pages 768-80 in vol. 6 of *TDNT*.

Longenecker, Bruce. 2004. Lukan Aversion to Humps and Hollows: The Case of Acts 11:27—12:25. *NTS* 50:185-204.

Longenecker, Richard N. 1981. The Acts of the Apostles. Pages 205-573 of vol. 9 in *The Expositor's Bible Commentary*. 12 vols. Edited by Frank E. Gaebelein. Grand Rapids: Zondervan.

Löning, Karl. 1990. Das Verhältnis zum Judentum als Identitätsproblem der Kirche nach der Apostelgeschichte. Pages 304-19 in *"Ihr alle aber seid Brüder": Festschrift für A. Th. Khoury zum 60. Geburtstag*. Edited by Ludwig Hagemann and Ernst Pulsfort. Würzburg: Echter.

Lüdemann, Gerd. 1989a. *Early Christianity According to the Traditions in Acts: A Commentary*. Translated by John Bowden. Philadelphia: Fortress.

————. 1989b. *Opposition to Paul in Jewish Christianity*. Translated by M. Eugene Boring. Minneapolis: Fortress.

Lyons, George. 2012. *Galatians: A Commentary in the Wesleyan Tradition*. New Beacon Bible Commentary. Kansas City: Beacon Hill Press of Kansas City.

Lyons, William John. 1997. The Words of Gamaliel (Acts 5.38-39) and the Irony of Indeterminacy. *JSNT* 68:23-49.

MacDonald, Dennis R. 1999. The Shipwrecks of Odysseus and Paul. *NTS* 45:88-107.

————. 2003. Paul's Farewell to the Ephesian Elders and Hector's Farewell to Andromache: A Strategic Imitation of Homer's *Iliad*. Pages 189-203 in *Contextualizing Acts: Lukan Narrative and Greco-Roman Discourse*. Edited by Todd Penner and Caroline Vander Stichele. Atlanta: Society of Biblical Literature.

MacMullen, Ramsey. 1974. *Roman Social Relations: 50 B.C. to A.D. 284*. New Haven, CT: Yale University Press.

Maddox, Randy. 1994. *Responsible Grace: John Wesley's Practical Theology*. Nashville: Kingswood Books.

Maddox, Robert. 1982. *The Purpose of Luke-Acts*. FRLANT 126. Göttingen: Vandenhoeck & Ruprecht.

Malherbe, Abraham J. 1989. *Paul and the Popular Philosophers*. Minneapolis: Fortress.

Malina, Bruce J., and Jerome H. Neyrey. 1991a. Conflict in Luke-Acts: Labelling and Deviance Theory. Pages 97-124 in *The Social World of Luke-Acts: Models for Interpretation*. Edited by Jerome H. Neyrey. Peabody, MA: Hendrickson.

———. 1991b. Honor and Shame in Luke-Acts: Pivotal Values of the Mediterranean World. Pages 25-65 in *The Social World of Luke-Acts: Models for Interpretation*. Edited by Jerome H. Neyrey. Peabody, MA: Hendrickson.

Malina, Bruce J., and John J. Pilch. 2008. *Social-Science Commentary on the Book of Acts*. Minneapolis: Fortress.

Marguerat, Daniel. 1993. La mort d'Ananias et Saphira (Ac 5.1-11) dans la stratégie narrative de Luc. *NTS* 39:209-26.

———. 1999. The Enigma of the Silent Closing of Acts (28:16-31). Pages 284-304 in *Jesus and the Heritage of Israel*. Edited by David P. Moessner. Harrisburg, PA: Trinity Press International.

Marin, Louis. 1970. Essai d'analyse structurale d'Actes 10:1-11:18. *RSR* 58:39-61.

Marshall, I. Howard. 1970. *Luke: Historian and Theologian*. Grand Rapids: Zondervan.

———. 1980. *The Acts of the Apostles*. TNTC. Grand Rapids: Eerdmans.

———. 1998. How Does One Write on the Theology of Acts? Pages 3-16 in *Witness to the Gospel: The Theology of Acts*. Edited by I. Howard Marshall and David Peterson. Grand Rapids: Eerdmans.

Marshall, I. Howard, and David Peterson, eds. 1998. *Witness to the Gospel: The Theology of Acts*. Grand Rapids: Eerdmans.

Martin, Francis, ed. 2006. *Acts*. ACCS. Downers Grove, IL: InterVarsity Press.

Mason, Steve. 1995. Chief Priests, Sadducees, Pharisees and Sanhedrin in Acts. Pages 115-78 in *The Book of Acts in Its Palestinian Setting*. Edited by Richard Bauckham. BAFCS 4. Grand Rapids: Eerdmans.

Matthews, Shelly. 2004. Elite Women, Public Religion, and Christian Propaganda in Acts 16. Pages 111-33 in *A Feminist Companion to the Acts of the Apostles*. Edited by Amy-Jill Levine. Cleveland, OH: Pilgrim Press.

———. 2010. *Perfect Martyr: The Stoning of Stephen and the Construction of Christian Identity*. New York: Oxford University Press.

Mattill, Andrew J., Jr. 1970. The Purpose of Acts: Schneckenburger Reconsidered. Pages 108-22 in *Apostolic History and the Gospel: Biblical and Historical Essays Presented to F. F. Bruce on His 60th Birthday*. Edited by W. Ward Gasque and Ralph P. Martin. Grand Rapids: Eerdmans.

McDonough, Sean M. 2006. Small Change: Saul to Paul, Again. *JBL* 125:390-91.

Mealand, David. 1977. Community of Goods and Utopian Allusions in Acts II-IV. *JTS* 28:96-99.

———. 1989. The Phrase "Many Proofs" in Acts 1,3 and in Hellenistic Writers. *ZNW* 80:134-35.

———. 1990. The Close of Acts and Its Hellenistic Greek Vocabulary. *NTS* 36:583-97.

Metzger, Bruce M. 1994. *A Textual Commentary on the Greek New Testament*. 2nd ed. New York: United Bible Societies.

Michaelis, Wilhelm. *procheirizō*. Pages 862-64 in vol. 6 of *TDNT*.

Miles, Gary B., and Garry W. Trompf. 1976. Luke and Antiphon: The Theology of Acts 27-28 in the Light of Pagan Beliefs about Divine Retribution, Pollution, and Shipwreck. *HTR* 69:259-67.

Mitchell, Alan C. 1992. The Social Function of Friendship in Acts 2:44-47 and 4:32-37. *JBL* 111:255-72.

Moessner, David P. 1988. Paul in Acts: Preacher of Eschatological Repentance to Israel. *NTS* 34:96-104.

———, ed. 1999. *Jesus and the Heritage of Israel: Luke's Narrative Claim upon Israel's Legacy*. Harrisburg, PA: Trinity Press International.

Moule, C. F. D. 1980. The Christology of Acts. Pages 159-85 in *Studies in Luke-Acts*. Edited by Leander E. Keck and J. Louis Martyn. Philadelphia: Fortress.

Moxnes, Halvor. 1991. Patron-Client Relations and the New Community in Luke-Acts. Pages 241-68 in *The Social World of Luke-Acts: Models for Interpretation*. Edited by Jerome H. Neyrey. Peabody, MA: Hendrickson.

Munck, Johannes. 1967. *The Acts of the Apostles*. AB 31. Garden City, NY: Doubleday.

Neale, David A. 2011. *Luke 1—9: A Commentary in the Wesleyan Tradition*. New Beacon Bible Commentary. Kansas City: Beacon Hill Press of Kansas City.

Neil, William. 1973. *Acts*. NCB. Grand Rapids: Eerdmans.

Neyrey, Jerome H. 1990. Acts 17, Epicureans, and Theodicy: A Study in Stereotypes. Pages 118-34 in *Greeks, Romans, and Christians: Essays in Honor of Abraham J. Malherbe*. Edited by David L. Balch, Everett Ferguson, and Wayne A. Meeks. Minneapolis: Fortress.

————. 1991a. Ceremonies in Luke-Acts: The Case of Meals and Table-Fellowship. Pages 361-87 in *The Social World of Luke-Acts: Models for Interpretation*. Edited by Jerome H. Neyrey. Peabody, MA: Hendrickson.

————, ed. 1991b. *The Social World of Luke-Acts: Models for Interpretation*. Peabody, MA: Hendrickson.

Nolland, John. 1980. A Fresh Look at Acts 15.10. *NTS* 27:105-15.

Novick, Tzvi. 2010. Succeeding Judas: Exegesis in Acts 1:15-26. *JBL* 129:795-99.

Oakes, Peter. 2009. *Reading Romans in Pompeii: Paul's Letter at Ground Level*. Minneapolis: Fortress.

Oropeza, B. J. 2011. *In the Footsteps of Judas and Other Defectors: The Gospels, Acts, and Johannine Letters*. Apostasy in the New Testament Communities. Eugene, OR: Cascade.

Oster, Richard. 1976. The Ephesian Artemis as an Opponent of Early Christianity. *JAC* 19:24-44.

O'Toole, R. F. 1977. Why Did Luke Write Acts (Lk-Acts)? *BTB* 7:66-76.

————. 1993. Parallels between Jesus and His Disciples in Luke-Acts: A Further Study. *BZ* 27:195-212.

Painter, John. 2004. *Just James: The Brother of Jesus in History and Tradition*. 2nd ed. Studies on Personalities of the New Testament. Columbia, SC: University of South Carolina Press.

Palmer, Darryl W. 1987. The Literary Background of Acts 1.1-14. *NTS* 33:427-38.

————. 1993. Acts and the Ancient Historical Monograph. Pages 1-30 in *The Book of Acts in Its Ancient Literary Setting*. Edited by Bruce W. Winter and Andrew D. Clarke. BAFCS 1. Grand Rapids: Eerdmans.

Panagopoulos, Johannes. 1972. Zur Theologie der Apostelgeschichte. *NovT* 14:137-59.

Pao, David W. 2011. Waiters or Preachers: Acts 6:1-7 and the Lukan Table Fellowship Motif. *JBL* 130:127-34.

Parker, Pierson. 1964. Three Variant Readings in Luke-Acts. *JBL* 64:165-70.

Parsons, Mikeal C. 1998. The Place of Jerusalem on the Lukan Landscape: An Exercise in Symbolic Cartography. Pages 155-72 in *Literary Studies in Luke-Acts: Essays in Honor of Joseph B. Tyson*. Edited by Richard P. Thompson and Thomas E. Phillips. Macon, GA: Mercer University Press.

————. 2006. *Body and Character in Luke and Acts: The Subversion of Physiognomy in Early Christianity*. Grand Rapids: Baker Academic.

————. 2008. *Acts*. PCNT. Grand Rapids: Baker Academic.

Parsons, Mikeal C., and Richard I. Pervo. 1993. *Rethinking the Unity of Luke and Acts*. Minneapolis: Fortress.

Parsons, Mikeal C., and Joseph B. Tyson, eds. 1992. *Cadbury, Knox, and Talbert: American Contributions to the Study of Acts*. Atlanta: Scholars Press.

Penner, Todd. 2003. Civilizing Discourse: Acts, Declamation, and the Rhetoric of the *Polis*. Pages 65-104 in *Contextualizing Acts: Lukan Narrative and Greco-Roman Discourse*. Edited by Todd Penner and Caroline Vander Stichele. SBLSymS 20. Atlanta: Society of Biblical Literature.

Penner, Todd, and Caroline Vander Stichele, eds. 2003. *Contextualizing Acts: Lukan Narrative and Greco-Roman Discourse*. SBLSymS 20. Atlanta: Scholars Press.

Perrot, Charles. 1981. Les décisions de l'assemblée de Jérusalem. *RSR* 69:195-208.

Pervo, Richard I. 1987. *Profit with Delight: The Literary Genre of the Acts of the Apostles*. Philadelphia: Fortress.

————. 1990. *Luke's Story of Paul*. Minneapolis: Fortress.

————. 2006. *Dating Acts: Between the Evangelists and the Apologists*. Santa Rosa, CA: Polebridge Press.

————. 2009. *Acts: A Commentary*. Hermeneia. Minneapolis: Fortress.

Pesch, Rudolf. 1986. *Die Apostelgeschichte*. 2 vols. EKKNT 5. Zürich: Neukirchener Verlag.

Peterson, David G. 1993. The Motif of Fulfilment and the Purpose of Luke-Acts. Pages 83-104 in *The Book of Acts in Its Ancient Literary Setting*. Edited by Bruce W. Winter and Andrew D. Clarke. BAFCS 1. Grand Rapids: Eerdmans.

————. 1998. The Worship of the New Community. Pages 373-96 in *Witness to the Gospel: The Theology of Acts*. Edited by I. Howard Marshall and David Peterson. Grand Rapids: Eerdmans.

————. 2009. *The Acts of the Apostles*. PiNTC. Grand Rapids: Eerdmans.

Phillips, Thomas E., ed. 2005a. *Acts and Ethics*. New Testament Monographs. Sheffield: Sheffield Phoenix.

————. 2005b. Paul as a Role Model in Acts: The 'We'-Passages in Acts 16 and Beyond. Pages 49-63 in *Acts and Ethics*. Edited by Thomas E. Phillips. New Testament Monographs. Sheffield: Sheffield Phoenix.

———. 2006. The Genre of Acts: Moving toward a Consensus? *Currents in Biblical Research* 4:365-96.

———. 2009. *Paul, His Letters, and Acts.* LPS. Peabody, MA: Hendrickson.

Plümacher, Eckhard. 1972. *Lukas als hellenistischer Schriftsteller: Studien zur Apostelgeschichte.* SUNT. Göttingen: Vandenhoeck & Ruprecht.

———. 1979. Die Apostelgeschichte als historische Monographie. Pages 457-66 in *Les Actes des Apôtres: Traditions, rédaction, théologie.* Edited by Jacob Kremer. BETL 48. Leuven: Leuven University Press.

Polhill, John B. 1992. *Acts.* NAC. Nashville: Broadman and Holman.

Poque, Suzanne. 1980. Une lecture d'Actes 11/27-12/25. *ETR* 55:271-78.

Porter, Stanley E. 2001. *Paul in Acts.* LPS. Peabody, MA: Hendrickson.

Powell, Mark Allan. 1991. *What Are They Saying about Acts?* New York: Paulist Press.

Praeder, Susan M. 1981. Luke-Acts and the Ancient Novel. Pages 269-92 in *SBLPS* (1981). Edited by Kent Harold Richards. Missoula, MT: Scholars Press.

———. 1984. Acts 27:1—28:16: Sea Voyages in Ancient Literature and the Theology of Luke-Acts. *CBQ* 46:683-706.

———. 1987. The Problem of First Person Narration in Acts. *NovT* 29:193-218.

Preisker, Herbert. *epieikeia ktl.* Pages 588-90 in vol. 2 of *TDNT.*

Radl, Walter. 1975. *Paulus und Jesus im lukanischen Doppelwerk: Untersuchungen zu Parallelmotiven im Lukasevangelium und in der Apostelgeschichte.* Europäische Hochschulschriften. Frankfurt: Peter Lang.

Ramsay, William M. 1895. *St. Paul the Traveller and the Roman Citizen.* London: Hodder & Stoughton.

Rapske, Brian M. 1994a. Acts, Travel and Shipwreck. Pages 1-47 in *The Book of Acts in Its Graeco-Roman Setting.* Edited by David W. J. Gill and Conrad Gempf. BAFCS 2. Grand Rapids: Eerdmans.

———. 1994b. *The Book of Acts and Paul in Roman Custody.* BAFCS 3. Grand Rapids: Eerdmans.

———. 1998. Opposition to the Plan of God and Persecution. Pages 235-56 in *Witness to the Gospel: The Theology of Acts.* Edited by I. Howard Marshall and David Peterson. Grand Rapids: Eerdmans.

Reid, Barbara E. 2004. The Power of the Widows and How to Suppress It (Acts 6:1-7). Pages 71-88 in *A Feminist Companion to the Acts of the Apostles.* Edited by Amy-Jill Levine. Cleveland, OH: Pilgrim Press.

Reimer, Ivoni Richter. 1995. *Women in the Acts of the Apostles: A Feminist Liberation Perspective.* Translated by Linda M. Maloney. Minneapolis: Fortress.

Reinhardt, Wolfgang. 1995. The Population Size of Jerusalem and the Numerical Growth of the Jerusalem Church. Pages 235-66 in *The Book of Acts in Its Palestinian Setting.* Edited by Richard Bauckham. BAFCS 4. Grand Rapids: Eerdmans.

Richard, Earl. 1978. *Acts 6:1-8:4: The Author's Method of Composition.* SBLDS 41. Missoula, MT: Scholars Press.

———. 1984. The Divine Purpose: The Jews and the Gentile Mission (Acts 15). Pages 188-209 in *Luke-Acts: New Perspectives from the Society of Biblical Literature Seminar.* Edited by Charles H. Talbert. New York: Crossroad.

Riesner, Rainer. 1994. James's Speech (Acts 15:13-21), Simeon's Hymn (Luke 2:29-32) and Luke's Sources. Pages 263-78 in *Jesus of Nazareth: Lord and Christ.* Edited by Joel B. Green and Max Turner. Grand Rapids: Eerdmans.

———. 1995. Synagogues in Jerusalem. Pages 179-210 in *The Book of Acts in Its Palestinian Setting.* Edited by Richard Bauckham. BAFCS 4. Grand Rapids: Eerdmans.

Robbins, Vernon K. 1999. The Claims of the Prologues and Greco-Roman Rhetoric: The Prefaces to Luke and Acts in Light of Greco-Roman Rhetorical Strategies. Pages 63-83 in *Jesus and the Heritage of Israel.* Edited by David P. Moessner. Harrisburg, PA: Trinity Press International.

Roloff, Jürgen. 1981. *Die Apostelgeschichte.* NTD 5. Göttingen: Vandenhoeck & Ruprecht.

Rosner, Brian S. 1993. Acts and Biblical History. Pages 65-82 in *The Book of Acts in Its Ancient Literary Setting.* Edited by Bruce W. Winter and Andrew D. Clarke. BAFCS 1. Grand Rapids: Eerdmans.

———. 1998. The Progress of the Word. Pages 215-34 in *Witness to the Gospel: The Theology of Acts.* Edited by I. Howard Marshall and David Peterson. Grand Rapids: Eerdmans.

Rowe, C. Kavin. 2007. Acts 2.36 and the Continuity of Lukan Christology. *NTS* 53:37-56.

———. 2009. *World Upside Down: Reading Acts in the Graeco-Roman Age.* New York: Oxford University Press.

————. 2010. History, Hermeneutics, and the Unity of Luke-Acts. Pages 43-65 in *Rethinking the Unity and Reception of Luke and Acts*. Edited by Andrew F. Gregory and C. Kavin Rowe. Columbia, SC: University of South Carolina Press.

————. 2011. The Grammar of Truth: The Areopagus Speech and Pagan Tradition. *NTS* 57:31-50.

Sakenfeld, Katharine Doob, et al., eds. 2006-9. *New Interpreter's Dictionary of the Bible*. 5 vols. Nashville: Abingdon.

Salmon, Marilyn. 1988. Insider or Outsider? Luke's Relationship with Judaism. Pages 76-82 in *Luke-Acts and the Jewish People: Eight Critical Perspectives*. Edited by Joseph B. Tyson. Minneapolis: Augsburg.

Sanders, Jack T. 1987. *The Jews in Luke-Acts*. Philadelphia: Fortress.

————. 1991. Who Is a Jew and Who Is a Gentile in the Book of Acts? *NTS* 37:434-55.

Sandnes, Karl Olav. 1993. Paul and Socrates: The Aim of Paul's Areopagus Speech. *JSNT* 50:13-26.

Sasse, Hermann. *kosmeō ktl*. Pages 867-98 in vol. 3 of *TDNT*.

Satterthwaite, Philip E. 1993. Acts against the Background of Classical Rhetoric. Pages 337-80 in *The Book of Acts in Its Ancient Literary Setting*. Edited by Bruce W. Winter and Andrew D. Clarke. BAFCS 1. Grand Rapids: Eerdmans.

Schaeder, Hans Heinrich. *Nazarēnos ktl*. Pages 874-79 in vol. 4 of *TDNT*.

Schille, Gottfried. 1979. *Das älteste Paulus-Bild: Beobachtungen zur lukanischen und zur deuteropaulinischen Paulus-Darstellung*. Berlin: Evangelische Verlagsanstalt.

————. 1983. *Die Apostelgeschichte des Lukas*. THKNT 5. Berlin: Evangelische Verlagsanstalt.

Schlatter, Adolf. 1948. *Die Apostelgeschichte*. Erläuterungen zum Neuen Testament. Stuttgart: Calwer Verlag.

Schlier, Heinrich. *anechō ktl*. Page 359 in vol. 1 of *TDNT*.

Schmidt, Daryl. 1985. The Historiography of Acts: Deuteronomistic or Hellenistic? Pages 417-27 in *SBLSP* (1985). Edited by Kent Harold Richards. Atlanta: Scholars Press.

Schmithals, Walter. 1982. *Die Apostelgeschichte des Lukas*. ZBK. Zürich: Theologischer Verlag.

Schnabel, Eckhard J. 2005. Contextualising Paul in Athens: The Proclamation of the Gospel before Pagan Audiences in the Graeco-Roman World. *R&T* 12:172-90.

————. 2012. *Acts*. ZECNT. Grand Rapids: Zondervan.

Schneider, Gerhard. 1980. *Die Apostelgeschichte 1-8*. HTKNT 5. Freiburg: Herder.

————. 1982. *Die Apostelgeschichte 9-28*. HTKNT 5. Freiburg: Herder.

————. 1985. *Lukas, Theologe der Heilsgeschichte: Aufsätze zum lukanischen Doppelwerk*. BBB 59. Königstein: Peter Hanstein.

Schottroff, Luise. 1993. *Let the Oppressed Go Free: Feminist Perspectives on the New Testament*. Translated by Annemarie S. Kidder. Gender and the Biblical Tradition. Louisville, KY: Westminster/John Knox Press.

Schrenk, Gottlieb. *dikē ktl*. Pages 174-225 of vol. 2 of *TDNT*.

Schwartz, Daniel R. 1983. Non-Joining Sympathizers (Acts 5, 13-14). *Bib* 64:550-55.

————. 1990. The End of the Line: Paul in the Canonical Book of Acts. Pages 3-24 in *Paul and the Legacies of Paul*. Edited by William S. Babcock. Dallas: Southern Methodist University Press.

Schwartz, Saundra. 2003. The Trial Scene in the Greek Novels and in Acts. Pages 105-37 in *Contextualizing Acts: Lukan Narrative and Greco-Roman Discourse*. Edited by Todd Penner and Caroline Vander Stichele. Atlanta: Society of Biblical Literature.

Schweizer, Eduard. 1980. Concerning the Speeches in Acts. Pages 208-16 in *Studies in Luke-Acts*. Edited by Leander E. Keck and J. Louis Martyn. Philadelphia: Fortress.

Scott, J. Julius, Jr. 1991. The Cornelius Incident in the Light of Its Jewish Setting. *JETS* 34:475-84.

Seccombe, David. 1998. The New People of God. Pages 349-72 in *Witness to the Gospel: The Theology of Acts*. Edited by I. Howard Marshall and David Peterson. Grand Rapids: Eerdmans.

Seifrid, M. A. 1987. Jesus and the Law in Acts. *JSNT* 30:39-57.

Seim, Turid Karlsen. 1994. *The Double Message: Patterns of Gender in Luke and Acts*. Nashville: Abingdon.

Shauf, Scott. 2009. Locating the Eunuch: Characterization and Narrative Context in Acts 8:26-40. *CBQ* 71:762-75.

Sheeley, Steven M. 1988. Narrative Asides and Narrative Authority in Luke-Acts. *BTB* 18:102-7.

————. 1992. *Narrative Asides in Luke-Acts*. JSNTSup 72. Sheffield: JSOT Press.

Shepherd, William H., Jr. 1994. *The Narrative Function of the Holy Spirit as a Character in Luke-Acts*. SBLDS 147. Atlanta: Scholars Press.

Sherwin-White, A. N. 1963. *Roman Society and Roman Law in the New Testament*. Oxford: Clarendon.

Skinner, Matthew L. 2003. *Locating Paul: Places of Custody as Narratives Settings in Acts 21-28.* Academica Biblica. Atlanta: Society of Biblical Literature.

Slingerland, Dixon. 1986. The Jews in the Pauline Portion of Acts. *JAAR* 54:305-21.

———. 1991. Acts 18:1-18, the Gallio Inscription, and Absolute Pauline Chronology. *JBL* 110:439-49.

Smyth, Herbert Weir. 1956. *Greek Grammar.* Cambridge, MA: Harvard University Press.

Soards, Marion L. 1994. *The Speeches in Acts: Their Content, Context, and Concerns.* Louisville, KY: Westminster/John Knox.

Spencer, F. Scott. 1992. The Ethiopian Eunuch and His Bible: A Social-Science Analysis. *BTB* 22:155-65.

———. 1994. Neglected Widows in Acts 6:1-7. *CBQ* 56:715-33.

———. 2004a. *Journeying through Acts: A Literary-Cultural Reading.* Peabody, MA: Hendrickson.

———. 2004b. Women of "the Cloth" in Acts: Sewing the Word. Pages 134-54 in *A Feminist Companion to the Acts of the Apostles.* Edited by Amy-Jill Levine. Cleveland, OH: Pilgrim Press.

———. 2011. Scared to Death: The Rhetoric of Fear in the 'Tragedy' of Ananias and Sapphira. Pages 63-80 in *Reading Acts Today: Essays in Honour of Loveday C. A. Alexander.* Edited by Thomas E. Phillips, Steve Walton, Lloyd Keith Pietersen, and F. Scott Spencer. London: T&T Clark.

Squires, John T. 1993. *The Plan of God in Luke-Acts.* SNTSMS 76. Cambridge: Cambridge University Press.

———. 1998. The Plan of God. Pages 19-40 in *Witness to the Gospel: The Theology of Acts.* Edited by I. Howard Marshall and David Peterson. Grand Rapids: Eerdmans.

Stegemann, Wolfgang. 1991. *Zwischen Synagoge und Obrigkeit: Zur historischen Situation der lukanischen Christen.* FRLANT. Göttingen: Vandenhoeck & Ruprecht.

Sterling, Gregory E. 1992. *Historiography and Self-Definition: Josephus, Luke-Acts and Apologetic Historiography.* Leiden: Brill.

———. 1994. "Athletes of Virtue": An Analysis of the Summaries in Acts (2:41-47; 4:32-35; 5:12-16). *JBL* 113:679-96.

Stoops, Robert F., Jr. 1989. Riot and Assembly: The Social Context of Acts 19:23-41. *JBL* 108:73-91.

Strelan, Rick. 2000. Recognizing the Gods (Acts 14:8-10). *NTS* 46:588-603.

———. 2001. The Running Prophet (Acts 8:30). *NovT* 43:31-38.

———. 2003. Acts 19:12: Paul's "Aprons" Again. *JTS* 54:154-57.

Stumpff, Albrecht. *zēlos ktl.* Pages 877-88 of vol. 2 of *TDNT.*

Sweeney, Michael L. 1995. The Identity of "They" in Acts 2.1. *BT* 46:245-48.

Tajra, Harry W. 1989. *The Trial of St. Paul: A Juridical Exegesis of the Second Half of the Acts of the Apostles.* WUNT 2, 35. Tübingen: Mohr.

Talbert, Charles H. 1974. *Literary Patterns, Theological Themes, and the Genre of Luke-Acts.* SBLMS 20. Missoula, MT: Scholars Press.

———, ed. 1984. *Luke-Acts: New Perspectives from the Society of Biblical Literature Seminar.* New York: Crossroad.

———. 1997. *Reading Acts: A Literary and Theological Commentary on the Acts of the Apostles.* Reading the New Testament. New York: Crossroad.

Tannehill, Robert C. 1985. Israel in Luke-Acts: A Tragic Story. *JBL* 104:69-85.

———. 1988. Rejection by Jews and Turning to Gentiles: The Pattern of Paul's Mission in Acts. Pages 83-101 in *Luke-Acts and the Jewish People: Eight Critical Perspectives.* Edited by Joseph B. Tyson. Minneapolis: Augsburg.

———. 1990. *The Narrative Unity of Luke-Acts: A Literary Interpretation. Volume 2: The Acts of the Apostles.* Minneapolis: Fortress.

———. 1991. The Functions of Peter's Mission Speeches in the Narrative of Acts. *NTS* 37:400-14.

———. 1996. *Luke.* ANTC. Nashville: Abingdon.

Taylor, Lily Ross. 1933. The Asiarchs. Pages 256-62 in *Additional Notes to the Commentary on Acts.* Edited by Kirsopp Lake and Henry J. Cadbury. The Beginnings of Christianity 5. London: Macmillan.

Thompson, Richard P. 1998. Believers and Religious Leaders in Jerusalem: Contrasting Portraits of Jews in Acts 1-7. Pages 327-44 in *Literary Studies in Luke-Acts: Essays in Honor of Joseph B. Tyson.* Edited by Richard P. Thompson and Thomas E. Phillips. Macon, GA: Mercer University Press.

———. 2000. "Say It Ain't So, Paul!": The Accusations against Paul in Acts 21 in the Light of His Ministry in Acts 16-20. *BR* 45:34-50.

———. 2004. Inspired Imagination: John Wesley's Concept of Biblical Inspiration and Literary-Critical Studies. Pages 57-79 in *Reading the Bible in Wesleyan Ways: Some Constructive Proposals*. Edited by Barry L. Callen and Richard P. Thompson. Kansas City: Beacon Hill Press of Kansas City.

———. 2005. "What Do You Think You Are Doing, Paul?" Synagogues, Ministry, and Ethics in Acts 16—21. Pages 64-78 in *Acts and Ethics*. Edited by Thomas E. Phillips. Sheffield: Sheffield Phoenix.

———. 2006. *Keeping the Church in Its Place: The Church as Narrative Character in Acts*. New York: T&T Clark.

———. 2007. Gathered at the Table: Holiness and Ecclesiology in the Gospel of Luke. Pages 76-94 in *Holiness and Ecclesiology in the New Testament*. Edited by Kent E. Brower and Andy Johnson. Grand Rapids: Eerdmans.

———. 2013. Living Words: Reading the Bible as Scripture. Pages 121-30 in *Missional Discipleship: Partners in God's Redemptive Mission*. Edited by Mark A. Maddix and Jay Richard Akkerman. Kansas City: Beacon Hill Press of Kansas City.

Thompson, Richard P., and Thomas E. Phillips, eds. 1998. *Literary Studies in Luke-Acts: Essays in Honor of Joseph B. Tyson*. Macon, GA: Mercer University Press.

Tiede, David L. 1988a. Acts 11:1-18. *Int* 42:175-79.

———. 1988b. "Glory to Thy People Israel": Luke-Acts and the Jews. Pages 21-34 in *Luke-Acts and the Jewish People: Eight Critical Perspectives*. Edited by Joseph B. Tyson. Minneapolis: Augsburg.

Towner, Philip H. 1998. Mission Practice and Theology under Construction (Acts 18-20). Pages 417-36 in *Witness to the Gospel: The Theology of Acts*. Edited by I. Howard Marshall and David Peterson. Grand Rapids: Eerdmans.

Trebilco, Paul R. 1989. Paul and Silas—"Servants of the Most High God" (Acts 16:16-18). *JSNT* 36:51-73.

———. 1994. Asia. Pages 291-362 in *The Book of Acts in Its Graeco-Roman Setting*. Edited by David W. J. Gill and Conrad Gempf. BAFCS 2. Grand Rapids: Eerdmans.

Trobisch, David. 2010. The Book of Acts as a Narrative Commentary on the Letters of the New Testament: A Programmatic Essay. Pages 119-27 in *Rethinking the Unity and Reception of Luke and Acts*. Edited by Andrew F. Gregory and C. Kavin Rowe. Columbia, SC: University of South Carolina Press.

Turner, Max. 1992. The Spirit of Prophecy and the Power of Authoritative Preaching in Luke-Acts: A Question of Origins. *NTS* 38:66-88.

———. 1998. The "Spirit of Prophecy" as the Power of Israel's Restoration and Witness. Pages 327-48 in *Witness to the Gospel: The Theology of Acts*. Edited by I. Howard Marshall and David Peterson. Grand Rapids: Eerdmans.

Twelftree, Graham H. 2009. *People of the Spirit: Exploring Luke's View of the Church*. Grand Rapids: Baker Academic.

Tyson, Joseph B. 1983. Acts 6:1-7 and Dietary Regulations in Early Christianity. *PerRS* 10:145-61.

———. 1984. The Jewish Public in Luke-Acts. *NTS* 30:574-83.

———. 1988a. The Emerging Church and the Problem of Authority in Acts. *Int* 42:132-45.

———, ed. 1988b. *Luke-Acts and the Jewish People: Eight Critical Perspectives*. Minneapolis: Augsburg.

———. 1988c. The Problem of Jewish Rejection in Acts. Pages 124-37 in *Luke-Acts and the Jewish People: Eight Critical Perspectives*. Edited by Joseph B. Tyson. Minneapolis: Augsburg.

———. 1992. *Images of Judaism in Luke-Acts*. Columbia, SC: University of South Carolina Press.

———. 1995. Jews and Judaism in Luke-Acts: Reading as a Godfearer. *NTS* 41:19-38.

———. 2006. *Marcion and Luke-Acts: A Defining Struggle*. Columbia, SC: University of South Carolina Press.

van der Horst, Pieter W. 1983. Hellenistic Parallels to the Acts of the Apostles: 1,1-26. *ZNW* 74:16-26.

———. 1985. Hellenistic Parallels to the Acts of the Apostles (2.1-47). *JSNT* 25:49-60.

———. 1989. Hellenistic Parallels to Acts (Chapters 3 and 4). *JSNT* 35:37-46.

———. 1994. The Altar of the "Unknown God" in Athens (Acts 17.23) and the Cults of "Unknown Gods" in the Graeco-Roman World. Pages 165-202 in *Hellenism, Judaism, Christianity: Essays on Their Interaction*. Edited by Pieter W. van der Horst. Kampen: Kok Paros.

van de Sandt, Huub. 1992. An Explanation of Acts 15.6-21 in the Light of Deuteronomy 4.29-35 (LXX). *JSNT* 46:73-97.

van Unnik, W. C. 1962. *Tarsus or Jerusalem: The City of Paul's Youth*. London: Epworth.

———. 1979. Luke's Second Book and the Rules of Hellenistic Historiography. Pages 37-60 in *Les Actes des Apôtres: Traditions, rédaction, théologie*. Edited by Jacob Kremer. BETL 48. Leuven: Leuven University Press.

Vielhauer, Philipp. 1980. On the 'Paulinism' of Acts. Pages 33-50 in *Studies in Luke-Acts*. Edited by Leander E. Keck and J. Louis Martyn. Philadelphia: Fortress.

Viviano, Benedict T., and Justin Taylor. 1992. Sadducees, Angels, and Resurrection (Acts 23:8-9). *JBL* 111:496-98.

Wagner, J. Ross, C. Kavin Rowe, and A. Katherine Grieb, eds. 2008. *The Word Leaps the Gap: Essays on Scripture and Theology in Honor of Richard B. Hays*. Grand Rapids: Eerdmans.

Walker, William O., Jr. 1998. Acts and the Pauline Corpus Revisited: Peter's Speech at the Jerusalem Conference. Pages 77-86 in *Literary Studies in Luke-Acts: Essays in Honor of Joseph B. Tyson*. Edited by Richard P. Thompson and Thomas E. Phillips. Macon, GA: Mercer University Press.

Wall, Robert W. Conscience. Pages 1128-30 in vol. 1 of *ABD*.

———. 1991. Successors to "the Twelve" According to Acts 12:1-17. *CBQ* 53:628-43.

———. 2000. The Function of LXX Habakkuk 1:5 in the Book of Acts. *BBR* 10:247-58.

———. 2002. The Acts of the Apostles: Introduction, Commentary, and Reflections. Pages 3-368 of vol. 10 in *New Interpreter's Bible*. 12 vols. Edited by Leander Keck. Nashville: Abingdon.

———. 2004a. Facilitating Scripture's Future Role among Wesleyans. Pages 107-20 in *Reading the Bible in Wesleyan Ways: Some Constructive Proposals*. Edited by Barry L. Callen and Richard P. Thompson. Kansas City: Beacon Hill Press of Kansas City.

———. 2004b. Toward a Wesleyan Hermeneutic. Pages 39-55 in *Reading the Bible in Wesleyan Ways: Some Constructive Proposals*. Edited by Barry L. Callen and Richard P. Thompson. Kansas City: Beacon Hill Press of Kansas City.

Walter, Nikolaus. 1983. Apostelgeschichte 6.1 und die Anfänge der Urgemeinde in Jerusalem. *NTS* 29:370-93.

Walton, Steve. 2000. *Leadership and Lifestyle: The Portrait of Paul in the Miletus Speech and 1 Thessalonians*. SNTSMS 108. Cambridge: Cambridge University Press.

Wedderburn, A. J. M. 1993. The "Apostolic Decree": Tradition and Redaction. *NovT* 35:362-89.

———. 1994. Traditions and Redaction in Acts 2:1-13. *JSNT* 55:27-54.

———. 2002. The 'We'-Passages in Acts: On the Horns of a Dilemma. *ZNW* 93:78-98.

Weiser, Alfons. 1984. Das "Apostelkonzil" (Apg 15,1-35): Ereignis, Überlieferung, lukanische Deutung. *BZ* 28:145-67.

———. 1986. *Die Apostelgeschichte*. 2 vols. OTNT. Würzburg: Echter.

Wenham, David. 1993. Acts and the Pauline Corpus. Pages 215-58 in *The Book of Acts in Its Ancient Literary Setting*. Edited by Bruce W. Winter and Andrew D. Clarke. BAFCS 1. Grand Rapids: Eerdmans.

Wesley, John. 1958. *Explanatory Notes upon the New Testament*. Naperville, IL: Allenson.

———. 1984. "Preface to *Sermons on Several Occasions*." Pages 103-8 in *Sermons I, 1-33*. Edited by Albert C. Outler. *The Works of John Wesley* (Bicentennial Ed.). Nashville: Abingdon.

Wilcox, Max. 1981. The "God-Fearers" in Acts—A Reconsideration. *JSNT* 13:102-22.

Williams, David John. 1990. *Acts*. NIBC 5. Peabody, MA: Hendrickson.

Wills, Lawrence M. 1991. The Depiction of the Jews in Acts. *JBL* 110:631-54.

Wilson, Stephen G. 1973. *The Gentiles and the Gentile Mission in Luke-Acts*. SNTSMS 23. Cambridge: Cambridge University Press.

———. 1979. *Luke and the Pastoral Epistles*. London: SPCK.

———. 1983. *Luke and the Law*. SNTSMS 50. Cambridge: Cambridge University Press.

Windisch, Hans. askeō. Pages 494-96 in vol. 1 of *TDNT*.

Winter, Bruce W. 1991. The Importance of the *Captatio Benevolentiae* in the Speeches of Tertullus and Paul in Acts 24:1-21. *JTS* 42:505-31.

———. 1993. Official Proceedings and the Forensic Speeches in Acts 24-26. Pages 305-36 in *The Book of Acts in Its Ancient Literary Setting*. Edited by Bruce W. Winter and Andrew D. Clarke. BAFCS 1. Grand Rapids: Eerdmans.

———. 1994. Acts and Food Shortages. Pages 59-78 in *The Book of Acts in Its Graeco-Roman Setting*. Edited by David W. J. Gill and Conrad Gempf. BAFCS 2. Grand Rapids: Eerdmans.

———. 1996. On Introducing Gods to Athens: An Alternative Reading of Acts 17:18-20. *TynBul* 47:71-90.

———. 1999. Gallio's Ruling on the Legal Status of Early Christianity (Acts 18:14-15). *TynBul* 50:213-24.

———. 2006. Rehabilitating Gallio and His Judgement in Acts 18:14-15. *TynBul* 52:291-308.

———. 2007. Carnal Conduct and Sanctification in 1 Corinthians: *Simul sanctus et peccator?* Pages 184-200 in *Holiness and Ecclesiology in the New Testament*. Edited by Kent E. Brower and Andy Johnson. Grand Rapids: Eerdmans.

Winter, Bruce W., and Andrew D. Clarke, eds. 1993. *The Book of Acts in Its Ancient Literary Setting*. BAFCS 1. Grand Rapids: Eerdmans.

Witherington, Ben, III. 1998. *The Acts of the Apostles: A Socio-Rhetorical Commentary*. Grand Rapids: Eerdmans.

Witherup, Ronald D. 1992. Functional Redundancy in the Acts of the Apostles: A Case Study. *JSNT* 48:67-86.

———. 1993. Cornelius Over and Over and Over Again: 'Functional Redundancy' in the Acts of the Apostles. *JSNT* 49:45-66.

Wordelman, Amy L. 2003. The Jerusalem Community in Acts: Mythmaking and the Sociorhetorical Functions of a Lukan Setting. Pages 205-32 in *Contextualizing Acts: Lukan Narrative and Greco-Roman Discourse*. Edited by Todd Penner and Caroline Vander Stichele. Atlanta: Society of Biblical Literature.

Wright, N. T. 2003. *The Resurrection of the Son of God*. Christian Origins and the Question of God 3. Minneapolis: Fortress.

Wycherley, R. E. 1968. St. Paul at Athens. *JTS* 19:619-21.

Zettner, Christoph. 1991. *Amt, Gemeinde und kirchliche Einheit in der Apostelgeschichte des Lukas*. New York: Peter Lang.

Ziesler, J. A. 1979. Luke and the Pharisees. *NTS* 25:146-57.

Zingg, Paul. 1974. *Das Wachsen der Kirche: Beiträge zur Frage der lukanischen Redaktion und Theologie*. OBO. Göttingen: Vandenhoeck & Ruprecht.

Zweck, Dean W. 1989. The Exordium of the Areopagus Speech: Acts 17:22, 23. *NTS* 35:94-103.

TABLE OF SIDEBARS

ACTS

ACTS

INTRODUCTION

The book of Acts, also known as the Acts of the Apostles, has had a variety of literary (and interpretive) "companions" since it first appeared. The book circulated before the creation of the NT canon, associated with the collection of General Epistles. Later, because it preceded the Pauline corpus, it often functioned as its historical introduction.

Because of a common addressee and other extensive similarities (vocabulary, style, characterization, themes, etc.) between the Gospel of Luke and the book of Acts, the use of the title "Luke-Acts" reflects a contemporary consensus about these two books: they were originally a single literary work of two separate volumes (see Cadbury 1927). This view has been assumed for nearly a century, despite their separation in the Bible and the lack of any extant MSS or canonical list that explicitly connects them.

External evidence of early usage indicates that the books were read separately (see, e.g., Gregory 2003; Rowe 2010, 43-65). The two texts deal with divergent materials: the Gospel of Luke depicts the life of Jesus and is placed with two other similar (Synoptic) Gospels; Acts depicts movements of the earliest believers, including Peter (chs 1—12) and Paul (chs 13—28). Its canonical position before communication among early Christian communities of faith corresponds with the general contexts depicted within Acts.

Yet the differences do not eclipse their literary links. Both books identify an addressee named Theophilus (→ "Addressee or Audience" in Introduction). Acts reminds Theophilus about the author's "former book" about Jesus (1:1), likely the Lukan Gospel. Luke 24 and Acts 1 join the two books together in numerous ways: the promise of the Father (Luke 24:49; Acts 1:4), the depiction of Jesus' followers as "witnesses" and the mention of "power" that they would receive (Luke 24:48; Acts 1:8), the emphasis on Jesus' ascension (Luke 24:51; Acts 1:9-11), etc. Characters in Acts (i.e., believers) often mirror characters in the Third Gospel (namely, Jesus). Most scholars consider the abundance of internal (literary) connections between the two books as sufficient reason for reading the two works together, despite the shortage of external evidence for doing so.

If readers approach Acts as the second part of the larger work "Luke-Acts" instead of a separate literary work, interpretive implications follow. First, intertextual connections are *primarily* between Luke's Gospel and Acts rather than between Paul's letters and Acts. Second, the Third Gospel and Acts are read differently, because (*a*) the former narrative does not end with the empty tomb (as do the other Synoptic Gospels) and ascension, and (*b*) the latter narrative presumes the *Lukan* story of Jesus. Third, these two texts *together* become the largest *single* contribution to the NT, comprising more than a fourth of the whole collection.

A. Authorship

Like the Third Gospel (and the other NT Gospels), the book of Acts is anonymous. Most of what is known about the author comes from narrative hints. Although persons may try to identify the "real" or "flesh-and-blood" author with textual evidence, the text itself only suggests what is known as an "implied author," constructed from textual cues about the author's knowledge, background, point of view, etc. From Acts, one may deduce that the implied author had significant literary skill (compared to other NT writers) and was adept in dramatic storytelling. The extensive use of the LXX, particularly the Torah, both in allusions and in vocabulary, suggests good knowledge of the Jewish Scriptures. Although commonly assumed that the author was a Gentile, this familiarity with the Scriptures points either to a Hellenistic Jew or a Gentile with significant exposure to the LXX. If the author was the latter, he was likely connected to the synagogue either as a Godfearer (→ sidebar "The Godfearers" with 10:1-2) or as a convert to Judaism before hearing the Christian gospel.

Most of Acts is narrated from a third-person perspective. But in chapter 16, that perspective changes to first person without warning: "After Paul had seen the vision, *we* got ready at once to leave for Macedonia, concluding that God had called *us* to preach the gospel to them" (v 10, emphasis added). This first-person narration continues through v 17 and then vanishes, only to reappear (and then disappear) again three more times (20:5-15; 21:1-18; 27:1—28:16). Some attribute this shift to Luke's source for this section. But it would seem strange that an author with polished literary skills who apparently had little difficulties editing other sources was unable to recognize and adapt these materials. Another plausible solution is that this perspective was inserted strategically at this point in the narrative for rhetorical or literary reasons (→ "Literary Features" in Introduction).

Still others see this as evidence that the author was a participant in the narrated events. This traditional view has understood the "we" passages to indicate that the author of Acts (and the Gospel of Luke) was a coworker or ministry companion of Paul (see Neale 2011, 23-24). According to early church tradition, Luke wrote both the gospel now ascribed to him and the book of Acts. Irenaeus cited these "we" passages as evidence that the author was Paul's associate (*Haer.* 3.14.1). But such information is corroborated by scarce NT references. Paul identifies Luke as one of two "fellow workers" (Phlm 24). Two other references refer to Luke as "the beloved physician" (Col 4:14 NRSV) who was still with Paul as he faced death (2 Tim 4:11). But these provide little support for Lukan authorship. These letters (whether or not from Paul's pen) place Luke with Paul during some periods but do not necessarily place them together during the critical "we" passages.

Such sparse evidence suggests caution is needed when drawing conclusions. Two considerations should be taken seriously. First, attempts to defend Luke the physician as the author of Acts (and the Gospel of Luke) by arguing that the narrator's style and perspective reveal someone from the medical profession often misinterpret both the specific textual details and the general work itself (see Cadbury 1920). Second, the different explanations for the "we" passages in Acts indicate that they may have an explanation unconnected to authorship. Other narrative issues such as differences between the portrait of Paul in Acts and Paul's self-descriptions in his letters (→ sidebar "Different Writers, Different Pauls?" with 13:46-47) also need to be considered before concluding that the pronoun "we" points to the author of Acts. At the very least, the differences in portrayals of Paul—in Acts and Paul's letters—raise questions about whether the author of Acts accompanied Paul or even knew him. Nonetheless, for convenience most scholars (as does this commentator) still refer to the author of Luke-Acts as Luke, although the mystery about his identity remains unsolved. Fortunately, the interpretation of Acts does not depend on the resolution of authorship questions.

B. Addressee or Audience

Both the Gospel of Luke and the book of Acts are addressed to "Theophilus," a name that means "friend / lover of God" or "beloved of God." But who is Theophilus? The honor with which Luke addresses Theophilus (1:1; see esp. Luke 1:3) suggests an individual of considerable social standing. Perhaps Theophilus was a wealthy patron who funded Luke's research. Because of the meaning of Theophilus' name, perhaps the book is addressed to all believers or all those "beloved of God." But the use of a name for such symbolic purposes was uncommon in ancient literary practice; thus, it is more likely that the original addressee was a specific person (see Alexander 1993, 132-33).

Yet Acts was not written only for an audience of one but for others who were also "beloved of God." Like authorship, the identity of this broader Lukan "implied audience" may be constructed from textual indicators. Clearly the readers of Acts understood Greek; the implied author also assumes that they are familiar with the LXX. Such an audience was probably quite diverse and found in varied locales. Given the issues in Acts, they may have included both Jewish and Gentile believers, perhaps dealing with similar issues of diversity themselves (see Esler 1987, 30-45). The references to various groupings of persons—wealthy and poor, men and women, Jew and Gentile, citizen and slave, prominent and marginal—suggest the possibility of diverse social composition (see, e.g., Tannehill 1996, 24-26).

C. Date of Composition

There are three viable options for the date of composition of Acts. The earliest date is shortly after the end of the book and Paul's house arrest in Rome (in the early 60s). Jerome, for instance, contended that Acts (and the Third Gospel) was written in the brief span between Paul's custody and his death a couple of years later.

This dating for the Lukan corpus still has a few adherents, for several reasons (see Hemer 1990, 365-410; Schnabel 2012, 27-28). First, the sudden ending of Acts tells nothing about Paul's release or subsequent death. Second, Luke mentions nothing about two noteworthy events: the emperor Nero's persecution (AD 64) and the destruction of Jerusalem (AD 70). Third, no place in Acts refers explicitly to any of the Pauline letters, which would have been collected several decades later.

The dominant view is that Luke-Acts was written as a two-volume work after the destruction of Jerusalem (AD 70), probably in the 80s. Such a view accounts for passages in the Gospel of Luke where Jesus alludes to the fate of Jerusalem (13:35a; 19:43-44; 21:20-24; 23:28-31)—words that would have greater significance after the city's destruction. But this position also explains the presence of passages in Acts that refer to the temple in Jerusalem closing its gates behind Paul after he was removed from the premises (21:30)—an act that would take on greater significance after the subsequent break between Judaism and the Christian movement. This date also precedes the likely time when the Pauline letters would have been collected and widely circulated, which explains the apparent lack of knowledge about them in Acts. Furthermore, this dating does not force historical explanations for an ending that may have better literary or rhetorical explanations.

A third hypothesis is that Acts was written during the first half of the second century. The classic formulation of this view came from Ferdinand Christian Baur in the nineteenth century, who contended that Acts played a pivotal role within early Christianity. Baur described the early church as having two competing sides. The Jewish Christians (first led by Peter) held to strict observance of the Jewish Torah. The Gentile Christians (first led by Paul) viewed the Torah as ineffective. Baur interpreted Acts as a document seeking conciliation and concessions between these two sides, whose conflict had extended into the second century (see 1876, 1:1-145). Few scholars today accept Baur's view without significant modification.

More recent proposals for a second-century dating of Acts consider other features of the book. One view contends the vocabulary of Acts, its possible intertextual links (e.g., Josephus, whose last volume dates about ca. AD 93), and Luke's depiction of "the other" (like the Jews) all point to an early second-century date, perhaps AD 110-120 (see Pervo 2006). Another proposal suggests that Acts may have been written as a response to the heretic Marcion (see Knox 1942). The suggestion is that the author of Acts edited and amended a pre-Marcionite version of the canonized Gospel of Luke to serve as a "prequel" to Acts, which was written to recover Paul from Marcionite teachings and distortions. This would date the composition no earlier than the 140s, which correlates with Irenaeus' first references to both the Third Gospel and Acts (see Tyson 2006; Matthews 2010, 27-53; also Trobisch 2010, 119-27).

These later dates for the composition of Acts are able to account for possible allusions to Pauline and deutero-Pauline letters in the narrative of Acts. In addition, they help to offer rhetorical explanations for some differences between the Lukan portrayal of Paul in Acts and the self-portrayal of Paul in the Pauline letters.

D. Genre of Acts

Different literary genres function differently, so the identification and assessment of the genre of Acts contribute to the interpretive task. Two issues complicate the matter. First, the possible association of Luke's Gospel and Acts as a two-volume work raises the question about whether the work's unity requires *generic* unity (see Parsons and Pervo 1993, 20-44). The differences in material make it likely that there are different genres for the two books, however interpreters determine the relationship between them. Second, ancient literary conventions often blurred genres. The study and imitation of different kinds of literature for learning composition were key aspects of Greco-Roman education. This results in literary features of different genres found in Acts.

Several proposals regarding the genre of Acts have been offered (see Phillips 2006, 365-96). Some who hold to the unity of Luke-Acts propose the genre of Acts as *biography*. Although this perspective typically focuses on parallels between NT Gospels and Hellenistic biographies (see, e.g., Burridge 1992), Luke-Acts has been compared to Diogenes Laertius' *Lives of Eminent Philosophers* (third century AD), which offers biographies of founders of religious schools or movements (Talbert 1974). Talbert notes that Laertius' *Lives* also depicts stories about those founders' successors or disciples, which he considers noteworthy when studying the genre of Acts. Such an understanding offers a proposal for reading Luke-Acts holistically, but more have been convinced of biography as a generic category for Luke's Gospel than for Luke-Acts (or Acts).

More scholars see Acts as *history* or *historiography*. They see both the preface of Luke's Gospel (1:1-4) as well as the beginning of Acts (1:1) as either consistent with prefaces that appear in Greco-Roman historiography or at least containing vocabulary emphasizing key themes from that tradition. Thus, Luke's description of his investigatory work and consultation of various sources in composing his work corresponds with similar statements by the Greek historians Herodotus (*Hist.* 1.1) and Thucydides (*War* 1.20.3; 1.22.2). For instance, the representation of his work as "accurate" (*akribōs* [Luke 1:3]) mirrors statements by other historians: Thucydides (*War* 1.22.2), Polybius (*Hist.* 1.14.6; 16.20.8; 34.4.2), Dionysius of Halicarnassus (*Ant. rom.* 1.1.2; 1.5.4; 1.6.3), Josephus (*J.W.* 1.2, 6, 9), and Lucian (*Hist.* 7, 24, 39-44).

Luke's characterization of his work as an "orderly account" (Luke 1:3) correlates with other historians who emphasize their role in arranging and unifying that work (see, e.g., Polybius, *Hist.* 1.3.4; 1.4.2-3). Luke links the stories about Jesus and the church both to the story of Israel and to the larger story of human history. He does this by alluding and referring to persons and events from the OT and from the Greco-Roman world.

This general understanding of the genre of Acts has several variations. Some consider it a popular form of *general history*, which focuses on the identity and emergence of a particular people (see Aune 1987, 77-157). Others classify it as *historical monograph*, a shorter work that focuses on narrated events in a more restricted period of time (see Plümacher 1979, 457-66; Palmer 1993, 1-30).

Since Greco-Roman historiography was concerned about its didactic or rhetorical purposes, others classify Acts as *apologetic history* because of its concerns to defend the Christian movement and its leaders from charges or accusations against them (see Sterling 1992). It could also be described as *biblical history* since Luke draws parallels between narrated events and biblical traditions of the LXX (perhaps more specifically Deuteronomistic or prophetic; see Rosner 1993, 65-82; Schmidt 1985, 417-27; Brodie 1990, 78-85). Still others have noted similarities between Acts and *political histories* of the Greco-Roman era, which seek to connect founder, ancestors, and successors through a common story (see Balch 1990b, 5-19).

Some features of the narrative do not coincide with more technical or formal characteristics of that tradition (see Pervo 2009, 17-18). The prefaces of the Third Gospel (Luke 1:1-4) and Acts (1:1) contain some vocabulary consistent with Greco-Roman historiography, but their literary conventions and style do not conform to the standards of *formal* Greco-Roman historiography. Rather, these prefaces were written in more accessible types of writing suitable for those of the "professions" or trades of that era (Alexander 1993; 1999, 9-26; Robbins 1999, 63-67). Thus, although the Gospel of Luke and Acts exhibit greater literary style than most NT texts, they are also more comparable to other NT texts in such accessibility. This would locate Acts on the "fringes" of the historiographical genre rather than in its mainstream (Alexander 1999, 23). This suggests that, although Acts is history, it is also written in a more "popular" form.

The popular form of Acts increases the possibility that features from different genres may contribute to this work. Since ancient literary education included the imitation of classic and dramatic literature, Acts has been studied to consider the creative aspects of its composition. In particular, Luke may write for dramatic effect and even the entertainment of his audience (i.e., telling a good story; see Pervo 1987), since keeping the interest and attention of an audience is an important element of composition. Similarities between episodes in Acts and ancient epics also suggest that these Lukan stories were told in familiar ways to heighten their impact (see, e.g., MacDonald 1999, 88-107; 2003, 189-203). Features in these and other types of literature were typically imported into more popular forms of history like Acts, as the author sought to compose a work in effective ways (see Aune 1987).

47

E. Sources and Intertextuality

Luke had sources in hand for writing Acts but states nothing about them (contrast Luke 1:1-4). The problem lies in determining what those sources may have been since Luke was skillful in shaping the final text with his own style and vocabulary (Dupont 1964). Some contend that the "we" passages in Acts reflect the authorial perspective of a source from which Luke draws in composing Acts, but other plausible explanations (→ "Authorship" in Introduction) make that argument less than compelling. A common view is that Luke had at least two sources—one from Jerusalem and another from Antioch of Syria—due to the shift in action from the holy city (chs 1—7) to the latter as the narrative focuses more on Paul's ministry (chs 13—21).

Were Paul's letters available to Luke as a source? Some contend that differences between those letters and Acts make their availability unlikely. Luke never mentions that Paul wrote a letter to one of the local churches that appear in the narrative. But such differences, which readers must take seriously, may have explanations other than Lukan unfamiliarity. In addition, some evidence in Acts 15 may suggest that Luke knew about and used Paul's Galatian letter but reversed the roles and views of Peter and Paul (Walker 1998, 77-86). Other matters in Acts, such as the accusations against Paul in ch 21, may also allude more to what Paul states in his letter to the Galatians than to what Luke himself narrates about Paul in Acts. If Acts was written in the first half of the second century (→ "Date of Composition" in Introduction), it is much more likely the collection of Paul's letters would have been available to the author.

One source that did influence Acts is the LXX (see Evans and Sanders 1993; Litwak 2005; also Neale 2011, 26-28). This intertextuality between the LXX and Acts is apparent in two distinct ways. First, Luke appropriates scriptural quotations at strategic points in Acts, such as Peter's explanation of what happened at Pentecost (2:17-21) and numerous instances when Jesus was proclaimed as the Messiah/Christ (see 2:25-28; 3:22-23; 4:11). Second, scriptural echoes occur throughout Acts as Luke draws from the story of Israel to continue that story among the followers of Jesus. Luke uses these intertextual connections to tell a *continuing* story of God's purposes of salvation as told in the Scriptures.

F. Textual-Critical Issues

Most variations among Greek MSS of Acts are relatively minor and exist in apparently random passages. These differences are due either to copying texts by hand or to attempts to clarify textual ambiguity. However, significant differences exist between two major textual traditions, the Alexandrian and Western traditions. The Alexandrian tradition includes copies of the Third Gospel and Acts from as early as the fourth century, with the oldest papyrus text of Luke's Gospel (P[75]) dating from AD 175-225. Texts of the Western tradition include parchment copies from as early as the sixth century as well as papyrus fragments and citations from early patristic writers (e.g., Tertullian, Cyprian, and Augustine) that go back to the third century.

Whereas the Western tradition *omits* materials from Luke 22—24 when compared to the Alexandrian tradition (Luke 22:19b-20; 24:3b, 6a, 12, 36b, 40, 51a, 52b), Western texts *expand* the narrative of Acts when compared to Alexandrian texts. These expansions amplify some stories, explain some textual ambiguities, emphasize the authority of the apostles, and accentuate Jewish rejection and the role of the Holy Spirit in a style that is different from the rest of Acts. This expanded version is about 10 percent longer than the Alexandrian one. Biblical translations of Acts are based on the Alexandrian tradition, since the Western tradition reflects consistent editorial revision through addition to the narrative of Acts (see Head 1993, 415-44). But because the Western text sometimes offers helpful clarification about textual ambiguity, readers should note such textual variations where they exist.

G. Literary Features

Literary-critical approaches to biblical studies developed during the last third of the twentieth century (including narrative criticism) and changed the study of Acts. This approach is concerned not only with *what* the text says but also with *why* something is stated or described and *how* the text may have functioned as the original audience heard and understood it. Two areas dominate: (1) textual features and cues of what may be described as the "narrative world" as shaped and defined by Luke, and (2) the role of the interpreter in making appropriate connections and conclusions (see Thompson 2004, 66-73). In light of this, interpretation of Acts must consider matters such as plot, narrative placement and sequence, characterization, and the place of various themes and scenes. It must also consider the role of the interpreter in making the connections between different narrative elements and in evaluating characters, actions, and plot in terms of the narrative progression.

When Acts is assessed from a narrative perspective, four features stand out. One is *the use of speeches in Acts* (including at least twenty-seven speeches and seven "partial speeches"; Soards 1994, 1), which accounts for over 35 percent of the entire work. Some speeches are similar in form and content and, because they call for repentance, are often described as sermons (see Acts 2:14-36; 3:11-26; 5:29-32; 10:34-43; 13:16-41). Because these speeches appear on the lips of different reliable characters, the similarities imply that Luke as narrator was responsible for their final form and content, not unlike the Greek historian Thucydides' comment about speeches in his own work (*War* 1.22.1). Some speeches (or sermons) are related to the narrative events where they are situated; others focus more directly on the respective event, thereby making them more analogous to speeches in ancient works of history (see Cadbury 1933d, 402-27; Dibelius 1956, 138-85).

In either case, speeches appear at strategic points in Acts. They function as commentary rather than verbatim record. Each speech offers a theological explanation for what happened, for what will happen, or both. The narrator thereby provides readers with needed information or insight to interpret scenes and characters appropriately, without addressing them directly. Thus, the speeches are particularly significant because of what they reveal about Luke's theological agenda. Since they are scattered throughout Acts, they also bring coherence to the narrative (see Soards 1994, 162-208).

A second feature is *the use of geography and travel motifs in the general structure of Acts*. Acts begins where the Gospel of Luke ends—in Jerusalem. The fulfillment of God's promises to Israel occurs there in the first seven chapters (see Acts 2:1-41). However, consistent with Jesus' commission to his apostles (1:8), this was only the beginning of their witness, which would extend beyond the city ("all Judea and Samaria") to "the ends of the earth." The narrative action returns to Jerusalem at strategic points: the introduction of the transformed Saul to the church leaders (9:26-30), questions about salvation and Gentiles (11:1-18; 15:1-35; 21:18-26), and legal proceedings against Paul (21:27—23:30). This grounds the story of the church (including the inclusion of Gentiles) within the story of God as seen in Israel. But Acts ends not in Jerusalem but in Rome, which suggests a shift in Jerusalem's narrative and theological role (see Parsons 1998, 155-71).

This use of geography is related to travel or journey motifs in Acts. Jesus' journey from Galilee to Jerusalem (Luke 9:51—19:27) is prominent in the Gospel; in Acts, Luke uses the journey motif to depict the spread of the gospel and the progress of the church's mission. Believers are on "the Way" (9:2; 18:26; 19:9, 23; 22:4; 24:14, 22), traveling first from Jerusalem to surrounding regions and then to the Mediterranean world. Particular attention is given to the journeys of Philip (8:4-40), Peter (9:32—10:48), and Paul (13:4—14:28; 15:36—18:22; 18:23—21:16; 27:1—28:16). In each instance, the journey was associated with Jerusalem or divine activity, thereby linking the Christian movement with the purposes of God.

A third literary feature is *characterization*. All authors depict their characters in particular ways that are appropriate for the broader narrative world that the author creates and the purposes for that world (see Neale 2011, 36-37). Thus, characterization must be interpreted within the narrative. In Acts, Luke paints his leading believers (e.g., Peter, Paul) in ways that are reminiscent of others. The episodes of Peter and John (3:1-10) and of Paul (14:8-10) healing a crippled man resemble a similar scene in Jesus' ministry (Luke 5:17-26), thereby connecting the story of the church with the story of Jesus. Luke also depicts characters in specific ways so that they stand in comparison or contrast to one another. Thus, readers must not only recognize the general nature of characterization but also its function in specific contexts.

A fourth distinctive feature is *the use of first-person narration in portions of Acts*. These sections after Acts 15 have provoked different explanations (→ "Authorship" in Introduction; see Praeder 1987, 193-218; Wedderburn 2002, 78-98). As a literary device, they may simply heighten the dramatic. Or they may indicate that Paul, the author, and the audience all shared a common perspective.

First-person narration also seems to make the claim of personal presence, despite improbabilities (due to details in Acts) that the author was a companion of Paul (see Wedderburn 2002, 78). The impression of personal presence is complicated by inconsistencies in shifts between first- and third-person accounts, which often obscure who was with Paul from scene to scene (see Kurz 1993, 111-24). Since this perspective reflects "the style of personal integrity and trustworthiness" consistent with prominent ancient historians (Campbell 2007, 89), it could encourage readers to view the narrative with confidence at these pivotal points in Acts. Despite the difficulties (see Pervo 2009, 392-96), the advantage of such literary interpretations is that attention centers on how these "we"-passages function in Acts.

H. Theology and Acts

Most interpreters consider Acts to be on some level a work of history. But that does not preclude Luke from shaping the work in theological ways. By writing a narrative, Luke went about the theological task very differently from Paul's letter to the Romans. Luke offers a "theological history" in Acts, so that readers of Acts may consider the theological orientation of this work or the theology that this book has to contribute alongside other biblical works. Yet "Luke's theology is intricately and irreversibly bound up with the story he tells and cannot be separated from it. An attempt to do justice to the theology of Acts must struggle to reclaim the character of Acts as a narrative" (Gaventa 1988, 150). Thus, interpreters must consider how narrative and literary features function *within* the work (→ "Literary Features" in Introduction), rather than simply interpreting or extracting theological images or ideas *apart from* that work.

Several theological themes resonate throughout the narrative. *First, God functions as the primary mover behind events and persons.* Throughout Acts (and the Gospel of Luke), the will and purposes of the God of Israel orient the scenes and their arrangement. Luke deliberately connects the story of the earliest Christians to the story of Jesus, both of which he connects to the story of God's people in the OT. From the beginning of Acts to its ending, Luke depicts the God of Israel as fulfilling God's promises and purposes for Israel as the people of God (see, e.g., 2:17-21; 26:12-23). This same God is the one who guides and initiates (often through the Holy Spirit) the mission of the church beyond its initial Jewish boundaries (see, e.g., 8:26-40; 10:1-48; 13:1-4; 16:6-10).

Second, Jesus is affirmed as God's Messiah/Christ on the basis of his resurrection and ascension. Luke's Christology has little to say about Jesus' death as sacrifice or atonement for sin (→ 20:28). Rather, Luke underscores the significance of Jesus' suffering and death in two ways: (1) as occurring due to the rejection and disobedience of the Jewish people, and (2) as the occasion by which God *resurrected* Jesus, thereby vindicating the faithfulness of Jesus' own life and ministry (2:22-24). Thus, God's actions of resurrecting and exalting Jesus confirm the latter's identity as "both Lord and Messiah" (2:36). With such affirmation comes the declaration that "everyone who calls on the name of the Lord will be saved" (2:21; see 4:12).

Third (and related to the previous theme), *the universality of salvation is affirmed as an essential characteristic of the people of God.* The affirmation of Jesus as God's Messiah/Christ carries with it a redefinition of the people of God to include both believing Jews and Gentiles. Acts (along with the Third Gospel) emphasizes the inclusion of Gentiles, but through the use of the LXX, this is always shown to be in continuity with Israel as the people of God. For example, Peter's Pentecost speech contains a quotation from the OT prophet Joel, which interprets the Pentecost phenomenon as God's fulfillment of God's promise to Israel (2:17-20). Also, Luke appropriates the term *ekklēsia* (usually translated "church" in the NT), which the LXX uses for the assembly of Israel as God's people. Thus, at the center of this theme of continuity is the activity of the God of Israel, who calls for and prompts repentance among the Jewish people (see Jervell 1972; 1996).

But this same God also steers believers to Gentiles: first to the God-fearing Cornelius (10:1-48) and Antiochenes of Syria (11:19-30), then to the eastern part of the Mediterranean world (16:6-10). Whereas the first quarter of the narrative focuses exclusively on salvation in Jewish contexts, the central half depicts the spread of the gospel in diverse situations. Proclamation typically begins in the Jewish synagogue, but the audience includes both Jews and worshiping Gentiles. And even there, Jewish opposition (likely over this inclusive understanding of the gospel) leads to ministry in increasingly diverse settings (see 18:7-11; 19:9-20).

Fourth, the call for repentance places the status of the Jewish people as the people of God in question. After World War II and the Holocaust, interpreters have wrestled with the difficulties posed by Luke's portrayal of the Jewish people (see, e.g., Tyson 1988b; Sanders 1987; Jervell 1996). Some interpret Luke's characterization of the Jewish people to be negative or even anti-Semitic. But others understand his portrayal of the Jews as having a rhetorical function to legitimize the church and her mission in light of the OT story of the people of God and the rejection of that mission by institutional Judaism. When viewed in the latter sense, the Jewish leaders at the beginning (chs 1—7) and end (chs 23—28) of Acts as well as other Jews in general during Paul's ministry (chs 9, 13—22) oppose the Christian gospel—a message about what the God of Israel had done in continuity with what God had *always* done on behalf of Israel. So as Luke depicts the Jewish people, they are disobedient and in need of repentance, with their ongoing resistance consistent with how their ancestors responded to the prophets (see 7:35, 39, 51-52; 28:26-27). There is also repentance early on in Jerusalem (2:38-41; 4:4; 5:12-16; 6:7), as well as most places where Luke describes the Christian mission at work (9:19*b*-25; 11:19-30; 13:16-52; 14:1-7; 16:11-15; 17:1-9, 10-15; 18:1-18; 19:1-20). Yet the universality of salvation and mission may be too much for the institutions of Judaism to accept, as this is a question of their identity as a people. Thus, the response and images of Judaism may be more tragic than negative in tone (see Tannehill 1985, 69-85).

I. Engaging Acts in a New Day

Across the centuries, Acts has had an awkward place within the theological discourse of the church. For some, Acts is a common source for basic information about the earliest Christians. Yet for others, it is often not appreciated for its theological contribution alongside Paul's letters and Jesus' teachings (within the Gospels).

The ambiguity about Acts' role is also apparent within Wesleyan and Wesleyan-holiness circles, from which many readers of this commentary come. John Wesley quoted Acts relatively little in his sermons in comparison to his favorite letter, 1 John (twice as much despite its comparative size). Conversely, many who worship in Wesleyan-related churches around the world today are drawn to Acts because of its dramatic descriptions of Spirit-empowered life within the early church.

To such diverse impressions and responses to Acts, this biblical book offers a needed scriptural resource that complements, nurtures, and challenges the spirit of the broader Wesleyan tradition . . . and of Christianity itself. But how may it be read or engaged in a new day?

I. Read Imaginatively

As with all biblical texts, it is not enough simply to "understand" the printed words on the page or even to imitate the actions of faithful persons in biblical stories. Rather, the task of interpretation demands "an integrative act of the imagination" analogous to a jazz musician making music through the improvisation of a composed musical score (Hays 1996, 6). Imagination engages creatively about what Acts may say to contemporary settings (see Adam 2006, 28-34;

Wall 2004a, 108-15). And this coincides with John Wesley's understanding of the inspiration of prayerful readers (or the church; see Thompson 2004, 57-79). Thus, engaging Acts in a new day does not mean replicating ancient images but imagining possibilities provoked by that reading. The question becomes how the church may live out or perform the narrative in a very different time (see Thompson 2013, 121-30). Plausible, faithful readings may result in responses that are surprisingly different but still embody the mission and purposes of the church as the people of God depicted throughout its narrative.

2. Read Soteriologically

The correlation between theological emphases throughout Acts (→ "Theology and Acts" in Introduction) and Wesleyan theological themes suggests this to be a natural resource for the Wesleyan tradition. Since Wesleyans read Scripture with a soteriological aim (see Green 2004, 130-32; Wall 2004b, 51-52), they see in Acts a focus on God and God's activity in offering salvation to all. The fulfillment of God's promises to Israel and the offer of salvation to the Gentiles, despite numerous obstacles, resonates with and contributes to Wesleyan understandings of God's grace.

Because such matters permeate all of Acts, Wesleyan readers are encouraged to view Acts holistically as a narrative. Thus, such readers have theological as well as narrative reasons to interpret *all* narrative elements—regardless of how powerful or wonderful those images or ideas may be—as having meaning *first* within the broader story of which they are a part.

3. Read Holistically

For contemporary Wesleyans, Acts should be read holistically as the story of God's salvific activity and work of grace. Sometimes, descriptions of the early church are lifted from Acts and interpreted *separately* from the broader story. But these should first be interpreted *within* that story so that readers may begin to imagine how the whole story may relate to the present day. For instance, several passages depict extraordinary growth in numbers among the believers (2:41, 47; 4:4; 6:7; 12:24). But one should interpret such descriptions along with many other descriptions and images of believers in Acts. Within that broader context, such references give evidence of God's presence and blessing because of the church's worship of God. As a result, contemporary engagement of such passages may have little to do with church growth strategies. Instead, a Wesleyan reading may look for different ways to recognize God's presence and grace at work in the midst of genuine worship offered to God by God's people.

For many Wesleyan contemporary readers, engaging Acts in a new day involves what Acts describes as persons "filled with the Holy Spirit" (e.g., 2:4; 4:8) or doing "signs and wonders" (5:12; 14:3; 15:12; see 2:43; 6:8). Such persons often interpret Acts through the lens of "personal Christian experience" or teachings about normative behavior for Christian discipleship. But when read holistically, Acts offers Wesleyans something at once greater and more significant in the mission of God. The power associated with the Spirit in Acts was given for the church's mission and witness, not for personal spiritual matters (1:8). The occurrences of "signs and wonders" were not mere accomplishments of extraordinary deeds by the faithful. These were *signs* of divine blessing upon those who set out to fulfill the divine mission as God called them. Such descriptions were reminiscent of Jesus (2:22). But these also echo OT descriptions of God's actions on behalf of Israel in Egypt (e.g., Deut 6:22; 7:19; 26:8; 34:11; Ps 135:9; Jer 32:20-21). So these images of extraordinary activities serve as literary and theological links between (*a*) the mission of the church in Acts, (*b*) the story of Jesus, and (*c*) God's broader mission and story.

When read holistically, Acts confronts Wesleyan readers with extraordinary descriptions within the story of that day as signs of God's grace at work. Thus, when thinking imaginatively about how such matters in Acts relate to the present day, Acts provokes Wesleyans to look for faithful ways to extend God's grace to those around them, rather than merely to seek the imitation of the extraordinary that accentuates the individual. As the church focuses on living out the gospel, her God-given mission, God's active grace continues to bring transformation in unexpected and extraordinary ways.

4. Read Experientially and Ecclesially

The primacy of Scripture has characterized the Wesleyan tradition from its beginning, as John Wesley described himself as "a man of one book" (1984, 105). Central to such claims is the belief that Scripture is sufficient for teachings necessary for salvation (see Jones 1995, 37-41). Yet Wesley and his theological forbears appropriated other "sources" in addition to Scripture, namely reason and tradition. Wesley and his successors also included experience. Although the precise relationship of these four sources (later described as the Wesleyan quadrilateral) continues to be debated, the primacy of Scripture among these sources affirms its authoritative role in shaping doctrine and practice within the church.

Wesley gave explicit attention to the complementary role of experience in doctrine and practice. Such experience, which assumes a church context, does not supersede Scripture. But it tests alternative interpretations or may even challenge assumed ones (see Maddox 1994, 44-46).

Many in Wesleyan circles are influenced significantly by theological traditions that focus on divine sovereignty, human depravity, and biblical inerrancy. Too often these emphases lead to a static and unchanging meaning attached to the Bible (i.e., "What the text meant is what it always means"). But the church's experience suggests otherwise. Acts *itself* challenges the church to look at and listen again to Scripture, because within Acts are numerous examples where believers' experiences clashed with their assumed/inherited understanding of Scripture (see, e.g., Acts 10:1—11:18; 15:1-35). So Acts not only challenges the church today but also offers a glimpse of how to wrestle, as the faithful people of God, with such issues.

5. Read Inclusively

Acts challenges all readers, Wesleyans and others, to see God's salvific work and grace that extends to all people. The struggles that faced the earliest Christians are defined by time, place, and customs. Jewish understandings of what it meant to be the people of God determined who was and was not considered an "insider." But numerous other boundaries or obstacles appear within Luke's narrative world: gender, socioeconomic, ethnic, political, geographical, spiritual, and others. Yet Acts offers a perspective that suggests that all such boundaries may be overcome by the good news of God's grace. It also challenges longstanding customs and traditions that kept "insiders" in and "outsiders" out.

Perhaps the book of Acts has not been adequately engaged by the Wesleyan tradition or the broader church because it still confronts and challenges her today about boundaries and obstacles that she directly or indirectly affirms in keeping individuals and groups apart from her. Acts offers a perspective that dares Wesleyans, if they really affirm God's grace at work in many different ways (even prevenient grace!), to begin expecting and looking for God at work . . . even within those persons or groups that the church had left behind or outside. And that perspective also encourages the church to read Scripture with such inclusion in mind. Unless the church is willing to read such biblical texts so that they question and challenge her, these texts will never truly become sacred Scripture through which God can speak to her (see Fowl and Jones 1991, 41-44).

Every commentary both comes from and assumes a particular kind of reading. As the volume title states, this work comes out of the Wesleyan tradition. Such influence will sometimes be more explicit and overt; more often it will be implicit and indirect. The assumption is that most readers will also find themselves in churches variously shaped by Wesleyan theology and practices. The hope is that such readings of Acts will result in faithful practices that extend God's love and grace to all.

COMMENTARY

I. PREFACE: CONTINUITY, COMMISSION, AND PROMISE: ACTS 1:1-11

BEHIND THE TEXT

Like the Gospel of Luke, the book of Acts begins with a preface that follows the advice and practice among historians of that day. Both the mention of the "former book" and the overlap in content from the end of that gospel (esp. Luke 24:36-53) subtly induce the recipient to read the ensuing narrative in light of the Lukan narrative about Jesus (→ also Introduction). Such expectations for the reader are not surprising, since Theophilus is the addressee for both works (→ "Addressee or Audience" in Introduction). The preface to Acts, however, lacks the distinct transition to the first narrative materials that accompanies the preface to Luke's Gospel. Thus, scholars disagree over where the preface ends and where the story of Acts begins. The general structure, literary connections, and shared content suggest that these first eleven verses form a literary unit that offers both a retrospective glance to the ending of the Lukan Gospel and a prospective glimpse of what will unfold in the narrative of Acts.

The narrator does not explicitly identify the exact location for what these verses mention. However, inferences here as well as information from Luke 24 suggest that Jesus and his apostles were in Jerusalem and in neighboring areas. In Luke's Gospel, Jesus appeared to the gathered followers in Jerusalem (24:33-49) and then ascended to heaven from Bethany (24:49-51), a village probably located about two miles east of Jerusalem. However, later in Acts 1:12, the stated location is the Mount of Olives, an area known for its abundance of olive trees between Jerusalem and Bethany. This location was known as a hideout for underground, Jewish revolutionary groups that opposed the religious establishment and the Roman occupation of Israel.

IN THE TEXT

■ **1-5** The narrator's first statement connects Acts with the Third Gospel, described as his **former book** (lit., *first word*). Here **Theophilus** is also addressed but, as in that gospel, no other information reveals his identity. Luke reminds him about that prior narrative of Jesus. The verb **began** (*ērxato*) in Luke 3:23 similarly indicates the inception of Jesus' ministry, which will then continue in Acts through the apostles and others.

The narrator or a character in the Third Gospel often describes Jesus as teaching (see Luke 4:15, 31; 5:3, 17; 6:6; 11:1; 13:10, 22; 19:47; 20:1; 21:37; 23:5). He frequently associates the believers as doing the same thing after the ascension (see Acts 2:42; 4:2, 18; 5:21, 25, 28, 42; 11:26; 13:12; 15:35; 17:19; 18:11, 25; 20:20; 28:31). Here Jesus is teaching the apostles. The phrase **through the Holy Spirit** appears ambiguously in Greek, between the mention of Jesus' instruction and his selection of apostles. Thus, it is unclear to which the phrase applies. The ambiguity suggests that the phrase describes *both* aspects regarding the apostles as dependent on the Spirit's activity.

Such matters continue until Jesus ascends to heaven, which only the Lukan corpus describes. The same verb, *analambanō*, describes Elijah being taken up to heaven (2 Kgs 2:11 LXX). This suggests that the author links these two incidents. He offers no other details here, content to summarize matters the Third Gospel developed more fully.

The remainder of that first statement (Acts 1:3-5) retains the reader's attention on Jesus and his apostles. The Lukan Gospel account seems to limit Jesus' appearances to one day (see Luke 24). Here, however, the author states that these extended over a period of **forty days**. The significance of this longer period may be found on at least two levels.

First, the extended time provides sufficient evidence for Jesus' resurrection. The noun translated **convincing proofs** (*tekmērios*) appears only here in the NT. In Greek rhetoric, it describes compelling evidence that results in defensible or irrefutable conclusions.

Second, the number **forty** probably links the beginning of Acts with OT stories of preparation and God's dealings with the people of Israel (see Exod 24:12-18; 34:28; Deut 8:2; 1 Kgs 19:8). Luke 4:1-13 describes Jesus' temptation as over forty days. Thus, as Moses prepared to receive God's commandments for the people, Jesus prepares his apostles and gives them his commandments (Spencer 2004a, 34-35).

This narrative includes little of Jesus' teaching. What little Acts mentions appears elsewhere. Several aspects of the teaching here are noteworthy.

First, the teaching is about **the kingdom of God**, a common but undefined expression for Jesus' message in Luke's Gospel (e.g., 4:43; 6:20; 7:28; 9:2; 10:9; 17:20-21; 18:16-17; 22:16, 18). This same expression also describes the message of the Christian preaching in Acts (e.g., 8:12; 14:22; 19:8; 28:23, 31). In Jesus' day, people hoped for the kingdom of God in the distant future. However, in both the Third Gospel and Acts (as in other NT texts), it expresses how God had *presently* entered into human experience through Jesus. The mention of this both here at the beginning of Acts and then later at its end (28:31) brackets the entire work with this theme as a literary *inclusio*. It lets the reader know without question "that the triumph of God's reign is the subtext of the narrative sandwiched between" (Wall 2002, 41). The term as used in both the Third Gospel and Acts also contrasts against its common reference to the Romans and the empire's imperial power.

Second, Jesus instructs the apostles to **not leave Jerusalem**, which reiterates the Gospel account (Luke 24:49). Luke offers no reason for these instructions. But he later describes the Pentecost scene in Jerusalem as the fulfillment of God's promises to Israel. Thus, at this stage Jerusalem is the geographical and theological center of the Acts narrative.

Importantly, the author places this instruction in the context of a meal, a common feature of the Third Gospel (see Luke 5:27-32; 7:36-50; 11:37-54; 14:1-24; 19:1-10; 22:7-38; 24:13-35). The participle *synalizomenos*, translated **while he was eating**, literally connotes the sharing of salt among persons. The social implications of shared meals point to what Jesus and the apostles hold in common. Their shared beliefs, values, practices, and traditions define the boundaries and rules that govern their meal and solidify their places within that group (see Thompson 2007, 77-78).

Third, Jesus tells his apostles to **wait for** or *expect*, as the verb *perimenō* often connotes, **the promise of the Father** (see Luke 24:49). He subsequently clarified this as being **baptized with the Holy Spirit**. There is no mention of Jesus saying anything resembling this in the Gospel of Luke. But the saying may reiterate the unfulfilled prophecy of John the Baptist (Luke 3:16). The Spirit is important here, because the promised Spirit baptism would establish continuity between Jesus and these apostles as well as enable them to serve as prophetic witnesses, as readers will soon see.

■ **6-7** Jesus' teaching about the kingdom of God probably precipitates the question about the restoration of **the kingdom to Israel** here. The dual conjunctions *men oun* typically link two events, with the latter event being dependent upon the first (Levinsohn 1987, 141). Thus, the participle *hoi synelthontes*—translated *those who came together*—probably refers to the eleven apostles, although a larger group of followers is not out of the question (Johnson 1992, 26). The imperfect tense of *ērōtōn* suggests that their questioning persists. That tense was typical in questions, since any inquiry was incomplete until it was answered (Barrett 1994, 75).

Jesus' reference to the Holy Spirit probably stimulates their questions, since Jewish tradition associated the Spirit's coming with the last days (see 2:17) and Israel's restoration (see Isa 32:14-30). No doubt, the apostles are speaking about the fulfillment of the messianic mission. They expect this would include both the reestablishment of a politically independent Israel apart from Roman rule and an accompanying conversion of Gentile nations to Israel's God (e.g., Isa 2:2-4; Mic 4:1-8). The indicative **restore** (*apokathistaneis*) in their question has a similar meaning in the LXX (Mal 4:6; Sir 48:10). There, it referred to Elijah and the restoration of all things associated with his return (Johnson 1992, 26).

Jesus' response in v 7 contrasts the *apostles'* misunderstanding with the *divine* understanding. This redirects the apostles' attention from *when* things would happen to *who* controls them. The apostles ask Jesus about the consummation of the kingdom with regard to **time** (*chronō*) in terms of chronology or dates on a calendar. Jesus' negative response refers both to such **times** (*chronous*) as well as to **seasons** (*kairous*) or specific times when God would act as falling under the *authority that uniquely belongs to the Father* alone.

■ **8** The conjunction **but** (*alla*) contrasts Jesus' refusal to grant the apostles' request with this ensuing promise. Jesus' followers did not receive the knowledge they sought. But he offers them other details. His promise of their reception of **power** (see Luke 24:49) correlates both with the Spirit's future coming and with their impending mission to be Jesus' **witnesses**. It is *not* concerned with matters of personal benefit or help.

To serve as Jesus' witnesses meant that the apostles would speak about Jesus from personal experience and conviction. That would be possible only as the promised Spirit enabled them. This power refers to a divine gift essential for them to be effective witnesses to these gospel events. It is not to make them and future believers "strong" in the faith.

This statement about their mission functions loosely as an outline of the Acts narrative. It would begin in Jerusalem (through 8:3), continue to the regions of Judea and Samaria (8:4-40 and perhaps ch 9), and then move on to other parts of the Mediterranean world.

One should not miss the radical overtones of this brief list. It includes places and persons most Jews considered outside the bounds of God's saving work. The phrase *heōs eschatou tēs gēs*, **to the end of the earth**, occurs four times in the LXX (Isa 8:9; 48:20; 49:6; 62:11; see *Pss. Sol.* 1:4). In Isa 49:6 (quoted in Acts 13:47), the phrase describes Israel's call to be "a light to the Gentiles," so they may share in God's salvation.

The singular *eschatou*, **end** (ends in most translations), may not refer to perceived geographical boundaries of the planet or the known world of that era. Commentators often conclude that the phrase refers to Rome. This corresponds with its role as the westernmost locale in Acts' list of locations from where Jewish pilgrims had come to Jerusalem (2:9-11). But Rome was typically regarded as the *center* of the world, not its *end*. Here, the phrase may not have a *geographical* reference as much as a *theological* one. God's purposes seek to bring salvation to *all* (Luke 1:46-55; 2:28-32), as represented by the capital of the Roman Empire.

■ **9-11** The ascension of Jesus is not a separate scene but immediately follows his commissioning of the apostles. Jesus' departure to heaven is reminiscent of the departure of significant prophetic figures in Jewish tradition, including Enoch and Elijah (see 2 Kgs 2:1-12; Philo, QG 1.86) as well as Moses (see Philo, *Moses* 2.291; Josephus, *Ant.* 4.326).

In the OT, a **cloud** typically symbolized God's activity and presence (see Exod 16:10; 19:9; 24:15-18; 40:34; 1 Kgs 8:10-11). The imagery may also remind the reader of the cloud that blanketed the transfiguration scene (see Luke 9:28-36). Thus, some argue that the **two men** who appeared with the apostles after Jesus' ascension were Moses and Elijah (Johnson 1992, 27; Wall 2002, 43-44). However, most scholars point to the similarities between these two men and the angelic messengers at the empty tomb (Luke 24:4, 23). What may be more significant than the identity of the messengers is their message. It helps the apostles grasp what takes place and how that relates to their commissioned role as witnesses.

Explanation of the significance of Jesus' ascension is left for later (→ 2:32-36). For now, the narrator highlights three matters.

First, Jesus is taken **into heaven**. The phrase appears four times in Acts 1:10-11. This redundancy probably explains why some MSS omit one of those phrases. However, the repeated mention of **heaven** clarifies the inferences of the cloud imagery. This and the passive voice of the two verbs translated **taken up** (vv 9, 11) indicate that God's presence captures Jesus and carries him heavenward.

Second, the five references to what the apostles *themselves* saw emphasize their commissioned role as witnesses. The first two references (v 9) reaf-

1:9-11

firm that the apostles could vouch for Jesus' departure because they were eyewitnesses.

The verb *atenizō*, translated **looking intently**, is a common Lukan term (see Luke 4:20; 22:56; Acts 3:4, 12; 6:15; 7:55; 10:4; 11:6; 13:9; 14:9; 23:1). It underscores that the apostles saw *everything* as Jesus departed. The two textual variants of the verb **looking** (*blepontes* or *emblepontes*) both fit the context. The first variant repeats the participle in Acts 1:9 and correlates with the verb **you have seen** later in v 11: the apostles saw Jesus' ascension as first-person witnesses, which was not the case with the resurrection. The second variant intensifies the verbal root, so that it conveys a gaze of intense consideration (BDAG 2000, 321-22).

Third, the messengers redirect the apostles' attention from Jesus' departure to his return. The expression **will come back in the same way** probably employs the imagery of Dan 7:13. It describes "one like a son of man, coming with the clouds of heaven." The question and assurance given to the apostles provoke them to embrace their mission as witnesses. Not only would they be Jesus' representatives, but their proclamation about him would declare God's primary role in the story of Jesus. This is the point of the statement "you will be my witnesses" (Acts 1:8). Thus, the message serves as a call to action for the apostles prior to Jesus' second return (Tannehill 1990, 18-19).

FROM THE TEXT

Like most texts, the opening of Acts offers an agenda for the rest of the narrative. It includes hints regarding what readers should bring to the table and expect as they engage this story. The author does not state such matters directly. But the literary imagery and connections in this introduction coax readers into making appropriate judgments about what this story is about and what (or who) is the driving force behind it.

This prefatory passage affirms that the unfolding story of Acts is a story of continuity on two interrelated levels.

First, the story of Jesus in both the Third Gospel and Acts is a continuation of the OT story of God. Both the OT literary allusions and the ascension scene in Acts point to God's presence and activity. Jesus' teaching about the kingdom of God and his twice-repeated promise of the Holy Spirit indicate that what happened in the forty days was consistent with what the Lukan Gospel presents: God was at work to fulfill God's promises to Israel. Readers must keep this important message and emphasis in mind as the narrative moves toward the Pentecost events of ch 2. There Peter's explanation will unpack these themes more fully (2:14-36). Ultimately, the ascension is about God's presence and fulfillment of divine promises.

Second, the story of Acts continues the story of Jesus as presented in the Third Gospel. There is an inherent theological and christological emphasis in Acts. The activities of the apostles and other believers are linked to the purposes and activities of Jesus as the Jewish Messiah (Christ), as presented in the Gospel of Luke. All else that happens in Acts begins with God's purposes as seen in Jesus as depicted in the Lukan Gospel.

Thus, when Jesus commissions his apostles to witness "to the ends of the earth" (1:8), no hint appears about the replacement of Israel as God's people with the church or about the creation of the church as a spiritual Israel. Rather, the cues about taking the gospel message about Jesus to the Gentiles come from the OT understanding of Israel as God's people. The story of Acts is a continuation of the story of God and the people of God. It is ultimately a part of God's plan of salvation from the beginning. The story begins with God and points back to God.

The continuity of these related stories emphasizes the apostles' role as witness *and* the Spirit's role as the power for witness. On the one hand, the apostles not only were called to be witnesses but also were prepared for their task. The extended time of preparation indicates that the experience of the extraordinary or divine occurrences was not sufficient. These verses imply the exercise of theological reflection: Jesus and the Eleven wrestled together with the implications of all Jesus embodied *as* the gospel. This reflection provided the context for them to discover the connections between their experience and God's purposes. At the beginning of Acts, Luke nudges us to be reflective in our reading and in our testimony regarding God's grace on our lives.

On the other hand, the words of Jesus in Acts 1 define the role of the Spirit in terms of witness rather than in terms of believers and their lives in obedience to God. Unlike Paul in Rom 8, Luke offers *nothing* here about the role of the Spirit in salvation, one's personal life, strength for living faithfully, or one's relationship with God. Rather, Acts describes the role of the Spirit in terms of empowerment for ministry as witnesses. The promise of the Spirit is to enable the church to fulfill God's purposes for God's people. It is not for the fulfillment of personal goals or aspirations for the Christian life. Luke redirects our attention again and again to God *alone*, rather than to what God can do for us.

II. GOD AND THE PEOPLE OF GOD: RESTORATION AND DIVISION IN JERUSALEM: ACTS 1:12—8:3

A. Gathering and Preparations (1:12-26)

BEHIND THE TEXT

The seamless transition from the first eleven verses to the next section leads some scholars to conclude that vv 12-14 also belong to the preface of Acts. In many ways, this unit moves the action from the Mount of Olives back to Jerusalem, where the focus will remain until ch 8. These verses also maintain the Jewish character of the narrative found in the opening of Acts.

The naming of the Mount of Olives as the location of Jesus' ascension and where he gave the promise of his return—*after* these things happened—underscores its significance. This was the location of Jesus' time of prayer prior to his arrest (Luke 22:39-46). It was also the same place Zech 14:1-4 identifies with the coming of Yahweh or "the Lord" (*kyrios* [LXX]) in victory over Judah's enemies on the "day of the Lord."

65

The distance that the apostles traveled back to Jerusalem was "a Sabbath day's walk"—about three-quarters of a mile (about a kilometer). This was how far people could walk without violating Jewish regulations regarding the Sabbath (Exod 16:29; Num 35:5). Jesus' ascension probably did not happen on the Sabbath, but the mention of this detail uses available imagery to present his followers as faithful Jews.

Throughout the biblical texts, a select group of images, stories, and numbers guides readers by linking events and concepts together. One of these is the number "twelve." It never appears *directly* in this passage, but it is inferred through the selection of Matthias as the twelfth apostle to replace Judas.

The number "twelve" is associated with Israel as the people of God—the twelve tribes of Israel. Jesus declared the *twelve* apostles would serve as judges over these *twelve* tribes (Luke 22:29-30). He commissioned them as his apostolic successors with distinct overtones regarding the restoration of Israel (Acts 1:4-8). The death of Judas meant that Jesus' "Twelve" must be restored so that they might fulfill that mission (Wall 2002, 48) and preserve the gospel tradition (see 2:42; 6:1-6; Luke 1:1-4).

Biblical accounts of the death of Judas are found only here and in Matt 27:1-10. Significant differences exist between them. In Matthew, Judas is remorseful (Matt 27:3-5); in Acts, he is not. In Matthew, the "blood money" Judas received and returned financed the purchase of the "Field of Blood" (Matt 27:6-8). In Acts, his ghastly death in the field he himself already purchased with that money leads the locals to label the land similarly. In Matthew, the account follows immediately after Peter's betrayal of Jesus (Matt 26:69-75), which contrasts the remorse of these two apostles. Acts places the account within the scene dealing with Judas' replacement, drawing attention to the theological significance regarding the needed restoration of the Twelve.

IN THE TEXT

■ **12-13** The first word, **then**, indicates that no momentous break in the action occurs between v 12 and the ascension scene. The apostles' return to Jerusalem is in direct obedience to Jesus' specific instructions (1:4). Apparently, they return to the place where they stayed during the forty days between Jesus' resurrection and ascension.

The location is only described as **an upstairs room** (*to hyperōon*; see also 9:37, 39; 20:8), which has traditionally been understood as the same room (*anagaion* [Luke 22:12]) where Jesus celebrated Passover with his apostles and others. Both the intensive form of the verb *katamenō* (**stay**) and its imperfect periphrastic construction (→ 1:14) underscore the apostles' obedience: they "stayed put."

The list of the apostles (v 13) is a conventional aspect of ancient succession narratives. These typically name those who assumed leadership after the death of a political figure or a movement's founder. Noting the apostles present reminds readers of the group's incomplete number without Judas and prepares for the next scene, which deals with his replacement.

The list's arrangement resembles that found in Luke 6:14-16. The two differences are that Andrew's name has been moved from second to fourth position, and the names of James and John have been reversed. Possible reasons for the shuffle may be: (*a*) to place Peter, John, and James first since Acts specifically mentions only these three subsequently; or (*b*) to record the names in order of their narrative prominence, from the greatest to the least.

■ **14** Acts mentions others with the apostles: **the women and Mary the mother of Jesus**. This is consistent with the Third Gospel's inclusion of women as followers of Jesus and participants in his ministry (Luke 8:1-3; 10:38-42; 24:1-11). However, the subsequent role of women in Acts is surprisingly minimal. Luke does not identify any women other than Mary. But the group probably included those who came from Galilee with Jesus, witnessed the crucifixion, and discovered the empty tomb (Luke 23:49, 55—24:9). Some interpreters think Jesus' **brothers** here were other disciples (some MSS have "disciples" [*mathētōn*]; see Luke 8:19-21). However, this likely refers to his blood brothers or relatives.

Acts summarizes what happened with these obedient followers of Jesus. It focuses holistically on the group rather than a collection of individuals. Both the adjective **all** and the adverb **together** highlight the communal bond between them.

The Believers "Together"

The adverb **together** (*homothymadon*) appears eleven times in the NT, ten of these in Acts. Six times (1:14; 2:46; 4:24; 5:12; 8:6; 15:25) the term refers to the unanimity of an early Christian group in positive ways. However, in three instances (7:57; 18:12; 19:29) the narrator uses the same term to describe the actions of opponents who joined ranks *against* the Jesus movement. Such usage of the term depicts the believers and their opponents in contrasting ways, a common ancient literary convention for emphasis of a key theme.

The expression **joined . . . constantly** (*ēsan proskarterountes*) describes an inner compulsion or persistent devotion that characterizes the entire context. This Greek imperfect periphrastic construction is a common stylistic feature of Acts. It underscores the ongoing, typical behavior of the believers.

Here, Luke mentions this devotion as observable in the group's practice of **prayer**. This is noteworthy, considering the connection between prayer and the Holy Spirit in the Lukan Gospel (see, e.g., Luke 3:21-23; 11:1-13). Such attention to prayer helps build anticipation in readers regarding the coming of the promised Holy Spirit (Acts 1:4-5, 8).

■ **15** The conjunction *kai*, **and**, links the subsequent scene to the previous paragraph. But the phrase **in those days** also indicates a distinct shift in time. The notation regarding the size of the group indicates that the gathered **believers** (lit., **brothers**) include not only the apostles but *many* others as well.

As is typical in Acts, the narrator employs numbers to indicate something about this now larger yet unspecified group. The particle translated **about** indicates that the number is an approximation. The number itself, **a hundred and twenty**, may represent an authentic gathering of God's people, especially since this was the minimum number of men required for a legitimate, local Jewish council (*m. Sanh.* 1.6).

The group's size probably necessitated a change in location from the upstairs room mentioned earlier (v 13). But the text itself mentions nothing about that. Most translations fail to translate the phrase *epi to auto*, which links this scene to the subsequent Pentecost scene. There, the same phrase reappears (2:1) and describes the believers as "together" or "in one place."

■ **16-20** Peter, as the spokesperson for the believers, addresses the dilemma regarding Judas. The opening address, ***Men, brothers***, may refer only to the apostles (see vv 17, 22). But this idiomatic expression may refer to everyone gathered, both men and women. Given Peter's failures before Jesus' crucifixion (see Luke 22:54-62), his interpretation of Scripture and discernment of God's purposes in ways reminiscent of Jesus are a surprising development. Specifically, he interprets both Judas' death and his vacant apostolic role in light of Scripture.

Peter's reference to the fulfillment of **the Scripture** (note the singular *graphēn*; Acts 1:17) resembles Jesus' words about himself (Luke 24:44-46). It implies that he has a specific passage in mind. In Acts 1:20, he combines *two* passages from the Psalms. The first portion adapts the LXX rendering of Ps 69:25. The term **place** may denote a house as well as a **field** (Acts 1:18) or homestead. Its curse seems to be linked to Judas' gruesome death, which Luke graphically describes in a side note (vv 18-19).

Unlike Matthew's version, there is no indication that Judas committed suicide. The Lukan version of Judas' death and the description of Judas' money in terms of **wickedness** or ***wrongdoing*** resemble similar Jewish stories of divine judgments bringing about the deaths of the wicked (e.g., 2 Sam 20:9-10; 2 Macc 9:5-9). The reason for Judas' judgment was his treacherous act against Jesus. Despite his inclusion among the Twelve and his apostolic **ministry** (Acts 1:17, 25), he betrayed Jesus by becoming a **guide** (*hodēgou*: ***one who leads the way***) for Jesus' captors (v 16).

The cited portion of Ps 69:25 refers to the judgment against Judas, even the field he purchased. But this does not explain the citation of a second passage from the Psalms in the same verse. It slightly adapts the LXX version of Ps 109:8, abruptly introducing the need to fill Judas' vacant place among the Twelve. On closer inspection, the first passage may suggest that Judas' apostolic **place** must remain vacant. Peter's interpretation resolves the contradictory imperatives of the two passages (Novick 2010, 795-99).

■ **21-22** The opening verb here, *dei*, **it is necessary**, introduces the divine necessity of finding a replacement for Judas. The number of the apostles must be restored to Twelve (see "Behind the Text" above). Peter presents two general but essential requirements for qualified candidates.

First, the replacement candidates needed to be associated with Jesus throughout his ministry. That this requirement is stated twice (vv 21, 22) underscores its importance (Gaventa 2003, 71). This requirement distinguishes all candidates from Judas himself, whose death preceded Jesus' ascension (v 21).

The wording of Peter's recommendation refers only to *male (andrōn)* followers of Jesus. This seems to reflect the characteristics of either (a) the apostolic group, including the predominant role of male characters in Acts generally (a characteristic that differs from the Third Gospel), or (b) a developing trend in the early church that did not reflect the inclusivity of Jesus.

Second, the chosen candidate must **become a witness** to Jesus' resurrection. The phrase **with us** probably refers specifically to the apostles rather than generally to the entire group of believers. All candidates must embrace Jesus' commission to be his witnesses (1:8) after the coming of the promised Spirit. Such a requirement implies that the group has embraced Jesus' commission and is responding in faithful obedience to that call (Tannehill 1990, 21).

■ **23-25** Based on Peter's recommendation, they nominate two candidates: Joseph called Barsabbas and Matthias. Although the whole group presumably offered the two names, the ambiguity leaves open the possibility that only the eleven apostles were involved in the nominating process. Both the ensuing prayer and the selection of the new apostle reflect the believers' faith in God. The prayer expresses their confidence that *God* would select the apostle (see 1:2) and make God's will abundantly clear, as the intensive imperative *anadeixon*, **show**, conveys.

Both the designation **Lord** (*kyrie*) and the descriptor *the one who knows everyone's heart* reflect common biblical understandings of God in terms of sovereignty and knowledge. The wording of their prayer reflects (v 25) that the believers recognize the irony of what happened to Judas: he gave up his *place* (*ton topon*) of ministry and apostleship for *his own place* (*ton topon ton idion*) of death. The verb translated **left** (*parebē*) suggests this occurred through Judas' transgression (*parabainō* is the root of the noun *parabasis*, "transgression").

■ 26 The Third Gospel mentions that the casting of **lots** decided the division of Jesus' clothes during his crucifixion (Luke 23:34). By this same means, the believers seek God's will. This was a common practice of discernment within Jewish circles (e.g., Lev 16:8; Josh 18:6; 1 Sam 14:42).

In this instance, casting lots probably involved writing the names onto stones or other objects, placing those items into a vessel or bag, and then either drawing one out or allowing one to fall out, as the verb *piptō* suggests (see Josephus, *Ant.* 6.62). Ironically, the group cast **lots** (*klērous*) to replace one who once obtained from Jesus a ***share*** or "lot" (*klēron*) in this apostolic ministry (1:17).

With that selection, the number of apostles was again restored to twelve. The verb **added** (*synkatapsēphizō*) appears only here in the NT. The term refers to someone added to a group by a vote. But the Lukan picture focuses on the believers' recognition of God's selection and their cooperation with God's purposes.

Some interpreters note with surprise that neither Matthias nor Barsabbas appears again in Acts. However, their hidden narrative role is not unlike most other apostles in Acts. The narrative focuses on the importance of God's restoration of the Twelve through the community of believers rather than the subsequent role of any specific individual in the narrative itself.

FROM THE TEXT

The extraordinary Pentecost scene that follows often overshadows this remarkable passage. However, one may rightly argue that Acts 2 depends on what Luke describes in the latter part of ch 1. Here he prepares his readers for a pivotal scene in his story by focusing attention on the gathered followers of Jesus.

The events on the Mount of Olives and later in the upstairs room seem to present believers as separated from and beyond the hostile reach of the temple officials (Spencer 2004a, 38-40). The narrator turns readers' attention to dynamics and activities among the believers themselves. One finds no hints of tension or opposition here. Rather, the believers gather obediently with a sense of quiet resolve and expectancy in prayer, which unites them when uncertainty could (should) have torn them apart.

Obedience, prayer, and unity cannot go unnoticed as the context of the dilemma Peter introduces to the larger group. Acts' placement of the account of Judas' death suggests that his betrayal of Jesus was not simply an individual failure. Rather, it fractured the Twelve, the group Jesus chose to represent God's purposes to restore Israel as the people of God. It threatened the mission Jesus had given to his apostles, the accomplishment of what Jesus had promised (1:8), and, as a result, God's saving plan (Johnson 1992, 38-39).

The faithful followers of Jesus recognize both the problem and the divine solution through prayer and Scripture. Even the casting of lots, within this context of unity and prayer, reflects this corporate sense of confidence in God, God's faithfulness, and God's plan. This enabled believers to discern the purposes of God and participate in the preparation for the events at Pentecost.

B. Pentecost and the Fulfillment of God's Promises to Israel (2:1-47)

1. The Coming of the Holy Spirit (2:1-13)

BEHIND THE TEXT

Jesus' promise of the coming Holy Spirit, the ascension, the gathering of believers in earnest prayer, and the restoration of the Twelve in ch 1 all anticipate divine fulfillment in ch 2. The abrupt transition of v 1 and references to persons and locations from ch 1 all suggest that one must read the Pentecost event in light of the preceding narratives.

The general setting of this chapter is the Jewish festival of Pentecost. The term "Pentecost" transliterates the Greek word *pentēkostē*, meaning *fiftieth day*. It does not appear in the OT but is used several times in nearly contemporary Jewish literature (Tob 2:1; 2 Macc 12:32; Josephus, *J.W.* 6.299) to identify the Jewish Festival of Weeks (see Exod 23:16a; 34:22; Lev 23:15-22; Num 28:26-31; Deut 16:9-12). This harvest celebration occurred fifty days after Passover. It was the second of three annual pilgrimage festivals in the Jewish calendar, which partly explains the crowds and diverse nationalities mentioned in Acts 2:9-11.

Such festivals included praise to God for blessing and provision. By the early second century, the festival was associated with covenantal renewal (see, e.g., Barrett 1994, 111-12; Conzelmann 1987, 15-16; but see *Jub.* 1:1; 6:17-19; 1QS1.8—2.5). These associations seem plausible and consistent with the perspective of Acts for two reasons. First, the Lukan imagery in Acts 2:2-4 alludes to multiple scenes in the Pentateuch of the formation of Israel as the covenantal people of God. Second, this imagery resembles Philo's description of the giving of the Jewish law (*Decal.* 46) from the late first century AD (see, e.g., Johnson 1992, 45-46; Fitzmyer 1998, 233-34).

IN THE TEXT

■ 1 The conjunction *kai* (*and*) connects this passage to the events of ch 1. The passive infinitive *symplērousthai* describing the coming of the **day of Pentecost** (v 1) conveys the idea of fulfillment. This parallels the beginning of Jesus' journey toward Jerusalem in the Third Gospel (Luke 9:51). In both instances, prophecies precede the fulfillment. With the concerns for divine fulfillment in Acts 1, this word provokes a sense of expectation of what will soon occur.

The narrator mentions those involved in vv 1-4 with only ambiguous third-person labels, implied by the verbs. Such literary cues encourage readers to refer back to the previous scene to identify who **they** may be. Some commentators think the implied pronouns with *pantes* (**all**) refer to the Twelve. But the mention of the 120 in 1:15 suggests that these pronouns refer to that larger group. The adverb *homou* (**together**) functions like its synonym, *homothymadon*, in 1:14, which describes the gathering of believers, including the apostles and others.

The phrase **in one place** (*epi to auto*) earlier describes the gathered group of 120 believers (1:15). Most interpreters assume the phrase here refers to the upstairs room (1:13). The phrase links the earlier setting with this one, but the location may have shifted to the outer courts of the temple. The term translated "house" (*oikos* [v 2]) is not a typical Lukan designation for the Jewish temple (*naos* or *hieron*), but it sometimes refers to it in the LXX (Isa 6:1, 4) and Luke's Gospel (2:49; see Williams 1990, 39-40). Several literary cues support this possibility: (*a*) the larger group mentioned in Acts 1:15; (*b*) the fulfillment language of v 1; and (*c*) the Jewish crowds that gather for the festival and then hear what transpires (vv 5-13). If the Lukan agenda includes the fulfillment of God's promises and purposes for Israel, the temple would be a plausible and significant location for that.

■ **2-3** The description of the event itself is cursory at best. Rather than fixating on specific details, Luke seems intent on introducing the Spirit's work among these believers. His rich OT imagery alludes to the Jewish Scriptures and the tradition of God's presence among the people of God.

The expression ***sound from heaven*** is reminiscent of the noise accompanying God's appearance on Mount Sinai (Exod 19:16-19). **Like** compares the sound to that of **wind**, which often symbolized the Spirit of God (e.g., Ezek 37:9-14). In both Hebrew and Greek, the terms referring to wind and Spirit share a common root. Blowing wind evokes thoughts of the creative and life-giving movement of the Spirit of God (see Gen 1:2; 2:7).

Jewish tradition associates **fire** (Acts 2:3) with the presence of God (see Gen 15:17; Exod 3:2; 13:21-22), particularly at the giving of the Law (Philo, *Decal.* 46). Sometimes, the combination of wind and fire in the OT depicts God's presence (Ps 104:4; Isa 66:15). The sound that those present ***heard*** and the tongues like fire that they **saw** provide firsthand evidence of the coming of the Spirit. Both Jewish and Greco-Roman writings of Luke's day associated fire with prophetic inspiration (Wall 2002, 54-55). Thus, the vision of ***divided tongues like fire*** on each believer hints that they all are inspired to speak as prophets (see Num 11:29).

■ **4** Consistent with various Jewish connotations of fire, this verse identifies the Holy Spirit as the source of their inspiration. The verb *apophthengomai* denotes that the Spirit enables believers to speak in bold and inspired ways (Haenchen 1971, 168). In addition, the imperfect tense of the indicative *edidou* (**was giving**) emphasizes that their prophetic proclamation continues. However, the narrator's evidence for the Spirit's inspiration is not through *what* they proclaim but *how* they do so.

Contemporary readers often associate the expression **other tongues** with the phenomenon of glossolalia, speaking in tongues, interpreted in light of Paul's mention of tongues in 1 Cor 12—14. However, the term *glōssa* (tongue) in Acts 2:4 and 11 is used synonymously with another noun, *dialektos* (**native language**), in vv 6 and 8. The literary context depicts believers speaking in human languages previously unknown to those speakers.

Verse 4 does not mention what they speak, leaving readers to infer from Jesus' commissioning statements (1:4-8) that their message witnesses about him. The mention of fire and the Holy Spirit indicates the fulfillment of the prophecy of John the Baptist (Luke 3:16). However, more significant is the fulfillment of *Jesus'* promise to his apostles (Acts 1:4-5, 8). They are all **filled with the Holy Spirit**. The indicative translated **filled** (*eplēsthēsan*) emphasizes fulfillment due to the Spirit's coming.

■ **5-12** Although Luke describes the extraordinary event in a mere four verses, he follows this succinct account with an additional nine verses of clarification. The gathered believers had witnessed distinctive aspects of the phenomenal event. But Luke focuses on bystanders whose words validate the narrator's cursory description of the atypical activity and proclamation. Luke introduces these other "witnesses" by noting four things about them in vv 5-6.

First, they were **Jews residing in Jerusalem**. The participle *kataoikountes* (**residing**) suggests they were not Pentecost pilgrims but residents of Jerusalem. That city residents were presumed to be Jewish may explain the omission of the word **Jews** from some MSS.

Second, the adjective *eulabēs* describes them affirmatively as **pious** or "devout" (NRSV) Jews.

Third, these inhabitants of Jerusalem apparently came **from every nation under heaven** (see Deut 2:25). This suggests they were Diaspora Jews.

The Diaspora

The word "Diaspora" derives from the Greek verb *diaspeirō* meaning "scatter." After the Babylonian Exile, many Jewish captives did not return to Israel. In the ensuing centuries, a large percentage of the Jewish populace "scattered" to other parts of the Mediterranean world. In the first century AD, over 80 percent of all Jews lived outside the land that had once comprised the Davidic kingdom. The present phrase provides a visual image of the Diaspora Jews.

Fourth, this group of pious Jews was quite large, as the noun *to plēthos* (**crowd**) denotes. Thus, the Lukan image is of a large gathering of the very best and most faithful of the Jewish people (Barrett 1994, 118).

The literary structure of vv 6-12 focuses readers' attention on three elements. Two elements frame the passage: various descriptions of reactions of the assembled crowd (vv 6-8, 11-12), and repeated references to hearing the believers speak in their own languages (vv 6, 8, 11). The third stands at the center between these elements: a list of nationalities and nations in vv 9-11.

The reason that the crowd gathers together is **this sound** that they hear. This expression may possibly refer to the **sound** like wind (v 2). But the change in terms and the context suggest that it is the sound of *speaking* believers. This point—that these Jewish people hear speaking in the native language of each person—is mentioned three times: first by the narrator (v 6) and then corroborated twice by the Jewish crowd itself (vv 8, 11).

The bystanders declare that believers proclaimed ***the mighty works of God*** (v 11), a familiar OT expression (e.g., Deut 11:2; Ps 71:18-19). They confirm what Luke has already presented regarding God's role in the coming of the Spirit. The added sense of surprise over the speakers being from Galilee (Acts 2:7) accentuates the miraculous event: those in Jerusalem may have had arrogant biases toward their unrefined fellow Jews from the north (Malina and Neyrey 1991a, 103-4; Spencer 2004a, 43-44).

Apparently, this speaking in other languages prompts mixed reactions. Luke describes these with four different verbs.

The first verb ***bewildered*** or ***confused*** (*syncheō* [v 6]) also appears in Gen 11:7, 9 (LXX), which describes the confusion during the Babel incident. However, unlike Babel and its *miscommunication* due to multiple languages, here the confusion is due ironically to the *communicative effect* through the languages.

The second verb **amazed** (*existēmi* [vv 7, 12]) conveys that the crowd is surprised and conflicted because they are having difficulty comprehending what just happened (BDAG 2000, 350).

The third verb ***astonished*** (*thaumazō*) is a favorite Lukan term, often depicting wonder and admiration (e.g., Luke 4:22; 7:9; 8:25; 20:26; 24:12, 41; Acts 3:12; 4:13). The imperfect tense of the last three verbs conveys these reactions as ongoing, alongside the believers' continuing proclamation.

The last verb **perplexed** (*diaporeō* [v 12]) connotes the crowd being at a complete loss over what has just occurred.

In the middle of these references to the crowd's reactions, Luke narrates that the observers themselves identify a list of nationalities represented among them (vv 9-11). The catalog includes fifteen places and groups, extending from the **Parthians** in the east (first in the list) to **Rome** in the west.

Although the list highlights the linguistic diversity represented by those at Pentecost, scholars have long debated about possible sources or influences behind the composition of this particular record. The Lukan list resembles other lists of nations in Jewish texts, which often functioned to describe the extent of the Diaspora (e.g., Philo, *Embassy* 281-82; also Philo, *Flaccus* 45-46; Josephus, *J.W.* 2.398; see Barrett 1994, 122). Others have understood the list to reflect the eschatological expectation articulated by OT prophets and in later Jewish tradition—that God would gather the scattered Jews of the world in Jerusalem (see, e.g., Isa 11:11-12; 43:5-6; see Krodel 1986, 77).

The general structure of the list roughly arranges the various locations according to compass directions. They start in the east, with **Jerusalem** as the earth's center. The list offers a verbal map of the global spread of salvation throughout the world through the restoration of Israel (Bauckham 1995b, 417-27; Gaventa 2003, 75; Spencer 2004a, 44). Surprisingly, Luke offers these hints to his readers about the significance of the event through the comments of baffled bystanders!

The mention of ***others*** may seem surprising if one misses the hyperbolic force of "all" in v 12 (CEB, NRSV). The narrated response in vv 5-12 is a mixture of confusion and wonder. This leads to the inquiry about the meaning of what has transpired.

■ **13** Some bystanders have already formed negative conclusions. The participle *diachleuazontes* connotes intense sneering (see NRSV) or ***mocking*** against the believers. This exposes the attitude behind what these say. The verb tenses, both of this participle and the indicative *elegon* (***were saying***), depict the continuation of this verbal abuse. These others malign the believers as intoxicated. The perfect tense of the verbal construction translated ***they are filled*** implies that they are feeling the side effects of having consumed too much ***new wine***. People tended to drink this in excess because of its sweetness.

From the Lukan perspective, the mockers misinterpret the event because they overlook what God had done. By including this latter group, the narrator leaves readers with an ambiguous picture of mixed responses from the Jews who gather and observe the extraordinary event.

FROM THE TEXT

This particular scene has received more attention than any other in Acts, with good reason. Only here (i.e., Acts 1—2) in the NT do we find any mention of *either* Jesus' ascension (1:1-11) *or* the subsequent Pentecost event (2:1-13). Only here in the NT do we find this vivid, memorable account of the coming of the Holy Spirit upon humanity, which Acts depicts as the fulfillment both of Jesus' promise to the apostles (1:4-8) and of God's promises to Israel (2:14-36).

Brevity of detail leaves much to readers' imaginations. Nevertheless, this dramatic encounter between the divine and Jesus' obedient followers resulted in a conspicuous display of God's faithfulness. This left other Jewish bystanders puzzling over what to make of it.

The inability to "avoid the obvious" may be precisely the function of the narration for ancient and contemporary readers of Acts. Spectacular phenomena allude to OT images of God and God's presence at the Pentecost event. But readers' attention is inescapably drawn to the workings of God. Rather than being enamored by the ability to speak in such remarkable ways, the Lukan narration coaxes faithful readers to recognize the movement of God among those who had faithfully gathered in obedience and prayer. Just as God breathed into the first human at creation, here at Pentecost readers observe God's creative work in the inbreathing of the Holy Spirit among the group of Jesus' followers (Haenchen 1971, 173-74).

In addition to the fulfillment of divine promises, two additional matters stand out in Luke's rendering of the Pentecost event.

First, the Holy Spirit came upon the *people*, not upon one or more *individuals*. Contemporary discussions about the role of the Spirit often focus on the individual. Luke concentrates instead on (*a*) the Spirit's coming upon the gathered community of persons, who represent the people of God through the restoration of the Twelve; (*b*) the unanimity among them; (*c*) the practice of prayer; and (*d*) obedience. The list of nationalities (vv 7-9) ultimately points to what God was doing for *all* Israel as the people of God. Thus, God's blessing and empowerment were corporate rather than private, collective rather than personal. Readings that privatize the coming of the Holy Spirit misunderstand the theological implications of this passage with regard to the people of God.

Second, the coming of the Holy Spirit resulted in believers speaking in extraordinary ways that baffled Jewish bystanders. But such divinely enabled speaking was for the sake of proclamation and salvation to all. It was for the Jewish Diaspora and, by implication, the rest of the world.

Contemporary readers sometimes attempt to interpret speaking "in other tongues" (v 4) in light of Paul's discussion in 1 Cor 12—14. However, Luke describes something rather different. He concentrates on how God's purposes and presence enabled faithful believers to proclaim what God was doing to others in known languages. Luke emphasizes the Spirit's role that enabled this gathering of believers to serve as Jesus' witnesses (Acts 1:8). That is, the Spirit did not come for the sake of the witnesses *themselves* but for the sake of their proclamation for others. The diverse crowd of bystanders came together not through a common language but as "the consequence of the generative activity of the Spirit" (Green 2008, 213).

One should not overlook the importance of Pentecost for the Christian faith. Pentecost occupies a key place in Acts, as one can readily see by its placement early in the narrative, the extended explanation of what happened that follows (2:14-36), and repeated references to the event—both direct (11:15; 15:8) and indirect (8:17; 10:45-46; 19:6)—throughout Acts. The place of Pentecost within the Christian calendar continues to affirm the importance of the event.

Some churches and theological traditions have looked to specific aspects of the Lukan narrative about Pentecost as a normative description for contemporary Christians. Some focus on distinctive Christian practices such as glossolalia or specific "steps" for the Christian experience of God's grace. The paucity of clear information in Luke's account tends to diminish the plausibility of such readings. This is especially true for those seeking theological precision out of narrative texts (→ "Engaging Acts in a New Day" in Introduction).

We should attempt to visualize from Luke's picture of Pentecost what God has done and is doing through the Spirit among God's people. If we do, the church will be in a better position to consider what it might mean for us to engage such a passage in faithful ways.

For many within the Wesleyan-holiness tradition, a close reading of the Pentecost account in Acts reveals something rather different from the commonplace exposition. Most teaching and preaching for the past two centuries focused on individualized notions of the baptism with the Holy Spirit. Some attempted to appropriate this particular scene to urge believers to seek a "personal Pentecost." Those who were willing to offer themselves completely to God and God's will might receive the Holy Spirit as had believers on that first Christian Pentecost. Others understood this passage as the equivalent of entire sanctification, a subsequent work of divine grace in the lives of believers after conversion. While such teachings may have biblical support, reading them here has often ignored specific aspects of the *Lukan* depiction of Pentecost. Specifically, they bypass Peter's explanation (2:14-36), which describes it in historic terms as God's fulfillment of God's promise to Israel.

Nonetheless, the emphases of this passage within the broader picture of the book of Acts ring true with important theological themes of the Wesleyan tradition. The scene concentrates, not on what God does on behalf of *individual* believers, but on what God accomplishes *through the gathered followers of Jesus*. The Pentecost scene in Acts may not spell out a sequence of works of grace through which Christians may experience God's sanctifying grace. But it does offer a powerful image of effective proclamation and ministry as a result of the Spirit's filling.

Rather than common emphases about the Spirit's role in strengthening believers for the sake of faithful living, this pivotal scene in Acts focuses attention on the Spirit's enablement of the faithful people of God to live as

God's servants on behalf of the rest of humanity. Seen in this light, the Lukan depiction of Pentecost corresponds with Wesleyan teachings about Christian perfection, which affirms loving others as a reflection of the love of God.

2. Peter Speaks to the Gathered Crowd (2:14-41)

BEHIND THE TEXT

Speeches from leading characters play a prominent role in the Acts narrative (→ "Literary Features" in Introduction). Like speeches in other historiographical works from the Greco-Roman era, the speeches in Acts do not simply recount what happened or restate in verbatim fashion what was declared (see 2:40, which summarizes undisclosed parts of Peter's explanation as "many other words"). Rather, through speech material the author provides the reader with selected comments or explanatory information about something that had or will happen in the narrative.

By using reliable characters to inform readers, the author remains "behind the scenes," assisting them and their interpretation of the narrative in more implicit than obvious ways. Thus, readers should interpret these speeches with due regard for their literary placement, not merely with historical concerns in mind. That is, when one interprets Peter's speech, one must consider its function not only for Peter's audience but also for faithful readers of Acts as they seek to understand the Lukan narrative.

A noteworthy feature of this particular speech is the central role and use of the Jewish Scriptures. On the one hand, Peter's speech draws from the prophet Joel and the Psalms to interpret this momentous Pentecost event. Thus, these passages provide interpretive lenses through which to view the event and understand it as the fulfillment of God's promises.

On the other hand, Peter offers a form of Jewish midrash or commentary on the OT. He does this directly on selected passages from the Psalms and indirectly on the Joel passage (see Wall 2002, 65). Peter's comments or interpretive remarks about these passages and his quotation of the passages contribute to the rhetorical purposes of the speech within Acts. Perhaps most significant is Peter's christological reading of the OT. This reading depends on the LXX rather than on the Hebrew text.

IN THE TEXT

■ **14-15** Both the question and sarcasm from some in the crowd prompt Peter to respond. Three aspects of the Lukan introduction of Peter's speech imply that both the crowd and Luke's readers should perceive it as authoritative.

First, that Peter **stood** is significant, since the Hellenistic orator took that posture when delivering a public speech.

Second, by mentioning the other eleven apostles, the author hints that Peter's imminent message represents the apostolic Twelve (see their importance in 1:15-26, also the crowd's response to them in 2:37).

Third, a form of the verb *apophthengomai*, used earlier to describe the believers' Spirit-inspired speech (2:4), describes Peter as he addresses the crowd.

Two questions come with the identification of Peter's audience. First, does he address only males, as the wording of the first part—*andres Ioudaioi*, (lit.) either **Men, Jews** or **Men, Judeans**—may suggest (see Seim 1994, 134-37)? Acts often employs the expression in speech material in formal addresses to audiences that include both men and women (e.g., 1:16; 3:12; 13:26, 38; 15:7, 13). Second, does Peter address **Jews** or "Judeans" (CEB)? The second Greek term could refer to either. The catalog of nationalities in vv 9-11 and the subsequent use of the term in Acts suggest the more generic translation.

Thus, Peter identifies himself with his audience as a fellow Jew. The more specific description of those **who live in Jerusalem** highlights two things: (1) the spiritual center of Israel where God's promise found fulfillment, and (2) those whom Peter would later incriminate for Jesus' death (2:23).

Peter's initial words declare his intentions: he would offer clarity to the crowd's confusion and correct their presumed misunderstanding (v 13). The idea of knowing or understanding frames the main body of the speech (vv 14, 36). The call for listening is crucial here: the verb translated **listen** (*enōtizomai*), only here in the NT, is used thirteen times in the LXX. It literally means "to put in one's ears."

Peter counters the assumption (as the verb *hypolambanō* connotes) that intoxication has occasioned the believers' unusual speaking. Some have suggested that **nine in the morning** (lit., *third hour of the day*) was the Jewish morning prayer time. So no meal with wine would have been served before then. However, Peter's remarks probably reflect the common sentiment that only the most disgraceful individual would be drunk at that early hour (see Cicero, *Phil.* 2.41.104). Given the sarcastic comments of v 13, Peter's response may simply and humorously assert, "It's just too early for that!"

■ **16-18** The conjunction *alla* (**No**) indicates that Peter's explanation rejects the skeptics' assumption about the believers' condition. The Pentecost happenings are not disgraceful; they fulfill OT prophetic descriptions regarding God's promise of the coming age of the Spirit. Although some MSS omit the prophet's name, the cited passage is Joel 2:28-32. It appears within a context that calls for Judah's repentance and offers hope for God's forgiveness.

These words *were spoken* [passive participle: *to eirēmenon*] *through the prophet*, who served as God's spokesperson and delivered God's message. The addition of the words **God says** to the quoted passage further affirms this. The phrase **in the last days** replaces the LXX phrase "after these things." This al-

79

lows Peter to link the OT reference to an undefined future time to what has just occurred in his time as part of God's eschatological acts of salvation.

By quoting this prophetic passage, Acts substantiates its narrative ascription of the believers' extraordinary speaking to the Spirit's work. The *Spirit's* activity, not unusual speech, prompts inclusion of this passage within the narrative. The indicative translated **pour out** (*ekcheō*) pictures a heavy deluge of rain to describe the dramatic fulfillment of *God's* promise by *God* (as the first-person form of the verb indicates).

The prepositional phrase *apo tou pneumatos mou*, quoting the LXX, does not literally render the Hebrew. Translations, however, typically reflect the Hebrew: **I will pour out my Spirit**. The LXX suggests that God will give "from" God's Spirit; the Spirit's fullness remains ultimately with God (see Bruce 1984, 89; Haenchen 1971, 179; Fitzmyer 1998, 252). Barrett considers the phrase a "surprising rendering" of the Hebrew, resulting in a partitive or material interpretation of the Spirit "hardly consistent with a developed view of the personality of the Spirit" (1994, 137). But this anachronistically evaluates the Lukan text in light of later theological developments.

The gift of the Spirit results in prophetic activity. This interprets the nature of the believers' speaking, including Peter's own speech. The verb translated **will prophesy** (*prophēteusousin*) appears in both vv 17*b* and 18*b*. The second instance is a Lukan addition to the Joel text (explaining its omission in some MSS). So the related images of prophetic activity and God's gift of the Spirit frame vv 17*b*-18.

The remainder of vv 17-18 elaborates on **all people** ("all flesh" [NRSV]) holistically. The entire community receives the divine gift of the Spirit, not only a few. In both Joel's and Peter's contexts, the immediate reference was probably the Jewish people. However, in the development of the Acts narrative, this reference includes all humanity, even Gentiles (e.g., 9:15; 10:43-46; 13:45-47; 15:12; 26:17-18; 28:28).

Joel expected both **sons and daughters** to engage in prophecy. This underscores the gender-inclusive nature of the gift of God's Spirit. However, Acts is mostly silent about the prophetic activities of women (except 21:9; see Seim 1994; Gaventa 2004, 49-60). Both **young** and **old** receive divine epiphanies and guidance, as **visions** and **dreams** frequently indicate in the LXX and even in the Greco-Roman world of the first century. Translations and commentaries often presume that these age distinctions refer only to men because of the gender of the respective Greek terms, but the literary context suggests that these specific terms indicate more generally how God's activity stretches across age groups and includes both men and women. The addition of the pronoun **my** reorients the reference to **servants** or ***slaves***, so that the emphasis is not on their socioeconomic status, but on God working through those *who belong to God*.

■ **19-20** In Joel, the cosmic **signs** are expressions of divine judgment, but not here. The words **above** and **below** are not part of the Joel passage; their addition underscores the full extent of the cosmic warnings. The Acts quotation adds the word **signs**. Paired with **wonders**, it reminds readers of Jesus' prophetic ministry (see 2:22) and of OT descriptions of Moses (Johnson 1992, 50). But signs and wonders in Acts function more generally as evidence of God's blessing and activity.

The triad of **blood, fire,** and **smoky clouds** evokes apocalyptic images of judgment, so one should not interpret them as literal representations. Some associate the sign regarding the sun with the solar darkening during Jesus' crucifixion in Luke 23:45 (e.g., Bruce 1988, 62). More generally, cosmic signs involving the sun and moon were associated with the day of God's judgment (see Luke 21:25). In particular, the imagery of the sun turning to darkness is reminiscent of Isa 13:10 and Ezek 32:7, both of which refer to God's judgment on the enemies of Israel.

Apocalyptic Imagery and Acts

Cosmic images regarding the workings of God were a common feature of apocalyptic thought in the ancient world. This perspective expected God to intervene in drastic fashion in the course of human history and to restore the people of God. Popular, contemporary interpreters sometimes assume that the dramatic, cosmic images characteristic of apocalyptic thought refer to literal, future events. But such views misunderstand the function of apocalyptic imagery in two basic ways.

First, apocalyptic imagery (like prophecy) typically interpret particular historical situations of the addressees themselves in terms of God's providence. Rather than speaking about events in the distant future, such images address contemporary contexts of the ancient people.

Second, apocalyptic imagery functions to evoke hope and confidence in the sovereignty and purposes of God. Grand, cosmic depictions of God emphasize lordship over the entire universe. Thus, these dramatic images of celestial bodies reflected God's cosmic purposes to bring salvation to pass, rather than precise, literal descriptions of what would happen in the last days.

Acts appropriates the Joel passage to interpret the Pentecost event, specifically here the sounds and sights of Pentecost (Fitzmyer 1998, 253). They reinforce the universal scope of what God has done (see Acts 2:17-18).

After these things, the **day of the Lord** comes, in which God's purposes are realized. The Hebrew text of Joel describes this day as "terrible" and in terms of judgment. But Peter's speech follows the LXX by using the adjective *epiphanēs* (**glorious**) to associate this day with the revelation of God's saving purposes.

The Lukan appropriation of the Joel passage interprets this Pentecost event in something akin to a "realized eschatological" perspective: God fulfills these prophesied promises at this particular time. Unlike common end-time scenarios today that urge readers to watch and wait for God's ultimate act of restoration, Luke offers Peter's explanation of Pentecost to show his readers that God's intervention in human history has already accomplished God's saving and transforming purposes!

Names for God and the Septuagint

In the Hebrew texts of the OT, several terms or names appear for God: *Yahweh* (God's personal or covenant name), *Elohim* (God), *Adonai* (Lord), and others. Due to their reverence for God and God's holiness, Jews avoid the pronunciation of God's personal name by speaking the name *Adonai* whenever the personal name *Yahweh* appears in a text. The Septuagint (the Greek translation of the OT from the second century BC) reflects this customary practice. It substitutes the Greek term *kyrios*, **Lord**, wherever *Yahweh* appears in the Hebrew text. Recent English translations render *Yahweh* as "LORD"—in capital and small capital letters—to distinguish these instances from those where the name *Adonai* appears in the Hebrew text. The LXX, however, obscured this distinction between the two Hebrew terms for God.

The Christian address of Jesus as "Lord" and the interpretation of OT texts with regard to Jesus rather than *Yahweh* reflect either this lack of clarity regarding the Hebrew term behind references to "the Lord" (*kyrios*) or a deliberate appropriation of OT language for *Yahweh* to describe Jesus as having "divine identity" (see Bauckham 2008, 1-59). In either sense, Christians often interpreted OT passages speaking about *Yahweh* as referring to Jesus, thereby depicting Jesus as God (*Yahweh*).

■ **21** This statement concludes not only the Joel citation but also this portion of Peter's speech. The inclusion of **everyone** within this promise of salvation corresponds with the earlier reference to "all people" (v 17). Peter probably understood this as a reference to the Jewish people. But later developments in the Christian movement, such as the inclusion of Gentiles (→ Acts 10), further explains and expands the full meaning of the promise.

The idea of calling or invoking the Lord's name focuses on a confession of faith in God. To invoke one's name is to draw on that one's authority. In Acts, similar expressions are repeated with reference to Jesus as the Messiah or Christ (9:14, 21; 15:17). Although **the Lord** (also 2:20) refers to Israel's God (Hebrew: *Yahweh*) rather than Jesus in Joel, Peter's speech declares *Jesus* also as Lord. The repeated references to Jesus' name and salvation through him in Acts 3—5 further explain this promise christologically (Tannehill 1990, 31).

■ **22-24** One may plausibly argue that the presence of the Holy Spirit is the distinguishing mark of Christianity and what makes a person Christian (Witherington 1998, 140). However, before v 22 little in Acts 2 supports this claim. The promise of the Spirit's outpouring in Joel extends to faithful Israel.

And Peter's speech clearly preserves this Jewish orientation. But what follows in Peter's speech clarifies the gift of the Spirit in christological terms.

Verses 22-24 form one complicated sentence in Greek. It begins with a second direct address of the audience. The form of that address—**Men, Israelites**—is similar to 2:14. It indicates a return to Peter's own words. The reference to Peter's audience as **Israelites** uses the sacred religious name for the Jews as the people of God.

Here, Peter first mentions Jesus in the speech. The emphasis on Jesus coming from Nazareth appears early in Acts (see 3:6; 4:10; 6:14) and later during Paul's legal defense (22:8; 24:5; 26:9). It probably counters those who insisted that the Christ could not come from there. However, Peter contends that the audience already has substantive evidence regarding Jesus' identity.

The verb translated **accredited** appears only three other times in the NT (25:7; 1 Cor 4:9; 2 Thess 2:4). It connotes something proven as true or genuine (BDAG 2000, 108). Such proof came *from God* and was evident in what God did through Jesus.

The term translated **miracles** or *powerful deeds* (*dynameis*) often describes the deeds of Jesus or his followers in both Luke (e.g., 4:14, 36; 5:17; 6:19; 10:13, 19) and Acts (3:12; 4:7, 33; 6:8; 8:10, 13; 10:38; 19:11). The pair **wonders and signs** is reminiscent of the same LXX expression that often depicts God's powerful acts on behalf of Israel (e.g., Exod 7:3; Deut 4:34; 28:46; Ps 135:9; Isa 8:18). In Acts, the expression describes God's activity through Jesus (and later through believers; see 2:43; 4:30; 5:12; 6:8; 14:3; 15:12). Peter's speech points to Jesus' divine activity during his earthly ministry as indicative of his identity. Nothing he says concerns the preexistence and incarnation of Christ.

The main part of the sentence focuses on Jesus' death (v 23). Here, the speech balances two apparently contradictory emphases. On the one hand, Peter's strong declaration places responsibility for his crucifixion squarely on his Jewish audience. Although they *personally* did not kill Jesus, the role of the Jewish leaders in the execution made the whole nation culpable (see Luke 22:1-6; 23:1-12; see Acts 2:36; 3:13; 4:10; 5:30; 7:52). However, the people were also included among those who persuaded Pilate to crucify Jesus (Luke 23:13-25).

The verb describing Jesus' crucifixion, *prospēgnymi* (**nailing**), appears only here (2:23) and in 1 Pet 1:2. It graphically depicts fastening someone or something to an object. This form of execution was reserved exclusively for Roman use. Technically, no Jew could have killed Jesus in this manner. Thus, the phrase *by the hands of the lawless* may ironically accuse the Jewish leaders for their evil complicity, hidden under the guise of religious scruples (Bock 2007, 121; Gaventa 2003, 78). The Gentiles, actually "those outside the law" (NRSV), merely served as accomplices who carried out the leaders' hostile intentions against Jesus.

On the other hand, Peter also declares that the handing over (*ekdoton*, only here in the NT) of Jesus (lit., **this one**; *touton*) to the Jews was part of God's **plan**. The emphasis on God's divine plan (*boulē*) in history appears several times in Luke (7:30) and Acts (4:28; 5:38-39; 13:36; 20:27). That plan was **established** ("definite" [NRSV]) and within God's **foreknowledge**, which underscores that nothing about these events took God by surprise.

Some theological traditions interpret this as an affirmation of predestination. However, a reading more consistent with the Lukan perspective perceives both the Jesus event and the Spirit's outpouring within the general "biblical script of God's salvation" (Wall 2002, 66). It takes for granted that God must have anticipated both before they happened. Together, the two segments of Peter's declaration introduce a paradox: the life-giving purposes of God and the life-taking (i.e., murderous) intentions of humans came together to bring about the death of Jesus.

The close of the complex sentence (v 24) that begins in v 22 contrasts God's response to Jesus' death with intentions of the Jewish leaders. Peter blames his Jewish audience for killing Jesus. But he asserts "the decisive contrast" (Marshall 1980, 75): God acted to reverse their murder of Jesus by raising him up (a common theme in Acts: e.g., 2:32; 3:15; 4:10; 5:30; 10:40; 13:30, 34; 17:31).

In Acts, the verb *anestēmi* often refers merely to someone standing up. But its noun form (*anastasis*) is the specific Greek term for resurrection. The phrase describing how God accomplished this employs a mixed metaphor.

The term translated **agony** actually refers to labor pains, so that its inferences regarding birth may seem incompatible with the death associated with it. However, the expression **the labor pains of death** likely quotes the LXX rendering of Ps 18:4 or 116:3, where the identical expression appears. The image suggests that God ended death's labor pains, thereby rendering death ineffective regarding Jesus (see Barrett 1994, 143-44; Peterson 2009, 147).

Peter offers no details explaining what made it impossible for death to **hold** or **restrain** Jesus (BDAG 2000, 564-65). But he probably refers back to the attestations of Jesus as God's agent (Acts 2:22) and later to Jesus' God-given role as the Christ (see v 36). In other words, death could not withstand the purposes and intervention of God.

■ **25-26** Peter's verbatim quotation and reinterpretation of Ps 16:8-11 (LXX) further clarify why God resurrected Jesus. Peter declares Jesus to be the subject of that portion of the psalm (v 25). But the first-person perspective of the psalm suggests that David was speaking about *himself*. Thus, interpreters must first consider the psalm in its original setting before evaluating Peter's use of it (vv 29-33). God's presence provided the basis of David's confidence and joy. That God was at David's **right hand** may depict God either as David's defender against an enemy or as his advocate.

The LXX verb quoted here, *saleuō* (**shaken**), often describes ships tossed by stormy seas or persons figuratively tossed in distress. Nearly half the LXX occurrences of this verb appear in the Psalter. These are often negated forms, declaring assurance that God would take away trouble or resolve distressing situations.

This psalm expresses confidence in the face of humanity's greatest dilemma: death. The verb translated "live" (*kataskēnoō* [CEB, NRSV]) offers a word picture of the **rest** and security of birds nesting in trees (BDAG 2000, 527; see Luke 13:19; Matt 13:32; Mark 4:32). Rather than accepting death as inevitable, the psalmist insists that even one's physical **body** (*sarx*) can **rest in hope**, the nature of which v 27 describes.

■ **27-28** The psalmist's confident assertion may have been that God would spare him from a premature death at the hands of his enemies. More likely, he believed he would ascend and be accepted into God's presence after death. He would not descend and have God reject him to ***Hades*** (the Greek equivalent of Sheol), the gathering place of the dead before judgment. Two aspects of these verses suggest this reading.

First, the latter half of v 27 seems to underscore this idea of resurrection soon after death with a parallel affirmation about not seeing *diaphthoran*—**decay** ("corruption" [NRSV]). This term appears in the NT only in Acts (also 2:31; 13:34-37). Peter proclaims Jesus' resurrection through a rereading of Ps 16.

Second, the image **paths of life** (Acts 2:28), following resurrection, focuses on what would lead from death to life. The description used for the recipient of this divine action is **your holy one**. In the LXX, this frequently describes priests or faithful persons dedicated to God. The original reference in this psalm was probably David. But later worshipers and readers of this psalm would have also identified themselves with that designation (Bock 2007, 124-25).

■ **29** Similar to vv 14 and 22, Peter's direct address of his audience signals an end to his quotation of Ps 16. He himself is speaking again. The address ***Men, brothers*** shifts to a familial expression that implies something about Peter's rapport and identification with his audience. As a fellow Jew, he was "one of them."

Peter offers a reinterpretation of the quoted psalm ***with confidence*** (*meta parrēsias*). **Boldness** (whether the noun *parrēsia* or the verb *parrēsiazomai*) frequently describes believers' proclamation of the gospel message in Acts (see 4:13, 29, 31; 9:27-28; 13:46; 14:3; 18:26; 19:8; 28:31).

The honorific title **patriarch** describes David (only here in the NT or LXX) confirms Peter's reverence for the former king and author of the quoted psalm. Nevertheless, David's death and burial contradicted David's own confidence as declared in the psalm. The verb describing David's death (*eteleutēsen*;

lit., **came to an end**) and the evidence of his tomb made his death undeniable (on David's tomb, see Barrett 1994, 146-47; Fitzmyer 1998, 257).

■ **30-31** Given the overwhelming evidence of David's death, Peter logically concludes that David was not speaking about himself. If David's words from the psalms may be interpreted as prophetic (see 1:16, 20), it is not surprising that Peter identifies David as a **prophet**, who knew when God had spoken. That designation authenticates the promise David received from God.

Both the verb *omnyō* (**swear**) and the noun *horkos* (**oath**) substantiate the certainty of that promise: God would **place** (**seat**, *kathisai*) one of David's descendants upon the throne. This alludes to Ps 132:11, which celebrates the Davidic dynasty. By bringing this psalm to bear on David's declaration in Ps 16, Peter's speech makes a strategic move in the argument. Jewish tradition had long understood the **Messiah**, the "anointed one," to be of Davidic descent. Peter declares that **the resurrection of the Messiah** is the actual subject of David's words quoted in v 27. The shift in verb tense, from the future (God **will not abandon** [*enkataleipseis* (v 27)]) to the past (aorist; the Messiah **was not abandoned** [*enkateleiphthē*]) indicates that this promise had been fulfilled.

■ **32** After Peter's reinterpretation of the Ps 16 passage, the focus of his speech returns to Jesus, whom Peter identifies again as *this one* (→ v 23), referring to the resurrected Christ (→ vv 30-31). The repeated declaration that **God . . . raised** Jesus (see v 24) frames Peter's treatment of the psalm. In v 24, he emphasized that *God* resurrected Jesus in contrast to the Jews, who murdered him. Here, the emphasis falls on *Jesus* as the one who was raised. He is, therefore, the subject of the Davidic psalm.

Peter further asserts that he and the other apostles (lit., **we**, *hēmeis*; see v 14) served as **witnesses** of the risen Jesus. This offers apostolic validation of Peter's understanding of what God had done. It also reminds readers of Jesus' promise before his ascension (1:8). It is unclear whether the apostles claim to be witnesses of *Jesus* or more specifically of Jesus' *resurrection*. The ambiguity and the context imply that they meant both.

■ **33** The conjunction *oun* (**therefore**) introduces some basic conclusions based on the previous remarks. The mention of Jesus as **exalted** moves Peter's argument beyond Jesus' resurrection to his ascension (1:9-11). **The right hand of God** may either identify God as the one who exalted Jesus (dative of instrument; see Barrett 1994, 149; Bruce 1988, 66) or identify the place of divine authority and favor to which he was exalted (dative of location; BDF 1961, §199; Conzelmann 1987, 21). The quotation of Ps 110:1 in Acts 2:34 makes the latter understanding more plausible here.

Both Jesus' exalted position and the phrase **from the Father** affirm the divine source of what Jesus received—the promise of the Holy Spirit. Here, Peter alludes to Jesus' own words (1:4-8). The use of the verb *ekcheō* ("pour out")—found in Joel 2:28 (LXX) and quoted in Acts 2:17—to describe what Jesus did establishes a direct link between Joel's prophecy and Jesus' actions.

Thus, Peter makes an essential assertion through this speech so that the Pentecost event is interpreted *christologically* as the fulfillment of God's promise to Israel. That is, that promise was fulfilled through God's Messiah or Christ, *Jesus*, the one whom the Jewish people killed through their Gentile accomplices. Ironically, Peter's audience is unaware that they *themselves* are witnesses to these matters, since the extraordinary Pentecost events that indicate the fulfillment of Joel's prophecy have drawn them together in the first place (v 6).

■ **34-35** The reminder that David himself **did not ascend to heaven** both reiterates what Peter had already declared (v 29) and contrasts him with Jesus (→ 1:9-11). Although there are OT examples of persons taken to heaven (Enoch, Gen 5:24; Elijah, 2 Kgs 2:11), no such stories exist about David. By quoting Ps 110:1, Peter reiterates the argument that David is not the subject of his own confident words in Ps 16 (see Acts 2:25-28).

Psalm 110, which is ascribed to David, is a royal psalm that celebrates the enthronement of a king from the Davidic dynasty. God had invited this king to ascend the throne and accept the place of honor and authority next to God. The LXX rendering of that verse describes **the Lord** (Hebrew: *Yahweh*) addressing not David but **my Lord**, a reference to David's descendant. Peter takes this to be the risen Christ, a christological interpretation of Psalm 110 found elsewhere in the NT (e.g., Luke 20:42-43).

The imperative **sit** repeats the prior image of the placement of a Davidic descendant on David's throne (Acts 2:30). That this position was at God's **right hand** reiterates v 33. From that exalted position of honor and authority in God's presence, Jesus as the Christ became the agent who dispensed the blessing of the Spirit.

Psalm 110:1 concludes with a reference to God's humiliation of the enemies of **my Lord**. In its original context, this referred to the victory of the newly crowned Davidic king. Here, it underscores previous descriptions of God's actions in raising Jesus to life in contrast to Jesus' enemies responsible for his death (vv 22-24).

■ **36** The conjunction *oun* (**Therefore**) indicates that Peter's speech has come to its conclusion. He does not direct these final remarks merely to the Jewish audience before him but to the *house of Israel*, a common biblical expression for the people of God. Given his explanation, they should readily recognize what God has done regarding Jesus.

Both the demonstrative pronoun **this** and the relative clause **whom you crucified** stress again that the Jesus whom Peter describes in his speech is the *same* one about whom he speaks. The adverb *asphalōs* connotes the general idea of certainty. It paints a word picture of having no question or doubt, so no one should stumble or fall because of his conclusions.

Peter has already described **this Jesus** as the Christ as seen in Jesus' resurrection and exaltation by God. So these remarks add that God's actions *confirmed* rather than established Jesus' identity as **Lord** by his resurrection (Rowe 2007, 37-56). This links Jesus explicitly with two references to the Lord in the OT passages cited in the speech: David's description of "my Lord" in Ps 110:1 (Acts 2:34), and the promise regarding salvation for those who call "on the name of the Lord" from Joel 2:32 (Acts 2:21). Thus, the emphasis here is not on a specific moment when God **made** or installed Jesus as **both Lord and Messiah**. Rather, it is on God's actions in contrast and opposition to the Jews' actions (Conzelmann 1987, 21). As a result, the Lord to whom one may call for salvation (v 21) is none other than Jesus.

■ **37** The crowd's initial response to **Peter and the other apostles** reiterates that Peter did not speak on his own but on behalf of the Twelve. This portrays Peter as an effective orator, due not to his gentleness (against John Chrysostom, *Hom. Act.* 7, cited in Martin 2006, 36), but to the Spirit's power (see 1:8).

The expression **cut to the heart** (only here in the NT) may allude to Ps 109:16 (a psalm from which Peter quoted earlier in 1:20). It conveys a sense of emotional turmoil due to the conviction of guilt over their now-recognized role in Jesus' crucifixion. They had placed themselves in a hopeless predicament by rejecting God's messenger and purposes. Their question is reminiscent of those asked in response to the preaching of John the Baptist (see Luke 3:10-14). The crowd addresses the apostles as **Brothers** (see Acts 2:29), reaffirming the common heritage they all share, and implying that their inquiry is sincere.

■ **38-39** Peter's response offers two specific instructions for the crowd.

First, the imperative **repent** echoes Jesus' preaching in the Third Gospel (e.g., Luke 5:32; 13:3, 5; 15:7, 10) and introduces a common theme in Acts (see 3:19; 5:31; 8:22; 11:18; 13:24; 17:30; 19:4; 20:21; 26:20). Typically, repentance in Acts is "the appropriate response to God's salvific work" (Green 1998, 104). It includes both the sorrow for regrettable deeds and the act of turning away from disobedience. Positively, it means turning toward God and obedience.

While both the verb (*metanoeō*) and the corresponding noun (*metanoia*) literally refer to a change of mind, these terms also depict in Greek philosophy the change of one's entire self in positive ways. The plural imperative extends the call to repent to the entire crowd. They all share culpability for Jesus' crucifixion. Indirectly, the call includes all the people of Israel (see Wall 2002, 68).

Second, the other imperative instructs them to **be baptized**. This further emphasizes the theme of repentance. Baptism was often associated with repentance, both in the preaching of John the Baptist (e.g., Luke 3:3) and of the earliest Christians (e.g., Acts 13:24).

88

Like John's baptism, the purpose (as indicated by the preposition *eis*) for this baptism is the divine forgiveness of sins. Christian baptism differs from John's practice in that it is **in the name of Jesus Christ** (*epi tō onomati Iēsou Christou*). This underscores Jesus as the authority for the practice (see BDAG 2000, 366). In Jewish tradition, the named person is also understood as present (e.g., 1 Sam 25:25; Fitzmyer 1998, 266).

This means that Jesus, whom the crowd is responsible for killing and whom God declared as the Christ, is the *same* one through whom Peter offers them forgiveness! The word **forgiveness** or ***pardon*** typically described the cancellation of financial obligation or debt. Here, it may suggest that the pardon of sins creates a community where financial debts may be forgiven as well (see Acts 2:42-47; Wall 2002, 67).

Those baptized would be identified with and belong to Jesus, God's chosen one whom they had rejected earlier. This is why Peter's instructions regarding baptism are directed not only to the whole crowd but also to individual Jews—**every one of you**—who accepted his message and its implications. From this point forward in Acts (see 8:12, 16; 10:47-48; 16:15; 19:5), baptism is associated with admission or acceptance into the fellowship of believers.

With Peter's instructions comes a promise. The plural verb translated **you will receive** (*lēmpsesthe*) suggests that it is offered to the community of believers that an individual joins through baptism. The language of promise echoes Jesus' assurances to his disciples (Luke 24:49; Acts 1:4) of **the gift of the Holy Spirit**. Repentant, baptized Jews would receive what both John (Luke 3:16) and Jesus (Acts 1:5) proclaimed. The same **Holy Spirit** the believers have *themselves* received earlier that day (2:1-4) in fulfillment of the prophecy from Joel (2:17) would be theirs.

The conjunction *kai* (**and**) connects the promise to the two imperatives. The promise is not merely a third element in a short list of directives. It is instead an introduction of what would follow when persons heed the imperatives to repent and be baptized. Peter delineates no other specifics.

The range of those included in the promise extends to those listening to Peter, their descendants, and **all who are far off**. Peter's subsequent actions in Acts 10 suggest that he initially understands the latter group to be Diaspora Jews, not Gentiles. However, the description creates the narrative anticipation of those Gentiles who would later accept the gospel message.

The final part of the promise seems to draw from the last portion of Joel 2:32, omitted earlier in Peter's speech (Acts 2:21). It reiterates that all who call (*epikaleō*) on the name of the Lord do so as a result of *God's* call (*proskaleomai* [v 39]). In other words, the promise concludes by concentrating on a divine summons to receive God's saving work. It does not offer the promise as merely an invitation from God, dependent on human decision alone.

■ **40** Luke does not claim to record everything Peter said. He acknowledges that Peter spoke **many other** things not specifically included here. In this, the narrator follows the rhetorical conventions of Greek historians (e.g., Polybius, *Hist.* 3.111.11; Xenophon, *Hell.* 2.4.42) to imply that he provides the most important matters (see Witherington 1998, 156).

The verb *diamartyromai*, although translated as "witness" or "testify," includes an intensive prefix that denotes the thorough, complete nature of Peter's testimony. Of the fifteen NT uses of this verb, nine appear in Acts (also 8:25; 10:42; 18:5; 20:21-24; 23:11; 28:23). This underscores the Lukan theme of witness. Permeating this complete testimony are repeated calls to respond (imperfect tense: *parekalei*). This saying (2:38) is representative of how Peter urges the crowd to respond. The passive voice of the imperative *sōthēte* calls for the crowd to **be saved**. In this context, it is an invitation to appropriate God's saving activity in Jesus.

A favorable response would separate them from a generation described as **corrupt** or "twisted" (Johnson 1992, 58). This adapts an abbreviated form of an OT depiction of unfaithful Israel wandering in the wilderness (Deut 32:5; Ps 78:8). The expression describes such a generation as "ethically crooked, spiritually off the path to God, and thus subject to judgment" (Bock 2007, 146). Although persons who aligned themselves with that generation would reject Peter's message, he repeatedly calls them to separate themselves from that generation by responding to God's gracious activity.

■ **41** The response to Peter's message is astounding. Many contend that the dual conjunctions *men oun* at the beginning of this sentence signals a shift in the Lukan narrative and introduces a new paragraph (e.g., Barrett 1994, 159-61). However, there are two reasons for thinking this verse concludes the paragraph rather than initiates a new one.

First, the conjunctions indicate that what Luke briefly mentions also continues and results from Peter's proclamation (see Levinsohn 1987, 141-50). Second, a shift to the imperfect verb tense begins in v 42 and extends through v 47, demarcating a different literary unit.

The participle *apodexamenoi* (**welcomed**, **accepted**) characterizes those who respond favorably to the message. They presumably repent, as their baptism suggests. The number of those baptized—**about three thousand** (*hōsei trischilia*)—is an approximation. The absence of logistical details (e.g., about how and where so many people could have been baptized) has provoked questions about the historical accuracy and plausibility of that number. It has also prompted attempts to defend the accuracy of Luke's account (see Reinhardt 1995, 237-65; Witherington 1998, 156).

Greek historians often used large numbers to highlight important aspects of an unfolding narrative. In this instance, Luke mentions this number of repentant Jews for two reasons: to underscore the initial success of the gospel message, and to offer an initial depiction of repentant Israel. His purpose is to provide a theological picture, not to provide precise historical details.

The verb translated **were added** (*prosetethēsan*) may be a divine passive (uncertain since the passive verb to which it is connected, *ebaptisthēsan*, suggests that the apostles performed the baptisms). If so, that large number offers tangible, convincing evidence for God's saving work on that day.

FROM THE TEXT

Luke devotes more than twice the narrative space to Peter's explanatory speech regarding Pentecost than to the description of that extraordinary event. This simple fact suggests both the event's significance and the importance the author gives it. He interprets the role of Pentecost in what theologians often describe as "salvation history."

Some contend that Luke merely recounts what happened on that day, as in a documentary. This would point to the role of Peter's speech for the bystanders who witnessed what happened that day. But it seems to offer far more than this. Consider the distinctive nature of the Acts speeches in the NT. Consider the attention given to this particular scriptural explanation of what happened at Pentecost in terms of God's activity. Consider the space provided for Peter's speech. All these suggest that Acts 2 offers readers valuable theological guidance as to how they should see and understand what God had done on behalf of the people of God (see Haenchen 1971, 189). In particular, four theological emphases emerge from this pivotal speech.

First, the speech continues to develop the theme introduced early in the chapter: the events of Pentecost were the fulfillment of God's promises and purposes for Israel as the people of God. The citation of the Joel passage, which was a promise to Israel, explains this from the Jewish Scriptures: what had occurred among Jesus' followers indicates that God had fulfilled that promise. The coming of the Spirit was part of God's eschatological acts of salvation on Israel's behalf. Peter's speech draws attention away from the extraordinary nature of the Pentecost event and to the simple fact that God acted as God had promised long ago.

Some describe the Pentecost event as signifying the birth of the church. But the Lukan perspective reflected in Peter's speech points instead to what God has done on behalf of all *Israel* as the people of God. Pentecost in Acts was entirely a *Jewish* event: during a Jewish festival, at the Jewish temple, with all Jewish participants and bystanders, with the God of the Jewish people initiating what happened and implementing what *this* God had vowed centuries before. Therefore, we do not find the significance of Pentecost for Christians in what God had done distinctly on behalf of Jesus' followers. Rather, its significance is in what God had done to fulfill God's promises and purposes *among the people whom God had first called.*

Second, a theological emphasis is closely related to that of the divine fulfillment of God's promises and purposes for Israel. It is the role of God in the crucifixion and death of Jesus. Peter's speech makes it clear that the Jewish response to Jesus was the rejection of God's purposes. But Peter also underscores several times that God responded by undoing their murder of Jesus by honoring Jesus. God exalted Jesus by placing him in the position of divine honor and authority. In other words, God had the final say, not human rejection.

Nothing specific in this speech explains the salvific importance of Jesus' death and resurrection (e.g., in terms of atonement). However, the Lukan focus on God's role in the reversal of what God's chosen people had done through their rejection of Jesus affirms the constancy and reliability of God's plans and purposes.

Third, the theological emphasis at the core of Peter's explanatory speech is the role of Jesus in God's fulfillment of the divine promises and purposes for Israel. The Lukan narrator depicts the Pentecost event in Jewish terms. The citation of the Joel passage at the beginning of Peter's speech maintains a similar orientation. However, the repeated accent placed upon the resurrected and exalted Jesus coaxes readers to see divine fulfillment in terms of Christology (see Turner 1998, 332-33) rather than pneumatology (as often in Wesleyan-holiness circles).

In other words, Peter's speech demands a radical change in perspective. Not only had God accomplished what God had promised, but the agent who accomplished this among the Jewish people was none other than Jesus, the same one whom they were responsible for murdering. The crucial role of Jesus in this divine fulfillment is the distinctive aspect of Peter's message and the gospel proclaimed by the believers to the Jewish people.

The gospel message declared to God's people how God had kept and accomplished those promises to them . . . through Jesus. Without this distinctively *christological* emphasis regarding Pentecost, there would be little if anything about this event that would be related to the Christian gospel. Thus, the Pentecost experience of the Jesus movement did not signify divine actions *apart* from the Jewish people but *within* them. The outpouring of the Spirit through Jesus as Christ and Lord signifies how God fulfilled God's purposes and promises within the people of God.

Fourth, Peter's speech emphasizes the divine call of God's people to mission. The quotation of the Joel passage reaffirms the call of prophetic, Spirit-enabled witness that Jesus placed upon his followers in Acts 1. The proclamation of the gospel message would make it possible that "everyone who calls on the name of the Lord will be saved" (v 21).

In Acts, the gift of the Spirit empowers prophetic mission rather than promotes personal piety. This is the kind of mission Acts describes: the proclamation of the gospel message about Jesus, beginning in Jerusalem and extending to the rest of the world.

Those who worship in Wesleyan communities of faith will recognize these emphases as consistent with our theological and missional trajectories. We understand that the Spirit empowers our mission to proclaim the gospel and transform society. Typically in holiness circles, the focus is on being "filled with the Spirit" so believers may truly love others as a faithful reflection of God's love toward us.

Yet in many ways, pneumatological images have been central to the proclamation of Christian holiness in our circles. We have sometimes ignored what is truly *Christian* about Pentecost: that Jesus as Christ and Lord provides the gift of the Spirit for the people of God, so that they might take the gospel in transforming ways into the world.

The kind of christological perspective regarding Pentecost offered by Luke takes the attention off personal matters such as piety, practices, and power for living. Awareness of this may free us to focus on living faithfully and missionally as the people of God—as those who embody the good news of God's love and grace.

3. The Spirit-Created Community of Believers (2:42-47)

BEHIND THE TEXT

A distinctive literary feature of the book of Acts is its usage of summary materials between narratives, rather than specific descriptions. These summary statements provide an overview of typical activities or conditions that describe believers in general ways (e.g., 1:12-14; 2:42-47; 4:32-37; 5:12-16). Some interpreters consider these materials of secondary importance, because they understand these summaries as mere connections between narrative sections. However, the explicitly selected images and themes found here offer readers additional information and perceptions from the narrator that they may need to assess the narrative.

Throughout this particular summary section (2:42-47), there is a distinct shift in verb tense from the Greek aorist to the imperfect tense. Acts characteristically uses the imperfect to describe continuing or typical actions; the aorist characteristically describes specific historical events.

These summary materials begin with v 42 rather than v 41 (→ 2:41) and comprise a distinct literary unit. But this section is also grammatically linked to the previous materials and to the next chapter by the conjunction *de* (v 42; 3:1). Thus, this description of the believers offers a generalized, yet conclusive, image of the restoration of Israel as the people of God. This is the result of Pentecost and the outpouring of the Spirit among the believers.

IN THE TEXT

■ **42** The first statement of this summary section broadly describes what believers do after Pentecost. These include not only the initial followers of Jesus from ch 1 but those from the Jewish people who responded with repentance to Peter's speech and were baptized. These converts comprised repentant Israel.

The expression translated **devoted themselves** (*ēsan proskarterountes*) repeats an earlier description of the ongoing compulsion of the apostles and others to the practice of prayer (1:14). Readers should perceive this larger group as similar to the obedient believers after Jesus' ascension.

Luke mentions four characteristic ways that these believers share a common religious life. The common interpretation is that these four characteristic activities of the believers and their life together present a simple list of what Luke understood as the basic activities of the church. However, since these characteristics are grammatically listed as two distinct pairs, with each pair linked together with the conjunction *kai* (**and**) but with no conjunction joining the two pairs, the connections within each pair may be more noteworthy.

In the initial pair, the first characteristic—**the apostles' teaching**—refers to the testimony or witness of the Twelve about Jesus' ministry and resurrection. This activity is described earlier as a significant aspect of their role as Jesus' apostles (see 1:21-22; 2:32).

The second characteristic, **fellowship**, *koinōnia*, was often mentioned in the Greco-Roman world and referred to the relation or bond between persons. The definite article that precedes the term suggests that this is a reference to what bonds the entire group of believers together.

The grammatical link of these two concepts invites readers to explore the possible connections between, on the one hand, this context of the proclamation of the gospel message and the worship of God and, on the other hand, the positive social bond among the community of believers.

Friendship in the Ancient World

Some of the vocabulary and concepts in the Lukan summary materials describing the community of believers (here and in Acts 4:32-35) reflect discussions in the Greco-Roman world about friendship. Aristotle offers the most extensive treatment of the concept (*Eth. nic.* 8-9; *Eth. eud.* 7). Both he and Plato draw from the friendship traditions the proverbial notion that friends have "all things in common" (Aristotle, *Eth. nic.* 8.1.4; Plato, *Critias* 110c; see Plato, *Resp.* 449c).

For Plato, such matters were important for the ideal city, which he characterized in terms of unanimity, since this would eliminate self-interest and affirm the collective interest of the citizens. For Aristotle, there were three types of friendship, based on utility or usefulness, pleasure, and virtue.

In all three types of friendship, there were three primary characteristics of friendship in varying degrees: (1) goodwill or the active seeking for the good or benefit of one's friend, (2) recognition of the goodwill or benefit that another has done on one's behalf, and (3) reciprocity or a response in the same proportion of goodwill that one has received from one's friend. In such cases, responses seek only the benefit of one's friend, and personal self-interest is never one's motivation for helping another.

Social boundaries limited this understanding of friendship to persons of equal status. Although persons of different status could become friends, their relationship often became more like a patron-client relationship. In such unequal friendships, different expectations of obligation and debt changed how they related to one another.

Acts' description of the community includes believers of different socio-economic strata (see 2:44; 4:34-35). Thus, the author appropriates the friendship tradition to portray the Spirit-created community with ideal terms. But he also suggests that the church transcended the social boundaries that normally limited or prevented such unequal friendships.

The second pair of characteristic activities invites similar connections. Interpreters often understand the expression **breaking of bread** to refer to the Lord's Supper. However, little here suggests such a specific reference. The subsequent mention of the believers eating together in one another's homes in v 46 lacks Eucharistic overtones. The expression probably refers simply to believers sharing meals with one another.

The final characteristic activity, *the prayers* (*tais proseuchais*), is both plural and accompanied by a definite article. Thus, the expression probably refers to the times of prayer at the temple (see 3:1). It may also refer to other times when believers met together to pray.

Like the first pair, the Lukan summary encourages readers to explore the connection between the worshipful activities of the believers and the social bond among them (Thompson 2006, 46-49).

■ **43** Identical forms of the same verb (*egineto*) frame this sentence. The imperfect tense of the verb highlights the ongoing effects of the community's activities in Jerusalem. The association of the apostles with **many wonders and signs** reminds readers that Peter similarly described Jesus' accreditation as a confirmation of divine power (v 22).

This description also reflects Joel's prophecy of the coming Spirit (v 19). This links the Spirit's ongoing work with what the apostles are doing within the community of believers. Thus, the narrative draws attention to the divine work among the believers. This should be the focus of contemporary interpretations, not the specific evidence per se (→ "Engaging Acts in a New Day" in Introduction).

It is no wonder that these activities evoked **awe** or reverence (*phobos*) among the people. Such wonders indicate that God was at work through the apostles! **Everyone** (*pasē psychē*) is a hyperbolic way of describing those in Jerusalem apart from the community of believers (lit., ***all who believe***: *pantes . . . hoi pisteuontes* [v 44]). Luke's language suggests that the entire city of Jerusalem recognized what God was doing among the believers.

■ **44-45** These two verses briefly describe typical aspects of the believers' fellowship (v 42). Their togetherness is underscored both by the word **all** and the phrase translated **together** (*epi to auto*). This phrase earlier describes the gathered believers after Jesus' ascension (1:15) and at the time of Pentecost (2:1).

Verse 46 depicts the believers meeting in one another's homes. But this general description has them together also in the temple courts (see v 46). However, this mentions nothing that implies that they lived together (against Fitzmyer 1998, 271).

The expression **had everything in common** reflects the friendship traditions of the day (→ sidebar "Friendship in the Ancient World" with 2:42). It particularly draws on themes of unity and harmony (see Mitchell 1992, 255-72). It is possible to interpret this to mean that believers pooled their possessions. But the next verse (with 4:32-37 and 5:1-11) suggests that their typical practice (note the imperfect verb tense) is the use of their possessions for the common good of the community.

Two different words indicate what they sold. The first, *ktēma*, often refers to parcels of land or property. The second, *hyparxis*, refers to possessions in general. The owners' sale of such items and the distribution of the sale proceeds are for the benefit of **whomever** had need.

This disposition of personal property reflects the unity affirmed by the friendship traditions. But the extension of such practices across social lines does not. Rather, it alludes to Jesus' call to minister to the poor (see Luke 4:16-19; 6:20-36; 12:33-34; 18:18-30). It also fulfills God's initial expectations for the people of God (see Deut 15:4, 11).

Luke mentions no rules or processes that governed such practices. The implied driving force behind such generous sharing is the Holy Spirit, who came upon and created that community.

Ancient Jewish Communities of Goods

The Lukan description of the community of believers in Jerusalem distinctly draws from the friendship traditions and popular philosophical discussions about community in the Greco-Roman world. But extant evidence from Palestinian Judaism suggests that the Essene sect adopted a communal lifestyle that also included the sharing of goods and property. The sect's *Rule of the Community* was part of the Dead Sea Scrolls discovery at Qumran. It outlines that particular community's process for prospective members regarding their relinquishment of property, first provisionally and later permanently.

The first-century Jewish philosopher Philo explains how the Essenes held property in common and shared their wages (*Hypoth.* 11). He implies that Essenes had settled in the most significant population centers in Palestine. Archaeological evidence from Jerusalem places what has been called the "Essene Quarter" on the southwest hill of the city in the first century AD. Interestingly, some early tradition-al Christian sites (such as the Upper Room) are located in the same general area, which suggests the possible influence of this branch of Judaism on the earliest com-munal practices of the fledgling Christian movement (see Capper 1995, 323-56).

■ **46-47** The major portion of these verses describes other activities of the be-lievers. The expression **every day** begins this section and reappears in the last sentence. It reiterates the ongoing nature of what takes place. This depiction of daily meetings in the temple alludes to earlier affirmative images of believers.

Both the adverb *homothymadon* (**together**) and the participle *proskarter-ountes* (**continued to meet**) have previously described the believers' unanimity and devotion to prayer (1:14). The participle also positively describes the be-lievers' commitment to various community practices (2:42).

The term used here for the temple, *hieron*, refers to the entire complex. Thus, believers probably gather in the temple courts for some of their wor-ship practices (see v 42; against Pervo 2009, 94). Their temple attendance represents the believers' claim to the temple as the true Israel (Conzelmann 1987, 24). But one should not be surprised that observant Jews continue their practice of temple worship. That they believe Jesus is the Messiah and experi-ence God's blessing through the outpouring of the Spirit does not change this.

Also consistent with common Jewish practice, believers extend their fellowship beyond the sacred precincts of the temple to ordinary meals in their homes (Jervell 1998, 157). The combination of the phrases **breaking bread** (v 42) and **receiving nourishment** does not suggest that they participate together in a Christian sacramental act per se. However, all Jewish meals are understood theologically as fellowship with God. Thus, these meals are still considered sacred. For believers, **gladness** and **sincerity** of their hearts are for more than daily sustenance; God is at work among them!

That is why they are continually **praising God**, a typical Lukan descrip-tion of those who recognize God in action (see, e.g., Luke 2:13, 20; 19:37; Acts 3:8, 9). Through the outpouring of the Spirit through Jesus, God is re-sponsible for the creation of this community of believers. Their various acts of fellowship cannot be separated from the fulfillment of that divine promise.

The final description of believers is ambiguous. Most English translations infer that believers developed a good reputation among the inhabitants of the city of Jerusalem. Those who look favorably upon them are identified as **all the people** (*holon ton laon*). Elsewhere in Acts, this refers to the Jewish people. Such a positive reception from the people seems consistent with the chapter's final sentence.

There are, however, several reasons for preferring an alternative translation: **having goodwill (or grace) toward all the people** ("they . . . demonstrated God's goodness to everyone" [CEB]). First, there is no grammatical support for translating the preposition *pros* in this construction (with an accusative noun as the object of the preposition) as "from" or "with." Second, in first-century texts written by the Jewish historian Josephus and the Jewish philosopher Philo, when this particular preposition follows the word *charis* (**favor,** the NT word for "grace"), it always describes the person *toward* whom *charis* is expressed (Andersen 1988, 604-10). Third, it fits the context, as those who praise God also respond in gracious ways to those around them. Fourth, such actions would account for the daily growth of the community of believers. The description of those added to the community, **those who were being saved,** brings to mind the promise of Joel's prophecy (v 21) and Peter's appeal to his Pentecost audience (v 40).

Luke makes it clear that divine activity is ultimately the moving force behind the church's growth. It is unclear, however, whether **the Lord**—*ho kyrios*—refers here to God (*Yahweh*) or Jesus (→ sidebar "Names for God and the Septuagint" with 2:19-20). But this divine activity does more than increase the numbers of believers. The phrase *epi to auto* appears again at the end of this sentence (as in 1:15; 2:1, 44). Most translations render this to complete the thought of the verb: the addition is **to their number** (i.e., of the believers). However, Luke typically uses the phrase to emphasize unity. This thought at the conclusion of this summary section emphasizes that God is behind the increasing unity of believers!

FROM THE TEXT

This brief summary section may be the one passage that most frequently comes to mind when Christians consider what the NT teaches about the nature of the church. In response, some ask, "Does this mean we should sell our possessions and give the proceeds to the church, like the first believers did?" This passage certainly has a *descriptive* function within the Acts narrative. But does it also have a *normative* function that determines what believers must do in today's church?

A few emphases stand out when one considers the role of this passage within the narrative and plot of Acts.

First, the passage accentuates the simple fact that *God,* not humans, creates and gathers the people of God. Everything that Luke mentions is the result of God's salvation and restoration of Israel. God fulfills the promise that God had given her long ago as the people of God. Everything that Luke mentions reflects the movement of God among the believers in bringing about God's purposes among the people of God. His description of the utopian ideals achieved within the early community could easily capture one's attention. But the last sentence reminds readers that what one sees here was the result of the faithfulness of God in fulfilling what God had promised.

Second, the believers responded to God and God's faithfulness by committing themselves in obedience to practices that were faithful responses to God. Their actions were consistent with what one would expect to find in a repentant and restored Israel, as they worshiped and prayed to God as faithful Jews. They reflected upon the gospel message as articulated by the apostles.

These common expressions of obedience and faithfulness gave the Christian community a common focus. These unified a group that was diverse both in background (see vv 5-13) and socioeconomic status (see vv 45-46). Luke describes the unity that humanity had often sought but failed to achieve through political ideals as happening among the believers through God's outpouring of the Spirit through Jesus. Such unity did not come because the people sought it. Unity happened among them because they had a common focus: being faithful to God.

Third, the faithfulness of the believers was evident in the ways they responded to others. As repentant Israel and believers in Jesus, these faithful Jews responded to one another as the people of God in ways consistent with their covenant with God by caring for the needs of the poor. One may affirm with John Wesley that their motive was the love for others (1958, 402) that the Holy Spirit placed in their hearts. Their identity and solidarity as God's people defined their priorities rather than the social system, classes, and values within which their everyday lives were immersed. Thus, they shared with others in need when society had its own ways of handling such things. Their day, not to mention our own, would have considered such behavior shameful.

Luke's descriptions of the church do not specify how contemporary Christians should live. But this passage still forces careful readers to ponder what it might look like to live faithfully before God. This is especially true in light of the reversal of priorities that comes with the movement of God among God's people through the Spirit.

C. A Healing that Leads to Opposition (3:1—4:31)

1. The Healing of a Crippled Man at the Temple (3:1-26)

BEHIND THE TEXT

After the brief description of the ideal community of believers, the narrative offers an extended scene that illustrates some specifics of what Luke had only mentioned in rather cursory ways. The narrative shifts from a "fast-forward blur" to a rather slow, dramatic episode (Dunn 1996, 39).

One should not be surprised that Peter and John go to the temple during a specified time for prayer and sacrifice, since the summary materials depict the believers as customarily involved in these practices (2:42, 46). The healing that takes place when they go to the temple also provides a tangible example of the "many wonders and signs" the apostles did (2:43).

This event is the first narrated instance of the believers' ministry following Pentecost. By this means, Luke provides an exposition of the final promise of Joel's prophecy: "Everyone who calls on the name of the Lord will be saved" (2:21). The striking similarities between this healing scene and the account of Jesus' healing of a crippled man in Luke's Gospel (5:17-26) draw parallels between the beginning of Jesus' ministry and the ministry beginnings for the post-Pentecost movement of these believers (Tannehill 1990, 48-51). In other words, Luke describes these apostles as doing what Jesus did. In both cases, healing became the opportunity to declare the vital claim about the saving power of Jesus.

The exact location of the healing has been a subject of debate, mainly because ancient Jewish accounts of the temple and its gates (e.g., Josephus, *J.W.* 5.190-221; *Ant.* 15.410-25) mention nothing of a gate called "Beautiful." There are two options for its identification and location. One option is the Shushan Gate, which was located in the east wall of the temple complex and gave access from the outside to the Court of the Gentiles. Early Christian tradition considered this the gate Luke identifies here. But it was an unlikely location for begging, because most pedestrian traffic from the city entered from the *west*. However, those entering from the Mount of Olives passed through this gate. Contemporary messianic beliefs often associated the Messiah's coming with the eastern gate to the temple, so this location could be linked to these beliefs (Malina and Pilch 2008, 38).

The other option is the Nicanor Gate, also known as the Corinthian or Bronze Gate due to its design and material (Josephus, *J.W.* 5.201-4; 6.293). This gate provided access into the Court of Women from the Court of the Gentiles somewhere inside the temple precincts on the eastern side. Most interpreters consider this as the more likely location because descriptions of this bright bronze gate correlate with Luke's identification of the gate as "beautiful."

However, what makes this conclusion less compelling is the repeated use of the term *hieron* to describe Peter and John entering the temple. In Lukan usage, *hieron* typically refers to the temple precincts or courts rather than to the sanctuary. Luke may have described the gate as he did because of the wonderful healing that occurred there rather than because that was its correct name (Fitzmyer 1998, 278). The possible ways that the Lukan description of the gate may function within the story may be of greater significance than precisely identifying the gate where the healing happened.

IN THE TEXT

a. The Account of the Healing (3:1-10)

■ **1-3** The conjunction *de* ("now") links the summary of 2:42-47 with this section. However, it offers no clear sense of the lapsed time between Pentecost and this event.

The opening of this scene introduces the major characters. Accompanying Peter is John, undoubtedly one of the Twelve and son of Zebedee rather than John Mark, who is not mentioned until ch 12. Although John's role is rather limited as Peter takes center stage, the need for two witnesses in Jewish tradition may explain why the narrator mentions his presence.

The two are heading to the temple precincts at **the hour for prayer**. Since Luke consistently associates prayer with subsequent divine activity, this should build a sense of anticipation in readers. The temple attendance of the two also indicates that the believers have not separated from Judaism. They continue to be faithful to Jewish religious practices as pious Jews.

The added detail regarding the specific time—**the ninth hour** or **three** o'clock **in the afternoon**—clarifies the time of the evening sacrifice known as the *Tamid*, which was offered for all Israel and included the reading of prayers (see Exod 29:38-41; Num 28:1-8; Josephus, *Ant.* 14.65).

The imperfect tense of the verbs **going up** and **being carried** indicate that the apostles' proceeding to the temple correlates with unidentified people carrying a "crippled" (CEB) man and placing him at a temple gate. The man is unable to walk, helpless, and desperate. He needs assistance from others. His malady has been lifelong—**from birth** or literally *from his mother's womb*. His helplessness is accentuated by him being placed at the gate **every day**. This stands in stark contrast to the daily practices of the believers and God's activities described by the same expression (2:46, 47*b*).

The crippled man sat at the gate for this purpose (see the genitive article *tou* preceding the infinitive *aitein*): to ask for **alms**. These were gifts or donations of charity done as acts of faithfulness to God and of provision for the poor as affirmed by the OT (e.g., Deut 24:10-22; Isa 58:6-7; Amos 8:4-8; Mal 3:5). By this time, Jewish thought regarded almsgiving as a key element of a faithful person's responsibility to share possessions as a means of doing justice (e.g., Sir 3:30; 29:12; Tob 4:7-11; 12:8-9). Thus, the man's location was probably determined more by expedience than anything else. However, the man also sat outside the temple because his condition likely meant he was banned from the temple and all it represented (e.g., Witherington 1998, 173-74; Wall 2002, 77).

When the man sees Peter and John and then asks them for a gift, he merely does as he had always done with entering worshipers. The imperfect tense of the verb *ērōta* suggests that the beggar begins to ask, which implies that he continues to repeat the request until they respond. However, there is no indication that the man knew the two apostles (against Williams 1990, 64-65).

Ancient Views of Body and Soul

In the Greco-Roman world, it was common to associate a person's physical traits with inner conditions and character. For instance, the depiction of Zacchaeus as "short" in the Lukan Gospel does more than merely add descriptive color to the story. Rather, his lack of physical stature was perceived as an indication that he was also "short" on character.

The crippled man at the Beautiful Gate was no doubt a social and religious outsider due to his physical condition. Most would have considered him weak in both body and character (see Parsons 2006, 109-22). Such ancient perceptions would have limited his participation in worship (see, e.g., Lev 21:16-23). However, it is unclear whether he would have been completely ostracized. Luke's description of the man's healing as the strengthening of his ankles and feet correlates with the ancient view that noble men had strong ankles (see Parsons 2008, 55-57).

■ **4-5** The repeated request from the crippled man captures the undivided attention of the two apostles, as the common Lukan verb *atenizō* suggests (see Luke 4:20; 22:56; Acts 1:10; 3:12; 6:15; 7:55; 10:4; 11:6; 13:9; 14:9; 23:1). The phrase **with John** rather awkwardly reminds readers that John is also present, but Peter alone responds to the beggar. His response piques the man's interest (as the imperfect indicative *epeichen* suggests): he anticipates (as *prosdokaō* connotes) that Peter would give him something. Since no specific accounts of Peter healing anyone have been included thus far in Acts, nothing here suggests the man expects anything other than money.

■ **6** Peter's initial words confirm that the beggar expects alms from him. The emphatic position of **silver or gold**, at the beginning of Peter's response, would have initially dashed the man's hopes, only to be replaced by something much greater. Later, Luke reports that the apostles received money from believers who sold property and gave the proceeds to the community (4:34-37). At this point, the two apostles have no economic resources. This may allude to ancient discussions that distinguished between having money and having virtue (e.g., Epictetus, *Diatr.* 3).

Some MSS omit the first part of Peter's command to **get up and walk**, probably because the same verb describes Peter helping the man up (3:7). However, in Acts there are no instances of healing in which the person was commanded only to walk (Pervo 2009, 100).

The premise of Peter's command—**in the name of Jesus Christ of Nazareth**, which precedes the command—reveals the divine power and authority behind that bold directive. Unlike the beggar, Peter does not beg. He does not plead for the exalted Jesus to act. Instead, he boldly commands the man to stand, after declaring Jesus' name (Haenchen 1971, 200).

This is the first of several invocations of Jesus' name in chs 3 and 4. The phrase does not function as a precise or "magical" formula (see 19:13-17). Rather, it acknowledges Jesus as the only source of salvation and healing (2:38). Thus, the authority in Peter's command does not come through Jesus' name per se but through the name(s) that his resurrection and glorification validated: Lord and Christ (2:36; Peterson 2009, 169).

■ **7** As in other healing stories in the Gospels and Acts, Peter helps the man stand up. The verb *piazō*, which depicts Peter taking the man's right hand, is typically used in the NT to describe one's apprehension or arrest (BDAG 2000, 812; see 12:4 as well as John 7:30, 32, 44; 8:20; 10:39; 11:57). Thus, the image is of Peter abruptly grabbing the beggar's hand and helping him up.

The adverb **instantly** in the Third Gospel often depicts the dramatic and immediate occurrence of miraculous events (see Luke 5:25; 8:47, 55; 13:13; 18:43). Here, it emphasizes the extraordinary nature of this particular event as consistent with the "signs and wonders" that are previously associated with Jesus (2:22) and the apostles (2:43). Rather than merely describing the man standing up, the narrator twice (here [3:7]; v 16) directs readers' attention to the wholeness and health (as *stereoō* indicates) that came to the man's feet and ankles. This is a sign of a dramatic healing and transformation (→ sidebar "Ancient Views of Body and Soul" above).

■ **8** The man's response is evidence of his healing and transformation. Twice, forms of the verb *hallomai* depict the man jumping or leaping around, perhaps an allusion to Isa 35:6 (LXX), where the same verb appears: "the crippled will leap like a deer."

Here and in the next verse, Luke reiterates three times that the man is walking. This may allude to Jesus' message to some disciples of John the Baptist (*the crippled are walking* [Luke 7:22]). This is a clear sign that the messianic age has dawned and made available the promised messianic salvation.

That the man is **praising God** is noteworthy, since the Lukan corpus typically reserves such a description for those who recognize the movement and activity of God among them (see, e.g., Luke 2:13, 20; esp. Acts 2:47). Thus, it is no surprise that the healed man accompanies Peter and John as they enter the temple to worship. Because of this healing in Jesus' name, a onetime outsider has become a symbol of Israel's restoration.

■ **9-10** The reference to **all the people** is reminiscent of the hyperbolic descriptions in the previous summary statement (see esp. 2:47; also 2:43). It suggests how widely known this event would become. It perhaps implies that news spread beyond those in the temple at the time to the other Jewish inhabitants of Jerusalem (see Gaventa 2003, 85).

By pointing out their recognition that the man who created the spectacle by jumping around is the same man who formerly sat and begged at the temple gate, the narrator highlights the radical transformation of that healing. The second reference to the **Beautiful** Gate of the temple suggests its importance to the Lukan account, despite the difficulties in its identification (see "Behind the Text" above).

There is a semantic connection between the terms *hōra* (as in the **hour** *of* *prayer* [v 1]) and *hōraia* (as in the **Beautiful** Gate, here with the connotation of "opportune" or "timely"). This wordplay insinuates the convergence of this time and location to offer the beggar this gracious moment of opportunity (see Hamm 1986, 317; Parsons 2008, 59).

The response of the people is a stereotypical Lukan description to a miraculous event. The narrator describes them as *filled with astonishment and surprise*. The verb **filled** is the same verbal form that describes how the Holy Spirit came upon the believers at Pentecost (2:4). This may suggest that readers should perceive this popular response in less-than-positive ways. Verbal forms (*existēmi*) of the noun *ekstasis*, translated as *surprise*, convey typical reactions to the Spirit's activity in Acts (see 2:7, 12; 8:9, 11, 13; 10:45). The narrator depicts Jewish ambivalence as to whether or not this is a divine encounter (see Wall 2002, 78-79).

b. Peter Explains What Happened (3:11-26)

The similarities between Peter's explanatory speeches at Pentecost and after the healing of the crippled beggar invite comparison. Both speeches call for repentance and briefly review the story of Jesus' death and resurrection. However, this speech introduces a more developed understanding of Jesus. Since the healing occurred in Jesus' name (v 6), its explanation depends on a more exalted Christology. Although both speeches address similar audiences about similar situations, they complement rather than repeat one another (Tannehill 1990, 58).

■ **11** The narrator introduces the post-healing portion of the scene by reminding the reader of the main characters. The healed man has joined the apostles Peter and John. The depiction of the man as holding onto the two implies that he would not let them leave at the conclusion of worship.

In v 12, Peter hints that the apostles had hoped to remain inconspicuous. However, the response of the crowd intensifies. The verb *syntrechō* implies that they quickly **gather together** by running toward the trio, giving them no means of escape. The intensive adjective *ekthambos* indicates that the people are **completely** astonished. They are at a loss to explain what just happened (see v 10). The repeated hyperbolic expression **all the people** (*pas ho laos*; see also v 9) underscores the widespread reaction of the Jews in the temple, who represent the Jewish people in general.

Solomon's Colonnade

Luke identifies the specific temple location where the crowd congregated around Peter, John, and the healed man as Solomon's Colonnade or Portico. The construction of this particular colonnade, like others that may have surrounded the temple precincts at this time, had occurred during the reign of Herod the Great.

The word *stoa*, "colonnade," normally referred to a columned, covered porch that provided shelter from the natural elements. Before and after worship and other sacred rituals, people gathered in these sheltered places to discuss Scripture and other religious matters. According to 5:12, Solomon's Colonnade became a customary meeting place for the earliest Christians. Its precise location is uncertain due to conflicting ancient sources (see, e.g., Josephus, *J.W.* 5.185; *Ant.* 20.221). But it probably was located on the eastern side of the temple, where Solomon's temple had stood.

■ **12** Peter begins his speech by addressing the people as **Men, Israelites**, one of the ways that he addressed the Pentecost crowd (2:22). The religious identification of the audiences as **Israelites** is an accurate assessment of that Jewish crowd that, like Peter and John, probably just came from worship. Peter's observation of the people's amazement (see vv 10-11) validates the narrator's perspective as reliable. Peter depicts the people as ***staring***, the same verb describing the apostles' undivided attention to the beggar (v 4). He diagnoses this reaction as due to their misunderstanding.

Acts has already made it clear that God was responsible for the "many wonders and signs" that first Jesus and now the apostles performed (2:22, 43; v 6). However, the reliable character Peter interprets their astonishment as based on the false assumption that the healing occurred because of the apostles' ***own ability or devotion to God.***

■ **13** Like his Pentecost speech (2:15), Peter begins with the refutation of the people's false understanding. He introduces a theme similar to that found in that earlier speech (see 2:22-36): God's purposes are accomplished through Jesus. In an adaptation of Exod 3:6, 15, he credits the miracle to ***the God of our ancestors.*** Peter abruptly shifts their attention from their false assumption about the *apostles'* role in the healing to *God.* This places their attention directly on God who entered into covenant with Israel. The theme of covenant reappears at the end of the speech (Acts 3:25-26), framing the entire speech.

The identification of Jesus as God's ***servant*** or "child" (*pais*) occurs in the NT only in Acts 3—4 (also 3:26; 4:27, 30). Since the speech later mentions suffering, this is probably an allusion to the suffering servant described in Isa 52:13 (LXX), where the same noun appears. Similar to the Pentecost speech, the actions of God and of the Jewish people are contrasted.

105

Repeated emphatic second-person pronouns (Acts 3:13-14) place the blame for Jesus' death squarely on Peter's audience. The Jewish rejection of Jesus before Pilate and their role in turning him over for execution echo the Third Gospel (Luke 23:1-25). Luke's concern is not to reduce Roman blame for Jesus' death (see Witherington 1998, 181), but to indict the Jewish people.

In stark contrast to what the Jewish people did, God **glorified** Jesus. That is, God resurrected and exalted him (2:24-26, 32-33). Jesus' authority in the healing suggests that God continues to glorify him in events like this (see Tannehill 1990, 53; Barrett 1994, 195).

■ **14** One may comprehend the gravity of the Jewish rejection of Jesus when one considers the title used here for Jesus, **the Holy and Righteous One**. This particular title is unusual because these adjectives seldom appear together in the NT to describe Jesus.

The OT reserves the title "Holy One" for God in relation to Israel (see, e.g., Pss 78:41; 89:18; Isa 1:4; 30:11, 12; 40:25; 49:7; 55:5; 60:9, 14). It is applied to Jesus in Luke 1:35 and in a demoniac's address to Jesus (Luke 4:34). The OT prophets' use of "Righteous One" as a messianic designation (e.g., Isa 32:1; 53:11; Jer 23:5) seems to be reflected here (and in 7:52; 22:14; see the centurion's declaration about Jesus in Luke 23:47). Ironically, the Jewish people rejected Jesus, God's servant and agent for salvation and life, in favor of an identified murderer (Luke 23:25).

■ **15** The tragic irony of the Jews' actions is reiterated in even starker terms with the charge that they **killed the author of life**. In the first century, the term *archēgos* (5:31; see also Heb 2:10; 12:2) typically connoted ideas of either leadership or origination (see LSJ 1996, 252). If it here describes Jesus as the *leader of life*, it suggests that he would lead others to new life by virtue of his resurrection by God (see, e.g., Pervo 2009, 105). If it identifies Jesus as the originator **of life,** the emphasis is on Jesus' role in *giving* salvation and new life to others, not merely in *leading* them to salvation and life (see, e.g., Peterson 2009, 175-76). The ambiguity allows readers to consider both connotations. However, the latter interpretation sharpens the contrast in this context between a murderer who takes life and Jesus who gives it (Johnson 1992, 68).

■ **16** Peter's speech makes a direct link between this summary of the gospel message (vv 13-15) and the healing that prompted it. The crowd had not witnessed the healing, but only its results. So Peter reiterates what he had already declared to the beggar (v 6): Jesus is the source of and authority behind that healing.

The term translated as **completely healed** or "perfect health" (NRSV; only here in the NT) describes unblemished animals acceptable for sacrifice to God in the LXX (e.g., Isa 1:6; Zech 11:16). Here, it may further clarify that the man's healing or salvation made him acceptable to God. **Faith** is twice mentioned to stress its essential role in what happened. But it is unclear whether this refers to the faith of Peter or of the healed man. In either case, it is faith in Jesus' name (Acts 3:6).

As Peter addresses that Jewish audience in the colonnade, he alludes to a prominent theme in Israel's worship: the power of the divine name to deliver God's people (e.g., Pss 20:1-7; 44:4-8; 54:1-7). Previously linked to Solomon's temple (1 Kgs 8:17), Peter now relates it to what has just taken place in Solomon's Colonnade (Spencer 2004a, 57).

■ **17-18** Peter's speech appropriates strong and emotionally charged language to convict his audience of what they have done, not to discredit them (Parsons 2008, 60). Peter refers to his audience as *adelphoi*, but the group likely included both men and women, ***brothers and sisters***. Such familial language affirms their shared identity as fellow Jews. Peter could relate with those who disowned Jesus (Acts 3:13-14); the same verb depicts both their acts against Jesus and his own denial of Jesus (Luke 22:34, 57, 61).

The audience's **ignorance** regarding Jesus' identity and mission did not excuse them or their ***rulers***, whose deeds transferred to the people. They did not know or understand the Scriptures on the subject of the coming Christ, particularly his suffering. The brevity of this comment leaves much unexplained. The narrator's succinct report was composed with the implied readers in mind.

Readers should understand the contention that God's announcement about the Christ came **through all the prophets** as rhetorical hyperbole. Few prophetic books explicitly mention the idea of a suffering Messiah. Peter probably refers to Isaiah's depiction of the suffering servant (Isa 52:13—53:12) as well as to Jesus' own teaching about why the Christ must suffer (Luke 24:25-27, 45-47).

■ **19-21** The disclosure about the people's ignorance opens the door for repentance and forgiveness. The conjunction *oun* (***therefore***) signals a conclusion in light of the preceding remarks. On this basis, Peter offers two challenges in the form of commands.

The first imperative, **repent**, repeats Peter's call to the Pentecost crowd (2:38) for a decisive change of mind, based on what he proclaimed about Jesus and his audience's role in his death. The second imperative, **turn**, reinforces the call to repent. The verb *epistrephō*, which often appears in Luke (1:16; 22:32) and Acts (9:35; 11:21; 14:15; 15:19; 26:20), refers to the turning around of one's life to God.

Together, the two imperatives declare that "genuine repentance involves a radical reorientation of life, turning back to God to seek reconciliation and to express a new obedience" (Peterson 2009, 179). However, the broader context implies that this is in response to God's initiative in the fulfillment of God's promises.

Three purpose clauses follow the two commands. The first clause functions as the primary purpose for repentance: sin's removal. The verb *exaleiphō* connotes wiping something away or eliminating it entirely. This expression may allude to Ps 51:1, 9, where the LXX uses the same verb to describe the removal or blotting out of sin. Through repentance, sins against Jesus as the Christ may be completely removed. This opens the way for what the other two clauses reveal.

The second clause speaks of coming **seasons of refreshment**, an expression found only here in the NT. In the LXX, a related noun depicts a cooling breeze, representing the reprieve from God's judgment through the plagues (Exod 8:11). Here, the expression announces the arrival of an eschatological period of salvation because of repentance. The phrase **from the face of the Lord** identifies God as the source of this refreshment. This speech does not explicitly mention the Holy Spirit. But the sense of "blowing wind" as the means of refreshment and the emphasis on God's presence offer subtle allusions to the outpouring of the Holy Spirit (Acts 2).

The third purpose clause focuses on the culmination of God's plan through the return of Jesus as the Christ (see 1:11). The perfect participle *ton prokecheirismenon* clarifies that the appointment of Jesus as the Christ happened in advance so that he would be ready to return after Israel's repentance. Thus, the restoration of Israel and **all things**, not Israel's judgment, would accompany his return. Appearing only here in the NT, the expression **times of restoration for all things** refers not only to Israel but also to all God's creation. This accentuates the significance of Israel's repentance.

Restoration recalls the question the apostles asked Jesus before his ascension: "Lord, are you at this time going to restore the kingdom to Israel?" (1:6). What is unclear is the precise relationship between the **seasons of refreshment** in the previous verse and the **times of restoration** here.

Some interpret these two expressions as distinct periods of God's saving work, with the first occurring before Christ's return, which would then bring about the second and the consummation of God's purposes (e.g., Peterson 2009, 179-81; Wall 2002, 82). Others interpret the two expressions as essentially synonymous, with the first indicating the beginning (*kairoi*) and the second indicating the duration (*chronoi*) of that eschatological period of messianic blessing, which will culminate with Jesus' return and final restoration (Fitzmyer 1998, 288-89; see Bock 2007, 177-78; Tannehill 1990, 55-56). The latter interpretation correlates better with the narrative tendencies of Acts.

■ **22-23** As in the Pentecost speech, Peter turns to Scripture in support of his message. The first portion cites Moses' expectation (Deut 18:15, 19) of a coming prophet similar to himself to whom Israel must listen. In its original context, Moses warned Israel to listen to that prophet rather than adopt the magical practices of other nations to discover God's will. At least in some Jewish circles (e.g., Qumran), they expected a Moses-like prophet who would come at the end times (see, e.g., 1QS1.9-11; 4Q175.5-8; John 1:21; 6:14; 7:40).

Slight changes in the wording here suggest that the people should not only listen to that prophet but also obey him (Johnson 1992, 70). Obedience would be a distinct mark of the people of God, since the prophet like Moses would speak to the people on behalf of God. Conversely, the added material from Lev 23:29 declares that disobedience would characterize those outside God's people.

The verb *exolethreuō* connotes complete destruction (LSJ 1996, 597; BDAG 2000, 351). Peter leaves little to the imagination regarding the devastating results of disobeying God's message through that prophet. The context clearly implies this prophet is Jesus. The disobedient Jews are ironically like their own perceptions of the crippled beggar: as outsiders to the people of God. This Petrine speech early in Acts allows the narrator to hint about a division among the Jewish people over the gospel message of Jesus as the Messiah/Christ, which will increasingly play itself out in the unfolding plot (see Jervell 1996, 34-43).

■ **24-26** As in v 18, the Petrine reference to **all the prophets** functions as rhetorical hyperbole. It claims that the message about the coming Moses-like prophet is found throughout the OT. The OT actually includes few sayings of Samuel and none about such a prophet. But the connections between Samuel (as the first prophet) and David may suggest an allusion to OT messianic promises. Such messianic hope, which appears from time to time in other prophets after Samuel, may be what was in mind here.

The conclusion returns to the theme of covenant that begins Peter's speech, one of only two places in Acts where the term **covenant** appears (7:8). The description of the audience as "children" or ***descendants*** has a dual function. On the one hand, their Jewish heritage implies that they, of all people, should receive the promises about the Christ that the prophets declared. *They* should take the prophets' message seriously. On the other hand, their heritage meant that God's promise to Abraham and their ancestors applies also to Peter's audience.

The cited promise from God to Abraham (Gen 22:18; 26:4) is a key scriptural text in Paul's justification of his Gentile mission (see Gal 3:6-14). Although the passage also has a missional function in its Lukan context, the substitution of the more generic term **peoples** or "families" (NRSV) for "nations" ("Gentiles") casts that mission in more neutral terms to refer to all humanity.

However, in this context the question remains whether the phrase **through your offspring** refers collectively to the Jewish people as Abraham's descendants, singularly to Jesus as *the* descendant of Abraham, or to both. Although the focus on God's servant (Acts 3:26) suggests Jesus as the reference, Jesus himself would have been included in the collective sense.

That this **servant**, Jesus (v 13), was **raised up** associates Jesus with the prophet Moses declared *God* would "raise up" (v 22). But this "raising up" may have a dual meaning. On the one hand, its combination with the verb **sent** may declare that God was responsible for Jesus' appearance and role on the stage of human history, as one sent **first** to the Jewish people. On the other hand, the verb often describes Jesus' resurrection, as in 2:24, 32 (see also 13:33, 34; 17:31). Although the "raising up" refers primarily to Jesus' mission to the Jewish people, the use of this "resurrection language" underscores the place of Jesus' resurrection in what amounts to his ongoing mission, as proclaimed through Peter's speech.

FROM THE TEXT

As the first specific example of the post-Pentecost ministry of the believers, the Lukan account of the healing of the crippled man offers *both* a vivid image of restoration to the people of God for one person *and* an opportunity to explicate the significance of Jesus and his resurrection. In many ways, at the heart of this healing scene is the healing of the people of God (Johnson 1992, 72). Thus, the dramatic transformation, seen in both physical and religious ways, opens the door to explore more fully what God has done through the outpouring of the Holy Spirit at Pentecost and what that may mean for the people of God.

A significant aspect of this story and subsequent explanatory speech is the correlation between worship and ministry. The Lukan account of this event depicts a cyclical pattern, in which worship leads to ministry and salvation, which in turn leads to worship and the acknowledgment of God's work, new opportunities for ministry, etc. The apostles' intent to worship leads them to a place where they encounter a person considered an outsider by the people of God. However, rather than ignoring the need of the outsider and thereby maintaining through worship the boundaries that separate insiders from outsiders, they engage the man in need of restoration through healing so that he, too, would be included among God's people.

Healing results in the man's worship, both by praising God and by joining the two apostles in worship in the temple (v 8). This is followed by a subsequent encounter between Peter and an audience of temple worshipers who *themselves* need restoration. This correlation between worship and ministry runs throughout Acts and suggests a more holistic understanding of salvation and the Christian life than is often seen in the Christian church today.

Another significant aspect of this story is the claim of Jesus as both the authority behind and the source of salvation. The speech makes the case that the resurrected Jesus is responsible for the crippled man's healing and restoration. The Pentecost speech emphasizes the resurrected Jesus' role as the agent of the Spirit's outpouring (see 2:32-36). Here, his role is, as in the Third Gospel, as God's prophet or spokesperson, to whom God's people must listen obediently (e.g., Luke 9:35).

To share in the promise God has given—to be a member of God's chosen people—means that one must turn to the one whom God sent. Thus, salvation comes in response to what God has promised, to what God has already done, and through the one whom God sent, Jesus. This understanding of salvation motivates the two apostles and defines the believers' mission, here in this scene and throughout the book of Acts.

This story also offers what may be characterized as the Lukan redefinition of "the people of God." This reconceptualization extends throughout the book of Acts. But two key elements stand out in this chapter.

First, Luke introduces through Peter the distinctive division among the Jewish people over the prophet whom God sent them. Those who refuse to obey him are excluded from the people who belong to and identify with God (vv 22-23).

Jewish responsibility for Jesus' death was already asserted in 2:23. Here, the citation of selected OT passages alters prevalent Jewish understandings of the people of God in two distinct ways. On the one hand, the words from Moses indicate that inclusion within this people requires obedience to God's message through God's agent (3:22-23). On the other hand, the promise to Abraham suggests a more inclusive understanding that potentially extends beyond the Jewish people to all humanity (v 25).

Second, the people of God have faith that (*a*) God truly resurrected and glorified Jesus, and (*b*) God fulfilled God's promise to the people of God by the outpouring of the Spirit through Jesus. This emphasis on God's dramatic acts of salvation through Jesus transforms the essence of the worship of God. Therefore, this becomes the foundational element in what becomes the Lukan redefinition of what it means to be the people of God.

2. Religious Leaders Oppose Peter and John (4:1-22)

BEHIND THE TEXT

Notably absent from the Lukan account of Peter's speech explaining the healing of the crippled man is any explicitly narrated response from the temple audience. The Pentecost speech and this one both implored the respective audience to repent (see 2:38; 3:19). Here, the narrator describes nothing about how they responded. One reason for this omission is the interruption of the scene that subsequently followed. A common Lukan literary device, the sudden interruption often functions as an abrupt means of introducing another significant component to the story, such as new characters, elements of contrast, an important theological question, etc. In this instance, the source of the interruption is a group of Sadducees, whose concerns and questions challenged the legitimacy of the apostles' actions and message.

According to the first-century Jewish historian Josephus, the group known as the Sadducees was one of three "sects" or schools of thought within Judaism (see *J.W.* 2.119; *Ant.* 13.171). The party was named after the priest Zadok (2 Sam 8:17; 15:24-36; 1 Kgs 1:32-40; 2:26-35), whose name is related to the Hebrew term for righteousness. He served as high priest during the time of Kings David and Solomon.

The priestly descendants of Zadok were granted the divine right to officiate as temple priests after the Jewish return to Jerusalem from their exile in Babylon (Ezek 40:46; 43:19; 44:15-23; 48:11). The Sadducees embraced that divine charge and believed that only such priests could speak authoritatively about spiritual matters.

By the first century AD, the Sadducees had become an aristocratic party including both priestly and lay members. They were the political and economic elites within Jewish society. Because of their favored position within Jewish life, they tended to cooperate with the Roman authorities to maintain their political and social status. Thus, they were often preoccupied with political concerns, reputation, and power.

There were several differences between the theological positions of Sadducees and Pharisees, a rival Jewish sect that will appear in Acts 4. Two distinct issues stand out. First, the Sadducees held to a strict interpretation of the Torah alone, whereas the Pharisees also embraced the oral interpretation of the Torah. Second, because the Torah mentions nothing about resurrection, Sadducees did not believe in resurrection (4:2; 23:8; see Josephus, *J.W.* 2.165; *Ant.* 18.16), but the Pharisees did. In Acts, the latter issue fuels the unfolding Sadducees' opposition, first against Peter and John in Acts 4 and then against the Twelve (5:17-42).

IN THE TEXT

■ **1-2** The sudden shift in action introduces a new issue into the narrative. Although Peter was earlier identified as the speaker (3:12-26), this section begins with both apostles as speakers. This implies one of two things: John contributes to Peter's message but Luke did not mention that earlier, or Peter speaks on behalf of the pair.

112

The interruption comes from the religious authorities, whom the narrator distinguishes in three ways: **the priests** as the temple authorities responsible for the temple; *the **commander of the temple***, probably the one in charge over temple security; and **the Sadducees**.

The narrator depicts the encounter negatively. The verb translated **came up** (*ephistēmi*) is a favorite Lukan term (eighteen of twenty-one NT occurrences of the term are in Luke and Acts) that connotes confrontation and opposition, as here. The leaders are **greatly disturbed** (*diaponeō* generally connotes annoyance or exasperation) by the apostles' action. There are two reasons for this.

First, **the apostles were teaching the people**, an activity Luke often associates with Jesus (see Luke 4:15, 31; 5:3, 17; 6:6; 13:10, 22; Acts 1:1). Jesus' teaching was the reason behind the temple leaders' opposition to him (Luke 19:47; 20:1; 23:5). This brief explanation depicts these apostles like Jesus (see Acts 5:21, 25, 28, 42; 11:26; 15:35; 18:11; 20:20; 28:31) and hints at ominous problems now facing them. That the two apostles are teaching **the people** (*ton laon*)—the term Luke reserves for the Jewish people of God (2:47; 3:9, 11)—suggests that these religious leaders are upset because the two have impinged on *their* authority as *temple* leaders (see Tannehill 1990, 59).

Second, it was impossible for these temple leaders to accept the apostles' proclamation about the resurrection **in Jesus** (or "by means of the story of Jesus," if the phrase *en tō Iēsou* has an instrumental sense; see Barrett 1994, 220). The Sadducees denied belief in resurrection.

■ **3-4** The contrast between the respective response of the Jewish *temple leaders* and the Jewish *people* is remarkable. The leaders' arrest of Peter and John—*they threw their hands on them*—suggests their violent seizure of the two. The late evening hour meant that the Jewish council (i.e., the Sanhedrin) could not hear their issue with the apostles until morning, since they only deliberated during the day (*m. Sanh.* 4.1; see Luke 22:66). It is unclear where they detained them until they could arrange for their hearing. They likely would not confine the two in a public prison.

Although a collectively small number of religious authorities respond with self-serving and hostile opposition, the general Jewish public respond very differently. The verb **believed** again depicts those who respond favorably to the gospel message (see 2:44). However, the verb's aorist verb tense focuses on the **many** who had come to believe in the gospel. The number of believers, which Luke estimates as *about five thousand men*, was probably much larger, since this only accounts for the males (*anēr*). The number itself specifies the community's extraordinary growth, not just after this second speech but during an extended period of time, from Pentecost to the arrest of Peter and John.

The Sanhedrin

The highest Jewish governing body in Palestine is commonly known as the Sanhedrin (from the Greek *synedrion*, lit., "sitting down with," "meeting with others"). The term in Greek literature often describes courts and legislative councils. Because the term also refers to a variety of meetings in ancient Jewish sources, precise description of the structure and function of such councils is nearly impossible. Historians are unclear whether such a council existed as a local or regional entity.

The Sanhedrin here was probably comprised of seventy-one members, including the high priest as convening officer. Although historical certainty is elusive, the NT Gospels and Acts consistently employ the term to depict a specific Jewish council located in Jerusalem.

The NT Gospels clearly associate the Sanhedrin with the hearing in which Jewish religious leaders falsely convicted Jesus, but they mention only members of the Sadducean party in their deliberations. Later in Acts, the Sanhedrin is comprised of members from the parties of the Sadducees and the Pharisees (5:33; 23:6-7). In these cases, the narrative depiction of the Sanhedrin functions as a symbol of rejection of Jesus and the gospel message about Jesus, particularly by the Jewish religious leaders.

■ **5-6** The narrator does not state whether the Jewish leaders assembled the next morning for this particular hearing or as their customary procedure. There is some question whether this assembly was of the whole Sanhedrin or a smaller Jewish council. However, the three mentioned groups correlate with typical understandings of the council's membership: the **rulers** are the chief priests and probably members of the Sadducees; the **elders** would include Sadducean laypersons, other priests, and heads of primary aristocratic families; and the ***scribes*** as experts on the Jewish law would be Pharisees.

That the pronoun ***their*** precedes the listing of these three groups insinuates that Luke distinguishes between this leadership of the "former" people of God and that of his redefined understanding of the people of God (Peterson 2009, 189). The reminder that this happens **in Jerusalem** keeps readers' attention on the role of this city as these initial events and responses to the gospel message unfold.

The list of specific individuals identifies some key figures included in the general list of v 5.

Annas, whom Luke identifies as the **high priest**, actually served in that capacity much earlier (AD 6-15) before the Romans deposed him. There are three possible explanations for this erroneous information: the use of a flawed source (see "Sources and Intertextuality" in Introduction), a passing comment on Annas' wrongful ouster, or a side note about his ongoing influence and legacy behind the scenes.

Caiaphas, Annas' son-in-law, was high priest (AD 18-36) at the time of this meeting. Nothing is known about **John**, whom some MSS identify as Jonathan the successor to Caiaphas (see Josephus, *Ant.* 18.95), or **Alexander**. By including these three high priests representing the past, present, and future of Judaism of that day, Luke implicates the Jewish religious leadership holistically for their opposition to these apostles.

■ **7** Since meetings of the Sanhedrin (and perhaps other similar legislative or judicial groups of that day) were typically arranged in a semicircle (*m. Sanh.* 4.3), the description that the council has Peter and John *stand in the middle* helps the reader picture what took place.

The specific wording of their opening (and only) question alludes to Peter's explanation after the healing. The anonymous query about the **power** behind their actions reminds the reader of Peter's observation that the bystanders thought the healing occurred because of the apostles' "own power" (3:12). The inquiry into the **name** behind their actions also reminds readers of Peter's declaration that Jesus' name was behind the healing (3:16; see 3:6). Thus, the narrative links between the apostles' authority and the name of Jesus have already been established.

In some ways, this line of interrogation mirrors the question about the authority behind Jesus' actions that the Jewish authorities raised after his arrival in Jerusalem (Luke 20:2). The leaders may have challenged the apostles' authority out of concern for their own authority in the face of the extraordinary healing and the attention the people gave Peter and John. Thus, they interrogate the apostles for an "on-the-record" answer, hoping to find reasonable cause to refute them.

■ **8-9** Luke's explicit description of Peter as **filled with the Holy Spirit** alludes to the Pentecost account, where the same verb refers to the Spirit filling and enabling them to speak as God's prophets (Acts 2:4). This does not suggest a "repeat performance" of Pentecost, which Jesus' promise conveys distinctly with baptism language (1:5). However, it does emphasize the ongoing role of the Spirit in the fresh enablement of the apostles' mission as witnesses (1:8) in particular instances (see Marshall 1980, 69).

Inspiration and wisdom were often associated with the Spirit's presence, reminiscent of Jesus' words that the Holy Spirit would provide the words to say when they faced religious authorities (Luke 12:11-12; see Luke 21:12-15). The verb that describes the apostles giving an account for their actions (*anakrinomai*) was often associated with the examination and cross-examination of witnesses and plaintiffs in legal proceedings (Barrett 1994, 227; BDAG 2000, 66). However, Peter offers the unavoidable irony that the religious leaders conduct a judicial investigation over "a good deed" (NRSV), something that should receive praise rather than scrutiny.

By raising the question about whether the formerly crippled man **was healed**, Peter's remarks introduce two significant ideas for the council's consideration. First, the verb's perfect tense not only confirms the restoration of the man's health but also points to its ongoing significance. Second, although he could have appropriated other verbs for healing (e.g., Acts 4:14), the verb *sōzō*, which means "save" in either a physical or spiritual sense, reiterates broader connotations of salvation that already appear (2:21, 40, 47). While the council members would have agreed that the source of ultimate salvation is the God of Israel, Peter's testimony about the man's healing confirms that the OT promises and calls for God's salvation declared in the previous chapters have been realized *through Jesus*.

■ **10** The declaration *let it be known* appears in several speeches in Acts to emphasize a significant thought (see 2:14; 13:38; 28:28). Because Peter directs his response to **all the people of Israel**, not only to the council members, this eliminates all ignorance (see 3:17) and questions about the source of the healing.

His answer to the council's question repeats the same phrase that preceded the command to the then-crippled man: the healing happened in **the name of Jesus Christ of Nazareth** (4:10; 3:6, 16). The phrase's instrumental sense answers the council's question by presenting Jesus as the power and authority by which the man, who had been "sick" and unable to stand, can now stand **healthy** before the council.

The two clauses—that declare the council's responsibility for Jesus' death and God's resurrection of Jesus from the dead—depict the council of Jewish religious authorities at odds with God's purposes. Peter, the accused, turns the tables on the council by raising serious accusations against them. Although Peter probably has more to say on these points, these succinct clauses take the reader back to his earlier speeches where he made similar points (2:22-24, 32; 3:13-15) and then urged the people to repent (2:38; 3:19).

■ **11** The citation of Ps 118:22 mirrors Jesus' use of the same verse against the Jewish religious authorities (Luke 20:17). However, the Lukan adaptation of the LXX's wording underscores noteworthy aspects of the verse. The addition of the second-person pronoun to the first line of the psalm redirects its reference to the corrupt builders so that it speaks directly to the council. In addition, the verb *exoutheneō* has replaced the LXX's *apodokimazō*, so that the stone is not merely rejected but scorned and despised.

These verbal changes may be dependent on the correlation between Jesus and the stone: a stone may be rejected but not scorned, whereas a person may be scorned as well. The verse's second line depicts divine reversal, as the rejected/despised stone has become the **cornerstone** of Israel's salvation, the result of God's inferred action. The shift in image accentuates the gravity of that rejection, as the stone became the most honored, essential component that kept the structure standing.

The council's rejection of Jesus means that they forfeit the messianic promises that God offers through him (see 3:17-26). This citation functions to reinforce Peter's indictment against the religious leaders (see Gaventa 2003, 93). The first line from the psalm complements the first clause in v 10. It places guilt for Jesus' crucifixion on the council. The second line complements the second clause, which depicts God's reversal of their rejection through Jesus' resurrection.

The Cornerstone and Psalm 118:22

The widespread citation of Ps 118:22 in the NT (Matt 21:42; Mark 12:10; Luke 20:17; Acts 4:11; 1 Pet 2:7) indicates its importance in the earliest christological reflection of the fledgling Christian movement. Today, a metaphoric "cornerstone" often represents an essential part of a building's foundation. It may also have an inscription of the date when it was set and other information. However, in the ancient world the cornerstone had other important functions in the architecture and construction of buildings.

In the LXX, the cornerstone was literally a "head of the corner," typically a large stone that joined and held together two walls or parts of a building. Unlike recent ceremonial functions, the cornerstone was essential for the structural integrity of a building (Fitzmyer 1998, 301).

Thus, for the earliest Christians, this picture of divine reversal in this psalm offers a theological lens that sharpens their focus regarding God's purposes, especially in light of Jesus' death and resurrection. That is, Jesus' death and resurrection pull and hold together the Christian vision of God's saving purposes.

■ 12 Rather than pronouncing judgment, Peter declares the possibility and necessity of **salvation**, the first time that this noun appears in Acts (see 7:25; 13:26, 47; 16:17; 27:34; see Luke 1:69, 71, 77; 19:9). The term broadly connotes the deliverance and restoration of a person or people from any evil, distress, or disability. This holistic understanding of salvation encompasses the healing of the crippled man (Acts 4:9). But Peter unpacks its christological implications.

The declaration that there is **no other name** through whom such salvation would come not only reiterates Joel's prophecy of salvation (2:21) but reinterprets it in light of Jesus' resurrection and exaltation. Thus, Peter identifies "the name of the Lord" upon whom one may call for salvation as none other than Jesus of Nazareth. It is not surprising that Peter's response ends by underscoring the redemptive significance of Jesus as the exclusive means by which salvation **must** (*dei*) come.

■ 13-14 What captures the council's attention is the two apostles' ***boldness***, a common Lukan expression (Acts 2:29; 4:29, 31; 28:31; for the verbal form, see 9:27, 28; 13:46; 14:3; 18:26; 19:8; 26:26). Boldness describes the believers' freedom to speak openly about the gospel message. This characteristic was often associated with philosophers and free citizens, not with persons of lower social status (see Johnson 1992, 78; Fitzmyer 1998, 302).

Two adjectives heighten the contrast between the apostles and the elite council. The first, **unschooled**, describes the two as lacking basic education, perhaps in rhetoric. The second, **ordinary**, depicts them as lacking professional skills. Given the council's perceptions of the apostles' lower social status, their boldness is most remarkable and by inference attributable only to the Spirit (see 1:8).

Like Pentecost bystanders confronted by the believers' Spirit-inspired speech (2:7) and temple worshipers by evidence of divine healing (3:10-11), Luke now describes the council as *amazed*. The council likely recognizes that the two were Jesus' former associates because of the similarities in their confident address of the council as well as their repeated references to Jesus' name.

In addition to the council's perceptions of the apostles, Luke briefly mentions the presence of the all-important "Exhibit A": the healed man standing with them. Except for this and Peter's passing comment about the man (4:10), the narrator indicates nothing about why he is there. However, his presence "stands" in stark contrast to him sitting crippled at the temple gate.

The perfect tense of the participle translated *the cured man* points to the indisputable evidence that he remains healed. Because of that evidence, the council cannot **contradict** them, perhaps an allusion to Jesus' promise (Luke 21:15). The hearing ends with the unexpected picture of the powerful, elite Jewish council silenced by the inspired rhetoric and healing power of two apostles of low social status.

■ **15-16** The council's recess provides opportunity for them to confer (see Luke 2:19; 14:31; Acts 17:18; 18:27; 20:14). It is noteworthy that the narrator offers readers inside information about the closed-door meeting without revealing his source. The members' initial question about what to do with the two apostles reveals the council's helplessness and anxiety (Haenchen 1971, 218).

Their assessment of the situation validates the Lukan account. Their exaggerated claim that **everyone living in Jerusalem** knew about the remarkable healing correlates with Luke's hyperbole that "all the people" saw the formerly crippled man walk (3:9-10). That the healing itself was *known* alludes to Peter's declaration to the council that what he had to say was to be known by "all the people of Israel" (v 10). Even their description of the healing as a "notable sign" (NRSV) attests to the divine encounter within the event and parallels the evidence in Joel's prophecy (2:19). The council's assessment offers nothing new, but it substantiates the Lukan perspective regarding this glimpse into the fledgling movement. In fact, the evidence is so compelling that even those

4:15-16

whom Peter describes as having "disowned" or "denied" Jesus (3:13-14) admit they cannot **deny** what has happened.

■ **17** Neither Peter's response nor the council's deliberations convince them to repent (see Wall 2002, 90). Rather, since they cannot discount the healing, they seek to squelch the prophetic voice of the two apostles. The intensive verb **spreading** (*dianemō*) conveys their fear that the gospel message would "blanket" the entire Jewish populace and threaten their own authority as religious leaders. Their agreed means of muzzling the apostles is a veiled threat of repercussions, as the verb *apeileō* (see 1 Pet 2:23) suggests.

Several aspects of the council's stated intention to silence Peter and John suggest their hope to eliminate all proclamation about Jesus. First, the verb *laleō*, which typically describes gospel proclamation in Acts, appears here in their warning that the two **speak no longer**. Second, the phrase **in this name** points back to Peter's repeated reference to Jesus' name (3:16; 4:10, 12), while the authorities appear averse to naming him themselves. Third, double negations (**no longer, *to no one***) emphasize that this proclamation must completely and forever stop—a gag order to ensure that things would not worsen (Pervo 2009, 118).

■ **18** Upon the hearing's resumption, the council summons the apostles and hands down the ruling. The reiterated threat intensifies the mounting tensions as Peter and John face the council's opposition. The threat generally corroborates the council's agreement (v 17). But two differences highlight aspects of the council's resolve. First, the warning against proclamation includes two verbs rather than one. One verb, *phthengomai* (see 2 Pet 2:16, 18; Wis 1:8), correlates with the council's complaints against public proclamation (see Barrett 1994, 236-37). A compound form of that verb (*apophthengomai*) earlier depicted the believers' Spirit-inspired speech at Pentecost (Acts 2:4) and Peter's subsequent speech to the bystanders (2:14). This implies that the council opposes the *Spirit*, not merely the apostles' message. The other verb reiterates the original problem of the apostles "teaching the people" (4:2), which led to their arrest. Second, the expression **at all** calls for the complete cessation of activities central to their commission as Jesus' witnesses (1:8).

■ **19-20** The pair's response dismisses the council's order. The two apostles characterize the dilemma as a question over obeying or disobeying God (→ sidebar "God or . . ." below). The underlying assumption is that both the apostles and the council members, as the religious leaders of the Jewish people, would affirm primary obedience to God.

Of course, the council would argue that God leads the people of God through their divinely chosen leaders, so that God's authority rests with them. Yet the two apostles, like the OT prophets who often stood up against leaders

119

whose directives opposed God's will, respond that the council's order ultimately demands that they *disobey* God.

Therefore, the suggestion that the council **judge** what is **right**, if taken seriously, could result in their self-incrimination and demise as legitimate leaders of God's people (Jervell 1998, 181; Wall 2002, 90). One should not miss the ironic picture contrasting the council and the apostles: the Jewish religious authorities who should obey God advocate disobedience; the two apostles outside the religious establishment seek to obey God (see Gaventa 2003, 94).

"God or  . . ."

The famous response of Peter and John to the Jewish council about choosing between God and another option resembles a saying from Socrates. He declared in his own defense before Athenian judges, "I will obey God rather than you!" (Plato, *Apol.* 29d). By the time of the writing of Acts, this saying was familiar enough to have colored an ancient reader's perception of this scene.

There are also several examples in Jewish history in which God's commands take precedence over other options pressed by adversaries. Perhaps the most notable OT example is of the three faithful Jewish men who exclaimed to King Nebuchadnezzar, "Be it known to you, O king, that we will not serve your gods and we will not worship the golden statue that you have set up" (Dan 3:18 NRSV). In 2 Macc 7, there is a story of members of a Jewish family who were forced by torture to eat pork. One of them declared, "We are ready to die rather than transgress the laws of our ancestors" (v 2 NRSV; see 4 Macc 7:14-21). Josephus mentions instances when Jews responded with similar dedication to obey God and God's law (e.g., *Ant.* 17.159; 18.268). These examples suggest that the reader should see the apostles' stance in similar ways.

The apostles' final statement explains their defiance of the council's instructions. Their appeal to what they had seen and heard probably refers in a general way to Jesus' ministry, including Jesus' commissioning of the apostles as witnesses (1:8). Their proclamation, as found thus far in Peter's speeches, underscores God's workings and purposes as these relate to Jesus and what is now happening among the believers. Hence, the emphatic first-person pronoun clearly identifies the apostles' stance in affirming obedience to God in contrast to the council, whose members suggest otherwise. For Peter and John, this is more than a matter of decision or will; the verb *dynamai* suggests that they are unable to or cannot do differently.

■ **21-22** As the scene closes, the helplessness of the council stands out as they either repeat the earlier threat (v 17) or add to it. However, their release of the men from custody indicates how little they can do. The stated reason behind their release—***finding no way to punish them***—does not mean that the council deems the gospel message legitimate. Rather, they find nothing that **the**

people would consider a punishable offense, since **all . . . were praising God,** thus affirming the apostles' message.

The division between the Jewish religious leaders and the Jewish people is evident in their different responses. The Jewish council tries to stifle the gospel message; the Jewish people affirm that message (see 2:47; 3:9). The council's actions put them in a precarious position. As those responsible for upholding God's law and mediating God's presence, further actions against Peter and John may cause the Jewish people to view them as antagonistic against God's work (see Spencer 2004a, 61).

Some have raised questions regarding the role of the tidbit of information regarding the healed man's age at the end of this scene. To be sure, that information provides one last touch to the picture, much like an artist finishing a painting, to clarify why the once-crippled-now-standing man offers such indisputable evidence that the healing occurred. One could argue that this information would function much more effectively in a number of narrative places prior to the end.

The man plays a narrative role as a symbol for *Israel's* restoration (→ 3:8). Thus, his restoration after more than forty years with his debilitating condition may offer one last clue. If readers missed this earlier, this detail may help them relate this healing story to Israel's wilderness story. "As God's saving purpose for ancient Israel was finally realized after forty years of stumbling and meandering through the wilderness, so the moment of fresh renewal—signaled by the dance of a forty-year cripple—has dawned upon the present Israel" (Spencer 2004a, 62).

FROM THE TEXT

For the first time in the book of Acts, the reader has opportunity to see more than a quick glimpse of one of the earliest members of the Jesus movement after Pentecost. As in everyday life, character and other inner traits become apparent when an individual or group faces adversity. Such is the case here, as the same powerful, authoritative group that condemned Jesus to death challenges these two faithful apostles. Yet in the end, the apostles do not crumple under the weight of threats from those who have both the power and the means to back them up. Instead, they stand strong.

The contrasting images of the apostles and the powerful Jewish council remain fixed in the mind's eye as the scene closes. The apostles, like Jesus, resemble the OT prophets. Filled with the Spirit, they have the courage to speak truthfully and openly about God's will. As John Wesley wrote, "God moves his instruments, not when they please, but just when he sees it needful" (1958, 406). However, the religious authorities attempt to intimidate the two while ironically acting in timid ways because the pair see things much differently from the Jewish people. The apostles act with resolve in the face of opposition that they do not initiate. The council creates division and reacts with hostility due to their concerns for preserving their power and religious authority. The apostles seek to obey God by fulfilling their divine commission, whereas these religious leaders give directives that call for disobedience. Thus, the apostles' lives reflect those qualities that one would expect to find in those leading the people of God, whereas the council members do not.

These contrasting images raise questions about what it means to be the people of God. Yet, it is not the negative image of the religious leaders but the positive image of the apostles that stands out. "This is a story about what happens when a purpose which is 'from God' is recognized by persons willing to obey God in spite of human hostility" (Tannehill 1990, 62).

3. The Believers' Response to Opposition (4:23-31)

BEHIND THE TEXT

This passage continues the larger literary section that began with 3:1. In many ways, it functions as a climax to the entire section. The believers' prayer articulates and clarifies major issues behind the composition of the scenes of this section. The narrative returns to a group of believers, reminding readers that Peter and John were not acting on their own but as representatives of the larger group. They all were probably aware of the prior developments regarding the temple leaders and the Jewish council.

IN THE TEXT

■ **23** The passage begins where the previous scene left off by referring to the release of Peter and John from the council's custody. The two apostles return to **their own people** (*tous idious*), a fairly common expression to describe family and close friends. This gathering of an unspecified number of believers may refer only to apostles (e.g., Johnson 1992, 83) or more generally to the believers. However, the gathering continues to function as earlier descriptions of the believers (e.g., 2:42-47).

■ **24** The believers respond to the council's threats (vv 17, 18) by turning to God in prayer. Both the adverb **together** (see 1:14; 2:46) and the singular *voice* (*phōnēn*) convey the ongoing togetherness and unanimity among the believers. One person probably prayed on behalf of all, who would have consented with the prayer.

The prayer addresses God in two distinct ways. First, they address God as **Sovereign Lord** or *Master*, using a rare NT term to refer to God (see Luke 2:29; Rev 6:10). *Despotēs* commonly describes one with complete ownership and power. Jews often used the title to address God (e.g., Tob 8:17; Wis 11:26;

122

Josephus, *Ant.* 4.40, 46; *J.W.* 7.323), including the LXX (e.g., Gen 15:2, 8; Jer 1:6; 4:10). Thus, the address depicts God as the one who controls all circumstances. Second, God is addressed as Creator of all things, reminiscent of OT descriptions of God (e.g., Exod 20:11; Neh 9:6; Ps 146:6; Isa 37:16). These are more than honorific ways of addressing God; they express the believers' faith in God.

Prayers for Deliverance from Israel's Past

The prayer of the believers following the first recorded incident of opposition to them resembles prayers for God's deliverance from Israel's history. The most notable example is the prayer of King Hezekiah, who prayed for the deliverance of God's people who were threatened by their Assyrian enemies (Isa 37:16-20; 2 Kgs 19:15-19). Hezekiah's address of God as Creator of all things and his description of the danger that they faced established a pattern that this prayer in Acts follows. However, one notable difference in Hezekiah's prayer is the specific request that God would deliver them from the Assyrian threat.

Other Jewish prayers, such as Josephus' account of Moses' prayer after Dathan and others charged him with failing to lead the Israelites into the land of promise (see Num 16:15 ff.), have a similar structure (*Ant.* 4.40-50). Did Josephus imitate this prayer's structure or use of a structure common for Jewish prayers? Either way, Jewish precedence for prayers like the believers' prayer in Acts 4 suggests that readers interpret it as an expression of Jewish faithfulness to God.

■ **25-26** There are difficulties with the Greek sentence regarding God speaking through David. Nevertheless, this introduction to the quotation of Ps 2:1-2 emphasizes the divine inspiration of David **by the Holy Spirit**. The identification of David as God's **servant** (see Ps 18:1; Isa 37:35) uses the same noun that Peter applied to Jesus (Acts 3:13, 26). It also reiterates David's role as God's spokesperson (like the prophets).

Having established David's prophetic role, Ps 2:1-2 is interpreted as a prophetic text through which the believers assess their particular situation. This royal psalm speaks of the coronation of a Davidic king facing hostilities from foreign kings. However, the psalm's messianic interpretation by the believers is not unprecedented, as some Jews had interpreted it in messianic ways before then (e.g., *Pss. Sol.* 17:26).

The first two lines, quoting Ps 2:1 (LXX), offer synonymous descriptions. Although the **nations** and **peoples** originally referred to Israel's foreign enemies, their reoccurrence (v 27) indicates their redefinition in light of Jesus' passion.

The verb *phryassō*, commonly translated **rage** to correspond with the Hebrew, often metaphorically describes the behavior of arrogant or insolent persons. Similarly, the expression *plot vain things* explains that these enemies not only thought but pursued unachievable goals. The remainder of the quotation, from Ps 2:2, depicts all non-Israelite political leaders in opposition to the Lord (*tou kyriou*; Hebrew: *Yahweh*) and **his anointed one**. These political leaders are paradoxically portrayed as both "gathered" (NRSV) and "unified" (*epi to auto*; 1:15; 2:1, 47) in their hostility against God and God's people. Common hostilities sometimes create strange alliances.

■ **27-28** The conjunction *gar* (*for*, **Indeed**) indicates that the following material (see Luke 4:25; 20:21; 22:59; Acts 10:34) interprets the cited passage. Several elements of the text—the repeated term **gathered**, the phrase **in this city** (Jerusalem), and the idea of God's anointed—all establish obvious connections with that particular psalm. However, the prayer interprets the passage and its depicted hostility in light of Jesus' passion. Its identification of Jesus as God's **holy servant** echoes earlier allusions to Isaiah's Suffering Servant (→ 3:13).

The names Herod and Pilate reflect the Third Gospel's passion account. Luke is the only NT Gospel that narrates Jesus' appearance before Herod (Luke 23:6-12). It is unclear how these two Roman officials joined the Jewish opposition to Jesus, since they both found him innocent (Luke 23:13-15). Still, Herod's narrative role as an antagonist to God's purposes fits the prayer's trajectories; he did mock and humiliate Jesus (Luke 23:11; see Darr 1992, 167). So Herod and Pilate represent those foreign "kings of the earth" (Acts 4:26) who stood in opposition of the Lord's "anointed one," whom the prayer identifies as Jesus.

The "nations" (*ethnē*) and "peoples" (*laoi*) in the psalm are reinterpreted through Jesus' passion as the **Gentiles** (*ethnesin*) and the **peoples of Israel** (*laois Israēl*). In the psalm, these two groups are depicted synonymously. Thus, this reading implies that those from Israel who reject Christ are no longer considered part of God's people and are numbered with the unbelieving Gentiles (Marshall 1980, 106). The "rulers" (v 26) would not include only those like Pilate (see Haenchen 1971, 227), but those leaders who comprised the Jewish council that condemned Jesus to death (Luke 23:13).

The prayer interprets all these events theologically as under God's authority (lit., *your hand*; see, e.g., Exod 3:20; Josh 4:24; Pss 10:12; 89:13; Acts 11:21) and purpose. The term *boulē* (**will**) in the NT appears mostly in the Lukan corpus. Here, it typically refers to God's plan (→ 2:23). The verb translated **decided beforehand** or "predestined" (NRSV) emphasizes God's sovereignty and plan, not God's manipulation of humans as cosmic pawns to accomplish God's purposes. Therefore, those who opposed Jesus as God's servant and chosen one were unwitting participants in God's grand plan of salvation (see 1:16-20; 2:23-36; 3:13-15).

■ **29-30** The opening words of v 29 not only signal a shift to the prayer's petitions but also interpret the believers' situation as corresponding to Jesus' passion. That is, the prayer interprets the opposition from the Jewish leaders in

Jerusalem through the lens of Jesus' passion and Ps 2. Although the anteced-ent for the pronoun **their** would be the enemies of Acts 4:27, the mentioned **threats** allude to the council acting as the believers' enemies by threatening Peter and John (vv 17, 21).

The enemies who gathered (v 27) in opposition to Jesus also gathered (v 5) to challenge the two apostles. The request for God to notice does not sug-gest that God was unaware of their plight. The term **consider** (*epide*) implies that God would note and respond favorably to the believers (see Luke 1:25).

The believers do not ask God for deliverance, as in Hezekiah's prayer (Isa 37:20). They pray instead for the courage to fulfill their assignment in the face of violent opposition. One part of their request, **to speak your word** (Acts 4:29), is a common Lukan expression for the proclamation of the gospel (e.g., 8:25; 11:19; 13:46; 14:25; 16:32). The phrase *with all boldness* alludes to what the Jewish council saw in the witness of Peter and John (4:13). It is ironic that they would ask God to give such boldness to God's **servants** or *slaves*, since it is a quality of free citizens or philosophers, not slaves (→ v 13). Nonetheless, the prayer suggests that the believers want God to continue doing what God has just accomplished through Peter and John.

The remainder of the prayer does not express additional petitions to God but reiterates what believers confidently assume is already happening. The biblical image of the stretching out of God's hand often describes God's power (e.g., Ps 138:7). The phrase that includes this image suggests that the proclamation would occur either *while* God acts with power and authority (a temporal function) or *by means of* God's activity (an instrumental function). However, the two listed examples for this divine activity—healing and doing **signs and wonders**—describe what is already happening (2:43; 3:1-10). As was evident in the case of Peter's healing of the crippled man, accomplishing such things in the name of Jesus opens the door for gospel proclamation.

■ **31** The narrator concludes this section by listing three things that happen after their prayer ends. First, the shaking of their location is commonly understood in Jewish circles as a sign of divine presence (e.g., Exod 19:18; Ps 18:7; Isa 6:4; *4 Ezra* 6:15, 29; Josephus, *Ant.* 7.76-77). This understanding was even prevalent in broader, Greco-Roman contexts (see van der Horst 1989, 44-45). In this instance, God's presence signifies confirmation and approval of their request.

Second, all those present are **filled with the Holy Spirit.** This essentially duplicates the description used for the believers at Pentecost (2:4) and for Pe-ter before the Jewish council (4:8). This does not suggest a repeat of Pentecost. It conveys a fresh moment of divine enablement for their mission signified and initiated by that momentous, divine event (→ 4:8).

Third, the imperfect tense indicative *elaloun* implies that *all* of them now begin to proclaim the gospel (lit., **the word of God**; see v 29) and con-

ACTS

4:31

tinue to do so. This does not mean that they had not engaged in such activity prior to this moment. However, the coming of the Holy Spirit empowers that entire group (→ v 23) to speak with the **boldness** that earlier characterized Peter and John before the council. This presents readers with convincing evidence that God answered their prayer.

FROM THE TEXT

The Lukan portrait of the believers who gather with Peter and John after the Jewish council interrogated and threatened the two goes against what one would expect to find with most (contemporary) Christians. Too often, when times are difficult or when society challenges the relevancy or credibility of the Christian faith, the common response among churchgoers is frustration and consternation. They "push back and fight" so that the Christian voice has its rightful place at the table of society's conversations about social values, practices, etc. So this picture of early believers may take today's readers by surprise. It reflects practices and issues that contemporary church contexts sometimes neglect or reject.

Notice, for instance, that the gathered believers turn to Scripture to understand their particular situation. That is, they seek to understand their life situation through the lens of Scripture. They recognize correspondences both between Scripture and their circumstances as well as between Jesus' life (and passion) and their circumstances. By doing so, these believers develop a sense of divine perception regarding their own situations. Thus, they discover God's purposes in the midst of whatever happens.

The Lukan author's inclusion of materials like this encourages faithful readers to make similar conclusions. However, in order for that to happen today, the sacred Scriptures must function in formative ways that transform and shape the identity, practices, and mission of those who consider themselves part of the Christian church.

Furthermore, these believers actively sought God's blessing and grace for faithful ministry through prayer. They were willing to accept their circumstances rather than expect deliverance from their less-than-desired circumstances. Their divergence from Hezekiah's prayer is noteworthy. Readers see their focus on God's purposes rather than their natural human reaction to the council's opposition. That does not mean there are no uneasy moments. Their gathering for prayer implies that concerns are there. However, their prayer allows the narrator to help readers see and hear what they may not expect. These believers request more of the same abuse rather than divine rescue from it. That prayerful focus reflects their desire to fulfill their divine mission and to see God's purposes achieved.

Finally, one should note the Lukan understanding of being "filled with the Spirit." It offers a distinctive voice in comparison with other biblical and contemporary understandings. The Spirit has often been the subject of books and sermons as a means of becoming better or more faithful Christians. However, the concern for power for ethical progress typically depends on other selected NT passages used to interpret Acts.

In Wesleyan circles, the activity of the Spirit has often been associated with sanctification—the transformation of believers' lives to be more like Christ. Thus, being "filled with the Spirit" is often understood within other contexts (see Eph 5:18) without adequate consideration of the *Lukan* usage in Acts. However, the careful, prayerful reader of Acts 4 may find evidence of what Jesus promised before his ascension: that the power to proclaim the good news about Jesus as the Christ would accompany the coming of the Spirit (1:8).

The Lukan description of Pentecost and later instances of believers being "filled with the Spirit" appropriate similar vocabulary and images. Competent readers should understand these latter instances as specific examples of God's fresh enablement for an appointed task. Here, the Spirit strengthened believers' resolve and faithful ministry in Jesus' name. John Chrysostom aptly observed, "'The place was shaken,' and that made them all the more unshaken" (*Hom. Act.* 11, in Martin 2006, 54).

D. Additional Images of the Community of Believers (4:32—5:11)

1. Unity and Sharing among the Believers (4:32-37)

BEHIND THE TEXT

This passage is the second of three major summaries in Acts about the believers' activities and the communal dynamics among them. Like the earlier summary (→ 2:42-47), this passage focuses on typical characteristics and practices of believers. Luke *tells* about them in a more direct, explicit fashion rather than *narrating* an event from which readers must make inferences and draw conclusions.

However, whereas the prior summary focuses more on connections between worship practices and fellowship (shared meals), here the narrator concentrates on the ways these believers care for one another's needs. This implicitly relates to the previous scene (4:23-31) and sets the stage for the following incident involving Ananias and Sapphira (5:1-11).

Because of the compassion depicted here, this passage was a favorite among early Christian interpreters. Augustine cites this passage over fifty times in his writings, often as evidence of the power of love in pulling the earliest Christian community together (see Martin 2006, 55-56)—although the term "love" never appears in Acts.

IN THE TEXT

■ **32** As often in Acts, the conjunction *de* ("Now" [NRSV]; untranslated in the NIV) links this summary section with the previous paragraph. This connection suggests that the divine presence and blessing among the believers are behind *everything* Luke describes here.

Luke introduces **the believers** (lit., ***the crowd of those who had come to believe***) so as to hint at the increasing size of their numbers (see Marshall 1980, 108). However, the sentence subject is the ***one heart and soul*** (*kardia kai psychē mia*) that characterized the group.

The expression ***one soul*** often described true friendship in Hellenistic circles (→ sidebar "Friendship in the Ancient World" with 2:42). Aristotle quotes a proverb, "Friends have one soul between them" (*Eth. nic.* 9.8.2; see Plutarch, *Frat. amor.* 478c; and Iamblichus, *Pythag.* 168).

The LXX frequently linked the terms **heart** and ***soul*** to describe the total person's response to God (see Deut 4:29; 6:5, 6; 10:12; 11:13, 18; 13:3; 26:16; 28:65; 30:2, 6, 10). This expresses the highest ideals of Israel in relation to God.

Thus, this Lukan description combines familiar expressions to indicate the divinely created bond that held believers together. The second part of the statement briefly mentions a consequence of this unanimity. Their renunciation of private ownership of possessions corresponds with holding ***all things in common*** (→ 2:44; see *Eth. nic.* 9.8.2). The connections between this passage and the previous summary (2:42-47) suggest that readers transfer the positive traits from that earlier section to these believers (Thompson 2006, 72).

■ **33** At first glance, the note regarding the apostles' ***witness*** or "testimony" (NRSV; *to martyrion*) seems to interrupt the descriptions of the believers' sharing. But a key narrative aspect of Acts is the correspondence between the believers' united, caring fellowship and their gospel proclamation. The emphatic position of the phrase **with great power**, which describes the apostles' witnessing, alludes to the resurrected Jesus' promise of power to be his witnesses (1:8; see 2:22; 3:12; 4:7).

The sequential emphases of heart, soul, and power reflect the Shema (Deut 6:5). In the LXX, these three identical nouns in the same order describe how God's people should love God (Pesch 1986, 1:181-82). Luke depicts the apostles as speaking specifically about Jesus' resurrection—doing *exactly* what the Jewish council warned them *not* to do. This builds suspense over the possibility of additional conflict (see Tannehill 1990, 64).

The corresponding description of **great grace** may allude to God's promise of favor upon the people in Exod 3:21 (Johnson 1992, 86). It reiterates the gracious divine work that enables their activities by framing the apostolic witness with references to God's provision (→ 2:47).

The ambiguous **them all** refers either to the apostles (mentioned earlier in the sentence) or to the community of believers (in v 34). In either sense, the narrative emphasis is on God and God's continual blessing on these believers.

■ **34-35** The conjunction *gar* (*for*, untranslated in the NIV), connects this sentence with v 33. It links God's provision of **great grace** with the absence of any needy person. The wording reflects Deut 15:4 (LXX), which identifies the elimination of need among God's people with God's blessing (see Luke 4:18-19).

A second occurrence of *gar*, for, indicates a major reason for the elimination of need. **Owners of properties or houses** often liquidated their assets and donated the proceeds to the community. All verb tenses throughout these two verses (imperfect indicatives, present participles) indicate typical activities within the community rather than communal requirements.

In that time and culture, persons who owned such resources were wealthy. However, the Lukan depiction of their donation of the sale proceeds radically departs from customary social practices. The picture of wealthy believers **placing** those funds **at the apostles' feet** contradicts conventional practices. The wealthy and powerful typically received honor from those with lower social status. Here, the wealthy take a position of humility by kneeling before the apostles, who serve as the believers' leaders due to their role as Jesus' witnesses. By giving those monies to the apostles for distribution rather than doing it themselves, the wealthy also relinquish all social expectations of receiving something in return (Malina and Pilch 2008, 46-47). Through such generosity, Luke reiterates what he mentions after Pentecost: the community cares for any need that arises (→ 2:45).

4:34-35

Reciprocity and Patronage

In the Roman Empire of the first century AD, an assumed cultural concept at the center of human interaction was reciprocity. All human actions toward others expected actions done in return. Reciprocity was an essential component of any two primary relationships within society.

For friends of equal social status, reciprocity as mutuality was essential, due to the inadequacy of one-sided friendships. The assumption of reciprocity among virtuous friends was not based on self-interest but on the good of one's friends.

However, for those who were not social equals, relationships took on characteristics of patronage. Here, reciprocity was defined in terms of a patron-client relationship. In such instances, gifts from the wealthy and powerful to those of lower social status always left the recipients (their clients) indebted to their patrons. Clients were both expected and obligated to give something in return and in proportion to what they received.

The Lukan depiction of the wealthy's donation of funds for use within the community of believers departs from social conventions. This indicates how God's blessing transcended the obligatory trappings of such patron-client relationships.

■ **36-37** The final part of this summary offers a brief, yet noteworthy example of such generosity. The narrator identifies **Joseph** and then adds three descriptors that aid the reader's interpretation of his actions.

First, Joseph was a **Levite**. He was a member of the Jewish tribe of Levi. They were dedicated to God and responsible for nurturing the spiritual well-being of Israel. Levites did not originally receive a portion of the promised land due to their sacred responsibilities among God's covenant people (see Deut 12:12; 14:27; Josh 14:3-4; 18:7). However, both Josh 21 and later in Josephus' writings (*Life* 68-83) indicate that they owned property.

Second, he was from **Cyprus**, the large island in the eastern Mediterranean. He was a Diaspora Jew who had moved to Jerusalem. Mention of his home region hints that he may have been among the Pentecost bystanders from the Greco-Roman world who witnessed what happened and then repented in response (Acts 2:9-11, 38-41).

Third, the additional nickname that the apostles gave Joseph—**Barnabas**—reflects an ancient practice. It signifies their authority over him, though his apparent wealth might suggest otherwise.

The problematic translation of the name "Barnabas" (lit., "son of Nebo") has provoked significant scholarly debate (see, e.g., Fitzmyer 1998, 320-21). The Lukan translation, **son of encouragement** or "Son of Exhortation" (Barrett 1994, 258-59), as the cognate verb *parakaleō* ("encourage," "exhort," "comfort") in Acts suggests, portrays Joseph's character and actions favorably.

It is unclear whether the field that Barnabas owned was in Cyprus, Israel, or elsewhere, but his generous actions mirror the general description in 4:34-35. Thus, this is one specific example of a person who responds to a need among the believers due to the oneness God's presence and blessing have created (Thompson 2006, 75).

FROM THE TEXT

The narrative placement of the second summary section about the community of believers further substantiates the correlation between God's workings within that community and the believers' activities. The community's existence and ability to fulfill her mission arise out of God's provision and blessing. Clearly, this group truly represents *God's* people—God's historic purposes for those chosen by God found fulfillment among them. As John

Wesley suggested, the believers' provision for the needs of one another is undisputable evidence of God's grace (1958, 409).

The balance in the Lukan perspective between internal and external dimensions of mission offers important elements to what may be called a developing Lukan ecclesiology. He portrays the character of the Christian church before he uses the term "church" (*ekklēsia*; first in Acts 5:11).

Narratives do not lend themselves to precise, systematic treatment of a theological topic like ecclesiology. However, this does not mean that the unfolding narrative has nothing to say about this matter. What one finds thus far is an understanding of the people of God that comes out of God's historic purposes as seen in Israel and ultimately through Jesus. Such purposes create the people of God, define who is and is not included in such a people according to their acceptance or rejection of those divine purposes, and empower the mission of that people as they embody God's saving purposes that bring deliverance and wholeness to humanity. Thus, the various ways that the believers respond to one another with care and compassion and to others through proclamation of the gospel cannot be separated from the Lukan depiction of the community as the people of God—as faithful Israel.

2. The Violation of Unity and Sharing—Ananias and Sapphira (5:1-11)

BEHIND THE TEXT

Interpreters have often suggested that Luke's insertion of Barnabas at the end of Acts 4 functions primarily to introduce this character into the narrative in which he reappears later in a prominent role. Luke seems to do something similar with Saul (later Paul), so there is some merit to this suggestion.

However, the noteworthy example of Barnabas as one who models and embodies what the narrator describes with generalities at the end of ch 4 provides readers with important images and concepts for evaluating what comes next: the incident involving Ananias and Sapphira. Their actions mirror much of what the narrator has just described in Barnabas' case. So both the similarities in actions and the divergent responses to those actions entice readers to ask some difficult questions about a dramatic and traumatic scene.

IN THE TEXT

■ **1-2** The couple Ananias and Sapphira appear to have done what Luke just describes Barnabas and other unnamed generous believers as doing (4:34-37; see 2:44-45). Like these faithful others, the narrator indicates that Ananias sold (see 4:34, 37) **a piece of property** (see 2:45). Like others who placed the proceeds at the apostles' feet, Ananias apparently does the same thing (see 4:35, 37).

131

In this instance, Luke assumes the role of an omniscient narrator. He supplies new information that implies Ananias' actions not to be as they initially appear. He mentions that Ananias **kept back** some of the proceeds from the sale, bringing only *a portion*.

The verb describing Ananias' withholding of the money (*nosphizomai*) commonly denotes embezzlement or the misappropriation of funds (see Titus 2:10). In its only appearance in the LXX, the verb refers to Achan's sin, when he kept some sacred objects from Jericho for himself, defying God's prohibition (Josh 7:1). The ominous tone of this verb colors readers' perception of these actions as a violation of the community's devotion to God.

In addition to informing the reader about Ananias' actions, the narrator also identifies Ananias' wife, Sapphira, as his coconspirator: Sapphira knew about him withholding some of the money. The wording (the verb *synoida*; related to the noun *syneidēsis*, "conscience") implies she not only *knew* about her husband's actions but fully *recognized* they were wrong.

Acts' descriptions implicate the couple, since they knowingly conspire as "partners in crime." Some interpreters debate whether or not the couple were believers. But their actions suggest that they probably had close ties with the community of believers. Paradoxically, the deceptive scheme that they plotted together contradicts the united nature of the community. These two characters provide a narrative "counter-community of avarice" opposite the "spirit-community" of generosity and sharing (Johnson 1992, 87).

■ **3-4** The narrator mentions nothing about where the meeting takes place or who is present to witness it. Nor does he explain the source of Peter's extraordinary insight into the mind of Ananias. However, Peter's narrative role is that of a reliable character and prophet who understands God's purposes because of the Holy Spirit. This provides the background for his rebuke of Ananias and confirms the narrator's explicit descriptions of Ananias' actions.

Peter addresses Ananias with a series of questions. These function in the narrative as an assessment of Ananias' actions. Ananias is the polar opposite of the Lukan depiction of believers thus far in Acts in three ways. First, Peter reveals that Satan **filled** Ananias' heart (see Luke 22:3) rather than the **Holy Spirit** (see Acts 2:4; 4:8, 31). Second, Peter's dual reference to what happened in Ananias' heart contrasts with the depiction of the united community as having one heart (4:32). He implicitly describes him as outside the community. Third, Peter accuses Ananias twice of lying: to the believers whom God has blessed (see 4:31), and more importantly to the **Holy Spirit** (5:3) and to **God** (v 4).

Luke does not state directly *how* Ananias lied, but Peter reiterates what the narrator already made explicit (v 2): Ananias only gave a portion of the funds from the property sale. Peter's comments suggest Ananias had the right to give all, a portion, or none of the proceeds. But his actions mirror (as the narrative implies) and imitate those who gave the entire sum from similar transactions. Thus, he is guilty of lying by pretense, at the least. Ananias, whose name ironically means "God is gracious," has removed himself from the community that Luke characterizes in terms of God's **great grace** (see 4:33).

■ **5-6** Peter's rebuke exposes Ananias' sin but does not pronounce judgment on him. Still, upon hearing Peter's words Ananias drops dead, an implicit result of his sin. Most interpreters view Ananias' death as a sign of God's judgment. The Lukan narrator indicates nothing about divine action or judgment as he often does (see 12:23). The narrative may draw from biblical precedence and well-known scenes of divine judgment for crimes of perjury (Harrill 2011, 351-69). The compound verb *ekpsychō*, describing that death, may suggest a subtle wordplay. The man whose actions imitate those of the community of "one soul" (*psychē mia*) has now "souled out" or become "soul-less," an outsider to that community (see Havelaar 1997, 64-82).

The reaction to what happened is similar to what is included in the summary section about the believers immediately after Pentecost. Many interpreters see the reaction as an indication that Ananias becomes a negative example that warns others about the sin of deception. But the addition of the adjective **great** describing the reaction of **fear** or ***awe*** (→ 2:43), like earlier expressions about "great power" and **great grace** (4:33), suggests a reverent awe toward God's presence among the believers (against, e.g. Spencer 2011, 63-80; Schnabel 2012, 285-88). However, here the response is not limited only to the believers, as **all who heard** apparently extends to others as well. The cursory details about Ananias' body being wrapped in a shroud, carried outside, and buried provide basic conclusive evidence for his death.

■ **7-8** Since many heard about Ananias' death (see v 5), it is surprising that his wife, Sapphira, is oblivious to it, especially since some buried her husband (v 6). Strangely, the one who knew all about the scheme and was her husband's accomplice (vv 1-2) is unaware of his premature death. However, Luke does not explain this, the delay of three hours, or the reason for her later appearance.

Since Peter could see through Ananias' actions, he does not interrogate Sapphira for needed information. Rather, his direct questioning gives Sapphira opportunity to repent or unwittingly expose her involvement in the scheme. Luke does not disclose the exact amount of funds that Peter specifies to Sapphira. But one presumes it correlates with what Ananias brought to the apostles (v 2). Her confirmation to Peter entraps her as an accomplice in the scheme as the narrator outlined (vv 1-2) and exposes her as guilty of lying like her husband (vv 3-4).

■ **9-10** As with Ananias, Peter's follow-up question uncovers the couple's plot. The agreement between Ananias and Sapphira makes the act more despicable. The verb referring to that agreement, *symphōneō* (the English de-

ACTS

5:5-10

133

rivative is "symphony"), means "to voice together" or "to be in harmony." The "harmony" of their joint plot is discordant with the believers' unity, evident in their faith and sharing together.

The characterization of the couples' actions as testing the Spirit of the Lord is reminiscent of Israel in the wilderness (e.g., Exod 17:2, 7; 20:20; Deut 33:8; Pss 78:41, 56; 95:9; 106:14). Since Acts often depicts Peter as "filled with the Holy Spirit" (4:8; see 2:4; 4:31), the couple's deception and dishonesty test the Spirit that enables *him* to discern their scheme as a prophet.

Thus, Peter rebukes Sapphira, as he had her husband. His disclosure about her husband's death serves as an antemortem account of what would happen to her. The similarity in vocabulary and basic details indicates Sapphira shares both her husband's deception in life and the ensuing consequences in death. However, one should note the irony of Sapphira collapsing in death at Peter's feet. This is the same place, along with the other apostles, where Ananias laid their pretentious offering (v 2). It was also a common ancient gesture of honor and respect (→ 4:34-35). This picture highlights (*a*) her failure to honor the community whom the apostles represent with her life, and (*b*) her inadvertent submission to them in death.

■ **11** Both the previous response of **great fear** or **awe** to Ananias' sudden demise and the particular description of those who reacted in this manner (**all who heard** [v 5]) are repeated here. This underscores the dramatic effect of the surprising turn of events.

In the middle of this sentence, the narrator inserts a specific reference to this fear or reverent awe that came upon **the whole church**, the first time that the term *ekklēsia* appears in Acts to describe Christian believers. In the LXX and Stephen's speech in 7:38, this family of words frequently refers to the assembly of Israel as the people of God (→ sidebar "Israel, the People of God, and the *Ekklēsia*" below). Most other occurrences of the noun in Acts (with the exception of 19:32, 39, 40) refer to the local gathering or assembly of *believers*. The author borrows a term that had been customarily applied in Jewish circles to themselves as the people of God. In this instance, the Lukan usage of *ekklēsia* and another general expression (**all who heard**) for the Jewish people in Jerusalem differentiate between the Jewish believers and nonbelievers. For Luke to call these believers *hē ekklēsia* suggests that this horrible event in Acts remarkably affirms God's presence among this group of Jewish believers, a characteristic reiterated throughout Acts 1—4 (Thompson 2006, 81-82).

Israel, the People of God, and the *Ekklēsia*

The Lukan (and Christian) appropriation of the term *ekklēsia* from Jewish tradition is often lost in translation. The translation of that noun as "church" points to a group or entity separate from Judaism and Jewish practices. However, the common use of this family of words (both noun and verbal forms) throughout

134

the LXX indicates it was a significant descriptor for the Jewish people as the people of God, either in worship or as a nation (e.g., Deut 4:10; 23:9; 31:30; Judg 20:2; 2 Chr 30:2, 4, 13, 17, 23-25; Ezra 10:1, 8, 12, 14).

The popular etymology of these words offers a picture of those "called out" and assembled. But the prefix to these words (*ek*) indicates the source or the one who called and assembled the people. Thus, this term as employed by Luke focuses on the presence of God among this people. As a result, in Acts the term *ekklēsia* depicts the community of believers both similar to and distinct from the rest of the Jewish people who also described themselves with that same term.

Some interpreters of Acts suggest that Luke presents the church as the "new Israel" or the replacement of Israel as the people of God. However, the church arises in these initial chapters as *restored* or *repentant* Israel. Thus, Luke uses the term *ekklēsia* to clarify rather than replace the concept "people of God" in terms of repentance and restoration.

FROM THE TEXT

After the exemplary response of Barnabas, the story of what appears at first glance to be the generosity of Ananias and Sapphira is shocking. The Lukan narrator clearly denounces the couple's actions as a despicable example of deception and disunity within a group characterized by trust and unanimity created by God's presence and grace.

However, what may be even more surprising than this unexpected turn of events is the Lukan characterization of the believers in the aftermath as God's *ekklēsia*, a scriptural term borrowed from the LXX (the Scriptures for most Jews of the first century) to refer to Israel as God's people.

How might one account for this astonishing claim about the community of believers, in light of an attack that challenges their unity (and ultimately their existence) from the inside? One way to explain this is to look again at Peter's fundamental indictment against the couple. Their sin of deception is not merely against humans but against God (v 4). In other words, the couple's actions challenge God and God's purposes, because they misunderstand the nature of the community of believers.

The critical error in the couple's ecclesiology is that they perceive the group in *human* terms. Luke offers a different perspective that identifies *God's* presence, blessing, and grace at the heart of everything in the church. The couple trivializes the Spirit's role among the believers by focusing more on *dynamic expressions* of the community than on *the Spirit's presence*. God is the divine, creative source of the community.

It appears that Luke has been holding this theologically loaded term, *ekklēsia*, in reserve for the right place within the narrative. Luke appropriates this term to make a theologically loaded claim about the rightful place of this movement of believers within the cosmic purposes of God. Therefore, at the exact moment when readers may think the community of believers would be at its lowest ebb, the narrator uses the vocabulary of the people of God to depict that community clearly as the inheritors and benefactors of God's promises and blessing.

E. Intensified Opposition from Religious Leaders (5:12-42)

BEHIND THE TEXT

Sometimes chapter and verse divisions give the false impression of distinct breaks in a narrative. These divisions were not in the original text of Acts. This is especially important to keep in mind with the summary section of 5:12-16, the last of three major summaries in Acts. All three depict typical actions and characteristics of the church in Jerusalem.

On the one hand, this section provides an important, albeit general, glimpse into activities indicating that the community of believers was indeed worthy of Luke's depiction as God's *ekklēsia*. On the other hand, those same activities provide the backdrop for escalating opposition from the Jewish religious leaders in 5:17-42.

IN THE TEXT

1. The Church's Mission Continues in Jerusalem (5:12-16)

■ **12-13** The summary begins by focusing on the apostles' activities, which Luke describes as **many signs and wonders**. The narrator has previously used this same expression to describe their activities immediately after Pentecost (2:43), which compares them favorably with God's affirmation of Jesus (2:22). This is also reminiscent of what the believers' prayer affirms after the Jewish council's interrogation of Peter and John (4:30). All of these features are indicative of both the fulfillment of Joel's prophecy regarding the coming of God's Spirit (2:19) and Jesus' saving power.

The association between these remarkable demonstrations of the Spirit's working *through the hands of the apostles* and the *great awe* (v 11) repeats similar connections in the summary sections of the believers after Pentecost (2:43). That these things occur **among the people** reiterates that their ministry continues in the context of the Jewish people, just as before the incident with Ananias and Sapphira.

This Jewish context provides the narrative stage for three descriptions about the communal relations between the Jewish believers and the Jewish people in general. First, the depiction of **all**, likely the believers, as **together** (1:14; 2:46; 4:24) again stresses the bond among the community of believers.

They gather in **Solomon's Colonnade**, the same place where Peter had addressed the people about the healing of the crippled man (see 3:11—4:4).

Second, the narrator mentions the hesitancy of many (lit., *no one from the rest*) to join or *associate* (see Luke 10:11; 15:15; Acts 8:29; 9:26; 10:28; 17:34) with **them**, which the context implies to be the community of believers. The Jewish people are mentioned before and after this. So some interpreters consider *the rest* to refer to believers (with "all" in 5:12 referring only to apostles) who are intimidated by what happened to Ananias and Sapphira (e.g., Johnson 1992, 95). Others think it refers to Jewish groups who, unlike the people in general, oppose the apostles (4:1; Fitzmyer 1998, 328).

However, the developing narrative plot suggests that the expression distinguishes between two Jewish groups: these who distance themselves from the believers and the people who generally respond favorably toward the believers (see Jervell 1972, 47; Sanders 1987, 240).

Third, the esteem of **the people** in general for the community of believers insinuates that they recognize God's role in what is happening. The Third Gospel and Acts elsewhere use this verb to describe such high regard (*megalynō*) as praise toward God (Luke 1:46, 58; Acts 10:46; 19:17).

■ **14** An increasing number of people are becoming believers as a result of their recognition of what God is doing, in spite of those who avoid the believers (v 13). As with earlier references to the numbers of believers (2:41; 4:4) and continuing growth of the group (2:47), such growth indicates the results of divine activity (→ 2:41, 47).

It is possible to associate the dative *tō kyriō*, **the Lord** (i.e., Jesus), with the verb describing the church's growth. But the sentence order suggests it probably refers to the participle *pisteuontes* (**believing**). This clarifies that their faith is **in the Lord**.

■ **15** What happens **as a result** (*hōste* with infinitive) seems unexpected to twenty-first-century readers. The association between these actions—the strategic placement of the sick to be in **Peter's shadow**—and believing in Jesus (see 3:16) distinguishes them from practices of magic in the ancient world. Behind such acts of placing the sick in public places is the ancient belief that a person's shadow was an extension of that person. Thus, the "touch" of a shadow was in essence that person's physical touch. Peter's role in healing the crippled man likely explains why he was singled out. The hope was that, if he passed these persons, his **shadow** (*skia*) might literally **overshadow** (*episkiasē*) the needy persons and extend healing to them.

■ **16** The final description lends credence to the Lukan descriptions. Not only those in Jerusalem but even large numbers (lit., **crowd**; see v 14) from surrounding towns came to Jerusalem and the temple, where these amazing things occurred through the apostles (v 12). In addition to the sick, Luke men-

137

tions them bringing those "tormented by unclean spirits" (NRSV), the first reference of this sort in Acts (see Luke 6:18). Like Jesus' ministry (e.g., Luke 4:33, 36; 8:29; 9:42; 11:24), the apostles' ministry healed and liberated persons from the oppressive work of Satan (Johnson 1992, 96).

FROM THE TEXT

This summary regarding the believers' actions—the third major summary about the community of believers in Acts—directs readers' attention to the evidence of God's presence through the Spirit among them. After the tragedy of Ananias and Sapphira, this summarizes how others responded to the apostles and believers. This reminds readers that God, through the gift of the Spirit, fulfills God's promise to Israel. God was responsible for this fledgling community of faith.

Thus, this summary functions within this narrative context to reiterate the divine role in all that had taken place in Acts. It draws on additional images of "signs and wonders," which confirmed Jesus' ministry (2:22). It also confirms the ministry of believers due to the Spirit's presence (2:43; 4:30).

Some theological traditions expect such extraordinary occurrences as present-day indications of the activity of the Holy Spirit. But such interpretations fail to consider the role of such descriptions within the narrative. Acts appropriates these materials in a *descriptive* rather than *normative* fashion (→ "Engaging Acts in a New Day" in Introduction).

This passage underscores the reality of the fulfilled promise about the outpouring of the Spirit, even in the aftermath of an internal crisis and challenge to that reality by Ananias and Sapphira. The apostolic "signs and wonders" had noteworthy connotations in that day. The expression indicated that God's presence through the Spirit was with them as with Jesus before them. To insist that such signs are indicative of the Spirit's activity in contemporary times blurs the *Lukan* perspective on the Spirit's creative role in empowering the community of faith to be the people of God.

2. Hostile Reaction by Jewish Leaders (5:17-42)

IN THE TEXT

■ **17-21a** The apostles' remarkable ministry in Jerusalem does not remain unnoticed by the temple authorities, since much of the believers' activities occurs within the temple precincts (see v 12). The temple courts were the realm of power and authority for these authorities, so they react strongly to the ongoing expansion of the Christian mission and the proclamation of the gospel message (including Jesus' resurrection). Whereas believers are filled with the Holy Spirit, the temple authorities are **filled** [2:4; 4:31] **with jealousy** (*zēlos* [5:17];

see 13:45). The term may also connote religious zeal, provoked by what is happening where these leaders have power and jurisdiction. But the mention of jealousy also warns readers of possible future problems; jealousy was often thought to incite murder (e.g., Plato, *Laws* 869e-870a; Plutarch, *Frat. amor.* 17; Philo, *Joseph* 12; Wis 2:24). Both the temple authorities and readers would remember their orders that the apostles cease such activity (4:17-18, 21).

The arrest of the apostles is reminiscent of the incident in 4:1-4. However, this time the narrator clarifies that the apostles were placed in custody **in the public jail** (5:18; see 16:37; 18:28; 20:20), although no explanation is offered for holding them in custody (see 4:3).

The arrival of an **angel of the Lord** (5:19) introduces the first of several occurrences in Acts of divine intervention on behalf of believers in custody. Although the temple authorities as Jewish religious leaders should promote God's purposes, the angel's release of the Twelve indicates God's endorsement of *them* rather than of the authorities. The references to the angel *opening the prison doors* and *leading them out* affirm the divine deliverance. However, the narrator highlights the angel's instructions: the apostles are to return to the temple precincts and continue doing what landed them in trouble. The explicit order from God's messenger contradicts the religious authorities (see 4:17-18). That they should continue to *proclaim* the **full message** (5:20; lit., *all the words of this life*) reiterates that they are to hold back nothing.

The description of that message as regarding *this life* has a double reference: to the life that comes from salvation (see 3:15), and to the resurrected Jesus through whom this salvation comes (to which these authorities would object; see 4:2; 23:8). Since the angel releases them sometime **during the night**, the notation that the Twelve respond *early the next morning* accentuates that they do *exactly* as the angel orders, once it is feasible. By resuming their practice of teaching (see imperfect tense: *edidaskon*) on the temple grounds, they ironically assume their *captors'* responsibility, who busy themselves with hearings about that same practice.

■ **21b-24** The Lukan narrator repeatedly depicts the temple authorities as oblivious to the apostles' divine rescue and ongoing obedience. As they arrive, presumably at the temple, there is no hint that they see or hear the apostles! The same is true as the **Sanhedrin (the full assembly of the elders of Israel [v 21b; see Exod 3:16; 12:21 LXX])** gathers. The summons of the apostles from their supposed place of custody makes these authority figures appear foolish and incompetent. The report from their *assistants* offers comic relief for the reader, as they inform the clueless leaders about seeming impenetrable security to ensure that no prisoner escapes, only to find no one there!

Since the *commander of the temple* (see 4:1) was responsible for keeping the apostles in custody and the **chief priests** (5:24; see vv 17, 21b) had summoned the entire council, the narrator notes their embarrassing reaction. The imperfect tense *diēporoun* (see 2:12) depicts them as completely baffled and trying haplessly to figure out what happened, all before a growingly impatient council. Ironically, the religious leaders have no awareness of what God has done, yet readers know that God rescued the apostles and sent them on a divinely ordered mission.

■ **25-26** A report from an unidentified witness about the apostles' activities provides additional evidence of their obedience. The apostles are **standing in the temple** and **teaching the people** (v 25). They are engaged in gospel proclamation, as ordered by the angel. All this is happening under the noses of an oblivious council!

This news provides the backdrop for the departure of some officials to reapprehend the apostles. The narrator offers no more details, as the reader could readily envisage them hurrying out to salvage their dignity from that embarrassing moment. However, they move from one awkward scene to another. Their fear that **the people would stone them** (v 26)—the penalty for blasphemy—is probably due to the apostles' continuing popularity and influence. Unlike the leaders, the people recognize God's hand upon the apostles. Unlike their earlier arrest (5:18; also 4:3), they muster enough restraint to escort the apostles *without force* to the council meeting place.

■ **27-28** The high priest begins the proceedings against the apostles by reminding them of the council's prior demands (4:17-18). The same verb, *parangellō* ("order," "demand"), as in 4:18, strengthened here with the dative noun form *parangelia*, makes it clear that they expected the apostles to obey their demands explicitly.

The council had ordered Peter and John **not to teach** in Jesus' name (5:28). But the high priest accuses them of doing the opposite. They have **filled Jerusalem with** their **teaching**, which blames the leaders for Jesus' death. The leaders may have interpreted these accusations of invoking divine vengeance on them or of inciting the people against them. The narrative offers little direct evidence for such an accusation, but the high priest's characterization of the apostles' actions fills in those gaps in ways that allude to Peter's proclamation to the people (3:13-18; see 4:10-11). Of course, the apostles could not deny that they had been teaching, since they were caught in the act!

Interestingly, the interrogation mentions nothing about their escape from custody or the validity of their teachings. Rather, the questioning expresses the concern that the apostles disregarded the authorities' orders. They seem *most* concerned about protecting their reputation and influence among the people.

■ **29** Peter probably delivers the apostles' response, which explains why the narrator points him out specifically. Rather than seeking exoneration from the charge, he confirms its accuracy. He offers a concise version of his previous response to the council (4:19). The verb *peitharcheō* (**obey** [5:29, 32; 27:21; Titus 3:1]) refers to doing what a ruler or person of authority commands (LSJ 1996, 1353). The use of *dei* (**must**) underscores the necessity for their obedience to God, something the council would surely not deny.

■ **30-31** What follows is an encapsulated version of Peter's gospel message. The repetition of God as the subject in these verses picks up the theme of obeying *God* rather than humans. Thus, Luke suggests that obedience to God includes believing the claims of the gospel as true (see Wall 2002, 106).

At the heart of Peter's message is God's resurrection of Jesus. By mentioning **the God of our ancestors** (v 30), a shortened version of his earlier description of God (3:13), he reminds the council that *their* God raised up Jesus, a common theme in earlier speeches (2:24, 32; 3:15; 4:10). As confirmation of the charge against the apostles, Peter affirms God's resurrection of Jesus as God's response to *their* murder of Jesus. Here, Peter emphatically blames the council for Jesus' death, described in graphic terms. The verb *diacheirizō* (**killed**, see 26:21) denotes the malicious abduction of a person that would often result in murder (BDAG 2000, 240).

The described means of killing Jesus—**by hanging him on a cross** (see 10:39)—mirrors Deut 21:22-23 (LXX), which requires the burial of the body of a criminal who had been executed and hanged on a tree as one cursed by God. According to Fitzmyer (1998, 337), the Qumran *Temple Scroll* identifies treason against Israel as a crime deserving this kind of death (11QT 64:7-8). Since Peter's previous speeches already declared how Jesus was God's anointed agent to restore Israel, the council's role in Jesus' death paradoxically made *them* guilty of such a crime rather than Jesus (see Wall 2002, 106).

The second reference to God, as exalting Jesus **to God's right hand** (v 31), is the same expression found in Peter's Pentecost speech. They shamed Jesus by killing him, but God honored him. This correlates with Jesus' reception of the promised Holy Spirit, which Jesus then poured out on the believers (→ 2:33). Here, Peter explains God's exaltation of Jesus in two ways. First, the term *archēgos* (see 3:15) refers to Jesus as **Prince** or "Leader" (NRSV). The second term, **Savior**, also refers to Jesus in Luke 2:11 and Acts 13:23. The title often refers to God, in Luke 1:47 and the LXX (e.g., 1 Sam 10:19; Pss 25:5; 27:1; 62:2, 6; Isa 62:11), as the source of Israel's salvation. But this title in the Greco-Roman world applied to gods, philosophers, emperors, and others (Foerster, *TDNT* 7:965-1024).

Together, these two terms depict the exalted Jesus as both the Helper and Savior of humanity. The subsequent construction further explains the purpose for God's actions and Jesus' role in God's salvific purposes. The pro-

ACTS

5:30-31

141

vision of **repentance** to **Israel** echoes Peter's Pentecost call for the people to repent, associated there with the forgiveness of sins (2:38; see 3:19).

■ **32** Peter's affirmation of the apostles' role as **witnesses** reiterates earlier claims (2:32; 3:15) of their commission from Jesus (1:8; Luke 24:44-48). The subject of their witness, **these things**, refers to God's exaltation of Jesus including the resurrection, which Peter addressed earlier (2:32; 3:15). The association of the apostles with the Holy Spirit underscores their divine calling as witnesses. However, Peter's crediting of God for giving them the Spirit in response to their obedience functions provocatively, as it links God and the apostles' activities of proclamation.

Peter concludes his comments by reiterating the same verb for obedience with which he began his rebuttal (5:29). Thus, the theme of obedience to God frames Peter's comments. His commitment to obey God stands in stark contrast to the council's staunch insistence that the apostles obey *them*.

■ **33-34** Not surprisingly, the council reacts strongly against Peter's message. The verb translated **furious** (*diaprio* [v 33]) literally means they are cut in two with rage (BDAG 2000, 235; see 7:54). Its imperfect tense depicts the council seething with anger over Peter's words. Their reaction against the apostles has multiplied in intensity, from threats to the desire to murder them. This confirms earlier hints about what may happen because of the council's jealousy (→ 5:17).

For the moment, **Gamaliel** suspends the leaders' hostile reaction (v 34). Unlike other council members whom the narrator identifies as Sadducees (4:5-6; 5:17, 21, 27), Gamaliel is a member of the **Pharisees**, the first mention of someone from that group in Acts. Later, Paul will identify him as his teacher (22:3).

The Pharisees and Gamaliel

According to the first-century Jewish historian Josephus, the Pharisees, like the Sadducees, were one of the three major "sects" or schools of thought within Judaism (see *J.W.* 2.119; *Ant.* 13.171). Their name comes from an Aramaic verb connoting separateness. They perceived themselves as separated from the populace because of their pious and strict adherence to the Jewish law. They emerged as a prominent group within Judaism during the Maccabean period, late in the second century BC.

In distinction from the Sadducees, who were identified with the clergy or priesthood, Pharisees were lay experts in the interpretation of the Torah, the Jewish law. They applied the law to everyday life. They sought to prepare the people of God for the coming messianic age by living holy lives. They also believed in the resurrection of the dead, the role of fate in governing all things, and human responsibility for behavior.

According to later rabbinic sources, Gamaliel—whom Luke identifies here as a Pharisee on the Jewish council—became the leader of the Pharisees. Later in

Acts (22:3), when Paul addresses the Jewish crowd after his arrest at the temple, he identifies Gamaliel as his teacher. This was offered as evidence of his high regard for the Jewish law and an affirmation of his faithfulness as a Jew.

The additional description of Gamaliel as a **teacher of the law** corroborates his membership among the Pharisees. His good reputation among **all the people** establishes him as an authoritative figure. He stands as a counterpoint to the narrative's presentation of the council's perspective toward the apostles as generally contrasting with that of the people. His request to dismiss the apostles gives him opportunity to address the council privately.

■ **35-37** The narrator offers inside access to the closed-door meeting without revealing his sources (→ 4:16-17). His address of the council as *fellow Israelites* (5:35) mirrors Peter's address of his Jewish audiences (2:22; 3:12) and affirms their heritage as the people of God. He cautions them to exercise caution before proceeding. Rather than addressing the specific concerns of the apostles' activities or message, he cites two examples of revolutionary figures and their respective followings that fizzled after their leader's death.

The first example refers to someone named **Theudas** (5:36), who appeared at an unspecified earlier time (*before these days*). The description of Theudas as **claiming to be somebody** resembles Josephus' description of a person by the same name who claimed to be a prophet (*Ant.* 20.97-98). In both cases, many followed him until his beheading (*Ant.* 20.98). The disbandment of Theudas' followers was probably due to their fear following their leader's death, especially if the Romans were responsible for his execution, and led to the group's end.

This raises chronological questions, since the events described by Josephus occurred ca. AD 44, at least ten years *after* this meeting. Some commentators attempt to reconcile this problem by proposing that Luke and Josephus refer to two different men with the same name (e.g., Barrett 1994, 293-95; Witherington 1998, 235-39). But it is equally possible that either Josephus, Luke, or their source was mistaken on this specific detail (e.g., Fitzmyer 1998, 339-40; Gaventa 2003, 109; Pervo 2009, 147-48). However one resolves this issue, Gamaliel's point still remains within the narrative: that movement's demise followed the death of the leader Theudas.

The second example refers to a person named **Judas,** who was a leader of some revolutionary group (v 37). The **census** in question may be the same one mentioned in Luke 2:1, which likely occurred at the beginning of Quirinius' reign as governor over Syria (ca. AD 6). Josephus twice mentions this incident about Judas (*J.W.* 2.118; *Ant.* 20.102), which he links to Jewish submissiveness in their compliance with that Roman census. The dating of this episode only complicates the chronological problems surrounding Theudas. This example is introduced as happening chronologically after Theudas. But the point remains: the death of Judas led to his band's demise. As with Theudas, the movement had no lasting impact.

■ **38-40** The expression *and now* indicates a conclusion to Gamaliel's brief speech (v 38). The verb *aphistēmi*, which depicts the rebellion that Judas incited (v 37), conveys the common idea of keeping far away from something or someone. He suggests that the council should have nothing to do with the apostles. Gamaliel advises the council either to release the apostles or to leave them alone.

Gamaliel's rationale resembles the criterion behind the apostles' declarations about whom they should obey (v 29): the *source* of **this plan** (*boulē*), not the council's ruling, determines failure or success. Throughout Luke and Acts, such plans refer to either divine (Acts 2:23; 4:28; 13:36; 20:27; Luke 7:29) or human ones (Acts 27:12, 42; Luke 23:51). Gamaliel's advice correlates with the evaluative options facing readers.

The term translated **work** (*ergon*) sometimes refers to the mission and ministry of selected Christians (Acts 13:2; 14:26; 15:38). Thus, Gamaliel's advice places the apostles' ministry under scrutiny, both for the council and for Acts' readers. At the heart of Gamaliel's proposal is the contrast between two potential sources (note the preposition *ek*) of the Jesus movement. If the movement is *human* in origin, it would fail completely, like the two cited examples. But if the movement is *divine* in origin, then the council would not merely oppose the *apostles* but also *God*. The term *theomachoi* conveys the idea of fighting God or taking God to battle. The repetition of the verb *katalyō*, which depicts the ultimate failure of a human-driven movement (5:38), heightens the contrast by emphasizing the council's inability to destroy any divinely empowered movement (v 39). In that case, they can do absolutely nothing to stop them.

The interpretive consensus affirms that Gamaliel's speech protected the apostles and revealed his favorable inclination toward the believers and the gospel. Such arguments lean heavily on the two conditional sentences in vv 38 and 39. They understand the second sentence (*ei* plus an indicative) as offering the more likely possibility, as Gamaliel assesses the situation.

However, the latter construction could also function simply to underscore the apostles' declaration about God in their response to the Jewish council (5:29-32). Gamaliel offers his advice *after* citing two negative examples of movements that eventually failed after the death of their respective leaders. This suggests his assumption that the Jesus movement and its proponents had "failure written all over them" (Darr 1998, 136; see Johnson 1992, 99-103). We should not miss the irony: Gamaliel offers advice to the council about how to discern God's involvement. But he himself is a member of the same council

144

that Luke depicts as blind to God's purposes and workings in both Jesus and his apostles.

Thus, through this recommendation from an *unreliable* character, Luke provides statements that actually *confirm* what the narrative has already presented: (*a*) God is on the side of the apostles and believers, and no one can stop them. And (*b*) the council's hostile opposition to the apostles is opposition to God.

The narrative offers no explicit reasons behind the Jewish council's acceptance of Gamaliel's proposal. Two reasons are possible. First, he shrewdly handled the delicate situation, appealing to the negative examples of Theudas and Judas to evaluate the Jesus movement. Second, Gamaliel's reputation among the Jewish people at large (v 34) may have swayed them, since the latter group was also favorably disposed toward the apostles (v 26).

That the council still had the apostles flogged after summoning them may seem contradictory to that advice. However, it gives teeth to their repeated orders that the apostles cease speaking in Jesus' name (4:18; 5:28). Oddly, the council also agrees to "wait and see" what would happen with the believers, yet they continue to dole out their hostilities against the apostles. The council's actions confirm themselves as those who fight against God (→ v 39).

The Ancient Practice of Flogging

The Bible refers to different cruel forms of punishment and discipline. One such practice was flogging, in which an offender was beaten in the back or the chest with a leather whip that had several strands embedded with hard materials that would bruise or tear the flesh.

In Jewish circles, this practice was reserved for serious offenses against the Law and was administered by religious leaders. The physical torture and loss of blood often left the recipient close to death. Thus, flogging was limited to thirty-nine lashes (*m. Mak.* 3.10-14; see Deut 25:3; 2 Cor 11:24; Josephus, *Ant.* 4.438). Such harsh treatment was intended as a deterrent to future offenses.

■ **41-42** The narrator concludes this section by inserting another summary statement that outlines the apostles' response to the council's hostilities. The description of the apostles with the participle **rejoicing** (v 41) reflects a common Lukan image associated with those who recognized God at work (8:39; 11:23; 13:48; see 2:47; 3:8, 9; 4:21; 11:18). Luke links this rejoicing with their departure, as they leave the council wounded. The reason for this is an oxymoron: the apostles are considered *worthy* by what society considers unworthy, dishonorable, and contemptible. In typical gospel fashion, the values of society are turned upside down (or right side up!).

Thus, the apostles continue to do what they had been doing before—what the council ordered them *not* to do. They continue to do two things: (1) teach (4:2, 18; 5:21, 25, 28) and (2) proclaim **the good news** (*euangelizomai* [v

145

42]). This is the first time this latter term appears in Acts. It frequently appears in later chapters to describe the sharing of the gospel message (8:4, 12, 25, 35, 40; 10:36; 11:20; 13:32; 14:7, 15, 21; 15:35; 16:10; 17:18).

Luke specifies that their message affirms Jesus as the Christ. This suggests that their proclamation echoes similar emphases in Peter's speeches (see 2:29-36; 3:17-26). Other descriptors highlight important aspects of those activities. **Every day** underscores their continuing obedience to God and disobedience to the council's orders. The phrase **in the temple** further stresses that the apostles pursue the *same* practices in the *same* location that landed them in prison. The phrase **from house to house** alludes to earlier practices associated with the fellowship among the believers (2:46). This connects the apostles' activities with the broader communal images of sharing meals and caring for one another.

Although the opposition from the Jewish religious leaders has intensified, the Lukan narrator depicts through the apostles a persistence in mission that these leaders cannot deter. However, that persistence also anticipates future clashes with the Jewish leaders. Their obedience to God, which was disobedience to the council and under the noses of hostile officials, means that they are "asking for trouble" (Barrett 1994, 301).

FROM THE TEXT

Some Christians in the contemporary world can readily identify with the apostles and the hostility that confronts them. But others cannot, because they have never dealt with religious opposition from persons of authority. As a result, passages such as this often become unintentionally trivialized in contemporary attempts to relate to them. However, when one allows the harsh realities of a passage like this to sink in, one may also begin to discover aspects of living a faithful life before God that defines what it means to be the people of God.

The apostles stand as exemplary models of what it means to live and serve God faithfully. Their divine call leads them to serve as conduits of God's salvation. They respond to the needs of others and proclaim the gospel message despite threats from the Jewish religious leaders. Their resolve to remain obedient to God and their God-given mission makes them vulnerable before those who have their own ideas about God's will and hold the power to stop them. The repeated threats and rage of the council members, not to mention the torturous flogging, all signify the cost the apostles pay for their faithfulness. Yet after all these things, they still respond with the courage to persist, because God instructs them to do so (see v 20).

Interpreters often focus on the apostles' suffering. But this is merely the result of their faithfulness in the face of threats. Their suffering merely reinforces what readers have already observed in the apostles and the community of believers thus far in Acts. In the process, the depicted chasm between these believers and the Jewish religious authorities widens. This begins to answer the question as to which group truly represents what it means to be the people of God.

The Lukan depiction of the apostles presents the church as the people of God. But we cannot ignore the role of God, largely behind the scenes, that motivates the apostles. The release of the apostles from custody makes it clear that God is in control and provides for them, although their predicament suggests otherwise. The confusion over the whereabouts of the apostles makes it clear that these human authorities are no match for God and God's provision. The futile attempts of the befuddled leaders to intimidate and coerce the apostles into submission reveal their ineptness in comparison to God's care.

Thus, the joy of the apostles is not due to their suffering per se but is the result of God's provision that leads them into and through their situation. Their continuation in ministry and mission reflects their deep confidence in God's care and provision, even when the odds seem against them. Such confidence in God is a fundamental characteristic of those identified as the people of God.

F. Internal Struggles and Caring for Widows (6:1-7)

BEHIND THE TEXT

In Acts 3—7, the narrative plot employs a common pattern with the following elements: miraculous acts, teaching, objections from Jewish leaders, a hearing or legal proceedings, and divine vindication of the believers' mission (see Pervo 1987, 19-21). Additional materials about communal dynamics and growth among the believers also consistently appear. All these depict the Jerusalem church in stark contrast to the opposition.

Certainly, these materials serve as narrative interludes between scenes. But more importantly, they usually reiterate significant aspects of previous portions of the narrative or introduce new developments and characters, or both. Such is the case with this brief passage involving the Hellenist widows. Both the conjunction *de* (**now**) and the phrase "in those days" (1:15; 6:1; 11:27) emphasize continuity with the preceding section, while also signaling a change in topic or scene.

The introduction of two groups, described simply as the **Hellenists** and the **Hebrews**, provides the broad context for this passage. In general, the first group was comprised of Greek-speaking Jews who had migrated to Jerusalem from the Diaspora. The latter group of Aramaic-speaking Jews was from regions surrounding Jerusalem. For over a century, the scholarly consensus understood these two groups to differ ideologically. The Hellenists were thought to have more "liberal" views; the Hebrews, more "conservative" views toward the Law and temple practices. Such views were consistent with where they lived, especially their interaction with non-Jewish (i.e., Gentile) people, ideals, and values.

On this basis, interpreters typically distinguished between Pauline Christianity and Palestinian Christianity. Acts interpreters often assumed these distinctions and concluded that unidentified ideological issues lurked behind the troubles mentioned here.

However, recent decades have experienced a revision of such interpretations, since ideological distinctions along these lines have little textual or historical support, especially given the complex nature of first-century Judaism. The narrative offers scant information about the two groups, apart from the obvious linguistic distinction. To note that language primarily distinguished these groups is both prudent and consistent with the text itself (see Hill 1992). Differences over language may have segregated these groups in other areas of everyday life. And it probably contributed to the problem facing the community of believers. How ironic that differences over language now threatened the community of believers in Jerusalem, which first came together at Pentecost when the Holy Spirit enabled the apostles and others to overcome language barriers to proclaim the gospel!

IN THE TEXT

■ I A problem arises in the Christian community apparently because of its continuing numerical growth. This stretches the limits of their organization and structure to handle everyday communal affairs. The verb *plēthynō* in Acts describes the numerical growth of believers or the spread of the gospel message (6:7; 9:31; 12:24). It connotes multiplication as a sign of divine blessing.

For the first time in Acts, believers are described as **disciples**, a term borrowed from the Greco-Roman world for learners or apprentices who followed a particular teacher. The Greek-speaking disciples raise a complaint against their Aramaic-speaking counterparts. Their grumbling (*gongysmos*) echoes the Israelites' grumblings and complaints in the wilderness (Exod 16:7-12; Num 14:27-29; Ps 106:25). This may hint at the potential danger facing the disciples (against Gaventa 2003, 113). And it reflects poorly on the Greek-speaking group (see also Luke 5:29-31; Pao 2011, 137-38). Their specific concerns are about the treatment of widows from their group.

The verb translated **being overlooked** suggests the Greek-speaking widows are being slighted in some way. The imperfect verb tense indicates that this is not an isolated incident. However, Luke never mentions the specific problem. The **daily distribution**, presumably of food (see v 2), has typically been interpreted to refer to the community's care for the poor or, in this case, the widows.

Such generosity is apparently in response to OT commands to provide for them (e.g., Exod 22:22, 24; Deut 10:18-19; 24:19-21; Jer 7:6; Zech 7:10).

Such a reading perceives this situation as the community's failure to meet the ongoing and increasing needs of their growing group, which threatens the unity among the believers. However, this **distribution** or "ministry" (*diakonia*) probably refers more generally to the daily meals shared by the believers (2:46; see Pao 2011, 135-37). Thus, these widows' collective role within that ministry may be the underlying problem (Finger 2007, 253-64; Reid 2004, 82-86).

Widows in Luke and Acts

The OT often mentions widows with orphans and aliens as persons who needed the care and provision of the community. So when a text such as the Third Gospel or Acts mentions widows, readers may assume that these women were destitute, the poorest and most vulnerable among a populace that *itself* was mostly poor and powerless.

Luke's Gospel mentions widows four times (2:36-38; 4:25-26; 7:11-17; 18:1-8). They also appear in this passage (Acts 6:1-7) and in 9:36-42. In all these instances, the author does not emphasize their poverty and helplessness. He stresses other qualities, such as piety and generosity. Since Acts has already described the community of believers as having "no needy persons among them" (4:34), a perception of the widows as needy may not be consistent with the emphases of Acts (Finger 2007).

ACTS

6:2

■ **2** Although Luke's Gospel identifies the apostles as the **Twelve** (Luke 6:13; 8:1; 9:1, 12; 18:31; 22:3, 47), this is the only place in Acts where that designation appears. They exercise their role as leaders of the church by summoning **all the disciples** to address the matter. The apostles' assessment of the problem implies two things.

First, they are not responsible for giving oversight to this aspect of the community. In light of 4:34-35, this would not refer to caring for the community's poor. In particular, they specify this not only as the "daily distribution" but as **waiting on tables** (*diakonein trapezais*). As mentioned in v 1, these descriptions refer to shared meals and table fellowship (see Pao 2011, 135-37).

Second, members of the community bring the problem to the apostles to solve. However, the apostles also state unequivocally their responsibility for **the word of God**, a common Lukan expression for the gospel message. So, as the apostles describe it, giving oversight of this area means that they would **abandon** (see the intensive verb *kataleipō*) their divinely commissioned role as apostles and witnesses to proclaim the gospel—just what the Jewish council ordered them to do (4:18; 5:28, 40)! In their estimation, the implied suggestion is **inappropriate** and unacceptable, given their calling as guarantors of the gospel tradition (see 1:21-22).

■ **3-4** The apostles' address of the community as **brothers and sisters** (v 3) reaffirms the close bond among them. Then they offer their recommendation to delegate this responsibility. The verb translated **choose** (*episkeptomai*) comes from a family of words referring to making wise decisions. This hints at the seriousness of the situation. The apostles outline several prerequisites.

First, they should nominate **seven men** for the task. Like the replacement of Judas as an apostle (1:21-22), the recommendation (without rationale) calls for the selection of *male* (*anēr*) believers for this role. This requirement reflects then current cultural assumptions regarding the role of men in public spheres and the role of women in private spheres. But it may also reflect the role change that Jesus advocated at the Last Supper: "as one who serves" (Luke 22:26-27; Finger 2007, 268). The number **seven** may arise from the role of seven leaders within Jewish tradition (e.g., Josh 6:4; Jer 52:25; Josephus, *Ant.* 4.214, 287; *J.W.* 2.571).

Second, the candidates should have good reputations validated by the "witness" of others (see Acts 16:2; 22:12). Third, each nominee should be **full of the Spirit and wisdom**. The Spirit plays a crucial role among believers (2:4; 4:8, 31), enabling them to speak authoritatively and effectively through divine presence. Given the situation, wisdom may be most essential in navigating the present difficulties. The combination of Spirit and wisdom conveys the notion of spiritual discernment.

The apostles direct the community to nominate this group of seven men to be responsible for the community meals. But the apostles as the community's leaders are responsible for their "official" appointment. ***This need*** refers specifically to the responsibility of caring for these meals. But the vocabulary echoes prior descriptions of the community's provision for "anyone who had need" (2:45; 4:35).

By delegating these duties, the apostles pledge to concentrate on praying and preaching—practices that have characterized the apostles from the beginning of Acts. However, this portrays the apostles rather ambiguously. On the one hand, their declared devotion (*proskartereō*; see 1:14; 2:42, 46) aligns with positive images of the church to this point in Acts (Thompson 2006, 100). On the other hand, the expression **ministry of the word** (*tē diakonia tou logou* [6:4]) oddly distinguishes gospel proclamation from tasks associated with their communal meals (*diakonein trapezais*; 6:2; → 2:42-47). Some interpret this distinction as a Lukan critique of the apostles' proposal, which separates proclamation and prayer from those communal practices Acts consistently joins (Spencer 1994, 715-33; 2004, 76-77; Finger 2007, 266; Pao 2011, 142-43).

■ **5** In contrast to the apostles' displeasure over the negative implications of the problem (v 2), their suggestion **pleased** the disciples. Both the acceptance of the apostles' idea by the *entire* group of disciples and their collective action in selecting seven men for this ministry depict the community responding again in unity, a Lukan characteristic of believers.

The primary function of listing the seven names is to confirm the community of believers for its problem-solving and preparation for proclamation. All seven have Greek names, a sign that they all come from the Greek-speaking Jewish believers that first raise the issue (→ v 1). However, since many Jews of that day also had Greek names, that conclusion is not certain.

Only the first two members of the Seven appear later in Acts. **Stephen** is probably mentioned first since he appears as the major character in the next passage. This may also explain why Luke attaches a brief descriptor to his name. The first part of the description, **full of faith**, identifies Stephen as a staunch believer. The second part—full **of the Holy Spirit**—identifies his qualifications in light of the apostles' proposal. Given the Spirit's role in empowering believers as prophetic witnesses of Jesus, this descriptor also identifies the source of Stephen's proclamation before his accusers in Acts 7.

The second person, **Philip**, is the major character in Acts 8. In 21:8, he reappears as "the evangelist."

We know little about the next four persons. Luke identifies the last person, Nicolas, as a **convert** or "proselyte" (see 2:11) **to Judaism**; that is, a circumcised former Gentile. That he was originally **from Antioch**, presumably in Syria, may explain why some Jerusalem believers later flee to that city, which will assume a prominent role later in Acts.

■ **6** The presentation of the Seven *before the apostles* indicates their authoritative role. Together, the prayer and the laying of **hands** upon them signify an OT practice of the invocation of God's blessing and the conferral of that blessing along with authority, office, etc., to another (e.g., Num 8:10; Deut 34:9). The text is unclear whether the gathered disciples or the apostles pray for and commission the Seven. The subject does not change from Acts 6:5, so the gathered disciples may commission the Seven (see Barrett 1994, 315-16). However, since the community presents the Seven to the apostles for their appointment to the specific ministry responsibility (v 3), the apostles likely perform these acts of commissioning on behalf of the entire community. Still, the cooperative actions of both apostles and the gathered group of disciples call attention on the church's collective commissioning. This is not the establishment of the ecclesiastical office of deacon (from the term for ministry, *diakonia*).

■ **7** A summary statement of what subsequently happens concludes this section. The three imperfect tense verbs in this statement all emphasize ongoing aspects of the community's life and successful resolution of the problem. That the gospel continues to **spread** offers evidence that **the word of God** is not abandoned (see v 2). By focusing on the message, the narrator shifts attention from the authority of the apostles to the authority and power of the message itself. The apostles' role diminishes as the gospel moves *to the end of the earth* (1:8; Wall 2002, 114).

The imagery of numerical growth here employs the same terminology as v 1, reiterating God's continued blessing of believers. The favorable response of many temple priests is most surprising. The apostles had faced their most hostile resistance from the religious establishment in Jerusalem, notably from the priestly ranks. However, a large number of priests in Jerusalem were financially independent of the temple establishment and had little to do with the temple leadership. Their obedience is a sign of their allegiance to **the faith** or the Christian community in both beliefs and practices, in contrast to the Jewish council that encouraged disobedience (4:19-20; 5:29). This may explain in part the negative narrative developments that follow.

FROM THE TEXT

In just a few verses, the narrative moves from a crisis threatening the unity of the church to a resolution that makes believers more effective than ever. Luke does not tell everything. His narrative directs readers' attention to some things and not others. This allows them to make discoveries that are crucial to the perspective and purposes driving Acts as a narrative.

Two aspects stand out in this brief section. On the one hand, the narrative focuses on the communal handling of a potential crisis. But this entire section is about the activity and purposes of God. Although the problem threatens the unity of the believers, the narrator repeatedly emphasizes God's presence at work among them. At the section's beginning and end, he stresses God's activity within the church. The potential problem is addressed within that context of divine blessing. Readers have come to expect the community to face problems directly, since God is already at work!

On the other hand, Acts consistently associates the church with God's presence, the proclamation of the gospel, the care for one another, and the unity that holds her together. The problem before them threatens not only their unity but also their mission (see 6:2-4) and identity as the restored people of God. The distinction between the "ministry of the word" and the "ministry of the table" helps the community care for the needy and outcasts like the widows. But it also keeps widows outside and works against the oneness of the community. Unwittingly, our acts of compassion and care often keep outsiders outside! And yet the actions that lead to the appointment of the Seven are instrumental both in caring for the widows' needs and in key future developments in the spread of the gospel (e.g., ch 8).

Interestingly, the apostles nearly disappear from Acts after this scene. Conversely, two of the Seven—Stephen and Philip—assume leading roles as the narrative soon moves out of Jerusalem. These two, associated with serving the needy and the excluded, now become the faces of the fledgling Jesus movement, for their ministry mirrors that of Jesus.

Note that Luke clearly frames this scene in terms of divine presence and activity. This Lukan theme of divine blessing provides balance and perspective to his hint about the church's misstep along the way. Perhaps Luke wants us to see that God can take even the church's missteps and bless them within the grand schemata of God's purposes!

G. The Persecution of Believers in Jerusalem (6:8—8:3)

BEHIND THE TEXT

The abruptness in transition to this section is due to the omission of information from the Acts narrative. For instance, the narrative mentions nothing about any of the seven members actually doing what the church appointed them to do. But Luke may implicitly present them as successors of Jesus' ministry. Jesus identified himself and his followers at "the table" (Luke 22:21; see Acts 6:2) as those who served (Luke 22:26-27; see Acts 6:8). There is no indication about how much time lapsed from their official appointment to the accusations raised against Stephen. Yet Luke gives the account of Stephen's arrest and death considerable prominence within Acts. His speech is the longest one in the book.

This extended section concludes a series of three instances of the Jewish council's interrogation of one or more leaders from the Christian community in Acts 4—7. The intensification of the hostile opposition and treatment of these leaders—first threats, then flogging, and finally murder—dramatically heightens the severity of crisis facing the earliest believers in Jerusalem. This persecution drove them out of the city. The entire incident involving Stephen functions as a narrative hinge in Acts. The focus of the story begins to turn from Jerusalem and the Jewish people to other areas that included Gentiles.

Most of this section concentrates on a speech from Stephen, one of the Seven, in response to accusations against him before the Jewish council. We might expect Stephen to defend himself against the charges. But his speech focuses on selected references to Israel's history.

Many interpreters conclude that the speech belonged to a source or tradition independent from those used in crafting the narrative materials (vv 8-15; e.g., Haenchen 1971, 286-89). However, it is more important to consider how the speech functions within its narrative context. Interpretations of the speech must consider how it functions in addressing three different groups: (1) the Diaspora Jews who brought the charges against Stephen; (2)

the members of the Jewish council who claimed to lead Israel faithfully; and (3) the Lukan audience, which receives this story about Israel as a means of understanding God's purposes and what it means to be God's people (Gaventa 2003, 120-21).

IN THE TEXT

1. Stephen's Arrest and Murder (6:8—7:60)

a. Stephen's Arrest (6:8-15)

■ **8** Additional descriptions of Stephen set the narrative stage for what follows. That Stephen is *full of grace* is consistent with earlier descriptions of believers (2:47; 4:33). That he is also full of **power** correlates with Jesus' promise of power for his witnesses (1:8; see 4:33). His practice (note imperfect tense: *epoiei*) of doing **great wonders and signs** among the Jewish people places him in the company of Jesus (2:22) and the apostles (2:43; 5:12*a*; see 4:30). Given what happened to them, this brief introduction builds anticipation for the opposition Stephen will face.

Synagogues in Ancient Judaism

"Synagogue" transliterates the Greek noun *synagōgē*, which refers to persons meeting or gathering together. It became a technical term for the meeting place of the Jewish people. But it referred initially to an assembly of Jews for the reading and interpretation of Scripture, prayer, and other social purposes.

Historians once debated whether the synagogue as an institution and building existed in Jerusalem and the surrounding region prior to the Roman destruction of the temple (AD 70). Before then, many activities of the synagogue were associated with the temple. However, evidence from various sources—archaeology, inscriptions, and literature—confirms that many synagogues were located in Jerusalem in the first century, perhaps over four hundred of them (Binder 1999; see Riesner 1995, 179-210).

■ **9-10** The narrator introduces an unspecified group of men. The ambiguity of the Greek has caused interpreters to speculate whether the group came from one or as many as five synagogues. However, the sentence structure suggests that the entire group was comprised of two distinct parties (with the definite article *tōn* appearing twice to distinguish those parties).

Some came from a particular synagogue identified with *the Freedmen, Cyrenians, and Alexandrians* (v 9). The latter two refer to Diaspora Jews who returned to Jerusalem from two cities: Cyrene, the coastal capital city of a Roman province in present-day eastern Libya; and Alexandria in Egypt. The designation **Freedmen** may refer to freed slaves who later became Roman citizens, including Jews and Jewish converts. However, since the specific term transliterates the Latin, it may refer to descendants of a specific Jewish group captured and enslaved by the Roman general Pompey in 63 BC.

The other party came from Cilicia and Asia, two Roman provinces in Asia Minor (modern Turkey) that will have greater significance later in Acts. Therefore, both groups were Diaspora (and therefore Greek-speaking) Jews. Since they begin to **argue** or **debate** with Stephen, he also must have been a Diaspora Jew, as one of the Hellenist group of believers (6:1; see Bruce 1979, 49-85).

Acts does not specify what these groups find questionable about Stephen. The verb *syzēteō* is the same term that describes the challenges to Jesus (Luke 22:23; 24:15-16). His opponents are no match for Stephen because his speech reflects **wisdom and the Spirit** (Acts 6:10; see v 3). Acts emphasizes that the Spirit enables believers to proclaim the gospel confidently and effectively. The verb used to describe Stephen speaking, *laleō*, in Acts 2—5 refers either to the proclamation by apostles and believers (2:4, 6, 7, 11; 4:1, 17, 20, 29; 5:20, 40) or to a message by God or God's messenger (2:31; 3:21, 22, 24).

■ **11-12** Because Stephen rebuffs the arguments of his opponents, they resort to underhanded tactics. The verb *hypoballō* (lit., "throw under") often describes the spreading of rumors or whispers about someone without that person's knowledge (LSJ 1996, 1875). Somehow, they convince others to accuse Stephen of **blasphemy** or slander against God (v 11). Strangely, they first mention **Moses**, a personified way of speaking about the Torah. Both the word choices and the lack of evidence for this accusation coax readers to evaluate the opponents' actions negatively. The consequence of these actions matches the apparent intentions behind them.

The verb *synkineō* conveys the sense of becoming overly worked up about something, often with a cumulative or "snowball" effect. As Luke presents it, public opinion throughout Jerusalem turns against Stephen because of the scandalous rumor. The **elders** (v 12), who had resisted the Jesus movement (4:5, 8, 23) and the **scribes**, the experts and teachers of the Jewish law, understandably lead the opposition.

However, the inclusion of the Jewish people within the generalized reaction against Stephen reflects a dramatic swing in public perception. The favorable perception from the general Jewish populace in Jerusalem has sheltered the apostles from hostile religious authorities (see 4:21; 5:26). Without this, Stephen is vulnerable to the opponents taking further action (see Tannehill 1990, 84). Thus, the verb *ephistēmi* suggests that they confront Stephen more forcibly than before (6:9). They haul him off (*synarpazō*) to the same Jewish council that threatened and punished the apostles earlier (4:1-22; 5:17-42).

■ **13-14** The introduction of **false witnesses** (6:13) confirms the illegitimacy of the prior accusation and reveals a new charge against Stephen. Ironically, his opponents bring Stephen before the council as one who has broken the Jewish law. But they *themselves* break its commands about bearing false witness (Exod 20:16; Deut 19:16-18). Like before, they accuse Stephen of something he supposedly said. This time, the charge is that he has been constantly speaking against the temple (**this holy place**) and the Jewish law (i.e., blasphemy against Moses [Acts 6:11]).

They supposedly based their claim on Stephen's teaching about Jesus. To be sure, that part of the claim referring to Jesus destroying the temple is reminiscent of Jesus' own predictions about the temple's destruction through judgment (Luke 21:5-6; Matt 24:1-2; Mark 13:1-2; John 2:19-22). The Matthean and Markan accounts of Jesus' trial include false witnesses who misrepresented Jesus' words and said that he *himself* would destroy the temple (Matt 26:60-61; Mark 14:57-58). However, the Lukan version omits this, reserving that charge for this particular scene. This associates Stephen with Jesus and intensifies the reader's sense of danger (Gaventa 2003, 118-19).

The term translated **customs** (Acts 6:14) may be synonymous with "law" and reflect Jesus' distinctive understanding regarding the Law. But this interpretation admits there may be some truth to the charge (Barrett 1994, 328-29). More likely, the term focuses on the oral interpretation of the Law, which was seen as authoritative as the Law itself (see Johnson 1992, 110; Fitzmyer 1998, 359-60). Thus, the charge from the false witnesses combines Jesus' teachings to claim that Stephen advocated the destruction of both the temple and the Law.

■ **15** The common Lukan verb *atenizō* (1:10; 3:4, 12) suggests that the Jewish council glare in anger at Stephen. After all, if true, the accusations were more serious than those the apostles faced. However, what the council members see is not the face of some religious "monster" but what resembles **the face of an angel**. This description may allude to Moses' shining face (Exod 34:29-35; see Spencer 2004a, 79-80; Peterson 2009, 242) or to Jesus' illumined presence at his transfiguration (Luke 9:29; see Johnson 1992, 110). Regardless, the comparison depicts Stephen as unmistakably reflecting God's glory and character. By associating Stephen with God's messenger, Luke prepares readers to hear Stephen's speech as a message from God.

b. Stephen's Speech before the Jewish Council (7:1-53)

■ **1-8** Stephen responds to the high priest's question about the charges against him, which Luke has already characterized as untrue (6:13). His formal address of the council as **brothers and fathers** (7:2) accords its members respect as fellow Jews (1:16) and requests that they listen to him. Stephen opens his remarks by recalling the story of Abraham, whom he identifies as *our ancestor* (again connecting him with his Jewish audience; see 7:11, 12, 15, 19, 38, 45). Stephen begins with Abraham. But the true subject of his remarks is **the God**

of glory, a rare expression found only in Ps 29:3 (anticipating his vision of "the glory of God" in Acts 7:55).

The first portion of the speech (vv 2-7) summarizes selected material from Gen 11—15. The account does not align chronologically with Gen 11:31—12:5 (which states that Abraham was *already* living in Haran when God called him and Abraham's father was alive when Abraham heeded that call). However, the focus is clearly on God's call for Abraham to **go to the land** (Acts 7:3) that God would indicate, as quoted from Gen 12:1 (LXX).

Historical Accuracy and the Bible

A close reading of texts such as Acts 7:2-4 raises questions about the historical accuracy of the Bible. Biblical accounts sometimes differ in their narration of specific details of the same events. This troubles some people. Such findings go against their preunderstanding of the Bible's authority as dependent on the Bible being completely without error (i.e., inerrancy), at least in the original manuscripts.

Wesleyans consider the Bible as authoritative regarding salvation (i.e., faith and doctrine, Christian life and practice, etc.). Accordingly, such questions should not challenge their views regarding the Bible. They understand God's inspiration of the biblical authors partially in terms of God working cooperatively with human persons (with their unique backgrounds and abilities) to compose these texts that the church has adopted as her sacred Scriptures.

In a case like this, in which historical details conflict, the obvious differences in the passage may actually *help* readers interpret the Bible better. Such discoveries in the text may coax them to consider *primarily* the text's theological message and purpose, *just as it is written*. In that sense, the Bible serves primarily to guide the church in her recognition of God's activity and grace that seek to save and transform humanity.

Stephen notes that God did not give Abraham any land, not even *space for his foot* (Acts 7:5), to be passed down from his generation to the next. Rather, alluding to Gen 17:8, Stephen stresses that God gave Abraham and his descendants the *promise* of land. That Abraham had no children at the time (see Gen 11:29-30) made both the promise and his obedience even more remarkable! Thus, Stephen emphasizes the link between Abraham's descendants and the promise of the land. But he focuses on God's covenant with the people.

By quoting Gen 15:13-14 about Israel's future enslavement in Egypt (see Exod 12:40-41, which refers to 430 years in Egypt), Stephen shows how God would fulfill that promise, even through a crisis that threatened the people.

The reference to worshiping God **in this place** (Acts 7:7) may paraphrase Exod 3:12, which looks forward to Israel's worship of God on Mount Sinai. This prepares Stephen's audience (and Luke's readers) for questions about worship and the temple, which appear later in Stephen's speech.

Circumcision (Acts 7:8), the ritual of removing the male foreskin, was the visible sign of God's covenant with Abraham (Gen 17:11) and with his descendants. Every male child of Israel was circumcised on the eight day (Gen 17:12). The cursory summary about Isaac, Jacob, and the twelve patriarchs (see Acts 7:8-9) reiterates the centrality of Israel's covenant relationship with God.

■ **9-10** The second major portion of Stephen's speech focuses on Joseph. Stephen moves immediately to the patriarchs' jealousy toward Joseph, which reminds readers of the council's jealousy toward the apostles (5:17) and reintroduces the Lukan theme of opposition toward God's chosen leaders. The mention of God's presence with Joseph underscores God's care and guidance (see Gen 39:2, 21). He refers to God delivering him **from all his troubles** (Acts 7:10), probably alluding to the incident involving Potiphar's wife (Gen 39:6-18) and the imprisonment that followed (Gen 39:19-20). He notes God's provision of *favor* and **wisdom**, which led to Joseph's appointment to rule Egypt and Pharaoh's household (see Gen 41:1-45). These qualities remind readers of Stephen's character (see 6:3, 8, 10).

■ **11-14** Stephen summarizes Gen 42—47, recounting Joseph's reunion with his brothers and father. As the earlier reference to Abraham, Stephen refers again to **our ancestors** (here, Jacob and his family [Acts 7:11]), reaffirming (see v 2) the Jewish heritage he shared with his council audience.

The verb *anagnōrizō* ("make known" or "recognize") is the same one used in Gen 45:1 (LXX) to describe Joseph's self-disclosure to his brothers. Joseph invited his family to move to Egypt. By this means, the Spirit of God (see Gen 41:38-39) enabled him to save his clan from certain death (Wall 2002, 126). The size of the family, **seventy-five**, reflects the LXX number (Acts 7:14; see Gen 46:27; Exod 1:5; MT: "seventy"). Thus, by God's provision, God's purposes for Israel as God's covenant people continued outside the promised land.

■ **15-16** Mention of the burials of Jacob and Joseph (vv 15-16) has baffled interpreters. These verses combine several OT accounts. According to Genesis, Jacob was buried in Hebron, in a plot that Abraham purchased (Gen 23:1-20; 49:29-33; 50:12-14). However, Joshua reports that Joseph was buried in Shechem, in a plot Jacob purchased (Josh 24:32; see Gen 33:18-20). Stephen's speech says that Jacob and his descendants were all buried at Shechem in a plot Abraham purchased.

Stephen twice mentions Shechem, which his listeners would know was in Samaria, near Mount Gerizim, the Samaritan worship center. This would not have endeared him to the council, as it links Israel's patriarchs with the Samaritans, whom traditional Jews despised.

As in Acts 7:7, Stephen contends that the worship of God cannot be confined to one sacred place. The mention of Shechem also prepares readers of

Acts for the inclusion of Samaritans among the people of God (ch 8; Spencer 2004a, 83-84).

■ **17-22** The longest portion of Stephen's speech (vv 17-43) concentrates on Moses as a prophet and leader of Israel. The speech divides the life of Moses into forty-year segments (see Deut 34:7):

- Israel's bondage and Moses' appearance on the scene in Egypt (vv 17-22), including his account of Moses' murder of the Egyptian who mistreated an Israelite and his flight to Midian (vv 23-29);
- God's appearance to Moses at Mount Sinai after his forty-year exile in Midian (vv 30-34); and
- Moses' leadership of the Israelites through the Exodus and wilderness wanderings (vv 35-38), and the consequences of Israel's rejection of Moses (vv 39-43).

Stephen's opening declaration about Moses identifies this portion of Israel's history as part of God's plan to save this people as the inheritors of God's promise. His description of the Israelites' situation in Egypt relies on the LXX account in Exod 1.

The verbs that describe the Israelites in Egypt—**grew** and **multiplied** (Acts 7:17)—come from Exod 1:7 (LXX). They are the same ones that just described God's blessing upon the church (see Acts 6:7). The quotation of Exod 1:8 (Acts 7:18) introduces the crisis facing the Israelites: Egypt's new Pharaoh was oblivious to what God had done through Moses. The descriptions of the Egyptian ruler's exploitation through deceit (see Exod 1:10) and harsh treatment (see Exod 1:11) allude to the broader story of Israel's hardship (Exod 1:8-14), including his orders to allow their newborn males to **die** without care (see Exod 1:15-22; Acts 7:19).

Although v 17 refers to a specific time in human history (*chronos*), v 20 describes Moses' birth as a strategic **time** (*kairos*) regarding God's purposes for the Israelites. Jewish tradition often speaks of Moses' physical attractiveness (e.g., Josephus, *Ant.* 2.230-32; Philo, *Moses* 1.9, 18) as **beautiful** (Exod 2:2). He enjoyed a favored status in God's eyes (see Luke 2:40, 52).

Stephen mentions the discovery of Moses by Pharaoh's daughter and her adoption of him (see Exod 2:3-10) to explain why Moses received the best of Egyptian education (absent from the Exodus account). That Moses received an education **in all the wisdom of the Egyptians** (Acts 7:22) is similar to references in Jewish tradition to his intelligence and education (e.g., Josephus, *Ant.* 2.229; Philo, *Moses* 1.20-24). But it also connects him with others in Acts who possess wisdom (v 10; 6:3). The depiction of Moses as **powerful in his words and deeds** resembles the Lukan portrayal of Stephen (6:8, 10), the apostles (2:43; 4:33; 5:12), and Jesus (2:22; Luke 24:19) as prophets of God.

■ **23-29** Stephen's description of Moses' adult life begins with an adapted account of Moses killing an Egyptian and then fleeing to Midian, an arid region northeast of the Red Sea. The speech introduces this second portion of Moses' life by stating that he was forty years old. Like the account in Exod 2:11-14, Stephen recounts Moses' intervention against an Egyptian who mistreated an Israelite (see Exod 2:11).

Stephen's account exonerates Moses, suggesting that he **avenged** the wrong by killing the Egyptian (Acts 7:24; see v 28). He deftly omits that Moses made sure that no one saw what he intended to do (see Exod 2:12). Stephen also explains that Moses assumed the Israelites understood his God-given mission, something *Moses* would not have known in Exod 2! The specification of Moses' mission—to *give them salvation* (Acts 7:25)—appropriates language associated with God's saving work in Jesus Christ (e.g., Luke 1:69; 6:9; 19:9; Acts 2:21; 4:9, 12).

According to Stephen, Moses' question to the two fighting Israelites (7:26) intended to reconcile them, much different from the accusatory tone of his question in Exod 2:13 (Pervo 2009, 185). However, the response of one Israelite (Exod 2:14) underscores their *mis*understanding of Moses' role and mission. This hints at the Jewish misunderstanding of Jesus (Acts 3:17). Stephen's rendition of the incident ascribes Moses' flight from Egypt to his fears over *Israelite* misunderstanding, not Pharaoh's attempts to kill him (Exod 2:15).

■ **30-34** The passing or "fulfillment" of another forty years signals the movement to the final stage of Moses' life. Stephen's account of God's appearance to Moses through the burning bush depends on the wording and quotation of Exod 3:1-7 (LXX). Omitted here are details about what Moses was doing when the angel appeared and his observation that the fire did not consume the bush (Exod 3:1-2). Stephen also identifies this theophany as at Mount Sinai rather than Mount Horeb (as in Exod 3:1).

One might account for this difference because of Stephen speaking or Luke writing from memory (e.g., Barrett 1994, 360). But even Josephus names Mount Sinai as the location (*Ant.* 2.264). This may reflect common assumptions in later Jewish tradition as well as typical associations of Moses and the Law with Sinai.

The reversal in chronology in Stephen's account, which first mentions God's self-identification followed by God's command for Moses to remove his sandals (see Exod 3:4-6), underscores the continuity of God's role throughout early Israelite history. This was the same God who called and guided the already-mentioned patriarchs (see Acts 7:2-16).

The omission of the extended account of Moses questioning God's call (Exod 3:13—4:17) does not seem coincidental: Moses' resistance would conflict with the speech's themes and emphases. For instance, Moses' self-description about inability to speak (Exod 4:10) would contradict Stephen's description of Moses as "powerful in his words and deeds" (Acts 7:22 NRSV). "It would also create problems for Luke's parallel between Moses and Jesus, if the forerunner were found to be stammering and timid" (Gaventa 2003, 126). By quoting Exod 3:7, Stephen's speech concentrates on God's response to the suffering of God's people and God's mission (*apostellō*) for Moses to go **back to Egypt**.

■ **35-38** Although the speech has been mostly descriptive of selected events in Israel's history, this section is comprised of a series of five declarations about Moses. Stephen refers to him each time with the demonstrative pronoun "this," which accentuates the specific declarations.

This Moses whom God called was questioned as their leader (Acts 7:35). The specific question had been raised by only one person (see v 27), but its use here generalizes it as a rebuke by the people of God.

God sent *this* Moses as their **ruler** and **deliverer** (v 35), the latter being an OT descriptor for God (e.g., Pss 19:14; 78:35; see 111:9).

This Moses led the people of Israel (Acts 7:36). The description of Moses doing **wonders and signs** compares him favorably to others associated with these indicators of God's blessing, namely Jesus (2:22), his apostles (2:43; 5:12), and Stephen himself (6:8). Collectively, the references to Egypt, the Red Sea, and the wilderness wanderings recount Moses' leadership under God's guidance throughout his life.

This Moses declared that God would raise up his prophetic successor. The quotation of Deut 18:15 repeats the same passage Peter quoted to his temple audience after the healing of the crippled man (Acts 3:22) with reference to Jesus. However, Stephen does not yet make such associations.

Finally, *this* Moses received the **living words** from God (7:38), a likely reference to the law of Moses, which Stephen had been falsely accused of deprecating (6:8, 13). That Moses received the Law while he was **in the assembly** during the wilderness period is noteworthy. The use of the term *ekklēsia* (see 5:11) here suggests that the people of Israel, redeemed out of their Egyptian bondage, had assembled to affirm their covenant with God through obedience to God's word (Exod 19:5-6).

■ **39-43** This last section begins with a relative clause, grammatically connected to v 38. But the focus shifts from Moses to the rejection of Moses by Israel—**our ancestors** (vv 11, 12, 15, 19, 38), even though Moses was obviously led by God.

Stephen characterizes the people's actions as both disobedience and rejection (see v 27). Of all instances of disobedience in Israel's history, Stephen focuses on the ultimate act of disobedience and disloyalty to the covenant: idolatry as seen in the incident of the golden calf (Exod 32). Their request to

Aaron, a quotation from Exod 32:1 (or 32:23), provides Israel's self-incrimination for both their rejection of Moses and their apostasy.

Israel's ironic reference to *this Moses* underscores their rejection of *this one* whom God called and guided (Acts 7:35-38). Their joy over **what their own hands had made** (v 41) is reminiscent of OT language for idols (e.g., Lev 26:1, 30; Isa 2:18; 16:12; 46:6; Dan 5:4, 23). Ironically, the verb *euphrainō* that describes Israel's celebration is a common LXX term that typically conveys the people's rejoicing before God (e.g., Deut 12:7, 12, 18; 16:11, 14, 15; Pss 40:16; 43:4; 104:15; 105:3; Isa 25:9; 41:16; 61:10).

The transference of their rejoicing from God to an idol reveals their complete rejection of God. Israel turned back to Egypt (Acts 7:39), but God also **turned away** from them and *handed them over* to continue their idolatrous worship (v 42; see Rom 1:18-32). The quotation of Amos 5:25-27 (LXX) substantiates Stephen's assessment of Israel's past. The negative *mē* ("not") at the beginning of Amos' initial question (Acts 7:42d) expects Israel to answer "No": Israel *never* worshiped God during their wandering in the wilderness. They continued their idolatrous practices. Amos related these to the situation in his own day.

Significant difficulties exist regarding the identification of the deities **Molek** (v 43; perhaps the Canaanite-Phoenician god of the sun and sky) and the star-god **Rephan**. These provide specific examples of the Israelites' worship of the *heavenly host*, an OT expression Jeremiah associated with idolatry (Jer 7:18; 19:13).

Two adaptations to the Amos quotation reveal the reason for its use here in Stephen's speech. First, the addition of **to worship** highlights how Israel's making of idols signifies her failure to worship *God*. Second, his substitution of Babylon for Damascus (the capital of the Assyrian Empire, which threatened the northern tribes of Israel that Amos addressed) relates the message of judgment to his Jerusalem audience. They knew well that the Babylonians had destroyed Jerusalem centuries before. The speech expands the scope of God's judgment to include *both* the exile of Israel (eighth century BC) *and* the exile of Judah (sixth century BC).

Amos associated God's judgment and exile with idolatry. Similarly, Stephen's appropriation of that material here takes matters one step further. He associates judgment through exile with both idolatry and *all* Israel's rejection of Moses.

■ **44-50** To this point in the speech, Stephen has not mentioned the temple, although the accusation on the table states that he often spoke against it (6:13-14). Rather, the speech offers a swift account of Israel's history in moving from the tabernacle to the temple.

162

In contrast to Amos' reference to *the tent* of Molek Israel took with her for idolatrous worship, Stephen mentions Israel's tabernacle or *tent of testimony* (LXX Exod 27:21; 28:43; 33:7; Num 1:50; 12:4; Deut 31:14). This conveys its role in witnessing that "the God of glory" (Acts 7:2) was present in covenant relationship with Israel (Exod 25:8). Thus, its function was not unlike the prophetic role of the apostles and even Stephen as witnesses (see Acts 1:8, 22; 2:32; 4:20; 5:32; Wall 2002, 128).

The construction of the tabernacle **according to the pattern** (7:44) from God contrasts with Israel's idolatry, which Stephen consistently associates with the work of *human* hands (see vv 40, 41, 43). Incongruously, Moses received God's directions at the same time when the Israelites formed their idol (Peterson 2009, 261).

Stephen gives only scant attention to the conquest. He relates Israel's success in possessing the land with (*a*) Israel taking the tabernacle with them and (*b*) God's activity in driving out the other nations from the land. The phrase **until the time of David** (v 45) may refer to the removal of non-Israelite groups from Canaan. But it more likely speaks of the tabernacle's ongoing place within Israel through David's time (see, e.g., 2 Sam 6:17; 7:2, 6). He emphasizes the tabernacle's longstanding role within Israel's history as the place of God's presence among the people of God.

Although Peter's Pentecost speech gives considerable attention to David, Stephen's speech accords him only a mere glance. The description of David as one "who found favor with God" (Acts 7:46 NRSV) is somewhat consistent with OT depictions of him (e.g., 1 Sam 16:12; 2 Sam 15:25). But nowhere in the OT is David described exactly this way. This is also similar to Lukan portrayals of persons such as Jesus (Luke 2:40, 52), Mary (Luke 1:30), and Stephen (Acts 6:8). It suggests that we should perceive David's request favorably (against the negative implications of 2 Sam 7:5-7). Manuscripts differ as to whether he requested **a dwelling place for the God of Jacob** or *the house of Jacob*. The former is the easier reading and reflects the wording of Ps 132:5. The latter is the more difficult reading and likely original version. However, the two readings are similar in meaning: the first refers to a temple in which God would dwell, the second to a dwelling place that Israel would use as a temple (Barrett 1994, 372).

Textual Variations and the Bible

Persons are often surprised to learn that the text of the Bible, as translated, bound, and printed, is a compilation of numerous materials containing portions of biblical texts. The vast majority of materials agree. However, some differences exist, sometimes over one word or phrase, sometimes over a longer section (e.g., Mark 16:9-20).

Textual criticism is a specialized discipline within biblical studies that analyzes different manuscript variations and attempts to evaluate which wording is most likely the original version. Such work is important, since what the church reads today as sacred Scripture depends on its processes of authentication. Within the highly technical work of textual criticism, several basic criteria stand out.

First, what kind of evidence from manuscripts, papyrus documents, and fragments is there to support one reading over another variation? The textual critic takes into account "families" of documents that may be traced to a common source, so that the quantity of support does not override support from better quality sources in terms of dating and reliability.

Second, which version is shorter? Copyists tended to insert words or phrases for clarity or explanation. So the shorter version is often considered the probable, original one.

Third, which variant creates the more difficult reading? Since scribes tended to prefer greater clarity, a variant that is more difficult to understand within its context is typically considered the more authentic (→ "Textual-Critical Issues" in Introduction).

The reason for mentioning Solomon here is that he, not his father David, built the temple for God (see 2 Sam 7:1-17; 1 Kgs 5—7). However, the conjunction *de* (**but** [Acts 7:47]) signals that Solomon's actions marked a change. Those from priestly circles listening to Stephen would have embraced this move from the portable tabernacle to the permanent structure of the temple as an epical moment in Israel's history (Spencer 2004a, 88).

However, Stephen immediately dumps cold water on any collective joy that may have welled up inside his audience. The adversative conjunction *alla* (***rather*** [v 48]) indicates something much different: God—identified as **the Most High** (e.g., LXX Gen 14:18, 19, 22; Ps 46:4; mostly in the Lukan corpus in the NT—Luke 1:32, 35, 76; 6:35; 8:28; Acts 16:17)—**does not live in *places built* by human hands.**

The Israelites' celebration over what they made with their hands (7:41) compares Jewish pride in the temple with idolatry. However, Stephen does not just condemn the temple as Israel's center of worship (see 2:46; 3:1, 8; 5:12) or even Solomon, who fulfilled David's sincere wishes, but rather criticizes *all* human or institutional attempts to place theological claims upon God that ultimately limit God or diminish God's greatness. His quotation from Isa 66:1-2 buttresses this argument.

Stephen's accusations challenge all who refuse to believe the divine message delivered by God's prophets: first by Moses, then by Jesus as the Christ, and now Jesus' apostles and Stephen (Wall 2002, 129).

■ **51-53** To this point, most of Stephen's speech is only an indirect critique of the Jewish council. The accused invites his judges to join him (note the

164

repeated *our ancestors*) in examining their shared history as Jews and the chosen people of God.

However, the speech's tone suddenly changes from the first person plural—we—to an accusatory, second-person stance. As Stephen moves to his contemporary situation, the accused becomes the accuser. He lodges three charges of his own.

First, he calls them **stiff-necked** (v 51), which is what God called the disobedient Israelites after they made and worshiped the golden calf (Exod 33:3, 5; Neh 9:16-17). Since Stephen already mentioned this incident from Israel's past, he now condemns his audience for repeating their ancestors' sins.

Second, by describing the audience as **uncircumcised in hearts and ears**, Stephen compares them to those Jeremiah condemned as unfaithful to the covenant (Jer 6:10; 7:1-17) by practicing idolatry and then desecrating the temple when they participated in temple rituals.

Third, his depiction of the council as **always *resisting* the Holy Spirit** echoes Isa 63:10. This also reflects on Israel's rebellion and disobedience after God's deliverance from her bondage in Egypt. By referring to these ancestors in a second-person perspective (**your** ancestors [Acts 7:52]), Stephen distances himself from his audience. He charges them with the same unfaithfulness of Israel's checkered past before their exile.

After associating his audience with their ancestors' sins of idolatry and unfaithfulness, Stephen compares those same hearers with their ancestors who persecuted God's prophets. This theme appears in both the OT (e.g., 1 Kgs 19:10, 14; 2 Chr 36:15-16; Neh 9:26; Jer 26:20-23) and on Jesus' lips (Luke 6:22-23; 11:47-50; 13:34).

From this generalized condemnation, Stephen refers more specifically to their rejection of prophets who spoke about the coming **Righteous One** (→ Acts 3:14)—Jesus. The innocence associated with such a description stands in stark contrast to what Jesus received from those who opposed him: betrayal and murder (see 3:14).

By addressing his audience directly, Stephen places full responsibility for Jesus' death on these religious authorities. Peter had earlier allowed for ignorance playing a role in Jesus' death. But Stephen makes no such concession, as these leaders continued to resist God's purposes by opposing the apostles (see Johnson 1992, 134, 138).

Thus, Stephen declares that these religious leaders who gathered to see if he was guilty of speaking against the Law actually failed to keep it themselves (*phylassō*; see Exod 12:17; 19:5; 20:6; Deut 4:2; Ps 119:8-9, 44; also Luke 11:28; 18:21; Rom 2:26; Gal 6:13). This was most obvious in their role in Jesus' death. That is, the ones entrusted with guarding the Law had *themselves* failed to guard or obey it. Conversely, the one facing accusations of speaking ill against the Law *affirms* its divine authority by noting a Jewish belief that angels had put it into effect (see Deut 33:2; *Jub.* 1:29; Josephus, *Ant.* 15.136; Philo, *Dreams* 1.141-43; see Gal 3:19; Heb 2:2).

c. Stephen's Murder by the Jewish Council (7:54-60)

■ **54-56** There is no indication that Stephen has concluded his speech. The council's reaction may have interrupted him and cut him short. Although his speech provides indisputable evidence of his innocence, rage consumes the members of the Jewish council (→ 5:33). They are intent on killing him.

The imagery of these leaders gnashing their teeth at Stephen borrows from the OT. There, it is a sign of the wicked's anger and hostility against the righteous people of God (e.g., Pss 35:16; 37:12; 112:10; Lam 2:16).

Conversely, Luke describes Stephen as **full of the Holy Spirit** (Acts 7:55). This common Lukan description of believers confirms that God has enabled him to speak authoritatively as God's prophet or spokesperson (6:3; see 2:4; 4:8, 31). His heavenly vision, as he *stared into heaven* (see 1:10), offers divine confirmation of his testimony in the face of the growing antagonism.

After beginning his speech with a reference to "the God of glory" (7:2), Stephen now sees the **glory of God** for himself (v 55). This confirms that God is in heaven, not in the temple (vv 48-49; Gaventa 2003, 131). He exclaims that he could see Jesus as the **Son of Man** [the only NT use of this title outside the Gospels] **standing at the right hand of God** (v 56). Jesus has assumed a position of authority and honor (see 2:33-34; Ps 110:1).

The significance of Jesus' posture of standing rather than sitting (Acts 2:34; Luke 22:69) has been interpreted in various ways: the welcome or acceptance of Stephen as a persecuted prophet, the assurance of Jesus' advocacy on Stephen's behalf, or the judgment that these religious leaders as God's opponents are about to receive (see Isa 3:13; see Bock 2007, 311-12).

■ **57-58** The scene had opened as a judicial hearing—witnesses and testimonies, the council as jury, and the high priest presiding. But it suddenly turns into a chaotic mob scene after Stephen's declaration about his vision of Jesus. The covering of ears and the shouting are attempts by these dignified leaders of the Jewish people to squelch Stephen's words. Perhaps they consider his words about Jesus in heaven as blasphemy.

Stephen's reference to the council's "ears" being "uncircumcised" (Acts 7:51) depicts them as stubbornly refusing to accept his message, and thereby rejecting God's word (Johnson 1992, 120). Their rage against Stephen bonds them "together" (v 57 NRSV: *homothymadon* in 1:14; 2:46; 4:24; and 5:12 describes the "unity" of believers). As one body, they charge him (see 19:29), overwhelmed with hostility. They proceed to "throw" him forcefully out of the city (*ekballō*).

Luke mentions no formal verdict against Stephen, but the mob action exposes their intentions. Jewish law prohibited a person's execution within Jerusalem (see Lev 24:11-13; Num 15:35; see *m. Sanh.* 6.1). Since there was no guilty verdict or Roman involvement (Rome alone held the "rights" to capital punishment), these actions against Stephen are nothing less than an unauthorized lynching. However, Jewish law did allow stoning for convicted offenses such as the worship of other gods (Deut 17:2-7), child sacrifice (Lev 20:2-5), and blasphemy (Lev 24:14-16), among others (Fitzmyer 1998, 393; see Hill 1992, 29-31).

The brief mention of a **young man named Saul** (Acts 7:58) at the scene of Stephen's stoning is consistent with Lukan tendencies to introduce a character who appears later in the narrative. At this stage, Luke offers few details about **Saul**, other than that persons placed garments at his feet. This is perhaps a sign that he is a leader (see 4:35, 37; 5:2). Recall that some of the original opposition to Stephen (see 6:9) came from Cilicia, Saul's home region (22:3).

The term translated **young man** suggests that Saul is in his late twenties or thirties. Since witnesses to an offense were the first to stone the offender (Deut 17:7; *m. Sanh.* 6.4), the ones who laid down their garments (Acts 7:58) were either the false witnesses that originally accused Stephen (Johnson 1992, 140) or those who heard his speech. It is unclear whether they removed these articles of clothing to participate in the stoning or as some other kind of symbolic act (Fitzmyer 1998, 394).

■ **59-60** The Lukan description of Stephen's stoning and death is filled with implicit theological connotations and allusions to the scene of Jesus' death in the Third Gospel. The verb *epikaleō* ("to call upon") describing Stephen praying at his stoning, coupled with the address **Lord Jesus** at the beginning of that prayer (v 59), echoes Peter's quotation of Joel 2:28 in his Pentecost speech that "everyone who calls on the name of the Lord will be saved" (Acts 2:21). Stephen's prayer indicates that he trusts Jesus (whom he saw standing in heaven [7:56]) for his salvation, even in the throes of death. His brief request, **receive my spirit** (v 59), parallels Jesus' dying words (Luke 23:46; see Ps 31:5). Luke presents him as a model disciple, who dies like Jesus.

Stephen's posture, as he *fell to his knees*, indicates the physical toll that the stoning takes on him as well as his prayerful posture in the face of his enemies (see Luke 22:41). Like his opponents and Jesus (see Luke 23:46), Stephen *cried out with a loud voice* (see Acts 7:57). Unlike his opponents, he does so not to drown out God's word but to offer one last word to God. His prayerful petition on behalf of those stoning him is similar to Jesus' request that God forgive those who crucified him (Luke 23:34, although some MSS do not include that saying).

Stephen's enemies close themselves off from any call to repentance and forgiveness (Acts 7:51, 57). But his prayer turns matters over to divine mercy. He expresses hope in the future possibility of their salvation (Tannehill 1990, 86).

The verb describing Stephen's death, *koimaō*, literally refers to falling asleep. This was a common expression for dying in the ancient world (see, e.g., Gen 47:30; 2 Sam 7:12; 1 Kgs 11:21; 14:20; 1 Cor 15:6, 18; 1 Thess 4:13-15). By not elaborating on his death, Luke calls attention to Stephen's life as a witness (*martyr*), not his death as a martyr.

2. Persecution Extends to All Believers (8:1-3)

BEHIND THE TEXT

Most translations attach the added notation regarding Saul's role in Stephen's death (v 1a) to the previous materials. The expression *egeneto de* (**now it happened**) in Acts commonly signals the beginning of a new literary section.

However, the startling turn of events that led to Stephen's horrific demise and the subsequent persecution of the believers in Jerusalem suggests that this summary section serves a transitional function. It wraps up the loose ends regarding Stephen's death and sets the stage for the narrative trajectories that follow.

IN THE TEXT

■ **1** A second hint regarding Saul's role in Stephen's death implies greater involvement than 7:58 might indicate. The periphrastic construction translated "giving approval" (*ēn syneudokōn* [NIV84]) emphasizes both the duration of his involvement (at least as long as the stoning) and his direct involvement as an accomplice.

Since Saul was from Cilicia (see 22:3), from where some of Stephen's initial challengers came (6:9), he may have been involved from the beginning (see Johnson 1992, 141). At the very least, Luke portrays Saul as having Stephen's blood on his hands.

The noun referring to Stephen's death, *anairesis*, is a particularly strong term. It connotes not merely death, but a wrongful death, by killing or murder. This is what the council had wanted to do with the apostles (see *anaireō* in 5:33).

Linked to Stephen's death, as the phrase **on that day** suggests, is a **great persecution** brought **against the church in Jerusalem**. In the NT, the term **persecution** (*diōgmos*) refers only to activities intended to force adherents to give up their religious beliefs and practices.

The verb *diaspeirō* describes the ensuing scattering of believers. It is from this term that "Diaspora" is derived (→ sidebar "The Diaspora" with 2:5-

12). That these believers scatter throughout the regions of Judea and Samaria reminds readers of Jesus' promise about where his witnesses would go (1:8).

The narrator does not explain the apostles' exemption from the scattering of the believers. Some argue that this persecution did not really affect every believer, as the Lukan hyperbole **all** implies (8:1). They assume that it was limited to Greek-speaking or Hellenistic Jewish Christians, most likely instigated by unrest among fellow Greek-speaking Jews (e.g., Bruce 1988, 162; Hill 1992, 32-40).

This explanation does not answer historically how the Jewish religious authorities or the general Jewish populace responded to the ongoing presence of non-Greek-speaking Jewish believers in Jerusalem. Nor does Luke address this question. But we would not expect them to be immune from similar treatment (see Bauckham 1995a, 428-29; Witherington 1998, 278).

Nonetheless, the apostles' presence in Jerusalem remains important to the narrative, at least for now, for two reasons. First, their presence maintains continuity between Judaism and the Christian movement. Second, their presence enables them to lead the Jerusalem church. This remains the mother church and serves within Acts to validate the results of the gospel's proclamation (see Fitzmyer 1998, 397).

■ **2-3** Before moving the narrative to places beyond Jerusalem, the narrator offers one last glimmer of hope for the city. The mention of those who buried Stephen is reminiscent of Joseph of Arimathea (Luke 23:50-54). Their **great mourning** suggests intense grief and lamentation over what happened. The narrator does not identify these **godly men**, but they were probably nonbelieving Jews who were sympathetic toward Stephen (Acts 8:2; see Luke 2:25; Acts 2:5; see Dunn 1996, 106; Witherington 1998, 277; against Marshall 1980, 151-52; Fitzmyer 1998, 397).

Conversely, Saul's assault against the church illustrates nothing less than complete rejection of the gospel message. The imperfect tense of the indicative *elymaineto* ("destroy," "ravage") suggests an ongoing practice of inflicting both physical harm and verbal abuse. Just as the believers were characterized earlier as going "from house to house" (2:42) for fellowship, now Saul goes **from house to house** to destroy it (8:3).

Saul's assault against the church includes dragging believers off to prison, apparently with little or no regard for who they are. But why did Saul take such drastic measures? He must have thought that these believers "were not merely misguided enthusiasts whose sincere embracing of error called for patient enlightenment; they were deliberate impostors, proclaiming that God had raised from the tomb to be Lord and Messiah a man whose manner of death was sufficient to show that the divine curse rested on him" (Bruce 1988,

163). The persistence of Saul's opposition illustrates Israel's division in its response to the gospel.

FROM THE TEXT

As mentioned in the Introduction, the speeches in Acts have an important function of explaining to readers what happens in the narrative. Through a speech from a reliable character, the narrator may offer such explanation while remaining hidden from the readers' view. Because the speech from Stephen is the longest of the entire book, the inference is that the issues raised here are significant to the developing plot and narrative of Acts.

Thus, this speech does not appear to be a defense speech, although the setting would suggest that. Rather, it is instead an indictment against Israel: she has rejected God and God's law, so that she has failed to live as the people of God.

Stephen's speech appears to focus on the history of Israel. But the primary subject of that story is God. God's call and promise of a people provided the impetus behind the outlined periods in this selective history. God constantly acted to empower the people, thwart evil against them, and redeem Israel when she faltered in her covenant with God.

However, Stephen's description of Israel's history returns repeatedly to Israel's embrace of idolatry, the worship of what their own hands made. The move from tabernacle to temple itself underscores Israel's persistent attempts to domesticate God. They treated sacred site and religious prescriptions as idols. Their continued disobedience and lack of repentance were evident in their resistance against God's repeated calls to repentance and warnings about judgment, as prophets like Moses spoke to them as God led them.

Thus, the focus of Stephen's speech is not the denunciation of the temple or the Jewish law per se, as his accusers alleged. Rather, he speaks against Israel's ongoing disobedience, as seen in her leaders' use of these religious fixtures to hide the truth about God's saving purposes in Jesus. The Jewish religious leaders expected God to conform to their religious institutions and entities. They tried to domesticate God, to exercise authority and political power, even over God.

Conversely, Stephen's speech serves "to challenge their presumption that a transcendent God, the only God, can be contained with a sacred place or particular parcel of land and regulated by a powerful group of self-appointed people," revealing instead this God to be "making choices at every turn in fulfilling the promise of salvation" (Wall 2002, 125).

We see this in Stephen's death, as he prays on behalf of these very same, unrepentant people, voicing to Jesus his hope for their possible, future salvation. "It is what and for whom he prays, and not that he prays, that gives his death its most profound meaning" (ibid., 133). Thus, he prays for those "inside" the religious establishment that had turned the *worship* of God into the *domestication* of God but could not tell the difference. And Luke has left that prayer for the church to consider as part of Stephen's legacy, because she, too, has had vulnerabilities in such areas across the centuries.

Excursus: God and the People of God (Acts 1:12—8:3)—The Narrative Portrait of the Church in Jerusalem

This first major narrative unit generally presents the believers in Jerusalem with ideal imagery. They were blessed by God, unanimous, caring toward others, and unstoppable in the proclamation of the gospel (2:42-47; 4:32-37). The speeches, the large numbers of those accepting the gospel, and the excitement in Jerusalem among the Jewish people implicitly present a picture of compatibility between the Christian gospel and the fulfillment of God's promises and purposes for the Jewish people as the people of God (see 2:41, 47; 4:4; 5:14; 6:7).

These positive images of the believers provide a literary paradigm or an ideal model that assists in the evaluation of the Christian community in subsequent portraits. However, alongside these positive descriptions are also increasingly negative images of the Jewish leaders and some of the Jewish people that lead to the murder of Stephen and the scattering of the believers from Jerusalem.

Luke applies the term *ekklēsia* ("church") to Christian believers (5:11), which the LXX applies to Israel as the people or the assembly of God. Thus, these two contrasting groups present two opposing views or understandings of the people of God.

On the one hand, the narrative presents the believers as those in whom God was at work and among whom was unanimity. On the other hand, Acts describes the Jews, the historic people of God, as increasingly becoming God's *opponents* (see 5:39) and divisive in their actions. Acts does not offer an image of God establishing the church apart from the historic people of God on Pentecost. Rather, Luke portrays the unbelieving Jews as those who rejected God's promise and whose divisive actions implicitly placed *them* outside the realm of God's saving activity and purpose (Jervell 1972, 41-74; 1996, 34-43).

The Lukan depiction of the believers as the *ekklēsia* of God does not distinguish them as a separate group or as God's people apart from the Jewish people. They are those faithful to what God had been doing all along. These contrasting images in this narrative unit affirm that Jewish believers in Jerusalem were the people who belonged to and were called by God.

III. GOD AND THE SPREADING GOSPEL: THE PEOPLE OF GOD AND OTHER "PEOPLES": ACTS 8:4—14:28

The persecution of believers in Jerusalem scattered them outside the holy city, the narrative setting of everything thus far in Acts. Luke has established several important emphases regarding the Christian message and God's purposes for the people of God in that city, the sacred center of Jewish religious practice and identity as the people of God:

- God fulfilled God's promises to Israel through Jesus the Christ.
- God called Israel to repentance and restoration through this good news delivered by prophetic spokespersons, beginning with the apostles and extending to other Spirit-filled believers.
- God's faithfulness and blessing were extended to those who responded favorably to the gospel. Such respondents comprised repentant and restored Israel.
- God's judgment was pronounced upon Israel's religious leaders for their role in creating division among Israel by their disobedience and rejection of God's saving purposes.

Thus, Luke's account indicates the fulfillment of Jesus' commission of the witnesses to Jerusalem (1:8). The scattering of the believers opened the door for that witness beyond Jerusalem, as his commissioning words directed.

173

With the scattering of believers comes a geographically scattered narrative, with several trajectories out of Jerusalem in chs 8—11. The narrative sequence leads some readers to assume that the sequential order of these accounts matches the chronology of these events. However, these materials may draw from incidents that came from the same general period after the persecution of the believers in Jerusalem. The connections between these episodes have more to do with their emphases and contributions to narrative developments than with historical chronology.

A. The Ministry of Philip (8:4-40)

Both Stephen and Philip were nominated and appointed as part of the seven-member group assigned with responsibility and oversight of the ministry of tables (6:1-6). This allowed the apostles to continue their collective role as witnesses to Jesus and his resurrection, the proclamation of the gospel (6:4). Only these two subsequently appear in Acts, but neither is distinguished by the responsibilities to which they were appointed. Their narrative roles are in different capacities. Philip serves as the first narrative example of what happened to scattered believers.

I. Philip and the Samaritans (8:4-25)

BEHIND THE TEXT

The geographical neighbors of Judea and the Jews were the Samaritans, who lived between Judea and Galilee. Samaria was so named by the Assyrians who typically identified a region by its capital or primary city. The notorious rift between the Jewish people and the Samaritans made for a rather unsettling coexistence of mutual animosity. Their mutual hatred had its roots in Israel's history.

As part of the northern kingdom of Israel, the Samaritan region was devastated by the Assyrian invasion of the eighth century BC. Many Israelites not scattered elsewhere in the Assyrian Empire intermarried with persons from other displaced nations relocated in former Israelite territory. After returning from Babylonian exile, the Judeans (now called Jews) considered their northern relatives, the Samaritans, "half-breeds." Their mixed ancestry made them peripheral to the Jewish people.

Growing hostilities between the Samaritans and Jews as well as the religious significance of Mount Gerizim within Samaria (Deut 11:29; 27:12; Josh 8:33; see John 4:20-21) eventually led to the establishment of a rival temple there. However, the Jewish king John Hyrcanus destroyed it in 128 BC (Josephus, *Ant.* 13.254-58; *J.W.* 1.62-63). Samaritans accepted the Pentateuch, but they did not accept other portions of the Jewish Scriptures that were added later, including the Psalms and the Prophets.

174

Because of their common ancestry and religious practices, interpreters have debated whether the Samaritans in Acts are seen as Jews, Gentiles, or somewhere between. The narrative progression of Acts has not yet included any references to the gospel extending to Gentiles. So it seems best to conclude that Philip's ministry among the Samaritans functions as a middle ground, as the gospel begins to challenge the religious boundaries the city of Jerusalem symbolized.

IN THE TEXT

■ **4-5** The opening reference to **those who had been scattered** (8:4) connects this new section with the summary about the new "Diaspora" (see v 1) created by persecution. The dual conjunctions *men oun* confirm that connection, while also indicating a new direction to the story.

Luke associates one particular practice with the travels of the persecuted believers. They proclaimed the gospel message wherever they went (see v 25). He singles out Philip as one who began to preach (see imperfect tense: *ekēryssen*) about Jesus as the Christ.

Nothing about Philip's activity seems out of the ordinary in light of Acts 1—7, except that his proclamation was to Samaritans, not to the Jews. Manuscript evidence is divided over whether this happened in an unidentified city of the region of Samaria or specifically in the city of Samaria. Herod the Great rebuilt Samaria and named it Sebaste in honor of Augustus (Greek for "Augustus"). Textual evidence supports the latter reading, but the largely Gentile demographics of that city favor the former reading.

On either reading, it was a radical departure to preach to an audience most Jews considered apostates (see Jervell 1972, 113-32). They rejected Samaritan claims that they worshiped Israel's God and followed Moses' law.

■ **6-8** The large **crowds** (8:6) indicate an overwhelmingly positive response by the Samaritans. The adverb ***together*** (*homothymadon*), which often depicts the united believers (1:14; 2:46; 4:24; 5:12), appears here to describe the attentiveness of the Samaritans to Philip's message. The verb *prosechō* connotes the Samaritans listening attentively, hanging onto every word Philip speaks.

Accompanying Philip's message are **the signs** that he accomplishes, a description reminiscent of Jesus (2:22) and the apostles (2:43; 4:30; 5:12). The message itself, not these extraordinary actions, is effective in prompting faith, as people could easily misunderstand signs. The selected examples of Philip's ministry provide dramatic proof of the saving transformation of his actions, which correspond to the apostles' actions (5:16).

The **shrieks** (lit., ***shouting with a loud voice***) from **unclean spirits** demonstrably indicate their defeat (see Luke 4:33-36, 41; 6:18; 8:2, 29; 9:1, 6, 42; 11:24). The curing of paralyzed people is reminiscent of Jesus' ministry (e.g.,

Luke 5:17-26). The healing of disease and crippling ailments was an antici-pated sign of the messianic age (Luke 7:22; see Acts 3:1-26).

Luke does not indicate whether the Samaritans' **great joy** (8:8) came from relief from their suffering or from recognition of what God was doing through Philip. That these signs accompany and aid their attentiveness to Phil-ip's gospel message suggests that joy is their initial response to that message (see Fitzmyer 1998, 403; against Barrett 1994, 404; Dunn 1996, 108). Thus, Philip's ministry resembles that of Jesus and the apostles.

■ **9-11** The introduction of Simon into the scene briefly interrupts the ac-tion. He serves as an interesting character whom Luke employs to clarify the impact of the gospel. According to Luke, Simon was a magician who, like Philip, had *himself* captured the people's complete attention and devotion. The same verb that describes the Samaritans' attentive listening (v 6) appears twice (vv 10, 11) describing how Simon enthralled them. Their amazement over what Simon could do (vv 9, 11) echoes earlier responses to divine occur-rences among the believers in Jerusalem by those uncertain about what had happened (see 2:7, 12; 3:10).

The Samaritan belief that Simon was *the power of God* indicates that they thought he was a divine person, perhaps by his own suggestion (see 8:9). Both the word **all** and the expression *from the least to the greatest* (v 10) un-derscore how widespread his reputation was before Philip appeared. Luke's introduction of Simon builds suspense, as he offers a glimpse of conflicting powers (gospel vs. magic) and allegiances (Philip vs. Simon).

Magic and the Ancient World

For twenty-first-century Western readers, references to magic seem foreign and obtuse in light of contemporary scientific knowledge. However, the practice of magic was fairly common in the ancient world. Magicians were be-lieved to possess abilities to use a variety of techniques, chants, and spells to exert control over divine reactions of one sort or another. For instance, Deut 18:9-14 describes a number of forbidden magical practices because of their as-sociation with idolatry.

In Matthew's Gospel, those who came to see Jesus in Bethlehem were described as magicians (*magoi* [Matt 2:1]), probably astrologers, since they fol-lowed a star (Matt 2:2). Some ancient magicians were highly respected, as in Simon's case. However, some were viewed suspiciously as deceivers (e.g., Philo, *Spec. Laws* 1.100-1). Because both magicians and these spokespersons for God were often viewed as doing divine work, the lines between the two realms were often blurred.

This may help explain why Luke depicts Philip's ministry and Simon's magi-cal practices in contrasting ways. Magicians sought to control God, whereas God controlled and directed these servants of God.

■ **12-13** The action picks up where v 8 left off. Following the Samaritans' initial response of joy is the Lukan notation that they came to believe (see aorist tense: *episteusan*) in the gospel message (see *euangelizomenoi*; v 4). **The kingdom of God** (v 12) echoes the theme of Jesus' teaching (1:3; e.g., Luke 4:43; 6:20; 7:28; 8:1, 10). The mention of **the name of Jesus Christ** recalls previous emphases on the importance of Jesus' name for healing (Acts 3:6, 16) and salvation (4:12; see 2:21). Thus, Luke makes it clear that the Samaritans now believe in the same gospel Jesus and the apostles proclaimed. Their subsequent baptism signifies their inclusion into the community of believers. These actions also disclose that Philip's gospel won over the Samaritans from Simon's tantalizing grip through magic.

The additional information about Simon's coming to faith and baptism accentuates the effectiveness of Philip's message. Luke depicts him as "*qualitatively* superior" to the magician (Spencer 2004a, 96; 1992, 92-103). Interpreters often question Simon's sincerity due to what occurs later (8:18-24). But Luke depicts his response like that of other believers. Simon shadows Philip (see 1:14; 2:42, 46; 6:4). His firsthand observation of *the signs and great miracles* parallels what Peter stated about Jesus (2:22) and what the Samaritans also witnessed (8:6-7). Ironically, this one whom others associated with "great power" (v 10) now recognizes the "great powers" that Philip accomplished. This one who had "amazed" (*existēmi* [vv 9, 11]) the Samaritan masses now is *amazed* by what he sees Philip doing! However, in Acts amazement is usually associated with unbelievers (2:7, 12; 3:10). So Luke may hint that something is defective in Simon's faith.

■ **14-17** For the moment, the narrative shifts from Simon and Philip in Samaria to the apostles in Jerusalem. The narrator does not explain how they heard about events in Samaria. The generalization that **Samaria**, rather than one group or city, **had accepted** the gospel message (lit.: **the word of God**; see 4:31; 6:2, 7) prompts the dispatch of **Peter and John**. These actions establish "official" connections between Jerusalem and the fledgling Samaritan ministry. Considering the animosity between Jews and Samaritans, this is remarkable!

The apostles' prayer for the Samaritans to **receive the Holy Spirit** and the narrator's parenthetical explanation about that prayer in 8:16 do not conform precisely to earlier descriptions regarding baptism and the coming of the Spirit (2:38-41). In particular, Luke does not explain the delay in the Spirit's coming, which finally occurs when the two apostles **placed their hands** (8:17) on the Samaritan believers (see 6:6).

Some conclude that a deficiency in the Samaritans' baptism required supplemental action (e.g., Dunn 1996, 110-11). This reflects a diminished view of the Lukan description of their baptism as **in the name of the Lord Jesus** (8:16). Others contend that the apostles' approval of the Samaritan ministry was necessary for validation and authentication by the Jerusalem church (e.g., Fitzmyer 1998, 400-401).

However, the apostles' actions represent two things. First, the apostles' actions join the Samaritan believers with those in Jerusalem in solidarity and equality. This may have been as necessary for the Jerusalem believers as for the Samaritans, given their entrenched mutual hostility (see Marshall 1980, 157-58; Bruce 1988, 168-70). Second, these actions remind all readers of Acts that any community's participation in God's call to proclaim the gospel requires the gift of the Holy Spirit (1:4-8).

▪ **18-19** Simon's return to the story suggests he was among the Samaritan benefactors of the two apostles' actions, despite the error of his subsequent request (see Wall 2002, 139). The narrator does not mention what Simon saw when the apostles conferred the Holy Spirit upon the Samaritan believers. However, he probably interpreted it as a secret magical ability or skill he could simply purchase. The word translated **ability** typically denotes the authority that gives someone the right to do certain actions or make particular kinds of decisions.

Simon's request reveals his theological failure to recognize the gift of the Spirit due to God's gracious activity. Simon desires power or authority he could appropriate as *he* determines, whereas Luke depicts the sharing of resources within a trusting partnership or community among the believers (see 2:42-47; 4:32-37).

▪ **20-21** Peter's response to the request is a strong rebuke of Simon (lit.): *May your silver be to destruction with you* (8:20). *Destruction* in the LXX is often associated with Hades and death. The force of this wish (optative mood: *eiē*) of condemnation was, "May your money burn with you in hell!"

Peter immediately explains: Simon thought he could purchase this divine **gift** (see 2:38). He tried to secure for *himself* what belongs *only* to God. "Magic seeks a craft that can rationally control the divine powers; it has no real place for 'gift' as the free disposition of the divine apart from human manipulation" (Johnson 1992, 149). Simon may also be challenging Peter's honor to regain some of his former honor (see 8:9-11) at the expense of Peter and John (Spencer 2004a, 98-99).

Since the term **share** (v 21) echoes descriptions of the apostolic ministry (1:17, 21-22), the phrase *in this matter* (*logos*) implies Simon to be unfit to proclaim the gospel (6:2, 4, 7; see Johnson 1992, 149; Wall 2002, 139-40). Using the term *logos* as a synonym for gospel (e.g., 4:31; 8:14) suggests that Simon has not truly embraced the message. Thus, he is now an apostate. He has made himself an outsider to the community of believers despite his earlier coming to faith (v 13; see Haenchen 1971, 305; Barrett 1994, 414-15; Peterson 2009, 289).

As one whom Luke has repeatedly characterized as God's prophet, Peter could discern the inner person (see 5:1-4). Peter's assessment of Simon alludes to Ps 78:37. The term translated **right** (*eutheia*) describes something that is straight—honest and open. Simon's offer is offensive, not only to Peter, but ultimately to God.

■ **22-23** Earlier, Peter did not offer Ananias an opportunity for repentance (see 5:1-5). But he calls for Simon's repentance here. That call, if heeded, would open the door to forgiveness. "If possible" (NRSV) implies that forgiveness does not come *automatically* through repentance and prayer but through God's gracious response to the penitent who prays. The truly repentant seek forgiveness by placing themselves at the mercy of God.

Peter's instructions specify the manifestation of the **wickedness** that requires Simon's repentance (8:22). **Thought** (*epinoia*) connotes more than mental processes; it refers to a person's intentions. Peter negatively evaluates Simon's motives in making the offer.

Peter's reference to Simon being *in the gall of bitterness* (v 23) recalls Deut 29:18. It compares the person who worshiped other gods and led others to do so to a root that produced bitter poison. **Captive to sin (*chained to unrighteousness*)** may reflect Isa 58:6. There it describes the enslavement to injustice God wished to end. If so, the allusion behind Peter's words to Simon offers implicit hope for his salvation by God.

■ **24** Simon's response to Peter's call does not precisely follow the apostle's instructions. Some question Simon's sincerity and view him as seeking only to escape the consequences of his sin (see Peterson 2009, 290). However, his response may be a recognition of his sinfulness and his unworthiness to pray for himself (see Klauck 2003, 22-23).

That Luke offers no resolution to this matter leaves the scene open-ended, a common aspect of Luke's literary style. We are left with the final image of a Samaritan man—who once spoke of himself in extravagant ways, who had been revered as the embodiment of divine power (v 10)—now humbled and powerless before God. In light of the Christian gospel, he realized his dependence upon others to intercede before God on his behalf.

Whatever Happened to Simon?

Although Simon the magician never reappears in Acts or the NT, the ambiguity that surrounds him may be one reason why the early church fathers mention him often. Simon Magus (from the term *magos*, "magician"), as he came to be known, was blamed for the promotion of various controversial teachings that plagued the second-century church.

Justin Martyr, himself from Samaria, ascribed Simon's magical powers to demons. He reported that Simon accepted honor as a god in Rome (*I Apol.* 26; *Dial.* 120.6). Irenaeus associated Simon with various heretical teachings, particularly those associated with a gnostic sect known as the Simonians (*Haer.* 1.23). In the third century, Hippolytus wrote of Simon's death. He had earlier promised he would raise himself on the third day to prove that he was a (false) Christ (*Haer.* 6.2-15).

Even the term "simony," which the church later coined to describe the practice of purchasing ecclesiastical offices, suggests how his notoriety lived on. Solid historical evidence about him is scarce. Such ecclesial depictions are based more on *impressions* about Simon than on Luke's characterization of him in Acts 8.

■ **25** This episode's conclusion summarizes the ongoing ministry of Peter and John. First, the two continued to minister for an unspecified amount of time before leaving town. The expression *speaking the word of the Lord* refers to their proclamation of the gospel. The intensive verb *diamartyromai* depicts them as fulfilling their commission as witnesses (see 1:8; 2:32; 3:15) and providing that gospel message in its entirety (see 2:40).

Second, the two apostles *were proclaiming the gospel* (see 8:4) in several Samaritan villages as they returned to Jerusalem. This is a mirror image of the opening statements about Philip's ministry as he left Jerusalem for Samaria. Mention of this activity confirms and endorses his ministry that took the gospel message to the Samaritans and incorporated Samaritan believers within the Christian community.

2. Philip and the Ethiopian Eunuch (8:26-40)

BEHIND THE TEXT

Contemporary readers of Acts often miss the author's role in composing a text to capture the reader's attention. In the first century, descriptions of exotic lands and people often piqued public interest. The use of such detail makes for greater effectiveness as a text.

Luke's account about Philip's encounter with a eunuch from Ethiopia reflects some of these artistic, compositional touches. Ethiopia means "the land of a people with burnt faces." At that time, it included most of modern Ethiopia and the Sudan. It attracted considerable attention in ancient Greek historiographical works because of the distinctive racial and ethnic features of her people.

Historians equated Ethiopia with the ends of the earth (see, e.g., Herodotus, *Hist.* 3.114; Strabo, *Geogr.* 1.1.6; 1.2.24). Those located on the earth's fringes also received the least honor (see Herodotus, *Hist.* 1.134; Parsons 2006, 132). The Roman Empire imported many commodities from Ethiopia: exotic spices, incense, ivory, ebony, and gold. The Ethiopian language was Semitic in origin, and so her people related to the Hebrew and Aramaic languages associated with Jerusalem and the surrounding region (Fitzmyer 1998, 412). By introducing this story in this manner, Luke seeks to capture readers' attention, recounting a mission that extended as far as Ethiopia, *to the end of the earth* (1:8).

IN THE TEXT

■ **26-28** References to divine guidance for Philip frame the introductory part of this story (vv 26-29): **an angel of the Lord** (v 26) and **the Spirit** (v 29) guided him. True to the tendency in Acts thus far, the narrator depicts God as orchestrating the ministry of believers.

God directs Philip, who last appeared north of Jerusalem in Samaria, to the road that stretched southwest from Jerusalem toward the city of **Gaza**, 50 miles (80 km) from Jerusalem near the Mediterranean coast. The road Philip was to take did not pass through a *wilderness* or **desert** area. The mention of this terrain must refer to Gaza. The phrase *kata mesēmbrian* might have directed Philip to go down that road "at noon." But it seems here to point him to the more southerly route, which the noonday sun in the northern hemisphere would indicate.

These initial instructions move Philip from a place of successful ministry to an isolated location with little potential for effective work (see Marshall 1980, 161; Gaventa 2003, 141). Yet Philip goes without objections, obedient to God's guidance.

These details were essential to Philip's providential encounter with one particular man on that road. The narrator describes him as both *a man of Ethiopia* and a **eunuch** (v 27). In the ancient world, eunuchs were castrated males who often served in positions of significant responsibility, including governance of royal harems.

Luke notes his powerful position as the official responsible for the treasury of the queen—the meaning of the dynastic name **Kandake** or "Candace" (CEB, NRSV)—of Ethiopia. The eunuch's devotion to God is evident in his extended travel to *worship in Jerusalem*. Interpreters debate whether readers should view him as a Jew, a proselyte to Judaism, or a Gentile worshiper of God (not a full convert to Judaism; like Cornelius in 10:1-3).

Luke does not state whether the eunuch was Jewish or Gentile. If he was a Gentile, the importance of the subsequent event involving Cornelius diminishes the narrative role of this episode. But his physical condition as a eunuch would have excluded any possibility or hope of him being a practicing Jew or a convert to Judaism (see Deut 23:1; Josephus, *Ant.* 4.290-91). Circumcision may also have been out of the question.

As a Gentile, the man would have had limited access to some courts of the temple (see Josephus, *J.W.* 2.409-16). But as a eunuch, he (and foreigners) could hope for a *future* place in the house of God (Isa 56:3-8). Thus, the narrator depicts the man in a liminal position between insider (Jew) and outsider

(Gentile). In this sense, he is similar to the Samaritans (Acts 8:5-25; see Shauf 2009, 762-75).

Eunuchs in the Ancient World

In many ways, eunuchs occupied a socially ambiguous place in the Greco-Roman world. Like the Ethiopian eunuch, they often held important offices and were both literate and wealthy. However, in a world with clearly defined gender roles, the sexual ambiguity of eunuchs caused them to be a socially maligned group.

Eunuchs were prohibited from temple worship in Jerusalem because they were considered sexually defective (see Deut 23:1; Josephus, *Ant.* 4.290-91). Polemo described them as "evil people" (*Physiogn.* 1.162F). Lucian of Samosata contended that a eunuch was an "ambiguous sort of creature . . . alien to human nature" (*Eunuch.* 6-11; see Spencer 1992, 156-57; Parsons 2008, 119-20).

Luke mentions only the eunuch's influential position in this passage. But these unstated assumptions would have contributed to the implied Lukan audience's perceptions of this character. *None* of this could prevent his baptism—his full entrance into the people of God (Parsons 2006, 123-41).

The story illustrates the movement of God's saving purposes. The Ethiopian eunuch transcends Jewish categories (people and places) and geography, as the gospel encompasses those from *the end of the earth* (1:8; see Shauf 2009, 762-75).

That the eunuch is reading from the book of Isaiah further indicates his piety toward God. It also implies that he is wealthy, since he possesses a personal copy for reading. He may have been attracted to Isaiah because of its references to Ethiopia (Cush) receiving God's blessings (Isa 18:1; 45:14; Wall 2002, 143).

■ **29-31** Next, the Spirit instructs Philip to approach the chariot of this high-ranking official. The verb *kollaō* connotes joining the chariot's riders. It would have been inappropriate for him to climb uninvited into the chariot of such an official. The instructions suggest that Philip should accompany the traveling party on foot.

The narrator's description of Philip running serves two purposes. It depicts Philip in ways reminiscent of the prophets (e.g., Elijah in 1 Kgs 18:46; Strelan 2001, 31-38). And it places him in proximity to the moving chariot. This explains how Philip heard the eunuch reading from Isaiah (people seldom read silently in antiquity). Repeated references to Isaiah emphasize the centrality of this text in what follows.

Philip's question may seem offensive at first. Who is this one who appears out of nowhere and abruptly inquires whether this man of high social status—literate, powerful, and wealthy—*really* (*ara ge*) understands what he

182

is reading (*ginōskeis . . . anaginōskeis*)? But the eunuch's response reflects no hint of offense.

The eunuch's counter-question—**"How can I . . . ?"** (Acts 8:31)—is entirely appropriate, both for a person of elevated status and for the situation. The rare Greek construction, a potential optative (interrogative *an* followed by optative; BDF 1961, §385; Smyth 1956, §1824), conveys a future possibility as an opinion of the speaker.

The eunuch expresses his hope of understanding the text someday, if someone would **lead the way** (*hodēgeō*, explain) for him. The narrator offers no explicit reason for the eunuch's invitation for Philip to join him in the chariot. Given the divine guidance that prompts this encounter, it is plausible that the pious man recognizes Philip as God's prophet.

■ **32-35** The quotation of only one portion (Isa 53:7-8) of the Servant Song of Isa 52:13—53:12 suggests that it functions here as its summary or an allusion to its central emphasis. Unlike previous citations of OT passages, Luke offers no interpretation. This is perhaps because the one who quotes it *himself* needs someone to interpret it. Philip interprets this passage as referring to Jesus rather than the prophet.

The quotation came directly from the LXX. Divergences from the Hebrew text as well as previous speech materials in Acts (see 3:13) offer clues regarding Philip's interpretation. Instead of the servant being "cut off" (*gazar*) from the earth, the LXX speaks of him being **taken** or "lifted up" from the earth (see 1:9-11). Luke offers the first part of these verses as a description of Jesus' death and this last portion as a reference to his exaltation.

■ **36-38** The narrator offers a subtle hint about the eunuch's reception of Philip's interpretation. He had hoped for someone to **lead the way** (v 31). Now Luke describes the two as traveling together **along the way** (v 36). This may refer not only to their literal traveling but also to "the Way" as the Christian journey (see 9:2).

The eunuch's inquiry about baptism suggests that, at some point, Philip mentioned the importance of baptism with regard to repentance and incorporation into the community of believers (see 2:38, 41; 3:26). The availability of water for baptism may also be seen as an additional sign of God's provision and guidance, which brought the two men together (Peterson 2009, 296).

Given the eunuch's physical condition, his question about anything that may hamper his baptism conveys the liberating sense of the gospel message (see Isa 56:3-8; see Parsons 2006, 133-36). Philip's baptism of the eunuch fully incorporates the Ethiopian into the community of faith.

Most MSS, including the earliest ones, do not include Acts 8:37, in which Philip asks the eunuch to affirm his faith, followed by the eunuch's confession. One may assume this affirmation of faith occurs in light of prior emphases in

Acts. Its secondary insertion here provides consistency with earlier descriptions of believers.

■ **39-40** Philip's sudden disappearance from the scene leaves readers with the lasting image of the eunuch's baptism in their minds. Like Jesus' ascension, the narrator offers only a brief statement regarding Philip's hasty departure. The verb *harpazō* suggests that the Spirit carries him off or snatches him up in a vigorous manner (see 6:12). But the text does not linger on specific details as to how this happens.

Acts 8 and Common Features with the Account of Jesus' Appearance to the Couple of Emmaus (Luke 24:13-35)

Sometimes Luke makes literary associations between Luke and Acts. This invites readers to draw comparisons and to bring aspects of earlier materials into the reading and interpretation of later materials. Several features of the Emmaus story (Luke 24:13-35) reappear in Acts 8, including:

- Travelers meeting as they traveled
- Conversation about the death and resurrection of Jesus
- Interpretation of Scripture in light of Jesus
- An invitation or request, followed by response
- Disappearance of the one who was teaching
- Emotional reaction of the one(s) left behind (See Spencer 1992, 141-44; Pervo 2009, 219-20.)

By recognizing these similarities, recurring narrative elements take on added significance as the narrative continues to unfold.

The remaining description of the eunuch focuses on his response. His joy is a typical response in the Lukan corpus to God's activity. The present participle indicates that his joy is not momentary but characterizes the rest of his journey. The reference to his journey may have the same double meaning here as in v 36. Not only did he return to Ethiopia, but he also continued on "the Way" as a member of the community of believers (→ 9:2).

One may infer from Philip's reappearance in **Azotus** (8:40), a coastal town 20 miles (32 km) northeast of Gaza, that divine guidance took him there to *continue proclaiming the good news* in towns along the Mediterranean coast. He eventually arrived in **Caesarea**, 50 miles (80 km) north of Azotus. Here he reappears in the narrative in 21:8-9. But when Caesarea becomes a center of the narrative in ch 10, there is no mention of Philip. His coastal mission must have occupied him and delayed his arrival there.

FROM THE TEXT

At a critical juncture in the narrative, the persecution of the believers scatters them from Jerusalem. Readers might wonder whether Gamaliel's comparison of the Jesus movement to other failed Jewish factions (5:36-37) was an accurate assessment after all. Like those other short-lived movements, the scattering of the followers happens after the death of their leader.

Luke clearly portrays the community of believers in Jerusalem as created and empowered by God's presence and blessing. But the question remains: Does Luke's perspective hold true, especially since the image of scattering challenges his portrayal of the unity of believers in Acts 1—7?

The example of Philip shows how God's saving work continues in areas beyond Jerusalem. The scattering contributes to the fulfillment of Jesus' promise to his apostles (1:8). Believers apparently do not make conscious plans to take the gospel to others outside the holy city. The reality of persecution forces them to go elsewhere, so that they (minus the apostles who remained in Jerusalem) proclaim the gospel wherever they go.

It is one thing to share the good news with those of similar background but quite another to do so with those who are "different." Through Philip's ministry, Luke offers two instances of the gospel extending to places and persons on the margins, to the periphery of the Jewish understanding of the "people of God."

On the one hand, the Samaritans were a peripheral people due to the history and "bad blood" between the Jews and their northern relatives. On the other hand, the eunuch was a member of a peripheral group, excluded from full participation within Israel as God's people because of physical conditions Jews considered indicative of a deficiency in their character.

Yet in both instances, God confirms their inclusion in God's people:

- The Samaritans' conversion through the coming of the Holy Spirit, and
- The Ethiopian eunuch's conversion through the Spirit's guidance of Philip, making their providential meeting possible.

Through the apostles Peter and John, Luke offers readers a glimpse into how God's purposes can bring reconciliation between parties with deep-seated estrangement. Through the Scriptures and its Spirit-guided interpretation, the narrator prepares readers to see how God's purposes can extend to persons and groups who may be marginalized by society or even by God's people (see Shauf 2009, 769-75).

Therefore, the narrative has taken a significant step forward in showing what it might look like for God's promise—the gospel—to be extended to "all who are far away" (2:39 NRSV).

B. The Transformation of Saul—from Persecutor to Persecuted Preacher (9:1-31)

BEHIND THE TEXT

One of the most memorable NT stories is the account of God's transformation of Saul from the persecutor of the church into the persecuted preacher who becomes the central figure (known as Paul) in the second half of Acts. The story is so important that Paul himself refers to it in several of his letters (1 Cor 9:1; 15:8-10; Gal 1:11-17; Phil 3:3-11), while Luke tells it three times! The three versions (Acts 9; 22; 26) of the story are similar, yet distinct.

Interpreters sometimes struggle to reconcile their divergent materials historically (e.g., Witherington 1998, 308-14). However, the more pertinent questions focus on *how* the narrator shapes and tells the story in three specific contexts. Careful attention to the ways in which the repetition contributes to the portrayal of Paul is more fruitful than attempts to harmonize the details (see Hedrick 1981, 415-32; Gaventa 1986, 52-95).

IN THE TEXT

1. The Healing and Call of Saul (9:1-19a)

■ **1-2** The narrative abruptly shifts to a different character—the scoundrel Saul—who continues (**still** [v 1]) his persecution of the believers (see 8:1-3). As Pervo notes, an ancient audience would perceive his unruly rage as a sign of a serious character flaw (2009, 240).

The association of Saul with **threats** and ***murder*** is reminiscent of the Jewish council's actions against the apostles (4:17-21; 5:27-33) and Stephen (7:54-60). The participle translated **breathing** (*empneōn*, a cognate of "Spirit") subtly depicts Saul as filled with hostility **against the Lord's disciples** rather than the Holy Spirit that characterizes believers in Acts. This antithetical description seems to be more significant than an explicit explanation for Saul's reaction against them. Perhaps, Saul understands them to be an apostate movement that is unfaithful to God, the Jewish covenant, and Israel.

It is unclear which high priest authorized Saul's intended activities or what authority the high priest had to sanction Saul's imprisonment of others. However, the request further implicated Saul with the Jewish religious leaders and their resistance against the believers in Acts 4—7.

Damascus (9:2; see 8:3) was an ancient Syrian city and strategic economic center of the Roman Empire. Located nearly 135 miles (217 km) northeast of Jerusalem, it had a significant Jewish population (see Josephus, *J.W.* 2.559-61).

186

Luke does not explain why Saul intended to go *there*. But his request assumes that some Jewish believers had been scattered there (see 8:2). For the first time, the narrator describes believers as those of **the Way** (18:25-26; 19:9, 23; 22:4; 24:14, 22). This metaphorical designation may have adapted a similar OT description of those who lived faithfully for God and the covenant (e.g., Exod 18:20; Deut 26:17; Pss 1:1, 6; 119:1, 30; Isa 40:3). Perhaps a particular way of life distinguished the Christian movement (see 2:42-47; 4:32-35; Johnson 1992, 162; Fitzmyer 1998, 423-24).

■ **3-6** As Paul approaches Damascus, his extraordinary encounter occurred without warning (see adverb *exaiphnēs*; see Luke 2:13; 9:39). The appearance of light that **flashed** (Acts 9:3; see 22:6) *around* Saul makes it impossible for him to avoid it. Light (e.g., Pss 4:6; 36:9; 78:14; 89:15; 104:2; Isa 2:5; 60:19) and lightning (e.g., Exod 19:16; 2 Sam 22:15; Pss 18:14; 77:18; 97:4; Ezek 1:4, 13-14) are often associated with God's presence. This was a theophanic moment. That is, God appears in what seemed a strategic "natural phenomenon." Saul's falling to the ground was probably a response of reverence (see Ezek 1:28; Dan 8:17; Rev 1:17), rather than a result of being knocked down.

Neither the narrator nor the voice initially identifies the speaker. However, the double address—**Saul, Saul** (Acts 9:4)—reflects OT instances when God addressed someone by repeating the person's name (e.g., Gen 22:11; 46:2; Exod 3:4; 1 Sam 3:4, 6, 10).

Saul's initial inquiry exposes his confusion. Those confronted by God typically respond with an exclamation ("Here I am!"), not a question ("**Who are you . . . ?**" [Acts 9:5]). Because of his confusion, his address of the speaker as **Lord** indicates either his reverent response to God (as the speaker in a theophanic encounter) or simply an address of respect, *"Sir."* Readers know God gave Jesus the designation "Lord" (2:36). Thus, the irony is that the confused Saul unwittingly identifies the speaker correctly and validates the gospel he vigorously opposes!

The repeated accusation that Saul is persecuting Jesus establishes two points. First, the crucified leader of the Jesus movement is alive, not dead. Second, the risen leader identifies himself with his followers as recipients of Saul's harsh attempts to suppress them.

The encounter concludes with a familiar Lukan theme about God's purposes (see verb *dei*, "it is necessary"). He instructs Saul to enter the city, not to do as he had planned, but to hear what he must do as part of that divine plan.

■ **7-9** Saul's traveling companions probably accompanied him to assist in his intended mission and to provide security. They also hear the voice but, unlike Saul, are not addressed. They do not observe **anyone** with their eyes (*theōreō* [v 7]; against Gaventa 2003, 150). Saul sees **nothing** (v 8; including Jesus). His companions stand there **speechless** (v 7), at a complete loss to explain what just happened. Or, perhaps, they are unaffected by the direct, divine confrontation Saul experienced. Some details differ from the two subsequent accounts (→ 22:8-9; 26:13-14).

Saul responds as the risen Jesus instructs, only to find that he cannot see anything or find his way into the city. Ironically, the one who intended to "lead" believers out of Damascus as prisoners is rendered so helpless that he himself must be led . . . by the hand (9:8; see 13:11).

The specific duration of his blindness—three days (9:9)—underscores the physical and emotional trauma Saul endured. Interpreters understand the reference to Saul not eating or drinking anything as descriptive of penance or fasting (e.g., Neh 1:4; Jer 14:12; Joel 1:14) or preparation to receive divine instruction (see Exod 34:28; Deut 9:9; Dan 9:1-3).

Abstinence from eating and drinking in the Third Gospel and Acts is associated with various practices besides penance and fasting (e.g., Luke 4:2; 7:33; Acts 23:12). Saul likely engaged in some serious soul-searching, which would prepare him for what would follow. Given the Lukan description of salvation as recovery of sight to the blind (Luke 4:18), his blindness hints at the transformation taking place.

■ 10-12 Thus far in Acts, Jesus' prophecy (1:8), angels (5:19-20; 8:26), and the Holy Spirit (8:29) have been cited as sources of divine guidance for the believers. To this list Luke has now added Jesus' appearance before Saul.

The double visions—to Saul and Ananias—accentuate the role of divine intervention and guidance. In this case, they explain the transformation in Saul's life. They also legitimize his later role within Acts as a catalyst in the expanding ministry of the church.

The first vision mentioned is of the Lord (9:10), the risen Jesus. Luke infers that Jesus also appeared to Ananias, described simply as *a certain disciple*, an ordinary believer in Antioch (see 22:12, which describes him as a devout observer of the Jewish law).

Luke makes no attempt to compare or contrast this Ananias with the dishonest believer of ch 5. Nor does he offer information about how believers arrived in Damascus. Ananias was simply representative of those who were targets of Saul's original plans. The narrator gives attention only to what Ananias heard and his response, not to what he saw. His initial response echoes the faithful responses of Abraham (Gen 22:1, 11) and Samuel (1 Sam 3:4) and signals his willingness to obey.

The specific details about Saul's address on Straight Street were of importance for Ananias. However, the narrator likely offers a play on words: in a house on a street called Straight (9:11), Saul was "straightened out" about the gospel, Jesus, and Jesus' followers. This contrasts with Simon the magician whose heart was not "straight" before God (8:21; Spencer 2004a, 108).

Saul/Paul and the City of Tarsus

Although the book of Acts mentions several times that the hometown of Saul/Paul was the city of Tarsus (9:11, 30; 11:25; 21:39; 22:3), nothing about this appears in the NT letters attributed to him. Tarsus was the principal city of the Roman colony of Cilicia, in southeastern Asia Minor (modern Turkey) along the Mediterranean coastline. The cosmopolitan city prospered from its strategic location on a major trade route between Syria and the rest of Asia Minor.

By the first century AD, Tarsus had become a leading intellectual and cultural center, rivaling Athens and Alexandria. Neither Luke nor Paul/Saul mentions anything about his education in the city. Many scholars assume that the Hellenistic culture of that city would have significantly influenced him during the years he lived there.

The mention of Paul **praying** (9:11), introduced by the words *idou gar* (*For, look!*), builds anticipation. In Acts, such activity has been associated with believers and has been followed by the coming of the Spirit (e.g., 1:12-14; 4:24-31).

The reference to a *second* vision, this one experienced by Saul, underscores the divine role in leading *both* characters. Some MSS omit the phrase **in a vision** (9:12), but the opening of the sentence, *and he saw a man*, suggests the same thing (see Metzger 1994, 319). The focus here is on what Saul sees, not on what he hears. This provides indirect instruction for Ananias about what he is to do. The image of Ananias laying his hands upon Saul (see 6:6; 8:17) implies that Saul's restoration of sight would come through the believer Ananias.

13-14 Ananias' objection is surprising in its emphatic tone and challenge (i.e., not a question) to Jesus' instruction. But it is understandable, given Saul's reputation. It reiterates basic information about Saul in 8:3 and 9:1-2. Luke does not explain how Ananias knows this.

Ananias' reference to reports *from many* about **how much evil** (v 13) Saul had done and his intention to arrest **all who call on your name** (v 14; see 2:21) underscores Saul as an enemy of "your holy ones." Ananias would not want Saul the persecutor to regain his sight with him standing in front of Saul! This disciple's grave reservations about Jesus' instructions help readers understand how incredible and extraordinary Saul's transformation is (see Barrett 1994, 455).

■ **15-16** The Lord's response repeats his command (9:11) and outlines an alternative identity for Saul that Ananias has not envisaged. Rather than an enemy to be shunned, Jesus identifies Saul as **my chosen instrument** or "vessel" (v 15). This refers to a particular function he would perform (BDAG 2000, 927-28). That he was **chosen** (see 1:2, 24; 6:5) indicates Saul's divine calling to serve in a role not all believers would share. This one (see genitive article

9:13-16

189

tou before *bastasai*) who had intended to arrest those who invoked Jesus' name would ironically be the one to *carry* that name.

The arrangement of **Gentiles** (or ***nations***), **kings**, and **the people of Israel** offers a programmatic look into the rest of Acts, including the ministry of Saul/Paul. Both non-Jews and Jews are included in the subsequent ministry of the church and Saul.

The suffering that is a necessary (*dei*) part of Saul's new identity reverses Ananias' depiction of Saul. The one who came to do harm would now receive such harm (Haenchen 1971, 325). Suffering would align Saul with Moses and Jesus in the line of suffering prophets (see Luke 9:22; 17:25; 22:37; 24:7, 26). By suffering in Jesus' name, Saul would do so as Jesus' representative (see Luke 6:22; 21:12, 17; Acts 5:41; Johnson 1992, 165). The persecutor would become the one others persecuted. Luke does not indicate that Saul hears these words from Jesus (see 26:16-18) or even from Ananias (see 22:14-15). But the message to Ananias implies that the risen Lord would tell Saul about such matters.

■ **17-19a** Ananias' response conveys his obedience (9:11-12). That obedience and his address of Saul as **brother** (v 17) indicate Ananias' own transformed perceptions about the former persecutor and his acceptance of Saul. Ananias' message to Saul makes two additions to the vision material.

First, Ananias speaks about Jesus' appearance to Saul. Although he does not specifically mention that Saul actually saw Jesus, a later reference does (26:12-18, esp. 26:16; see also 22:17-21).

Second, Ananias declares that he came so that Saul may **be filled with the Holy Spirit** (*plēsthēs pneumatos hagiou* [9:17]; see 2:4; 4:8, 31; 6:3, 5; 7:55). God would empower him to witness. This serves implicitly as a sign of Saul's commission to proclaim the gospel (9:15-16). The gesture of laying his hands on Saul indicates the community's role in his healing.

The metaphorical description of **something like scales** falling from Saul's eyes may reflect common notions about blindness (v 18; see Tob 3:17; 11:13), which Ananias' touch reversed.

Saul's baptism signifies his incorporation into the Christian community. Luke does not mention the coming of the Spirit, but readers may infer from Ananias' words and actions, as well as from other episodes in Acts, that this happens.

Fellowship and meals in Acts figure prominently in Acts (see Acts 2:42, 46; 6:1-7). The grammatical connection between Saul's baptism and what follows indicate that the strength he gained comes not only from the food he eats but also from the disciples with whom he shares the meal (see Brawley 1990, 153; Heil 1999, 245-47).

2. The Initial Ministry of Saul in Damascus (9:19b-25)

■ **19b-20** The most visible sign of Saul's inclusion within the believing community of Damascus was the **several days** (v 19b) he spends with them. This small detail implies something significant: the Christian community accepted Saul.

The conjunction *kai* ("and") grammatically links believers in Damascus to the activities mentioned next: Saul's preaching in the city's Jewish synagogues. As in preceding chapters, the proclamation of the gospel comes out of the community of believers, which Luke has consistently depicted as blessed by God's presence, united in worship, and motivated to care for one another.

Thus, like Philip, Saul's ministry begins (imperfect tense: *ekēryssen*) with preaching (8:5). The synagogue setting corresponds to the apostles' proclamation within the temple. He proclaims Jesus as **the Son of God** (9:20), the only time this common NT title for Jesus appears in Acts (see 13:33, which quotes Ps 2:7).

We should not assume that the title's meaning corresponds with that found in the Pauline letters or even in the Third Gospel. It may be better to understand it as synonymous with the designation "Christ" or "Messiah" (9:22). This was often the case in Jewish literature (Bruce 1988, 190; see, e.g., 2 Sam 7:14; Pss 2:7; 89:26-27; *1 En.* 105:2; *4 Ezra* 7:28-29; 13:32, 37, 52).

■ **21-22** Saul's preaching provokes an ambivalent response from everyone (*pantes*) who hears him. The verb *existēmi*, which often connotes surprise or amazement, suggests that they are unable to accept what they hear, given Saul's notoriety. Their skeptical questions mirror Ananias' initial response (Acts 9:13-14).

The verb *portheō* describes Paul's persecution (v 21; see Gal 1:13, 23). It conveys violent actions intent on destroying its victims or plundering something. Their reference to **this name** (v 21) points back to Saul's proclamation of Jesus as the Christ. Surprisingly, this man who had targeted **those who call on this name** (see Acts 9:14; 2:21) now speaks as if he belongs to that same group! The one who came to capture believers in Damascus now sounds as if he is the target of his own manhunt!

Luke depicts Saul as becoming ***increasingly more powerful*** or effective in proclaiming the gospel (9:22). The verb *endynamoō* in both the LXX (Judg 6:34; 1 Chr 12:18) and the NT (Rom 4:20; Phil 4:13; Eph 6:10; 1 Tim 1:12; 2 Tim 2:1; 4:17) describes divine enablement for ministry. This description alludes to earlier glimpses of believers. It implies some degree of acceptance among those who heard him speak (see Acts 4:7, 33; 6:8; 8:13; Thompson 2006, 123).

The verb **baffled** or ***confused*** conveys the same reaction to the initial hearing of the gospel as that of the Pentecost bystanders (2:6). It suggests that conflict was growing among the Jews (Tyson 1992, 119). Luke ascribes that confusion to Saul **proving** or literally "bringing together" (see 16:10; 19:33; 1 Cor 2:16) convincing evidence that Jesus was the Messiah. He probably draws from the OT to make the case in a manner similar to earlier speeches in Acts.

"The Jews" in Acts

For the first time in Acts, Luke mentions a general group designated the Jews (9:22). They resisted and opposed the followers of Jesus. Prior to this reference, opponents in Acts were specific Jewish religious leaders or groups, such as the Sadducees, the chief priests, the elders, or scribes. In the Gospel of Luke, that list also included the Pharisees.

In v 22, the designation is modified to refer specifically to the Jews living in Damascus. From this point forward, Luke identifies "the Jews" in a generalized manner as opponents of the Christian movement, without further specification.

However, repeated references to *both* Jewish acceptance of the gospel *and* Jewish resistance later in Acts indicate that readers should not conclude that the church had severed all ties with Judaism and the Jewish people. Rather, ambiguity and tension signal the ongoing struggle regarding the definition of what it meant to be the people of God.

■ **23-25** The vague reference to the passing of **many days** (v 23) correlates with the imperfect verb tense describing Saul's ongoing practices in vv 20 and 22. Thus, it is unnecessary to find consistency regarding basic chronology between Luke's version and Paul's in Gal 1:17-18 (against Peterson 2009, 314).

The Jews' involvement in a conspiracy (*symbouleō*) to murder Saul (see also Acts 9:24; see 5:33; 8:1) places them in opposition to God's plan (*boulē* [2:23; 4:28; 5:38-39; 13:36; 20:27]). By not offering any explicit explanation, the narrator subtly emphasizes the danger that Saul faces from the Jews who oppose him. Perhaps it also marks the beginning of suffering the risen Jesus declared that Saul would endure (Fitzmyer 1998, 436).

Somehow, Saul found out about their sinister **scheme** (*epiboulē* [v 24]; see 20:3, 19; 23:30). An anonymous source probably informed him (as the passive voice of *egnōsthē* suggests).

Luke tells about the activities of two very different groups.

On the one hand, Jewish opponents **kept close watch** (*paratēreō*). In the NT Gospels, this verb always conveys suspicion (Mark 3:2; Luke 6:7; 14:1; 20:20; see Gal 4:10). Both its imperfect tense and reference to **day and night** characterize the Jews as so intent on murdering Saul that they watch the city gates around the clock to prevent his escape.

On the other hand, Saul is protected by another group, which Luke describes as **his** [i.e., Saul's] **disciples** (v 25). This is an unusual expression; elsewhere in Acts disciples belong to Jesus (or the Lord). Some MSS and interpreters omit the pronoun "his" and suggest that "the disciples" is the original wording. The expression may simply refer to those who responded favorably to Saul's message. However, this may also be another indication of Saul's transformation: the one who came to hunt down disciples of the Lord now could claim these same disciples as his own in some limited sense (Gaventa 2003, 154).

Whoever they are, Saul's partisans smuggle him out of the city. The details parallel Paul's account in 2 Cor 11:32-33. Saul was **lowered** (Acts 9:25; 2 Cor 11:33) to safety *through the wall* in a *large basket* (*spyris*) to safety. Paul describes this as an escape from the governor of Damascus (2 Cor 11:32). His Jewish opponents may have colluded with the political leaders against him (see Act 13:50; 14:5-6, 19-20; see, e.g., Marshall 1980, 174; Barrett 1994, 466). Luke depicts Saul's escape from Damascus as similar to the believers' flight from Jerusalem to escape Saul's hostile pursuits (8:3-4). Saul the persecutor has truly become the persecuted preacher!

3. The Introduction of the Transformed Saul in Jerusalem (9:26-31)

■ **26** Saul's return to Jerusalem would remind both readers and the narrative characters of his role in the persecution of believers in the holy city. This reputation thwarts his overtures to become part of the community of believers, the existence of which Luke does not explain after the persecution in Jerusalem had scattered all believers except the apostles (8:1).

The verb **join** (see 5:13; 8:29) implies that Saul wishes to identify himself with them, yet the imperfect tense of the verbs translated **tried** and *feared* suggest that his *repeated* attempts at doing so are *consistently* met with skepticism from **all** (*pantes*) the disciples in Jerusalem. According to the narrator, they suspect that Paul may have resorted to covert means in his mission to crush the movement. Their hesitation is like that of Ananias (9:13-14; Brawley 1990, 151; Tannehill 1990, 123). However, their persistence is more like that of those who first heard Saul in the Damascus synagogues (v 21; Thompson 2006, 127).

■ **27** The reemergence of Barnabas as an intermediary on Saul's behalf is consistent with his earlier characterization as the "son of encouragement" (4:36). His confidence in Saul counters the initial response of the Jerusalem believers. No reason is offered for Barnabas taking control of the situation (as *epilambanō* connotes).

Barnabas personally escorts Saul to meet the apostles, who probably had similar reservations about Saul. He *recites them Saul's story* (*diēgeomai* refers to narration). Readers are left to fill in the gaps regarding the source of Barnabas' information. Barnabas makes three points.

First, Saul saw **the Lord** (see v 17). This provides evidence of divine initiative and validation about Saul's drastic change.

Second, Saul heard from the Lord, a reference to what Jesus said to him initially (vv 4-6). It may imply whatever else he may have heard during or after

193

that encounter (v 16; see 22:14-15; 26:16-18). Perhaps this implies that Saul spoke with Jesus. Saul is the implied subject of all three verbs. However, the conjunction *hoti* ("that") makes it more likely that Barnabas underscores Jesus' call of Saul.

Third, Saul had **spoken boldly** about Jesus (see 4:13, 29, 31). Luke repeatedly links the reference to **the name of Jesus** to the promised salvation (see 2:21). Thus, Barnabas' narration reiterates what readers of Acts already know: the risen Jesus confronted Saul and called him to be his spokesperson. This resulted in Saul's transformation. The Spirit empowered him for effective proclamation of the gospel.

■ **28-30** The periphrastic constructions about Saul **going in** and **going out** of the city refer to ordinary life activities in the company of the apostles (**with them** [v 28]). Barnabas' intervention convinces them to accept Saul without further reservation. Since Luke portrays the community of believers in Jerusalem as acting in unanimity, the others likely join in accepting the transformed Saul.

Saul's bold proclamation continues (v 27). Saul's ministry included **the Hellenists** (v 29; see 6:1)—Greek-speaking Jews or Jews from the Diaspora (see 2:5-11), likely the same group that opposed Stephen (6:8-11) and that once included Saul himself (→ 7:58). Like Stephen, Saul becomes embroiled in debates with these Jews (see 6:9). They probably see Saul as a threat, perhaps angered that their ally has defected to the "enemy," the Jesus movement.

Their persistent attempts (see imperfect tense: *epecheiroun*) to murder (see 9:23-24; 5:33; 8:1*b*) Saul are foiled by "the brothers" (9:30 [NIV84]). This probably refers more generally to **believers**, not just the apostles (see v 25). The verb referring to such attempts (*epicheireō*) depicts persons placing their hands upon a specific task they wished to accomplish. In contrast to the Christian practice of laying hands on others for divine blessing or empowerment, these Jewish opponents put their hands to a deadly mission—to murder God's chosen instrument (9:15).

They took Saul to Caesarea, about 65 miles (105 km) northwest of Jerusalem. Then they sent him to Tarsus. He could travel by land or sea from there. Caesarea increasingly becomes a strategic location for the expansion of the Christian mission in Acts. This becomes obvious in the next chapter.

■ **31** The conjunctions *men oun* indicate that this summary functions as a transition. The subject is **the church** (*hē ekklēsia*). Here, it refers not to a local assembly of believers (see 5:11; 8:1, 3) but to Jewish believers scattered over a larger area. This may explain why some MSS have **the churches** (Metzger 1994, 322-23). The area of Judea, Galilee, and Samaria approximately comprises the territory of ancient Israel. Luke's description corresponds with the geographical boundaries of ancient Israel, the historic people of God. **Galilee**, not previously mentioned in Acts, was where Jesus' ministry began in Luke's Gospel.

Luke describes the general situation in two ways. First, the church experienced **peace**. This may be due to the transformation of her archenemy, or to the removal of Saul as a target of Jewish opposition. In the Third Gospel, peace is linked with the good news (e.g., Luke 1:79; 2:14, 29; 7:50; 8:48; 10:5-6; 19:38, 42; 24:36).

Second, the church *continued to grow in numbers*, as it had before Stephen's death and the ensuing persecution (Acts 6:1, 7). God's blessing continues (see imperfect tense: *eplēthyneto*) to characterize the Christian community.

The participle translated *was being built up* (*oikodomoumenē*) metaphorically speaks about strengthening a person in faith or a group in size (see esp. 1 Cor 2:9-14; 8:1, 10; 10:23; 14:3-5, 12, 17). The passive form implies that this is the work of God.

They lived in **the fear of the Lord**. This is a common OT expression referring to living in ways that show holy reverence for God (e.g., Pss 19:9; 34:11; 111:10; Prov 1:7; 8:13; 10:27) that is appropriated later in Acts (e.g., 10:2, 22, 35; 13:16, 20). Here, "Lord" likely refers to the risen Jesus, as is usual in Acts. And they lived in *the encouragement of the Holy Spirit,* which may refer either to the Spirit's encouraging (see John 14:26-27; Wall 2002, 154) or more likely the encouragement of one another as the Spirit enabled them (Barrett 1994, 474).

Luke depicts the regional church holistically in glowing terms, not just at one specific moment but in an ongoing manner (see the imperfect tense indicatives and the present tense participles).

FROM THE TEXT

Of all the episodes in Acts, the account of Saul's dramatic encounter with the risen Jesus may be the most memorable, due to the radical transformation of Saul from the leading antagonist against the believers to the most ardent protagonist of the Christian gospel. His life drastically changed in its mission and direction due to that encounter. Saul became in many ways the "poster child" of evangelistic calls to accept the gospel message. This story of Saul's "conversion," as it is often described, has become a paradigm in many circles for those who become Christian converts.

As readers within the church consider this significant portion of Acts as Scripture, there are two aspects of this extended section that may continue to shape Christian understandings regarding salvation and Christian practices.

First, the transformation of Saul cannot be limited to contemporary understandings about conversion—entering the Christian faith—prevalent in many Christian circles. This is one reason why scholars debate whether or not Saul's encounter with the risen Jesus should be considered a "conversion."

Contemporary experiences and evangelistic calls for such experiences often read ideas into the Acts story that go well beyond what the text itself implies.

Luke's account does mirror conversion stories of his day (e.g., Talbert 1997, 93-103). But conversion may take one of several forms:

- from one general way of life to another,
- from a lack of knowledge to a particular philosophy,
- from one school of thought to another,
- from paganism or polytheism to monotheism,
- even from one form of Jewish thought and life to another (as may be true regarding Saul).

Saul did not convert to belief in the God of Israel, since that was already central to his Jewish beliefs. He did not disavow the Jewish law, as Acts will subsequently reveal. Saul/Paul continued to live as a faithful Jew. However, Saul *did* experience conversion with regard to Jesus, in that the encounter with the *risen* Jesus disproved Saul's contention that the believers were mistaken about the *dead* Jesus of Nazareth. Nonetheless, for Luke's telling of this story, there was more to Saul's transformation than simply whether or not he was identified with the believers.

Luke does not employ conversion terminology to describe Saul's transformation. He describes a healing (typically associated with salvation) and a divine commission. The result for Saul was not merely a change in ideas but a change in life and mission. The evidence of his transformation is in those glimpses into Saul's post-encounter settings in which the tables were turned—in which the persecutor became the preacher. His initial steps into Christian ministry in response to his call from the risen Jesus led to his persecution.

Luke describes Saul's salvation consistently in other scenes with other persons throughout Acts. "Personal transformation never collapses into sanctified self-absorption. Rather, conversion prepares the believer for performance of concrete tasks in the service of God" (Wall 2002, 155). The sense of mission that accompanies Paul's about-face is inseparable from conversion. This provides an important corrective to contemporary emphases, which too often focus on confessional declarations with little attention to a faithful life of service and ministry.

Second, an important aspect of Saul's conversion may be observed in the role of the Christian community in his transformation and ensuing ministry. Saul was alone for three days after his encounter with the risen Jesus near Damascus. But Saul's fledgling ministry began only as he entered the Christian faith community. The church provided the context for the confirmation and strengthening of his faith. His ministry in both Damascus and Jerusalem came out of his participation in the community of believers. Even his safety was ensured by the believers, who cared for his needs when those opposing him seemed to have him trapped and vulnerable to their death wishes.

As in earlier chapters in Acts, images like these contribute to the Lukan depiction of the church as the people of God. Transformation entails more than the experience of God's salvation and presence. Salvation must be lived out in tangible, missional ways.

It is a mistake to view Saul's conversion in purely individualistic or personal ways. The Lukan account suggests that the story of this transformation of Saul's life and mission may not have been told apart from the role of the Christian community in accepting and nurturing him from the beginning. The church prepared him to move into contexts of effective ministry.

Acts' emphasis upon the communal dimensions of salvation and mission were recovered in the eighteenth-century Wesleyan movement. The stories of both Paul and the Wesleys may remind today's church of her essential role in enabling transformation. This is possible only as she embodies God's salvation through her ecclesial life and ministry.

C. The Extension of Peter's Ministry outside Jerusalem (9:32—11:18)

BEHIND THE TEXT

The reintroduction of Peter returns attention to apostolic activity and its importance in authenticating the movement of the gospel beyond Jerusalem. In many respects, the two appearances of the apostles since their appointment of the Seven (6:1-6) function merely to authenticate the faith of others and their inclusion within the community of believers (→ 8:14-25; 9:26-30).

As the narrator recounts the church's ministry beyond the holy city and in the surrounding regions, he also associates this activity with the apostolic commission of Jesus. God's plan and purposes through Jesus were the catalyst of this expanding ministry. By focusing again on Peter, the narrator reestablishes these emphases. As leader and representative of the apostles, his presence helps readers recognize past and upcoming activities as within that divine plan.

One prominent literary feature of the Lukan corpus is the travel narrative. He depicts Jesus and his disciples as traveling from one place to another (see Luke 9:51—19:27). Paul's ministry will be narrated as a series of journeys (13:1—14:28; 15:36—18:22; 18:23—21:16). Similarly, Peter traveled about the general region surrounding Jerusalem and then returned to the holy city. These trips were in areas in proximity to the Mediterranean coast, where Philip had ministered (8:40). Philip's ministry may have paved the way for Peter's journey, including his momentous meeting with the Gentile Cornelius in Caesarea.

I. Peter's Miracles among Some Believers (9:32-43)

a. Peter's Healing of Aeneas (9:32-35)

■ **32** Since the apostles remained in Jerusalem after the persecution following Stephen's death, the vague description of Peter's travels "here and there" (NRSV) probably refers to the general region around that city. The reference to "God's holy people" (CEB; see v 13) who lived in the town of **Lydda** suggests that Peter was visiting and supporting believers whom he found in the area, much like he did in Samaria (8:25). **Lydda** was located in the coastal plain of Sharon, about 25 miles (40 km) northwest of Jerusalem on the road to Joppa, a town about 15 miles (24 km) further up the road on the Mediterranean coast.

■ **33-34** The abbreviated account of Peter's encounter with Aeneas resembles Jesus' healing of a paralyzed man (Luke 5:17-26; ‖ Mark 2:1-12; Matt 9:2-8; → Acts 8:7). Like the previous account of Peter healing the crippled man, the stated duration of the condition underscores its debilitating effects (→ 3:2; 4:22).

As in the previous healing of the cripple at the temple, Peter attributes this healing to Jesus as the Christ, God's anointed one (see 3:6). Here, Peter merely declares that Jesus healed the man and did not call upon Jesus to do that. The command *make your bed* emphasizes that Aeneas should do this *himself*; he responds **immediately** as evidence of his healing (9:34).

It is unclear whether Aeneas was already one of the believers in Lydda when he was healed. The narrative focuses on the healing power of Jesus through the apostle Peter, not on Aeneas and his faith. The favorable image that links the healing to the community of believers contrasts with the controversy that Jesus' healing of a paralytic stirred up among the Pharisees and scribes (Luke 5:17-26; see Wall 2002, 161).

■ **35** The residents of the city and the surrounding coastal plain of Sharon confirm the divine source of Aeneas' healing. **All** of them saw what happened and responded favorably. This obvious hyperbole conveys the overwhelming response to God's gracious act.

The verb **turned** (*epistrephō*) is the same conversion language employed earlier in Peter's address to Jewish temple worshipers (3:19). Some interpreters suggest that all these converts were Jewish, since in Acts Gentile conversions occur only after Peter's meeting with Cornelius (e.g., Barrett 1994, 482; Dunn 1996, 129; Haenchen 1971, 338; Weiser 1986, 1:243). But this included both Jewish and Gentile populations. The general description of conversions to Jesus as **to the Lord** implies that some converts were Gentiles (e.g., Bruce 1988, 198; Marshall 1980, 179).

ACTS

9:32-35

In this short section, the narrative depicts the gospel spreading to persons and places of ambiguous status with regard to traditional Jewish understandings of the concept "people of God."

b. Peter's Raising of Tabitha (9:36-43)

Luke often pairs scenes, with one featuring a male character and another a female character. The story of Peter raising Tabitha from the dead has more detail, however, suggesting that important developments lay ahead.

■ **36** Joppa, the setting of this section, is a Mediterranean port city 10 miles (16 km) from Lydda.

The City of Joppa within Biblical History

Joppa's (now Jaffa) place within biblical history is easily eclipsed by better known cities. But its strategic location as a port on the eastern Mediterranean coast made Joppa an economic and cultural connection between Palestine and the broader Mediterranean.

For centuries, the city's population was largely Gentile. When Solomon constructed the temple in Jerusalem, and when it was rebuilt after the Babylonian exile, timbers from Lebanon were shipped by way of Joppa (2 Chr 2:16; Ezra 3:7). From Joppa, Jonah boarded a ship bound for Tarshish (Jonah 1:2-3). In Acts, the narrator identifies Joppa as the setting of Peter's divine call to accompany the messengers of the Gentile Cornelius back to Cornelius' house (Acts 10:5-23a). That divine call formally opened the door in Acts to the inclusion of Gentiles within the Christian mission.

Luke describes Tabitha in greater detail than Aeneas. The term *mathētria*, only here in the NT (*Gos. Pet.* 12.50 uses the term for Mary Magdalene), identifies Tabitha as a female disciple. Most interpreters and translators treat the term as a feminine counterpart to a male disciple (*mathētēs*). But its rarity suggests it may be a title for her role among the believers in Joppa (Anderson 2004, 45). This would explain why the other disciples in Joppa sent representatives to summon Peter upon her death (v 38).

The inclusion of her Hebrew/Aramaic and Greek names, both meaning "gazelle," also hints of her stature within the Christian community and the city itself. As with Lydda, the population of Joppa included both Jews and Gentiles (Barrett 1994, 483).

The term *plērēs*, "full" (see 6:3, 5, 8; 7:55), signals something about Tabitha's character. Her reputation for ***good works and alms*** (→ 3:2-3 about alms) identifies her as a woman of financial means. She embodied her Jewish piety by generously caring for those in need. Such a description also mirrors previous images of the believers' provision for the needy (2:44-45; 4:32-35).

■ **37** The beginning of the next sentence (*egeneto de*, "now it happened") introduces what made this particular story noteworthy. Tabitha became ill and died while Peter was in the vicinity (**in those days**; 9:32-35).

Mention of those (perhaps women; see Keener 1993, 349) who washed the body reflects then contemporary Jewish and Roman practice in preparation for burial. Anointing of the body, also common, is not mentioned. This detail confirms Tabitha's death.

The laying of the body in an **upstairs room** may allude to the story of Elijah and the dead son of the widow in Zarephath (1 Kgs 17:17-24), since Elijah carried the dead son to an upper room (1 Kgs 17:19). However, in Acts Luke only refers to this type of room as a location where Christians assembled (Acts 1:13; 20:8). Since only the homes of the wealthy had two stories, it is plausible that believers in Joppa regularly met at Tabitha's home. This further supports the conclusion that she was a church leader (Spencer 2004a, 117-18).

■ **38-39** The care the disciples extend to the deceased Tabitha also includes their summons of Peter. It is unclear how they knew Peter was in the area. Their brief request offers no explanation for the summons or any hint that they hope for something miraculous (against Marshall 1980, 179; Longenecker 1981, 382). Their polite request that Peter not delay implies only that he may not want to travel to Joppa, so as to avoid its predominantly Gentile populace. However, it may also indicate the need for him to come before the corpse began to decompose.

Peter returns with them. Upon arrival (presumably later that same day), they (either the two messengers or other unidentified believers) escort Peter into the same upstairs room where they have placed Tabitha's body. Since Luke mentions only **the widows** in the room (v 39), Tabitha probably had no surviving immediate family. The weeping widows create a sense of pathos and reveal the tremendous loss felt over her death.

The widows' display (as the verb *epideiknymi* suggests; see LSJ 1996, 629) of Tabitha's handiwork offers tangible evidence of her benevolence (v 36). The two terms for clothing—*chitōn* ("inner garment") and *himation* ("outer garment")—suggest that Tabitha was responsible for fully clothing others. Perhaps these widows were poor and beneficiaries of her generosity. However, the text states simply that she made the clothing while she was still **with them**. Tabitha may have led the widows in a ministry of "good works" (v 36 NRSV) or employed them in a shop that enabled them to support themselves while also caring for the needs of others (Finger 2007, 260).

■ **40-41** The participle *ekbalōn* conveys an abrupt, forceful removal of **all** those gathered in the upper room (v 40). This includes the widows and other believers (see Mark 5:40). Luke offers no reason for Peter clearing the room. The elimination of the commotion may have been part of it.

200

Luke instead directs readers' attention to Peter. He knelt to pray, much like Elisha in 2 Kgs 4:32-34. What happens next is the obvious result of divine intervention, not Peter's inherent abilities. The specific command to Tabitha is identical to the first part of Peter's instructions to Aeneas (Acts 9:34). However, in this instance, the wording takes on greater significance, since the root verb *anistēmi* often appears in Acts with reference to Jesus' resurrection (see 2:24, 32; 3:26; 13:33, 34).

Tabitha's physical response confirms the divine answer to Peter's prayer. After helping her stand up (the verb *anistēmi* again), Peter summons the **saints** as well as the widows, and **presented her to them alive** (9:41; compare the Lukan description of Jesus' resurrection appearances in 1:3; Johnson 1992, 178). The repeated verb *paristēmi* ("stood around" [v 39]; **presented** [v 41]) underscores the remarkable event: to the widows "present" to mourn Tabitha's death (v 39), Peter **presented** her very much alive!

Peter's Raising of Tabitha and Jesus' Raising of Jairus' Daughter (Luke 8:40-42*a*, 49-56)

Commentators often note the similarities between this account of Peter raising up Tabitha and the account in the Third Gospel of Jesus raising Jairus' daughter from the dead (Luke 8:40-42*a*, 49-56; || Mark 5:21-24*a*, 35-43; Matt 9:18-19, 23-26). Basic similarities include the following:

- The presence of mourners (*klaiō*),
- The clearing of the room where the deceased was located,
- The command to "get up" directed to the deceased,
- The offering of a helping hand,
- The person's response of "getting up,"
- The response by others to the miracle.

Although there are also differences between the accounts, the similarities encourage readers to see Peter as one who resembles Jesus (see also Luke 7:11-17). In fact, similarities between this story and OT stories of Elijah (raising the widow's son [I Kgs 17:17-24]) and Elisha (raising the Shunammite's son [2 Kgs 4:18-37]) depict Peter in the line of these OT prophets (see Tannehill 1990, 126-27). However, Peter does not accomplish these things because of his inherent divine power. Rather, his prayer signifies that he continues to seek God's power and salvation by calling on "the name of the Lord" (2:21).

■ **42** Given Tabitha's standing in Joppa, it is likely that news of her death had already made its way through the city. Reports of the miraculous restoration of her life would spread even more quickly. Again, the result of this healing was that **many people believed in the Lord.** In both instances, the summaries omit details about what brought the people to the point of faith. Readers are allowed to fill in those details by inference from previous episodes in Acts.

Elsewhere, the proclamation of the gospel typically accompanied healings. This led persons to faith (see 3:12-26 followed by 4:4; 5:12-14; 8:5-12).

■ **43** A vague time reference makes it difficult to reconstruct a precise historical chronology. However, the **many days** (see 9:23) that Peter stayed in Joppa fits the basic pattern in Peter's ministry in Acts 8 and following: the proclamation of the gospel led to conversions, after which an unspecified time follows (perhaps for instruction and nurture in the faith). The repeated references to Joppa (vv 36, 43; 10:5, 23) suggest its importance, perhaps in contrast to traditional negative associations of the city with Jonah (→ sidebar "The City of Joppa within Biblical History" with 9:36).

Reference to Peter's place of lodging concludes this section with a detail that raises more questions than it answers. A tanner's work with animal hides brought him in contact with dead animals, animal blood, and urine used in the tanning process. Jews typically considered those in such occupations perpetually "unclean." They ridiculed them for the unpleasant odors associated with their work.

The narrator does not explain why Peter lodged with *this* man of questionable status instead of a socially respectable believer in Joppa. This concise notation may be another example of someone of ambiguous purity status connected to the people of God. These categories will become the major point of contention for Peter in the next chapter.

2. Peter, Cornelius, and the Salvation of Gentiles (10:1-48)

No other single event receives more attention in Acts than the conversion of Cornelius. After this account of the conversion and acceptance of Gentiles into the Christian community, much of the remaining narrative deals with issues and questions that arose because other Gentiles, along with some Jewish individuals, accepted the gospel message. The salvation of Gentiles indicates the fulfillment of Joel's prophecy Peter quoted on Pentecost (2:21). Undoubtedly, Peter himself did not appreciate all this entailed when he first cited it. The inclusion of Gentiles may have been the most problematic issue that the Christian church had faced so far, since she was comprised entirely of *Jewish* believers.

a. An Angel Appears to Cornelius (10:1-8)

■ **1-2** The narrative setting shifts to **Caesarea** (v 1), a Gentile city about 30 miles (48 km) north of Joppa. It had been rebuilt by Herod the Great in honor of Augustus Caesar on the site of Strato's Tower, an ancient trading station and settlement between Egypt and the Fertile Crescent. The construction of its harbor (see Josephus, *Ant.* 15.331-41) made Caesarea a commercial center and the seat for the Roman military in that part of the world.

This explains why Cornelius lived in Caesarea. He was a **centurion**, a Roman military official in charge of one hundred soldiers. The entire *Italian Cohort* of which he was a member would have had around six hundred soldiers. Because he was a Roman military official, Cornelius was not Jewish. But he would have had significant social and financial standing. Centurions were expected to be good leaders who possessed wisdom (Polybius, *Hist.* 6.24.8).

The name **Cornelius** was common in the first century (after Cornelius Sulla freed thousands of slaves in 82 BC). But the narrator depicts him as having uncommon character and religious piety. Luke describes Cornelius and those of his household—his family members and servants—in four ways more expected of *Jews* than Gentiles.

First, he was **devout** (v 2) or pious, devoted to God. The specific term (*eusebēs*) appears only in this context (see v 7) and 2 Pet 2:9 to describe Jewish reverence for God (e.g., Sir 11:17; 13:17; 27:11; 2 Macc 12:45).

Second, he *feared God* (see also Acts 10:22), an OT theme of allegiance to God (e.g., 2 Chr 5:6; Pss 115:9-11; 118:2-4; 135:19-20; Prov 1:7; 3:7, 9:10). Luke reserves this description for Gentiles who worshiped the God of Israel.

The Godfearers

In Acts, the narrator depicts some Gentiles as those who feared God (10:2, 22; 13:16, 26). No evidence exists to suggest this was a technical term for Gentiles associated with the God of Israel. Luke uses it for Gentiles drawn to Jewish beliefs, worship, faith, and practice (presumably at Jewish synagogues), but who had not become circumcised Jewish proselytes (see 2:11; 6:5; 13:43). Although still considered Gentiles and outsiders to the Jewish people as the people of God, they regularly attended synagogue and sought to live according to the ethical aspects of the Jewish law.

In Acts, "Godfearers" were often prime candidates for conversion to the Christian gospel. In fact, this "Godfearer" designation would apply to most Gentile converts in Acts (see Tyson 1995, 19-38; Levinskaya 1996, 51-126; Barrett 1994, 499-501; Witherington 1998, 341-44).

Third, Cornelius gave *much alms* or charitable donations for those in need, an OT sign of faithfulness to God and God's call to provide for the poor (→ 3:2-3 and 8:36). That he directed such acts toward the Jewish people (*laos* as Acts uses the term) indicates his concern to follow God's commands about the vulnerable among God's people.

Fourth, Cornelius **prayed to God**, a characteristic of faithful Jews and particularly Jewish believers in Jerusalem (1:14; 2:42; 3:1; 4:24-30; 6:6). The phrase *dia pantos*, **always** or "constantly" (NRSV), clarifies that prayer was a regular or habitual practice of the Gentile Cornelius.

These last two life practices of this *Gentile* reflect traditional *Jewish* piety and faithfulness to God (see Tob 12:8; Matt 6:2-6; 1 Pet 4:7-11; *Did.* 15:4; 2

Clem. 16:4). Overall, Cornelius is like the centurion who sent Jewish elders to request that Jesus would return with them and heal his servant (Luke 7:1-10).

■ **3** Cornelius' vision occurs at approximately *the ninth hour* or **three in the afternoon**, one of the Jewish times of prayer (see 3:1). The text implies that he is praying, as he himself later confirms (10:30). Although the term translated **vision** may refer generally to any object of sight, in Acts it refers to supernatural or divine sightings (7:31; 9:10, 12; 10:17, 19; 11:5; 12:9; 16:9-10; 18:9; see Matt 17:9). The vision during a time of prayer underscores its divine origin. Cornelius is the only *Gentile* recipient of such a vision in Acts. The adverb translated *clearly* indicates that Cornelius could not possibly misinterpret this vision of **an angel of God**, signifying divine guidance and help (see 5:19; 8:26; 12:7; 27:23).

■ **4** Cornelius' response is typical for someone who had a divine encounter in Acts. The verb *atenizō* (1:10; 3:4, 12; 6:15; 7:55; 11:6; 13:9; 14:9; 23:1) describes Cornelius as staring at the angel, giving him complete attention. His response may have been out of terror, but more likely it was out of reverent awe (see 10:2).

He addresses the angel as **Lord**, conveying respect for God's messenger, and then asks about the purpose behind the meeting. The angel notes Cornelius' practice of praying and giving alms (see v 2), reaffirming his piety and faithfulness. The image of such practices having gone up **as a memorial . . . before God** is reminiscent of grain offerings burned and presented to God (see Lev 2:2; Sir 35:6; 50:16; Tob 12:12).

■ **5-6** The angel instructs the *Gentile* Cornelius much as if he were a devout *Jew*. His representatives are to **summon** (*metapempō* [Acts 10:5]) one Simon called Peter, to distinguish him from Simon the tanner, Peter's host (see 9:43). The house of Simon the tanner may have been outside the city, due to the stench and "uncleanness" associated with his occupation (see Bruce 1984, 216).

Later rabbinic literature (e.g., *m. Ketub.* 7.10; *m. B. Bat.* 2.9) offers considerable disparaging comments about tanners. Peter's stay with someone of marginal religious and social status may have helped prepare him for the next step in the Christian mission (see Spencer 2004a, 123). The angel did not explain why Cornelius should summon Peter or what he should expect upon Peter's arrival.

■ **7-8** The promptness of Cornelius' response underscores his obedience to the angel's instructions. He commissions three trusted representatives to go to Joppa in his behalf: two household servants and a **devout soldier** (10:7; see v 2; participles of the same verb, *proskartereō*, describe the believers in 1:14; 2:42, 46; 6:4).

As the verb *exēgeomai* (Luke 24:35; Acts 15:12, 14; 21:9; John 1:18) connotes, Cornelius fully informs his envoys of his vision and the angel's instructions before sending them off to Joppa to find Peter. They also know about the divine prompting behind their mission (as the verb *apostellō* implies).

b. Peter's Heavenly Vision (10:9-16)

■ **9-12** Luke again employs double visions to accentuate the divine guidance. The second instance occurred during the day after the departure of Cornelius' representatives. Like Cornelius, Peter is praying.

The location **on the roof** (v 9), presumably something like a terrace, provided some privacy for Peter to pray (see 2 Kgs 23:12; Neh 8:16; Jer 19:13; 32:29; Fitzmyer 1998, 454), but that setting also lent itself well to the vision (see Acts 10:11).

The *sixth hour* or **noon** was a time for a meal rather than prayer, which explains why Peter became **hungry** (v 10) and associated the vision with this time and context. While unidentified persons prepared the meal, a **trance** comes upon Peter, an experience synonymous with a vision (see v 17). However, the verb translated **saw** (*theōrei* [v 11]) suggests that Peter acts merely as a spectator. The opening of heaven was associated with divine revelation or visions in the Lukan corpus (Luke 3:21; Acts 7:56) as in Jewish writings (e.g., Isa 64:1; 3 Macc 6:18; *2 Bar.* 22.1).

What *descended* from heaven was an object or *vessel* like a *large linen sheet* let down by its four corners. Early interpreters understood this image as representing the earth (e.g., John Chrysostom, *Hom. Act.* 22, and Bede, "Commentary on the Acts of the Apostles" 10.11B, in Martin 2006, 126). Although the noun *othonē* may refer to fine linen (LSJ 1996, 1200), the suggestion that this was a tablecloth (e.g., Witherington 1998, 349) may be anachronistic. The list of creatures within the sheet parallels lists of creatures representing all the earth's animals (e.g., Gen 1:24; Lev 11:46; Rom 1:23).

■ **13-16** The exchange between Peter and **a voice** (Acts 10:13) constitutes the critical aspect of this experience. Readers infer that the voice comes from heaven and is divine. The first part of the command—for Peter to **get up**— echoes his own directives to Aeneas and Tabitha in the previous chapter (9:34, 40). Peter, like those whom he healed, needs to arise from his own needy condition (see Spencer 2004a, 120).

The second part of the command—to **kill**—has cultic connotations of sacrifice. But here, the verb (*thyō*) refers only to the slaughter of animals.

The third part of the command—to **eat**—invites the famished Peter to dine on the animals that he first must butcher. However, Peter completely rejects the divine command, which two negative adverbs emphasize. *By no means* (*mēdamōs* [v 14]; only here and in 11:8) denotes an absolute refusal (see Ezek 4:14 [LXX]; Johnson 1992, 184). **Never** (*oudepote*) rejects the notion that Peter had ever eaten **anything** that could be deemed *common* (*koinon*) or

unclean. Animals and food outside the boundaries and practices of the Jewish people of God had never passed his lips.

Peter's refusal reflects the kosher laws of Lev 11:1-47, which deal with clean and unclean animals (see Dan 1:8; Tob 1:10-11; Jdt 12:2; 2 Macc 5:27; see Spencer 2004a, 120-21). Barrett argues that the command still allowed Peter to select clean animals, which made his response somewhat puzzling (1994, 508). Witherington suggests that the unclean animals polluted the clean animals, making them unfit for consumption (1998, 350). Either way, like Ananias before him (see Acts 9:13-14), Peter thinks he knows more than God (Gaventa 2003, 166).

By reversing two key words from Peter's objection, the response from the heavenly voice offers an antithetical challenge to his stated concerns (see Tannehill 1990, 132). First, the voice refers to what **God has made clean** (10:15). Second, the voice suggests that God had declared all creation clean, so Peter must stop insisting that it was profane (*sy mē koinou*). "What is at issue between Peter and the heavenly voice is not Peter's luncheon menu but the way he applies the terms 'profane' and 'unclean.' The subject is not his practice, but his assumption that he knows what is clean and what is unclean" (Gaventa 2003, 166).

The threefold repetition of the exchange between the heavenly voice and Peter accentuates both the divine guidance and persistence and Peter's misunderstanding and stubborn refusal to heed (v 16). Neither Cornelius nor Peter completely understands their respective visions. But Peter's initial resistance contrasts sharply with the Gentile Cornelius' immediate obedience to God's guidance.

c. Cornelius' Representatives Meet Peter (10:17-23a)

■ **17-20** The vision ends without resolving its meaning. This depends on narrative developments. The imperfect verb *diēporei* suggests that Peter's perplexity is interrupted only by the arrival of Cornelius' party, which finds Simon's house through persistent inquiry (*dierōtaō*; LSJ 1996, 426). The narrator does not specify whom they asked about Peter's whereabouts. Luke focuses instead on Peter's ongoing confusion over the vision, which so consumes his attention (as the intensive verb *dienthymeomai* indicates) that he does not hear the voices at the house's gate.

Coupled with Peter's befuddlement is divine guidance, this time through the Spirit, which informs Peter of the party's appearance at the gate. Two aspects are noteworthy:

- First, not hesitating (*mēden diakrinomenos*) acknowledges Peter's initial hesitancy about meeting these Gentiles (see vv 27-28; 11:12). But the verb *diakrinō* also refers to distinctions between persons due to social/economic status or ethnic/religious categories (e.g., between Jews and

Gentiles). This dual meaning may reflect ancient rhetoric, which utilized ambiguous expressions to emphasize something of importance (Parsons 2008, 147; *Rhet. Her.* 4.53.67).

- Second, both the emphatic first-person pronoun I (10:20) and the perfect tense indicative *apestalka* make it clear that these three men were not sent on a *human* mission (from Cornelius) but sent on a *divine* one (from the Spirit). This meeting is divinely orchestrated.

■ **21-23a** Although Peter had resisted the divine voice during his vision, he obeys the Spirit's instructions. Upon seeing the three men, he identifies himself. Peter's question about the reason for the men seeking him may seem unnecessary to readers, who know of the angel's instructions for Cornelius. Their response allows them to reiterate Cornelius' exemplary character (→ vv 1-2).

The messengers hyperbolically describe the respect the centurion enjoys as among **the entire nation of the Jews** (v 22; see Luke 7:5). They reaffirm his piety and positive standing, at the very least in Caesarea and the surrounding region. This may allay Peter's Jewish concerns about returning with them to Caesarea and Cornelius' house (Esler 1987, 94).

Their explanation of their mission repeats the angel's basic instructions to Cornelius (Acts 10:5). The verb *chrēmatizō* denotes divine instruction or disclosure (e.g., Matt 2:12, 22-23; Luke 2:25-26; Heb 8:4-6; see Haenchen 1971, 349; Bock 2007, 392). They emphasize God's role in prompting Cornelius' actions.

Subtle shifts in emphases diminish Cornelius' role and accentuate God's role (Witherup 1993, 45-66). The representatives also mention another reason for the summons: to hear a message from Peter. No details are offered. Readers may assume that this message would be Peter's proclamation of the gospel, but now to a *Gentile* audience.

The conjunction *oun*, **therefore**, suggests that Peter's invitation for the Gentile envoys to enter the premises (*eiskalesamenos*) is because of their explanation about the divine guidance Cornelius had received. The verb *xenizō* (Acts 10:23a; showing hospitality to strangers, including a meal or lodging) also describes Simon the tanner's hospitality to Peter (v 6).

Peter's invitation to the three Gentiles would not expose him to the same risks of "uncleanness" as would a Jew staying in a Gentile's home. However, strict observers would have still frowned upon such association, especially if a meal was involved. This is likely, since the three stay overnight before departing with Peter the following day (v 23b). Peter's response reflects both his obedience to the Spirit's leading (v 20) and his recognition of God's orchestration of their meeting (see Johnson 1992, 185; Pervo 2009, 273).

d. Peter at Cornelius' House (10:23b-48)

■ **23b-26** Their departure for Caesarea is probably delayed until **the next day** (v 23b) because Cornelius' envoys arrive during the late afternoon, too late to conclude the return trip before dark.

The significance of **some of the believers** from Joppa who accompany Peter only becomes clear in 10:45 and in Peter's subsequent explanation of the incident (11:12). Luke depicts the party's arrival in terms of anticipation (as the verb *prosdokaō* connotes [10:24]), with Cornelius himself greeting Peter upon his entrance into the house. Manuscripts differ as to whether the verb depicting that entrance is singular (referring to Peter alone) or plural (referring to the entire party). The singular verb keeps the narrative focused on Peter, whose apostolic role continues to have prominence.

The centurion had invited **relatives and close friends** to join him (v 24). Such persons along with household servants (see v 7) would have comprised Cornelius' extended family or household. Like Cornelius, these would have been Gentiles whom Luke described as "God-fearing" (v 2).

Both the image of Cornelius falling at Peter's feet and the verb *proskyneō* (v 25) are puzzling. They convey the centurion's honor and reverence for his apostolic visitor (vv 5-6). But they also describe acts of worship, offered to a mere human. Peter's emphatic reminder about his humanity (v 26) indicates its inappropriateness (see Barrett 1994, 513). Peter deflects Cornelius' reverence from himself and to God, who was responsible for bringing them together.

■ **27-29a** Peter responds favorably to Cornelius. Although the verb *synomileō* connotes two persons in conversation (BDAG 2000, 974), its root verb, *homileō*, also refers to two who converse as equals (see LSJ 1996, 1222; Marshall 1980, 188). The extraordinary responses of both men—of a Roman centurion toward a political "subject" from the area, and of a Jew toward a non-Jew—remind readers that divine guidance led to this unlikely meeting. God set the stage for Peter's interpretation of his vision (vv 9-16) before the assembled Gentile guests.

Peter assumes the assembly is aware of Jewish customs regarding their association (*kollaō*; see also 5:13; 8:29; 9:26) with non-Jews, but he still reminds them. The rare adjective translated **unlawful** (*athemiton*; see 1 Pet 4:3) refers to something that a custom or decree prohibits (esp. purity laws, at the center of the Maccabean conflict; see 2 Macc 6:5; 7:1; 10:34; 3 Macc 5:20). The Roman historian Tacitus (*Hist.* 5.5) and later rabbinic works (see references in Larkin 1995, 161) mention Jewish customs that governed contact with Gentiles. Such customs were intended to keep God's people separate from other nations (see Lev 20:24-26).

However, these regulations often dealt with meals, especially the uncleanness of certain kinds of food associated with sacrifices to idols (e.g., Lev

ACTS

10:23b-
29a

208

11; Dan 1:8-17; Jdt 10:5; 12:1-2; Tob 1:10-13). The emphatic **you** underscores the unlikely nature of this meeting (Acts 10:28). Peter's vision explains his presence despite his Jewish scruples.

Earlier, the meaning of Peter's vision (vv 9-16) was unclear (v 17). But now Luke interprets it. Peter understands the vision with regard to Jewish distinctions of persons, not food. He cites this revelation rather than the Spirit's guidance as his primary reason for coming. Peter emphasizes his obedience to divine instruction, diminishing his prior, strenuous objections to the heavenly voice during his visionary experience.

■ **29b-33** The repetition of Peter's question (v 21) and Cornelius' response (vv 3-8, 22) accentuate significant themes and introduce Peter's subsequent speech.

Cornelius echoes elements of the initial account: the angel's appearance and divine instructions while praying. The reference to "four days ago" (v 30 CEB, NASB, NRSV) probably includes the portion of four different days inclusively. However, the mention of *the ninth hour* suggests only seventy-two hours had actually elapsed between his angelic vision and this meeting with Peter. This is why some manuscripts refer to **three days ago**, probably to accommodate the actual time span (see Metzger 1994, 330-31). Thus, the basic chronology would be as follows:

- *Day 1*: the angelic vision and the sending of the party;
- *Day 2*: the party arrived in Joppa and met Peter;
- *Day 3*: the return departure with Peter and others;
- *Day 4*: the group arrived at Cornelius' house.

By noting God's acceptance of Cornelius' prayer and alms rather than specific details about those prayers and actions, the narrator focuses on *God's* role in the story rather than on *Cornelius'*. The LXX often uses the verb translated **remembered**, *mimnēskomai* (v 31; see noun *mnēmosynon*, meaning "remembrance," in v 4), to convey God's intervention on behalf of the righteous or the people with whom God had entered into covenant (e.g., Gen 9:15; Exod 2:24; 6:5; Lev 26:42; Pss 106:45; 136:23).

Cornelius reiterates that he summoned Peter so those gathered may hear Peter's message (see Acts 10:22). The mention of **the Lord** as the one behind Peter's message is probably a reference to God rather than Jesus, since Cornelius had not yet heard the gospel message about Jesus as the Christ. Since an angel delivered the instructions to Cornelius, he assumed God gave Peter his message. This gathering of God-fearing Gentiles *before God*, an OT expression describing *Israel* worshiping God (e.g., Exod 23:17; 34:23; Deut 16:16; 31:11; Judg 21:2; Ps 68:3), suggests their readiness to accept the divine message.

■ **34-35** Peter's fourth speech in Acts repeats a number of themes sounded earlier. Here, Peter begins with a confession about God as one who **does** not show favoritism or "partiality" (Acts 10:34 NRSV; *prosōpolēmptēs*). Although this specific term appears only here in the NT, a related noun form (*prosōpolēmpsia*) describes God similarly (Rom 2:11). These terms, found nowhere outside the NT, were probably derived from an LXX phrase (*prosōpon lambanein*) describing God as "receiving a face" or "lifting up a face" (e.g., Lev 19:15; Deut 10:17; 2 Chr 19:7). The imagery reflects ancient customs of honoring another by bowing one's head and then lifting up one's face as a sign of acceptance and respect (Lohse, *TDNT* 6:779-80; Fitzmyer 1998, 462-63).

Thus, God's impartiality has to do with God's favorable response toward both Jews *and* Gentiles who worship God. This is in stark contrast to Peter's earlier defiant response to the heavenly voice (Acts 10:14-16). The conjunction **but** (*alla*) suggests that God's favor is not limited to a particular people (Jews) but extends to persons *in every nation* (Gentiles [v 35]).

The adjective *dektos*, conveying God's acceptance of such persons, in the LXX describes worshipers and sacrifices God found suitable and pleasing (e.g., Lev 1:3-4; 19:5; 22:19-21, 29). In Isa 56:7, Gentiles are included among such worshipers, which Peter's initial comments echo.

The specific wording of Peter's description of the one whom God accepts—**the one who fears him and does what is right**—parallels an earlier description of the *Gentile* Cornelius (Acts 10:22). Thus, Peter's opening remarks affirm worshiping Gentiles like Cornelius and his household (→ vv 23*b*-26) in the eyes of God.

■ **36-38** These three verses form one complex sentence. Textual variations attempt to clarify its meaning (see Barrett 1994, 521-22). The placement of **the message** at the beginning of v 36 emphasizes what Peter had just declared about God (vv 34-35). Unlike his previous speeches, Peter here does not quote the OT but alludes to it. **The good news of peace** echoes Isa 52:7, which Peter related to Jesus' preaching. **Peace** is often associated with the blessing of salvation and comprehensive well-being (Hebrew *shalom*) that would come through God's Messiah (Luke 1:79; 2:14; 7:50; 8:48; 10:5-6; 19:38, 42; 24:36; Acts 9:31). Here, it may refer to cordial relations between Jews and Gentiles.

However, the exclamation that Jesus is **Lord of all** indicates that **peace** came through him to all peoples (v 36). It summarizes what Peter has already stated about God's impartiality (vv 34-35). This declaration has important religious and political inferences: the similar expression "Lord of all the earth" often describes the God of Israel (e.g., Josh 3:11, 13; Ps 97:5; Zech 6:5; Josephus, *Ant.* 20.90) as Master of all other supposed gods (e.g., Plutarch, *Is. Os.* 355e). Imperial propaganda applied "Lord of all" to the Roman emperor (e.g., Epictetus, *Diatr.* 4.1.12).

The remainder of the sentence (Acts 10:37-38) succinctly summarizes Jesus' ministry. Peter assumes his audience knows something about Jesus'

210

ministry. This was based on either (*a*) the relative proximity of Caesarea to **Judea** and **Galilee**, where these activities occurred, or (*b*) the possible ministry of Philip (8:40) or Saul (9:30) there (Johnson 1992, 181). Peter highlights two things about Jesus.

First, Peter describes Jesus as God's anointed one, since God anointed him **with the Holy Spirit and power** (10:38), two indicators of his messianic role and status (see Isa 61:1; Luke 4:18). The linking of power to the Spirit reiterates the divine source of the extraordinary things Jesus accomplished.

Second, Peter characterizes Jesus' ministry for the audience. The participle translated **doing good** (*euergetōn*) often described patrons and benefactors in the Greco-Roman world. Jesus' healings offer an example of such public activities. The verb *katadynasteuō* (see Jas 2:6) often refers in the LXX to the rich who oppressed the poor (e.g., Exod 1:13; 21:16; Neh 5:5; Jer 7:6; 22:3; Ezek 18:7; Amos 4:1; 8:4). This contrasts Jesus' ministry to the devil's opposition to the kingdom of God. The declaration that **God was with him** describes God's protection and empowerment of God's servants (e.g., Gen 21:20, 22; 39:2; Exod 3:12; Isa 58:11), like Joseph (→ Acts 7:9). God's presence enabled Jesus to fulfill his divinely ordained role within God's saving purposes.

■ **39-41** Peter affirms his role as one of the divinely appointed apostolic **witnesses** to Jesus' ministry (v 39; see 1:21-22; 2:32; 3:14-15; 5:32), which validates his message. Peter had been with Jesus throughout his entire ministry. He had the perspective to make reliable observations as a witness to Jesus' death and resurrection.

Peter's description of Jesus' death mirrors his description before the Jewish council (5:30; see 2:23) and emphasizes its murderous and shameful nature (see Deut 21:22-23; Acts 13:29). The implied subject, **they,** refers either to the Jewish inhabitants or to the Jerusalem authorities (10:39*a*; see 2:23; 3:14-15; 4:10; 5:30). As in previous speeches, Peter emphasized God's intervention by resurrecting Jesus, in contrast to the Jewish murderous rejection of him.

This is the only place in Acts that mentions Jesus' resurrection **on the third day** (10:40). This counts inclusively the Friday of Jesus' death, the Sabbath, and the day after the Sabbath. God orchestrated both Jesus' resurrection and his postresurrection appearances, not to the whole Jewish **people** (*laos* [v 41]), but only to those witnesses (including Peter) whom God selected beforehand (see 3:20).

The risen Jesus' eating and drinking with his apostles as eyewitnesses appears only here and in Luke 24:41-43 (see Acts 1:3-4; John 21:13-15). Jesus' hosting of a meal may be especially noteworthy within this incident of hospitality (see Acts 11:3) toward Gentiles (Gaventa 2003, 171). The focus on God's role underscores the significance of this testimony about God's plan of salvation.

ACTS

10:39-41

211

■ **42-43** The remainder of Peter's message reiterates themes found in Luke 24 and Acts 1. Commentators differ over the subject of the verb **commanded** (10:42). The previous verses suggest that God gave these directives (see Barrett 1994, 527). But the broader context depicts Jesus as doing such things (see 1:4, 8; see Marshall 1980, 193; Fitzmyer 1998, 466).

The gospel came first **to the** [Jewish] **people** (*tō laō*; see 3:26; 13:46), as Acts 1—7 indicates. The intensive verb *diamartyromai* (see 2:40; 8:25) reiterates the apostles' role as Jesus' witnesses (1:8, 21-22). In particular, they were witnesses that God appointed Jesus as **judge** (see Luke 9:26; 10:13-16; 11:29-32; 12:41-48; 13:22-30; 17:25-37; 18:8; 22:69; Acts 17:31) of **the living and the dead**. This suggests a universal understanding consistent with Peter's earlier declaration about Jesus as "Lord of all" (10:36).

The message of **all the prophets** (v 43) echoes what Jesus declared prior to his ascension (Luke 24:45-49). Peter does not identify or quote any specific OT prophet. Believing in Jesus becomes increasingly emphasized as the narrative unfolds (see Acts 5:14; 8:12; 9:42; 11:17; 13:39; 16:34; 18:8; 19:4; 24:14; 26:27; 27:25).

Linked to belief in Jesus' **name** (3:16; 4:10, 12) as the Christ is the **forgiveness of sins** (see 2:38; 3:19; 5:31; 13:38; 22:16; 26:18; see Luke 24:47). **Everyone who believes** (see Acts 10:35-36) follows Peter's notation about the divine command to preach to the Jewish people (v 42). He may not have fully realized the implications of his universal tone (→ 2:21). Nevertheless, such comments set the narrative stage for further developments, which disclose the inclusive nature of that message (see Haenchen 1971, 353).

■ **44** Since **Peter was still speaking,** he probably had not concluded his address when the Holy Spirit came upon the assembled Gentiles. This may also explain why Peter mentions nothing about the gift of the Holy Spirit, which he previously associated with forgiveness (→ 2:38).

The Spirit's interruption is both the divine fulfillment of that message and its validation. It reiterates God's initiative—seen throughout this chapter—in the realization of the plan of salvation. And it confirms his inclusive declaration from the OT prophets about God's salvation for "everyone who believes" (10:43), both for the gathered Gentiles and for him!

The significance of this momentous occasion, for these Gentiles and Peter, extends into subsequent portions of Acts. Peter was the only person in Acts to experience and witness the Spirit's work among the believers at Pentecost (2:1-4), the Samaritans (8:16-17), and this initial group of Gentiles. Thus, Peter alone had a unique vantage point from which to interpret these events later for their soteriological significance (→ 11:15; Wall 2002, 167).

■ **45-46** For reasons that later become apparent (→ 11:11-18), the narrator offers initial conclusions about what just happened from the *spectators'* perspective (see Johnson 1992, 194). *The faithful ones from the circumcision* (10:45; see 11:2) is the first mention in Acts of circumcision as a Jewish identity marker (see 15:2; 21:21; Spencer 2004a, 127). This reminds readers about the distinction between Peter's *Jewish* companions and his *Gentile* audience.

The divine intervention caught them all by surprise. This insinuates the reliability of their conclusion that God has just **poured out** (see 2:17-18) **the gift of the Holy Spirit** (see 2:38) on these Gentiles. The emphatic position of the phrase **even on Gentiles** underscores the reason for their astonishment (see 2:7, 12): the recipients of this divine blessing are still uncircumcised *Gentiles* and outsiders to God's chosen people ($\rightarrow$ 8:26-40).

Luke explains (*gar*: **For** [v 46]) their conclusion by offering two observations about the Spirit's coming.

First, the expression **speaking in tongues** alludes to Pentecost ($\rightarrow$ 2:4). Some interpreters contend that this particular scene, unlike Pentecost, did not require proclamation in different languages (see 2:5-11). Thus, this must refer to glossolalia similar to what 1 Cor 12—14 describes (see Haenchen 1971, 354; Peterson 2009, 340). However, such readings tend to diminish rather than accentuate the *Lukan* narrative connections between Pentecost and this event at Cornelius' house. Luke's description appropriates Pentecost imagery to underscore that these pious Gentiles, like the Jewish believers at Pentecost, were recipients of the Holy Spirit, blessed by God's saving work. To make this specific description normative for contemporary Christians misunderstands its basic role in Acts, which links what happened here with the earlier Pentecost event.

Second, the description of these Gentiles as praising God (*megalynontōn ton theon*) parallels Pentecost. There, Spirit-filled believers spoke about "the mighty works of God" (CEB; *ta megaleia tou theou*; 2:11). Here, the verb *megalynō* suggests (see Luke 1:46, 58; Acts 5:13; 19:17) that their praise of God indicates their recognition of what God had just done.

■ **47** Since Peter functions as a reliable character in Acts, the narrator appropriates his question and comment as confirmation for the observations and conclusions from the last three verses. Some interpreters contend that Peter acted out of apostolic authority by suggesting baptism for these Gentiles, since his rhetorical question expected a negative response—*No one!*

Peter favorably compares these Gentiles believers with their Jewish counterparts. His explicit reference to these Gentiles now sharing the same gift of the Spirit as his Jewish companions reiterates that God responded similarly to the repentant, whether Jew or Gentile. The Spirit's coming demonstrates that God has already saved them ($\rightarrow$ 11:14, 18). To deny these Gentiles baptism—a Christian rite of inclusion in Acts—would be to refuse to recognize God's obvious inclusion of them among the people characterized by God's saving work.

Peter's role, both within the narrative and for readers of Acts, is significant. He identifies direct connections between God's saving activities among the Jewish people and now among this group of believing Gentiles. Both groups now find themselves included within the messianic community as the people of God.

■ **48** The command to baptize these Gentile believers **in the name of Jesus Christ** corresponds with previous references to Christian baptism (→ 2:38; 8:16). The wording suggests that Peter himself does not baptize them, but the text also does not say who does. The account's final detail is vital: Peter is invited to stay with them for a few days. This presumes table fellowship between the *Gentile* believers and the *Jewish* Peter. The text makes no mention of the Jewish believers who accompanied him (10:45). Luke's interests are not merely in the Gentiles' admission into the Christian community but in the establishment of fellowship between Jewish and Gentile believers (see Esler 1987, 95-97). This latter issue, rather than the baptism of Gentiles, becomes the subject of Peter's interrogation upon his return to Jerusalem (→ 11:1-18).

3. Peter's Response to Questions from Jerusalem Believers (11:1-18)

BEHIND THE TEXT

The city of Jerusalem and the church there continue to play a significant role in Acts. Although Peter's ministry after Acts 9 placed him outside Jerusalem, Luke mentions his return to the city without explanation, undoubtedly since the apostles remained there after persecution following Stephen's murder (8:1*b*-3).

Consistently after the first seven chapters (all of which are located in the city), the narrative either returns to Jerusalem or includes responses by the church there to events elsewhere. Acts has already established the importance of Jerusalem in the fulfillment of God's promises to Israel. But Jerusalem does not function as the center of the Lukan symbolic world (see Parsons 1998, 155-71), nor does Luke wish to establish the ongoing authority of the Jerusalem church.

IN THE TEXT

■ **1-3** The reference to apostles and other believers in Judea does not explain from where the latter group had come, given the scattering of the believers after Stephen's death (8:1*b*-3). Nor does Luke indicate how news of Peter's escapades in Caesarea reached them (→ 8:14). His stay in Caesarea for "a few days" (10:48) gave adequate time for them to hear the news.

214

Luke reported that Peter was accompanied to Caesarea by believers *from the circumcision* (10:45). The same description of those who question Peter in Jerusalem (11:2) may indicate that some from Peter's entourage were the informants. As Luke describes it, only Peter received an invitation to stay behind with the Gentile believers in Caesarea (→ 10:48). Perhaps some of Peter's *Jewish* companions, who traveled there with him and witnessed the Spirit come to the gathered Gentiles, left that meeting in protest and informed the believers in Jerusalem of Peter's "shenanigans."

The interrogation of Peter may not have come from the entire Jerusalem church but from a smaller, vocal minority. The phrase *from the circumcision* could describe the entire Jerusalem church as *Jewish* believers. But it may describe a smaller, more rigid group concerned with strict adherence to the Torah. Their objections are over Peter engaging in table fellowship with Gentiles. Apparently, they raise no objection to the baptism of Gentiles. Their description of these Gentiles as **uncircumcised men** (11:3) labels Peter's dinner companions as outsiders to his *circumcised* Jewish interrogators.

Table Fellowship and the Jewish People

An important feature of Jewish life was table fellowship. In the ancient world, the rules and boundaries associated with meals reflected the beliefs, traditions, and values of broader social and religious systems, including worldviews. Thus, concerns about purity and persons with whom one ate came from understandings regarding life itself. In the minds of observant Jews, there was a correlation between what one ate and who one was.

For Jewish people, such concerns were ultimately about identity and solidarity as the covenant people of God. These issues were at play in the Third Gospel when Jesus was censured for eating with "sinners" (see, e.g., Luke 5:27-32). Jesus' Jewish critics perceived these actions as making him unclean and, therefore, an outsider to the faithful people of God. They failed to see that Jesus' presence redefined these traditional rules and values by calling these "sinners" to repentance (see Thompson 2007, 76-94).

Peter's own critics not only reflected customary Jewish views in contrast to Jesus' teachings and practice but also held invalid assumptions that all non-Jews were alike. Jewish concerns about fellowship focused on food and customs tainted by idolatry. But the *Godfearer* Cornelius would have known such Jewish concerns, distanced himself from such associations, and demonstrated respect and sensitivity regarding these matters (see Barrett 1994, 533-35).

Peter's interrogators' actions subtly contradict God's instructions given earlier to Peter. The verb *diakrinō*, which describes their critique of Peter's behavior, is the same term that denotes how Peter should *not* react toward Cornelius' representatives (→ 10:20; see 11:12). Luke ironically compares their initial response toward Peter with similar attitudes and actions that God told Peter were invalid toward Cornelius' envoys.

■ **4-10** Peter's explanation (*ektithēmi* [v 4]) in vv 4-17 never explicitly addresses his critics' concerns about table fellowship. Instead, he rehearses what happened in detail (*kathexēs*; see Luke 1:3). He emphasizes God's initiative in all that took place (see Witherup 1993, 45-66).

Luke begins with Peter's vision that came while he was **praying** (Acts 11:5; → 10:9). He reiterates its divine source, adding that it came **from heaven** (→ 10:11, "let down to earth"). The list of unclean creatures in the vision is expanded to include **wild beasts** or beasts of prey (11:5; see Lev 11:13-40; Deut 14:11-18). Both the command for Peter to **kill and eat** (Acts 11:7; → 10:13) and Peter's resistance reiterate the unexpected reversal God demanded. No doubt, Peter's questioners agreed with his staunch refusal to consider *any* demands contrary to Jewish scruples (see Spencer 2004a, 128).

■ **11-14** Peter's account never mentions the centurion by name or his piety. Instead, he refers only to *a man.* Perhaps the problematic issue extended beyond that particular situation. Peter mentions nothing about staying in Joppa at the home of a tanner (9:43; 10:6) nor that he hosted the Gentile's three envoys overnight (10:23*a*). This would certainly complicate an already-contentious meeting. That Peter singles out the six (noted first here) who accompanied him to Caesarea insinuates that they could verify his testimony.

Significantly, the stated reason for summoning Peter is given. This is absent from the initial narrative (10:4-6) and Cornelius' own account (10:30-33). The message has to do with Cornelius and his "entire household" (11:14 NRSV) being **saved.** Acts' previous references to salvation (2:21; also 2:40, 47) applied to Jewish people. The incident at Cornelius' house signals the inclusion of *Gentiles* in God's saving plans as well. The angelic message indicates that God initiated everything that led to that meeting in Caesarea.

■ **15-17** Peter does not repeat the content of his message; readers already know it (10:34-43). The wording (**As I began to speak** [11:15]) emphasizes that Peter had more to say but was interrupted by the Spirit bursting onto the scene (10:44; see Kilgallen 1990, 405-10). Both the divine interruption and the repetition of the identical description of that divine activity—*the Holy Spirit fell upon them*—underscore Peter's explanation that all this happened by *divine* initiative, not *his.* God was responsible for Peter's presence in Caesarea and for the gift of the Spirit to those Gentiles.

Peter equates this gift of the Spirit with the apostles' Pentecost experience and perhaps that of others **at the beginning** (2:1-4; see 10:45-46). He recalls Jesus' promise (1:5), which referred to the *Jewish* followers of Jesus and echoed the message of John the Baptist (Luke 3:16). But here, Peter appropriates that promise to include *Gentiles.*

216

Memory and recent events interact, producing new understanding. Recent events are understood on the basis of their correspondence to past experiences and promises, and the promise is newly understood on the basis of recent events. A growing understanding of the breadth of God's purpose and the depth of God's power is the result. (Tannehill 1990, 145)

Both the equality and nature of the gift received by Jewish and Gentile believers alike obliterated ethnic distinctions. The people of God in the messianic age were one. Peter's rhetorical question about his ability to **stop** or "hinder" (NRSV) again accentuates the divine role. Peter uses the same verb (*kōlyō*) here as in his earlier question about baptizing the Gentile believers at Cornelius' house (10:47). So his concluding remarks may also refer to impeding the baptism and incorporation of Gentiles into the community of believers. To stand against solidarity with and inclusion of *all* believers, both Jew and Gentile, due to their common gift of the Spirit, would be to oppose God (see 5:39).

■ **18** Peter does not directly explain his behavior, nor does the response of his critics exonerate him. But the Jerusalem believers calm their contentious tone. The verb *hēsychazō* refers to neutralizing the emotionally charged situation. Nagging issues remained unaddressed, and later questions would lead to another debate in Jerusalem (15:1-29).

Still, their praise of God correlates with other instances in Acts in which people affirmed what God had done (see 2:47; 3:8-9; 4:21). Their pronouncement that God had granted **repentance** to Gentiles mirrors Peter's declaration before the Sanhedrin that God offered repentance to Israel and the Holy Spirit to those obedient to God (5:31-32). This association between repentance, obedience, and the gift of the Spirit affirms Jewish beliefs. God took the initiative, and Peter was obedient to God.

Their agreement refers to "the Gentiles" (NRSV; note the definite article: *tois ethnesin*) in general, rather than to specific Gentiles (Cornelius and those with him). The emphatic position of that reference implies that the event had broader implications that they had yet to understand. Subsequent events confirm their lack of full comprehension. "Whether the acceptance of such a God-fearing Gentile as Cornelius counted as an anomaly or as the beginning of a new pattern had not yet been demonstrated" (Dunn 1996, 198).

FROM THE TEXT

That Acts gives more attention to this account involving Peter and Cornelius than any other indicates its importance to the narrative. The expansion of the gospel to include Gentiles is nothing less than a "game changer." It forced reconsideration of a host of preconceived ideas about God, salvation, and what it meant to be the people of God.

The coming of the Spirit on Gentiles in Caesarea had profound significance for the self-understanding and mission of the church. This becomes clear in the repetitive aspects of the broader passage, as the narrator hammers home images of divine guidance and purpose. As Johnson aptly states:

> The struggle Luke seeks to communicate to the reader is the process of *human* decision-making as the Church tried to catch up to God's initiative. And it is precisely this struggle that gives the narrative its marvellous tension. The reader is a privileged observer, knowing far more than the characters about what God wills and what God is doing. But the reader is also drawn sympathetically into the poignancy of the human confusion and conflict caused by God's action. The struggle of Peter and his fellow believers to understand what God is doing works subtly on the reader, shaping a sharper sense of the enormity and unprecedented character of the gift. (1992, 186-87)

Contemporary interpreters cannot deal with these events as merely historical moments from the church's past. The narrator has skillfully crafted these materials so that readers of Acts will be caught up in the struggle to recognize what God is doing and challenged to partner with God's saving purposes.

Luke's account depicts an inclusive understanding of the church with both Jewish and Gentile believers. His narrative points the reader again and again to the divine initiative that led to that understanding. The inclusive nature of the church was the result of God's purposes and guidance. It did not result from human instigation or political correctness.

The brief scenes involving Peter prior to the Cornelius incident, the visions, and the meeting in Caesarea all make one thing perfectly clear: the same God who facilitated Peter's healing of the sick and raising of the dead carefully orchestrated events that brought strangers together in a divinely ordained moment. Neither the Gentile Cornelius nor the initially resistant, Jewish Peter planned it.

Luke offers his readers several glimpses into the divine workings of what Wesleyans describe as "prevenient grace." Like Peter and the Jewish believers in Jerusalem, Wesleyans can mistakenly assume that the promises and purposes of God involve only those currently identified with God and God's people.

Such a dramatic sense of God's initiative is essential when God's purposes move outside traditional boundaries and assumptions. The purity codes and laws associated with Judaism provided the boundaries and definitions needed to distinguish and maintain the identity of the Jewish people as the covenant people of God.

As Israel faced the risk of extinction during the exilic and postexilic periods, such boundaries were effective and necessary. They defined who was included within the people of God. And they kept the "lost" lost, the "sinner" sinful, and the "outsider" outside.

But these same labels and distinctions restricted what God's people were able to perceive to be the persons and places where God was at work. These dividing walls minimized God's redemptive purposes outside these predefined categories.

Luke has already shown how God fulfilled God's promise to Israel outside the religious authorities and institutions of Judaism. So one should not be surprised that God's purposes would also extend beyond these Jewish categories.

But what if the divine purposes extend beyond the categories to which we tightly cling? What does the coming of the Spirit in Caesarea say to contemporary readers? Do we fail to recognize God at work because our generalizations and labels define (sometimes too specifically) who is and is not Christian, orthodox, Spirit-filled, evangelical, liberal, conservative, or whatever else ends up blocking divine activity from our view?

Perhaps a passage like this offers a radical alternative. We, too, need prayerful discernment and perspective to recognize God's grace and purposes at work among those we might least expect. We should not limit, much less oppose God, by stubbornly holding on to our preconceived ideas.

If we endorse such an understanding regarding the ways in which God may work, other questions arise: What legitimate sources of authority may the church appropriate in her theological reflection? Many theological traditions claim the Scriptures as the exclusive source of divine revelation and, therefore, the only authoritative source of theology. But in the Wesleyan tradition, the so-called Wesleyan quadrilateral identifies not only Scripture, the primary source of authority, but also reason, tradition, and religious experience. These complementary sources of authority allow the church to reflect theologically in response to what God seems to be doing in our day. From this reflection, she pursues her task of proclaiming the gospel faithfully in both word and deed.

These "secondary" sources of authority are often downplayed by other theological traditions because of human depravity. But the present passage may offer insights from how some of the earliest believers wrestled with theological issues that challenged the norms of their faith. In this instance, it is noteworthy that believers did not turn to Scripture in working through this issue, as was often the case in Acts (see, e.g., 1:15-26; 2:14-36).

Peter's Pentecost speech had already cited the Joel prophecy and its inclusive tendencies regarding God's purposes ("all flesh" [2:17 KJV]; "everyone" [2:21]). But Peter did not explicitly reiterate these scriptural passages here. Instead, he turned to the recognition of divine activity through the collective experience and discernment of the community of faith. This forced them to rethink their scriptural understanding and traditional views regarding the people of God (see Wall 2002, 171-72).

It must be noted, however, that the appropriation of religious experience to discern what was (or was not) divine guidance and activity occurred in a *collective* rather than *individualistic* way. Although Peter responded individually to what he perceived as divine guidance, the corporate recognition and endorsement of what God had done ultimately provided the decisive theological assessment. This opened the door in subsequent chapters of Acts to the inclusion of Gentiles within the Lukan redefinition of the people of God.

Perhaps this provides a window through which we can see an ecclesial hermeneutic at work. In this, the church reengages sacred Scripture alongside her careful discernment of the corporate experience of God's activity and purposes among her as the people of God. Today's church may need to ask: What groups have we excluded that God would include? What contemporary ecclesial understandings resist others, rather than recognizing God's grace at work within them?

D. The Beginnings of a New Church in Antioch (11:19-30)

BEHIND THE TEXT

After the contentious meeting in Jerusalem, an abrupt shift in narrative setting returns the reader's attention to the persecution after Stephen's death. Like Philip in Samaria, others took the gospel elsewhere in the eastern Mediterranean where they fled. The present narrative picks up another story line leading from that earlier persecution.

Here, the proclamation to non-Jews in Antioch is an implication of the previous scene: God had opened the door to include Gentiles within God's purposes of salvation (see v 18). Thus, this passage functions as a strategic narrative link between the preceding and subsequent materials (see Longenecker 2004, 185-204).

IN THE TEXT

■ **19-20** The conjunctions *men oun* indicate the beginning of a new section, which connects with previous events. The scattering of believers "throughout Judea and Samaria" (8:1) after Stephen's death sent others further north. Some went to Phoenicia, a Mediterranean coastal region. Others traveled to Cyprus, Barnabas' homeland (4:36) located south of Asia Minor and west of Syria, probably because it had a significant Jewish colony. Still others went as far as Antioch, the major city of Syria.

Antioch  of Syria

The prominent Roman city of Antioch would have been a logical destination for at least some Jewish believers who fled Jerusalem. Although the city was over 300 miles (483 km) north of Jerusalem, it included a sizable Jewish population. Several long-established synagogues were there, with the right to practice their customs without official resistance.

Antioch's location as a crossroads between the east and west contributed to its growth in size, wealth, and influence in the Roman Empire. Only Rome and Alexandria exceeded it in population by the first century. The city's assets provided a natural springboard for the mission of the Jesus movement. It was to become a leading center of Christianity in the next few centuries. Early Christian tradition identifies Antioch as the location from which the Gospel of Matthew was written.

Since these unidentified believers fled the persecution in Jerusalem, their proclamation had been to "no one except Jews" (v 19 NRSV), probably in synagogues. Luke specifically mentions some other refugee believers proclaiming the gospel in Antioch, but they were Diaspora Jews (see 6:9), **men from Cyprus and Cyrene.** Their preaching practice (see imperfect tense: *elaloun*) **also** (*kai*) extended **to the Hellenists.** These were Gentiles rather than Greek-speaking Jews (see 6:1), as the textual variant **Greeks** reinforces (see Metzger 1994, 340-41).

11:21-24

■ **21** The reference to *the hand of the Lord* draws from OT images (see, e.g., 1 Kgs 18:46; 1 Chr 28:19; Isa 41:20; see Luke 1:66). Here, **the Lord** refers to Jesus, another instance of Luke identifying the activity of God with Jesus (see Gaventa 2003, 179). The success of their ministry, *a large number* becoming believers, links to previous positive responses to the gospel as a sign of divine blessing (Acts 2:41, 47; 4:4; 6:7; 9:31). These new believers who **turned to the Lord** (see 3:19; 9:35) included *both* Jews *and* Gentiles. This is the first time Acts reports large numbers responding, including Gentiles.

■ **22-24** As before (→ 8:14), reports reached Jerusalem and prompted the church's decision to send a representative. Again, this established continuity between the successes in Antioch with what God had done in Jerusalem. The church may have sent Barnabas since he, like some who proclaimed the gospel in Antioch, was from Cyprus (4:36; 11:23). His reputation for offering encouragement may have also been a factor. However, concerns over Peter's prior association with Gentiles may have led the church to send Barnabas instead. His assignment was to look into the reports (see Bruce 1988, 226-27; Barrett 1994, 552).

The narrator mentions three things upon Barnabas' arrival in Antioch. First, he recognizes among the believers there the effects of **the grace of God** (v 23; see 2:47; 4:33). Second, his rejoicing corresponds to earlier responses

ACTS

of praise to God (e.g., Luke 1:47, 58; 2:20, 28, 38; Acts 2:47; 3:9; 4:21; 5:41). Third, his encouragement of believers is consistent with his Lukan introduction as the "son of encouragement" (4:36).

Barnabas' message focuses on their complete commitment (lit., **with purpose of heart**) to the Lord (i.e., Jesus [11:21]). Luke's summary of his exhortation affirms both the ministry and the resulting group, including both Jewish and Gentile believers. The characterization of Barnabas as **a good man, full of the Holy Spirit and faith** (v 24) is reminiscent of prophetic figures such as Stephen (6:5, 8; 7:55) who served as witnesses that the risen Jesus was the Christ. This description validates his assessment and the divine source of his exhortation. Many people respond favorably to Barnabas' ministry, continuing the image of divine blessing of these Antiochene believers (see v 21).

■ **25-26** Barnabas is again responsible for introducing Saul to the community of believers (see 9:27). Luke states no explicit reason why Barnabas brings Saul to Antioch from Tarsus (see 9:30). But the ensuing teaching suggests that Barnabas recruits him to assist in this extended time of ministry.

Significantly, Luke employs the term **church** (*ekklēsia* [11:26]) to describe these Antiochene believers. Until now, the term has referred exclusively to *Jewish* believers (5:11; 8:1, 3; 9:31). In Antioch, both Jews *and* Gentiles comprise the contingent of believers. This epitomizes Luke's redefinition and expansion of the concept "people of God."

A new designation, **Christians**, now identifies believers in Antioch simply as persons associated with Christ. It is unclear whether the believers took this term upon themselves or others gave them the name (perhaps in derision). Because the growing numbers of believers included Gentiles as well as Jews, this label may reflect this group's distinctiveness. This distinguished them both from unbelieving Jews and from the Jewish believers in Jerusalem (see Fitzmyer 1998, 477-78; Pervo 2009, 294-95). How fitting that those who preached and served "in the name of Jesus Christ" in Acts now carried that name (see 9:15) in a new way (see Fitzmyer 1998, 474; Gaventa 2003, 180)!

■ **27-28** The arrival of other prophets from Jerusalem, probably near the end of the year of teaching by Barnabas and Saul (11:26), reinforces the role of Barnabas as a prophet as well as Jerusalem's representative (see vv 22-24). The one prophet identified by name, **Agabus** (v 28), reappears later (21:10-11). The explicit mention of the Spirit as the source of his prediction clarifies why the Antioch church takes it so seriously.

In an age when most people lived from hand to mouth, food shortages due to poor harvests or insufficient food distribution created economic and social havoc. Ancient records mention no food shortages of widespread proportions during that time. Thus, this prediction probably refers to one of several regional shortages during the reign of the emperor Claudius. The reference to

the entire Roman world or "all the world" (NRSV) underscores the gravity of this looming crisis (see Winter 1994, 59-78).

■ **29-30** The response of the Antioch church resembles the sharing of resources that earlier characterized the Jerusalem church (2:44-45; 4:34-35), including Barnabas their teacher (4:36-37). This crisis would have also affected believers in Antioch as well as Jerusalem. The church develops a plan to collect financial resources. The wording (*euporeō*) suggests that these funds come from those who had plenty (see Tannehill 1990, 148; LSJ 1996, 727). The purpose of this ministry (*eis diakonian*) is to meet the needs of *Judean* believers.

The funds are delivered to **the elders** (*presbyterous* [11:30]), the authorities in the Jewish community (4:5, 8, 23; 6:12; 23:14; 24:1; 25:15). Elders are also mentioned in non-Jewish Christian circles (14:23; 15:2, 4, 6, 22, 23; 16:4; 20:17; 21:18), sometimes along with the apostles. This suggests that the designation may have drawn from its Jewish use. However, nothing in Acts defines their role or distinguishes them from the Twelve or the Seven.

What stands out here is that this church—both Jewish and Gentile believers in Antioch—responded for the sake of the *Jewish* believers in Judea. This response is even more remarkable considering the initial resistance in Jerusalem to Peter's meeting with the *Gentile* Cornelius (11:1-17). The reciprocity between believers indicates the common, divine bond uniting them, despite their differences in demographics and location.

Collection for the Poor and Paul's Letters

Because Paul refers several times to a collection for the poor, many have correlated them with this instance in Acts. Paul's instructions to the Roman and Corinthian churches (Rom 15:25-29; 1 Cor 16:1-4; 2 Cor 8—9), like Acts 11, refer to a collection on behalf of "the poor among the Lord's people in Jerusalem" (Rom 15:26; see 2 Cor 8:1-4; 9:1). His rationale was that the Gentile Christians should give "material blessings" in response to their privilege of sharing in the Jews' "spiritual blessings" (Rom 15:27).

Although the similarities suggest a common emphasis in Acts and the Pauline letters, these actually refer to different collections. The one mentioned in Paul's letters would have occurred later in Paul's ministry than this particular collection in Antioch. Acts does not mention Paul's later collection (→ sidebar "Interpreting Acts 20—21 in the Absence of Paul's Collection for the Poor" with 20:4-6).

In Gal 2, Paul describes a meeting with church leaders in Jerusalem about his ministry to the Gentiles and their instructions that he should "continue to remember the poor" (Gal 2:10). Paul also mentions an unpleasant encounter with Peter and Barnabas in Antioch (Gal 2:11-13). Many equate these matters with the Acts 11 collection (see Bock 2007, 486-93; Bruce 1988, 231; Marshall 1980, 244-45; Witherington 1998, 86-97, 375, 439-445).

The problems in reconciling the Lukan materials with the Pauline letters on historical matters make definitive conclusions difficult. Thus, the *differences* between Gal 2 and Acts 11 render this equation unsatisfactory for many scholars, especially since the basic data of Gal 2 seem to correlate more with the so-called Jerusalem Council of Acts 15 (see Phillips 2009, 51-82, 125-55).

Still, this image of the generosity of the Antioch church toward Judean believers remains.

FROM THE TEXT

In some ways, the introduction of the gospel mission in Antioch interrupts the narrative flow of Acts. Almost without warning, Luke returns his readers to the days when persecution forced Jewish believers to flee the holy city. Like the account of Philip's ministry, the narrator focuses a spotlight on a group of believers—unnamed ones, this time—who were simply faithful in taking the good news where their life circumstances thrust them. In both cases, the Christian gospel rather than the ethnicity of an audience took center stage. That gospel was more than the message they proclaimed; the good news was that divine activity transformed their unplanned encounters into providential moments of grace and redemption.

For the Antioch church, the evidence of God's saving work among Jews and Gentiles mirrors Luke's earlier presentation of the church in Jerusalem. Their care for fellow believers extended beyond ethnic, religious, and geographical boundaries. This validates what the Jerusalem church concluded earlier: God had truly given **even to Gentiles repentance unto life** (11:18). What happened in Antioch illustrates the implications of that realization.

From a theological perspective, "that Luke describes no cause-and-effect relationship between the mission in Antioch and the conversion of Cornelius is important" (Gaventa 2003, 181). What happened in Antioch was not the culmination of an official mission strategy developed by church leaders in Jerusalem. Rather, the birth and growth of the church in Antioch were the result of God's saving work within a context cultivated by faithful proclamation.

This may serve as a reminder to the contemporary church and its emphases on the "missional church." We must not confuse mission strategies with faithful living. "The emergence of a church in Antioch is God's doing through the Holy Spirit, not that of any individual or group" (Gaventa 2003, 181). The same is true today.

E. Politics and Persecution of the Church (12:1-25)

BEHIND THE TEXT

Like the previous section, the materials of Acts 12 take the narrative stage without clear indication of their roles. Some suggest that this chapter contributes little, either to the developing story or to the message of Acts itself. But it clearly provides an important narrative transition. Luke shifts attention from Peter and the apostles to Saul (later Paul) and the beginning days of the postapostolic church, and from Jerusalem to Antioch as the new center of the Christian mission.

Peter's miraculous prison escape is his second divine deliverance from captivity (→ 5:17-20). Both the imminent death facing Peter and the extraordinary divine intervention accentuate God's role in leading and enabling the church against overwhelming human odds. Miraculous prison-escape stories were fairly common in the ancient world (e.g., Homer, *Il.* 5.749; Ovid, *Metam.* 3.690-700). They typically depicted divine power and supremacy over malevolent rulers. This escape occurs just after Passover (12:4) and the Festival of Unleavened Bread (v 3), Israel's paradigmatic story of the Exodus. Its timing accentuates this deliverance (Tannehill 1990, 153-55). The episode strikingly resembles an account by the Jewish historian Artapanus of Moses' prison escape (Frag. 3.22-26; Holladay 1999, 179-83).

Acts depicts the experiences of Jesus' followers in ways that mirror Jesus' arrest and trials (esp. Acts 4—5). It is not surprising, therefore, that Luke notes Peter's arrest just prior to Pentecost and involving someone named Herod.

The Herods, Jesus, and the Church

Most people correctly associate the name "Herod" with Herod the Great (see Matt 2:1-18), who ruled Judea for thirty-three years (37-4 BC) and expanded the temple in Jerusalem. His son Herod Antipas inherited the family name and the rule over the territories of Galilee and Perea (4 BC—AD 39). He was responsible for John the Baptist's arrest and death (Luke 3:19-20; 9:7-9). Pilate sent the arrested Jesus to him for questioning (Luke 23:6-12). Thus, mention of the name "Herod" signifies an enemy of God and God's purposes.

Herod in Acts 12 refers to Agrippa I, a grandson of Herod the Great, a friend of the emperors Caligula and Claudius, and the ruler of Judea for three years (41-44). A Roman politician, he tried to live and rule the territory as a good Jew, thereby receiving the praise of the Pharisees (see Josephus, *Ant.* 19.292-316). His son, Agrippa II, appears later in Acts (25:13—26:32).

These arrests link to Jesus' prophecy about what would happen to his disciples (Luke 21:12). Peter's rescue from certain death (see Acts 12:1-4) is reminiscent of Jesus' resurrection. The divine intervention through the angel secures new life for Peter. Readers of this passage should attend to the literary overtones that connect this episode with the passion of Jesus and Israel's Exodus stories (see Garrett 1990, 656-80).

IN THE TEXT

■ **I-5** Opposition up to now has been from Jewish religious leaders. Now it comes from the political authorities. This signals a new phase in the narrative. It is unclear exactly why or when this happened. The phrase *at that time* merely indicates the resumption of an undefined narrative thread. Barnabas and Saul probably were not in Jerusalem at the time (see 11:30), so the phrase may refer to a time before the prophesied famine (11:28).

Luke depicts Herod as acting violently and harmfully against some from the church, presumably in Jerusalem. There is no indication why Herod was in that part of his territory (see 12:19). The image of *throwing [his] hands* upon some believers mirrors the hostile actions taken earlier in arresting Jesus (see Luke 20:19) and the apostles (Acts 4:3; 5:18; see Luke 21:12).

The term referring to the mistreatment of these believers (*kakoō*) is the same one used twice in Stephen's speech describing Israel's enslavement and abuse in Egypt (7:6, 19). Of course, Herod did not personally execute James. The sentence simply identifies the ruler *alone* as ultimately responsible for the atrocity. Like Jesus' death, Luke characterizes this as murder (*anaireō*; Luke 22:2; 23:32; Acts 10:39; 13:28; see 5:33; 9:23, 24, 29) and resistance to God's purposes. The mention of the sword implies that James was beheaded, a Roman means of execution for those considered political threats. The Jewish people considered this the most shameful of all deaths.

Nothing in Acts accounts for James' execution. Apparently, the church took no action to replace this apostle (contrast 1:15-26). However, "inside information" about Herod notes that this was *pleasing to the Jews*. This connects his actions with others who sought to exterminate the Jesus movement (see Marshall 1980, 207). This also signals a shift in Jewish public opinion toward believers. Animosity has replaced their previous respect (see 4:21; 5:26).

Luke accentuates the desperation of Peter's situation by using the same verb to describe his arrest (*syllambanō*) that earlier described Jesus' arrest (1:16; also Luke 22:54). The timing of the events is ironic—during the weeklong **Festival of Unleavened Bread** (Acts 12:3). This immediately follows Passover and continues the celebration of Israel's deliverance from captivity (Exod 12:1—13:16). Now it highlights *Peter's* own captivity and need of God's deliverance.

The extraordinary security measures for Peter's imprisonment accentuate the gravity of his hopeless situation. Four squads of four soldiers provide around-the-clock security. With four watches during the night, each squad covers one watch, with two soldiers flanking Peter and two others guarding entrances. Such provisions seem excessive. However, "Peter's notoriety for nocturnal jail-breaks has obviously preceded him" (Spencer 2004a, 135)!

ACTS

12:1-5

The delay of his hearing until **after the Passover** (Acts 12:4) explains the lag behind Peter's expected execution. The grim prognosis for Peter's future prompts the church to pray **earnestly** (v 5; see Luke 22:44) on Peter's behalf for several days (the imperfect tenses denoting ongoing action).

■ **6** According to Luke, Herod is responsible for opposition to the church (Acts 12:1-4) and specifically Peter. Peter's situation is perilous. The reference to *that night* is a reminder of Herod's intention to press charges against Peter and then execute him after the conclusion of Passover week (v 4). The security team makes escape humanly impossible—a notable characteristic of ancient prison escape stories. Even the mention of Peter's sleeping, which some interpret as a remarkable sign of tranquillity and confidence in the face of imminent death (e.g., Pervo 1987, 62; Bruce 1988, 235; Peterson 2009, 363), accentuates the likelihood of Herod's resolve becoming reality.

■ **7-10** The sudden appearance of **an angel of the Lord** again shatters the prevailing conditions of the situation (12:7; see 5:19; 8:26; 10:3, 7, 22; 11:13). It resembles Jesus' earlier appearance to Saul (9:3; 22:6, 9; 26:13). The light signifies a divine encounter. Strangely, no one in the prison seems to notice. Peter is so oblivious that the angel must strike Peter to awaken him. The verb *patassō* connotes something much stronger than a nudge or tap on the shoulder (see 12:23). Given the hopeless situation, the wording suggests that the angel "resurrects" Peter from certain death, as the term for Peter's awakening (*egeirō*) often depicts Jesus' resurrection in Acts (4:10; 5:30; 13:30, 37; see Luke 24:6, 34).

Similar to God's instructions to the Israelites (see Exod 12:11), the angel initiates Peter's escape. The angel's guidance builds suspense. Inexplicably, Peter and the angel exit the prison without resistance. None of the four guards detects their departure. Even the imposing **iron gate** (Acts 12:10) at the prison's entrance opens for the pair **by itself** (*automatē*). The Western text's additional detail about them descending seven steps adds color to the story, but little else.

Once Peter is safely outside the prison grounds, the angel deserts him (*aphistēmi*) as abruptly as he entered the scene. The apostle now must fend for himself. Luke presents both the directives for the stupefied, still half-asleep apostle and the subsequent prison break as nothing less than a divine rescue from the hands of human authorities.

■ **11** Peter's full recognition of what just happened comes only after the angel's departure (see v 9). Luke provides Peter's assessment of the episode through interior monologue, a common literary device (e.g., Luke 7:39; 12:17-19; 15:18-19; 16:3-4; 18:4-5). He offers no reason for Peter's sudden conviction (*nun oida alēthōs*, **now I know for certain**), in contrast to his prior lack of understanding (*ouk ēdei*, **he did not know** [v 9]).

The assessment confirms the narrator's perspective: God's actions thwart human attempts to hinder God's purposes. The expression **rescued from the hand of Herod** recalls Exod 3:8 and 18:4, 10, which describe God's deliverance of the Israelites from Pharaoh and the Egyptians (see Garrett 1990, 656-80). The mention of **the expectation of the Jewish people** may refer generally to Peter's anticipated hearing before the people (Acts 12:4; Wall 2002, 179). Or it may connect them more negatively to Herod's plan of execution. Either sense falls woefully short of the Jewish messianic expectation mentioned early in Luke's Gospel (Luke 3:15).

■ **12** Luke does not explain why Peter visits **the house of Mary**. The prayer meeting there parallels the church's response to Peter's incarceration (v 5). The location clarifies this group to be only part of the larger church in Jerusalem (v 5), perhaps where one of the city's house congregations met.

John Mark and His Mother Mary in Acts

Luke introduces a character into Acts who will reappear later. John, also called Mark, will later accompany Barnabas and Saul (later Paul) on part of their first ministry excursion in ch 13, only to return to Jerusalem without explanation.

Acts 12:12 introduces John Mark to identify the location of the meeting of praying believers. His father is not mentioned. Many conclude that Mary was perhaps divorced or widowed but also wealthy, with a large enough house to accommodate that meeting. That meeting also suggests this family's prominence within the Jerusalem church.

The ambiguous role of John Mark in Acts 13 and 15 has puzzled interpreters. This is especially so in light of his assumed historic role within the fledgling Christian movement. He reappears after the so-called Jerusalem Council of ch 15, when Barnabas sought to convince Paul to reinstate Mark to the ministry team. Their disagreement on the matter caused the two to go separate ways (see Black 1998, 101-20).

John Mark was also a follower of Peter (see 1 Pet 5:13). Early in the second century, Papias identified Mark as the author of the gospel that now bears his name (Eusebius, *Hist. eccl.* 3.39.15). If John Mark was part of the praying group, this episode is the only instance Acts offers in which the two crossed paths. This only adds to the mystery.

■ **13-14** Peter's troubles in gaining access to the prayer meeting are both ironic and comical. The outer gate where he begins knocking probably separated the house's courtyard from the street. Strangely, this gate prevents his entrance, yet the prison's iron gate with its guards could not prevent his escape (v 10).

Luke identifies the one who answers the gate as Rhoda, a **servant** girl (*paidiskē* [v 13] may refer simply to a young girl; see Luke 22:54-62). She may have recognized Peter's voice because she belongs either to Mary's household, to the group gathered to pray, or to both. Rhoda's understandable joy causes (the preposition *apo*) her to run inside to announce the news, leaving Peter standing on the street and vulnerable to recapture.

The character Rhoda mirrors stereotypical slaves in ancient comedy, providing comic relief to hopeless situations (Harrill 2000, 151-57). But here, the angel has already miraculously delivered Peter from his hopeless confinement and impending death. Instead, the girl becomes the first female character in Acts to prophesy or deliver good news (see 2:18). In this instance, the message is that Peter is alive and well (see Spencer 2004a, 137).

■ **15-16** Just as the apostles did not believe the women's report of Jesus' resurrection (Luke 24:10-11), the gathered believers do not believe Rhoda. Their disbelief may reveal their skepticism about the outcome of their prayers (given James' demise) or their intercession for something other than deliverance. Their harsh response toward Rhoda (see Acts 26:24-25) may be due to her low social status. But it also emphasizes how extraordinary and unexpected was Peter's rescue. Nonetheless, she sticks to her story (imperfect tense: *diischyrizeto*; also Luke 22:59).

Rhoda's news about Peter's appearance prompts the believers to offer another plausible explanation: it is Peter's angel. This reflects an ancient understanding about guardian angels, often believed to resemble those they protected. Ironically, an angel led Peter through a locked prison gate, yet no one would open the house gate because the believers have mistaken him for an angel (see Johnson 1992, 218)!

Amid the confusion, Peter continues knocking. This would potentially attract attention, especially during the night (see Acts 12:6). *Finally*, someone opens the door only to discover Peter, perhaps because of the incessant rapping at the door or because someone took Rhoda's message seriously. The amazement of the assembled believers parallels other instances in Acts of people encountering signs of divine activity (2:7, 12; 3:10; 8:13; 9:21; 10:45).

Thus, the servant girl Rhoda, often taken to be a comedic character in Acts, ends up having the last laugh. The gathering confirms her message about Peter as both delivered and alive (see Chambers 2004, 89-97).

■ **17** Peter's gesture quiets the ecstatic believers and signals his intention to speak (see 13:16; 19:33; 21:40). Peter's remarks reiterate God's role in delivering him. His instructions to inform *James and the brothers* about these remarkable events abruptly introduce James without further details, implying that Luke's audience would know about him. James is likely the brother of Jesus, who later became the leader of the Jerusalem church (see Gal 1:19; 2:7-10) and reappears in leadership roles (Acts 15:13-21; 21:18). *The brothers* may refer to the broader Christian community (see 6:3; 9:30), but their association with James suggests the leaders of the Jerusalem church, perhaps the other apostles.

The dangers for Peter prompt his quick exit from Jerusalem to an unidentified location. Some contend that this passage indicates the transfer of leadership and authority in the church from Peter and the apostles to James and others (see Bauckham 1995b, 427-50; Wall 1991, 628-43). However, its narrative setting suggests broader issues central to the plot of Acts, namely the transition from Jerusalem to Antioch as the center of the Christian mission (see 13:1-3).

■ **18-19** By returning to the situation at the prison, this vignette ties together a few loose ends. Since it was the next morning, clearly Peter is already out of harm's way. That there is **no small commotion** (v 18) among Peter's guards is an understatement, given the harsh Roman punishment that would likely follow: those responsible for an escapee received that prisoner's sentence (Code of Justinian 9.4.4).

Herod's personal involvement in the investigation is consistent with his role in Peter's arrest (vv 1-4). The intense search (see the intensive verb *epizēteō*) turned up nothing (v 19). The interrogation (see the legal term *anakrinō*; see 4:9; 24:8; 28:18; Luke 23:14) and torture of the guards were intended to find out who shirked responsibilities (fell asleep?) or were accomplices. Their inability to explain what happened probably contributed to their severe punishment. Luke specifies only that the guards were led away (*apachthēnai*) for punishment. But since Herod intended to execute Peter (Acts 12:1-4), that was likely their penalty. Whatever his reason for being in Judea, Herod returned to Caesarea, his administrative capital and the same coastal city where Peter met Cornelius.

■ **20** Some dispute between Herod and the residents of Tyre and Sidon led them to seek a meeting with the ruler. These were the two most important cities of Phoenicia, the coastal region north of Caesarea. These tensions infuriated (*thymomacheō* denotes violent rage) Herod. Perhaps, he may have withheld food or grain exports from them. Palestine's ability to export grain also suggests that this episode preceded the famine that Agabus predicted in Antioch (→ 11:27-30). Representatives of the cities convinced (probably by bribery) the king's **personal** *attendant* to arrange a meeting with Herod so they could end the dispute.

■ **21-23** Luke's account focuses only briefly on the royal pageantry of Herod. He donned royal robes, sat on a raised **throne** (12:21) signifying his authority. Those in attendance are presumably Caesareans and others from Tyre and Sidon. As Herod addresses them (imperfect tense: *edēmēgorei*), the audience begins exclaiming repeatedly (imperfect tense: *epephōnei*) that they hear a god speaking rather than a human being. The Western text's inclusion of a phrase marking the occasion of the reconciliation between Herod and the two cities implies that the newly formed peace prompts their response to Herod. The

230

swift action against Herod by **an angel of the Lord** (v 23) resembles God's judgment of Pharaoh (Exod 12:12, 23, 29) and other Jewish stories describing the gruesome death of those who persecuted the people of God (e.g., Jdt 16:17; 2 Macc 9:5-9; and Josephus, *Ant.* 17.168-70; see Allen 1997, 46-65).

The stated reason for Herod's death is that he *did not give the glory to God*. This mirrors other OT pronouncements of death reserved for kings whose pride caused them to accept the honor reserved for God (e.g., Isa 14:12-20; Ezek 28:1-20; see Dan 4:26-34). The nature of this ailment is not as important as the image of the horrific death deserved by tyrants opposed to God's purposes (see also Isa 51:8; 66:24; Allen 1997).

Ironically, the agent of Herod's divine judgment parallels Peter's divine rescue from Herod's captivity: **an angel of the Lord** initiates both by striking (both *patassō*) the person in question, but with drastically different results. For Peter, the angel delivers him *from* death; for Herod, the angel delivers him *to* his sudden death (see 5:5, 10; *ekpsychō* also describes the deaths of Ananias and Sapphira).

The Death of Herod Agrippa I according to Josephus

The death of Herod Agrippa I is one of the few specific events in Acts also described in a nonbiblical source. Josephus provides a fuller account of Agrippa's death (*Ant.* 19.343-52). So comparisons with Acts may help interpreters discover possible emphases in the Lukan account. Josephus also places this episode in Caesarea. The setting was a gathering of political leaders for a festival celebrating Caesar in AD 44. Josephus similarly depicts Agrippa wearing luxurious garments. The Jewish historian notes that, when the sun reflected off his silvery garments, the radiance captured the onlookers' attention, who then addressed him as a god.

Josephus explains that Agrippa's failure to denounce such deification and flattery was soon followed by an ominous sign of doom. An abdominal ailment immediately struck and killed him after five days of intense pain. Josephus, like Luke, depicts Agrippa's death as God's judgment. But Acts more explicitly underscores the divine role in his horrific demise.

■ **24-25** Two summary statements conclude this section. Whereas Herod's authority ceased at his death, the gospel message—**the word of God** (v 24; 4:31; 6:2, 7; 8:14; 11:1; 13:5, 7, 46; 17:13; 18:11)—continued to spread. The brief description echoes what happened earlier after the resolution of the controversy over the Hellenist widows (6:7). The imperfect tense verbs suggest that Herod's attempts to thwart the Christian movement, like others before him, did nothing to hamper the church's mission and her message's effectiveness.

Luke also reminds readers about the mission of Barnabas and Saul to Jerusalem and its successful completion. The chronological problems associated with this chapter (→ vv 1, 20) may suggest that their ministry (*diakonia*; see

231

11:29) occurred at some point after Herod's death, another sign of the ruler's inability to impede God's purposes through the believers.

The confusing word order of 12:25 suggests that the pair returned **to** (*eis*) Jerusalem after completing their mission, which does not correlate with 11:30. This apparent discrepancy may have led some manuscripts to state that they returned **from** (*ek* or *apo*) Jerusalem, presumably to Antioch (see 13:1). The most plausible solution to this textual problem is to understand this phrase as a reference to **their mission** or **ministry** of offering financial assistance to the believers *in Jerusalem* (see 11:27-30; Metzger 1994, 350-52; Barrett 1994, 593-96; Parker 1964, 165-70).

Upon completion of their mission, Barnabas and Saul **returned** to the place that sent them, Antioch, as the next episode implies (see 11:27-30; 13:1-3). That John Mark accompanied them explains his presence in the next chapter.

FROM THE TEXT

The bleak images of death at the beginning and ending of this section raise questions for contemporary readers. Why did God *not* intervene to rescue James from the death grip of Herod Agrippa? How is it that the quasi-believing prayers of the believers appear to be effective in Peter's case, when their prayers on James' behalf did not? Why have many tyrants and abusers of power and authority across the centuries not experienced the kind of judgment that one sees in the writhing death of Herod?

Reading narrative texts in light of such large, complex theological issues can be as difficult and troubling as readings of miracle stories. We must hesitate to draw universal claims regarding God, the gospel, and the Christian life based on stories alone. Too often, such readings result in cliché-like expressions that may sound correct at first hearing but create more questions than they answer. Problems occur because materials are extracted from their narrative context for their theological or interpretive value. We must first interpret materials *within* their narrative context to see what they may indicate about God and God's purposes.

Within Acts, the major conflicts of this chapter are not Herod vs. the apostles James and Peter. They are the Roman ruler vs. God. Throughout this chapter, the contrast between human and divine power clarifies where true power is found (see Parsons 2008, 170).

The allusions to two central stories regarding God's saving purposes and the covenant people of God affirm that those divine purposes are still in play. Allusions to the Exodus, both in Peter's rescue and Herod's death, point to God's deliverance of God's people, despite all indications about popular or political opinion to the contrary. Likewise, allusions to Jesus' arrest, death, and resurrection suggest "the story of Jesus is continued in the story of his followers, and the power at work in Jesus is now even more powerfully at work in his Church" (Johnson 1992, 219).

Understood in such terms, one may best understand Acts 12 in terms of the Lukan perspective that God "has brought down the powerful from their thrones, and lifted up the lowly" (Luke 1:52 NRSV). Sometimes, the church responds to perceived political or social opposition to the gospel or the church's mission in general by mounting counteroffensives of various means: petitions, boycotts, picketing and demonstrations, email campaigns, political involvement, etc. Such actions often imply that the church's mission involves the resistance of all opponents of the gospel or the forces of evil.

However, Luke offers the contemporary church another perspective. The God of the Exodus has the power to deliver God's people from any bondage and overcome any opposition to God's purposes, as vividly witnessed in Jesus' resurrection.

This is not to say that the church should become passive toward society and its story about reality. But it *does* mean that the church should respond faithfully in the midst of society as those who recognize and believe that God is truly the Lord of all creation who has called her to be God's people and, therefore, God's transforming agents within society.

F. The Ministry Journey of Barnabas and Saul/Paul (13:1—14:28)

1. Call, Commission, and Contention (13:1-12)

BEHIND THE TEXT

The shift from Jerusalem to Antioch at the end of ch 12 represents a major change. To this point, Jerusalem has been the center of the Christian mission from which the gospel message has spread. Confirmation has come from Jerusalem regarding the legitimacy of new people—groups who experienced God's salvation. Now, the church in Antioch becomes the hub of the so-called missionary enterprise to the broader Roman world. In Acts 1—12, Peter and the other apostles, along with Stephen and Philip, were the primary witnesses to God's expanding saving work through Jesus the Christ.

From ch 13, the apostles appear only once more (15:4-11). Saul/Paul takes the prominent role in what appears as the postapostolic portion of the narrative. This does not completely eliminate either the Jerusalem church or Peter from view. But the expanded narrative focus clearly indicates a broadening understanding of the Christian mission and the Lukan perspective of what it means to be the people of God.

IN THE TEXT

■ **I** Luke's list of the **prophets and teachers** in the church at Antioch establishes a direct connection of this group with Jesus and the apostles (see 2:42; 4:2, 18; 5:21, 25, 42; 11:26). Most recently, in Antioch the prophet Agabus delivered the message about the famine (11:27-30). The identity of the five men indicates their diverse backgrounds. The Diaspora Jews **Barnabas** (from Cyprus [4:36]) and **Saul** (from Tarsus [9:11]) have already appeared in the narrative. Simeon's Latin surname **Niger** ("black") has led interpreters to believe he came from Africa. More speculative suggestions that identify him as Simon of Cyrene (Luke 23:26) have scant textual support. **Lucius** was of Cyrenian descent (see Acts 6:9; 11:20). Although **Manaen**'s home region is not mentioned, his association with **Herod the tetrarch** (or Herod Antipas; → sidebar "The Herods, Jesus, and the Church" before 12:1; Luke 23:6-12) places him among the social and political elite. The term *syntrophos*, which describes that relationship, may refer to them growing up together (as friends or foster brothers) or serving together in a court (LSJ 1996, 1729).

■ **2-3** It is unclear whether only these five or the whole Antioch church were **worshiping** and **fasting** (Acts 13:2; see also 14:23). This corporate reflection on God or on serving God (see 2:42-47) provides the context for instructions from the **Holy Spirit**. Given the common understanding of the Spirit speaking through prophets, this message likely comes through one of the listed prophets (13:1).

The verb translated **set apart** (*aphorizō*) appears in the NT only here and in Gal 1:15. But its frequent LXX use refers to choosing something or someone for a holy purpose (e.g., Exod 19:23; Lev 27:21; Num 8:11; Isa 52:11). The task assigned to Barnabas and Saul is not defined here. The previous description of Saul's future (→ Acts 9:15-16) comes into play. The perfect tense of the verb referring to the calling of Barnabas and Saul (*proskeklēmai*) indicates that this mission had not yet been fulfilled (Larkin 1995, 191). However, that mission or **work** (see Gamaliel's warning about opposition to the **work from God** in 5:38-39) implies that their divine task would be as unstoppable as the Christian proclamation thus far in Acts (Lohfink 1975, 87-88).

The immediate response (*tote*, **then** [13:3]) of the church captures the urgency of the untranslated particle *dē* near the beginning of the Spirit's guidance. The reiteration of them having **fasted and prayed** suggests how significant these corporate practices were, both in the church's reception *and in validation* of the divine command.

By praying, the church seeks divine strength and continued guidance for the pair. By placing their hands upon them (see 6:6), the church invokes the same divine presence for the two that characterizes their community (as seen

234

in their recognition of the Spirit's guidance). The church does not send off the pair so much as they **release** (*apolyō*, not *apostellō*) them to fulfill what God sent them out to do. The Antioch church recognizes and validates the divine call of Barnabas and Saul.

■ **4-5** The reminder that the two have been **sent . . . by the Holy Spirit** (13:4) reiterates the divine source of their mission. Their first stop, **Seleucia**, was west of Antioch and near the Mediterranean Sea. From there, they could easily sail to Cyprus (Barnabas' origin).

Ancient Israelites viewed islands from their landlocked perspective as the locale of far-flung Gentile nations (see Gen 10:5, 32; Isa 49:1; Spencer 2004a, 152-53). The port of **Salamis** (v 5), on the eastern coast of Cyprus, was the island's major commercial center and included a significant Jewish population with multiple **synagogues** (see also Philo, *Embassy* 282; Josephus, *Ant.* 13.284-87).

As has often been noted, Luke begins his typical pattern of portraying the Christian ministry as going first to the Jews and proclaiming the gospel to them (e.g., Lüdemann 1989a, 148-51). Luke offers no indication about how they received the message (which later becomes a common narrative feature) or how long Barnabas and Saul stayed there.

The mention of **John** (or John Mark [12:25]), who was an assistant or helper to Barnabas and Saul (Black 1998, 105-8), is the first indication that someone else accompanied the ministry pair. However, this side note provides basic information only for what happened later (13:13).

■ **6-8** Luke mentions only in passing the journey across Cyprus to **Paphos** (v 6), a port city on the southwest coast (see Gill 1995, 219-28). There, they encountered a man named Bar-Jesus, whom Luke describes as a **Jewish sorcerer** (or magician; → 8:4-24) and a **false prophet** (in direct contrast to OT prophets and believers who served as prophets in Acts). The narrator does not indicate how the party met him, perhaps at a synagogue. This also partly explains the interest of Sergius Paulus, the proconsul of that Roman province (AD 46-48). He is with Bar-Jesus and is eagerly seeking (see the intensive verb *epizēteō*) to hear the gospel (i.e., **the word of God** [13:7]). The proconsul's intelligence may explain his openness to the Christian message.

Ironically, the magician with the name "son of Jesus" begins to oppose (imperfect tense: *anthistato*) the pair who are proclaiming God's salvation through Jesus. This charlatan, who had the ruler's ear, repeatedly tries (present participle *zētōn*) to turn him away from the gospel by misleading him and twisting the pair's message (*diastrephō*; BDAG 2000, 237).

The translation of the magician's name as Elymas continues to baffle interpreters—the names have very different meanings. Regardless, he is portrayed as an opponent of the divinely ordained ministry of Barnabas and Saul (see Klauck 2003, 47-50).

■ **9-12** The narrator sometimes notes second names for certain characters in Acts. The mention of another name for Saul without explanation falls in line with this Lukan tendency.

Why Now *Paul* Rather than *Saul?*

Without warning, in 13:9 Luke introduces a second name for Saul—Paul. He then uses the latter for the remainder of the narrative, offering no explicit reason for doing so. He does not indicate why this shift in name occurs here.

Since Saul is a Hebrew name and Paul is a Greek name, the widely accepted explanation is that the narrator initially appropriates the Hebrew name to continue the associations of the Jesus movement with Israel. He switches to the latter name as the mission of the two Christian evangelists took them into predominantly Gentile territories. However, the lack of any corresponding name change for Barnabas (also Hebrew in origin; see 4:36) reveals this rationale as incomplete.

The OT stresses that King Saul was a man of imposing physical stature (1 Sam 9:2; 10:23). But the name "Paul" literally means "small." The name change may illustrate the dramatic transformation from the haughty "big man" among those who persecuted the church to the "small" servant of the Lord Jesus (Mc-Donough 2006, 390-91).

But the delayed shift in name from Saul to Paul long after his Damascus road encounter may underscore the differences between the two Sauls, so that the one Acts reference to the king (13:21-22) may represent those Jewish opponents to the gospel in contrast to Paul, whose transformation led him to proclaim a more inclusive message (see Chapman 2008, 214-43).

The Greek form of the Hebrew name Saul was also an adjective that sometimes described the walk or behavior of prostitutes (as "prancing" or "loose"). So the use of a different Greek name may have sought to avoid those unfortunate connotations (see Leary 1992, 467-69; Fitzmyer 1998, 502-3; LSJ 1996, 1586).

Depending on the time of composition of Acts, the Lukan audience may have been familiar with at least some Pauline letters. A later dating for that composition, even in the early second century AD, makes this a relative certainty. This shift helped that audience to associate the author of those letters with this character.

For the first time, Luke focuses specifically on *Paul's* actions rather than on those of the pair. The depiction of Paul as **filled with the Holy Spirit** (v 9) mirrors earlier images of prophets (2:4; 4:8, 31; see 7:55) and corresponds with Ananias' words (9:17).

Given Elymas' staunch antagonism, Paul does not merely direct his full attention toward him; he glared (*atenizō*; see 1:10; 3:4; 6:15; 7:55) at this opponent of God. Paul's threefold address of Elymas makes it clear that, in contrast to the Spirit-filled Paul, the magician is filled with everything associated with the devil (see 10:38) and evil. This "son of Jesus" is nothing more than a "son of the devil" (13:9 NRSV). The term translated **deceit** generally denotes cleverness. But this context suggests a more sinister nuance, given Elymas' distortion of the gospel (v 8) and *wrongdoing* (see Deut 27:24; Ps 23:4; Wis 5:5; Sir 1:30; 19:26). The same verb describing his attempts to turn Sergius Paulus away from the Christian faith (Acts 13:8) appears in Paul's condemnation. It echoes LXX descriptions of disobedience (e.g., Isa 59:8; Mic 3:9) and opposition to the *straight ways* of God's purposes (Isa 40:3; Hos 14:9; see Luke 3:4).

The imagery of **the hand of the Lord** in Acts typically refers to God's power and purposes (13:11; 11:21; see 3:7; 4:28, 30; 7:25, 50). However, Paul's pronouncement draws from its OT usage to describe God's judgment (e.g., Exod 9:3; 16:3; Judg 2:15; 1 Sam 5:6, 9; 7:13; 12:15; see Garrett 1989, 81-85).

The blindness that overcomes Elymas as divine judgment may be significant on three levels. First, the magician likely practices astrology and needed to see the sun (Klauck 2003, 48). Second, his helpless condition signifies God's defeat of the evil marking his life (see Garrett 1989, 79-87). Third, Paul *himself* endured three days of blindness and needed others to **lead him by the hand** (Acts 13:11; see 9:8) after his encounter with the risen Jesus.

Elymas' temporary condition may have had a redemptive (*kairos*: *for a season*) rather than a punitive purpose. After this dramatic turn of events, the proconsul comes to believe. His astonishment over **the teaching about the Lord** (the gospel) indicates that he believes because of the truth of the message demonstrated in this divine encounter, not because of this extraordinary exchange.

FROM THE TEXT

The transition from the Christian mission centered in Jerusalem to an expanded mission centered in Antioch does not occur separate from the first part of Acts (chs 1—12) but is dependent on it. In this initial scene, God guides the worshiping believers in Antioch as in the opening chapters: God orchestrates and directs the believers as those who are obedient and belong to God.

Importantly, the church in Antioch functions as the context within which God's guidance was heard and confirmed. As Wesley noted, the mission did not originate in the church but came from God, with the obedient church serving as the corporate confirmation of that mission (1958, 443).

The contemporary church must listen to and obey the prophetic voice of God, if it is to be the people of God. God can still guide the *church* in her mission as partners with God in bearing the good news of salvation.

This narrative challenges individualistic understandings of salvation and the Christian life. God's guidance and call are not the possessions of individuals but belong to the church as the people of God (see 1 Cor 12—14). Individuals have often mistaken their own thoughts or wishes for the voice of God. When subjected to the wisdom and discernment of the collective group of believers, such erroneous conclusions may be recognized and corrected.

The clarification about the proconsul's coming to faith in v 12 also challenges the view that Acts expects supernatural occurrences and miracles to be the normal indication of the Spirit's presence among all "Spirit-filled" Christians. This initial scene of the ministry of Barnabas and Paul is an extraordinary validation of God's presence and power upon the pair.

But even in Acts such instances are relatively rare, restricted to signs of God's work in strategic places within the narrative (e.g., transition, opposition, new locations, etc.). Thus, the message of Acts is not that *all* proclaimers of the gospel did or will do such remarkable things. Rather, Acts affirms that God will continue to accomplish God's purposes through obedient people, whose existence is dependent on the empowering presence and grace of God. God enables the church to proclaim the gospel through word and deed (see Peterson 2009, 382-83).

2. Proclamation in Antioch of Pisidia (13:13-52)

BEHIND THE TEXT

In Acts, most accounts of Paul's ministry provide only sketchy details about what happened in a given city. Antioch of Pisidia is an exception. Here, the narrator includes another speech for which Acts has long been noted (→ "Literary Features" in Introduction). Such extended accounts provide a narrative paradigm for what happened in other places. Like the earlier Petrine speeches, Paul's speech coheres with the apostolic teachings: the life, death, and resurrection of Jesus; the role of witness by the earliest believers; the emphasis from Scripture; and the call to repentance (see Dibelius 1956, 165).

In many respects, this Pauline speech seems very different from what Paul himself wrote in his letters. However, the speech is consistent with both the synagogue context where Paul delivered it and the broader Lukan emphases of the unfolding Acts narrative. Thus, readers must interpret this speech within *Acts*, rather than forcing correlations between the speech and the canonical Pauline letters.

IN THE TEXT

■ **13-15** Luke's subtle change from "Barnabas and Saul" to naming Paul first and his dominant role throughout the rest of Acts 13—14 indicate that Paul

238

stepped out of the shadow of his advocate and partner. The partners traveled northwest from **Paphos** (v 13) in Cyprus to **Perga**, an important river port off the Mediterranean coast in the region of Pamphylia in southern Asia Minor (modern-day Turkey). From here, John Mark **return[ed] to Jerusalem**. Luke does not explain why. Interpreters often suggest that Mark was homesick. But **left** translates a term (*apochōreō*) with stronger connotations of desertion (→ see 15:38). His departure may reflect the increasingly Gentile contexts of their travels or Paul's increasing role in leading their ministry efforts.

From there, the ministry party continued north about 90 miles (145 km) to **Antioch** (v 14), a city located in the southern part of Galatia, near the region of Pisidia. This city was located on an important east-west trade route, where a group of Babylonian Jews had once settled (Josephus, *Ant.* 12.147). Thus, as became the pattern for Paul's ministry in Acts, as faithful Jews, the team went first to the synagogue on the Sabbath to worship. Luke mentions only the reading of **the Law and the Prophets** (v 15), which includes the recitation of the Shema (Deut 6:4-9).

An official invitation to speak from the leaders of a local synagogue was typically reserved for those qualified to interpret the Scriptures (see Philo, *Spec. Laws* 2.62). A **word of exhortation** is likely synonymous with a sermon (see Heb 13:22) for the gathered people of God (as *laos* suggests). Since synagogues normally had one leader or synagogue ruler, the mention of plural leaders may indicate a larger synagogue (Barrett 1994, 629). They address Paul and Barnabas as *Men, brothers* (see Acts 1:16; 2:29, 37; 6:3; 7:2, 26; 11:12) and give them a favorable initial reception.

■ **16-20** By standing and gesturing (see 12:17), Paul indicates his intention to speak. His twofold address of the crowd—*Men, Israelites* (see 2:22; 3:12; 5:35; 21:28) and *those who fear God* (13:16; also v 26; 10:2, 22)—addresses both Jewish worshipers and those "God-fearing" Gentiles present. Unlike Stephen's speech, Paul's speech does not mention historic Jewish persons. Instead, he begins with an outline of God's formation of Israel as God's people: election; exaltation (the same term that described Jesus' resurrection and ascension [2:33; 5:31]) during their time in Egypt; and deliverance by God's "uplifted arm" (13:17 NRSV), an OT image depicting God's **mighty power** (see Exod 6:1, 6; Deut 6:21; 7:8; 26:8; 2 Kgs 17:36; Ps 136:12). Perhaps, Paul's speech to his synagogue audience includes more detail, but such information would have been redundant for the *Lukan* audience after Stephen's speech (see Acts 7:2-34).

Two textual variations of the reference to the wilderness wanderings of Israel (13:18) offer broadly different images regarding God's actions. One reading reflects Deut 1:31 (LXX) and is more consistent with this specific context. It states that God nourished (*trophophoreō*) the people during this time. However, the more difficult reading (with slightly better textual support) depicts God as having put up (*tropophoreō*) with the people (see Acts 7:35-44). God patiently tolerated Israel during that dark period of unfaithfulness.

Verses 19-20 continue with God as the subject. God is responsible for Israel's defeat of the seven nations in Canaan (see Deut 7:1) that made possible the gift of the promised land. The LXX portrays this as fulfillment of the covenantal promise of that land for Israel (Num 33:54; 34:18; Deut 3:20, 25; Josh 12:1; 24:8; Ps 37:34; Ezek 34:13; see Acts 7:3-5). The Western text links the 450 years to the period of the judges. The approximation refers either to (*a*) the time period beginning with Israel's 400-year enslavement in Egypt (see 7:6), her 40-year wandering in the wilderness (13:18), and the time of the conquest (v 19); or (*b*) the time of Israel's possession of the land of Canaan (Conzelmann 1987, 104).

■ **21-22** The shift from God to Israel as the subject reminds the audience of a negative phase within Jewish history. They asked for a king (1 Sam 8), so God gave them Saul as their first king (1 Sam 9—10), whom God removed from the throne (1 Sam 13).

The stated duration of Saul's reign as **forty years** (Acts 13:21) may coincide with Jewish tradition (Josephus, *Ant.* 6.378; but *Ant.* 10.143 has twenty years). Besides, the number "forty" plays a significant role in many stories of God's dealings with Israel (→ 1:3-5).

In contrast to that time of testing, the description of God's act of ***raising up*** David as king appropriates a common verb (*egeirō*) associated with Jesus' resurrection (see 13:30, 37; also 3:15; 4:10; 5:30; 10:26, 40). In addition, the citation (combining 1 Sam 13:14, Ps 89:20, and Isa 44:28; see *1 Clem.* 18:1) about God's own perspective of David depicts him as faithful and obedient to God's will. This explains God's actions. Paul's quotation excludes the second half of Ps 89:20 (which refers to God's anointing of David). But it sets up the next stage of his remarks. The last part of this combined citation, which referred originally to the Persian king Cyrus (also described as God's "anointed" [Isa 45:1]), associates God's ultimate purposes with David.

■ **23-25** Now that Paul has established a sense of God's purposes and introduced King David, he focuses on David and God's promise. The promise itself was about David's descendant (***seed*** [Acts 13:23]) through whom God would establish "the throne of his kingdom forever" (2 Sam 7:1-16, esp. 13; see Ps 89:29). Paul will return to this in Acts 13:32-33.

The pivotal move of Paul's speech occurs here. Passing over centuries of Jewish history, he identifies Jesus as that messianic descendant (see 2:32). He appropriates the title **Savior**, which only the Third Gospel among the Synoptics applies to Jesus (Luke 2:11). This links Jesus to God's saving purposes (→ on Acts 5:31) assumed in that promise.

13:21-25

Paul next makes a surprising reference to John the Baptist and his message (Paul's letters never mention him and seldom refer to repentance). He describes John as **before the face of his coming** (alluding to Mal 3:1; see Mark 1:2). He summarizes the essence of John's message as **a baptism of repentance** (echoing Synoptic descriptions; Luke 3:3; Mark 1:4; see Matt 3:2, 6) and reiterates his call for radical change (see Acts 2:38).

The hyperbolic **all the people of Israel** stresses that John's call extends to all Jews who would listen. The clarification of John's mission (lit., "race," *dromos*; see 2 Tim 4:7) assumes knowledge of the Third Gospel if not also the Synoptic tradition (see Luke 3:16; Mark 1:8; Matt 3:11). John's repeated message (imperfect tense: *elegen*) pointed humbly—during his ministry and in Paul's speech—to Jesus as the Coming One, for whom John considered himself unworthy to do even a slave's task.

■ **26-31** Paul's readdress of his audience indicates the importance of this new section. As before (Acts 13:16), he speaks not only to the Jewish majority (***Abraham's descendants*** [v 26]) but also to the **God-fearing Gentiles** present.

The ***message of this salvation*** refers back to Paul's identification of Jesus as Savior (v 23). It also introduces the basic Christian gospel message that follows. His assessment of the role of **the people of Jerusalem and their rulers** (v 27) in Jesus' death corresponds to Peter's perspective: they failed to recognize Jesus (through "ignorance" [3:17]). They were complicit in Jesus' sentencing (see 2:23-24; 4:10, 25-28; 5:30). This, nonetheless, fulfilled the Scriptures regarding Jesus as the Davidic Messiah (see 3:18; Luke 24:44-46).

The lack of justification for Jesus' death sentence (see Acts 3:13; Isa 53:8) and the demands for his execution echo Luke's Gospel. There, Pilate states three times that Jesus was innocent (Luke 23:4, 14, 22). This is followed by Jewish insistence that Jesus be crucified (Luke 23:23-25). The explicit reference to Jesus' removal **from the cross** (lit., "from the tree"; Acts 13:29; see 5:30; 10:39) underscores both the shamefulness of his death by crucifixion and its centrality in the teachings of the earliest believers.

The narrator includes nothing here from Paul that directly interprets the significance of the cross as atonement (see Green 1998, 97-101). However, the allusions to Isa 53 and the Suffering Servant encourage some readers to view Jesus' death accordingly (e.g., Peterson 2009, 75-79, 391).

The mention of Jesus' body being **laid . . . in a tomb** underscores the certainty of his death. However, in dramatic reversal, Paul proclaims that God vindicated the innocent Jesus by raising him from the dead (see Acts 2:24, 32; 3:13-15; 4:10; 5:30-31; 10:40).

The brief reference to Jesus' postresurrection appearances reiterates 1:3. The apostles were those Galileans who first followed Jesus to Jerusalem and served as the **witnesses** of his resurrection (13:31; see 1:8, 22; 2:32; 3:15; 5:32; 10:39) to the Jewish people (*laos*; see 10:3).

■ **32-33** This sentence opens with the emphatic pronouns **we** and **you**, accentuating the role of Paul (and Barnabas). They extend the apostolic witness (v 31) to this synagogue audience. This occurs, even though the two are usually not depicted as apostles in Acts.

By returning to the theme of promise (v 23), Paul now interprets Jesus' resurrection through Scripture as validating and fulfilling the promise of a Davidic Messiah. Psalm 2:7 was originally part of a royal psalm composed for the enthronement of Israel's king. But Paul applies it to Jesus, as did most other early Christians (see esp. 4:25-26; see also Heb 1:5; 5:5; see some MSS of Luke 3:22).

Paul affirms that God fulfilled the declaration about the promised "anointed" in Ps 2:2 **by raising up Jesus** (Acts 13:33). God functioned as Father by giving Jesus life. Some interpret this to mean that Jesus became Messiah at his resurrection (e.g., Pervo 2009, 338-39). But this speech and Acts in general see resurrection as confirmation of Jesus' messiahship (see Gaventa 2003, 200). This corresponds with what Luke 4 depicted in the programmatic scene at the Nazareth synagogue. There, Jesus read from Isa 61 about being "anointed . . . to proclaim good news to the poor." His announcement—"Today this scripture is fulfilled in your hearing" (Luke 4:18-19, 21)—declares that the Spirit-empowered Jesus *himself* fulfilled this promise.

■ **34-37** Paul contrasts Jesus' resurrection and the **decay** or "corruption" (NRSV) of death. This underscores the claim that God fulfilled the promises given to David for Israel through Jesus (see 2:25-33). Two scriptural citations support that claim. Paul links them with the shared adjective "holy" (*hosios*): the **holy . . . blessings** (v 34*b*) and **your holy one** (v 35*b*).

Isaiah 55:3 refers to the covenantal blessings God promised David, accompanied by an expanded view of that covenant as including a call to the Gentiles (Isa 55:5). This brings to mind the blessings to David Jesus received.

Psalm 16:10 (see Acts 2:27) distinguishes David and Jesus. Paul contends that David could not be the referent through whom God fulfilled those promises, since he died and was buried (13:36; see 2:29). Although Jesus was also buried (13:29), God's resurrection of Jesus did not leave him in the tomb and spared him the decay that would naturally occur (13:37; see 2:31).

■ **38-41** Paul's remarks are to help the synagogue audience recognize Jesus as God's chosen one—the one through whom God's promises were fulfilled. By doing so, they would not duplicate the failures of their fellow Jews in Jerusalem (Witherington 1998, 413).

Thus, the speech's shift to exhortation corresponds with the invitation that prompted it (13:15). The subject of the proclamation—**forgiveness of sins** (v 38)—repeats common themes associated with Jesus and the Christian message (2:38; 3:19; 5:31; 10:43), including the call to repentance (which some MSS include). Accompanying this is the language of justification by faith, a dominant theme in the Pauline letters, which appears only here in Acts.

Paul affirms that, by means of Jesus (instrumental *en*), "everyone who believes is justified" (NIV84), put in a right relationship with God (13:39). Grammatically, it is unclear whether the middle part of these two verses refers to the inability of the Mosaic law (as *ouk ēdynēthēte* suggests) to deal with *some* or *all* sins. Commentators typically interpret this in ways that reflect thoughts expressed in the Pauline letters (e.g., Bruce 1988, 262-63; Fitzmyer 1998, 518-19; Johnson 1992, 236). But nothing *here* places the Law in antithesis to salvation through Jesus (through whom God fulfilled God's promises to Israel).

In Acts, the Law functions as the sign that Israel is the historic people of God (Jervell 1996, 54-61). Even so, the inclusive **everyone who believes** reiterates the expanding purposes of God to save all people (see 2:21; 10:34-35).

Paul's remarks to the synagogue audience conclude with a warning (13:40-41) against responding like those in Hab 1:5, **scoffers** or those unfaithful to the covenant who rejected what God was doing. Like those in Jerusalem (Acts 13:27), those in the synagogue of Pisidian Antioch also hear the reading of Scripture (v 15), which Paul proclaims as referring to Jesus as the promised Messiah. Yet they, too, can fail to recognize this message and reject what God is doing. The quotation of this declaration was notably applicable in that synagogue setting (see Wall 2000, 247-58).

In Habakkuk's original setting, the term "work" (v 41 NRSV) emphasized *God's* historical activity (note the emphatic I) of judgment (about Nebuchadnezzar's rise to power). However, here it accentuates those divine actions on behalf of Paul's *current* audience (present indicative: *ergazomai*, **I am doing**): God is offering the choice of salvation and/or judgment through Jesus through the ministry ("work") of Paul and Barnabas (see v 2; 14:26).

■ **42-43** The abrupt ending to Paul's address shifts attention to the repercussions. Although the Habakkuk quotation anticipates disbelief from the synagogue audience, their initial response suggests differently. As the pair leaves the meeting, some in attendance were ironically exhorting *them* (note the imperfect tense: *parekaloun*; see v 15: "word of exhortation") to return **the next Sabbath** so they may continue to proclaim **these things** (i.e., the gospel [v 42]).

In Acts, the verb translated **followed** (v 43) typically describes someone physically accompanying another. In Luke, it refers to someone who followed because of interest, devotion, or calling (such as Jesus' command that Levi follow him [Luke 5:27]). The group following Paul and Barnabas substantiates the general description about the favorable response (13:42).

The ambiguous reference to **devout converts to Judaism** (v 43) combines one description (**devout**) associated with God-fearing Gentiles (10:2) with another associated with full Jewish proselytes (2:11; 6:5). The latter were Gentiles who had converted to the Jewish religion, including full acceptance of the Jewish law (see Cohen 1989, 13-33).

By mentioning that **many** responded favorably, Luke offers a positive picture of both Jews and others attracted to the Christian message. Such responses consistently reappear in subsequent chapters (see Tyson 1992, 133-34). The wording suggests that the two continue speaking about the gospel (the root of the verb *proslaleō* typically refers to such activity in Acts). Their instructions to **continue in the grace of God** allude to earlier scenes where grace was indicative of gospel acceptance and divine blessing among believers (2:42; 4:33; 11:23; against Sanders 1987, 259-63).

■ **44-45** Luke gives a hyperbolic image of **almost the whole city** (v 44) arriving at the Jewish synagogue the **next Sabbath**. The Jewish assembly is overrun by the Gentile populace. They had all **gathered** (*synagō*, the verbal root of "synagogue") with the expressed purpose of hearing **the word of the Lord** (i.e., the gospel). These **crowds** provoke a Jewish backlash, which Luke describes in two related ways (v 45).

First, **the Jews** in general (→ sidebar "'The Jews' in Acts" with 9:21-22) are **filled with jealousy** (see reaction in 5:17). Jewish jealousy or zeal (*zēlos*; Stumpff, *TDNT* 2:877-82) may reflect their concern for their unique status as God's chosen people, which the Gentile crowds now threatened.

Second, they "contradicted" (NRSV)—actively and persistently speaking against (see imperfect tense: *antelegon*)—Paul's proclamation of the gospel (lit., **what was being said by Paul**). Luke considers this "blasphemy," not speaking merely against *Paul* but also against *God* (see 5:39). The message was not the problem (see 13:42-43). Rather, they believe that the overwhelming Gentile response threatens their identity as the people of God. Ironically, however, they distance themselves from the one upon whom that identity was based.

■ **46-47** The bold or courageous response of Paul and Barnabas alludes to earlier images of believers who faced similar hostility (see 4:13, 31). Their statement about the necessity of proclaiming the gospel (**the word of God**) first to the Jews (lit., **to you**) probably reflects the divine election and promise Paul asserts in his synagogue speech. However, the pair assesses Jewish rejection (see 7:39) of the gospel as consistent with their staunch opposition to the gospel and Paul's warning about the rejection of what God offers them (13:40-41).

The ministry team's response may seem harsh after the favorable response they received just a week before. But the Lukan portrait is of *general* Jewish rejection, leading to the declaration that the Jews of Pisidian Antioch *in general* considered themselves unfit for **eternal life** (v 46). This expression is common in the Johannine writings and first-century Judaism. But it is rare in the Lukan corpus (see v 48; Luke 10:25; 18:18, 30). Here, it probably refers to the salvation Paul proclaimed through the life of the resurrected Jesus (Acts 13:32-39).

People often interpret the dramatic pronouncement that Paul and Barnabas would turn their attention to the Gentiles as the beginning of Paul's ministry to the Gentiles as the "apostle to the Gentiles" (Rom 11:13; see Gal 2:8). Two similar pronouncements occur later (Acts 18:6; 28:28).

But Acts consistently depicts Paul as starting his ministry in a new city by proclaiming the gospel first in the Jewish synagogue. Here, Paul ends his synagogue preaching, not simply because of Jewish opposition but because of the divine purposes articulated in Isa 49:6—that the offer of salvation should also be extended to Gentiles—*to the end of the earth* (→ 1:8). Because Jewish opposition sometimes made this (see 9:15; 26:22-23) impossible within the synagogue setting, Paul's stated intentions indicate that such opposition could not hamper those divine purposes.

Different Writers, Different Pauls?

Next to Jesus, Paul may have been the most prominent and influential person within the early Christian movement. The central place of the Pauline letters within the NT canon and his role in the second half of Acts both attest to his influence in early Christianity. All too frequently, interpreters have assumed correlations between these different NT materials, with Acts functioning as a source of background information for the Pauline letters. Often, interpretations of the Pauline materials in Acts are filtered through the thought reflected in those letters.

However, the portrayals of Paul, by Paul himself and by Luke, often include details that depict him differently. Such differences could be related to the two authors' different rhetorical purposes. For instance, the title "apostle" that Paul freely uses to describe himself is almost entirely absent in the Lukan depiction of Paul (except 14:4, 14). Also, there is no mention in Acts of Paul writing any letters, which is most surprising given the collection of his letters in the NT. In the Pauline letters themselves, Paul sometimes distances himself from the Jewish law, whereas the Lukan Paul consistently ministers in Jewish contexts and consistently lives as a faithful, law-abiding Jew (contrast Paul's comments on circumcision in Gal 5:2-11 with Paul's actions of circumcising Timothy in Acts 16:1-5).

These and other differences naturally prompt questions about Paul as a historical figure (see Phillips 2009; Witherington 1998, 430-38). Readers of Acts are well advised to interpret the nuanced Pauline materials of Acts as contributions to *this* specific narrative. They would do well to avoid interpreting the Lukan Paul through the Pauline autobiographical materials in his NT letters.

■ **48-50** The general response to Paul's announcement was mixed. On the one hand, **the Gentiles** (v 48) who had gathered at the synagogue and heard the news were favorably disposed (*chairō* [5:41; 8:39; 11:23; e.g., Luke 1:14; 6:23; 13:17; 19:6, 37]; *doxazō* [3:13; 4:21; 11:18; e.g., Luke 2:12-20; 4:15; 5:25, 26; 18:43; 23:47]). These Gentiles become believers.

Some theological traditions interpret the description of these Gentile believers—those **appointed for eternal life**—as a reference to predestination (e.g., Barrett 1994, 658; Peterson 2009, 399-400). But within Acts, the phrase simply depicts believers as within the saving purposes of God due to their faithful response to the gospel. Wesley concluded that this description of the believers does not indicate that these divine purposes were predetermined or prescriptive for those who believed. Rather, it describes the offering of divine grace that made possible "working faith" in them (1958, 449).

These Gentile believers were probably responsible for the **spread** (v 49; lit.: *carrying*) of **the word of the Lord** (gospel; → v 44) throughout **the whole region**. This generalization does not suggest that all Gentiles, either in the city or from that gathering, responded favorably to the Christian message. However, Luke does depict an overwhelmingly favorable response from the Gentiles in Pisidian Antioch.

The general Jewish opposition to Paul and Barnabas (v 45) continues. **Incited** (*parotrynō* [v 50]) negatively connotes stirring up intense emotions or working others up into a frenzy. This leads to hostile actions against the two. They are expelled (lit., "thrown out"; *ekballō*) from the city.

The agitators may have targeted Gentile women who were attracted to the synagogue (as **devout** suggests; → v 43). They were prominent within the city because their husbands held positions of political authority and could challenge the legitimacy of the Christian ministry on political grounds (see 18:12-17; see Levinskaya 1996, 117-26).

This portrayal of Jewish rejection is also general in nature. It does not negate the earlier favorable Jewish response (13:42-43). Nonetheless, these two generalized pictures stand in juxtaposition, with one depicting favorable response and the other opposition.

■ **51-52** The gesture of Paul and Barnabas shaking the city's **dust** from their feet is an act of defiance (v 51; see Luke 9:5; 10:11) against the Jewish opposition. It symbolizes their resolve to separate themselves from everything associated with their opponents. Paradoxically, their actions resemble a common Jewish practice of similarly ridding themselves of all association with a given Gentile region.

Their departure to **Iconium**, a city about 80 miles (129 km) southeast of Pisidian Antioch, sets the stage for the next episode. The constant, final images of the chapter—about those **filled with joy and with the Holy Spirit** (Acts 13:52; note the continual sense of the imperfect tense *eplērounto*)—allude to earlier positive images of divine presence and blessing among the believers (2:4; 4:8, 31; 5:41; 11:23; 13:9).

Although some interpreters identify these **disciples** as Paul and Barnabas, Luke probably refers to the believers in Pisidian Antioch (→ 14:21-23 on "disciples"), both Jews and Gentiles (see 13:43, 48; against Dunn 1996, 185). Thus, the narrator concludes this episode with a positive portrait of believers in contrast to the Jewish opposition in the city. This demonstrates the unstoppable nature of the gospel.

FROM THE TEXT

Most interpreters recognize the prominence of this episode within Acts. But the variety of opinions regarding its narrative function suggests a greater complexity to the passage than is often acknowledged.

This extended episode reiterates Lukan themes first proclaimed in earlier speeches by Peter and Stephen. All notably stress the role of Jesus as the Jewish Messiah and the function of God's resurrection of Jesus. The risen Jesus fulfilled God's promises to Israel as the people of God. The overwhelming response by the Gentiles is consistent with the narrative's expanding vision regarding God's purposes of salvation as inclusive of Gentiles.

But for the first time in Acts, the early Christian mission turned away from the Jewish people and toward the Gentiles. *Both* the declaration of judgment in response to Jewish opposition *and* the receptivity of Gentiles raise questions. What will be the direction of the Christian mission and the subsequent place of the Jews within God's saving plan for humanity?

These critical issues are significant to the task of interpreting Acts. They need careful consideration as the narrative unfolds. However, readers must also consider how these general images of Jewish and Gentile response to the Christian mission relate to broader narrative emphases. In light of the Lukan themes of God's saving purposes and God's people, the substantive issue in this episode may involve the difficulties in moving from the *recognition* of God's purposes through Jesus to the *acceptance* of their results.

What seems apparent is that the Jewish people, as their initial responses indicate (vv 42-43), readily endorsed Paul's message about God's activities with regard to Israel, even as this related to Jesus as *their* Messiah. However, problems arose when the *implications* of that message resulted in the Gentile populace of the city overrunning the Jewish congregants in the synagogue. This was the one place where Jews maintained their unique identity as God's people.

As emphasized elsewhere in Acts, God's purposes ultimately extended God's blessing to all humanity (e.g., 2:17, 21; 3:25; 10:34-35). Yet, in general, the Jews in Pisidian Antioch did not fully comprehend or accept the consequences of these divine intentions. Hence, the Lukan narrator may have concentrated on these concerns for two reasons:

- First, to underscore the divine initiative in the Lukan redefinition of the people of God.
- Second, to remind them of the divine purpose to save others whom the church viewed as "outsiders."

This suggests that the episode functions in Acts as an appeal to recognize and embrace the purposes of God as inclusive of all. They are not the exclusive property of the few whose religious categories and self-perception blinds them from seeing God's grace at work among the unlikeliest persons around them.

3. Continuation and Confirmation of Ministry (14:1-28)

BEHIND THE TEXT

Ancient narrators often described the first episode within a sequence of similar scenes in detail to avoid repetition. This literary technique helped readers (and esp. audiences) maintain interest and focus on significant elements of the work. The extended account of the ministry of Paul and Barnabas in Pisidian Antioch in ch 13 provides the basic reference point for their subsequent work elsewhere.

Up to this point, Acts has depicted ministry within mostly Jewish contexts (the temple, Jerusalem, synagogues) or with persons associated with the Jews (Samaritans, God-fearing Gentiles). Now, for the first time, one of the settings has no Jewish associations. In Lystra, the gospel extends into the broader context of Greco-Roman culture and politics, especially their religious practices. Thus, the narrative expands beyond the Jewish people to include all peoples.

IN THE TEXT

■ 1-2 The ministry of Paul and Barnabas in Iconium generally mirrors events in Pisidian Antioch. The repetition of three specific occasions in this new city underscores Lukan narrative emphases.

First, the setting of the Jewish synagogue reaffirms the place of the Jewish people in the Christian mission. After the partners' declaration that they would turn to the Gentiles (13:46), their return to the synagogue to proclaim the gospel indicates that the basic mission had not changed.

Second, as before, a mixed group of both Jews and Gentiles responds favorably by becoming believers. The **great number** is again a sign of divine blessing (14:1). Luke does not indicate from where these believing Gentiles come. The synagogue setting implies they are God-fearing Gentiles (→ 13:16, 26).

Third, in contrast to the believing Jews, other Jews refuse **to believe** (14:2; see, e.g., Lev 26:15; Deut 1:26; 32:51; Isa 30:12) the gospel message. This is evidenced in their opposition among Gentiles believers (→ Acts 5:39). The verb translated **poisoned** (*kakoō*) earlier referred to the oppression of the Israelites in Egypt (7:6, 19) and to Herod's hostility against some believers (12:1). Here, the roles are reversed, as the *Gentiles* of Iconium are the targeted victims of *Jewish* opposition. Like in Pisidian Antioch, the concocted problems are apparently political in nature (see 14:5; 13:50).

■ **3-4** The conjunctions *men oun*, introducing 14:3, indicate how Paul and Barnabas respond to this latest adversity. Unlike the previous episode, which ended with their defiant exit from the city, they stay in Iconium for a *sufficient season* (*hikanon chronon*) to accomplish their mission.

The boldness of Paul and Barnabas' proclamation alludes to earlier positive images of the believers (4:13, 31) and themselves (13:46). As before, the reference to God's gift of **signs and wonders** they perform (lit.: *through their hands*) offers divine confirmation of their message and mission (see 2:22, 43; 4:30; 5:12; 6:8).

Again, the Jewish people are divided over the gospel: some believe, others do not. Here, Luke extends the image of division to the whole city, spilling over among the Gentiles, due to the tactics of the Jewish opposition (14:2). Surprisingly, Luke calls Paul and Barnabas **apostles** (v 4; also v 14). Acts elsewhere avoids this designation, presumably since they did not meet the qualifications (1:21-22). However, the pair's activities mirror much of the apostolic mission in earlier chapters. They function as those "sent out" by the Holy Spirit (13:4) to take the gospel *to the end of the earth* (1:8; see Clark 1998, 184-86; Barrett 1994, 671-72).

■ **5-7** Paul and Barnabas somehow hear about a developing **plot** (*hormē*; see LSJ 1996, 1253) to harm them (14:5). **Both Gentiles and Jews**, who had rejected the Christian message, were behind the scheme (vv 2, 4). The involvement of Iconium's **rulers** in the plot hints at the political dimensions of this opposition. The intent to mistreat the pair is reminiscent of what happened in Pisidian Antioch (see 13:50). But the plan to stone them signals a rapid escalation in danger and the potential for death (see 7:58-60). The term describing their flight from the city (*katapheugō*) in the LXX depicts fleeing to another location for refuge (e.g., Gen 19:20; Exod 21:13-14; Ps 143:9).

The city of **Lystra** (Acts 14:6) was a Roman colony about 25 miles (40 km) south of Iconium on a major east-west trade route. **Derbe** was another 55 miles (89 km) to the southeast. The Lukan summary of the ongoing proclamation (imperfect periphrastic *euangelizomenoi ēsan*) of Paul and Barnabas stresses the unstoppable nature of the gospel. Luke does not mention where this ministry occurs; when the setting is the Jewish synagogue, that is typically stated (→ 13:5, 14, 43; 14:1).

■ **8-10** The pair encountered a disabled man in Lystra. This is reminiscent of the episode of the healing of the lame man in the temple (3:1-10). Both may echo Jesus' healing of a crippled man (Luke 5:17-26). In both Acts' episodes, the narrator emphasizes the crippled man's inability to walk since birth (see 3:1). Like Peter, Paul gives the man his full attention (*atenizō*; 3:4). Also, Luke mentions that Paul recognizes that the man possesses *faith to be healed* (14:9; see 3:16; 4:9-12), probably prompted by Paul's preaching. The infinitive *sōthēnai*, which denotes not only his healing but his salvation, reiterates the Lukan theme of universal salvation (2:21, 40, 47; 4:12; 11:14).

That Paul addresses the man *in a loud voice* (v 10) is a common feature of Greco-Roman stories about the appearance of the gods. This prepares for the subsequent reaction of the Lystran people (vv 11-13; see Strelan 2000, 588-603). The man's remarkable response to Paul's command to **stand up** (*anistēmi*, a verb often associated with Jesus' resurrection; see 2:24, 32; 3:22, 26; 10:41; 13:33-34; 17:3) mirrors the jumping and walking of the healed crippled man in Jerusalem (3:8).

■ **11-13** The reaction of the witnesses to the healing reflects their cultural and religious contexts. The notation about the crowds speaking in their Lycaonian dialect adds local color to the story (v 11). It may also represent them as "primitive and rustic" and in need of sage-like guidance from someone like Paul (Béchard 2001, 84-101). However, in the narrative it accounts for the pair not understanding what the people were saying.

From the crowd's perspective, this healing indicates that gods have descended to their city. Thus, they begin *to call* (imperfect tense: *ekaloun*) Paul and Barnabas by the names of two Greek gods. The familiar mythological stories about the appearance of Zeus (Roman: Jupiter) to humans probably explain their identification of Barnabas as Zeus. That they identify Paul as Hermes correlates with his role as the chief spokesperson for the party; Hermes was the messenger of the gods.

Acts 14 and the Tale of Philemon and Baucis

Lukan scholars widely assume that behind the Lystran response to Paul and Barnabas was a familiar, ancient myth. Philemon and Baucis were a poor, elderly couple who lived near Lystra. Ovid (*Metam.* 8.611-724) reports that two Roman gods, Jupiter and Mercury (Greek: Zeus and Hermes), disguised themselves as humans and entered the couple's village. The general populace treated them rudely.

The lone exception was this poor couple. They did not know the true identity of the divine visitors. But they welcomed the gods as guests and provided for them from their limited resources. In time, the gods revealed themselves to the couple before punishing the village for its inhospitality and turning the couple's humble dwelling into a temple. The Lystrans responded to Paul and Barnabas so as to avoid the divine retribution recounted in this well-known story.

Homer tells similar tales (e.g., *Od.* 1.96-324, 405-19; 17.484-87). So Ovid's account and the Lystran response may reflect broader Greco-Roman influences (Wordelman 2003, 205-32).

This interpretation of the dramatic healing is confirmed by the priest of a small local shrine dedicated to Zeus located just outside Lystra. His intent to **offer sacrifices** to Paul and Barnabas is the appropriate response to any appearance of the gods (v 13; against Haenchen 1971, 432). Both the parading and sacrifice of **bulls** or "oxen" (NRSV) adorned with woolen **wreaths** or "garlands" (NRSV) were common practices (see Gill and Winter 1994, 81-85).

As a Christian, Luke knows the people are confused, wrongly seeking to honor and deify the two men. Throughout Acts, healings offer evidence of God's empowerment and blessing (→ 3:12). If the faith of the crippled man demonstrates the promise of the church's expanding mission to the known world, the crowd's response indicates the problems of diverse religions and practices the mission faced (see Krodel 1986, 257).

■ **14-18** Luke may have mentioned the strong reaction from Barnabas first because the crowd associates him with Zeus. Both he and Paul seek to correct the city's erroneous views about them. The violent tearing of their own garments is an ancient gesture of intense grief and despair (vv 14-15; e.g., Gen 37:29; Num 14:6; Josh 7:6; 2 Sam 1:11; Esth 4:1; Jer 36:24). It is also a response to blasphemy (see Matt 26:65; Mark 14:63), as the two would understand the city's actions.

Unlike Herod (Acts 12:21-23), they refuse to accept divine honor and act quickly to squelch the festivities. Their question about what the people are doing is an implicit demand for them to stop. They identify themselves as humans, not gods. The term *homoiopathēs* refers to common human experiences and dispositions (see Wis 7:3; 4 Macc 12:13; Jas 5:17).

The pair's denial stops the proceedings, since the gods would not remain disguised after being recognized. This transforms the scene into an opportunity for proclamation. Their gospel message (*euangelizomenoi*) to the Lystrans has a distinctly Jewish focus. They call for the people to turn *away from* the **worthless things** associated with the idolatry of Greco-Roman religions (Acts 14:15; see 1 Cor 8:4-6) and *to* the **living God** (see Acts 3:19; 9:35; 11:21; 15:19). "Idolatry diminishes the divine to human size . . . and makes God dependent on human actions and subject to human control" (Tannehill 1990, 179).

The description of God as Creator of all things echoes Jewish references to God (Exod 20:11; Ps 146:6) *alone* as worthy of worship. The Lystran confusion revealed their ignorance about God (see Acts 17:30). Their actions confirm that God had formerly allowed **all nations** (14:16; or "Gentiles") to go their own separate ways (see Rom 1:24-32). But this was the case only *in past generations*. God had insinuated a change.

Barnabas and Paul affirm that God had, nonetheless, left a **testimony** or "witness" (v 17 NRSV) about God through the gifts of nature (**rain** and **crops**; see Ps 147:8; Rom 1:18-20) and other blessings (see Ps 145:13-17). This made pagan ignorance deplorable.

Unlike other messages in Acts, the narrator mentions nothing about the Lystran audience's response to the gist of the message. Luke indicates only that the two barely succeed in stopping the sacrifice.

■ **19-20** A dramatic reversal in the Lystrans' perception and response to Barnabas and Paul follows immediately. The narrator refers to Jewish opponents who arrive from Antioch of Pisidia and Iconium (see 13:50-51; 14:6). Some traveled nearly 100 miles (161 km) in pursuit of the two. They are successful in *persuading* the **crowds** (*ochlos* [vv 11, 13, 14, 18]) in Lystra against the two. The pair's critique of the city's idolatrous practices would have turned their way of life upside down. Thus, the crowds were amenable to criticisms against Barnabas and Paul to eliminate such threats (Rowe 2009, 23-24).

Luke does not specify whether the Lystrans or Jewish opponents stone Paul (→ v 5). However, he clearly links this attempted murder to what seems to be a group of persistent, unrepentant Jewish vigilantes. As in the stoning of Stephen (see 7:58), accomplices treat Paul with further contempt by dragging him out of the city and leaving him for dead.

The appearance of some **disciples** implies that some Lystrans respond favorably to the gospel message Paul and Barnabas proclaimed before the healing (see vv 6-7) and before the arrival of the Jewish opposition (between v 18 and v 19). These **disciples** arrive and *encircle* (see Heb 11:30) Paul. With only minimal details, Luke reports the unexpected arising of the presumed-dead Paul within this gathering of believers. This stands out as the most important image of this otherwise ambiguous scene. As in 14:10, the verb *anistēmi* describes Paul getting up by alluding to God's resurrection of Jesus. His return to the city where these hostilities began underscores that *nothing*, including opposition, can stop God's purposes through the Christian mission. In no small part, the community of disciples that came into existence because of the ministry of Paul and Barnabas enables that mission to continue (see Johnson 1992, 256).

■ **21-23** Paul and Barnabas leave Lystra the next day and travel to Derbe. They minister there as they have throughout that region (see vv 6-7). Again, there is no mention of a Jewish synagogue from which the partners could proclaim the gospel. But perhaps it may be assumed. Nevertheless, they *made many disciples* (v 21; a rare verb in Acts, but common in Matthew; see Matt 13:52; 27:57; 28:19). Their mission was a success.

Luke is silent about what prompts them to return to the three cities, where opposition led to their premature departure. However, readers remember the Spirit's role in calling and guiding them (Acts 13:2). Both confirmation and encouragement were especially essential for believers who lived in cities that were demonstrably hostile to the gospel they had embraced.

The missionaries call for believers to *remain in the faith* (14:22). A past decision to believe was insufficient. Ongoing faithfulness and loyalty, both to their belief in the gospel itself and to the community of faith, were necessary.

The instruction about **many hardships** compares their experience to the persecution in Jerusalem that scattered the believers and assisted in the spreading of the gospel (11:19; see 8:1-3). The divine necessity (*dei*) of persecution does not mean that such difficulties are required to **enter the kingdom of God**. The point is that persecution is consistent with God's saving plan, which often leads to opposition from the unrepentant and unfaithful.

Within this context, the appointment of church leaders (**elders**, → 11:30) is particularly significant. Paul and Barnabas would not be present personally to help ensure that Christians remain faithful within hostile contexts.

■ **24-28** Paul and Barnabas retrace their itinerary (see 13:4-14) back to Antioch in Syria. The reminder that their mission began there (13:1-3) brackets the entire account of their journey. Upon their return, the pair reports to the Antioch church that their mission has been *God's* work: God's initiative—**the grace of God** (14:26)—made their mission possible. God's active presence *among them* (v 27) enabled people to respond in faith to the gospel.

The metaphor of a **door of faith** corresponds generally with the idea of entering the kingdom of God (v 22). The missionaries' report emphatically declares that God had opened this door **to the Gentiles**. This by no means suggests that their ministry was limited to the non-Jewish populace. It is true that ch 14 mentions nothing about favorable Jewish response after v 1. The point of their affirmation highlights the dramatic spread of the gospel beyond the Jewish people alone (1:1—8:3) to both Jews *and* Gentiles. With that door opening to Gentiles, Paul and Barnabas were fulfilling Israel's call to be "a light for the Gentiles" (13:47; Isa 49:6).

FROM THE TEXT

Readers of Acts often overlook the significance of this chapter within the unfolding narrative. The sketchy episodes of these ministry stops in out-of-the-way places often hide in the literary shadows of more fully developed scenes before (in Pisidian Antioch [13:14-52]) and after it (in Jerusalem [15:1-29]). And the dramatic Lystran response reflecting their Greco-Roman religious contexts takes readers' attention away from Lukan concerns. They turn instead to contemporary issues, such as the relationship between Christianity and other world religions. However, the material in Acts 14 offers additional perspectives about the purposes of God.

First, suffering and opposition may be expected when obedient servants to God's mission face opposition that seeks to quiet their message and stop their ministry. Nothing in Acts equates the gospel and obedience with prosperity or a life free from hardships. However, it does demonstrate that attempts to oppose God's purposes are futile as the gospel is lived out and shared by divinely called and empowered believers.

The obstacles these early missionaries faced became increasingly formidable as political pressure was added to religious resistance. But the gospel continued to move forward. The mission of Paul and Barnabas seemed doomed to fail in Lystra. The narrative mentions no success among Gentiles unfamiliar with the God of Israel. Instead, readers are confronted with the apparent murder of Paul. Then, unexpectedly, a circle of believers surrounds Paul's lifeless body. And, even more remarkable, Paul stands alive. The narrative reminds readers that God's resurrection power seen in Jesus also extends to the faithful people of God! In the end, this story is not about the ministry journey of Paul and Barnabas. It is about the God of Israel. God cannot be stopped in reaching out to Jews and Gentiles alike.

Second, this chapter makes a contribution to a more holistic understanding of the church's task of evangelism. "Evangelism" in the last two centuries has narrowly referred almost exclusively to the church's attempts to win converts to the Christian faith. The methods may vary from public preaching to more private, one-on-one sharing of a simple gospel message. Not surprisingly, Christian readings of Acts 14 understand Paul and Barnabas as doing something similar.

However, Luke portrays these ministry partners as proclaiming the gospel not only through preaching but also through other ministry practices that required extended time (vv 3, 28). These other practices included what Luke mentions as part of their return trip—the encouragement of believers to remain faithful and the establishment of spiritual leaders to oversee and guide local groups of believers (see Gaventa 2003, 209-10).

The ministry of John Wesley similarly sought to balance public proclamation with the nurture and accountability of his converts. Wesley's spiritual descendants have sometimes neglected the nurturing dimensions provided by his small bands and societies. He would not understand evangelism as "saving souls" without the essential follow-through of making disciples.

The Lukan understanding of evangelism does not limit the Christian gospel to proclamation or to instruction of a list of theological propositions. Rather, evangelism for Luke extends "gospelizing" to the entire arena of human life. Not only words of preaching but all other speech and actions by believers may potentially extend the gospel's work, demonstrating God's presence and love (see Twelftree 2009, 179-203).

Third, the return of Paul and Barnabas to the Antioch church underscores a significant role of the church with regard to their mission. Luke begins and concludes his account of their ministry journey with scenes of commissioning and reporting. These associate the extension of the gospel among the Jews and Gentiles of Asia Minor with the faithfulness of this church in "releasing" the pair to accomplish the work to which God called them (13:2-3).

"Nothing can be farther from Luke's theological point than for a congregation to gather in isolation from its surroundings without any interest in reaching out to diverse populations or institutions" (Wall 2002, 202). Political agendas, economic hardships, and theological squabbles often tempt local congregations and denominations to focus on self-preservation to the neglect of identity and mission as the people of God.

Acts 14 reminds the church who we are and to whom we belong. It calls us to live faithfully according to God's mission and compels us to extend God's grace accordingly.

Excursus: God, the People of God, and Other "Peoples" (Acts 8:4—14:28)—The Developing Narrative Portrait of the Church

The second major narrative unit of Acts presents several episodes recounting the spreading of the gospel to regions surrounding and beyond Jerusalem. The geographical movement of the narrative is linked to the associated ethnic and cultic changes in these episodes.

As the narrative progresses, the plot thickens to include another line of action. With the continuing Jewish opposition, which has become common in Acts (see 9:23-25, 29), tensions arise. Not only Jews but also Gentiles accept the gospel message and change the face of the church. While unanimity is a characteristic among *Jewish* believers in the first seven chapters, it is notably lacking when the church seeks to be inclusive of both Jewish and Gentile believers (see 10:44-48; 11:1-18).

Luke explicitly identifies God, not believers, as the instigator of the proclamation of the gospel to non-Jews. God is also working to save Gentiles. They, too, are included as a part of those called to be the people of God.

So far, Acts has illustrated two possible understandings of the "people of God." In its first narrative unit appears the historical understanding, which includes all the Jewish people. The second understanding includes all Jewish *believers.* Here, Luke introduces a third understanding, which includes *both Jewish and Gentile believers.* The idealistic description of the Antioch church

(11:19-30), composed of both Jewish and Gentile believers, best illustrates this distinct *third* portrait or understanding of "the people of God."

Acts 11 juxtaposes the ideal, positive portrait of Antioch believers with the mounting questions of Jerusalem believers. This suggests that the unanimity and blessings from God that transcend ethnic and cultic boundaries are characteristic of the church. Those who belong to and are called by God are not defined by race or culture but by the empowering work of the Holy Spirit.

IV. GOD AND THE EXPANDING MISSION: TENSION AND RECONSTITUTION OF THE PEOPLE OF GOD: ACTS 15:1—19:41

A. The Jerusalem Council (15:1-35)

BEHIND THE TEXT

The movement of the gospel beyond Jerusalem was into uncharted territory. The church struggled with Peter's association with Gentiles, although they recognized that God had granted repentance to Cornelius and his household (11:18). But this did not prepare them for the ministry of Paul and Barnabas.

Their ministry typically began in Jewish synagogues and resulted in the acceptance of the message by *both* Jews *and* Gentiles. The *Gentile* response stood out, as the ministry pair reported to the Antioch church (14:27). This troubled those concerned to maintain the religious identity of the Jewish people as the people of God. Luke mentions nothing about what Paul and Barnabas required of Gentile converts. But their successful ministry among Jews and Gentiles set the stage for what is known as the Jerusalem Council or apostolic council.

Interpreters have long emphasized the significance of this meeting, both in Acts and in the history of the church. Literarily, its account is at the center of Acts, with nearly as many words preceding as following it (Fitzmyer 1998, 538). Although technically not a "council" like the ecclesiastical councils convened in subsequent centuries, it *is* a "turning point" in Acts for several reasons (Haenchen 1971, 461-62).

First, from this point forward Jerusalem no longer occupies the central role. Second, Peter and the apostles no longer appear in the narrative after this meeting. Third, James and the elders now lead the Jerusalem church. Fourth, the council's decision pronouncedly influences the church's future as it expands to other parts of the Roman Empire.

The Christian movement would have probably remained a secluded Jewish sect if they heeded the demands of those who provoked the controversy. Some issues were resolved in the story of Cornelius. But this episode tackles additional questions about Gentiles, salvation, and the people of God.

Most interpreters correlate the Jerusalem Council in Acts 15 with Gal 2:1-14. Both texts note a meeting in Jerusalem over the requirement of circumcision for Gentile converts, but some significant differences in detail remain (see Lyons 2012, 100-127). Among the differences are the following:

- Acts 15 states that the problem was created by some who "came down from Judea" (15:1) from "the party of the Pharisees" (15:5). Galatians 2 describes the culprits as "false believers" (Gal 2:4).
- Acts 15 describes the controversy as originating in Antioch (15:1), whereas Gal 2 depicts the controversy as arising in Jerusalem.
- Acts 15 depicts the Antioch church sending representatives to Jerusalem to consult with leaders (15:2). Paul declares in Gal 2:2 that he went to Jerusalem "in response to a revelation."
- Acts mentions only the so-called apostolic decree (15:20, 29; 21:25) as stated requirements for the Gentile believers. Paul mentions only the requirement to "remember the poor" (Gal 2:10). And
- Acts 15 does not mention Titus or John; Paul mentions both (Gal 2:3, 9).

Those who understand these two passages as referring to the same general events see these differences as a reflection of different contexts, perspectives, and rhetorical purposes (see, e.g., Barrett 1998, xxxvi-xli; Fitzmyer 1998, 539-41; Pervo 2006, 79-96). Others relate Gal 2 with Acts 11:29-30 (→ sidebar "Collection for the Poor and Paul's Letters" with 11:29-30). Besides these differences, they stress the incongruities between the Pauline chronologies in Acts and the Pauline letters. These are important *historical* questions. But for the *interpretive* task, readers of Acts must first consider the details and perspective provided by the narrative itself.

IN THE TEXT

1. The Problem (15:1-5)

■ 1 The arrival of some people **from Judea** stirred up controversy among the believers in Antioch. Luke does not say who they are (see v 5) or why they come. The verb **came down** implies that they may have come from Jerusalem to set things straight in Antioch (Peterson 2009, 419). Their concern is that Gentile converts had not been circumcised, as Luke's silence on the subject in the preceding chapters implies. These Judean believers (see v 5) begin **teaching** (imperfect *edidaskon*) Gentile believers that they needed circumcision *according to the custom of Moses* (see 6:11, 14; actually Abraham, Gen 17:9-14, 23-27; see Exod 12:43-49).

This is the only instance in Luke or Acts where "teach" describes actions the narrator does not affirm. The visiting teachers insist that Gentile believers can only be **saved** (*sōzō*; see 2:21, 40; 4:12; 11:14; 14:9) if they become Jewish. This entails males taking circumcision as the sign of belonging to the people of God. They directly challenge what constitutes conversion and salvation, contradicting the church's affirmation of what God has done (14:27). These Jewish believers think it best to teach these **brothers and sisters** (*adelphous*), but they clearly do not view them that way (Barrett 1998, 699).

Circumcision, Covenant, Jews, and Gentiles

Circumcision, the removal of a male's foreskin, was the longstanding sign of the covenant people of God. The practice was not unique to the Jewish people, but its adoption and continuation were significant to their cultural and religious identity. The OT frequently refers to circumcision—both physically (e.g., Gen 17; Exod 4:24-26; Josh 5:2-9) and metaphorically (e.g., Deut 10:16; 30:6; Jer 9:25-26; Ezek 44:7-9)—as central to Israel's covenant with God.

Two centuries before the Common Era, the Maccabean crisis dramatically bolstered the importance of circumcision for Israel. The Syrian rulers over Israel sought to eliminate Israel's unique identity by banning it. This led to Israel's revolt (1 Macc 1:48-61) and the reassertion of circumcision as essential for all Jews (1 Macc 2:46). Abandoning circumcision was regarded as apostasy (1 Macc 1:11-15; Philo, *Migration* 89-92). By the first century AD, some Diaspora Jews may have understood circumcision as only symbolic of religious identity and did not have the actual surgery performed (Philo, *Migration* 92; *Spec. Laws* 1.8-11, 304-6; 1QS5.5, 28; Johnson 1992, 259).

There was some debate about the status of Gentiles in relation to the Jewish people, particularly pertaining to circumcision. The book of *Jubilees*, a Jewish text from the first century BC, states that *no* Gentile who had not been circumcised as an infant on the prescribed eighth day could convert to Judaism (see *Jub.* 15:26-27). The general Jewish populace held a more moderate position, affirming that a Gentile could convert to Judaism. However, such proselytes needed to be circumcised as adults to enter the Jewish covenant community (see Josephus, *Ant.* 20.38-48; Parsons 2008, 208-9).

■ **2** The question—"Must a Gentile become Jewish to be a Christian?"—provokes a heated argument between these teachers and the ministry pair of Paul and Barnabas. The term *stasis* refers to a **sharp dispute** or serious difference of opinion (BDAG 2000, 940; Delling, *TDNT* 7:568-71; see Acts 23:7, 10; Josephus, *Ant.* 18.374), even hostility (see Plato, *Resp.* 470b). It sometimes referred to civil strife and division (see 19:40; 24:5; Luke 23:19, 25). The Western text explains Paul's adamant opposition to the teachers: he believes Gentile believers should remain as they are (Metzger 1994, 376-77).

Antioch's failure to resolve the issue led to the selection of representatives to consult with leaders in Jerusalem. It is unclear who selected these representatives (the verb *etaxan*, **appointed**, has no subject). Grammatically, the antecedent *autous* suggests that the Jerusalem *teachers* decided who would go. The Western text has Paul and Barnabas sent to Jerusalem to stand trial (Barrett 1998, 701). But since the Antioch church provides support (*propempō*, v 3; BDAG 2000, 873) for the journey to Jerusalem, believers there probably appointed them.

■ **3-4** The party travel the 300-mile (483 km) journey south to Jerusalem, passing through two regions mentioned earlier. **Phoenicia** (v 3) was where some Jewish believers fled to escape the persecution after Stephen's death (11:19). **Samaria** was where Philip and the apostles Peter and John ministered (8:4-25). At each stop, the group reports in detail *the conversion of the Gentiles* (see 14:27; in the LXX and Acts, *ekdiēgeomai* describes only what God had accomplished; see Ps 118:17; Hab 1:5; Acts 13:41). In contrast to the resistance to Gentile conversion from the Judean believers, these reports prompt *great joy* from **all the believers** in those mentioned regions. These would presumably include at least some Jewish believers (see 11:19).

Upon their arrival in Jerusalem, the envoys from Antioch receive a warm reception, not only from **the church** (15:4) but also from **the apostles and elders** with whom they would consult (v 2; see 11:30). Their report before the entire church in Jerusalem encompasses **everything God had done through them** (see 14:27). Unlike in 15:3, they report on their entire ministry, including the conversion of Gentiles (chs 13—14).

■ **5** A group of believers Luke describes as belonging to the **party** or "sect" (NRSV) **of the Pharisees** (→ 5:33-34) soon raises the circumcision question. This is the first time Acts associates this Jewish group with the believers. Luke typically portrays Pharisees as opponents to God's plan (e.g., Luke 7:30; Acts 5:34-39; see Darr 1992, 120-21; Tyson 1992, 146; Johnson 1992, 260). That these *stood out* (*exanistēmi*) from the rest of the church suggests that theirs was a minority position (see Barrett 1998, 705).

The proponents of circumcision understand their demands as a divine necessity (*dei*). They further want to require Gentile believers to **keep the law of Moses**. These demands clearly defined the religious and social boundaries of the people of God and would have impacted the church's table fellowship.

2. The Debate and Evidence (15:6-12)

■ **6-7** The meeting of **the apostles and elders** (v 6) was probably somewhat separated from the broader church group (vv 4-5), so that the larger group merely observed their proceedings. This allowed the smaller group to examine (*idein*) the issue more fully in a legal sense (Barrett 1998, 713; Wall 2002, 208). As in Antioch, the issue led to considerable **discussion** or "debate" (vv 2, 7 NRSV).

As the **discussion** wore on or people wore out, Peter stands to speak. His contribution was critical, because he alone among the Jerusalem leaders had experience in dealing with Gentiles. Thus, he refers to his experiences with Cornelius a decade earlier (**some time ago**). Peter summarizes the material from ch 10, as he did for the Jerusalem believers (11:5-16). Here, he moves beyond personal recollection and offers some distinct theological conclusions. He affirms God's initiative in the election or **choice** (→ *eklegomai* in 1:2, 24; 13:17) to include the Gentiles among those to hear the **gospel** (see also 20:24, the only other appearance of this noun in Acts) and *come to believe* (aorist tense of *pisteusai*; see 13:8, 12, 39, 41, 48; 14:1, 9, 22, 27). Peter underscores God's work through him without mentioning his earlier resistance or that of the Jerusalem believers.

■ **8-9** Peter continues to accentuate all God had done. God is the one **who knows the heart** (15:8; see 1:24; also 1 Sam 16:7; 1 Kgs 8:39; Ps 7:8; Jer 17:10; Luke 16:15; Rom 8:27; 1 Thess 2:4; Rev 2:23). Thus, God alone was capable of discerning the human condition and, more specifically, the Gentiles in question. With the gift of the Holy Spirit, God offered witness (*emartyrēsen*) to God's own redemptive actions among the Gentiles, just as God had done among the Jewish believers (see also 13:22). God confirmed the acceptance and inclusion of Gentiles in God's saving purposes, to the Gentiles themselves *and* to these Jewish Christians.

Peter's final reflection reiterates more forcefully the theme of God's impartiality (see 10:34; 11:17; compare Rom 2:11; 3:22; 10:12; Gal 2:6; Eph 6:9; Col 3:25). The use of the verb *diakrinō* reminds readers of two previous instances in Acts. One is when the Spirit instructed a confused Peter after his heavenly vision in Joppa to go with Cornelius' representatives "without hesitation" (*mēden diakrinomenos* [10:20]; see 11:12). The other is when the circumcised believers in Jerusalem "criticized" (*diekrinonto*) Peter for staying at Cornelius' house for several days (11:2). As in ch 11, Peter understands the vision to be about the salvation and acceptance of Gentiles.

ACTS

15:6-9

261

At this point, Peter makes a significant theological move. The evidence of God's refusal to discriminate was God's "cleansing" (*katharisas* [NRSV]) of the Gentiles. This recalls the voice in Peter's vision: "Do not call anything impure that God has made clean" (*ekatharisen* [10:15]). This "heart-knowing" God (15:8) cleansed their hearts **by faith** (v 9; see v 7). Obviously, some Jewish Christians still thought that social contact with Gentile Christians made them ritually "unclean," even after the conclusion of 11:18. Thus, they demanded that Gentile Christians become Jewish converts through circumcision and obedience to the Mosaic law (15:5).

Peter's conclusion trumps this contention: God made these Gentile Christians clean by removing what made them "outsiders" to the people of God. Faith, rather than circumcision, Jewish law, or other regulations governing who was "insider" and "outsider," was the criterion for the salvation of this people (see Thompson 2007, 77-79).

■ **10** Although Peter's audience (see v 6) had not voiced those Pharisaic demands, his pointed question addresses them as though they support such measures (Pervo 2009, 373-74). The idea of "putting God to the test" (NRSV) or "challenging God" (CEB) draws from OT examples of mistrusting God and opposing God's purposes (see Exod 17:2, 7; Num 14:22; Deut 6:16; Ps 78:18, 41, 56; Isa 7:12), something Jesus condemned (Luke 4:12; Matt 4:7). Within Acts, this idea is reminiscent of Ananias and Sapphira, whom Peter accused of conspiring to "test the Spirit of the Lord" (5:9). Peter, echoing the Pharisee Gamaliel's warning (5:39), had spoken earlier about the dangers of opposing God (11:17).

The **yoke** was a common Jewish metaphor for the Mosaic law. Placing (*epitithēmi*; see v 28) it on the necks of Gentile *disciples* refers figuratively to imposing it on Gentiles. The addition of circumcision and Jewish law to the faith God deemed sufficient for salvation (see v 9) constitutes "testing" or opposition to God and God's purposes.

The Jewish/Mosaic Law as a Yoke

In the ancient world, the yoke—an instrument used to restrain and control domesticated animals—was often used as a metaphor to describe political or social oppression (see, e.g., 2 Chr 10:10; Ps 2:3; 1 Macc 8:31). However, in Jewish teachings, the metaphor of a yoke often described the *benefits* of the Jewish or Mosaic law. The Hebrew term for law, Torah, refers to teaching and guidance rather than legal codes and regulations. Thus, the metaphor of a yoke emphasized the direction and guidance that the Torah provided (*m. Ber.* 2.2; *m. 'Abot* 3.5; Sir 51:26; *Pss. Sol.* 7:9; 17:30). Like a yoke, the Law enabled obedience to God. Therefore, the Law was not an unbearable burden to endure but made faithful living possible (see Nolland 1980, 105-15). This was a quite different comparison from what Paul expressed to the Galatians: "Stand firm, then, and do not let yourselves be burdened again by a yoke of slavery" (Gal 5:1b).

The verb translated **bear** seldom has negative connotations of something oppressive in the NT, LXX, Pseudepigrapha, and the writings of Josephus and Philo (Nolland 1980, 113-15). Peter denies that the yoke of the Law was an unbearable burden neither they nor their ancestors could fulfill (against, e.g., Haenchen 1971, 446; Fitzmyer 1998, 548; Witherington 1998, 454). Rather, at issue is Israel's failure to fulfill the demands of the Law (see 7:53). The problem is not a deficiency in the Law God gave Israel, but Israel's disobedience to God through the Law (Nolland 1980, 105-15; Gaventa 2003, 216; Jervell 1998, 392-93).

■ **11** Peter's rhetorical question (15:10) addresses the Pharisaic demands (v 5). His final statement emphasizes (at the beginning of the Greek sentence) the requirements for salvation (v 1; see Richard 1984, 191; Tannehill 1990, 185). Salvation occurs **through the grace of our Lord Jesus**, not through circumcision or Jewish law (see 13:38-39). *All* believers—both Jewish and Gentile—are the people of God solely on the basis of grace.

Surprisingly, Peter does not compare the Gentiles' salvation to that of the Jewish believers. Instead, Peter reverses the order and underscores the *Gentiles'* salvation to disclose the basis of the *Jewish believers'* salvation. By doing so, the focus remains on them sharing a common salvation. With these words, Peter's role in Acts concludes.

In many respects, this sentence includes themes more common in the Pauline letters than in Acts (see Rom 3:21—5:11; Gal 2:15—3:14). Several explanations exist. Some contend that, by noting these similarities, Luke indicates that the criticism against Paul's message is unfounded, as this is the same apostolic message proclaimed by Peter. Others suggest that this passage encourages an *intracanonical* reading, in which the interpretation of Peter's testimony takes into account these prominent themes from the Pauline letters. If Acts was written in the second century, even the original readers of Acts would have known those Pauline letters that would contribute to their reception of this passage.

■ **12** After raucous debate (v 7), silence (*esigēsen*) comes over the **whole assembly** (vv 4, 6). Peter convinces them about the salvation of Gentiles and that circumcision and Jewish law are unnecessary requirements.

Then **Barnabas and Paul** speak. Barnabas probably appears first due to his prominent role among the Jerusalem believers (see 4:36-37; 11:22). They report about their specific experiences of ministry among the Gentiles, which prompted this meeting.

Readers should not confuse the brief summary of the pair's contribution to the meeting as "passivity" (Conzelmann 1987, 116) or a small role (see

Witherington 1998, 456). Luke merely summarizes what the narrative already describes (chs 13—14) by reiterating three things.

First, God was the source of everything that happened, a repeated theme in the reports about their ministry journey (→ 14:27; 15:4). This theme underscores God's role as Creator (4:24, 28) who enabled Jesus' ministry (2:22, 36). Second, the **signs and wonders** that were evidence of God's activity in the ministry of Jesus (2:22), the apostles (2:43; 5:12), and Stephen (6:8) also validated the ministry of Paul and Barnabas (see 14:3). This description does not appear again in Acts. Third, they tell about God's saving work **among the Gentiles,** because *Gentile* salvation is under challenge. The focus is on God as Savior, not on the human agents or the Gentiles as those being saved.

3. The Assessment by James (15:13-21)

■ **13-14** Like Peter's message, the report from Barnabas and Paul silences (*sigēsai*; see v 12) the audience. James (see 12:17) then responds. His role as a leader within the church is obvious, both by his participation in the meeting and his handling of the situation.

James, a Leader of the Early Church

The abrupt entrance of James into the Acts narrative takes contemporary readers by surprise. However, Luke assumes his readers are familiar with James and his role in the early church. He is not the apostle, James the son of Zebedee, whom Herod executed (12:2), but the brother of Jesus (Gal 1:19) and one of the three "pillars" of the Jerusalem church (Gal 2:9). James probably did not become a follower of Jesus until sometime after the resurrection (see 1 Cor 15:7).

It is unknown how James rose to such prominence within the Jerusalem church. However, his leadership correlates with traditional accounts that emphasize his devotion to the Jewish law (see Eusebius, *Hist. eccl.* 2.23.4-18). This devotion to the Law is one reason why early Christian tradition associated him with the letter that bears his name (see Jas 1:25). According to Josephus, James was executed by stoning prior to the Roman destruction of Jerusalem (ca. AD 70). In Josephus' account, the high priest Ananus accused James of breaking the Law and then carried out the sentence when no Roman official was present to oversee the region (*Ant.* 20.197-203; see Painter 2004).

Interestingly, James refers only to what Simeon (the Hebrew spelling of **Simon;** see 2 Pet 1:1) said. He almost certainly refers to Simon Peter. But nowhere else is Peter called Simeon (see, e.g., Acts 10:5, 18; Luke 4:38; 5:3-5, 8, 10; 6:14). Two other possibilities exist.

It could refer to Simeon Niger (see 13:1), who may have been one of the representatives who accompanied Barnabas and Paul (15:2) and may have participated in the earlier debate (v 7; see Fitzmyer 1998, 553). Less likely, following John Chrysostom, it could be the elderly Simeon who prophesied that the salvation Jesus brought would be "a light for revelation to the Gentiles, and for the glory of your people Israel" (Luke 2:32; see Riesner 1994, 263-78).

James summarizes Peter's message as a visitation from God, a common OT image of God's intervention and deliverance (see, e.g., Gen 21:1; 50:24-25; Exod 3:16; 4:31; 13:19; 32:34; 1 Sam 2:21; Jer 5:29; 9:8, 24; 11:22; see also Luke 1:68, 78; 7:16; 19:44). The same verb (*episkeptomai*) earlier describes God's intervention through Moses to deliver Israel from their Egyptian oppression (Acts 7:23). Now God is creating **a people from the Gentiles** (or "nations"). The idea of God choosing Israel as a special people *apart* from the nations is common in the Pentateuch (see, e.g., Exod 6:7; 19:5; 23:22; Deut 4:20; 7:6; 14:2; 26:18-19). However, the phrase **from the Gentiles** (*ex ethnōn*) paradoxically specifies from where the chosen came (see Zech 2:11; Dupont 1985a, 321-35). Although they were not Jews, God also chose them from among the Gentiles to be known by God's **name** (see Dahl 1957-58, 319-27).

■ **15-18** James' citation of Amos 9:11-12 correlates these divine actions with Amos' depictions of divine restoration. His introduction is significant, as he understands **the words of the prophets** to **agree** (see Acts 5:9) with God's inclusive actions outlined in the previous verse. God's actions provide the context for understanding this passage of Scripture (Johnson 1992, 271). The citation itself adapts the LXX version. Similar to Peter's citation of the Joel prophecy (see 2:17), the opening phrase **after these things** replaces the original "in that day" (Amos 9:11). So the fulfillment of Amos' prophecy occurred in the church's mission after Pentecost.

James underscores the divine restoration of Israel, which Amos describes as God "raising up" the fallen Davidic dynasty. The first verb in Amos 9:11 (LXX)—from *anistēmi* (see 2:24)—has been changed, perhaps influenced by Jer 12:15-16. This alteration was to prevent James' audience or Luke's readers from directly linking this to Jesus' resurrection. Rather, it underscores God's restoration of Israel as God's people—the **fallen tent of David** (Gaventa 2003, 219; Jervell 1998, 395). Or it may be interpreted more specifically as the eschatological temple (or the end-times people of God, comprised of both Jews and Gentiles) over whom the Davidic Messiah reigns as Lord (Bauckham 1996, 164-67; Wall 2002, 219). Either way, Luke proclaims Jesus as the fulfillment of those divine promises through the prophet to Israel (see Dupont 1985b, 19-32; Tannehill 1990, 188-89).

The purpose (*hopōs*) of the divine restoration, according to the Hebrew text of Amos 9:12, is that Israel would "possess the remnant of Edom" and other nations as a restored kingdom. But the cited LXX verse offers a different promise: the **remnants from humanity** will **seek the Lord**. These are **all the Gentiles** upon whom God's "name has been called" (NRSV). This expression signifies divine ownership (Deut 28:10; 2 Chr 7:14; Jer 14:9; Dan 9:19). All belong to God and are the intended recipients of God's saving initiative (see Acts 13:48). God's call of both Jews and Gentiles creates a people belonging to God.

This adapted LXX version of Amos 9:11-12 validates the testimonies of Peter, Barnabas, and Paul: the divine plan of restoring Israel includes the salvation of uncircumcised Gentiles apart from becoming Jewish proselytes. The last phrase in Acts 15:18, alluding to Isa 45:21, accentuates the inclusion of Gentiles as a long-established part of God's salvation purposes.

■ **19-20** On the basis of the Amos passage (*dio*, **therefore**), James addresses the ecclesiological rather than soteriological implications of the debate (see Löning 1990, 315-17). The assembly must not harass (*parenochlein*—see LXX: Judg 14:17; Job 16:3; 1 Macc 10:35; 2 Macc 11:31) Gentiles **turning** [*epistrephousin*; see v 3: *epistrophēn*] **to God** by requiring circumcision and the Law (Acts 15:19).

Instead (*alla* [v 20]) signals James' concern to address the other side of the debate. They should send Gentile believers some instructions by letter (*epistellō*) consistent with their deliberations (vv 6-18). Three things complicate the interpretation of the following list: (1) three slightly different versions of the list (vv 20, 29; 21:25); (2) the rare terminology and brevity of the description; and (3) early MSS of Acts differ over the wording of 15:20.

James' instructions do not require Gentiles to become Jewish proselytes through circumcision and Law-keeping. But they are completely to avoid four things:

First, Gentile believers should avoid **whatever has been polluted by idols**. Idolatrous practices were commonplace in Greco-Roman culture and politics. Verse 29 refers to "things sacrificed to idols" (NASB; 1 Cor 8:1-10; 10:19-30; Rev 2:14, 20; 4 Macc 5:2). This prohibits eating or drinking things consecrated to a god (see Lev 17:7-9; Dan 1:8; Mal 1:7, 12; Sir 40:29).

Second, they should avoid **sexual immorality** (*porneia*). This broad term refers to sexual irregularities such as forbidden marriages and banned sexual practices (Lev 18:6-23), and possibly sacred prostitution. Jewish tradition often associated these with idolatry (see Jer 3:1-10; Ezek 16:15-46; Hos 5:3-4; Wis 14:12; *Jub.* 22:16-23; 1 Cor 10:7-8; Rev 2:14, 20).

The third and fourth prohibitions, against **whatever has been strangled** and **blood**, may be similar. The former likely refers to the consumption of meat from which the blood had not been properly drained (see Exod 22:31; Lev 17:13-14; Philo, *Spec. Laws* 4.122). Some magical papyri indicate that choking sacrifices was thought to transfer their spiritual life to the idol. Again, idolatry was the issue (Witherington 1998, 464).

The fourth refers to the consumption of an animal's blood (see, e.g., Lev 17:10-12; Deut 12:23-35; 1 Sam 14:31-35; Josephus, *Ant.* 3.260). This was often associated with idolatry (see Wis 12:3-5). The similarities of these two prohibitions may explain the Western text's omission of the third ban. Some interpreters combine these as redundant (e.g., Johnson 1992, 267). Others suggest the latter to be a prohibition against murder (e.g., Barrett 1998, 733; Cohen 1987, 77).

Several suggestions about the function of this apostolic decree have been made. It bears striking similarities to later rabbinic prohibitions against idolatry, murder, and incest (see Barrett 1998, 734-35; Cohen 1987, 77). It may also reflect the Holiness Code of Lev 17—18, especially those that refer to "resident aliens," Gentiles living among the Jewish people (see Lev 17:7, 10, 13, 15; 18:26; see, e.g., Callan 1993, 284-97).

Some interpreters downplay connections between the decree and Leviticus, contending either (*a*) there is little direct correlation between the two texts (Lev 17—18 is about Gentiles in a largely Jewish context, not the other way around) or (*b*) there are many other Jewish laws resident aliens were obliged to follow (see, e.g., Wilson 1983, 68-102; Witherington 1998, 462-67).

These four specific prohibitions depend upon James' reading of Amos in light of Jer 12:16. The focus shifts from Gentiles living *in* Israel to them living *among* Jews without a specific location (Bauckham 1996, 172-78). James' instructions reflect pragmatic issues Gentile believers faced daily. Idolatry was a persistent problem, especially celebrations and festivals at pagan temples. This is consistent with Luke's concerns about idolatry (Acts 7:40-41; 14:15-17; 17:22-31; 19:23-41; see Gaventa 2003, 222-23). Everything in the list was associated with such contexts (Witherington 1998, 462-67).

ACTS

15:21

These different understandings are closely related, as James' proposal is concerned with three things:

- Jewish believers' perception of uncircumcised Gentile believers as part of the people of God,
- Gentile believers' protection from the idolatrous practices of their world, and
- Jewish believers' protection from the contamination of their world they feared threatened their identity as the people of God.

■ **21** James concludes his proposal by offering an explanation (*gar*). Other Jewish writers made similar claims about the long-standing influence and tradition associated with Judaism (see, e.g., Josephus, *Ant.* 16.43; *Ag. Ap.* 2.175; Philo, *Spec. Laws* 2.62). But James' instructions are to help Gentile believers live in harmony and fellowship with the many Jewish people who were "deeply committed to Mosaic law" (Tannehill 1990, 190). Many Gentile believers, already associated with the Jewish synagogue, would be familiar with the requirements Moses provided for "resident aliens" and would already follow them, especially in their fellowship with the Jewish people.

4. The Letter to Gentile Believers (15:22-29)

■ **22-23a** James' proposal receives a favorable response. Acts gives no indication how the church arrived at its decision (the indicative *edoxe* portrays a formal decision; also vv 25, 28). Two things stand out.

First is its support, not only from the "inner circle" of **the apostles and the elders** but also from **the whole church** (v 22). This need not mean that this moderating view completely won the day (against, e.g., Marshall 1980, 254). Still, the church agrees about offering guidance to Gentile believers.

Second is the selection of two representatives to accompany Paul and Barnabas back to Antioch. Their presence would counter those who initially went to Antioch and created the controversy. Although **Judas** had the same surname (**Barsabbas**) as Joseph who was nominated to replace the apostle Judas (1:23), there is no indication of any connection between the two. **Silas** will soon become an important character in Acts: Paul will ask him to accompany him on his next ministry journey (v 40). Their place as **leaders** within the Jerusalem church also lends credibility to the letter they personally deliver.

Embedded Letters in Ancient Narratives

Ancient historical narratives—both from the broader Greco-Roman context and those from Jewish circles—often included letters embedded within them (e.g., Herodotus, *Hist.* 3.40; Thucydides, *War* 7.11-15; Josephus, *Ant.* 16.162-73; 1 Macc 10:11—12:23; 3 Macc 3:11-30). Acts includes two: the one here, and one to the Roman governor Felix about the transfer of the prisoner Paul from Jerusalem to Caesarea (23:26-30).

Like speeches, these letters have specific rhetorical functions. Narrators use letters to authenticate accounts by accentuating important aspects of the plot. They also provide opportunity to repeat key emphases of the narrative. They may also minimize or downplay other aspects of the narrative that have little importance.

All these functions are visible in the Jerusalem church's letter to Gentile believers. It accentuates the Spirit's guidance (v 28), repeats the decision (v 29), and downplays the debate (see vv 25, 28). Thus, the letter clarifies their important decision and authenticates James' role as leader of the Jerusalem church (see Aune 1987, 128; Parsons 2008, 215-18).

■ **23b-27** Since the church approves James' proposal, the **apostles and elders** (v 23b) serve as official spokespersons. They call both the Gentile believers and themselves **brothers**, affirming their shared relationship in Christ.

The letter distances the Jerusalem church from the troublemakers. In v 1, it is unclear whether they went to Antioch on their own or the church sent them. But the letter characterizes their message as both unauthorized and subversive (*anaskeuazō*; Bruce 1984, 302). The verb translated **disturbed**

ACTS

15:22-27

268

(*tarassō* [v 24]) connotes confusion (see 17:8, 13; for noun, see 12:18; 19:23). It sometimes characterizes false teaching (see Gal 1:7; 5:10).

In contrast to the nameless group of Acts 15:1, the letter names the party that will deliver it and affirms the collective stance of the council (*homothymadon*, **together**; see 1:14; 2:46; 4:24; 5:12) behind it. The acknowledgment of Barnabas and Paul as **our dear friends** (15:25) who have "devoted their lives" (v 26 CEB) to the cause of Christ reinforces that unified front. By introducing Judas and Silas in the letter (v 27), it clarifies their role that Luke leaves for readers to assume (v 22).

■ **28-29** For the second time (see v 25; also v 22), the letter refers explicitly to the church's decision. Here, it refers for the first time to the **Holy Spirit**'s role in the proceedings. The image of unity (v 25) implicitly alludes to previous scenes of the Spirit's presence (see, e.g., 2:42-47; 4:32-37). But the mention of the Spirit underscores the divine role in these human deliberations (Shepherd 1994, 218; Twelftree 2009, 160-62).

The letter combines Peter's ardent plea (15:10) with James' proposal (v 20). James interprets and responds to what Peter, Barnabas, and Paul shared. The stated concern that they place (*epitithēmi*; see v 10) **not one burden** (v 28) on the Gentile believers seems to address the issues both James and Peter raised (vv 10, 19). However, the letter lists the four prohibitions as **necessary things** or "essentials" (NRSV), not for salvation (as in vv 1, 5) but for fellowship between Jewish and Gentile believers.

The decree itself is similar to the proposed version in v 20, with three notable differences. First, the wording for the first prohibition differs, but its meaning seems unaffected (→ v 20). Second, the prohibitions in the letter appear in a different order. Here, the arrangement mirrors that found in Lev 17—18, which further indicates the plausible role of this OT text in crafting the decree (Bauckham 1996, 180). Third, the encouragement to abstain from these things (*diatēreō*) uses LXX language for contexts dealing with covenantal faithfulness (see Gen 17:9-10; Num 18:7; Deut 7:8; 33:9; Sir 1:26; Johnson 1992, 277). These instructions would facilitate Gentile fellowship with Jewish believers, who related such avoided things to the polytheism of their day. Observing them would also nurture their own faith and devotion to the God of Israel.

5. The Delivery and Reception of the Letter (15:30-35)

■ **30-31** The joyful response in Antioch to the letter corresponds to the joy the gospel evokes in Luke (see, e.g., 1:14; 2:10; 8:13; 10:17; 15:7, 10; 19:37; 24:41) and Acts (see, e.g., 5:41; 8:8, 39; 11:23; 13:48, 52; Gaventa 2003, 225). It specifically reflects the joy expressed about Gentile conversions (15:3). For Gentile Christians who already had more-than-casual ties with Jewish syna-

ACTS

15:28-31

gogues, these prohibitions would have been both familiar and readily acceptable to them (v 21).

■ **32-35** Luke closes this extended episode by summarizing the activities of the four named persons who deliver the letter to Antioch.

Judas and Silas as **prophets** (v 32) function as divine spokespersons (see 11:27-28; 13:1), including those filled by the Holy Spirit (see, e.g., 2:4; 4:8, 31; 6:5; 11:24). What they say to **encourage and strengthen** the church in Antioch corresponds with the earlier ministry of Paul and Barnabas (see 14:21-22).

The **blessing of peace** (15:33) reiterates the community's favorable response to the decree. Some MSS include "it seemed good to Silas to remain there," likely a later insertion to account for Silas' presence in Antioch in v 40 (Metzger 1994, 388).

The description of Paul and Barnabas continuing to teach (see, e.g., 2:42; 4:2, 18; 5:21, 25, 28, 42; 11:26; 13:1-3) and proclaim the gospel (see, e.g., 5:42; 10:36; 11:20; 14:7, 21) corresponds with earlier images in Acts also associated with God's presence and blessing.

FROM THE TEXT

Although the extended account of the so-called Jerusalem Council functions as a narrative hinge of Acts, interpretations often focus on secondary issues. To be sure, this episode has much to teach the contemporary church about conflict resolution and decision-making. But this is not the primary reason for its placement here in Acts. Two related theological concerns are central.

First, how may the church discern God's saving activity and will? How do we recognize or discern what *is* divine activity, blessing, and guidance and distinguish it from what we *think* or *hope* to be divine activity, blessing, and guidance? Here, the church's task was to discern what God was doing among the Gentiles. Was this truly God at work? If so, what did that mean with regard to the church and her mission?

In essence, this is the difficult task of doing theology. In the church's deliberations, they turned to Scripture. But they did so in a context where they had already heard the debates and the reports of what God had done among the Gentiles. That is, much of what Wesleyans consider in terms of tradition, reason, and experience was already at work in the meeting when James brought up the Amos passage for consideration.

We should also note how the church went about this discernment process. Peter's personal experience was placed before the *collective* discernment of the community as he described how God provided testimony to what God was doing (v 8). In this way, the personal experience of what God was doing was evaluated within the corporate context. James' proposal also ensured that tradition played a vital role in the process by making sure that their endorsement of the "new" did not inadvertently make the "old" extraneous (see Wall 2002, 211-12).

Throughout Acts and affirmed here by the council, there was a continuity of God's saving plan that extended throughout the story of God's covenantal people to that moment. Their fresh reading of Amos came out of this emerging, collective understanding of God's saving activity among the Gentiles.

Nonetheless, the ongoing theological challenge of discernment regarding God's purposes and those among whom God is working ultimately has to do with the mission of the church. Debates over contemporary philosophies of church ministry often end up wrestling over this theological question. While Wesleyans optimistically see God's grace at work throughout the world, other theological traditions often do not. The result is that situations similar to what we find in Acts 15 often face the missional church. As Dunn aptly states,

> What we have here, then, is a . . . classic confrontation between old revelation, confirmed by centuries of history, and a new insight, given not through Jesus himself but in the course of an expanding, developing mission. It would have to take clear indication of divine approval and tremendous confidence in the agreed judgment of the leadership for such an epochal step and breach with unbroken tradition to be taken. With the Christian mission continuing to develop today, the church cannot avoid being confronted with similar hard questions in the resolution of which not all will be satisfied. (1996, 199)

Such discovery and discernment concerning God's activities will breathe life and vitality into the church and her mission.

Second, what is the nature of the church? What does it mean for God *to take from the Gentiles a people* known by God's name? Some contend that the narrative depicts one people that is Jewish (i.e., Israel) and another that is Gentile. However, there are three reasons why it seems more likely that the narrative portrays *one* people of God, which include both believing Jews and believing Gentiles:

- Such an image is consistent with earlier depictions of believers in places like Antioch in Syria (11:19-30).
- Luke makes it clear that God granted salvation to Jews and Gentiles alike on the basis of faith alone (see 15:7-9). God's grace, not Jewish law or circumcision, is the common criterion for salvation and being part of God's people.
- Acts indicates that the people of God are not defined by their ethnic background but by their worship of God and God alone.

The prohibitions in the apostolic decree guarded Gentiles from the polytheistic practices of idolatry that could detract them from worshiping the God of Israel. The common worship of the God of Israel brought Jews and Gentiles together as one people. This needs to be remembered when political preferences, family or friendship ties, consumerism, or many other allegiances often take our attention away from, if not take precedence over, our common Lord.

B. Changes to Paul's Ministry after the Jerusalem Council (15:36—16:10)

BEHIND THE TEXT

Since the Jerusalem Council confirmed that the people of God included Jews and Gentiles, the ministry to both groups could continue through Paul and Barnabas. However, at this point the church has not separated from its Jewish context, so observant Jews will continue to oppose the place believers give to non-Jews.

IN THE TEXT

1. A Serious Disagreement between Paul and Barnabas (15:36-41)

■ **36-38** Paul's suggestion about visiting the believers in the cities where they previously ministered came after an unspecified period of time teaching and preaching in Antioch (see v 35). Barnabas is *wanting* (*ebouleto* [v 37]) to take John Mark with them. No reason is offered; given Barnabas' portrayal in Acts, he probably wished to give him a second chance (Col 4:10 identifies Mark and Barnabas as relatives). But Paul is insistent (*ēxiou*) that they *not* take John Mark with them.

The imperfect tense of these two verbs, indicating continuous action, portrays persistent, opposing viewpoints. Luke specifically offers Paul's perspective about John Mark's earlier unexplained departure (→ 13:13): he **deserted them in Pamphylia** (15:38). The verb *aphistēmi* connotes desertion or apostasy (see, e.g., Luke 8:13; Acts 5:37-38; 19:8; 1 Macc 11:43). No reasons appear for John Mark's departure. But the timing (after a Gentile official's conversion) and his Jerusalem church ties suggest that he may have resisted the inclusion of Gentiles within the Christian mission (see Black 1998, 112-20).

■ **39-41** Rather than resolution, the disagreement intensifies. The word describing their rift, *paroxysmos*, conveys growing mutual exasperation ("having a pungent odor"; see LSJ 1940, 1342-43; Black 1998, 114). This results (*hōste*) in their split. Barnabas takes John Mark with him to Cyprus (see 13:4-12). Neither Barnabas nor John Mark appears again in Acts.

Paul selects Silas, one of the representatives from the Jerusalem church. Luke does not explain how either John Mark or Silas arrived in Antioch. By describing the believers' blessing of Paul (and not Barnabas) before his departure, Luke implicitly endorses Paul as well. His ministry with Silas in **Syria and Cilicia** (15:41) places them in the same area James' letter addressed (see v 23). Their activity of **strengthening the churches** correlates with earlier descriptions of the believers (14:22; 15:32), which implies they overcame the problem that temporarily sidelined their ministry.

2. An Addition to Paul's Ministry Team (16:1-5)

■ **1-3** Since Paul is now the major character, the narrative focuses mostly on him. The subsequent naming of Silas (v 19) implies that he accompanies Paul here. Their arrival in the cities of Derbe, Lystra, and Iconium recalls Paul's prior ministry there (see 14:1-23). Timothy and his mother (Eunice [2 Tim 1:5]) may have become believers then. Timothy became a prominent figure in the early church. He is identified as the co-author of several undisputed Pauline letters (see 2 Cor 1:1; Phil 1:1; 1 Thess 1:1; Phlm 1) as well as two "disputed" Pauline letters (Col 1:1; 2 Thess 1:1). Paul mentioned him in favorable ways on several occasions (Rom 16:21; 1 Cor 4:17; 16:10; 1 Thess 3:2), and the first two Pastoral Letters are addressed to him.

Luke does not explain why Paul decides that Timothy should join his ministry team, but the sentence structure and wording highlight two qualities about *this one* (*touton*). One was Timothy's mixed family background, with a Jewish mother and a Greek (Gentile) father. Timothy embodied the diversity of the developing church. The other was his good reputation among the believers in both his hometown (Lystra) and Iconium. The short distance between them suggests he may have ministered in both.

Given the Jerusalem Council's debate about circumcision and Gentiles, the account of Paul's ministry (chs 13—14), and Paul's own statements about circumcision (see, e.g., Gal 2:3-4; 5:2-11), his circumcision of Timothy has puzzled many. Clearly, he does not circumcise Timothy to assure his salvation.

Does Paul (and Luke) regard Timothy as Jewish or Gentile? The preceding debates dealt with the exemption of circumcision for Gentile believers only. As the child of intermarriage, Timothy would have been considered a Jew because of his Jewish mother, according to later Jewish law (*m. Qidd.* 3.12). Timothy's Gentile father may have prevented his circumcision earlier (see, e.g., Barrett 1998, 761-62). By having him circumcised now, Paul clarifies Timothy's identity as a faithful Jew (and not an apostate) and his place within the "mixed" context of the church. Early exegetes, however, such as Jerome and Augustine, considered Timothy a Gentile (see Cohen 1986, 251-68; Pervo 2009, 388). However, it seems unlikely that Luke would depict someone who actively affirms the decisions of the Jerusalem Council (16:4) but who is also a "walking contradiction of the very thing the decree said" (Bryan 1988, 293).

The narrative ambiguity of Timothy's status is not unique in Acts (see, e.g., the Samaritans [8:4-25], the Ethiopian eunuch [8:26-40], and Cornelius [10:1-48]). Its attention is on the pragmatic reason behind Paul's actions: **the Jews who lived in that area** (16:3). Paul prepares Timothy for their upcoming mission. Paul's ministry in Acts typically began in Jewish synagogues, so his circumcision of Timothy is about Jewish reception of the gospel (Conzelmann 1987, 125). Paul's action here anticipates questions about his faithfulness to Jewish law (see 21:21, 28).

■ **4-5** The last two sentences of this paragraph summarize the general ministry activities of Paul, Silas, and Timothy (imperfect tense). The distance between the three cities (→ 14:6) required them to spend considerable time in the region. These cities were located outside the regions addressed by James' letter. The delivery of the council's decisions implies that they were applicable to all Gentile believers (see 21:25). Perhaps the letter was a beneficial tool for addressing the problems over circumcision of Gentile believers that Paul addressed in Galatians (see Gal 5:1-12; 6:12-16). But if so, Paul never mentions it directly there.

The term translated **decisions** (*dogmata* [v 4], from the verb *dokeō* in the apostolic decree) describes what they officially decided to recommend (15:25, 28; see 15:22; Johnson 1992, 284). Both the task of **handing over** these decisions (*paradidōmi*)—a verb often associated with tradition (see, e.g., Luke 1:2; Acts 6:14; 1 Cor 11:2, 23; 15:3; 2 Pet 2:21)—and the reference to the **apostles and elders** emphasize the continuity of the Christian teachings.

The positive descriptions about the growth and strengthening of the church confirms (*men oun*; Smyth 1956, §2899) those actions and the function of the instructions within the churches. The verb translated **strengthened** (*stereoō* [Acts 16:5]) also describes the healed crippled man (3:7, 16). In the LXX, this verb affirms God as Creator and Lord of the universe (see, e.g., 1 Sam 2:1; Isa 42:5; 44:24; 45:12; 48:13; 51:6; Hos 13:4; Amos 4:13). The growth of the churches is reminiscent of earlier descriptions of divine blessing (see, e.g., Acts 2:41, 47; 4:4; 5:14; 6:7; 9:31; 12:24).

3. The Vision of the Macedonian Man (16:6-10)

■ **6-8** The group's westward movement eventually takes them beyond those areas in south central Asia Minor where Paul ministered previously (see 13:13—14:25). The narrative includes nothing specific about what they do there. But a passing reference to disciples in that same area (18:23) suggests that they lived out their mission wherever they went (Tannehill 1990, 194-95).

It appears that they planned to continue west into **the province of Asia** (16:6), a highly developed and wealthy area with several prominent cities, including Ephesus. They planned **to proclaim the word** (gospel message; see *lalēsai* and *laleō* with *ton logon* in 4:29, 31; 8:25; 11:19; 13:46; 14:25). But divine guidance changes their itinerary. Luke does not state how they are **prevented by the Holy Spirit** from fulfilling those well-intentioned plans. The verb **prevented** (*kōlyō*) earlier affirms that God's saving purposes through the church's mission cannot be stopped (8:36; 10:47; 11:17). So Luke hints that such divine purposes were at work in this "closed door."

Their modified itinerary takes the group north. They arrive at a point where **Mysia** (16:7), in northern Asia, is on their left, and **Bithynia**, on the coast of the Black Sea northeast of Mysia, is on their right. Their attempt to enter Bithynia is also inexplicably thwarted by divine intervention. This time, Luke describes that guidance as coming from **the Spirit of Jesus** (only here in Acts; see Phil 1:19; also Rom 8:9; Gal 4:6; 1 Pet 1:11). Although this is synonymous with the Holy Spirit, it also alludes to Jesus' prior active role in Acts (7:56; 9:1-16).

So the group travels through Mysia to **Troas** (16:8). It is a large seaport on the northeastern Aegean Sea opening into the Black Sea. It serves as a launching point for sailing to Greece.

■ **9-10** Paul had a **vision** in Troas signifying divine guidance (see 9:12; 10:3, 17, 19; 11:5; 12:9; 18:9). Perhaps it is a dream since it happens **during the night** (16:9; see Gen 46:2; Dan 7:13). In the vision, Paul sees an unidentified man from **Macedonia**, the Roman province in the northern part of the Greek Peninsula.

Visions of persons giving traveling instructions were common in the ancient world and understood as divine communication (see references in Talbert 1997, 147-48). The man is **standing and begging** for help, which implies urgency. The verb used in his call for help (*boētheō*), may allude to the LXX of Second Isaiah, where it describes God as the one who helps in Israel's redemption and restoration (see, e.g., Isa 41:10, 14; 44:2; 49:8; 50:9; 60:15). Those who hear Paul recount the vision are convinced (*symbibazō*; BDAG 2000, 957) this is God's call.

The verb depicting that calling (*proskaleō*) alludes to early Lukan emphases on God's initiative in salvation (see Acts 2:39; Joel 2:32). They promptly prepare to go to Macedonia, obedient to the divine calling. In Acts, such direct divine involvement leads to extraordinary things.

First-Person Narration in Acts

A characteristic feature of Acts is its shift from third-person to first-person plural narration. This first appears here in v 10 and continues through v 17. It reappears in 20:5-15, 21:1-18, and 27:1—28:16. There are several plausible explanations for this (→ Introduction). The first-person plural may reflect the author or the sources that the author used. In either case, this would have obvious implications for authorship.

However, a more helpful and shared trait is that this offers credibility and additional corroboration alongside Paul. This first-person perspective may implicitly identify the narrator with the narrated events. But it also tends to draw readers into the story, so that they relate more closely with the story's events as the narrator presents them (see, e.g., Kurz 1993, 111-24; Byrskog 2003, 257-83; Campbell 2007).

FROM THE TEXT

Because of the obvious importance of the Jerusalem Council, readers can easily miss the significance of these episodes. The fact that Paul and Barnabas went their separate ways is itself significant. However, it was not because the two were able to accomplish twice as much. This may be true, but it is not Luke's emphasis. Nor was it because they simply wanted to part agreeably (see Chrysostom, *Hom. Act.* 34, quoted in Martin 2006, 193-94). Rather, it allows Paul to take center stage. However, in these three sections are also distinct issues faithful readers need to consider.

First, the complicated issues involving understandings of the people of God, salvation, and relations among Jews and Gentiles were not all neatly resolved by the Jerusalem Council. Questions remained, as the tensions between Barnabas and Paul over John Mark imply. And we should not expect the Jewish synagogue, which has been the primary location of the church's ministry, to endorse such conclusions.

The rift between Paul and Barnabas might suggest that Paul took a more "liberal" stance, favoring Gentile believers. But both his selection of Silas and his circumcision of Timothy indicate his awareness of and sensitivity for other perspectives. Both the Jewish heritage and the extending mission continue to be played out.

Silas may represent the Jerusalem church's active partnership with the Antioch church through Paul's mission (see Tannehill 1990, 196). The recognition of tradition as dynamic rather than static is essential in creative missional leaders. In this instance, it allowed for the expansion of mission without excluding Jewish believers or the Jewish people. These actions also incorporated persons for ministry who were particularly suited for Paul's divine mission (see 9:15-16).

Second, discernment is necessary regarding divine guidance. Discernment of divine activity was central to the Jerusalem Council in general terms of mission. Here, discernment is needed when God seems to be guiding in particular ways. Certainly, Paul and Silas were prophets, which in Acts meant that the Holy Spirit offered them divine insight (see, e.g., 9:18; 13:9; 15:32). The team's mission placed them where the Spirit blocked or thwarted their plans. We can only imagine the mounting frustration as God blocked their attempts to go both left and right! Yet these divine obstacles also served God's purposes by putting them in the right place to receive a divine call as prominent and unmistakable as the one that initiated Peter's visit to Cornelius (10:1-20) and the first ministry journey of Paul and Barnabas (13:1-3).

Third, the first-person plural narration suggests the importance of what transpired in those moments. The narrator directs the reader's attention to the divine calling of Paul to embark on this mission to Macedonia. Paul and the others had other worthy plans, yet God steered them to Troas and gave them an unmistakable message. The serious challenges they would face would make it imperative for them and the readers of Acts to know with certainty (see Luke 1:4) that God initiated their mission to Europe, as in earlier instances in Acts.

C. The Ministry of Paul in Philippi (16:11-40)

BEHIND THE TEXT

The movement from Asia to Europe signals a new chapter in the story of the emerging Christian movement. Set in motion by divine guidance, Paul and his entourage arrive in Philippi to obey their divine mandate. As the story moves farther from Jerusalem, fewer Jewish characters appear. Here, the group encounters three different non-Jewish characters. Drastically different social statuses color each meeting. The conversions of both Lydia and the jailer (and their households) provide a general framework for interpreting the broader passage.

IN THE TEXT

1. The Conversion of Lydia (16:11-15)

■ **11-12** The first two legs of the trip were about the same distance. The verb translated **put out to sea** appears often in Luke's description of Paul's journeys (v 11; see 13:13; 18:21; 20:3; 21:1; 27:4, 12, 21; 28:10-11). The main verb, "took a straight course" (NRSV; see 21:1), is not a nautical term. It implies not veering to one side or the other.

The first destination was **Samothrace**, a mountainous island in the far northeastern Aegean. Homer mentioned the island (*Il.* 13.12), stating that Poseidon (Greek god of the sea) surveyed the city of Troy from the island's tallest mountain. Since the island has no harbor, the travelers probably stayed onboard. The second leg took them to **Neapolis**, the port for Philippi. Philippi was located inland and northwest about 10 miles (16 km).

The group probably travels to **Philippi** the following day (v 12). Textual problems complicate Luke's description of the city. The oldest MSS read that Philippi was a **leading city of that district of Macedonia**. The adjective *prōtē* commonly describes *capital* cities, which Philippi was not. An alterna-

277

tive reading is that Philippi was "a city of Macedonia's first district" (CEB; see Metzger 1994, 393-95). This correlates with the Roman division of Macedonia into four districts (see Livy, *Hist.* 45.29).

Philippi was a **Roman colony** established by Octavian (31 BC). It was originally a small gold-mining town, named after Philip II of Macedonia, father of Alexander the Great. Its importance was due to its location on the Via Egnatia, the main road between Asia and the West. In either sense, Luke affirms the city's stature in its corner of the empire, perhaps because Roman customs and citizenship later affect the story line.

The peculiar mention of the party *spending some days in this city* fills the time gap between their arrival in Philippi and the Sabbath. The verb translated *spending* (*diatribō*) or "staying" has connotations of wasting time (BDAG 2000, 238; LSG 1996, 416). Luke offers no explanation for this delay, which calls attention to what would happen on the Sabbath.

■ **13** On the Sabbath, the group goes outside the city to the Gangites river, where they expect to find **a place of prayer**. The location may be due either to Philippian suspicions of Jews in general (see v 20) or to convenience near the river for ceremonial washings. Many understand this to be a Jewish meeting place for prayer and worship in the absence of a synagogue. (*a*) Only women meet with Paul and his companions (a minimum of ten Jewish males were required for the institution of a synagogue). (*b*) Luke uses the term "synagogue" whenever he refers to the building or institution.

However, Luke's silence about Jewish men in Philippi should not be pressed. Jewish writings (including inscriptions) often used **place of prayer** as a synonym for a Diaspora synagogue (e.g., 3 Macc 7:20; Philo, *Flaccus* 45-49; Josephus, *Ant.* 14.258; *Life* 277-93; Binder 1999, 111-18; Levinskaya 1996, 207-25). In effect, Paul continues his pattern of starting his ministry in a Jewish synagogue. Here, it may begin among some prominent women leaders. Since prayer is an emphasis in Acts (see, e.g., 1:12-14; 2:42; 3:1; 4:23-31; 10:1-20; 13:1-3), the Lukan use of this terminology may anticipate God's working.

■ **14-15** Luke introduces one woman, whom he identifies as **Lydia** from **Thyatira** (v 14). Since this city was in the region of Lydia, her name may simply mean "the one from Lydia." This may indicate that she was a freedwoman (i.e., a freed slave), since freedwomen and men as well as slaves often took the name of their homeland. She was a **dealer in purple cloth**, a luxurious commodity for which her hometown was famous. Such a trade could generate considerable income, although those in elite circles would have looked down on those in such trading professions (see Matthews 2004, 126). That Lydia was the leader of her own household also suggests she had some financial means.

Lydia, Her Profession, and Social Status

Contemporary readers of Acts often assume that Lydia's financial means defined her social status. However, social standing was more complicated than that. Luke offers only one Greek word, *porphyropōlis*, which refers to someone who sold purple cloth. Some interpreters claim that those in this profession were wealthy and enjoyed high social standing, since rulers and the rich coveted the luxurious fabric (see Gill 1994b, 114-18; Witherington 1998, 492-93; Williams 1990, 282). Others correctly note that dyers and weavers were often despised (as were tanners; → 9:43) because of their dirty and odorous conditions, often involving the use of animal urine (see Schottroff 1993, 131-37; Reimer 1995, 101-9; Spencer 2004a, 175; Malina and Pilch 2008, 117).

Luke associates Lydia with a trade that brought low status. But he mentions nothing about her living outside the city, indicating that she sold *and* produced the purple fabric (against Spencer 2004a, 175; 2004b, 148-49). Yet her economic achievements would have provided her some level of respectability.

Lydia's status probably fell somewhere between the two extremes. As a narrative character, Lydia joins a growing group of ambiguous figures in Acts, including the Samaritans (8:4-25), the Ethiopian eunuch (8:26-40), Simon the tanner (9:43), Cornelius (10:1-48), and Timothy (16:1-3). Rather than an unnamed woman remaining in the shadows of the plot, Luke offers Lydia an identity transformed by the gospel.

Lydia is reminiscent of the Godfearer Cornelius. First, she is a **worshiper of God** (16:14; see 13:50; 17:4, 17; 18:7). Second, the imperfect verb **listening** underscores her prayerful concentration on Paul's gospel message (present participle *laloumenois* [16:14]; imperfect indicative *elaloumen* [v 13]). Third, Lydia's conversion is due to God's actions. God *completely* opens (*dianoigō*; see Luke 24:45) her heart to embrace (*prosechō*) the gospel. This leads to her baptism (see Acts 10:47-48) and that of her entire **household** (16:15; see also 11:14; 16:30-34; 18:8), which would have included family members and slaves. Fourth, her hospitality to Paul's party involves accepting responsibility for their provision. Lydia's invitation to stay at her **house** (*ton oikon mou*) with her household (*ho oikos autēs*) indicates her faithfulness to God.

Lydia is a *Gentile* offering table fellowship to the *Jewish* Paul and his cohorts. This resembles the *implicit* Lukan depiction of Peter's table fellowship with Cornelius (see 10:48; 11:2-3; Matthews 2004, 126-27; Pervo 2009, 404). Lydia, as the first convert in Europe, appears and functions much like the new "Cornelius" of the European portion of Paul's ministry in Acts.

2. The Conversion of the Philippian Jailer (16:16-40)

a. The Conflict and Arrest over a Slave Girl (16:16-24)

■ **16** After an unspecific period of time (*egeneto de*), there is an encounter between Paul's entourage and a **female slave** (see 12:13) on their way to the **place of prayer** or the synagogue (→ 16:13). **Prayer** reminds us of the healing of the crippled man at the time of prayer (3:1-10) and anticipates God's working.

This girl has a **spirit** that enables her to do **fortune-telling**. The word used to describe this spirit refers to the mythical snake Python of Delphi. Unlike the respected oracles at Delphi, the girl's owners exploited popular beliefs for profit (*ergasia*; see 19:24), probably using her as a fortune-teller in the marketplace.

Python, Oracles, and Fortune-Telling in the Greco-Roman World

In Greek mythology, Python was the great snake that lived at Delphi as a representative of the underworld. The god Apollo defeated Python and founded at Delphi what became the most famous oracular center in antiquity (Ovid, *Metam.* 1.438-47). A woman from Delphi served as the prophetess. She descended within the temple of Apollo to pursue spiritual insight to provide answers to questions posed to her. Such consultation of the gods was highly revered (see, e.g., Herodotus, *Hist.* 1.51, 66-67; 5.42-43). Many believed the gods spoke through such human instruments.

Popular belief led to distorted practices and abuses (see Plutarch, *Def. orac.* 414e), including charlatans who exploited the gullible for profit. One such abuse was the use of ventriloquism to "declare" divine messages in exchange for money. Gifted ventriloquists could make lifeless images appear to speak. The OT associated oracular practices with idolatry and witchcraft (e.g., Deut 18:9-14; Isa 8:19; 29:4). Judaism prohibited such practices (see, e.g., *Sib. Or.* 3.224-26; *T. Jud.* 23.1; Philo, *Dreams* 1.220; see Levison 2009, 318-20).

■ **17-18** The girl not only **followed** (v 17) the Pauline party but was practically "under foot" (*katakoloutheō*). She was incessantly crying out (imperfect *ekrazen*) her message. Her description of God as the **Most High God** echoes those found in Acts (7:48), the Third Gospel (1:32, 35, 76; 2:14; 6:35; 8:28: 19:38), and the OT (e.g., Gen 14:18-22; Num 24:16; Deut 32:8; 2 Sam 22:14; Isa 14:14; 57:15; Mic 6:6). People within the polytheistic context of first-century Philippi would have used the same description for many of their gods.

Two small differences distinguish the girl's message from Paul's. First, she uses a generic verb (*katangellō*, "declare") rather than *euangelizomai* ("proclaim the good news"). Second, there is no definite article before the noun **way**, so that the girl refers to "a way of salvation" (CEB; NRSV), implying this

280

to be merely one path among many. Thus, the girl's message would ultimately lead to misunderstanding (Klauck 2003, 68-69).

Paul's slow response may have been due to his foresight of negative consequences (see Acts 16:19-24). In the end, he probably acts to prevent confusion among new converts (Klauck 2003, 69) rather than from impatience. The verb *diaponeō* is also used to describe the Sadducees' response to Peter and John in 4:2.

Paul's response is directed to the spirit, not to the girl. He, like Jesus, commands the spirit to depart. Luke does not describe this spirit as evil or unclean, or as tormenting the girl (contrast, e.g., Luke 4:35-36; 8:32-33). Paul commands the spirit **in the name of Jesus Christ** (Acts 16:18), emphasizing the authority of Jesus (see, e.g., 3:6, 16; 4:10, 12, 17, 18, 30).

■ **19-21** The girl's **owners** (Acts 16:9) remain her masters (*kyrioi*; also v 16) after the exorcism. But they recognize (*idontes*) that Paul's actions rob them of future profits from her. They are masters of the girl, not that spirit. Their rough treatment of Paul and Silas (Luke mentions no others) before the governing officials suggests how livid they are. Taking the pair to the **magistrates** initiates legal proceedings (v 20). The **marketplace** was used for various public purposes (commercial and legal).

On the surface, the charges appear to have little to do with the situation, other than the identification of Paul and Silas as **Jews**. Their charge reflects general Roman suspicions of Jews as disloyal to the empire, since they refused to worship the popular gods (associated with politics). The first part of the charge—about them **throwing our city into an uproar**—labels the pair as creators of social chaos and confusion (see *ektarassō*; Josephus, *J.W.* 7.41; *Ant.* 17.253). However, the only noted upheaval comes from those pressing charges!

The second part of the charge concerns **unlawful** customs (v 21). This seems ambiguous, since the narrator never mentions Paul advocating *any* custom. Some consider this a fabricated charge intended to cover up the plaintiffs' actual complaints—their economic losses. More likely, these charges reflect the deeply disruptive character of Paul's exorcism. By expelling the pythonic spirit from the slave girl in the name of Jesus Christ, Paul exposes the weaknesses of the popular religious system and attacks the economics and power associated with it (Rowe 2009, 23-27; see also Peterson 2009, 436).

■ **22-24** Not surprisingly, the Philippian crowd sides with the plaintiffs who are probably well known to them. Luke mentions nothing about formal legal proceedings. The magistrates move immediately from hearing the charges to having Paul and Silas **beaten** with wooden rods (v 22; see 2 Cor 11:25; also 1 Thess 2:2), a means of public humiliation depriving them of an opportunity for defense (see Keener 1993, 369). They are then placed in custody to await sentencing.

281

Like the account of Peter's incarceration (Acts 12:4), Luke notes the security detail intended to restrain the prisoners. The jailer **put** [lit., **threw**] **them in the inner cell** (16:24). This would have been so completely dark that no one could see to escape. The **stocks** were instruments of both confinement and torture, with several holes to lock the prisoner's feet for maximum security and discomfort. With such security arrangements, escape seemed impossible. This scene reminds readers that Paul would suffer for the Lord's name (9:16), here for an exorcism "in the name of Jesus Christ" (16:18).

b. The Earthquake and the Conversion of the Jailer (16:25-34)

■ **25-26** Since Acts includes stories of miraculous escapes, readers may anticipate that possibility again (but James' execution warns against this assumption [12:1-2]). Paul and Silas continue **praying** [present participle *proseuchomenoi*] **and singing hymns** [imperfect *hymnoun*] **to God** around **midnight** (v 25), which conveys their trust and confidence in God. Antiquity considered such resolve in the face of suffering the sign of true philosophers (see, e.g., Epictetus, *Diatr.* 2.6.26-27; Plato, *Phaed.* 60e; Pervo 2009, 408-9). The other prisoners may have heard them if they were in the same inner cell (see Rapske 1994b, 202-4).

In divine response to their prayer, an **earthquake** subsequently comes that is strong enough to shake the prison's **foundations**, open all its **doors**, and free all the prisoners of their **chains** (v 26; see 4:24-30). The prison that confines Paul and Silas, not to mention all the other prisoners, is rendered incapable of holding these divine witnesses.

■ **27-30** Luke says nothing about the effects of the earthquake. He focuses only on the exchange between the two believers and the jailer. Upon awakening and discovering the doors of his secure prison wide open, the jailer assumes the worst. His decision to commit suicide may be prompted by the Roman punishment for dereliction of duty by jailers—the punishment of the escaped prisoners (→ 12:19). Ancient literature often depicted such dramatic moments for characters facing loss or shame (see, e.g., Chariton, *Chaer.* 1.5.2; 3.1.1; Xenophon of Ephesus, *Eph.* 2.4.6; Apuleius, *Metam.* 6.12, 17).

Paul's knowledge of what the jailer is about to do and of the prisoners' whereabouts, given his pitch-black location (see 16:24) and his inability to see anything, implies divine insight. Ironically, Paul's assurance that no one has escaped places Paul the prisoner in charge of the situation. The jailer asks for a lamp (needed in the total darkness of the inner prison) and **fell trembling** before the imprisoned pair (v 29).

The strong emotion seen in his **trembling** (see 7:32; Pss 18:7; 77:18; also Isa 66:2, 5; Luke 8:47) may indicate his fear that the earthquake reveals divine displeasure of his treatment of the two. In a reversal of roles, the one who treated them as common criminals (Acts 16:24) now honors them by bowing before them (see 4:34-37; 10:25) and addressing them as "honorable masters" (*kyrioi*; 16:30 CEB). His question about how **to be saved** focuses on his fears for his life, not on salvation in Christian terms (compare 16:17).

■ **31-34** The jailer's question opens the door to the gospel message. Their message reverberates with themes common in Acts. The call to **believe in the Lord Jesus** (v 31) alludes to Peter's Pentecost message (2:14-37) and repeated references to believing and faith (see, e.g., 2:44; 3:16; 4:4; 8:12-13; 10:43; 14:27). The declaration that the jailer would **be saved** (16:31) echoes throughout Acts (see 2:21, 40, 47; 4:9, 12; 7:25; 11:14; 13:26, 47; 14:9; 15:1, 11). The association of faith and salvation is central to Peter's articulation of the gospel (15:7-11).

Luke does not explain how Paul and Silas meet the jailer's **household** (16:31; see v 15) before entering his house (v 34). But the jailer treats the pair as guests by caring for the wounds from their beating (vv 22-23). In turn, they baptize the jailer and his household (see v 15; also 10:47-48 and earlier), confirming their membership in the people of God. Like Lydia, the jailer responds by providing a meal for the two men. He would know they had not eaten while in custody.

The verb conveying their joy (*agalliaō*) alludes to the "gladness" (*agalliasis* [2:46]) enjoyed by the earliest believers in Jerusalem when they ate together as a celebration of salvation (see Tannehill 1990, 200). This jailer was the first convert who came from the Gentile masses rather than the so-called Godfearers who were already attracted to the God of Israel. This makes his response all the more remarkable (see Heil 1999, 278-83).

c. The Release and Departure of Paul and Silas (16:35-40)

■ **35-37** The order that comes in the morning to release Paul and Silas is probably the direct result of the earthquake (the Western text explains this inference). Presumably, the jailer has already returned the pair to the prison, where he delivers what he considers to be the good news.

Paul's response turns the tables on the magistrates, as their treatment amounts to illegal actions against **Roman citizens** (v 37), whose citizenship offers them the right to legal proceedings and protection from harsh treatment (see, e.g., Cicero, *Verr.* 2.5.66; Livy, *Hist.* 10.9.3-6).

Paul's Roman Citizenship

Paul's mention of his Roman citizenship is the first reference to it in Acts. Its role within Acts is significant, as it gives Paul opportunity to proclaim Christ before kings (9:15; 25:23—26:32) and in Rome (19:21; 23:11; 25:25-27; 28:14-31). Paul referred to his rights as a Roman citizen to avoid the use of torture to force him to divulge information (22:22-29). His appeal for a legal hearing before the emperor as a Roman citizen (25:10-12, 21, 25; 26:32; 28:19) becomes the impetus for the last four chapters of the book.

Because the Pauline letters mention nothing about Paul's Roman citizenship, questions about the historical Paul often surface in relation to this issue. Readers of Acts may recognize the significant role Paul's Roman citizenship plays in Acts, without assuming this in the interpretation of the Pauline letters.

Ironically, this means the *magistrates* are proponents of unlawful practices—the exact charge against Paul and Silas (see 16:21)! Paul's refusal to go quietly contains a wordplay: **publicly** they **threw** [*ebalan*] **us into prison** and *now privately they are throwing us out* [*ekballousin*]? (v 37). The demand for the officials *themselves* to **escort** the two out of the prison forces a public acknowledgment of their mistreatment.

■ **38-40** The magistrates' fear of Roman retribution forces them to comply with Paul's demands. The inference of **requesting** (*ērōton* [v 39]) is that the magistrates beg the pair to leave town. Paul and Silas first return to see **Lydia**—the person with whom their ministry in Philippi began—and the believers at her home (v 40). The latter group would include believers of her household (see v 15) and perhaps the fledgling Philippian congregation that grew out of Paul's ministry before v 16.

FROM THE TEXT

Most people read narrative episodes with little regard for the broader context in which they appear. When this happens, we interpret them as short stories without considering how the episodes that frame them shape their meaning.

What happens when we do this with this portion of Acts? Innumerable sermons and Bible studies have focused on the response of joy and praise by Paul and Silas in the midst of the horrible conditions of their Philippian incarceration. Their songs in the night serve as notable examples for Christian living.

However, several features of this extended passage suggest the Lukan account of Paul's ministry in Philippi to be an epochal period in the westward movement of the church and her mission through the Roman Empire.

Importantly, the Spirit led Paul and his ministry party to Macedonia (vv 6-10). As in the divinely orchestrated encounter between Philip and the Ethiopian eunuch (8:26-40) or Peter and the God-fearing Gentile Cornelius (10:1-48), God's guidance initiated these latest episodes. Divine involvement occurred throughout the ministry in Philippi as well. This makes it clear that this stage of the church's mission was part of God's plan and purposes.

But this passage marks the movement of the church and the gospel into the European portion of the Roman Empire. The similarities (and differences) between the devout, God-fearing Gentile man Cornelius and the devout, God-fearing woman Lydia suggest this movement to be as dramatic and as potentially "world changing" as what transpired at Cornelius' house.

What happened in Philippi illustrates that the gospel message not only has an impact on Judaism but also had profound implications for the social and political structures of the Roman Empire. The gospel's reach extended beyond so-called spiritual or religious realms and affected economic and power systems as well.

As a result of the westward advance of the gospel, even the Philippian jailer and his household responded to the gospel. Importantly, this is the first noted instance in Acts of Gentile converts who had not previously attended the Jewish synagogue. The use of two conversion stories to bracket Paul's ministry in Philippi underscores the transformative role of the gospel in such a Roman setting.

Such a message has contemporary implications. Too often, the proclamation of the gospel is presented in ways that focus exclusively on spiritual matters, without addressing the many ways that the gospel also addresses the sin and sinful practices embedded in the systems and practices that structure much of human existence. Too much contemporary preaching is like the message of the girl with the pythonic spirit. It is so ambiguous as to have no discernible *Christian* distinctives. In such cases, we should not be surprised that she marches to the beat of the same drummer as our society. The church's call is to be the people of God, which requires us to proclaim and live out the transforming gospel in the midst of society. Are we willing to do so, even if it means stepping on toes and getting in trouble?

As in Acts, the church will recognize and appropriate baptism as an initiatory rite (or sacrament) that incorporates believers into the life of the church as the people of God. Often, we delay in offering baptism until believers receive some basic Christian teachings. But perhaps the church needs to initiate believers through baptism sooner. Baptism may even be extended to others who cannot make a confession of faith, including infants and persons with restricted mental capacities. Then, their "place" within the church allows for them to be shaped by the church's worship, teachings, and practices. Baptism may help people discover and become people who embody the transforming gospel of Jesus Christ.

D. The Ministry of Paul in Macedonia and Greece (17:1-34)

BEHIND THE TEXT

Like other stops along Paul's itinerary, Luke offers only minimal details about what transpired in the cities mentioned in the first half of Acts 17. Even in Athens, he notes only in passing Paul's activities in the Jewish synagogue, consistent with his previous practices. Based on the extended description of

Paul's ministry in Antioch of Pisidia (13:13-52), the pattern of his practices includes the following:

- Upon arrival in a city, Paul went to the Jewish synagogue on the Sabbath;
- In the synagogue, Paul proclaimed Jesus as the Jewish Messiah;
- Some Jews and some Gentiles (Godfearers) responded favorably to the gospel, others did not; and
- Opposition arose, not over proclamation of Jesus as the Christ, but in conjunction with Gentiles being included among those responding favorably to the gospel.

This pattern provides general background for Paul's ministry, especially when Luke mentions, even in passing, the Jewish synagogue as the context for some of these activities.

IN THE TEXT

I. Paul and Silas in Thessalonica (17:1-9)

■ **1-3** Upon leaving Philippi, Paul and Silas continue on the Via Egnatia (→ 16:11-12), which leads them about 30 miles (48 km) southwest of Philippi to **Amphipolis** (17:1), near the Aegean coast. From there they continue southwest on that major land route about 27 miles (44 km) to **Apollonia**, and then another 30 miles (48 km) west to **Thessalonica**. Thessalonica was the capital of one of the four Roman districts of Macedonia. Perhaps they stop there because of Thessalonica's prominence and its synagogue.

Thessalonica: A City of Strategic Importance

Luke highlights prominent cities in Acts and glosses over insignificant towns and villages, as he draws on the knowledge and familiarity of his readers. Thessalonica was founded by Cassander in 316 BC and named after his wife, Alexander's stepsister. He was a general under Alexander the Great.

The prominence of Thessalonica grew because of its location at the intersection of two major transportation routes: the Via Egnatia (which ran through the heart of the city) and its port, the beginning of the main route from the Aegean Sea to the Danube River.

During Paul's day, mystery religions and emperor worship were particularly strong in the city. However, archaeological evidence from the city is minimal, since the present city is located on the ancient site.

Paul continues his **custom** of going to the **synagogue** (v 2; → 13:5, 14; 14:1; 16:13). Here, Luke varies the terms depicting Paul's activity. The verb *dialegomai* suggests that he is leading discussions **from the Scriptures** (also 17:17; 18:4, 19; 19:8, 9; 20:7, 9; see 24:12, 25). The verb for Paul's explanations of Scripture (*dianoigō*) earlier refers to the opening of Lydia's heart to the gospel

(16:14) and the opening of the disciples' minds to understand the Scriptures (Luke 24:32, 45). The verb translated **proving** suggests laying out the facts or argument (Acts 17:3). The verb *paratithēmi* often describes the preparation of the table for a meal (e.g., Luke 9:16; 10:8; 11:6; Acts 16:34). Metaphorically, Paul lays out the gospel of the necessity of a suffering and risen Christ, whom he identifies as Jesus (see 3:18; also 2:22-36; 13:26-37), to feed his synagogue conversation partners (see Wall 2002, 238).

■ **4** The favorable response from both Jews and Gentiles mirrors previous episodes. The passive voice of **joined** implies that God is ultimately responsible for bringing them to faith. God-fearing Gentiles comprise most of this group, whom the narrator describes as **God-fearing** or "devout" (NRSV), the same adjective used for Lydia (16:14; see 10:2; 13:50). Unlike in Pisidia Antioch (13:50), **quite a few prominent women** of Thessalonica are responsive. Other than Lydia (16:14-15, 40), Luke has mentioned nothing specifically about the response of women or women of prominent social standing (see Tannehill 1990, 208; Reimer 1995, 245).

■ **5-9** The misguided zeal (see Larkin 1995, 246-47) of the Jews mirrors earlier instances in Acts (5:17; 13:45). Luke offers no reasons for such reactions. Some suggest Paul's interpretation of the Scriptures in terms of a suffering and risen Messiah is the problem (Fitzmyer 1998, 594; Wall 2002, 238). But the issue is likely over Paul's converts, particularly among Gentiles who frequented the Thessalonian synagogue.

Ironically, in order to counter Paul's successes, the Jewish opponents join forces with persons of questionable character (v 5). They create a mob and start a **riot** to make the case that *Paul* is "disturbing the peace" (v 6 [CEB]) or "subverting the empire" (Johnson 1992, 307; see 21:38).

The Jewish opponents' futile search for Paul and Silas ends in the apprehension of Jason and other believers. They see Jason as an accomplice, since he **welcomed** the missionaries into his home (17:7). The charge of crimes against **Caesar's decrees** is partially true: Paul's teachings about Jesus as Lord and Christ have significant political and social implications.

But what troubled the Thessalonian **crowd** and **city officials** are the actions of the Jews (v 8; the implied subject of *etaraxan*; see Thompson 2006, 202). The bond that Jason and the others post probably serves to guarantee their own civil behavior as well as that of Paul and Silas (v 9; Barrett 1998, 816-17).

2. Paul and Silas in Berea (17:10-15)

■ **10-12** The posted bond (v 9) may have necessitated the Thessalonian believers sending Paul and Silas away under cover of darkness (see Williams 1990, 296; Pervo 2009, 421). This hasty exit is apparently done out of concern for their fellow believers' need (see 2:42-47; 4:32-37; 11:27-30).

The pair arrives in **Berea** (17:10), a fairly large and prosperous city about 50 miles (81 km) west of Thessalonica. There they go as usual **to the Jewish synagogue**, presumably on the Sabbath. The initial response is more favorable than in Thessalonica. The narrator depicts Bereans as having **more noble character**, because they were "more receptive" (NRSV) to Paul's new teachings (v 11).

Since most people in antiquity were illiterate, their examination of Scriptures would have been corporate rather than individual in nature. The verb *anakrinō* typically describes the interrogation of witnesses (see 4:9; 12:19; 24:8; 28:18), but it never refers to the study of Scripture in the NT (Barrett 1998, 818). Here, the verb likely refers to the Bereans asking Paul questions to test his teachings against their own scriptural understanding (Ciampa 2011, 527-41).

This dialogue results in **many** from the Berean synagogue coming to faith (17:12). Those who **believed** would likely include both Jews and God-fearing Gentiles (Jervell 1998, 438; Peterson 2009, 484; against Pervo 2009, 422). The latter group includes a significant number of **prominent Greek women** (see v 4) and men.

■ **13-15** News from Berea somehow reaches Paul's Thessalonian Jewish opponents. Their arrival brings the same civil disturbance they stirred up earlier (*etaraxan . . . ton ochlon* [v 8]; *tarassontes tous ochlous* [v 13]).

Again, the believers respond **immediately** (*eutheōs* [v 14]; see v 10) to secure Paul's safety by sending him away **to the coast**. Silas and Timothy (who inexplicably reappears here) temporarily stay in Berea. A group escorts Paul safely over 200 miles (322 km) south to **Athens** (v 15).

Paul gives **instructions for Silas and Timothy to join him as soon as possible**. Luke never mentions the two meeting Paul in Athens, but only later in Corinth (18:5). However, in 1 Thess 3:1-2, Paul indicates that Timothy came to Athens and then returned to Thessalonica.

3. Paul in Athens (17:16-34)

The Lukan account of Paul's activities in Athens is one of the most familiar stories in Acts. Paul's speech to the Athenians has perhaps provoked more attention than any other passage in Acts, due to its engagement with popular and philosophical concepts from the Gentile world. Dibelius considers this speech "a climax of the book" (1956, 26). It certainly sets the stage for Paul's ministry in the next two chapters, which are largely set outside the synagogue.

■ **16-17** Athens was no longer the prominent city it was four centuries earlier. But it still enjoyed its reputation as an intellectual and cultural center (see Cicero, *Flac.* 62). Paul's initial response to what he observes there is "gut-wrenching." He (lit., **his spirit**) is *personally* **distressed** over the idolatry he witnesses (v 16). The verb *paroxynō* (→ 15:39) connotes utter exasperation, even anger (see Deut 9:18; Isa 65:3; Hos 8:5 [LXX]). The description of Athens as **full of idols** ("a veritable forest of idols"; Wycherley 1968, 619-21) is consistent with ancient references (see, e.g., Pausanias, *Descr.* 1.14.1-7; Strabo, *Geogr.* 9.1.16; Livy, *Hist.* 45.27.11). Luke's description of Athenian idolatry (*kateidōlon*, from *eidōlon*) reflects Jewish sentiments concerning such practices (Wis 14:11-12, 27-30).

The conjunctions *men oun* suggest that Paul's subsequent activities stemmed from his observations of the Athenians' idolatry. His activity in the synagogue mirrors his initial ministry in Thessalonica (Acts 17:2), but Luke notes no response. However, unique here is Paul's daily activity extending into the **marketplace** (v 17; see 16:19). This is the economic, political, and cultural heart of the city. In Athens, it is surrounded by colonnades (stoas). One part includes the idols that so disturb Paul (see Gill 1994a, 444-45).

Here, Paul speaks with Gentiles with no Jewish background (see 14:8-9). Luke depicts Paul as typically (present participle *paratynchanontas*) in "dialogue" (*dialegomai*) with any who would talk with him. His marketplace conversations are reminiscent of an Athenian philosopher five centuries earlier: Socrates.

Paul as Socrates?

Numerous parallels between Luke's description of Paul in Athens and ancient references to Socrates suggest that Luke was alluding to the ancient philosopher. These parallels include:

- The use of the verb *dialegomai*, which was famously associated with Socrates (e.g., Plato, *Apol.* 19d; 33a), describes Paul's activity in Athens;
- The marketplace was the location for Socrates' dialogues with whomever he met (Plato, *Apol.* 29d; Dio Chrysostom, *Socr.* 3);
- The accusation against Paul proclaiming *foreign deities* (v 18) or "bringing" such matters to their hearing (v 20) echoes the charges against Socrates (Plato, *Apol.* 24b-c; Xenophon, *Mem.* 1.1.1-2); and
- The appearance of Paul *in the middle of* the Areopagus (v 22) places him before the same council that sentenced Socrates to death.

Because Paul did not suffer Socrates' fate, interpreters should not seek *exact* correspondence between the Lukan depiction of Paul and Socrates. Still, these parallels encourage readers to view Paul in ways that are reminiscent of the philosopher (see Sandnes 1993, 13-26).

■ **18** Among those whom Paul meets in the marketplace are *some Epicurean and Stoic philosophers*, the only time either group is mentioned in the NT. They were most influential at that time, largely due to their emphasis on practical or "pastoral" rather than speculative matters. However, they were quite different.

The Epicureans

The philosophers known as the Epicureans, founded by Epicurus (341-270 BC), were not advocates of the idolatrous system that Paul discovered in Athens. Central to Epicureanism was their view of the universe. They understood the world, human bodies, and even the gods as comprised of atoms that came together by chance and could not change. Epicureans thought the gods lived outside the world system. So they denied divine involvement in either the creation of the world or in human affairs.

Epicureans denied the existence of any moral order in the universe and of an afterlife. They believed people should seek pleasure and happiness, but not in selfish, hedonistic ways. They viewed pleasure as the absence of pain and the anxieties of life caused by the fear of the gods and death.

The Stoics

The philosophers known as Stoics were founded by Zeno (340-265 BC). They were named after the *Stoa Poikilē*, the painted porch on the northwest side of the Athenian marketplace, where he taught. They believed in a divine rational order that created and permeated the entire universe, and could be observed in nature. The secret to a good life for individuals and society was to live in harmony with the rational order. This was to "live according to nature."

Central to Stoic ethical teachings was obedience to reason and duty. This included the recognition and acceptance of what was and was not within one's power to control. They believed human passions caused people to make false judgments about good or evil. So they emphasized freedom from passions as a result of virtue. They equated virtue, worthy of being achieved for its own sake, with happiness.

Their responses to Paul are mixed. Some dismiss him with the insult that he is a **babbler** (*spermologos*). The Greek term describes birds picking up scraps—used as a metaphor for gossip. Thus, they malign Paul as a religious charlatan, one who ignorantly pieces together borrowed ideas (LSJ 1996, 1627; BDAG 2000, 937; see, e.g., Dio Chrysostom, *Alex.* 9). The demonstrative pronoun **this** accentuates the insult. This not only leads readers to distrust these accusers but also prepares them to understand Paul's subsequent references and allusions to philosophers and poets suspiciously (see Rowe 2009, 28-29).

Others misunderstand Paul. Their description of Paul as a proclaimer (*katangeleus*) is accurate enough (*katangellō* [13:5, 38; 15:36; 16:17, 21; 17:3, 13]). But their reference to *plural* **foreign deities** is a misunderstanding of the monotheist Paul. The narrator's explanation (*hoti*) suggests that the Athenians, who are unfamiliar with the concept of resurrection, have mistaken Paul's message about **Jesus** and his *anastasis* (**resurrection**) as a reference to a male-female pair of deities (John Chrysostom, *Hom. Act.* 38.1). This response may at least reflect curiosity about or less resistance to Paul. Yet this, too, may have been dismissive. This was the accusation that led to Socrates' execution (see also v 20; Plato, *Apol.* 24b-c; Xenophon, *Mem.* 1.1.1-2). So there may be a hint of danger here, given the potential political, economic, and social implications of Paul's message. Such tensions appear throughout chs 16—19.

■ **19-20** Whether Paul's marketplace debates result in a trial, a formal legal hearing, or an informal appearance before an Athenian audience is a matter of scholarly contention. Paul is led to **the Areopagus** or *the hill of Ares*—the Greek god of war ("Mars Hill," after the Roman counterpart)—west of the Acropolis (v 19).

The Areopagus also refers to the council that once met there (but probably did not in Paul's day). Since this passage later mentions Paul standing *in the middle of* it (v 22) and mentions Dionysius as an "Areopagite" (v 34 NRSV), the council rather than the hill must be the primary referent. This council, which was the high court of first-century Athens, could intervene on *anything* regarding Athenian public life, including education, philosophy, morality, and religion (Barnes 1969, 413).

Paul is escorted before the Areopagus council—they **took** (*epilabomenoi*) and **brought** (*ēgagon*) him there. This resembles his Philippian arrest (Schwartz 2003, 125-26) in 16:19-20 (see 18:17; 21:30, 33; Luke 23:26; compare Acts 9:27), but without the violence. It also resembles the charges brought against Socrates, again reminding readers of the infamous story of his trial and execution for introducing other new gods (→ sidebar "Paul as Socrates?" with 17:16-17; see also Josephus, *Ag. Ap.* 2.263-68). These echoes depict Paul's situation as tenuous, even if the outcome (vv 32-34) was a hearing and not a trial.

In either case, the request—**May we know?** (v 19*b*)—is effectively a summons to appear before the Areopagus council. Perhaps the council would offer a formal ruling about the accusations against Paul (Winter 1996, 80-84; Rowe 2009, 31).

The repetition of the word **know** (vv 19, 20) underscores what the Athenians do *not* know, a theme of Paul's subsequent speech (see vv 23, 30). Their last statement about wishing to know *what these things mean* (v 20*b*) echoes what the Pentecost bystanders asked: "What does this mean?" (2:12). This offers opportunity for Paul's speech.

■ **21** In this narrative aside, Luke describes a typical perception of the Athenians in the ancient world (see, e.g., Thucydides, *War* 3.38; Demosthenes, *1 Philip.* 10; Chariton, *Chaer.* 1.11.6-7; Strabo, *Geogr.* 10.3.18). Paul's audience was not comprised of inquiring minds. This anticipates their response to his message (17:32-34).

Ironically, the council accuses Paul of teaching "some strange things" (*xenizonta . . . tina* [v 20 CEB]), yet the **Athenians** and **foreigners** (*xenoi*) living there talked about and listened to the kinds of things that Paul preached (see Rowe 2009, 32-33)! That is, their general behavior violated the standards they were charged to protect (see Talbert 1997, 161). So Luke turns the tables on these Athenians, making them the "charlatans" or "babblers," not Paul (see v 18)!

■ **22-31** In some respects, the themes of Paul's speech before (lit., *in the middle of* [v 22]) the Areopagus council build upon his earlier comments in Lystra (14:15-17). There he also spoke to a "Gentiles only" audience. This speech fits the context as Luke describes it. It appropriates and challenges both the language and the ideas of the Epicureans and Stoics (see, e.g., Balch 1990a, 52-79; Klauck 2003, 81-95).

Given its formal setting, it is noteworthy that Luke presents Paul standing (v 22), the posture of a Greek orator (see Peter in 2:14). He delivers a speech that conforms to the general form of Hellenistic oratory (see Zweck 1989, 94-103). The speech has the following basic chiastic (X-shaped) structure (see Parsons 2008, 245; Polhill 1992, 370):

> A Introduction: The Ignorance of False Worship (17:22-23)
>> B The Focus of True Worship: The Creator God (vv 24-25)
>>> C The Proper Relationship between God and Humanity: Seeking after God (vv 26-28)
>> B' The Focus of False Worship: Idols (v 29)
> A' Conclusion: The Removal of Ignorance (vv 30-31)

Introduction: The Ignorance of False Worship (vv 22-23)

The opening of the speech begins like other speeches in Acts, with the formal **Men, Athenians** (see, e.g., 2:14; 3:12; 7:2; 13:16; 15:7, 13). But women were probably there as well (see 17:34).

Paul's initial statement about what he observed in Athens (*theōrō*) reflects his prior observations (*theōrountos*) about the city's idols (minus the exasperation of v 16). The word translated **very religious** (*deisidaimonesteros* [v 22]) has a double meaning. It could be complimentary of the city's proverbial reputation (see Pausanias, *Descr.* 1.17.1; Sophocles, *Oed. col.* 260; Josephus, *Ag. Ap.* 2.130). But, it could also be an insult, characterizing their excess as mindless superstition.

With v 16 in mind, readers will take "superstitious" as more accurate. "With a wink (so to speak) Luke lets the reader understand that the allegedly so intelligent Athenians have not even noticed how poisoned this praise was" (Klauck 2003, 81-82; see Rowe 2011, 39-40).

Verse 23 offers grounds (*gar*) for Paul's assessment of the Athenians. What caught his attention (*anatheōreō*; see LSJ 1996, 105) were their numerous sacred altars and statues. Although the term translated **objects of worship** had little significance for Paul's live audience, in Jewish and Christian circles it was often used negatively to refer to idols (see 2 Thess 2:4; Wis 14:20; 15:17; Josephus, *Ant.* 18.344).

Paul refers specifically to an altar with the inscription, TO AN UNKNOWN GOD, as evidence of their superstition: they even worshiped a god they did not know! Ancient sources refer to altars dedicated to unknown *plural* gods (see, e.g., Pausanias, *Descr.* 1.1.4; Philostratus, *Vit. Apoll.* 6.3). So it seems plausible that altars were dedicated to unknown individual gods (see van der Horst 1994, 165-202; Witherington 1998, 521-23).

The inscription provides the "text" for Paul's comments in two significant ways. First, he uses the singular form in monotheistic terms. Second, he starts with the idea of the UNKNOWN and addresses the charge that he was spreading a "new teaching" (v 19). From this, Paul infers that his message about new "foreign gods" (v 18) is actually about what the Athenians themselves unknowingly attribute to God already in their acts of worship (see Marshall 1980, 286).

Thus, the problem is not the newness of Paul's teaching but the Athenians' ignorance. They do not understand their own worship or Paul's teachings. Because Luke depicts Paul as the proclaimer (*katangeleus* [v 18]) in earlier debates (see vv 19, 20), the narrator links those previous teachings to what he is about to **proclaim** (*katangellō*) to the council. The theme of ignorance frames Paul's speech to the Areopagus council and recurs later (vv 30-31).

The Focus of True Worship: The Creator God (vv 24-25)   17:22-31

Paul begins his refutation by turning his audience's attention to this so-called UNKNOWN GOD. Two descriptions frame these verses. The opening declaration about the one true God as Creator (v 24a) is the crucial theological point of the entire speech. It assumes both God's existence and nature (see 14:15) without offering additional proof or testimony (see 14:17). The basic Jewish background of this assertion is evident (see, e.g., Gen 1:1; Exod 20:11; Pss 115:15; 124:8; 134:3; Isa 42:5; 45:18; 2 Macc 7:28).

However, Paul's emphasis on God's creative work in its grandeur—using the word **universe** (*kosmos*) rather than **earth** (*gē*)—establishes common ground with the Greek philosophers. Although the Greeks had different beliefs about God, they often referred to God as the Creator or "Maker" of the universe (see, e.g., Plato, *Tim.* 28c; Epictetus, *Diatr.* 4.7.6; see Sasse, *TDNT* 3:880-82).

God is also the source of **life** and **breath** for humanity (see, e.g., Gen 2:7; Isa 42:5; 2 Macc 7:22-23). The gift of **all things** points ahead to Paul's explanation of God's creative purposes: that humanity might seek after God (Acts 17:26-27; Dibelius 1956, 46). However, **gives** also emphasizes God's *ongoing* providential role in sustaining human life (for **all**, *pasi*). By linking the Athenians' UNKNOWN GOD and his proclamation to the God of creation, Paul refutes the claim that he was teaching something new. The God Paul describes not only created Athens and the universe but also gave the Athenians their present life (see Rowe 2009, 34).

Within this context, Paul describes God as both the Creator and Sustainer of life. Thus, God is the **Lord of heaven and earth** (see, e.g., Isa 42:5; 44:24; Jer 10:12; Tob 7:17). This underscores God's sovereignty and providence, in line with Stoic philosophy (e.g., Dio Chrysostom, *Dei cogn.* 27-34; Balch 1990a, 75-76). In light of these affirmations, two misunderstandings about God are laid to rest.

First, God does not live in buildings constructed by humans (Acts 17:24*b*). The term translated **built by human hands** (*cheiropoiētos*) reflects the LXX's criticism of idolatry (see Lev 26:1, 30; Isa 2:18; 10:11; 16:12; 19:1; 21:9; 31:7; 46:6; Jdt 8:18; Wis 14:8; see also Acts 7:48; Mark 14:58). Similar sentiments about **temples** or "shrines" (NRSV) as the dwelling for the Creator God are found in both Jewish (e.g., 1 Kgs 8:27; Isa 57:15; 66:1-2; Josephus, *Ant.* 8.114, 227-29) and Greek (e.g., Plutarch, *Stoic. rep.* 1034b) circles.

As universal Creator and Lord, God cannot be confined or defined, controlled or manipulated by any sacred space that humans set up and control. Nor can any creature place the divine Creator under any religious lock and key.

Second, God's existence does not depend on humans or what humans do (v 25*a*). Human existence depends on God. So it is illogical that God's existence would depend on humans (see Ps 50:9-12; see also 2 Macc 14:35; 3 Macc 2:9; Josephus, *Ant.* 8.111). Greek and Roman philosophers often made similar statements about God's self-sufficiency (e.g., Plato, *Euthyphr.* 12e-15e; Plutarch, *Stoic. rep.* 1052d; Euripides, *Herc. fur.* 1345-46; Seneca, *Ep.* 95.47, 50). Yet everyday religious practices in the ancient world often included the veneration of idols and other religious relics. Pagans considered idol worship as offered directly to the gods that the idols represented. People viewed these images as participating in some way in their existence and essence.

The verb translated **served** (*therapeuō*) refers in the NT to healing (in Acts, see 4:14; 5:16; 8:7; 28:9). In Greco-Roman circles, it described one person serving another in the context of worship (see Beyer, *TDNT* 3:128-32). Thus, Paul's comments indicate the foolishness of the Athenians' religious practices in light of God as Creator. In this part of the speech, Paul "upholds God's transcendence . . . by understanding God's role in creating and giving as irreversible. God gives and creates for humanity; humanity may give and create, but not for God" (Tannehill 1990, 215).

The Proper Relationship between God and Humanity: Seeking after God (vv 26-28)

As the central part of the chiastic structure, this section is the focal point of Paul's speech. The reiteration of God as Creator (God **made** [see v

24]) builds continuity with the previous theme. In particular, God was responsible for the creation of *every nation of humanity*. God began with **one**, which the text leaves unnamed (see Philo, *Creation* 134-47). Paul's audience may have understood this as a unifying principle for all humanity (see Dibelius 1956, 35-37; Balch 1990a, 77). But Luke's readers would have probably understood this as a reference to the first human, Adam (Gen 1:27-28; 2:7; see Luke 3:38). The Greeks often distinguished themselves from barbarians. But Paul contends for an essential unity of the human race.

The first purpose behind God's creative work is that humanity would **inhabit the whole earth**. The divine design and purpose are central to human existence. Interpreters wrestle over whether the **appointed times** and **boundaries** refer to historical periods (see, e.g., Acts 1:7; 3:20) and national boundaries (see Deut 32:8; Fitzmyer 1998, 609; Pervo 2009, 436), or to the earth's seasons (see Acts 14:17) and inhabitable zones (see Ps 74:17; Dibelius 1956, 29-32; Haenchen 1971, 523; Balch 1990a, 54-67). In either case, these images affirm that God has created and placed all humanity under God's gracious provision.

The second stated purpose is that all persons might also **seek** or *search for God* (Acts 17:27). The theme of seeking God is common in the OT (see, e.g., Deut 4:29; Pss 27:8; 105:4; Prov 28:5; Isa 51:1; 55:6). However, the focus here is on the human reflection upon the divine organization of the world (Acts 17:26b). Nature suggests something about God (i.e., natural theology; see Philo, *Spec. Laws* 1.32-40; Dio Chrysostom, *Dei cogn.* 60-61).

Paul downplays human attempts to search for God as insufficient *alone* for finding God. The conditional clause (*ei* with two optative verbs) metaphorically compares the uncertainty of such efforts at finding God to someone groping in the dark (*psēlaphaō*; see Deut 28:29; Judg 16:26; Job 5:13-14; 12:25).

Yet Paul also affirms that God **is not far** from anyone, a concept shared by Greeks/Romans (see, e.g., Seneca, *Ep.* 41.1; Dio Chrysostom, *Dei cogn.* 27-28) and Jews alike (see, e.g., Ps 145:18; Isa 55:6; 65:1; Jer 23:23-24; Josephus, *Ant.* 8.108; Philo, *Spec. Laws* 1.31). Thus, Paul describes God as available to those who seek God, yet ultimately depicts humans as unable to find God apart from divine revelation (see Acts 17:30-31). "When one is blind, even an object right in front of one's face can be missed. The sentence does not encourage us to think the speaker believes that the finding of the true God is actually going on. . . . To the contrary, the true God remains unknown apart from such revelation" (Witherington 1998, 529).

Verse 28 provides the basis (*gar*) for the argument dealing with God's nearness. The Stoics may have understood **in him** according to their pantheistic beliefs: that God is near them since humanity lives *in* God. However, for

Luke's readers the phrase has an instrumental sense in light of vv 24, 26-27: human life is created and sustained *by* God. Interpreters and translators alike debate whether this saying is quoted or paraphrased.

The verbal triad of **live, move,** and **being** (compare Plato, *Soph.* 248e; *Tim.* 37c) encompasses the totality of human life, which is completely dependent upon God. All three verbs appear in Jewish polemic against idolatry (see Wis 13:6-19; 15:16-17; *Jub.* 20:7-8; Ep Jer 8, 24, 26; Bel 5; Gärtner 1955, 197, 219-20). The grounding of human life in God establishes all humanity as God's **offspring,** part of God's *family* (*genos*; see Acts 4:6; 7:13, 19; 13:26). This finds support in the biblical account of creation (Gen 1:27).

Paul's citation of a familiar saying from the Greek poets reiterates his argument against the novelty of his preaching. Paul's quotation resembles a saying found in two Stoic sources from the third century BC: the poet Aratus of Soli (*Phaen.* 5) and the philosopher Cleanthes (*Hymn to Zeus* 4-5). Both refer to Zeus. Of course, the Jewish Paul affirms the place of Israel as the covenant people of God. But such claims could not be understood exclusively, since he also affirms before the Athenians that God as Creator draws *all* humanity into God's family (see Tannehill 1990, 219).

The Focus of False Worship: Idols (Acts 17:29)

For Paul, idolatry directs attention *away* from God rather than focusing on God in light of humans being **God's offspring**. In idolatry, humans falsely assume they can capture and represent the *living* God in their *own* likeness because of their relationship with the divine (vv 28-29). Out of ignorance, they create gods in their own image (see vv 23, 30).

It is impossible for humans adequately to express the reality of the divine from their limited, human perspective. All such attempts will result at best in partial or distorted images of God. The listed materials—**gold, silver,** and **stone**—may offer splendor or beauty, yet these all stand in stark contrast to the *living* God, who gives life to all humanity (vv 25, 28). Every humanly crafted **image** is merely the product of human technical or artistic skill (*technē*). They may reveal human thought or imagination (*enthymēsis*). But idols ultimately confuse human creations for the true God, who is Creator of all and alone worthy of worship.

Such arguments against idolatry resemble those found in the OT (see, e.g., Deut 4:28; Pss 115:4-8; 135:15-18; Isa 40:18-20; 44:9-20; 46:5-7; Jer 2:26-28; 10:1-5; Hab 2:18-19) and in later Jewish writings (e.g., Wis 13:10-19; 15:7-17; Philo, *Contempl.* 7; *Decal.* 66-81; Josephus, *Ag. Ap.* 2.65-67). But some ancient Greek and Roman philosophers argued similarly against the images of the gods (see, e.g., Plutarch, *Stoic. rep.* 1034b; *Superst.* 167d-e; Cicero, *Nat. d.* 1.36.101-2; Seneca, *Ep.* 31.11; see Balch 1990a, 67-72). This may explain why no objections are raised to this aspect of Paul's message. This passage explains why the apostolic decree was so concerned about idolatry (→ 15:20, 29). Paul's argument goes beyond the Jerusalem church's concern to maintain Jewish identity (see Wall 2002, 247).

Conclusion: The Removal of Ignorance (vv 30-31)

The last portion of Paul's speech shifts from a universal perspective regarding God and humanity to particularities of the gospel. Paul's description of the Athenians' idolatry as *times of ignorance* is reminiscent of his opening remarks (v 23; → 3:17-26; 13:27). That God **overlooked** this (*hyperoraō*; see 14:16; Rom 3:25-26) does not imply God's approval. The verb has the sense of looking down on and ignoring something for a time (Barrett 1998, 851). In contrast to God's former tolerance, the adverb **now** indicates the urgency of God's call to **repent** in response to the gospel message (Acts 17:30; see 2:38; 3:19; 5:31; 8:22; 11:18; 13:24; 19:4; 20:21; 26:20; see also Luke 24:47).

Repentance is necessary because of the Athenians' restriction and confinement of God to human form and space—by their religious institutions, practices, and philosophical concepts. The inclusive language—**all people** [*pantas*] **everywhere** (*pantachou*)—reiterates five earlier references to "all" (*pas* in Acts 17:24-26).

Paul emphasizes not only humanity's common ancestry and Creator but also its common need for repentance. In Acts, such universal emphases allude to promises of universal salvation (e.g., 2:21; 10:34-35; 13:38-39). "Rather than invite his hearers to change and join the party (cf. Luke 15:25-32), Paul demands that they repent or face the music" (Pervo 2009, 430).

Verse 31 offers the rationale (*kathoti*) for this urgent call to repent: God had already determined **a day** when the world will be judged (Acts 17:31). The expression **judge the world with justice** or "righteousness" (NRSV) refers to the culmination of human history (see, e.g., Pss 9:8; 96:13; 98:9). **Justice** reflects Jewish emphases regarding God's nature (e.g., Pss 11:7; 31:1; 35:24; Isa 45:8, 21) and expectations for ethical behavior (e.g., Isa 26:2; Amos 5:24; Zeph 2:3). Of course, Greeks were also concerned about the place of justice within society.

The declaration about **a man** whom God **has appointed** and through whom God would judge the world echoes Peter's description of Jesus before Cornelius (Acts 10:42). Paul does not explicitly name Jesus. But the passage clearly implies him, since his message about Jesus and the resurrection prompted this hearing before the Areopagus court (see 17:18). Nonetheless, the focus remains on the God who created and will ultimately judge the world. Paul mentions resurrection as specific **proof** or "assurance" (NRSV) that God exalted Jesus to serve as God's agent for divine judgment.

Not surprisingly, this understanding of Jesus' resurrection differs from earlier speeches to Jewish audiences (see 2:24, 32; 3:15; 13:30-39). There, his resurrection provides evidence that Jesus is Israel's Messiah. In all instances, however, the resurrection provides validation of God's plan, whether that involves the coming of the Messiah or impending judgment (see Gaventa 2003, 253).

Interpreters often note the distinctively Christian tone to the ending of this speech, especially given the more universal emphases leading up to these last two verses. This may be good rhetorical strategy, which recommends the deferral of references to misunderstood subjects (e.g., Jesus and the resurrection; see 17:18) until the latter portion of the speech (see Quintilian, *Inst.* 4.1.42-50; Parsons 2008, 248).

Theologically, however, these particularities define the vantage point from which God judges humanity (see Conzelmann 1987, 146). Through the resurrection of Jesus, God reveals God's saving purposes for humanity. This event removes the ignorance that had hampered humanity's search for God.

■ **32-34** A mixed response from the audience is common in Acts. Most hearers would have found Paul's radical message of resurrection unimaginable. They would have needed to destroy their established belief systems completely. Common Greek thought was that the dead remained forever dead (see, e.g., Aeschylus, *Eum.* 647-48; Wright 2003, 32-84).

The negative response of those who **sneered** (*chleuazō* [v 32]) at or "began to ridicule" (CEB) Paul resembles the initial reaction of the Pentecost bystanders (*diachleuazō* [2:13]). The suggestion by others for another hearing may indicate either their genuine interest or polite rejection of Paul's message. It is unlikely that the Epicureans comprised the former group and the Stoics the latter. Paul's Areopagus audience would not have been limited to those two groups of philosophers (against, e.g., Haenchen 1971, 526; Neyrey 1990, 118-34; Croy 1997, 21-39).

Important for the Lukan perspective is that Paul departs *from the middle* (see 17:22) of the Areopagus council. Paul successfully countered the claims that he spread "new teaching" (v 19) about "foreign gods" (v 18). Conviction could have led to more serious legal troubles, potentially the death penalty.

Nonetheless, Paul's encounter with the prestigious council also produces some fruit for the Christian mission (contrast 1 Cor 16:15, in which Paul states there were no converts in Achaia prior to his visit to Corinth). However one interprets the second group in Acts 17:32, the narrator closes the episode in Athens by mentioning those who responded favorably to Paul's Areopagus speech. The word translated **became followers of** or "joined" (CEB) Paul refers in Acts to how the believers associated together within the community of faith (see 5:13; 9:26; 10:28). The narrator, however, mentions no church being founded in Athens.

Luke does mention two specific individuals. The first, **Dionysius** (17:34), is significant because of his prominent social standing as a member of the

Areopagus council. The second, **Damaris**, may have been present at the Areopagus meeting as a council member or because of her participation in one of the two mentioned philosophical schools (v 18), since both included women as members (see Reimer 1995, 246-48).

There were also **others** who *came to believe* (*episteusan*), presumably Gentiles (against Malina and Pilch 2008, 129). Thus, from the Lukan perspective, "neither Paul nor the gospel failed in Athens; only those who heard the good news and did not respond in faith failed" (Parsons 2008, 250).

FROM THE TEXT

Much of the narrative drama and tension that characterized the previous chapter lingers in the three distinct episodes of Acts 17. Mob scenes and accusations of actions against the emperor followed Paul's proclamation of the gospel. In the first two cities, he had to be rushed out of town for his own safety. Even in Athens, Paul's personal safety was in jeopardy. Yet throughout this chapter, Paul's faithful resolve in the face of imposing obstacles reminds readers of the Spirit's guidance (16:6-10) that had led him westward into increasingly Gentile circumstances.

The Athenian speech appears at a strategic location in Acts, because it contributes a programmatic perspective of how Paul dealt with Gentiles who had no Jewish background, just before the Lukan account of Paul's ministry in Corinth (18:1-17) and Ephesus (19:1-41). Both of these included extended time outside the synagogue setting.

The speech relates the Christian tradition and mission to her "mission field." It offers theological commentary for interpreting this portion of Acts. But it also suggests ways for considering contemporary issues, such as the church's mission in what some call our "post-Christian era." Three characteristics in Paul's Areopagus speech offer insight into the Christian mission and enable him to articulate the Christian message with clarity.

First, Paul finds *common ground* where he can speak and communicate. He starts where his audience lives, recognizing what Wesleyans affirm as the workings of God's prevenient grace (i.e., God always takes the initiative, "going before"; see 17:23; Rom 1:18-32).

Paul did not quote Scripture before his Areopagus audience, although he typically did in synagogues. These Gentiles would simply not know it. But, recall that there are no explicit biblical quotations in 1 Thessalonians either. Paul's descriptions of God—as Creator and Lord, the Giver of life, the Sustainer of all things, and the Judge of all (see Acts 17:24-28)—are thoroughly biblical. But he communicates these themes in ways that are understandable and suitable to his audience, stressing their common ground. This needs to be considered when attempting to correlate this speech with other Pauline materials (e.g., Rom 1:18-32; see, e.g., Witherington 1998, 533-35; Peterson 2009, 486-87).

Second, the speech includes the *critical engagement* of the Athenians' worldview. Paul not only *appropriates* but also *challenges* concepts that the Athenians accepted. The speech exposed misunderstandings of God, who does not live in temples "built by human hands" (v 24), is not "served by human hands" (v 25), and is not like "an image made by human design and skill" (v 29)—misunderstandings that stood out when Paul first toured the city (v 16).

However, the more significant critical engagement occurred in Paul's brief articulation of the gospel at the speech's conclusion, when he mentioned the resurrection of Jesus. His call to repentance essentially invited the Athenians to abandon their former interpretive framework(s) in favor of this Christian one. This would then disrupt all the other systems (social, political, economic) that ordered human existence (see Rowe 2009, 40-41). Without such critical engagement, the "fundamental structures of the old life remain standing, and the gospel loses its culture-transforming power" (Tannehill 1990, 215). Paul's approach in Athens has profound implications for the contemporary church as she seeks to proclaim the Christian gospel in increasingly diverse contexts and to persons who lack basic biblical and theological background (see Flemming 2002, 199-214).

Third, this speech contributes significantly to the ecclesiology of Acts. Its inclusive tone—that all humans are "God's offspring" (v 29) and that God commands "all people everywhere to repent" (v 30)—speaks into the developing theme that the people of God are comprised of *all* people who repent and believe in God's saving purposes accomplished through Jesus Christ. Before this point in Acts, Peter's Pentecost speech (2:21) and Paul's speech at Pisidian Antioch (13:38-39) raised this inclusive aspect of the people of God among the Jewish people. This speech in a Gentile-dominated context underscores the universal, inclusive aspect of that ecclesiology. The God of the church is the Creator and Sustainer of all. As such, the speech provides both the strategy and legitimation for Paul's subsequent ministry activities outside the Jewish synagogue.

E. The Ministry of Paul in Corinth (18:1-17)

BEHIND THE TEXT

This portion of Acts focuses on Paul's ministry in founding the church in Corinth. Interpreters of the Pauline letters of 1 and 2 Corinthians often consult Acts for supplemental, background information about the Corinthian congregation. Similarly, Acts interpreters often look to these Pauline letters for assistance in filling in gaps in this Lukan account. Acts and the Corinthian correspondence agree on several key points:

- the correlation of a few members of the congregation, including Priscilla and Aquila (18:2; 1 Cor 16:19), and Crispus (Acts 18:8; 1 Cor 1:14);
- Paul's practice of a trade to earn a living (Acts 18:3; 1 Cor 4:12; 9:3-18); and
- Paul's vision of the Lord (Acts 18:9-10), likely due to his experience of "great fear and trembling" (1 Cor 2:3) caused by Jewish opposition (Acts 18:6; see 2 Cor 11:1-15).

However, either Acts or the Corinthian correspondence is silent on some issues:

- Acts mentions nothing about the internal issues that plagued the Corinthian church or the rift between Paul and some of the Corinthians addressed in the NT letters.
- The letters mention nothing about issues related to Jewish opposition and the apparent conflict between church and synagogue that characterize the Acts account.
- Acts fails to mention some people Paul apparently considered important: Stephanus (1 Cor 1:16; 16:15) and Gaius (1 Cor 1:14). And the Corinthian letters never mention Silas, who arrived in Corinth with Timothy to serve as his ministry partner there (Acts 18:5).

These differences indicate that the author of Acts may not have used the Corinthian letters as sources. But they also remind contemporary readers that the two authors have specific and different purposes and agendas for their respective texts. Their texts may appear in general ways to refer to the same group of people, but in reality have rather different things to say.

Luke offers no reason for Paul's departure from Athens to Corinth, about 40 miles (64 km) west. But the increasing prominence of the latter city was the likely reason for his interest in ministering there. The original city was destroyed by Rome for its leadership among Greek cities in the attempt to stop Roman expansion (146 BC). However, a century later Julius Caesar recognized the strategic location of the isthmus that connected the northern Greek mainland (or Macedonia) to the Peloponnesian peninsula (which the Romans designated as the region of Achaia; see 18:12). Thus, he restored Corinth (44 BC), and the bustling city later became the capital of Achaia (27 BC).

Its geographical location made Corinth a wealthy commercial center with dual ports accessing both the western Adriatic Sea and the eastern Aegean Sea. There, ships' cargo could be transferred by land (for a tariff) to avoid the dangerous voyage around the southern tip of the Greek peninsula (see Pausanius, *Descr.* 2.1-5; Strabo, *Geogr.* 8.6.20-23).

The ethnically diverse, rapidly growing city included a Jewish community (Philo, *Embassy* 281-82). Interpreters often note the gross immorality of the city, although its reputation was founded on centuries-old Athenian slander, not on first-century Corinthian practices (see Winter 2007, 186). But this has nothing to do with the conflict between Paul's Christian mission and his Jewish opposition, which occupies Luke's attention.

IN THE TEXT

■ **1-3** Upon his arrival in Corinth, Paul finds **Aquila** and **his wife Priscilla** (v 2). Luke describes Aquila as **a Jew**, which explains why the couple recently left Rome and arrived in the city: an edict by the Roman emperor **Claudius** forced all **Jews to leave Rome** (→ sidebar "Claudius and His Edicts against the Jews" with 18:1-3). Both Acts and the Pauline letters mention the couple (18:18, 26; Rom 16:3; 1 Cor 16:19; see also 2 Tim 4:19), but the Pauline letters use "Prisca" (CEB, KJV, NASB, NEB, NRSV) rather than the diminutive **Priscilla** ("little Prisca"). Priscilla's name is always listed first, which may reflect her superior social status or her notable reputation in Christian circles. They were probably believers before coming to Corinth, since Luke mentions nothing about them becoming believers under Paul's ministry. However, nothing in Acts indicates that they started a congregation in Corinth before Paul's arrival (see 1 Cor 3:6).

Claudius and His Edicts against the Jews

Upon becoming emperor, Claudius (AD 41-54) upheld religious privileges Julius Caesar had granted the Jewish people (Josephus *Ant.* 14.190-230; 19.278-91). However, two separate reports indicate that he issued official edicts against the Jews in Rome. Dio Cassius (ca. 160-230) reports that in AD 41 the emperor banned Jewish assemblies, because of their rapidly growing numbers (*Hist.* 60.6.6). The second-century biographer Suetonius notes that Claudius expelled the Jews from Rome because of "disturbances at the instigation of one Chrestus" (*Claud.* 25.4).

Interpreters typically associate the edict expelling the Jews from Rome with the one Luke cites in Acts 18. Most date it in AD 49, although Suetonius does not specify when Claudius acted. The name "Chrestus" (a common slave name) may be a misspelled reference to Christ or a reference to another. It seems likely that a serious inter-Jewish dispute in Rome, perhaps over early Christian teachings, precipitated the expulsion of Jews.

Since nearly 50,000 Jews lived in Rome at that time, it is likely that only those involved in or blamed for the controversy were expelled, not "all Jews" (18:2). If Priscilla and Aquila were believers involved in that dispute, this would explain both their departure from Rome and their friendship with Paul. They shared similar experiences of Jewish conflict.

In addition to their Jewish heritage and Christian faith, Paul and the couple share the *same trade*: they are *tentmakers*. Tents then were usually made of leather. Unlike the Pauline letters, the narrator notes not only Paul's use of manual labor to support himself but also his specific trade (see 1 Cor 4:12; 1 Thess. 2:9). This kind of manual labor would not endear Paul or the couple to the Corinthian elite, who looked down on the working classes (→ Acts 16:13-15). Tradespersons or artisans often lived and worked together. In this instance, Aquila and Priscilla demonstrate hospitality toward Paul by allowing him to stay with them—a sign of Christian discipleship.

■ **4-5** Whereas Paul apparently works at his trade during the week, his **Sabbath** (18:4) activities **in the synagogue** of Corinth mirror previous scenes upon entering a city (see, e.g., 13:14; 14:1; 17:1-3, 10). Paul is in dialogue with synagogue goers, as in both Thessalonica and Athens (see *dialegomai*; 17:2, 17). The audience includes both **Jews and Greeks** (see 17:4, 11-12).

The narrative does not indicate how much time passes before **Silas and Timothy** arrive from **Macedonia** (18:5; see 17:14-16). But Luke correlates their arrival with the onset of Paul's full-time (*synechō*; BDAG 2000, 970-71) preaching of the gospel (*the word*; → 4:29, 31; 6:2, 4; 8:4). Most interpreters suggest that Paul's partners bring funds with them, which enable Paul to give up his manual labor and focus solely on ministry. The Pauline letters may encourage such a reading (e.g., 2 Cor 11:8-9; Phil 4:15; but see 1 Cor 9:12-15), but Acts does not (see Gaventa 2003, 257).

Luke focuses instead on Paul offering his complete testimony, using the same vocabulary reserved earlier (*diamartyromai*; → 2:40; 8:25; 10:42) for the apostolic witness to Jesus as the **Messiah**. According to Luke, Paul proclaimed the same gospel message as Peter—a message that affirmed salvation for all (see 2:21; 10:34-35; 15:9, 11).

■ **6-8** Both the Jewish response and Paul's reaction mirror the episode in Pisidian Antioch (13:43-52). As before, no explicit reasons appear for the Jews' resistance. However, based on a cumulative reading of Acts, this opposition likely arises because of (*a*) the inclusive nature of Paul's gospel message (see 18:5) and (*b*) the likely favorable response from *some* Gentile synagogue attendees (see 13:43-48; 14:1; 16:14; 17:4, 12). The conversion of **Crispus**, because of his prominence as **synagogue leader** (18:8), may have contributed to increasing tension between Judaism and the Christian mission (Haenchen 1971, 539-40). By describing Jewish resistance not merely as **abusive** behavior or words but as "blasphemy" (v 6; see 13:45), Luke again suggests their opposition to be not only against *Paul* but against *God* (see 5:39).

How long this continues is unclear; the verb tenses (imperfect: *dielegeto* [v 4]; *syneicheto* [v 5]; present: *diamartyromenos* [v 5]; *antitassomenōn*, *blasphēmountōn* [v 6]) indicate this goes on for a while. Paul finally responds to this Jewish opposition by shaking out his clothes as a symbolic act of defiance against and complete separation from them (→ 13:51; also Neh 5:13; Matt 10:14; Mark 6:11).

Paul's declaration—**Your blood be on your own heads!** (Acts 18:6)—echoes OT ideas regarding blood and responsibility (see, e.g., Judg 9:24; 2 Sam 1:16; 1 Kgs 2:32-37), especially judgment in Ezek 33:4. His Jewish opposition in Corinth aligns with those in Jerusalem who endured exile centuries earlier. As in 13:46, Paul states his intention to **go to the Gentiles**. This, of course, applies only to his time in Corinth (see 18:19). However, he no longer proclaims the gospel in *that* Jewish setting (i.e., the synagogue of Corinth) because of their rejection.

Paul leaves the synagogue in favor of **the house of Titius Justus** (v 7). Two details are significant. First, Titius Justus is a Gentile **worshiper of God** (see 13:43, 50; 16:14; 17:4, 17). So Paul moves to the house of a Gentile Godfearer (see 10:1-48). Second, his house is located **next door** to the synagogue; they share a common wall ("adjoining"; Bruce 1988, 350) or boundary. Such a move replacing the Jewish synagogue as Paul's mission center could not have promoted good relations with institutional Judaism. Opposition may have forced Paul from the synagogue, but his location still leaves the door open for Jewish individuals who may have a change of heart. As a result, Crispus (see 1 Cor 1:14) may have come to faith after Paul's move, a notable occurrence since Jewish religious leaders typically opposed the gospel in Acts. The conversion of Crispus' **entire household** (Acts 18:8) mirrors earlier instances involving Cornelius (10:44; 11:14-15), Lydia (16:15), and the Philippian jailer (16:31-34). The narrative emphasizes the ongoing success of Paul's ministry (present tense: *akouontes*; imperfect tense: *episteuon, ebaptizonto*) among **many** other Corinthians (likely both Jews and Gentiles).

■ **9-11** Luke does not explicitly indicate that Paul is in danger. But the nocturnal **vision** (18:9; see 7:31; 9:10, 12; 10:3, 17, 19; 11:5; 12:9; 16:9-10) and its assurances suggest that he is (see 1 Cor 2:3). In a similar scene in Pisidian Antioch, Jewish opposition ran him out of town (Acts 13:50-51; see also 14:1-6, 19; 17:5-9, 13-15). Elsewhere, public charges against Paul (e.g., 16:19-40; 17:1-10; see 18:12-13) forced him to leave town earlier than expected. Thus, this type of scene (see also 22:17-18; 23:11; 27:23-24) provides divine assurance to Paul, as **the Lord** (i.e., Jesus) appears before him and keeps him there.

The heart of the divine message echoes common OT themes. The call **do not be afraid** often accompanies epiphanies. It was also frequently paired with assurances of God's presence (see, e.g., Gen 21:22; 26:24; 31:3-5; Exod 3:12; Deut 31:6; Josh 1:5-9; Isa 41:10; 43:5; Jer 1:8, 19), as it is here. Because of Jesus' presence, the present tense of the command tells Paul, ***Don't be afraid any longer!*** (see Culy and Parsons 2003, 347). Similarly, the present imperative *lalei* calls for him to persist in proclaiming the gospel, and the command **do not be silent** reminds readers that earlier threats from powerful leaders in Jerusalem could not silence the apostolic voices (4:1-31; 5:17-42).

With these commands comes the promise of divine protection from harm, which is linked here with the additional assurance that **many people in this city** belong to God (v 10). This **people** (*laos*) is Luke's usual term for the Jews as God's chosen people. Here, for only the second time in Acts, it refers to persons outside that exclusive context (→ 15:14). It identifies both Jews and Gentiles, those who have already responded in faith and those yet to respond (see Dupont 1985a, 327-28; Jervell 1998, 461). "The scriptural style conveys meaning: the Lord's 'large people' in Corinth is now part of the one covenant people that began with Israel, not by accepting Israel's circumcision but through being cleansed by faith (15:9)" (Tannehill 1990, 225).

The final sentence of this paragraph summarizes the results of Paul's vision. Luke notes that Paul remains in Corinth for an eighteen-month period, probably his entire stay in the city, not only the time after the vision. More importantly, it signifies his obedience to Jesus' instructions. The description of his ongoing activity as **teaching** (present *didaskōn* [v 11]) as elsewhere (4:2, 18; 5:21, 25, 28, 42; 11:26; 15:35) refers to sharing **the word of God** (the gospel; 4:31; 6:2, 7; 8:14; 11:1; 12:24; 13:5, 7, 46; 17:13). In Acts, such activities result in more favorable responses. Jesus' comment about having **many people in this city** (18:10) is both descriptive and prophetic.

■ **12** As in 16:19-24 and 17:5-9, **the Jews of Corinth** stand *together* (*homothymadon*; → 7:57 and sidebar "The Believers 'Together'" with 1:14) as plaintiffs in opposition (*katephistamai*) to Paul. **Gallio**, as **proconsul** (see 13:7), ruled the Roman province of Achaia and had legal jurisdiction over the city. The **place of judgment** ("tribunal" [NRSV]) was a central, raised platform in the city marketplace where public pronouncements and important legal cases were settled.

Gallio and Pauline Chronology in Acts

The appearance of Gallio is noteworthy for the study of Pauline chronology in Acts. Unlike most characters, historical information about this individual is available outside the NT. Gallio was the brother of the Stoic philosopher Seneca (4 BC-AD 65; on Gallio's pleasant disposition, see Seneca, *Nat.* 4a). Like his adoptive father, a Roman senator, Gallio also became a politician. The emperor Claudius appointed him as Roman proconsul of the province of Achaia. Such appointments took effect in June and typically lasted one year.

An important piece of historical evidence regarding Gallio's political career, particularly his tenure as Roman proconsul over Achaia, is a reconstructed inscription from a temple of Apollo in Delphi (i.e., within his jurisdiction). It contains a letter from the emperor Claudius to the people of Delphi. The letter deals with a report about a depopulating situation in Delphi from Gallio, whom the emperor describes as his friend and proconsul over the area. This information with other historical data from extant sources dates the beginning of Gallio's office in Corinth and Paul's appearance before him to AD 51 or 52 (see Fitzmyer 1998, 621-23).

■ **13** The emphatic position of the phrase **contrary to the law** (*para ton nomon*) underscores "the law" as a central issue in the accusers' complaint. But it is unclear whether their concern is with *Roman* or *Jewish* law. Luke may depict the Jewish instigators as not only ambiguous on this point but deceptive so that Gallio may rule against Paul (see Conzelmann 1987, 153). However, the phrase has multiple meanings that remain in play within this episode.

On the one hand, the Jewish accusers draw on the phrase's *Roman* connotations. The verb translated **persuading** (*anapeithō*) often had negative connotations of corruption by political leaders (e.g., Herodotus, *Hist.* 3.148; 5.66; Xenophon, *Cyr.* 1.5.3; Aristophanes, *Pax* 622; LSJ 1996, 115). Paul's alleged seditious practice involves promotion of the worship of a *single* God (a Jewish vs. Roman idea). But the litigants charge Paul with deceptive practices against the Corinthian **people**. This is an issue of *Roman* concern. Thus, his accusers charge him with crimes that undermine the political and social stability of the state.

On the other hand, from the perspective of his Jewish accusers, Paul in his ministry practices does *exactly* as they inform Gallio in their complaint with regard to the *Jewish* law. Luke, however, presents Paul as obedient to divine instructions. Since Paul established his ministry center and taught next door to the synagogue (where the Jewish people studied the Jewish law and worshiped God), Luke's readers should understand that his accusers would perceive those actions as **contrary to** or literally "beside" the *Jewish* law (*para ton nomon*). Although Paul lives as a faithful Jew, his new ministry setting places him *outside* the synagogue, where Jews worshiped God and nurtured their identity as the people of God through obedience to the Jewish law. The logic of Paul's accusers is that he had set up a rival "institution" *beside* or *outside* such a Jewish setting. Thus, he must not obey the Jewish law but must be *against* it. Similar concerns over Paul's relation to the Jewish law will continue to play a significant role in Acts.

■ **14-15** Paul is about to offer a rebuttal when Gallio addresses Paul's accusers. The first half of his response (v 14) is a second-class condition: the protasis (condition) is contrary to fact, so the apodosis (result) describes what would have been the case only if the false condition were true. Gallio dismisses the issue as neither a **misdemeanor** nor **serious crime**. He infers that it involves no aspect of Roman law. Consequently, he had no legal obligation to listen to the complaint (*anechō*; see Schlier, *TDNT* 1:359). He would not tolerate their pettiness (see BDAG 2000, 78; LSJ 1996, 136-37). Gallio's uncaring response to Sosthenes' beating at the episode's end (v 17) suggests the dismissive tone of his comments.

Gallio's further clarification (v 15) about the **questions** raised before him has implications he does not anticipate.

First, Gallio's reference to *a word* (*logou*), which could refer to the Jews' "legal immunity" from observing the imperial cult, may suggest that the Jewish litigants argue that Paul's group is ineligible for protection under this provision for the Jewish people (Winter 1999, 219). However, since the common Lukan term for the gospel is the *word* (*logos*) or "message" (CEB), readers of Acts may hear from Gallio the (correct) suggestion that the dispute is over the Christian gospel.

Second, the reference to **names** or titles implies the Christian teachings about Jesus as the Messiah, something with which a Roman official would have been completely unfamiliar. However, Luke's readers would recognize the authoritative role of the name of Jesus throughout the narrative.

Third, Gallio emphatically describes the Jewish law as distinct from the Roman law. He understands the controversy to be theological in nature and wants no part of it.

■ **16-17** After Gallio delivers his ruling, he expels the litigants from the "place of judgment" (v 12). Importantly, he releases Paul unharmed, true to the Lord's promise (vv 9-10). The same cannot be said about **Sosthenes** (v 17), a **synagogue leader** in Corinth (see v 8). He is captured and beaten before Gallio by a group identified only as *they all*. Other MSS insert "of the Greeks," suggesting that this is an instance of anti-Semitic action against the Jewish accusers who failed to have Paul indicted (see Metzger 1994, 411). But nowhere else in this episode does Luke mention Greeks. It is possible that Sosthenes is caught in the middle when Greek evictors move in and the Jewish delegation push back (see Hubbard 2005, 416-28). Yet this would not correspond with emphases in Acts or this passage. Here, the only plural antecedents are Jewish opponents. This suggests that they are the culprits who turn on **Sosthenes**, who may have led the Jewish delegation.

No textual evidence identifies Sosthenes with Paul's colleague with the same name (1 Cor 1:1). Nor is there evidence to explain Sosthenes' beating from Jewish hands on the possibility that he had become a Christian or Christian sympathizer, as is often suggested. Gallio is indifferent to what happened to Sosthenes (*none of these things*: *ouden toutōn*), because he refuses to become involved as a *judge of these things* (*kritēs . . . toutōn* [v 15]). He considers this an intra-Jewish matter (see Winter 2006, 302-3).

FROM THE TEXT

The narrative of Paul's ministry in Corinth builds on the theological foundation of Paul's Areopagus speech. It offers an inclusive strategy for extending the gospel to all humankind, not only to those with Jewish backgrounds or interests. Although the narrator leaves much to inference, it seems likely that the Jewish opposition to Paul's ministry in Corinth arose because he proclaimed a gospel message offered inclusively to Jews and Gentiles alike. The narrator depicts Paul's ministry as an expression of his obedience to God. But most Jews viewed this differently, seeing the inclusion of Gentiles as creating a serious theological and identity crisis, challenging their self-understanding as God's people.

A people of God that was no longer exclusively Jewish was nearly impossible for Jews to comprehend. But Luke insists that Paul's inclusive concept had divine endorsement. In Paul's vision, Jesus speaks of the people of God in universal terms—both Jews and Gentiles in Corinth belong to the chosen people (see Towner 1998, 426). The mission location of that people outside the Jewish synagogue further clarifies that the Jewish people did not have an exclusive claim to this ecclesiological understanding.

However, Luke is concerned throughout Acts to depict the Christian movement in continuity with Israel and God's purposes through Israel. Thus, this separation from the Jewish synagogue was no small matter and created numerous issues. On the one hand, Jewish Christians were separated from a synagogue context that nurtured Torah observance. This had the potential to throw into question the future role of the Jewish law (see 21:18-26). But separation allowed believers to read the Jewish Scriptures in the ways illustrated by the Jerusalem Council. They could remain faithful to Jewish traditions and still remain open to fresh, inclusive readings of the Scriptures (see Wall 2002, 252). The speeches in Acts illustrate how Jewish believers read their Scriptures differently in light of the Christ event.

On the other hand, the departure of the Christian mission from the Jewish synagogue has serious theological implications for the place of Israel within Luke's theology. Up to this point in Acts, Luke has portrayed various Jewish characters as resistant to what God was doing through the Jesus movement. He refers, first, to the religious leaders in Jerusalem; then, to "the Jews" in general.

Nonetheless, Luke portrays the Jesus movement as *also* very Jewish. Jewish leaders, initially Jewish believers, then both Jewish and Gentile believers, meet in Jewish synagogues, read the Jewish Scriptures, etc. Even Gallio admitted as much! The departure of believers from the synagogue signifies Judaism's refusal to embrace God's inclusive purposes to save Gentiles as well as Jews. It is true that, in Paul's vision, "my people" describes Corinthian believers rather than synagogue goers (v 10). But the narrator never appropriates an aside or a speech by a character to explain what leaving the synagogue might mean for Israel as God's chosen people. He clearly keeps his emphasis on mission.

Finally, subtleties in a text often open new windows through which to view possible ways of reading. Luke's passing reference to Paul as a "tentmaker" (v 3) offers a detail that may seem to contribute little to the unfolding plot. However, his reference to Paul's trade may allude to James' earlier quotation of Amos during the Jerusalem Council. There, he referred to the rebuilding of the "fallen tent" of David that would include the Gentiles (→ 15:16-18).

Perhaps Luke's depiction of Paul's exit from the synagogue to the house of a God-fearing Gentile next door functions as a reminder of this "rehoused" Israel that James affirmed before the church in Jerusalem (Wall 2002, 252). If so, this narrative detail about tentmaking may link Paul's ministry practices in Corinth to the fulfillment of Amos' prophecy. His separation from the synagogue "extended his tent" to include both Jews and Gentiles. Paul shared James' insight that God had chosen "a people for his name from the Gentiles" (15:14).

F. The Ministry of Paul in Ephesus (18:18—19:41)

BEHIND THE TEXT

Paul's ministry strategy typically focused on the important cities of the northeastern Mediterranean world. One city was conspicuously absent from his itinerary thus far: Ephesus. According to Luke, Paul planned earlier to go that direction, only to face a divine detour (→ 16:6). How fitting that the final Lukan depiction of Paul's ministry in specific city settings would be in this renowned ancient city.

Ephesus was one of the largest cities of the Roman Empire, surpassed in population by only Rome and Alexandria. Located in Asia Minor at the mouth of the Cayster River on the Aegean coast, it had become the prominent crossroads of that part of the world, especially between Persia and the West.

By the first century AD, Ephesus had become a vibrant commercial and cultural center (Philostratus, *Vit. Apoll.* 8.7.8) as well as the political capital of the Roman province of Asia. The city was most noted for its religious temples, especially the spectacular temple of the Greek goddess Artemis (Roman Diana; see Strabo, *Geogr.* 14.1.20-26). It was one of the "Seven Wonders of the Ancient World" (→ sidebar "Artemis and Her Temple in Ephesus" with 19:23-27).

Ephesus had a sizable Jewish population (see Josephus, *Ant.* 14.225-27; 16.160-73; *Ag. Ap.* 2.38-39). But no archaeological evidence remains for synagogues from that era. Ephesus eventually became a major center for Christianity. Its bishops were among the more influential church leaders during important Trinitarian and christological debates through the fifth century AD.

IN THE TEXT

I. Paul's Travels, with a Stop in Ephesus (18:18-23)

■ **18** This section introduces the transition of Paul's ministry away from Corinth. Gallio's refusal to rule against Paul gave him freedom to stay longer in the city. That sea travel was limited to specific seasons would have factored into the timing of Paul's departure.

The mention of **Syria** as Paul's destination serves as a reminder that his journey started there in Antioch (15:40). **Priscilla and Aquila** accompany Paul as he leaves, perhaps due to business in Ephesus. However, Luke mentions nothing about Timothy or Silas (see 18:5), who may have remained in Corinth to continue ministering there.

Interpreters differ about the significance of Paul's haircut and vow. The narrator mentions them only in passing as taking place in **Cenchreae**, the eastern port of Corinth on the Aegean Sea. It is possible that Aquila takes the vow and receives the haircut, since he is the last person named before they are mentioned. But the most likely reference is to Paul, the subject of the verse. The nature of the vow is unclear.

- Most consider it to be a Nazirite vow (see Num 6:1-21; *m. Naz.* 1.1-9.5). This was accompanied by one haircut at its beginning (or perhaps several during the period of the vow). But it was distinct from the shaving of one's head at its conclusion at the temple in Jerusalem (→ 21:24).
- Others speculate that it was a Jewish vow of petition or thanksgiving (see Josephus, *J.W.* 2.309-14). Paul's haircut was either the culmination or commencement of his vow.
- Still others suggest that such actions reflect Greek responses to divine guidance (see Barrett 1998, 877).

Common threads among these different interpretations are (*a*) the Lukan perspective of Paul as God's agent for spreading the gospel and (*b*) Paul's recognition of God's providential care.

■ **19-21** These verses merely introduce Paul to Ephesus. Their arrangement is awkward. That **Paul left Priscilla and Aquila** in the city precedes any description of what he does there (v 19). It implies that he acts alone.

This statement focuses attention solely on Paul: he enters the **synagogue** (→ 13:14; 14:1; 17:1-3, 10; 18:4) and engages the worshipers in discussions (*dialegomai*; 17:2, 17; 18:4), presumably about the gospel. The Ephesian Jews' invitation for Paul to extend those conversations is an encouraging sign after the Corinthian opposition. But it also mirrors the initial response at the synagogue in Pisidian Antioch (13:42-43), which was followed by hostilities (13:44-52).

The Western text explains why Paul declines their offer: he wants to attend the festival (probably Passover) in Jerusalem (see Metzger 1994, 412). However, his stated desire to return anticipates what Luke recounts in ch 19. The expression **if it is God's will** (v 21) was a conventional way of affirming God's providence in human affairs (see, e.g., 1 Cor 4:19; 16:7; Heb 6:3; Jas 4:15; Josephus, *Ant.* 2.333; 7.373; Plato, *Alc.* 1.135d; *Phaed.* 80d; Epictetus, *Diatr.* 1.1.17). On that note, Paul resumes his return voyage to Antioch.

■ **22-23** Readers might expect Paul to disembark in Seleucia, the port for Antioch (see 13:4), rather than **Caesarea**, about 250 miles (402 km) south of Antioch. Perhaps weather conditions were to blame. Although the text does not directly mention Jerusalem, that Paul **went up** and then **greeted the church**, and then **went down to Antioch** (18:22) suggests that Jerusalem was his intended destination all along (see the Western text's addition to v 21).

This apparent visit to the Jerusalem church does not coincide with any of those mentioned in the Pauline letters. Luke's sketchy account of this visit may hint that there were tensions in the Jerusalem church over Paul's ministry practices (Dunn 1996, 247-48; Barrett 1998, 880-81). If this trip to Jerusalem was essential for Paul's vow (v 18), this stark description offers little information.

From Jerusalem, Paul makes his way north to **Antioch**, the location of his sponsoring church (v 23; see 11:26-30; 13:1-3; 14:26-28; 15:30-35, 40). After spending an undefined period of time there, he leaves to embark on another ministry journey. By mentioning that Paul travels **from place to place** (*kathexēs*; 3:24; 8:4; Luke 1:3; 8:1) through **Galatia and Phrygia** (see 16:6) where he is **strengthening** [see 14:22; 15:32, 41; 16:5] **all the disciples**, Luke recalls previous ministry excursions by Paul and others, followed by pastoral nurture and encouragement.

2. Apollos in Ephesus (18:24-28)

■ **24-26** **Apollos** (18:24), an abbreviated form of the name Apollonius that was derived from the Greek god Apollo, arrived in Ephesus some time after Paul's departure (v 21). He was a Diaspora Jew, born in **Alexandria**, the intellectual and cultural center of the Hellenistic world and the empire's second largest city. It was the home of the first-century Jewish philosopher Philo. A large, well-established Jewish presence in that city was responsible for the translation of the LXX (→ sidebar "Names for God and the Septuagint" with 2:19-20), widely used by the earliest Christians.

The narrator mentions several additional qualities about Apollos. First, he was **learned** ("eloquent" [NRSV]). This is consistent with his Alexandrian background and was an asset for his ministry.

Second, his ability to interpret the Scriptures (→ 18:28) caused him to stand out among his peers.

Third, his instruction (*katēcheō*; see Luke 1:4) in **the way of the Lord** (Acts 18:25; see 9:2; 18:26; 19:9, 23; 22:4; 24:14, 22; see also Isa 40:3; Jer 5:4) suggests that Apollos received Christian teaching, perhaps in Alexandria. The narrator gives no hint as to when that happened or who his teachers may have been.

Fourth, he speaks "stirred up by the Spirit" (CEB; see Rom 12:11). Some interpreters and most translations understand this expression to describe Apollos' dynamic personality. But it resembles Luke's description of Stephen's Spirit-enabled speech (Acts 6:10; see Tannehill 1990, 233).

Priscilla and Aquila do not baptize Apollos (Acts 18:26), as Paul later baptizes twelve Ephesian disciples (→ 19:1-7). These disciples resemble Apollos in some respects, but they know nothing about the Spirit. This reference to the Holy Spirit rather than his fiery disposition explains why no baptism is needed.

Fifth, Apollos teaches **about Jesus accurately**, a practice Luke consistently associates with believers. Still, he knows **only the baptism of John** (18:25; see 1:22; 10:37). So his instruction is incomplete.

Sixth, Apollos begins to **speak boldly in the synagogue** (v 26), a practice that mirrors the apostles and Paul (see 4:13, 29, 31; 9:27-28; 13:46; 14:3) and indicates the Spirit's presence (see 18:25).

The Lukan characterization of Apollos is not dissimilar to that of other ambiguous characters in Acts. It prepares readers for his initial meeting with Priscilla and Aquila, who must have heard him while attending the same synagogue. His teachings, based on John's baptism alone, are consistent with other traditional Jewish teachings in Acts. He may not have emphasized salvation inclusively by calling Gentiles to repentance and baptism (see Hedlun 2010, 48-49).

Rather than speaking with Apollos publicly in that context, the wording suggests the couple **invited him to their home** (or "took him aside" [NRSV]) to address the deficiency in his preaching (BDAG 2000, 883). The verb **explained** (*ektithēmi*; see 11:4; 28:23) connotes laying things out in detail so that someone is more fully informed (BDAG 2000, 310). Priscilla and Aquila offer some helpful clarification to Apollos' teaching and doctrine.

As a result, this one whom Luke depicts in "Christian" ways becomes identifiable with the Christian movement. He does not need (re)baptism (→ 19:5). Luke places Apollos within the scope of Paul's ministry (an important point in the relationship between Apollos and Paul in 1 Cor 1; 4; and 16).

Priscilla and the Role of Women in Ministry

The role of women in Christian ministry settings has often been defined by passages from NT letters, notably 1 Tim 2:11-12 and 1 Cor 14:34-35. Interpretations of such passages as *universal* prescriptions typically fail to account for the *specific* historical situations the respective letters addressed. The biblical examples of women who served in various ministry roles, often against the prevalent social and cultural norms of their times, are particularly significant.

Priscilla is a notable example. Although she was considered an artisan or tradesperson as a tentmaker with her husband (see 18:3), she took on the role of teaching the more educated Apollos (v 26). Unfortunately, Luke does not offer any direct speech from Priscilla or any specific content of her teaching. Nonetheless, the effectiveness of Apollos' ministry that followed in Corinth (see vv 26-27) validates Priscilla's role as his teacher (see Reimer 1995, 195-226).

The other NT references to her outside Acts (Rom 16:3; 1 Cor 16:19; 2 Tim 4:19) also list her name before her husband's. This underscores her standing in the NT church. Her example, along with others like her, affirms the role of women in Christian ministry, as do the countless women through the centuries who have faithfully responded to God's call to minister in the church and in the world.

■ **27-28** At some point, Apollos hoped to travel to **Achaia** (v 27), the region from which Paul, Priscilla, and Aquila had just come. Luke offers no explanation for his plan. The Western text adds that visiting Corinthians who heard him speak extended an invitation for him to return with them (see Metzger 1994, 414).

Apollos' plans are supported by **the brothers and sisters** (*adelphoi*; "the believers" [NRSV]). This may refer to Priscilla and Aquila alone but probably points collectively to a larger, unidentified group of believers in Ephesus (perhaps the result of the couple's ministry). They provide a letter of recommendation on his behalf, a common practice of that time (see 9:2; 2 Cor 3:1; Rom 16:1-2).

Upon his arrival in Corinth, Apollos picks up in ministry where Paul left off (see also 1 Cor. 1:12; 3:4-6, 22; 4:6; 16:12). He also squares off with "the Jews" and proclaims the same message (Acts 18:5; see 9:22; 17:3, 7) as Paul.

> For Apollos to go to Corinth and engage in open disputation with Jews in the synagogue on the basis of Scriptures is to make the point once more that the Pauline mission was not one exclusively and definitely directed to the Gentiles, but remained engaged in the effort to win a "people for his name" among the Jews as well. (Johnson 1992, 335-36)

3. Summary of Paul's Ministry in Ephesus (19:1-10)

■ **1-3** Apollos' time in Ephesus overlaps with Paul's travels to Jerusalem and Antioch (18:22-23). Luke relates the next episode to Apollos' *absence* from Ephesus and ministry in Corinth (18:27—19:1a). Paul's journey **through the interior** of Asia Minor (19:1a; 18:23) mirrors his previous one (16:6), except for the inference that *this* time God allows him to proceed to Ephesus (see 16:6; 18:21). Upon his arrival, he meets **some disciples** (19:1b), perhaps in one of the city's synagogues, since Luke typically describes Paul going to the synagogue on the Sabbath after entering a city.

Paul's interaction with them (vv 2-4) implies that he attends a different synagogue than where Priscilla and Aquila attend (see 18:26). The initial description of this group suggests they are Christians. Elsewhere in Acts, the term "disciple" refers only to believers (6:1-2, 7; 9:1, 10, 19, 25-26, 38; 13:52; 14:20, 22, 28; 15:10; 16:1; 18:23, 27; 19:9, 30; 20:1, 30; 21:4, 16). But their startling response to Paul's question—whether they received the Holy Spirit upon believing—indicates their unawareness of **a Holy Spirit** (19:2). This is not a contradiction of the OT and John's teachings (1:5; 11:16; Luke 3:16), but an indication that they do not know about Pentecost.

Like the precorrected Apollos, these disciples are ambiguous characters. They are familiar with **John's baptism** (Acts 19:3; 18:25; see 1:22; 10:37; 13:24-25), but lack the Spirit. Yet Luke associates discipleship with being filled with the Spirit (→ 2:38; 4:31; 6:3, 5; 8:15-16, 19; 9:17; 10:44; 11:15-16; 13:9). Most interpreters differentiate whether or not they are "Christian" disciples. The narrative focuses on Paul's attempts to bring them "into the fold."

■ **4-5** One would expect Paul to respond to the group's shortcomings by emphasizing that John baptized with water, whereas Jesus baptized with the Holy Spirit (1:5; 11:16; Luke 3:16). However, Paul focuses instead on the importance of their **baptism** and its characteristic call to **repentance** (Acts 19:4; see Luke 3:3, 8). John indicated that this prepared them for the Coming One, who would baptize with the Holy Spirit (Luke 3:15-16).

The cursory identification of Jesus with **the one coming after him** need not mean that Paul offered no further explanation of the centrality of Jesus. Paul undoubtedly helped his small audience "connect the dots." But readers of Acts already possess sufficient information to make that connection. Their baptism **in the name of the Lord Jesus** (Acts 19:5; see 2:38; 8:16; 10:48) signifies both their belief (19:4) in the gospel and incorporation into the Christian community of faith. This is the only instance of rebaptism in the NT (although it is not *Christian* rebaptism).

■ **6-7** After their baptism, Paul **placed his hands** on the group (v 6), like other leaders had done in Acts (→ 6:6; 8:17; 13:3). Similar to what happened when Peter and John prayed for the Samaritan believers (8:17), **the Holy Spirit came on them**. Without the Spirit, this group could not continue the prophetic mission of John and Jesus.

In this instance, Luke notes that the coming of the Spirit is accompanied by two activities. First, the group begins to speak (imperfect *elaloun*) **in tongues** (or "languages" [CEB]), an activity reminiscent of Pentecost (2:4) and what happened at Cornelius' house (10:46). Second, they begin to prophesy (imperfect *eprophēteuon*), which also reminds readers of Pentecost (→ 2:4) and of the praise proclaimed at Cornelius' house (→ 10:46; see Levison 2009, 336-43).

314

Such narrative interconnections in Acts focus on God's saving work. They do not address contemporary questions about glossolalia or 1 Cor 14. Pentecost functions as the epochal event inaugurating the Christian mission throughout Acts. The Cornelius event reiterates that mission inclusively among the Gentiles. Just so, the Ephesian episode extends that mission to the rest of the empire.

Luke does not again mention this group of **about twelve men** or its size after v 7. So there is probably no formal symbolism to the number "twelve" (against Johnson 1992, 338). However, Ephesus is the last location where Paul takes the gospel, so this group may provide an opposite bookend to the twelve apostles, whose mission was to extend throughout the known world (1:8). Like Apollos, these disciples respond faithfully to the instruction offered them.

■ **8** After the encounter with the twelve Ephesian disciples, Luke summarizes Paul's ministry as he returns to the Ephesian **synagogue**. This recalls his earlier brief visit and the invitation extended to him then (→ 18:19-21). His bold speech is reminiscent of the Spirit-enabled confidence of the apostles (2:29; 4:13, 29, 31), his own practice elsewhere (9:27-28; 13:46; 14:3), and that of Apollos (18:26).

As Paul had done earlier in Ephesus, he enters into dialogue (*dialegomai* [18:19]) with people in the synagogue (as in Thessalonica, Athens, and Corinth [17:2, 17; 18:4]). In addition, he is also ***persuading*** (*peithō*; → 13:43; 17:4; 18:4; 19:26; 28:23-24) them by proclaiming the gospel.

The expression **kingdom of God** is not a common theme in the Pauline letters (Rom 14:17; 1 Cor 4:20; 6:9-10; 15:24, 50; Gal 5:21; 1 Thess 2:12). However, in Acts (1:3, 6; 8:12; 14:22; 20:25; 28:23, 31) it summarizes the gospel and ties it to Jesus the risen Christ. This particular description may suggest the political implications of Paul's gospel (as later complaints imply; → 19:23-41).

Three months pass before opposition arises, a relatively long time of positive response (compare, e.g., 17:1-9). Both the earlier invitation from the Ephesian synagogue goers (18:20) and the apparent "tolerance" of different groups in that synagogue (e.g., John's disciples in vv 1-7) make this setting more open to Paul's message (see Pesch 1986, 2:167).

■ **9-10** Not surprisingly, opposition arises eventually. In contrast to the united Jewish opposition in Corinth (18:12), the resistance involves only a minority (**some** [v 9]) of the synagogue. There is no mention of God-fearing Gentiles here. But Paul's inclusive understanding of salvation and the people of God probably provokes discontent. This is a robust response.

Hardening the heart or being stiff-necked (*sklērynō*; see 7:51) alludes both to Pharaoh in the Exodus stories (see, e.g., Exod 7:3; 9:12; 13:15; 14:17-18) and to Israel's rebellion against God (Deut 10:16; 2 Chr 30:8; Neh 9:16;

Ps 95:8; Isa 63:17; Jer 7:26; 17:23). The imagery signifies the stubborn refusal to acknowledge God when God appears or acts (see Rom 2:5; Heb 3:8, 13, 15; 4:7). In contrast to those Paul is **persuading** (*peithōn* [Acts 19:8]), these others are not convinced (*ēpeithoun* [v 9]; see 14:2). Instead, they are disobedient to the gospel and to God (see 5:39).

The unconvinced make their opposition public (**before the crowd** in the synagogue [19:9]). There, they are **speaking evil** (*kakologeō*) against or slandering (→ 13:45; 18:6) **the Way** (18:25-26; see 9:2; 19:23; 22:4; 24:14, 22). The verb tenses (two imperfect indicatives and one present participle) indicate ongoing opposition. Luke mentions nothing else about the resistance. But readers may assume similar situations as in previous episodes (see 1 Cor 15:32; 2 Cor 1:8-11).

Paul's response to the vocal opposition is equally pointed and abrupt. As in Corinth, Paul leaves the synagogue. The opposition made civil discourse impossible. The participle *apostas* (source of the word "apostasy") does not suggest that Paul merely left the synagogue for another location. The verb *aphistēmi* connotes complete separation (LXX Deut 7:4; Jer 6:8; Dan 9:9; Wis 3:10) or revolt (in political settings: Herodotus, *Hist.* 1.95; Thucydides, *War* 8.35; Josephus, *Ant.* 20.102). Paul did not just depart the building. He refused to identify with them and separated **from them** (*ap' autōn*), his Ephesian opponents. The verb referring to Paul taking **the disciples** with him connotes separation (*aphorizō*; see Luke 6:22; LSJ 1996, 139; BDAG 2000, 158).

Paul reestablishes his ministry in **the lecture hall of Tyrannus**. Nothing is known about Tyrannus. The building was likely a place where pupils and teachers met and philosophers lectured. It may have extended Paul's influence into Ephesus beyond the synagogue. The Western text precisely sets Paul's discussions there between 11:00 a.m. and 4:00 p.m. daily. Perhaps Paul worked at his trade early in the morning (→ 20:34). The **lecture hall** would be more publicly accessible than a private residence and provides a preferred venue for Paul's ongoing ministry. As a result, Paul's opponents only succeed in amplifying Paul's ministry, which continues for the next **two years** (19:10).

In typical Lukan hyperbole, **the word of the Lord** (the gospel; → 4:4, 31; 6:2, 7; 8:4, 14, 25; 11:1; 12:24; 13:5, 49; 15:7, 36; 16:32) reaches not only all the Ephesians but **everyone living in Asia**. Although Luke leaves much left unsaid, he directs readers' attention to the phenomenal success of Paul's ministry among both **Jews and Greeks**. This is not despite the separation from the synagogue, but perhaps because of it.

4. Effects of Paul's Ministry in Ephesus (19:11-22)

■ **11-12** In Acts, Luke cites God's presence and activity through individuals as evidence of divine endorsement (see 2:22, 43; 3:1-10; 5:12-16; 9:32-43; → 14:8-20). Readers of Acts would know—but the Ephesians would not—that the **unusual deeds of power** (miracles [19:11]; → 2:22; 8:13) associated with Paul are actually accomplished by God. Paul's notoriety for miracles leads people to take articles that have physically contacted Paul to cure those with **illnesses** and **evil spirits** (19:12). This parallels previous healings occasioned by touching the fringe of Jesus' garment (Luke 8:44) or by Peter's shadow passing over the sick (Acts 5:15).

Most interpreters understand the **handkerchiefs** and **aprons** to be common materials used in tentmaking. The cloth was used to wipe perspiration from one's brow; the apron, belt, or towel was worn around the waist for protection. Luke has not mentioned Paul's craft since his arrival in Ephesus. He has characterized him as a lecturer or orator (19:9), whose customary attire would also include a similar cloth around the neck for perspiration. People may have wanted access to these specific pieces of clothing they believed would exude the special powers that Paul possessed (see Strelan 2003, 154-57).

Ancient Beliefs and Narrative Interpretation

Although the healings associated with Paul in Ephesus should not surprise readers of Acts, aspects of this specific account reflect particular beliefs common in the Greco-Roman world. People believed healing power resided in or came from certain individuals and was transmitted to other individuals through objects or specific words (e.g., Plutarch, *Quaest. nat.* 916d).

Jesus' use of spittle to heal an individual (see Mark 7:31-37; 8:22-26) draws on ancient notions about the curative powers of bodily fluids. That Jesus possessed divine powers conveys particular theological ideas about his identity.

The use of Paul's "handkerchiefs and aprons" (19:12) for the sake of others in need came out of that same general milieu. Luke makes it clear that this was God's doing (19:11). This differentiates these unusual occurrences from what was often associated with other religions or magic.

Yet church history is littered with examples of misapplications of this passage. Some have confused Luke's *description* for contemporary *prescription*. These and other descriptions of ancient beliefs and actions mentioned in Acts must *first* be interpreted as contributing parts of the narrative. It is a mistake first to export them into a different world, where they may be foreign (→ "Engaging Acts in a New Day" in Introduction).

ACTS

19:13-14

■ **13-14** The departure of evil spirits due to Paul's ministry (v 12) sets the stage for the peculiar episode involving seven itinerant Jewish exorcists. Luke identifies their father as **Sceva** (v 14). His name appears on no extant list of Jewish high priests. He is probably a *chief priest*—a member of an aristocratic, priestly family (→ "chief priests" in 4:23; 5:24; 9:14, 21; 22:30; 23:14; 25:2, 15; 26:10, 12; see Fitzmyer 1998, 649-50, for a less plausible explanation).

Exorcism was common in Jewish circles (see Luke 11:19; Matt 7:21-23), and Jesus even endorsed it when outsiders practiced it (Luke 9:49-50; Mark

9:38). Josephus describes Jewish exorcism as derived from Solomon's extraordinary wisdom (*Ant.* 8.42-49). Persons in need or desperation often sought such highly respected men.

In a wordplay reminding readers of Paul placing his hands upon the Ephesian disciples (Acts 19:6), these men **tried** or "put their hands" to work (*epicheireō* [v 13]; see BDAG 2000, 386; LSJ 1996, 307). They use **the name of the Lord Jesus** like a magic formula (see Origen, *Cels.* 1.22), referring to **Jesus** as their authority under false pretenses. Their hope is to share some of Paul's success (vv 10-12).

Their use of the verb **command** (*horkizō*; "adjure" [NRSV]) is different from Jesus' practice in Luke's Gospel. It only refers in the NT to an evil spirit's scheming command *of* Jesus (see Mark 5:7). These would-be exorcists have a different agenda: to manipulate and control both Jesus and God (Garrett 1989, 92). In this respect, this episode resembles Peter's encounter with Simon the magician in Samaria, who wrongly believed that the power of Jesus' witnesses could be manipulated (→ Acts 8:18-24). They command the evil spirit under the authority of **Jesus**, not the **Lord** Jesus. This underscores their ironic failure to grasp the essence of Paul's preaching.

■ **15-16** The humorous response of the **evil spirit** (v 15; singular, perhaps speaking for *all* the spirits) confirms what readers of Acts already know. The people of God are identified as those who "call on the name of the Lord" (2:21 NRSV), not merely those who cite the name of Jesus.

The two different verbs translated **know** here have no substantive difference in meaning. These seven Jewish exorcists are not at all like Jesus and Paul. The evil spirit implies that, if Paul had offered the command, the evil spirits would have complied.

Unfortunately for these exorcists, Jesus was not summoned through their magical use of names. Rather, the opposite occurs. The scene turns suddenly serious as the man with the evil spirit attacks the seven. The verb *katakyrieuō* conveys his complete submission and mastery of the group (used of God's authority in the LXX: Num 32:22; Ps 72:8; Jer 3:14). The evil spirits **overpowered** (*ischyō*) the exorcists. Nakedness here may indicate that they leave only clothed with their undergarments (Lake and Cadbury 1933a, 242). Their shameful departure accentuates their complete failure to confront the evil spirits.

■ **17** The response in Ephesus resembles that in Jerusalem after Pentecost (2:43) and after the deaths of Ananias and Sapphira (5:5, 11). In these earlier instances, the **fear** or reverent **awe** (*phobos*) that captivated the cities was due to the power associated with **Jesus** as **Lord**. After this latest incident, people recognize Jesus' name has a character completely different from the names that magicians routinely invoked. In typical Lukan hyperbole, the narrator

318

claims that the entire Ephesian populace, **Jews and Greeks**, offer **the name of the Lord Jesus** praise (normally reserved for God alone: *megalynō*; → 5:13; 10:46; Luke 1:46, 58).

■ **18-19** As a result, many believers renounce their magical practices. Ephesus was a renowned center for magic. Perhaps some believers still engaged in magic after their conversions. Rather than "still hedging their bets by seeking to balance faith in Jesus with reliance on magic" (Malina and Pilch 2008, 139; see Peterson 2009, 541), this is evidence of their need to grow and mature in the faith (→ sidebar "Magic and the Christian Faith" with 19:20). So now they recognize the need to abandon such practices.

Typically, this particular nuance of the verb **confessed** (v 18; see Matt 3:6; Mark 1:5) is associated with the acknowledgment of one's sin. In this case, their sin is related to *their magical practices* (v 19). Accompanying their confession is the disclosure of these practices before the community of faith. Since mystery and secrecy were essential aspects of magical practices, this rendered those practices ineffective (see Bruce 1988, 369). These believers became convicted of the incompatibility of such magical practices with the Christian faith and life, which prompted their repentance before the fledgling church in Ephesus.

In the ancient world (as today), the public burning of literature was an open condemnation of the contents (e.g., Josephus, *Ant.* 10.88-95; Diogenes Laertius, *Vit. phil.* 9.52; Livy, *Hist.* 39.16.8; Lucian, *Alex.* 47; Suetonius, *Aug.* 31). The Ephesian believers gather and burn **scrolls** that probably contained magical formulas or incantations (on "Ephesian letters," see Plutarch, *Quaest. conv.* 7.5). This is an emphatic and demonstrable break from the systems and values that defined Ephesian life. The believers' former lives literally go up in smoke. In contrast to an earlier magician, Simon, who tried to buy the powers of the Spirit (→ 8:18-20), these believers forfeit their wealth as part of their transformation (see Spencer 2004a, 197).

The text does not specify the exact value of the documents they destroyed. *Myrias* may simply refer to a huge number. Readers are left to imagine a "ridiculously" large sum of money. To interpret this on the basis of either the Greek drachma or Roman denarius, both approximately a day's wage for a common laborer, the total would roughly equal about two hundred years of income!

■ **20** The summary statement concluding the description of Paul's ministry in Ephesus reiterates several Lukan emphases. The **word of the Lord** (→ 19:10) frames this section and underscores that the gospel and its inclusive mission— as embodied by Paul and his ministry—are the focus of this section.

The reference to its **spread** is a strategic narrative marker, signaling the advance of the gospel and its mission: first in Jerusalem (6:7), then just before Paul's journeys began (12:24). Here, it emphasizes that same success with reference to this epochal setting for Paul's ministry (see Krodel 1986, 364)—the last time this description appears in Acts.

Ironically, the same verb that describes the evil spirit "prevailing" over the seven exorcists also depicts **the word of the Lord** "prevailing." However, this "powerful" verb (*ischyō*) reinforces the emphasis of the prepositional phrase that introduces the sentence: *In power* (*kata kratos*). Historians often used this phrase to refer to military power. Here, it refers to divine power, seen most distinctly in the Ephesian battle against magic. Thus,

> the echoes of the apostles' successful work in Jerusalem and Samaria in the early days of the mission suggest that the word of the Lord is equally powerful in Paul's Ephesian ministry and that the Christian mission can be equally successful in the pluralistic world of Greeks and Diaspora Jews represented by Ephesus. (Tannehill 1990, 238)

Magic and the Christian Faith

The confession of magical practices in Ephesus (19:18-19) is the third instance involving magic in Acts (→ 8:9-24; 13:6-12). These intersections between practices described as "magic" and the Christian faith in Acts often surprise contemporary readers.

But in the ancient world, magic, like religion in general, attempted to deal with what seemed to be supernatural or spiritual forces beyond normal, everyday experience. Boundaries between magic and religion were nebulous. Interpreters may label practices as "magical" that those engaged in such practices might not. Jesus and the early Christians were criticized by their opponents for dabbling in magic.

Confusion abounded over practices and rhetoric about such practices. This may explain in part why early Christian writings condemned magic and its practices for the church (see, e.g., *Did.* 2:2; Ign. *Eph.* 19:3; *Barn.* 20:1). Justin Martyr distinguished between the church and magic: "we who formerly used magical arts, dedicate ourselves to the good and unbegotten God" (*I Apol.* 14).

■ **21-22** There are striking similarities between the beginning of v 21 and Luke 9:51, which concludes Jesus' Galilean ministry and begins his journey toward Jerusalem. By similarly "closing the circle" begun in ch 13, Luke depicts Paul's ministry as coming to an end (see Sanders 1987, 76-77).

The reference to the fulfillment (*plēroō*) of *these things* (*tauta*) may refer to what just occurred in Ephesus (vv 1-20), including the establishment of a mature community of faith that overcame various obstacles to the Christian faith (see Wall 2002, 269-70). However, this fulfillment language suggests that Luke may be looking more retrospectively over Paul's entire ministry. He characterizes it in terms of divine guidance (e.g., 13:1-3; 16:6-10; 18:9-10).

Given Luke's depiction of Paul, readers of Acts would likely perceive the phrase *in the Spirit/spirit* (*en tō pneumati*) with regard to Paul's travel plans as another reference to the Holy Spirit's guidance rather than his own personal decision (against Fitzmyer 1998, 652; Barrett 1998, 919). Such divine guidance is accentuated by Paul's insistence that he **must** (*dei*) also travel to Rome, using the vocabulary of divine purpose characteristic of Acts (→ 1:16, 21-22; 3:21; 4:12; 5:29; 9:6, 16; 17:3). God will continue to direct events in upcoming chapters (23:11; 27:24; see Krodel 1986, 364). This is the first time in Acts that Paul mentions Rome. The narrator gives no indication how he learned this from God.

Paul's itinerary for this return trip to Macedonia, Achaia, and Jerusalem is reminiscent of previous travels in chs 16—18. As before, the purpose behind these trips includes pastoral nurture and encouragement (→ 14:21-22; 15:36, 41; 16:5; 18:23). Some of Paul's letters offer other possible reasons for Paul's itinerary: to deliver the collection for the poor to Jerusalem (see Rom 15:25-28; 1 Cor 16:1-8; 2 Cor 8:1—9:15); and to reconcile with the Corinthian church (see 2 Cor 2:12-13). However, Luke is silent about these.

Paul sends **Timothy** (19:21; last seen in 18:5; see 1 Cor 4:17; 16:10) and **Erastus** (probably not the same person mentioned in Rom 16:23) ahead of him to Macedonia. These associates (*diakoneō*; see 6:2) are to serve as an advance party to initiate Paul's pastoral work before his arrival.

5. Controversy: Ephesian Defenders of Artemis (19:23-41)

Some interpreters question the historicity and purpose of this section. Paul plays a minimal role in the narrative. His letters offer firsthand references to life-threatening situations in Ephesus (1 Cor 15:32; 2 Cor 1:8-11) that Luke does not mention (see, e.g., Haenchen 1971, 576-78; Pervo 2009, 486-90).

Surprisingly, the narrator only offers a mere summary of Paul's ministry of more than two years in duration. Yet this last glimpse of Ephesus barely includes the lead character! This episode depicts the impact of the gospel upon society in general and contrasts society's gods and ideals with the one true God and those Luke presents as "the people of God."

■ **23-27** The understatement *no little disturbance* (v 23; → 12:18) introduces this episode. It signals the onset of troubles Luke has downplayed thus far in Ephesus (see Thompson 2006, 215). The threat is directed against **the Way** (see 9:2; 18:25-26; 22:4; 24:14, 22). This refers to the church as "a socially cohesive movement . . . arising out of and grounded in their shared faith in Jesus" (Cassidy 1987, 95). In Acts, the expression is typically associated with persecution or resistance (Gaventa 2003, 270).

This trouble is instigated by **Demetrius** (v 24), who convenes fellow "artisans" (NRSV) and other **workers** (v 25) associated with the silversmith craft, perhaps as a leader of their guild. Their chief products were **silver shrines of Artemis** (v 24), probably replicas of her Ephesian temple for housing small statues or figures of the goddess. Replicas made of terra-cotta or marble have

321

been discovered. But, not surprisingly, no silver ones survive. They were likely melted down for other uses in later years.

Both Luke's introduction of Demetrius and his brief speech refer to the silversmiths' **business** or *profit* (*ergasia* [16:16, 19]) coming from these religious artifacts. Their ultimate concerns are mercenary and economic rather than religious. The narrator consistently depicts such motives in contrast to God's saving purposes (→ 1:17-20; 5:1-11; 8:20-22; 16:16-18). These people have little credibility in readers' eyes from the start.

Demetrius' accusations against Paul (19:26) function like earlier ones (16:20-21; 17:6-7; 18:13) to incite angry reactions from the audience. His claims of Paul's overwhelming success in Ephesus and (*almost all*) Asia stir up the crowd (and echo 19:10). He is dismissive of Paul (*this Paul*), but his description of Paul's persuasive powers corresponds with Luke's depiction of the preacher (*peithō* [13:43; 17:4; 18:4; 19:8]).

Demetrius' recounting of Paul's message expresses views consistent with Paul's earlier Athenian speech (17:24-25, 29), although Paul condemned making *images* of God, not making gods per se (19:26). By offering Paul's message as evidence of false or misleading teaching, Demetrius indicts himself and his fellow silversmiths as "greedy artisans encrusted with superstition" (Pervo 2009, 491).

The inherent danger or risk (*kindyneuō*; see v 40) that Demetrius outlines (v 27) suggests that the economic threat to their business also had potentially serious cultural, civic, and religious implications. In an honor-shame culture, Demetrius identifies different ways in which honor would be lost in an ascending hierarchy of values: trade, temple, and goddess (see Spencer 2004a, 197). Collision rather than coexistence is inevitable. Luke depicts "the profound incompatibility between the way of Christ and the ways of being that commonly defined pagan life, precisely as such incompatibility breaks violently into the public sphere" (Rowe 2009, 46).

Artemis and Her Temple in Ephesus

It is difficult to overestimate the importance of the cult of Artemis for Ephesus. It held a central place in the city for centuries (Herodotus, *Hist.* 1.26; Strabo, *Geogr.* 14.1.22-23; Achilles Tatius, *Leuc. Clit.* 7.13—8.14). The Greek goddess Artemis (Roman: Diana) was the daughter of Zeus and Leto, the sister of Apollo. As a virgin huntress and "queen of the wild animals" (Homer, *Il.* 21.470), hers was a role of protection. Her name literally means "safe and sound" (see Strabo, *Geogr.* 14.1.6; LSJ 1996, 248). She protected particularly the young, women in childbirth, and those who sought refuge in her temple (see Pausanias, *Descr.* 7.2.7; Achilles Tatius, *Leuc. Clit.* 7.13), including the poor and outcasts. It is no wonder that, according to Pausanias, "all cities worship Artemis of Ephesus, and individuals hold her in honor above all the gods" (*Descr.* 4.31.8).

19:23-27

Other worship sites for Artemis were scattered throughout the Mediterranean world, but the renowned Ephesian temple was this cult's worship center. The magnificent structure in Paul's day dwarfed the Parthenon in Athens. It was about four times larger: about 225 feet wide (69 m) by 425 feet (130 m) long, with 128 pillars over 65 feet (20 m) tall. The temple, adorned with sculptures and other artistic works, attracted worshipers and travelers from all over the empire.

Perhaps due to the goddess's reputation for protection, the temple also functioned as the banking center of Asia (see Dio Chrysostom, *Rhod.* 31.54). The temple and cult of Artemis in Ephesus were deeply embedded in the economic, political, and social structures of the city and the region. Thus, threats to this religious institution could affect Ephesian and Asian society (much like the world banking and debt crises in the opening decades of the twenty-first century; see Oster 1976, 24-44; Trebilco 1994, 316-31).

■ **28-29** Demetrius outlines no course of action. His speech merely provokes his colleagues to riot before he disappears from the stage. Their reaction to the perceived threat is not unexpected. Artisans and other manual laborers are not beneficiaries of prominent social status. Any threat to their income endangers whatever status they had gained financially (see Witherington 1998, 593).

The **furious** (v 28; lit., *full of rage*) crowd is reminiscent of the response to Jesus at the synagogue at Nazareth (Luke 4:28; Schneider 1982, 275) and similar to the Jewish leaders' response to the apostles and Stephen in Jerusalem (Acts 5:33; 7:54). Their repeated acclamation (imperfect tense: *ekrazon*) in honor of Artemis takes on a familiar ring. Such chants typically functioned as liturgical or hymnic cries proclaiming the greatness of a god or goddess and invoking its power. Much like a short chorus, the acclamation reminds them of the entire mythology that bonds Artemis and Ephesus together.

The Western text inserts that they shout this as they are "running into the streets." This helps explain the "confusion" (*synchysis* [19:29 NRSV]; compare Babel; Gen 11:9 LXX) that comes over the city. The rest of the populace would have no idea what is provoking the clamor. Ironically, in contrast to that confusion, Luke depicts a large, growing crowd from the city: **together** (*homothymadon*; see 7:57; 18:12) they rush (see 7:57) **into the theater** of Ephesus. This is reminiscent of the Jewish leaders' hostile response to Stephen's speech. The natural location for mass demonstrations in ancient cities was the theater. In Ephesus, this 25,000-seat stadium was carved out of a hillside overlooking the city.

The mob's capture of **Gaius and Aristarchus** (→ 6:12) is probably due to their association with Paul. If Paul was unavailable for abuse, his partners would suffice (see 19:37). This **Gaius** is not the Gaius of Derbe mentioned later (20:4). Since he is a Macedonian, this Gaius may be the one whom Paul mentions (1 Cor 1:14). **Aristarchus** appears later on (20:4; 27:2; see Phlm 24; also Col 4:10).

That both men are **from Macedonia** reminds readers that Paul's travel plans are to begin there (19:21). Such hostilities against Paul's ministry partners could delay that trip. But the divine guidance behind those plans implies the delay would be temporary.

■ **30-31** Generally speaking, the term *dēmos*, which describes the people gathered in the theater, refers to a local assembly of citizens from a free Greek city. However, Luke reserves it for those out of control and acting like a mob (also 12:22; 17:5; 19:33; Penner 2003, 96 n 96). The narrator offers no reason for Paul's desire to go there. Is he concerned for the welfare of his friends? Does he want an opportunity to respond to the complaints? In Acts, these always become opportunities to proclaim the gospel!

Two different groups block his noble intentions. Some unidentified **disciples** refuse to let Paul get involved (v 30; imperfect tense: *eiōn*; → 9:25, 30; 17:10, 14-15). Some **friends** from circles of significant social standing, wealth, and political power also advise him to stay away. Luke identifies them as **Asiarchs**, officials involved with civic administration within the Asian province (Kearsley 1994, 363-76). Although officials' duties were not primarily involved with the imperial cult (against Taylor 1933, 256-62), the religious and political structures of the city intertwined significantly. Their friendship and persistent attempts (imperfect tense: *parekaloun*) to protect Paul stand out and reveal his increasing influence and growing reputation in the city.

■ **32-34** Back at the theater, the turmoil continues. The scene is chaotic, with groups offering different perspectives (→ 2:12-13), shouting them aloud in confusion (*syncheō*; see noun, 19:29; see LXX: Gen 11:7, 9; 2 Macc 10:30).

Luke notes that **most** of those present do not know the reason for the gathering (Acts 19:32). He depicts this **assembly** (*ekklēsia*) as a clueless mob that should not be taken seriously! The ironic difference between this mob-like assembly of Ephesians and Luke's descriptions of the church (*ekklēsia*) or "assembly" of God's people in Acts should not go unnoticed.

The situation with **Alexander** only compounds the confusion (v 33). Questions surround the Jewish presence in the crowd and their reasons for thrusting Alexander forward to speak before the people. He probably offers his defense (*apologeomai* [24:10; 25:8; 26:1, 2, 24]) before the mob (*dēmos*; see v 30) on behalf of his fellow Jews rather than the two believers in custody, since the Ephesians probably associate the Christian movement with Judaism.

Certainly, the Jews were well-established opponents to idolatrous practices, both here and elsewhere in Acts (→ sidebar "'The Jews' in Acts" with 9:21-22). But they also opposed the Christian movement. So they probably want, through Alexander, to dissociate themselves from the entire debacle, including Paul and the believers. Yet the Ephesians, steeped in idolatry, seem to recognize the theological solidarity between Jews and Christians more clearly than do the Jews themselves (Wall 2002, 272-73). The attempt of the Jewish Alexander to speak becomes an opportunity for the crowd to channel their hostility and allegiance.

Ironically, Alexander serves as a catalyst to unite the tumultuous crowd, which had been screaming *different* things, into a crowd shouting **in unison** (lit., with **one voice**) for nearly **two hours** (19:34). They refuse to listen to Alexander's message. This may be a rather serious threat to the broader Jewish community (see Philo, *Flaccus* 24; Stoops 1989, 86-87). The crowd chants what the silversmiths shouted in response to Demetrius' speech (v 28), which initially prompted that gathering in the theater. By framing vv 28-34 with these chants, Luke associates this unruly assembly (*ekklēsia*) with the polytheistic practices of the Artemis cult.

■ **35-36** The crowd's chants are also pleas for Artemis to intervene. Of course, she never did. This opens the door for other intervention. The **city clerk** (v 35), the city administrator and leader of official assemblies, was knowledgeable in legal issues and civic procedures. He brought order to the situation. Possessing "transferred omniscience" about the entire situation despite just coming onto the scene (Pervo 2009, 487), the clerk's assessment offers a more realistic, "third-party" perspective. His description of Ephesus as the **guardian** (*neōkoros*) of Artemis' temple appropriates a title given to cities with official temples of the imperial cult. He affirms the city's status and reputation within the cult and empire.

Along with the temple was Artemis' **image** ("statue" [NRSV]), which **fell from heaven** or from the god Zeus (*diopetēs*; see Euripides, *Iph. taur.* 87-88, 1384-85; Trebilco 1994, 351-53). This may reflect an ancient view of meteorites as sacred objects from the gods. It was often thought that the statue itself appeared in that form from heaven (see Cicero, *Verr.* 2.5.187; Herodotus, *Hist.* 1.11.1).

The clerk's view of Artemis' statue counters any suggestions attributed to Paul that the goddess was crafted by human innovation (19:26). His confidence that such matters are **undeniable** (passive: *anantirrētos* [v 36]; cf. 10:29; "not to be contradicted," BDAG 2000, 68-69) is not a suggestion that Paul or his ministry partners *could* not refute his argument. He merely contends that these issues are not open to debate (Barrett 1998, 936). Based on this common knowledge about Artemis and Ephesus, the clerk warns the crowd against overreaction, which is precisely what Demetrius' speech encouraged and provoked.

■ **37-39** The town clerk both clarifies and refutes the reason for the capture of Gaius and Aristarchus (v 29). The Romans would perceive temple robbing and blasphemy against Artemis as a threat against the social order. Such charges were not uncommon when tensions arose between Jews and Gentiles in the Roman Empire.

According to Josephus, the Jewish law prohibited such overt activities (*Ant.* 4.207; *Ag. Ap.* 2.237; see Exod 22:28; Philo, *Spec. Laws* 1.53; *Moses* 2.205), as did the decrees of the emperor Claudius in ensuring the Jews' status within the empire (see Josephus, *Ant.* 19.283-85). The clerk's comments discern the two captured believers (and implicitly Paul, too) as not guilty of such blatant disregard for the Artemis cult. Yet on a more basic level, Paul and the pair *are* guilty as charged, despite the clerk's attempts to put things in the best possible light.

An Ancient Rumor about Jews as Temple Robbers

At the end of the first book in his work *Against Apion*, Josephus responds to several false rumors about the Jewish people. One rumor deals with the city of Jerusalem. The Greek name for the city, *Hierosolyma*, is remarkably similar to the Greek term for temple robbing or theft, *hierosylia*. Josephus recounts how the similarity of these two terms had resulted in Jerusalem being wrongly described as a city full of temple robbers and built on plundered wealth (*Ag. Ap.* 1.309-11).

The Jewish historian points out that the similarity of terms was mere coincidence, since the city's name originated from Hebrew rather than Greek (*Ag. Ap.* 1.318-20). This rumor, along with reminders to Diaspora Jews to treat other religions with due respect (→ v 37), suggests the accusations raised against Gaius and Aristarchus were consistent with general perceptions toward the Jewish people in the Roman Empire (see Rom 2:21-22).

The town clerk concludes (*oun*) that the crowd should consider two alternatives (*men . . . de*). The first relies on due process in the Roman court system. Individuals or groups could press charges in the courts (*agoraioi*) located in the city marketplace (*agora*; → 16:19-21). Since those courts were available immediately to Demetrius and his colleagues, they should not take matters into their own hands regarding their complaint.

The second alternative involves regular meetings of citizens that dealt with larger issues, including religious matters. Such meetings were convened three times a month. So important issues could still be handled promptly. The description of such a meeting as a **legal assembly** (v 39) suggests in not-so-subtle fashion that the gathered crowd is an *illegal* assembly—another negative image in contrast with the positive images of the Christian "assembly" in Ephesus and elsewhere.

■ **40-41** In distinction from Demetrius' warnings (v 27), the use of the same verb (*kindyneō*) in the town clerk's warning suggests that the *real* danger is the crowd's disorderly behavior. Ironically, they are guilty of doing what Demetrius accused the believers of doing (see 16:19-24, 37; 17:5-9). Two aspects of the clerk's description of the crowd's actions underscore the seriousness of the situation.

The term translated **rioting** (*stasis* [v 40]; see Luke 23:19, 25) connotes not only strife and discord but also rebellion (Delling, *TDNT* 7:568-71). The term translated **commotion** (*systrophē*) often depicts seditious gatherings (BDAG 2000, 979; LSJ 1996, 1736; e.g., Herodotus, *Hist.* 7.9; Polybius, *Hist.* 4.34.6; Dionysius of Halicarnassus, *Ant. rom.* 5.31; Josephus, *J.W.* 4.601).

To such a situation, Rome would respond quickly and harshly (see, e.g., Dio Cassius, *Hist.* 54.7.6; Tacitus, *Ann.* 14.17; Dio Chrysostom, *2 Tars.* 34.39). The Ephesian assembly remains as confused in their dismissal as in their gathering (v 32). Both the lack of resolution and the open possibility of the silversmiths (unsatisfied with the town clerk's ruling) pursuing legal charges against Paul may lead to Paul's quick departure from the city (20:1).

FROM THE TEXT

This portion of Acts has long left interpreters struggling to make sense of these materials within the broader context of the developing plot of the book. On the one hand, these materials are held together by their general location: Ephesus. On the other hand, the various scenes and topics are so vastly different and scattered in nature that interpreters have disagreed as to the central focus of these materials.

This portion of Acts concludes the Lukan account of *both* Paul's ministry *and* the Christian mission. Therefore, multiple emphases converge at this critical narrative juncture.

First, the coming of the Holy Spirit upon the Ephesian disciples reiterates that the entire Christian mission, including Paul's ministry, was characterized by obedience to the command of God to be Christ's witnesses (1:8) and mirrored the experience of Pentecost (2:1-4).

The narrative allusions to the Pentecost scene, as well as the event at Cornelius' house (10:44-48), underscore the continuity between God's saving activity and the Christian mission. These descriptions of the Spirit's coming create an inclusio that characterizes the entire mission. That is, the coming of the Spirit on the Ephesian disciples serves as the closing parenthesis that Pentecost opened.

By alluding back to Pentecost and also minimizing Paul's role in this portion, Luke reminds readers of Israel's God as the divine mover, not only behind Paul's ministry but also behind the entire Christian movement. Given the religious practices with which Luke depicts the movement as being increasingly in conflict, this reiteration about God's role reaffirms God's ongoing blessing upon them.

Second, there is incongruity between the Christian faith and the prevalent way of life that structured much of the first-century Roman Empire. Although some interpreters argue that Acts offers a perspective of Christianity that the Romans would find amenable, this section suggests something more like a collision of theologies, values, and ways of life. Despite the Ephesian town clerk's clarification after Demetrius' speech, his assessment was essentially accurate: Paul's proclamation of the gospel posed a threat to their trade, the goddess Artemis, the local economy, and the city in general (see Gaventa 2003, 275).

Religion in the ancient world did not exist as a separate entity apart from culture. It was closely intertwined with other dimensions of life such as politics and economics. No "common ground" was to be found between the gospel and the Ephesian way of life. Christianity appeared on the scene as a "force for cultural destabilization" (Rowe 2009, 51). It would ultimately undermine the entire empire.

Even if Paul had been allowed to address the Ephesian crowd (like he did the Areopagus in Athens; → 17:22-31), he could not have convinced the Ephesians otherwise. For the Ephesians, the recognition of the "far-reaching and profoundly troubling effects of Christianity" (Rowe 2009, 51) meant that the gospel would turn their world upside down.

The last image at the chapter's end is of an unhappy crowd dismissed to their homes. This leaves readers with this tension in mind. Haenchen suggests that "Paul is victorious, without himself setting foot on the field of battle" (1971, 579). But a more plausible conclusion suggests differently. Paul's lack of response to the speeches by Demetrius and the town clerk and his prompt departure from Ephesus (20:1) soon thereafter underscore the existential dilemma among the Ephesians that the gospel created.

Third, the Ephesians' response to Paul and his proclamation reaffirms other depictions of the church in Acts. The term *ekklēsia* typically refers to the church in Acts (nineteen of twenty-three instances; → sidebar "Israel, the People of God, and the *Ekklēsia*" with 5:11). It was used in the LXX to refer to the assembly of Israel as the people of God (see 7:38).

However, after this consistent use of *ekklēsia* in Acts, the narrator suddenly appropriates the term three times at the end of Acts 19 (vv 32, 39, 41 [v 40 in Greek text]) to depict the unruly, confused assembly of Ephesians that gathered in the Ephesian theater over the perceived threats to their goddess and way of life.

Since other terms were available within the Lukan vocabulary, this unusual use of "assembly" terminology in this last episode encourages a comparison between two very different assemblies in Acts: the unruly type observed in idolatrous Ephesus, and those of the church (see Stoops 1989, 86-91).

Earlier sections of Acts distinguish the church as the faithful people of God from other segments of Judaism. This is reiterated in Paul's departure from the Ephesian synagogue (19:8-10). Here, Luke distinguishes between the church and the broader, cultural understanding of *ekklēsia*. The scene in Ephesus illustrates the challenge the Christian mission faced as it moved into the heart of the Roman Empire.

This raises questions about the nature of the "kingdom of God" (v 8; see 1:3; 20:25; 28:23, 31) in the context of human kingdoms or empire (see, e.g., Luke 20:20-26 and parallels). The contrast in characterization between the Ephesian assembly and the developing church in Acts highlights the role of the Spirit among the believers in creating the kind of model community depicted earlier in the narrative (see, e.g., 2:42-47; 4:32-35), albeit now in the more diverse context of the Roman Empire.

For contemporary readers, these episodes serve as reminders that the Christian gospel does not easily assimilate when it confronts the prevailing values and systems of society. Incongruities between the gospel and society are far more prevalent than many contemporary Christians seriously consider, even in places where Christian influence has left its mark on the history of a given people or nation.

Too often, little attention is given to exploring and acting upon the relationship between the values of the Christian faith and the realities of the social, political, economic, and ecological networks of our world. Thoughtful Christians know full well that gospel values and worldly realities are often discordant.

At times, some Christians have been overly cautious. They remind us that matters of faith and religion are personal in nature, not issues to be aired in the marketplace. Yet the fact remains that the gospel has broad implications that affect all aspects of life. However, those implications may not correlate with what society itself values.

Excursus: God, the People of God, and the Expanding Mission (Acts 15:1—19:41)— The Portrait of the Church within the Roman Empire

This third major narrative unit portrays the church in terms of the expanding mission into the Roman Empire. After the question of Gentile inclusion within the people of God was addressed by the leadership of the Jerusalem church during the Jerusalem Council of ch 15, the remainder of this unit describes Luke's account of what became of the church when the proverbial door had now been opened to Gentiles (14:27).

It should be noted that human initiative was not responsible for this important development. Rather, Luke makes clear that divine guidance prompts the Pauline ministry team to move into Europe (16:6-10), remain in Corinth (18:5-11), and return to Ephesus (18:21). The coming of the Holy Spirit upon the twelve Ephesian disciples (19:4-7) serves as divine confirmation of this expanding mission.

The importance of this divine guidance and confirmation cannot be underestimated, given the escalating conflict that the Christian mission faced. Two points must be emphasized.

First, there is no indication that Jewish opposition intensified beyond previous levels. This unit describes for the first time the move of the center of Paul's ministry from the context of the Jewish synagogue to another location, both in Corinth (18:7) and Ephesus (19:9). The move was probably necessitated by the inclusive nature of Paul's message. At least in the former case, such actions prompted additional Jewish opposition, undoubtedly due to the theological (especially ecclesiological) implications of leaving the synagogue context. This new location depicts the people of God in more inclusive ways than the Jewish synagogue would indicate.

Second, opposition now comes increasingly from resistant Gentiles rather than Jewish opponents. With the exception of Corinth, the other major episodes in this unit—in Philippi, Athens, and Ephesus—all include significant resistance against Paul and his message.

Such strong resistance was not due merely to conflicting ideas over Luke's depiction of the church and the Christian "spiritual" mission. Rather, this inclusive understanding of the people of God and the gospel has significant overtones that impacted valued social systems and structures of the Roman world. Not only did Luke's depiction of the church as the people of God intersect with Jewish understandings, but its articulation of the gospel as the "kingdom of God" had distinct religious, economic, and political connotations that could not be missed or ignored by the larger Greco-Roman world.

ACTS

20:1—
28:31

V. GOD AND THE PURPOSES OF GOD: SCRUTINY AND VALIDATION OF THE RECONSTITUTED PEOPLE OF GOD: ACTS 20:1—28:31

Although Paul's ministry in Acts may have come to an end (→ 19:20), the narrative of Acts continues. Nearly a third of the book remains. Luke focuses readers' attention on God's purposes for the Christian mission throughout the first nineteen chapters. These chapters usually capture interpreters' attention as well.

The narrative attention has shifted to Paul revisiting established churches and his extended legal troubles. Readers must now consider how these subsequent chapters contribute to Acts' narrative progression. These materials provide opportunity to evaluate and validate:

- the Christian mission as embodied by Paul, and
- the resultant reconstituted people of God as evidenced in the churches he established.

A. Paul's Journey to Jerusalem: Revisiting the Churches (20:1—21:17)

BEHIND THE TEXT

The disruptions from the Ephesian concerns over Paul's proclamation of the gospel subsided (19:23-41). As a result, Paul is free to pursue his divinely guided journey to Jerusalem (19:21). He travels by way of the same regions where his earlier ministry concentrated (chs 16—18). However, Paul's declaration that he would "see Rome" offers readers an important, long-range perspective. The narrator also offers some rather ominous information about what Paul might face in Jerusalem (20:22-24; 21:4, 11-14). But readers know God will continue to guide Paul toward that outcome, as God has throughout Paul's ministry.

Two additional characteristics of this section contribute to the larger picture.

First, Paul's journey to Jerusalem mirrors Jesus' journey to the holy city in the Third Gospel, including (a) announcing his intentions (19:21; see Luke 9:31); (b) sending representatives before him (Acts 20:3; see Luke 10:1); (c) moving ahead despite obvious opposition and obstacles (Acts 20:3, 6, 16; see Luke 13:31-35) with an entourage of followers (Acts 20:4); and (d) finally arriving at the destination (21:17; see Luke 19:28). There are also notable allusions to Jesus' passion (e.g., his farewell to his disciples [Luke 22:14-38]) and resurrection (see Acts 20:7-12), which depict Paul's initiatives within the broader redemptive purposes of God.

Second, four shorter, alternating passages report mostly general information about Paul's journey and little else (20:1-6, 13-16; 21:1-8a, 15-17). His traveling companions (20:4) come from the churches to which Paul's ministry gave birth. Within these passages, three additional passages focus specifically on local gatherings of believers (20:7-12, 17-38; 21:8b-14). Luke depicts these in ways consistent with earlier images of the Jerusalem church (see Gaventa 2004, 42-43; Thompson 2006, 217-27). These local congregations had no formal connections between them. And yet the Lukan narration both depicts the relation between these scattered groups through the Christian mission and clarifies the nature of these groups through Paul's speech to the Ephesian elders (20:17-38), which appears at the heart of this section. "Even as the Spirit pulls Paul to Jerusalem and Rome, and therefore away from these small groups of Christians, the journey itself pulls them together" (Gaventa 2003, 282).

I. Travels from Ephesus to Macedonia, Greece, and Troas (20:1-6)

■ **1-3** The **uproar** of the "riot" (CEB) in the Ephesian theater (19:23-41) ceases for the moment as the crowd disperses (20:1). Tensions undoubtedly would continue, if Paul remained in Ephesus (see 2 Cor 1:8-11). Luke links his departure to divine guidance (19:21), not the lingering danger. Paul's encouragement (see 2:40; 11:23; 14:22; 15:32; 16:40) of the disciples must have included urging and teaching them to remain faithful when faced with opposition (see 20:2, 12). This is a message he repeated often in his travels throughout **Macedonia** (see 16:11—17:15; see also 14:21-22; 16:4-5; 18:23). But he travels first to Troas (2 Cor 2:12-13), mirroring his earlier route to Macedonia (Acts 16:11-12).

After an unspecified time in Macedonia, Paul continues on to **Greece** (Achaia), probably Corinth (20:2; 2 Cor 12:14). He stays there for **three months** (Acts 20:3), probably during the winter when travel was difficult. Most interpreters think Paul wrote Romans at this time.

Paul's discovery of a "plot" (NRSV; *scheme, epiboulē*; see v 19; 9:24; 23:30) by *the Jews* leads him to revise his travel plans. The Western text attributes this change to the Spirit (Metzger 1994, 420). Luke offers no details of the conspiracy. Paul probably had planned to sail **for Syria** with other Jewish pilgrims bound for Passover in Jerusalem. Some of them had conspired to attack him while they were at sea and he could not escape (see Ramsay 1895, 287). But Paul spoils the plot by backtracking to Macedonia to begin his return to the holy city from there.

■ **4-6** Scholars debate both the composition of the group that **accompanied** Paul and the function of the list (20:4). Of the seven group members, four names appear only here in Acts. Only **Timothy** (see 16:1-3; 17:14-15; 18:5; 19:22) and **Aristarchus** (19:29; 27:2) have recurring roles in Acts. The narrator mentions **Trophimus** as a reason for Paul's troubles later in Jerusalem (21:29; see 2 Tim 4:20). This group may include representatives from the churches that contributed to the collection for the poor in Jerusalem (see 1 Cor 16:3-4; Rom 15:26-27; 2 Cor 8:1—9:15). But there is no mention of this particular collection in Acts (except perhaps in 24:17). Nor are there representatives from notable churches in Corinth and Philippi. Since this entourage comes from different locales of Paul's ministry, they represent the fruit of his labors—evidence of what God has done. That *seven* persons comprise the group signifies the completion of that phase of Paul's ministry (→ 6:1-7; see Parsons 2008, 286; Pervo 2009, 507).

ACTS

20:1-6

Interpreting Acts 20–21 in the Absence
of Paul's Collection for the Poor

Most historical chronologies of Paul's life include something about his collection for the poor in Jerusalem after his departure from Ephesus (20:1). Paul certainly emphasizes it in letters written to churches in this time period (Rom 15:26-27; 1 Cor 16:3-4; 2 Cor 8:1—9:15). Thus, most commentaries interpret Acts 20:1-6 with a particular historical context in mind as reconstructed from Paul's letters. But these verses mention *nothing* about Paul's collection for the poor in Jerusalem (→ 11:27-30 for a similar collection).

This omission in Acts puzzles interpreters, especially since *Luke* emphasizes care for the poor. A common historical assumption is that Paul's later meeting with the Jerusalem church did not bring reconciliation between them. That is, the Jerusalem leaders did not accept the offering that came from the churches of Paul's ministry (see, e.g., Haenchen 1971, 611-14; Johnson 1992, 357-58, 377-80).

Narrative interpretation is interested in *historical* questions like this, but it must also evaluate a selected passage within its broader *literary* context. Elements of shared perspective and emphasis provide "boundaries" for interpreting a specific passage. The latter part of Acts does not mention a Pauline collection for the poor in Jerusalem. So, the interpretation of Acts should focus on *Lukan* narrative emphases, not historical data from Paul's letters that the narrative itself does not include. The question about what happened to that collection and how it was received when Paul met with the Jerusalem church leaders is much different from Luke's narrative purposes and perspective.

Most of Paul's entourage continue their travels to **Troas** (20:5), where Paul received his call to minister in Europe (16:6-10). Some suggest that only the last two, Tychicus and Trophimus, make that trip to Troas, since they were from that area (Asia) and could make advance preparations (e.g., Lake and Cadbury 1933a, 253; Schneider 1982, 282).

Meanwhile, Paul himself returns to **Philippi** (20:6), where he remains until after Passover and **the Festival of Unleavened Bread** (see 12:3-4). Paul likely celebrates these Jewish festivals with believers, which underscores his fidelity to Jewish tradition. The trip from Philippi to Troas reverses Paul's earlier excursion that introduced him to Macedonia (16:11-12).

Significantly, the beginning of Paul's journey is accompanied by a shift in perspective. Here, the narrative returns to the anonymous first-person narration ("we" as in 16:10-17). Since such previous narration occurred in this same region, some contend that the source of this information remained in Philippi and now rejoins Paul upon his return. The first-person style helps draw readers into the story to share particular experiences, including preparation for Paul's absence and embracing his legacy (see Tannehill 1990, 247; → sidebar "First-Person Narration in Acts" with 16:9-10).

2. Believers in Troas (20:7-12)

■ **7-8** Luke says nothing about the origins of the believers in Troas. Their gathering with Paul and others to **break bread** (v 7) signifies Christian fellowship (not Eucharist) and worship (→ 2:42-47). The **first day of the week** associates Christian meetings with Sunday, the day of Jesus' resurrection (see 1 Cor 16:2; also *Did.* 14:1; *Barn.* 15:9).

It is unclear whether Luke considers the beginning of a calendar day according to Jewish (i.e., sunset) or Roman (i.e., sunrise) standards. Thus, commentators are divided over whether this meeting occurs during what would be, according to contemporary standards, Saturday evening or Sunday evening.

The narrator uses the same verb, *dialegomai*, to describe Paul's "discussion" (NRSV) with believers as with unbelievers (→ 17:2, 17; 18:4, 19; 19:8-9). This implies that the conversation centers generally on the Christian gospel (that the risen Jesus is the Messiah) and its implications.

Two logistical details contribute to the unfolding scene. First, the meeting lasts **until midnight** since Paul **kept on talking** (*parateinō* describes protracted speech; LSJ 1996, 1328), perhaps concerned to offer encouragement (see vv 1-2) before leaving the **next day**. Second, **many lamps** keep the **upstairs room** (*hyperōon* [20:8]; see 1:13; 9:37; also Luke 22:12) well lit. This may be to avoid suspicions from those who associated nocturnal meetings with political conspiracy or bizarre religious practices (see Talbert 1997, 183-85). The scene is reminiscent of Jesus' last supper with his disciples, whom he prepared for his departure (Luke 22:14-38), and of them falling asleep (Luke 22:39-46).

■ **9-10** The narrator introduces a **young man named Eutychus** (20:9; "Fortunate" or "Lucky"). Is he to fulfill the promise of Joel that "young men will see visions" (2:28)? How *fortunate* that he has opportunity to listen to Paul so he may fulfill such potential! However, Luke twice notes (using *katapherō*) Eutychus' unsuccessful struggle to stay awake. Finally, overcome ("brought down") by that sleep, he falls out of the window where he was seated.

Luke twice mentions **sleep** as the culprit for Eutychus' demise, perhaps aided by the "many lamps" (v 8) and Paul's long-winded farewell. However, sleep often served metaphorical roles in Jewish and Christian texts, including describing moral laxness (Judg 16:14-20; Jonah 1:1-9; Nah 3:18*a*; see also *Pss. Sol.* 16:1-4) and spiritual negligence (Rom 13:11; 1 Thess 5:4-6; *Barn.* 4:13).

Luke's readers may have seen in Eutychus' condition a deficiency in his moral or spiritual condition, much like the sleeping disciples at the Mount of Olives (Luke 22:39-46; see Arterbury 2009, 201-21). This could explain the subsequent pastoral instructions to "watch" (Acts 20:28) and "be alert" (v 31 NRSV). *Unfortunately*, his fall and subsequent death separate Eutychus from the community. The detail of the **third story** (v 9) indicates that he fell from a sufficient height to cause his death.

ACTS

20:7-10

Paul's response echoes two familiar OT stories: Elijah's raising of the widow's son (1 Kgs 17:17-24), and Elisha's raising of the Shunammite's son (2 Kgs 4:18-37). Similar to these OT prophets, Paul embraces the youth and restores his life. His declaration—about Eutychus' life (*psychē*) being "in him" (Acts 20:10 NRSV)—announces the miracle that has just taken place.

Like Peter (9:36-43), Paul resembles Jesus (Luke 7:11-17; Luke 8:40-42*a*, 49-56) by demonstrating God's power and salvation (see 2:21). He commands the others, **"Don't be alarmed"** (*Mē thorybeisthe*)—"Don't create such commotion!" (*thorybos*; → 17:5; 20:1; 21:34; 24:18). His words restore calm to what is understandably a chaotic situation. The community, gathered on the day commemorating Jesus' resurrection, now celebrates the power of the resurrection in fresh ways!

■ **11-12** After Eutychus' restoration to life, Luke focuses again on the community's teaching, fellowship, and worship rather than their reaction to the miracle. Paul rejoins the original, upstairs gathering, continuing like nothing has happened until his departure at daybreak.

Since the response to Eutychus' restoration appears at the episode's end, many assume he is taken **home** (v 12). In fact, he is returned to the gathered community (see Bulley 1994, 171-88). This one who had fallen from the community now has the good fortune of restoration. This **encouraged** them (*parakaleō*: see vv 1-2) "not a little" (NRSV), a typical Lukan understatement.

3. Travels from Troas to Miletus (20:13-16)

■ **13-15** A second travel itinerary reflects typical sea travel in that era. Whenever possible, sea voyages would make their way along the coast from one port to another, in short one-day journeys. The first stop on the trip, **Assos** (v 13), was about 20 miles (32 km) southeast of Troas in northwest Asia Minor. The trip by sea was much longer around the coastline and treacherous at times. This may explain Paul's arrangements to travel by foot (see Lake and Cadbury 1933a, 257).

As planned, Paul rejoins his traveling party in Assos. Presumably the next day, they embark by boat for **Mitylene** (v 14), a major port city about 45 miles (72 km) southeast of Assos on the eastern side of the Aegean island of Lesbos. Their third stop, **Chios** (v 15), was a mountainous island with a city and harbor by the same name about 60 miles (97 km) southwest of Mitylene. The fourth stop, **Samos**, was an island 60 miles southeast of Chios. The fifth stop, **Miletus**, was a short distance further southeast.

Miletus was an ancient, prosperous city with a Jewish population over 30 miles (48 km) south of Ephesus. Ephesus had exercised considerable economic and political influence over it for centuries. Although Ephesus surpassed it in prominence, Miletus was one of the major cities of Asia Minor.

■ **16** Before continuing, the narrator explains why Paul does not return to Ephesus on this journey. According to Luke, Paul had earlier decided (pluperfect tense: *kekrikei*) to **sail past Ephesus**. The stated reason (*hopōs*) is so he would not "spend too much time" (CEB) in Asia. The verb *chronotribeō* connotes wasting time or loitering (LSJ 1996, 1092; see Aristotle, *Rhet.* 3.3.3; Josephus, *Ant.* 12.368). Paul's concern is to be in Jerusalem by **the day of Pentecost**, another indication of Paul's ongoing faithfulness as a pious Jew. The festival of the firstfruits would also be an appropriate time for Paul to introduce his seven traveling companions (v 4) as the firstfruits of his mission (Talbert 1997, 186). However, time is running short, since at least seventeen days have already elapsed since the Festival of Unleavened Bread ended (v 6).

Many question this as a valid reason for Paul's avoidance of Ephesus. His alternative plan—the summons of Ephesian church leaders to meet him in Miletus (v 17)—would take four to six more days. And Luke never mentions whether Paul arrived in Jerusalem in time for Pentecost.

The consensus among interpreters is that Ephesus posed too great a danger for Paul to reenter (see 2 Cor 1:8-11), although Luke never admits that. After Paul's long ministry there, the *real* danger facing Paul may have been that his plans of reaching Jerusalem would be "held hostage to an affectionate, vigorous and ultimately extended hospitality" by the Ephesian believers, which could have lasted weeks (Rapske 1994a, 15-17).

4. Paul's Speech to the Ephesian Elders (20:17-38)

Paul's speech to the Ephesian elders at Miletus offers an appropriate conclusion to Paul's ministry in Ephesus. Circumstances did not allow a fitting farewell when he left the city in haste (20:1).

This is the third major speech by Paul in Acts and the only one addressed to Christians (the first speech was addressed to Jews [13:16-41]; the second to Gentiles [17:22-31]). It stands in a pivotal location within the narrative of Acts, offering both a retrospective view of Paul's ministry and a prospective view of his future. At the heart of this section (20:1—21:17), it assesses Paul's ministry and, more particularly, the church as depicted within the broader Pauline portion of Acts.

Noteworthy in this speech are a number of distinctive emphases found in Paul's letters, but not emphasized elsewhere in Acts. Paul's stated disinterest in protecting his own life, his statements on working with his hands, and grace stand out. Of particular interest is the relation between this speech and the Pastoral Epistles (see Barrett 1998, 964-65). Nonetheless, while this speech appears to appropriate Pauline thought if not language at times (see Porter 2001, 117), it still addresses broader Lukan concerns.

Paul's Miletus Speech and the Pauline Letters
of the New Testament

The Pauline letters of the NT are generally categorized as either "authentic" or "disputed," due to questions about the authorship of part of that collection (Ephesians, Colossians, 2 Thessalonians, 1 Timothy, 2 Timothy, Titus). In the case of the "disputed" Pauline (or deutero-Pauline) letters, most NT scholars view their respective authors as seeking to interpret and apply Paul's thought to later times and for different situations.

Not surprisingly, Paul's speech to the Ephesian elders in Miletus does not reflect this kind of differentiation. It draws more broadly from selected themes and emphases found in the letters that would later form the Pauline corpus of the NT.

The significant parallels between this speech and emphases in the Pastoral Epistles (especially 1—2 Timothy) and Ephesians are noteworthy. These three letters are all traditionally associated with the church in Ephesus. Some suggest this feature indicates *Lukan* authorship of the Pastoral Epistles (e.g., Wilson 1979) or of this speech functioning as a source for the composition of those letters. However, if the Lukan author of Acts consulted these letters, a later date for the composition of Acts (i.e., early second century AD; → "Date of Composition" and "Sources and Intertextuality" in Introduction) allows for sufficient time for both the composition and dissemination of those letters.

20:17-38   Paul clearly states that the elders would not see him again (20:25) and refers to a time after his departure (v 29). Thus, the occasion and content of Paul's speech (esp. vv 25, 29) are consistent with a farewell address, which was a common literary form in ancient literature. Such a speech typically occurred in a setting of immanent separation (usually death) within an intimate gathering of family and/or close friends. Farewell speeches often shared these common elements:

- recollection of the speaker's past service (often as an example);
- mention of the present situation;
- future predictions;
- instructions to future successors; and
- exhortation to faithfulness. (See Kurz 1990, 33-51; Fitzmyer 1998, 674; Walton 2000, 55-65)

Multiple examples of farewell speeches exist in the OT (e.g., Gen 49:1-33; Josh 23:1—24:30; 1 Sam 12:1-25), other Jewish literature (e.g., *Jub.* 36:1-16; 2 Esd 14:28-36; *2 Bar.* 77:1-16; Josephus, *Ant.* 4.309-26), and Greco-Roman literature (e.g., Homer, *Il.* 16.844-53; Sophocles, *Oed. col.* 1518-55).

Paul's speech does not conform precisely to *all* aspects of conventional farewell addresses. For example, Paul does not emphasize his impending death. This suggests that Luke uses the speech for his broader purposes in

338

Acts. This particular literary form does not hide the *Lukan* emphases within the speech, especially those that correlate with the ecclesiological concerns of this broader section (20:1—21:17).

■ **17-18a** The Lukan account of Paul's ministry in Ephesus (19:1-20) offers few details about the church. His summons (see 7:14; 10:32; 24:25) of **elders** (see 11:30; 14:23; 15:6; 16:4; see also 1 Tim 5:1, 2, 17, 19) is the first indication that he appointed leaders there. Several days would be needed for the message to reach the group, for them to travel to Miletus, and then to assemble with Paul.

■ **18b-35** The structure of Paul's speech is a matter of ongoing debate. Some divide the speech in two halves: Paul's retrospective look (Acts 20:18b-27) and Paul's prophetic/futuristic view (vv 28-35) (e.g., Marshall 1980, 329; Wall 2002, 282-84). Others note the repetition of temporal references—**And now** (in vv 22, 25, 32)—that highlight changes in topic or emphasis. This suggests a fourfold structure:

vv 18b-21   Review of Paul's labors in Asia

vv 22-24   Paul's impending journey to Jerusalem

vv 25-31   Warning about the church's future

vv 32-35   The church commended to God (Gaventa 2003, 283; see Fitzmyer 1998, 675)

In addition to these temporal references, the repeated, emphatic references at the beginning of several sentences to "knowing"—Paul's knowledge ("I know" [vv 25, 29 NRSV]) and the knowledge of the Ephesian elders (**you know** [vv 18b, 34])—also seem to have a significant role in the speech. These two elements of repetition in the speech suggest a chiastic outline (see Talbert 1997, 186-87):

A Retrospective View (vv 18b-21): "You yourselves know" (*epistasthe* [v 18b NRSV])

   B Present Situation (vv 22-24): **And now** (*kai nyn* [v 22])

      C Prophetic Future (vv 25-27): **I know** (*egō oida* [v 25])

         D Key Instructions to Successors (v 28)

      C' Prophetic Future (vv 29-31): **I know** (*egō oida* [v 29])

   B' Present Situation (v 32): "And now" (*kai nyn* [v 32 NRSV])

A' Retrospective View (vv 33-35): **You yourselves know** (*ginōskete* [v 34])

Paul's opening comments are one sentence in Greek. They refer to his past ministry in Ephesus, offering Paul's perspective on events. There is little in common between this address and the earlier account. The emphatic declaration—"You yourselves know" (*hymeis epistasthe* [v 18b NRSV])—draws upon the leaders' collective memory (see also vv 31, 34) of how Paul lived. This confirms what he had to share.

339

Paul's description of his ministry as **serving the Lord** (*douleuōn tō kyriō* [v 19]) may reflect Pauline rather than Lukan terminology. In his letters, Paul often describes himself as a "servant [or slave: *doulos*] of Jesus Christ" (see Rom 1:1; Gal 1:10; Phil 1:1) or refers to the Christian life as serving or being enslaved (verb: *douleuō*) to Christ (see Rom 12:11; 14:18; 1 Cor 7:22; Phil 2:22; 1 Thess 1:9). Luke depicts Paul as an orator (Acts 19:9-10) and a renowned healer whom others wish to emulate (19:11-17). But he has Paul describe himself before the Ephesian church leaders as a mere slave, doing his Master's bidding. This emphasis at the outset is not coincidental. Paul acknowledges the divine authority that compelled and empowered everything that the Ephesians witnessed (see Soards 1994, 106).

Paul lists three things that accompanied his "slave-like" service to the Lord. This contrasts with the Lukan depiction of Paul's successes (19:10-20; see Spencer 2004a, 203).

First, he refers to **great humility** (20:19), a noun that appears only here in Acts. But this theme is common in Paul's letters (*tapeino-* terms in Rom 12:16; 2 Cor 7:6; 10:1; 11:7; 12:21; Phil 2:3, 8; 3:21; 4:12; see also in Eph 4:2; Col 2:18, 23; 3:12). Paul describes himself as unselfishly concerned for others' welfare rather than his own (see Grundmann, *TDNT* 8:1-26). He also experienced humiliation, contrary to the goals of his honor-shame culture (→ sidebar "Honor and Shame: A Different World" below).

Second, Paul's reference to **tears** (20:31; see 2 Cor 2:4; 2 Tim 1:4) offers a glimpse into his personal struggles and emotions.

Third, the **plots** (*epiboulē* [Acts 20:3, 19]) that Jewish opponents schemed against Paul were **testing** or **trials** (*peirasmos* [v 19]; see Gal 4:14; 1 Thess 3:15; also Luke 4:1-2, 13; 22:28, 40, 46) that challenged his divine calling.

Such plots may at first seem to correlate better with Paul's experiences in Corinth (Acts 18:6-17) and other earlier ministry locations (see 13:50; 14:2-7, 19; 17:5-9, 13-14) than in Ephesus, where his focus was on *Gentiles*. But they may also offer insight into the Jewish opposition that ultimately led to Paul's departure from the Ephesian synagogue (19:9).

Honor and Shame: A Different World

The status and identity of persons in the ancient Greco-Roman world were largely determined by social values such as honor and shame rather than by values often prevalent in contemporary Western culture (such as wealth). Honor involved a person's public reputation that came from living in accordance with one's roles and abilities. People incurred shame when others failed to acknowledge their worth or showed no concern for their honor.

Honor was often viewed in two ways. *Ascribed* honor may be inherited, a status into which one is born (e.g., family, state, group, etc.). *Acquired* honor may be sought or gained through achievement. However, honor was understood to be in limited supply. So one always gained honor at another's expense.

In an honor-shame society, the expectation was that persons would live in ways that honored their own human identity. This included their social status, gender roles, and social interactions with others (i.e., as equals, as superiors, or as inferiors). As a result, *all* social interaction involved various challenges to honor and the potential for dishonor or shame.

For those like Paul in the public's eye, honor was both "on display" and challenged by those who observed and listened. However, persons could also dishonor or shame themselves by aspiring to a certain status that public opinion denied them or by renouncing one's ascribed status (by "humility"; see Malina and Neyrey 1991b, 25-65).

In such a context, Paul's self-disclosure in 20:19 reveals the dishonor and shame that he faced and embodied during his extended time of ministry in Ephesus. This seems to contrast with the "successful Paul" of Acts 19. Or, it illustrates how honor and shame are redefined within the Christian community.

The second part of Paul's retrospective view (20:20-21) offers a summary of the gospel message he proclaimed. It is, perhaps, a form of self-defense typical of farewell speeches or a response to accusations. He claims to have **held back** (*hypostellō*; see v 27) nothing **beneficial** (see 1 Cor 6:12; 10:23; 12:7; 2 Cor 8:10; 12:1) from the Ephesians. This states negatively what Luke depicted earlier as the boldness or openness of the apostolic witness (→ Acts 4:29, 31; 9:27-28; 13:46; 19:8).

Paul's ministry in Ephesus occurred through both preaching and teaching, in both public and private (**from house to house** [20:20]) settings. He stresses that his proclamation in all these settings was consistent, regardless of mode, context, or audience. The use of the verb *diamartyromai* ("testify") to describe Paul's message draws correlations with the thorough, complete testimony associated with the apostolic witness in Acts (see 2:40; 8:25; 10:42; 18:5; also 23:11; 28:23).

The emphasis on Paul's offering the gospel to **both Jews and Greeks** (20:21) reflects both Pauline language (Rom 1:16; 2:9-10; 3:9; 10:12; 1 Cor 1:24; 10:32; 12:13; Gal 3:28) and the pattern of Paul's ministry in Ephesus (Acts 19:8-10, 17) and throughout Acts (→ 9:15; 13:44-48; 14:1; 17:4, 11-12, 17; 18:4-8).

The content of Paul's message as described here reflects Lukan emphases in Acts. These are not themes prominent in his letters. **Repentance to God** (20:21) in terms of turning away from rebellion to serve God on God's terms (Peterson 2009, 565) reflects a Lukan emphasis in both the Third Gospel (Luke 3:3, 8; 5:32; 10:13; 11:32; 13:3, 5; 15:7, 10; 16:30; 17:3-4; 24:47) and in Acts (2:38; 3:19; 5:31; 8:22; 11:18; 13:24; 17:30; 19:4; 26:20). It rarely appears in Paul's letters (Rom 2:4; 2 Cor 7:9-10; 12:21; see 2 Tim 2:25).

ACTS

20:18b-35

341

Faith is a prominent theme in the Pauline letters as well as Acts (e.g., 2:44; 3:16; 4:4; 5:14; 8:12-13; 11:17; 13:48; 14:1, 22-23; 15:7; 16:31; 19:2, 4, 18; 24:24; 26:18). But attention here is distinctly on faith **in** [*eis*] **our Lord Jesus** (20:21). Luke refers to what God had done in and through Jesus as Lord (→ 2:14-36). Throughout Acts, the people of God are distinguished both by the turning toward God indicative of repentance and by faith in what God has done in exalting Jesus as Lord (2:32-36).

And now (20:22) indicates a shift of perspectives from the past to the present. Paul is convinced **the Spirit** is leading him **to Jerusalem** (see 19:21; but see 13:2, 4; 16:6-10; 18:9-10). Ironically, he describes his compulsion as being **bound by the Spirit** to continue to the holy city. It is here, before his encounter with the risen Jesus, that he had hoped to bring "bound" believers as prisoners (9:2, 14, 21; see Johnson 1992, 361). Paul would end up "bound" or arrested in Jerusalem as well (see 21:11, 13, 33; 22:5, 29).

Paul's divine compulsion motivates him, not as a future prisoner or martyr but as a Jewish religious pilgrim. Rome is also on his long-term travel itinerary (19:21; see Wall 2002, 283). Yet the Holy Spirit reveals Paul's immediate prospects of **prison** (22:30; 23:29; 26:29, 31; Phil 1:7-17; Phlm 10, 13; see also Col 4:18; 2 Tim 2:9) and **hardships** (Acts 11:19; 14:22; 2 Cor 1:4, 8; 2:4; 4:17; 6:4; 7:4; Phil 1:17; 4:14; 1 Thess 3:7; see also Col 1:24; Eph 3:13) wherever he travels (**in every city** [Acts 20:23]). The language of the apostolic witness describes the Spirit's testimony (*diamartyromai*; see v 21) of what awaits Paul. Thus, his hardships are understood as part of the gospel.

Paul minimizes the value of his life (v 24) with the expression **finish the race**. In 2 Tim 4:7, this probably refers to his death, and some interpret it similarly here. But the first part of the sentence offers the purpose (*hōs* with infinitive) for this: for Paul to complete this **race** or **mission** (see Acts 13:25) and **ministry** (*diakonia*; see 1:17, 25; 6:1, 4; 11:29; 12:25; 21:19), as Luke depicts Paul in Acts 13—19.

Luke adds the description of that ministry as that which Paul **received from the Lord Jesus** (20:24). This takes the focus off Paul and places it on the one who called him (see 9:15; also 22:14-15; 26:15-18). His ministry was to involve the Christian witness (*diamartyromai*; see 20:24) **to the good news of God's grace.**

This rare mention of the specific noun translated **good news (gospel)** also summarizes Peter's message to Cornelius (only here and in 15:7). Peter's message at the Jerusalem Council characterizes the gospel as God extending salvation to both Jews and Gentiles by "the grace of the Lord Jesus" (15:11). This expression has Paul faithfully proclaiming the same message as Peter (see Tannehill 1990, 256). Paul's description of his current situation repeatedly redirects attention to the *Spirit's* working through him in his *Jesus*-given ministry. It is to proclaim an inclusive message of *God's* grace that seeks to create an inclusive people of God.

Once again, ***and now*** (20:25) introduces vv 25-27 (one Greek sentence) and signifies a shift in perspective. This time it is from the present situation to the future. Both here and in vv 29-31, Paul begins his comments about the future with an emphatic **I know** (*egō oida*), followed by conclusive remarks. Here (v 25), he informs the Ephesian elders that they would not see him again (see Gen 48:21; Luke 22:15-16).

This is not Paul's "last will and testament" as a reference to his impending death in Jerusalem. He plans to travel later to Rome (Acts 28:16-31; see 19:21). Paul indicates only that his ministry in Ephesus is complete.

Paul's subsequent declaration of being **innocent** ("pure" [20:26]) of anyone's **blood** initially sounds strange, given his involvement in Stephen's death (7:58) and violent imprisonment of believers (8:3). But his words are reminiscent of Samuel (1 Sam 12:2-5) and the prophetic watchman (Ezek 33:1-6). They also resemble Paul's words in Corinth (→ Acts 18:6). He fulfilled his divine responsibility to the Ephesians faithfully. Since Paul was faithful to his ministry call, the Ephesians now bear full responsibility for their response to God and the gospel (see Conzelmann 1987, 174).

Paul's use of terms associated with purity and worship (**innocent, blood**) links his mission to faithfulness, both to God and to others. Paul describes his ministry as "an act of worship, to be carried out faithfully" (Bock 2007, 629). Thus, Paul reiterates that he did not ***hold back*** in any aspect of his Ephesian ministry (see v 20). That is, he proclaimed **the whole will of God** (*boulē tou theou* [v 27]; see 2:22-23; 4:28; 5:38; 13:36; see *thelēma tou theou*: 1 Cor 1:1; Gal 1:4; Eph 1:9, 11). He refers to God's saving that is inclusive of all humanity (see Squires 1998, 19-39).

As the practical and theological center of the speech (Acts 20:28; Barrett 1998, 974), Paul both instructs the Ephesian leaders as successors to his ministry and articulates a theological understanding of the church that grounds that ministry. He instructs these leaders to serve metaphorically as **shepherds** over **all the flock** (v 28). This recalls similar OT imagery describing the guidance of God's people (e.g., Pss 78:52, 70-71; 100:3; Isa 40:11; Jer 13:17; 23:2-4; Ezek 34:1-24; Mic 5:4; Zech 10:3; see Luke 12:32; John 10:1-30; 21:15-17; 1 Pet 5:2-3). Leaders were to guard against anything that might do harm (imperative **keep watch**, *prosechete* [v 28]; BDAG 2000, 879; see Luke 12:1; 17:3; 20:46; 21:34; see also LXX: Gen 24:6; Exod 10:28; Deut 4:9; Hos 5:1).

Paul also refers to the Ephesian elders as **overseers**, *episkopous*. This is the only time this term appears in Acts (see 1:20, *episkopē*, an LXX quotation of Ps 109:8). This term would later refer to official church supervisory roles (bishops). A related verb (*episkeptomai*) often describes God's visitation to redeem God's people (see, e.g., Luke 1:68, 78; 7:16). This implies the *nature* of this ministry; it does not *define* a specific office (compare Phil 1:1; 1 Tim 3:2; Titus 1:7; also 1 Pet 2:25). However, like his own calling and ministry, Paul understands leadership responsibilities to be conferred by the **Holy Spirit**. This correlates with an earlier reference to the appointment of elders after "prayer and fasting" (14:23).

Two major questions saddle the last part of the verse. First, some MSS read "the church of the Lord" rather than **the church of God**. The former reading appears seven times in the LXX, but never in the NT. The latter is a common Pauline expression (1 Cor 1:2; 10:32; 11:16, 22; 15:9; 2 Cor 1:1; Gal 1:13; 1 Thess 2:14; see also 2 Thess 1:4; 1 Tim 3:5, 15).

Second, the last phrase may be translated **with his own blood** (i.e., God's own blood) or **with the blood of his own** (i.e., God's own Son). Theological caution about God shedding *God's own* blood may have led to copyists substituting "the Lord" for "God" in the former expression so that the latter phrase would *unambiguously* refer to Jesus' death (see Metzger 1994, 425-26). But even this reference to Jesus' death would be rare in Luke's writings, which seldom associate Jesus' blood or death and salvation (see Luke 22:20; Green 1998, 98-101). Even Paul, who emphasizes the cross, infrequently mentions Jesus' blood in his undisputed letters (Rom 3:25; 5:9; 1 Cor 10:16; 11:25-27; but see Eph 1:7; 2:13; Col 1:20).

Most significant here is the theological connection between the church and Jesus' death. The verb translated **bought** or **acquired** (*peripoieō*) was often associated in the LXX with God obtaining or securing Israel as an elect people (see 2 Sam 12:3; Isa 43:21; Mal 3:17). Such language, like the term *ekklēsia*, originally referred to *Israel* as God's people rather than to the *church* (→ sidebar "Israel, the People of God, and the *Ekklēsia*" with 5:11).

Paul's point here is that the Ephesian church belongs to God and is God's possession. "God's relation to the mixed church of Jews and Gentiles is being understood after the pattern of God's relation to Israel in Scripture" (Tannehill 1990, 259).

If God secured **the church of God** through the blood of *Jesus*, this offers a different understanding of Jesus' death from what has been presented thus far in Acts. Luke normally explains that Jesus died as a result of human error, ignorance, and rejection, but nevertheless as part of God's plan (see, e.g., 2:22-24; 3:13-17; 13:26-28).

The reference to Jesus' saving death is not developed or explained further (against, e.g., Bock 2012, 204). It simply leaves the church's nature and existence dependent on God's saving activity through Jesus' death to stand out prominently at the speech's center. At the same time, this stark image of Jesus' death also reminds readers of Peter's explanation on Pentecost: God

20:18b-35

responded to that death by raising Jesus and exalting him, and giving him the promised Holy Spirit to be poured out on God's people (2:32-36). Thus, from Pentecost through Paul's ministry in Acts, God's gracious activity has ultimately characterized the church in those various settings.

A second emphatic **I know** (20:29; see v 25) signals the return to additional, future pastoral concerns. Paul's instructions (v 28) and prior Ephesian ministry arose out of his theological understanding and experience of God's grace and workings. Thus, the beliefs and practices he established stood against the prevalent social norm (see Wall 2002, 284). Paul's departure would likely result in a challenge to what he established.

The imagery of **savage wolves** (v 29) correlates with the earlier metaphor of the **flock** for the **church** (v 28). Both the OT and early Christian literature often depict false teachers whose objective was to harm the community (see, e.g., Ezek 22:27; Zeph 3:3; Matt 7:15; John 10:12; *Did.* 16:3; Ign. *Phld.* 2:1-2; *2 Clem.* 5:2-4). In this context, such persons would be outsiders, perhaps like the Jewish opposition that regularly appears in Acts (see Parsons 2008, 294). However, others *within* the church could also pose similar threats by offering "perverse things" (Acts 20:30 KJV, NASB) or "twisting" (*diastrephō*; see 13:8, 10) Paul's teachings to gain their own disciples.

The verb translated **draw away** (*apospaō*) compares the actions of false teachers to these outsiders. Such distortion would have the effect of violently "tearing away" disciples from the group (see Herodotus, *Hist.* 3.1; compare 21:1 for positive sense). Such persons could be either Jewish or Gentile Christians influenced by Judaism (see 21:20-21; see Parsons 2008, 294), perhaps some from the elders themselves (**from your own number** [20:30]; see Walton 2000, 82; Oropeza 2011, 141).

The conjunction *dio*, **therefore** (v 31), indicates that the instruction to "stay alert" (CEB; present tense: *grēgoreite*; see 1 Cor 16:13; 1 Thess 5:6, 10) is an appropriate response to the dangers facing the church. Interpreters often consider Paul's call to remembering (present tense: *mnēmoneuontes*) part of the typical self-presentation in a farewell speech: he offers himself as an example to emulate.

But Paul refers to his specific activity of **warning** or literally "bringing things to mind" (*noutheteō*; LSJ 1996, 1182-83; see Rom 15:14; 1 Cor 4:14; 1 Thess 5:12, 14; also Wis 11:10; Josephus, *Ant.* 3.311). This suggests that the elders are to reflect on his teachings. "The repetition and variety of references to Paul's teaching in this speech underscore the importance of theological purity in maintaining and transmitting the Pauline legacy to the next generation of believers" (Wall 2002, 284).

The **three years** of Paul's Ephesian ministry is a rounded sum of his tenure there (three months [19:8]; two years [19:10]; "a little longer" [19:22]).

This conveys a generalized sense of the significance and scope of his teaching, perhaps in comparison to the duration of Jesus' ministry.

For a third time, **and now** (20:32) introduces a new section again focusing on the present situation. Paul earlier affirmed the Spirit's guidance upon his life and ministry, **testifying to the good news of God's grace** (v 24). He now blesses the Ephesian elders by reminding them that the church, her provision, and her future belong to God, not those who threaten it. The verb translated **commit** (*paratithēmi* [v 32]) connotes placing someone before another (in this case, God) for care or protection (BDAG 2000, 772).

Paul delineates this further by mentioning two aspects of *the message of God's grace*. First, Paul emphasizes how the gospel can **build . . . up** (*oikodomeō*) the church: by strengthening believers through spiritual formation and discipleship, similar to emphases in his letters (including the noun *oikodomē*: Rom 14:19; 15:2; 1 Cor 3:9; 8:1; 10:23; 14:3-5, 12, 17, 26; 2 Cor 10:8; 12:19; 13:10; 1 Thess 5:11; see also Eph 2:21; 4:12, 16, 29). The immediate context and the concerns for false teaching remind the elders of the essential role of gospel teachings. These enable believers to be faithful through discernment.

Second, Paul links the gospel to our **inheritance** in God, a theme in the Pauline letters (*klēronomia* and related terms: 1 Cor 6:9-10; 15:50; Gal 3:18; 4:30; 5:21; see also Eph 1:14, 18; 5:5). It refers generally to "transcendent salvation" (BDAG 2000, 548; see Hermann and Foerster, *TDNT* 3:781-85). It evokes thoughts of the promised land (e.g., Num 34:2; Josh 1:15; 11:23; Ps 105:11) and Israel as God's inheritance (e.g., Num 18:20; Deut 32:9; Isa 19:25; Jer 10:16; 51:19; Joel 3:2).

Paul identifies the Ephesian elders, as representatives of the entire church, as **sanctified** ("made holy" [CEB]; *hagiazō*: Acts 26:18; also Rom 15:16; 1 Cor 1:2). The church, like Israel, belongs exclusively to God. So its members are the "holy ones," "saints" of God (e.g., Deut 33:3; Pss 16:3; 34:9; Dan 7:18). Paul draws from vocabulary and imagery originating in the story of Israel and her covenant with God to address leaders of a mixed church of Jewish and Gentile believers. They fully share in the heritage of God's people. All the divine promises and purposes reserved for God's people belong to them (see Dunn 1996, 274).

Paul's speech concludes with a denial of ever acting out of greed or for selfish gain (Acts 20:33). Instead, he admonishes the Ephesians to respond to the needs of others as he did, thereby living out the gospel's concerns for building up (v 32) the whole church. The sudden raising of this issue is somewhat surprising, since only Paul's *opponents*—most notably the Ephesian silversmiths (19:25-27)—are portrayed as greedy (→ 16:16-19; Pervo 2009, 527). Paul similarly disavows being motivated by money in his letters (1 Cor

9:12; 2 Cor 7:2; 11:7-11). Such comments correlate with *Lukan* concerns about the appropriate use of possessions (see, e.g., Acts 2:42-47; 4:32-37; 11:29-30; 16:15) and the detrimental effects of greed (see, e.g., 5:1-11; 8:18-24).

Paul reminds the Ephesians that he worked with his own **hands** (20:34) to support himself and his ministry (see 18:1-3; perhaps 19:11; see also 1 Cor 4:12; 9:15-18; 2 Cor 11:7-11; 1 Thess 2:9). He preferred supporting himself and those with him over accepting financial support from others (contrast Phil 4:15-18).

Rather than urging, "Follow my example" (1 Cor 11:1*a*), Paul advises the believers: **We must** [*dei*; see, e.g., Acts 1:16; 3:21; 4:12; 5:29; 9:16; 14:22; 17:3; 19:21] *keep helping* [present tense: *antilambanesthai*] **the weak** (20:35; see Rom 15:1-2; Gal 6:2; 1 Thess 4:11-12). *Dei* here indicates that this is God's will. By sharing in this way, they actively remember (present tense: *mnēmoneuein* [Acts 20:31]) a saying of Jesus, which sets out the proper use of possessions. The saying does not value givers above receivers. Rather, it highlights the importance of seeking the benefit of others (*antilambanō*) over personal gain (receiving, *lambanō*).

The saying ascribed to Jesus does not appear in any extant Gospel (canonical or not). But parallels exist in a variety of other literature (see, e.g., Thucydides, *War* 2.97.4; Plutarch, *Reg. imp. apophth.* 173d; Seneca, *Ep.* 81.17; Sir 4:31; *Did.* 1:5; 4:5; *1 Clem.* 2:1).

The specific title **Lord Jesus** occurs frequently in the Ephesian portion of Acts (19:5, 13, 17) and in Paul's speech to the Ephesian elders (20:21, 24, 35). Here, it underscores Jesus' authority (see 2:36). This is the only citation in Acts of Jesus' teachings by someone other than Jesus himself. Thus, the saying ends Paul's speech on a divinely authoritative tone.

■ **36-38** A final prayer with the Ephesian elders is a fitting response before everyone departs. Luke mentions only Paul praying, interceding on behalf of the Ephesian church. The parting scene is reminiscent of similar emotional scenes in the OT (e.g., Gen 33:4; 45:14; 46:29) and reveals the elders' affection for Paul. The emotional scene, including *much weeping* over (Acts 20:37; see 9:39) and *kissing* (imperfect: *katephiloun*) of Paul indicates the depth of their grief, prompted by his revelation that they would not see him again (20:25).

After saying their final good-byes, the Ephesian leaders **accompanied** Paul to the ship (v 38). The verb *propempō* suggests that they also supplied him with provisions for his journey (see 15:3; also 1 Esd 4:47; 1 Macc 12:4; Rom 15:24; 1 Cor 16:6, 11). In this parting image of the church, they respond faithfully to the saying of Jesus (Acts 20:35).

5. Travels from Miletus to Caesarea (21:1-8*a*)

■ **1-3** After the difficulties of breaking away (*apospaō*; → 20:30) from dear friends, Paul and his companions (note resumed first-person plural **we** [21:1]) continue their journey. They sail **straight to Cos**, an Aegean island with a major port about 50 miles (81 km) south of Miletus. The next day's journey lands them in **Rhodes**, another island about 70 miles (113 km) southeast of Cos. The Colossus of Rhodes, a 100-foot (31-m) tall statue of the sun-god Helios, one of the Seven Wonders of the Ancient World, stood at the city's entrance.

The following day the party travels another 60 miles (97 km) west to **Patara**, a prominent port city on the Mediterranean coast of the province of Lycia, in southwest Asia Minor. There, Paul's party switches vessels, taking passage on a ship that would accommodate their schedule (see 20:16). Rather than hugging the coastline, this 300-mile (483-km) portion of the journey took a direct route south of Cyprus toward the coast of **Phoenicia** (v 2; see 11:19; 15:3), with its two major port cities of Tyre and Sidon on the eastern end of the Mediterranean.

■ **4-6** Delays due to unloading the ship's cargo in Tyre give ample time for Paul and his companions to "look up" (*aneuriskō*; see Luke 2:16) **the disciples** there, perhaps because Paul had not ministered in this area (Acts 21:4). But, ironically, he *was* partially responsible for the gospel spreading there, due to his persecution campaign that forced believers out of Jerusalem (→ 8:1*b*-3; see Spencer 2004a, 206).

After finding the Tyre disciples, they stay (see 10:48; 21:10; 28:12, 14) **seven days** with them (as earlier in Troas [20:6]). The disciples there repeatedly warn (imperfect: *elegon*) Paul **not to go on to Jerusalem**. Luke indicates that this warning does not come *directly* from the Spirit. Rather, they conclude this **through the Spirit** or as the result of a message from the Spirit.

Their warning contradicts the Spirit's guidance of Paul (see 19:21; 20:22-23), but it accurately reflects their concern for his welfare, based on what the Spirit revealed about the dangers facing him (→ 20:22-24). It is sometimes difficult to discern God's will and purpose (see Tannehill 1990, 262-67). Luke mentions nothing about Paul's response to these warnings.

Upon the traveling party's departure, two images are similar to the farewell scene in Ephesus. First, the believers escort (**accompanied** [21:5]) the travelers to the ship, perhaps offering provisions (*propempō*; see 15:3; 20:38) for the journey. Luke specifically mentions ***women and children*** among the disciples sending off Paul and his companions. This underscores the presence of the whole community and the importance of the occasion (Gaventa 2003, 293).

Second, before the travelers board the ship, everyone kneels together **on the beach** in prayer (see 20:36), a characteristic activity of believers throughout Acts (e.g., 1:14; 2:42; 4:24-31; 13:3; 14:23).

■ **7-8***a* The journey continues down the Mediterranean coast to **Ptolemais** (21:7), 25 miles (40 km) south of Tyre. Their one-day stay with the believers may have been the result of the ship's itinerary. From there, the ship continues another 30 miles (48 km) south to **Caesarea** (v 8*a*). This "crossroad" for the Christian mission (see 8:40; 9:30; 11:11; 12:19; 18:22) was the location for the epochal encounter between Cornelius and Peter (→ 10:1-48).

6. Believers in Caesarea (21:8*b*-14)

■ **8*b*-9** Upon their arrival in Caesarea, Paul and his colleagues go to **the house of Philip** (v 8*b*; → 8:40). Luke first introduced him as **one of the Seven** chosen to care for the Greek-speaking Jerusalem widows (6:3-6). He subsequently was busy "proclaiming the good news" (*euangelizomai*) to the Samaritans (8:12) and the Ethiopian eunuch (8:35). He later became known as the **evangelist** (*euangelistēs*).

Ironically, Paul, the former persecutor, stays in Philip's home, which is in Caesarea because persecution forced him out of Jerusalem (8:1*b*-3). Luke mentions nothing else about Philip or his hospitality, other than that he has **four unmarried daughters** (21:9) who regularly **prophesied** (present participle: *prophēteuousai*), fulfilling the Joel prophecy mentioned in 2:17. Such prophetic women would prepare that context for Agabus' prophecy (see Seim 1994, 181-83).

■ **10-11** **Agabus** (v 10) is probably the same prophet who earlier warned the Antioch church about an impending famine (11:27-28). Luke does not explain the occasion of his visit, noting only that he came **from Judea**. Like some OT prophets, Agabus not only speaks but acts out his God-given message (e.g., 1 Kgs 11:29-40; Isa 8:1-4; Jer 13:1-11; Ezek 4:1-17).

Agabus uses Paul's belt to bind "his own feet and hands" (Acts 21:11 NRSV). He refers to **the owner of this belt**, repeats the verb **bind** (*deō*), and identifies those responsible as "the Jews in Jerusalem" (NRSV). Careful readers recall Paul's earlier statement that he was "bound by the Spirit" to go to Jerusalem and that imprisonment awaited him (20:22-23). Agabus' comments from **the Holy Spirit** are consistent with the divine insights of both Paul (20:22-24) and the believers in Tyre (21:4) regarding Paul's future in Jerusalem (see Reimer 1995, 249).

■ **12-14** Those who witnessed Agabus' message attempt to convince Paul to cancel his travel plans to Jerusalem (see 21:4). The verb translated **pleaded** (v 12) is translated elsewhere as "encouragement" (*parakaleō*; see 14:22; 16:40; 20:1, 2, 12). The imperfect tense implies that Paul's traveling companions (**we**) and the *local believers* (*hoi entopioi*; against Pervo 2009, 538) continue to urge him to reconsider those plans.

According to Paul, they were **weeping and breaking [his] heart** (21:13). He undoubtedly appreciated their deep concern for his safety and well-being (see 9:23-35; 14:20; 17:10, 14-15; 19:30). They probably made it increasingly difficult for him to follow the Spirit's guidance. Nonetheless, Paul emphatically declares not only his willingness **to be bound** as Agabus announced (20:22) but even **to die in Jerusalem for the name of the Lord Jesus**.

Paul's statement reflects the motif of Jerusalem as the murderer of prophets (see Luke 11:49-51; 13:33-34). The expression **the name of the Lord Jesus** (*hyper tou onomatos*) recollects early scenes of preaching and healing in the holy city linked to the authority of Jesus' name (see, e.g., Acts 2:38; 3:6, 16; 4:10, 12; 5:28). It is also reminiscent of the apostles' response after being flogged by the Jewish authorities (5:41) and the risen Lord's own statement that Paul would suffer "for my name" (*hyper tou onomatos mou* [9:16]).

Despite Agabus' message, the believers' recognize Paul's resolve. The present genitive absolute (*mē peithomenou autou*) suggests that he would never be persuaded by anything they said. So they become "silent" (*hēsychazō* [21:14 NRSV]) and affirm with Paul, **"The Lord's will be done"** (see Luke 22:42).

This collective group represents several stages of the Acts narrative:
- Philip, a member of the Seven whom the apostles commissioned (6:1-6);
- Agabus, who came from Jerusalem and whose ministry had earlier extended to Antioch (11:27-28); and
- Paul's companions, who represent the fruit of his ministry among Jews and Gentiles (20:4).

Yet the narrator depicts this diverse group of believers as united together to support and encourage Paul to follow God's will (see Thompson 2006, 226-27; Pervo 2009, 539).

7. Travels from Caesarea to Jerusalem (21:15-17)

■ **15-16** After an unspecified period (*these days*) in Caesarea, Paul's party starts the final stage of the journey **to Jerusalem** (v 15): about 60 miles (97 km) over land. The presence of some **disciples from Caesarea** (v 16) would provide additional security and support for Paul. They are also responsible for Paul's lodging with **Mnason**, whom Paul may not have known.

Luke describes Mnason much like Barnabas: a *disciple from the beginning* whose homeland is **Cyprus** (→ 4:36). As a Diaspora Jew, he is open to hosting the traveling party that includes Gentile believers. The Western text adds that Mnason's home was located in a village between Caesarea and Jerusalem (Metzger 1994, 428; Fitzmyer 1998, 690). But his home was more likely in Jerusalem. If so, he provides lodging for Paul and his "mixed" party while they are in Jerusalem (see, e.g., Haenchen 1971, 607; Bruce 1988, 402-3; Barrett 1998, 1003-4).

■ **17** Interpreters have often understood the warm reception of Paul and his colleagues upon their arrival as an informal meeting with a few church members (*adelphoi*) before the official meeting the next day (21:18-25). More likely, this verse belongs with the previous paragraph. Paul's party is warmly welcomed upon arrival *at Mnason's home* in Jerusalem (see Marshall 1980,

350

341-42; Bruce 1988, 404). The scene *concludes* the section with Paul's successful journey to Jerusalem and his reception by those gathered believers. Their hospitality coheres with the depiction of the church throughout Acts (e.g., 2:42-47; 4:32-37; 6:1-7; 10:48; 14:20; 16:15; 17:10, 14-15; 20:37-38).

FROM THE TEXT

This passage generally tends to be overlooked. Dramatic scenes like Pentecost (2:1-13), divine jail breaks (5:17-26; 12:3-19; 16:19-34), healings (3:1-10; 14:8-10), and divine epiphanies that lead to drastic transformation (9:1-19a) better capture contemporary readers' attention. Ancient readers, who seldom traveled far from where they were born, probably found passages about sea voyages and exotic ports of call more engaging. Nevertheless, both the narrative placement and the contents of this passage assist readers in looking (a) *retrospectively* at Paul's ministry and its implications regarding God's saving purposes and the people of God, and (b) *prospectively* toward other issues potentially facing the Christian mission intent on spreading an inclusive understanding of the gospel.

On the one hand, both Paul's traveling party (20:4) and the churches along the journey serve as "exhibits" of his labors in ministry. Although they probably had no formal connection with each other because of distance, the narrative links them by these travelers, who themselves had little in common other than their leader (i.e., Paul) and the gospel. Nonetheless, Luke describes these local churches that would have included both Jewish and Gentile believers in ways that allude to images of the earliest Jewish believers in Jerusalem: breaking bread or fellowship (20:7, 11; see 2:42, 46), teaching (20:7-11, 18-35; see 2:42), prayer (20:36; 21:5; see 1:14; 2:42; 4:24-31), sharing possessions (20:35, 38b; see 2:44-45; 4:32, 34-37), and care for one another (20:37-38a; 21:8b, 12-13; see 2:46-47). Thus, these mixed churches, like the Jewish believers in Jerusalem, may be linked to the fulfillment of God's saving purposes as seen in Pentecost. Although many contend that Paul's farewell address to the Ephesian elders focused on emulating his example, both that address and this larger section redirect attention to God's purposes at work in the world, which were gathering together an inclusive "people of God" (see Tannehill 1990, 257-59). Paul's Miletus speech is not primarily about an *example* but about *ecclesiology*. God is the ultimate source, not only of the church's existence but of her faithfulness in the midst of erroneous teachings by some and conflicting visions of mission (20:28-30) and the future (see Gaventa 2003, 291).

On the other hand, it also addresses questions about the discernment of God's purposes and will. Different people sometimes respond to their understanding of divine revelation and guidance differently. For instance, the advice of well-meaning believers (21:4, 12-13), who learned about the dangers facing Paul in Jerusalem and who cared deeply about his safety, contradicted the Spirit's guidance to Paul (19:21; 20:22; 21:13). It is sometimes difficult to discern, interpret, and apply divine revelation (see Tannehill 1990, 263).

Some offer mistaken insights about one's mission (20:29-30) under the guise of "God's will." These may be inadequate or deficient because they limit the inclusive message and mission of the gospel. Since the destination of Paul's journey, Jerusalem, has also been a source of heated debate over the nature of Christian mission in the past, his arrival in the holy city hints of the possibility of upcoming difficulties. The contemporary church still needs discernment regarding divine purpose and guidance. We cannot assume we know God's will apart from thoughtful reflection and prayer.

B. Paul's Defense of His Ministry in Jerusalem (21:18—23:35)

BEHIND THE TEXT

For Luke, Paul's journey to Jerusalem is more than a religious pilgrimage by a pious, faithful Jew. Echoes of Jesus' journey to Jerusalem reverberate. Ominous references to serious trouble looming on the city's horizon (20:22-24; 21:4, 12-13) create both anxiety and anticipation for what Paul might face. After all, his personal history and reputation precede him. The city is "filled with the memories and possibilities of conflict" (Johnson 1992, 371; see 8:3). Yet Paul's driving passion for an inclusive welcome of both Jews and Gentiles into the people of God evokes questions, suspicions, and fear from believing and nonbelieving Jews alike. Identity issues for Jews as the people of God generate the dangers facing Paul.

IN THE TEXT

1. The Meeting with the Jerusalem Church Leaders (21:18-26)

■ 18-19 The day after their arrival, Paul and his colleagues seek out James, the leader of the Jerusalem church, and all the elders (v 18). Paul reports to them what God had done among the Gentiles through his ministry (v 19).

Luke emphasizes that God guided and enabled the Christian mission, including the gospel to the Gentiles (see 10:1—11:18). But Paul's ministry did not focus predominantly on Gentiles; Luke consistently has Paul in Jewish settings, seeking and prompting both Jewish and Gentile response. Since Paul is addressing a Jewish audience, this emphasis on his ministry to Gentiles simply assumes his work among his fellow Jews. Paul's "detailed" (*kath' hen hekaston*) report probably includes events in Acts 16—19, particularly in Corinth and Ephesus.

■ **20-21** The leaders' response of praise to God (4:21; 11:18; 13:48) confirms Paul's ministry as God's work. The imperfect indicative *edoxazon* may suggest that they praise God for quite some time (e.g., BDF 1961, §327; Barrett 1998, 1006).

However, the abrupt introduction of subsequent concerns within the same Greek sentence suggests that this initial response is squelched by interruption (→ 15:4-5). Before stating those concerns, a spokesperson (not explicitly named as James, as generally assumed) directs Paul's attention to the **many thousands** (21:20) of Jewish believers in Jerusalem, **all** (*pantes*) of them being **zealous for the law** (*zēlōtai tou nomou*; see *zēlos, zēloō*; 5:17; 13:45; 17:5).

These opening remarks about the Jewish believers stand in sharp contrast to the interruption, which reports accusations against Paul. Some allege that his customary practice in the Gentile world was teaching (present tense: *didaskeis*) **all** (*pantas*) Diaspora Jews to **turn away** or *apostatize* (*apostasia*) **from Moses**. They contend he specifically advised them against circumcising their children and against following Jewish customs. A similar accusation will also arise later (21:28).

Most interpreters suggest this accusation is invalid or unbelievable when compared to the Lukan portrayal of Paul as a devout, loyal Jew in Acts (esp. in light of his circumcision of Timothy; → 16:1-3; see, e.g., Johnson 1992, 375; Wall 2002, 293; Oropeza 2011, 124). Others suggest that the accusation merely depicts the Jewish Christians in Jerusalem much like the non-Christian Jews in general throughout Acts (e.g., Sanders 1987, 284; Tyson 1992, 162). Still other interpreters view this as a believable accusation that coheres with what Paul himself wrote and likely taught about circumcision (e.g., Gal 5:2-6; Bruce 1988, 405; Pervo 2009, 544).

The accusations are believable, not from a *Lukan* perspective, but from a *Jewish* perspective seen within the Acts narrative itself (see Thompson 2000, 34-50; 2005, 64-78). This fits Luke's account of Paul's ministry, especially in Corinth and Ephesus. Similar charges about Paul's alleged teaching against the Law were levied in Corinth by his Jewish opponents (18:11, 13; → 18:13).

The reference to Paul teaching apostasy (*apostasia* [21:21]) alludes to Paul's departure from the Ephesian synagogue (*apostas* [19:9]). From a Jewish perspective, this could be interpreted as nothing less than a radical departure and separation from anything and everything Jewish (see Jervell 1996, 88). But from the Lukan perspective, Jewish opposition precipitated this response (→ 20:19). Undoubtedly, Paul's message was more inclusive than the synagogue context condoned (see 20:21).

■ **22-24** The disparity between the Jewish believers' zealousness for the Jewish law and Paul's alleged disdain for it insinuates that the Jerusalem church leaders accept the rumor as true. Consequently, they would likely respond to him with resistance and hostility.

The leaders themselves ask Paul—"What about this?" (v 22 CEB; lit., **"What is it?"**). Suspicions about his activities call for his response before others find out of his arrival (see Lüdemann 1989b, 58; Porter 2001, 178). Interestingly, the leaders do not allow Paul opportunity to answer the question, nor do they address the rumor directly! Rather, they propose that he prove his Jewish fidelity by participating in a seven-day purification ritual with four other men and that he pay all their expenses. Left unexplained is the uncleanness from which Paul needs purification (perhaps his "apostasy" from Diaspora synagogues in Corinth and Ephesus!).

The references to the **vow** (v 23) and "shaving of their heads" (v 24 NRSV) lead most interpreters to understand this as a Nazirite vow (→ 18:18). The narrator offers few details. The leaders' rationale may have been simply pragmatic: Paul's proposed pious practice would negate the contrary reports about him (*katēchēntai peri sou*; see 21:21: *katēchēthēsan . . . peri sou*). But if the leaders believe the rumors are true, their comments about the potential outcomes for Paul's ritual practice may mask their skepticism about Paul's fidelity as a Jew (→ the sidebar "How Did the Jerusalem Church Respond to Paul?" with 21:30-33).

Jewish Law and the Church

Luke has consistently presented Paul as a devout, Law-observant Jew. But Paul's ministry increasingly took him outside the Jewish synagogue. Through Acts 20, the narrator scarcely touches upon the place of the Jewish law in either Paul's life or the church. The major exception is Acts 15 and the Jerusalem Council. It addresses the question of circumcision and Jewish law, but only as it impacts Gentile believers. It implicitly offers the general rubric for Paul's ministry from ch 16 forward.

The controversy in Jerusalem over Paul's teachings on the Jewish law becomes a "flashpoint" within Acts. On the one hand, there is the declared importance of the Jewish law for Jewish believers (21:20). The expectation is that Paul, as a faithful Jew, would follow the Law faithfully and teach others to do so. However, no reason for such ongoing demands within the church appears in Acts (see Pervo 2009, 544).

On the other hand, the church's decision not to require Gentiles to follow the Jewish law came from the recognition of God's saving purposes and workings for all people. The Law became associated with certain purely Jewish religious practices and customs (10:10-16), not with matters of salvation (13:38-39).

Paul's case became a problematic issue for the Jerusalem church because it brought the issues into conflict. Their concern for Jewish practices and customs threatened the Christian mission that God called Paul to live out. According to Acts, God's purposes, originally associated with Israel as the people of God, now extend more inclusively to both Jews and Gentiles. This reconstituted people of God throws the role of Jewish law into question within this mixed *ekklēsia* of God.

■ **25-26** The issue facing the Jerusalem church leaders and Paul has to do with *Jewish* fidelity to the Jewish law (vv 21-24). The leaders insist that the earlier decision regarding **Gentile believers** (v 25) and the Jewish law (15:22-29) still remains in effect. By mentioning it, they seem to question Paul's Jewish fidelity based on his ministry practices, which included Gentiles as well as Jews. The reiterated list of four prohibitions related to idolatry mirrors the one given in the earlier letter (→ 15:29). The tone of their remarks (with its emphatic and exclusive **we**, not including Paul) seems to reflect the leaders' escalating distrust of Paul and his advocacy of these policies affecting Gentile believers (see Spencer 2004a, 209).

Paul's compliance with the leaders' proposal—without comment or rebuttal—seems unlike the historical Paul (see Pervo 2009, 546; but see Bruce 1988, 407-8). It depicts him as conciliatory toward the Jerusalem church, affirming the rights of Jewish believers to live according to the Jewish law. His arrangement for the sacrificial **offering** (21:26) on behalf of all four men (vv 23-24) depicts Paul as someone with some financial means (to be able to cover such expenses) and beneficence for doing so (see Josephus' similar description of Agrippa I: *Ant.* 19.294).

2. Troubles at the Temple (21:27-36)

■ **27-29** Troubles arise for Paul as he nears the completion of the **seven days** (v 27) of the ritual observance the leaders required. This robs him of the opportunity to clear his name (v 24). This time, his adversaries are ***Jews from Asia*** who saw him in the temple. They are probably from Ephesus (the leading city of Asia), since they recognize Trophimus from that same city (see 20:4). He is in Jerusalem with Paul (21:29). Although Luke does not explain their presence, they may be religious pilgrims in Jerusalem for the festival of Pentecost (see 20:16).

The Asian Jews begin to create confusion and agitation (imperfect tense: *synecheon*; see 21:31; 19:29, 32; contrast 2:6) among the **whole crowd**. The result is a mob scene reminiscent of what had happened in Ephesus. The Asian Jews apprehend Paul (**seized**; lit., ***threw their hands on him***; see 4:3; 5:18; 12:1). Their accusation against Paul was twofold.

First, they complain that Paul taught **against our people and our law and this place** (21:28). This echoes the rumor reported a week earlier (v 21). The hyperbolic expansion of Paul's audience to **everyone everywhere** claims that he taught not only Jews but even non-Jews in anti-Jewish ways. This was the ultimate sign that Paul was a disloyal, apostate Jew, who had betrayed his own people. Teaching against the temple is added to the list of alleged offenses. This resembles the false charges brought against Stephen (6:11, 13-14).

Second, they also charge that Paul brought Greeks into the temple. It was by this means that he **defiled** or made **this holy place** ritually unclean.

Jewish Protection of the Temple

Strict guidelines protected the Jewish temple, including regulations about who could enter it. Gentiles were allowed only in the outer Court of the Gentiles. The stated penalty for violations of these restrictions was death (see Josephus, *J.W.* 5.193-94; 6.124-26; *Ant.* 15.417; Philo, *Embassy* 212). Engraved stone markers reinforced these guidelines and warnings within the temple grounds. Anyone accused of bringing a foreigner into the inner courts and desecrating the Jewish temple faced the same penalty.

The temple area was often the setting for Jewish social uprisings, created by perceptions that their customs had been slighted or violated by outsiders such as the Romans (see Josephus, *J.W.* 1.88-90; 2.8-13, 42-48, 169-74, 223-31, 315-20, 406-7, 449-56). Disturbances often arose during Jewish festivals such as Passover and Pentecost, when sensitivities to such religious matters would have been heightened. Since Paul intended to reach Jerusalem in time for Pentecost (20:16), the fervor of religious pilgrims in Jerusalem for that festival may explain the sudden, hostile response toward him because of these accusations.

In atypical fashion, Luke explains the opponents' accusation and zealous response. They earlier witnessed Paul and Trophimus together in Jerusalem and mistakenly assumed Paul had taken the Gentile believer beyond the Court of the Gentiles and into the inner courts of the temple.

■ **30-33** In typical Lukan hyperbole, the effects of the allegations are widespread, with the **whole city** (v 30) described as **aroused** or deeply *shaken* (*kineō*). This leads to the formation of a mob that first captures ("seized" [NRSV]; see 16:19; 17:19; 18:17) Paul and then drags (→ 16:19) him out of the temple. They may have **shut** the temple gates behind them to prevent further defilement or to carry out their intentions to execute Paul outside the temple area so as not to defile the temple. After this, Acts mentions no other believer entering the temple. So, the closed doors may signal a significant symbolic message: official Judaism's rejection of Paul and his Christian message (see Tyson 1992, 184). The mob's attempts to **kill** (21:31; see 3:15; 7:52) Paul suggests they believe the allegations against him to be true, making him deserving of death (→ sidebar "Jewish Protection of the Temple" with 21:27-29).

Ironically, this chaotic scene stands as a reversal of early scenes in Jerusalem, most notably the Pentecost episode. Earlier, the Jews of Jerusalem and the Diaspora came together in the temple, listened to Peter, and believed (→ ch 2). Here in another likely Pentecost episode, they have come together in the

356

temple, *refused* to listen, closed the temple doors to Paul (21:30), and tried to kill him (v 31; see Gaventa 2003, 301-2).

The Roman military was stationed adjacent to the temple in the Fortress Antonia. They were charged with the suppression of disturbances during Jewish festivals (Josephus, *J.W.* 5.238-47). Word about the continuing state of public confusion (present tense: *synchynnetai* [v 31; see v 27]) over Paul's alleged crimes would have spread over all Jerusalem. News would have easily reached the military **commander** or "tribune" (NRSV). Luke suggests that the Romans are concerned about quelling the uprising, not about Paul's well-being.

The detection of Roman military personnel rushing to the scene prompts Paul's attackers to cease **beating** (v 32) him, which prevents his death. Thus, the Roman military, known for its brutality, brings a semblance of order in the midst of the frenzy of Paul's Jewish assailants (see Béchard 2003, 249). However, the Romans' arrest and binding of Paul (v 33)—fulfilling Agabus' prophecy (21:11)—assume Paul to be the instigator of the chaos and a threat to the social order.

How Did the Jerusalem Church Respond to Paul?

The Lukan account of Paul's troubles at the temple leaves out numerous details. However, since Paul was at the temple in compliance with a suggestion from the Jerusalem church elders, Luke's silence about any assistance from the Jerusalem believers during his ordeal is surprising. Where were they when Paul was attacked while doing as they had instructed him? What, if anything, was their involvement in what transpired? Luke offers nothing specific. The Jerusalem church never appears again in Acts. However, the narrator's hyperbolic descriptions of the serious concerns and chaos of the "whole city" (vv 30-31) leave the impression that the Jerusalem believers, who apparently believed a similar rumor (vv 20-22), abandoned him to his fate.

The differences between Paul and the Jerusalem believers were over questions about the role of Jewish law for Jewish Christians in the church. Paul's ministry outside the Jewish synagogues in Corinth and Ephesus raised serious questions for Jewish believers, who apparently found no satisfactory answers. Luke's silence implicitly depicts the Jerusalem believers differently from earlier days, when they were concerned for Paul's safety (9:30). This may indicate a passive stance toward Paul, as they merely "washed their hands" of him and left him to "stew in his own juice" (Dunn 2006, 256). Some contend that these troubles were the direct result of a trap in which the Jerusalem elders were willing and active participants (Mattill 1970, 115-17; see Porter 2001, 179-80; also Johnson 1992, 377). It is plausible that the Lukan description of "all Jerusalem" includes the Jewish believers in the city, who joined the hostile mob in rejecting Paul and calling for his death (see Rapske 1998, 244-45; Thompson 2000, 34-50; 2005, 64-78).

■ **34-36** The commotion of the crowd, with persons shouting different things, is reminiscent of the scene at the Ephesian theater (19:32). They prevent the military official from finding out what led to the riotous **uproar** (*thorybos* [21:34]; 20:1; 24:18; see *thorybeō*: 17:5; 20:10). Paul's removal from the scene to the adjacent military fortress would allow an interrogation away from the hostile crowd. However, by the time the Roman soldiers escort Paul the short distance to the fortress steps (no more than about 300 to 400 feet [or 90 to 120 m]), the mob has become so unruly and violent that they must carry him through the chaos to safety. The continual shouting (present tense: *krazontes*) by the crowd—"Away with him!" (*aire auton* [v 36 NRSV]—is similar to the cries of those who sought Jesus' death (*aire touton* [Luke 23:18]).

3. Paul's Speech before the Jewish Crowd (21:37—22:29)

■ **37-40** Paul's inquiry to the Roman commander, Claudius Lysias (23:26), is met by initial surprise. This is not because Paul speaks Greek; people in Jerusalem were typically bilingual. It is because his accent is not of someone from North Africa. Lysias had erroneously identified Paul as an Egyptian revolutionary and leader of a large group of **terrorists** (v 38; political "assassins" [NRSV]) who hid from the Romans in the **wilderness**. Josephus mentions an Egyptian false prophet (ca. AD 54) who led as many as thirty thousand men to the Mount of Olives to take over Jerusalem. The Romans killed or captured thousands of his followers, but the leader himself managed to escape (*J.W.* 2.261-63; *Ant.* 20.169-72).

The Romans generally viewed Egyptians with suspicion (see, e.g., Philo, *Alleg. Interp.* 2.84; 3.37-38; *Dreams* 1.240; 2.255; Strabo, *Geogr.* 17.1.12; Lentz 1993, 29-30). Paul takes this identification as an insult. In response, he points out two contrasting things: (*a*) he is Jewish; and (*b*) he is a **citizen** from **Tarsus in Cilicia**, a prominent (lit., *not an insignificant*) city of the empire (v 39; → sidebar "Saul / Paul and the City of Tarsus" with 9:10-12).

Paul's identity and background convince Lysias that Paul could address the same Jewish crowd that just tried to kill him and followed him to the fortress. His reference to the crowd as **the people** (*laos*) implies a religious motive behind his remarks. Paul the Jew would address the Jewish people about his faithfulness to God on behalf of Israel (see Wall 2002, 298).

Paul's hand gesture to the crowd was typical of ancient orators calling for silence (v 40; see 13:16; 19:33; 26:1). By speaking to the Jewish crowd in either **Hebrew** or **Aramaic**, the sister Semitic languages most commonly used in that area, Paul would address them in the language of the temple and of the common Jewish people.

■ **22:1-3** Paul begins by describing his speech as his **defense** (*apologia* [v 1]), presumably against the charges pronounced against him (21:28*b*-29). Some interpreters question its suitability for the situation (because he never addresses the charge of bringing a Gentile into the temple). But the crowd's interruption of Paul allows Luke to let the speech attend to the major accusation: that Paul was an apostate Jew (21:28*a*; also 21:21; see Longenecker 1981, 524).

Paul's formal opening address of the audience as **brothers and fathers** echoes that of Stephen (7:2). After identifying with his audience as a fellow Jew, Paul offers basic autobiographical information. He follows a standard three-part formula (with three perfect participles) emphasizing (*a*) his place of birth (repeating 21:39), (*b*) his upbringing, and (*c*) his education.

By naming **Tarsus** as his birthplace (22:3; see 21:39), Paul allows the audience to identify him as a Diaspora Jew. However, his reference to **this city** (i.e., Jerusalem) as the place where he lived as a youth and received his upbringing affirms his traditional Jewish heritage at the center of the Jewish world.

Two phrases describe Paul's education in their ***ancestral law***. The first phrase, ***at the feet of Gamaliel***, associates him with the noted rabbinic teacher (see 5:33-39) but whose advice Saul ignored when he himself dealt with the believers (8:1-3).

The second phrase, *kata akribeian*, connotes something accomplished with precision as a goal (see words with the *akrib*- stem: 18:25-26; 23:15, 20; 24:22; 26:5; Luke 1:3; see LSJ 1996, 55). He underscores the strict adherence of his education in the Jewish law. Such emphases linked him to the Pharisaic tradition (see 23:6; also Phil 3:5-6). Paul's self-description as being **zealous for God** (see Rom 10:2) may contrast with those who were "zealous for the law" (21:20; see Gal 1:14). His audience's prompt actions against him show that they ironically shared the same passion.

Paul's Tale of Two Cities

Readers of Acts usually associate Paul with the city of Tarsus, since Paul (then Saul) returned there (9:30) when his life was in danger after his Damascus road encounter (9:1-19*a*). Pauline interpreters often assume that Paul was educated in Tarsus, since the city was a leading intellectual and cultural center of the Roman Empire, rivaling Athens and Alexandria.

But Paul's defense speech in Acts 22 indicates that, despite his birthplace, both his childhood and his religious education as a youth took place in Jerusalem, before he moved back to Tarsus (van Unnik 1962; against du Toit 2000, 375-402, who contends that Paul was raised in Tarsus).

This does not preclude the influence of the intellectual environment of Tarsus on Paul and his thought, particularly after his Damascus experience. Nonetheless, his speech accentuates the significant role of Jerusalem in his nurture and education as a Jew (see also Barrett 1998, 1034-36), thereby making his life a "tale of two cities."

■ **4-5** Paul's narration of his previous persecution of Christians illustrates the zeal that characterized his life. His self-disclosure largely repeats prior information (→ 8:3; 9:1-2). However, the curious reference to **the high priest and all the Council** (22:5; a likely reference to the Sanhedrin), who could verify Paul's story, assumes them to be the same group as before (although more than twenty years have passed). Nonetheless, this information reiterates Paul's activities against the followers of Jesus under the auspices of the Jewish religious authorities.

■ **6-11** Paul's account of his Damascus road encounter with the risen Jesus appropriates most of the details and vocabulary of Luke's first account (→ 9:3-9). But several differences stand out.

First, 22:6 indicates that the encounter happened **about noon**, which heightens how bright the light from heaven must have been to cause its effects.

Second, the additional description of Jesus in v 8 as *the Nazarene* (2:22; 3:6; 4:10; 6:14; 26:9) follows Luke's typical pattern. He refers to Jesus as coming from Nazareth in Jewish settings.

Third, Paul describes the response of his traveling companions differently. Here, Paul indicates that the men do not *hear the voice* of the risen Jesus speaking to him (22:9). But in 9:7, Luke's narrative states they *did* hear the voice but saw no one. The contrasting functions of these statements may account for their differences. In Acts 9, the men responded differently from Paul due to their lack of perception as to what happened, thereby highlighting Paul's response. Here, the mention of them not hearing Jesus' voice accentuates that Jesus' message is for Paul only, including his commission (v 10).

Fourth, Paul inserts his response—**"What shall I do, Lord?"**—prior to Jesus' instructions about going to Damascus. This offers a hint regarding his future calling.

■ **12-16** By mentioning nothing about the three days of fasting and prayer in Damascus (9:9) and moving to the arrival of Ananias, Paul focuses on dialogue that refers to his ministry. Paul's introduction of Ananias emphasizes his Jewish piety. He is **devout** (*eulabēs* [22:12]; 2:5; 8:2; Luke 2:25) *according to the law*, which the entire Jewish populace of the city could affirm.

The third-person account emphasizes the restoration of Paul's sight through Ananias but mentions no dialogue between the two about Paul's future (→ 9:17-18). Paul's account here only briefly mentions the restoration of his sight (22:13). This allows Ananias' articulation of Paul's calling (vv 14-15) to stand out more prominently.

Two aspects of Paul's call that Ananias declares to him are crucial to Paul's defense. Ananias grounds that call in the historic Jewish tradition by referring to **the God of our ancestors** (v 14; e.g., Exod 3:13; Deut 1:11; 1 Chr 12:17). This appropriates the LXX language common in other Acts speeches (see 3:13; 5:30; 7:32; 13:23). Being **chosen** (*procheirizō*; see 3:20; 26:16) is not only reminiscent of God's "appointment" of Jesus but also implies a particular task for Paul (see Michaelis, *TDNT* 6:862-64).

Three infinitives clarify the reason for God's selection of Paul. The first focuses on experiencing or discovering God's **will** (*thelēma* [22:14]). Acts describes this as God's plan (*boulē* [2:23; 4:28; 5:38; 13:36; 20:27]). The second and third infinitives refer to Paul's firsthand, dramatic encounter with the Messiah—Jesus, **the Righteous One** (→ 3:14; 7:52).

Ananias explains Paul's call as a **witness** (22:15). This depicts his mission similarly to the apostles' (see 1:8, 22; 2:32; 3:15; 5:32; 10:39). Jesus' words to Ananias are that Paul would "carry" his name to others (→ 9:15). The reference to **all people** (*pantas anthrōpous*) implies that Gentiles are part of Paul's mission (→ 9:15, where this is explicit). Paul avoids stressing this here to avoid provoking his volatile, Jewish audience.

Ananias' final instructions expand on Paul's baptism (→ 9:18). Although baptism has signified incorporation into the Christian community, Paul's Jewish audience would not have picked up on such connotations. They would associate this act with ritual cleansing, perhaps due to Paul's temporary blindness. The additional command to **wash away your sins** (22:16) recalls earlier calls of repentance linked to baptism (see 2:38) and interprets the symbolism of those actions. Even the last expression—**calling on his name** (see 2:21; 9:14, 21; 15:17)—would bring the God of Israel to the ears of the Jewish audience. Of course, Luke's readers would think of Jesus, both Lord and Messiah (2:36). But the entire exchange between Ananias and Paul presents Paul as a faithful Jew whom the Jewish people would find acceptable.

■ **17-21** The last portion of Paul's speech gives new information about Paul's Jerusalem visit after the Damascus episode. Not surprisingly, Paul mentions nothing about the Jewish opposition that forced him out of Damascus or Jerusalem. Rather, he recounts a divine vision or **trance** (22:17; see 10:10; 11:5) that occurred during his prayers in the temple. This is reminiscent of similar OT stories of temple visions (e.g., 1 Sam 3:2-14; 1 Kgs 3:4-14; Isa 6:1-13) and another sign of Paul's loyalty as a Jew. Surely a pious Jew who prays in the temple would not desecrate it!

The command that Paul received to **leave Jerusalem immediately** (Acts 22:18) reveals for the first time the tensions between his message and the Jews. His quick escape was due to the lack of Jewish acceptance of his **testimony** (*martyria*) about Jesus, as Jesus' witness (*martyr*; → 9:29-30).

Paul's response is not a refusal to comply with the divine commands. His review of his past as the ruthless persecutor may have encouraged some of his accusers to listen to him because of that past. The repeated stress on Paul's involvement in Stephen's death just outside the city implicates him as an accomplice (→ 7:58; 8:1). However, Paul's call was reiterated in different words, **"Go; I will send you far away to the Gentiles"** (22:17; → 9:15; Gal 1:15-17).

Such language comes as a surprise to Paul's audience. But Luke's readers will recall Paul's response to opponents in Pisidian Antioch (Acts 13:46) and Corinth (18:6) about turning to the Gentiles. This reflects the prophetic language of Isa 49:6. It is also reminiscent of Jeremiah's divine call as "a prophet to the nations" (Jer 1:5). Thus, Paul's self-presentation before his Jewish accusers portrays himself as an obedient, faithful Jew whose mission "embodies the vocation of a faithful Israel according to the prophets" (Wall 2002, 308).

■ **22-24** The frenzied interruption to Paul's speech indicates his failure to persuade the Jewish crowd of his innocence. Their response echoes both their earlier outcry (→ 21:36) and the crowd's demand for Jesus' crucifixion (Luke 23:18). Their judgment about Paul as not deserving to live reflects their fundamental rejection of Paul's attitude toward Gentiles. Ironically, they pronounce this before the *Gentile* (i.e., Roman) soldiers who hold him in custody (see Bock 2007, 663).

Three present participles (Acts 22:23) depict the crowd as persistent and spinning out of control. They keep **shouting** and **throwing off their cloaks**. This may simply reflect their rage or their willingness to ramp up their assault on Paul. It may also symbolically protest against Paul's message as blasphemous in its favoring Gentiles over Jews in terms of God's salvation.

The mob's actions of ***throwing* dust into the air** may have been defiant actions against Paul, since they could not actually stone him to death, because of the Roman presence. Their symbolic actions may have attempted to dispel what they consider as the potentially harmful effects of Paul's blasphemy (see Job 2:12; Cadbury 1933a, 269-77).

Because of this turn of events, Lysias gives orders for Paul to be taken inside the fortress so they can interrogate him apart from the chaotic mob scene. The Romans often used torture like flogging (→ sidebar "The Ancient Practice of Flogging" with Acts 5:38-40) to extract information when other means were unsuccessful or circumstances dictated. The move was *not* for Paul's safety. The commander hopes to discover the reason behind the "outcry" (22:24 NRSV) against Paul. He may have had only limited understanding of Paul's address, because it was spoken in Hebrew or Aramaic (v 2). Likely, so was the shouting of the Jewish mob.

■ **25-29** To this point, Paul's address and his audience share a common Jewish focus. However, in the hands of Roman soldiers, Paul's Jewish heritage and message count for nothing. Just as the soldiers finish preparations for Paul's flogging and interrogation, Paul raises a question about the legality of such torture for a Roman citizen (→ 16:35-37 and the sidebar "Paul's Roman Citizenship") who has not yet been found guilty by trial (*akatakritos*).

The reaction to Paul's unexpected announcement reflects their legal quandary. Roman law protected citizens from such cruel treatment, to which Romans often subjected non-citizens and slaves (→ 16:37; against Rapske 1994b, 139). Thus, Paul's inquiry dramatically allows him to seize control of the situation and gives him some legal ground he can use to his advantage (Keener 1993, 390).

The narrator mentions no confirmation of Paul's Roman citizenship. A false claim was punishable by death (see, e.g., Epictetus, *Diatr.* 3.24, 41; Suetonius, *Claud.* 25). Paul likely had official documents as proof in his possession (see Barrett 1998, 1048). The brief exchange between Paul and Lysias indicates that, as citizens, Paul actually had higher status than the Roman military commander due to differences between "ascribed" and "acquired" honor (Malina and Neyrey 1991b, 27-32; → sidebar "Honor and Shame: A Different World" with 20:18b-35). Paul's ascribed honor through family ties was greater than Lysias' acquired honor secured through bribing bureaucrats (see, e.g., Dio Cassius, *Hist.* 60.17.4-7).

Not surprisingly, the soldiers, who are preparing Paul for his impending torturous interrogation, quickly distance themselves from the situation. Claudius Lysias is himself concerned about his role and culpability in having Paul **bound** as a prisoner, in light of Paul's disclosure of his Roman citizenship.

4. Paul's Hearing before the Jewish Council (22:30—23:11)

■ **22:30** Lysias probably does not understand most of Paul's address to the Jewish crowd because Paul speaks in their native language (21:40; 22:2). The commander would not have known what provoked their animosity and calls for Paul's death (22:22). Nor could he interrogate Paul under torture as he originally intended. So in order to get some certainty (*to asphales*; see 21:34; cf. *asphaleia* [Luke 1:4]), his alternative plan is to assemble and consult the **entire Sanhedrin** (→ sidebar "The Sanhedrin" with Acts 4:3-4) about the charges (*katēgoreō*; see 24:2, 8, 13, 19; 25:5, 11, 16; 28:19).

Commentators often contend that Roman military officials had no authority to convene the Jewish council. Their presence may have been prohibited from such meetings. The meeting probably functioned in more of an advisory capacity. Paul's appearance before the council is reminiscent not only of Jesus' trial (Luke 22:66) but also of the apostles (Acts 4:15; 5:21) and Stephen (6:12, 15) before them.

■ **23:1** The account has two distinct parts. Luke depicts Paul in this first part as ironically seizing initial control of the meeting. The verb *atenizō*, a favorite Lukan term (→ 3:4), suggests Paul gazing intensely and confidently into the eyes of the council members. By addressing the council as **brothers**, Paul identifies them as fellow Jews.

The general description of how Paul lived his life (*politeuomai*; see Phil 1:27; 2 Macc 11:25; 3 Macc 3:4; 4 Macc 5:16; Culy and Parsons 2003, 438) briefly summarizes his previous speech (22:3-21; see Gaventa 2003, 313). Paul describes his life with two dative expressions. The first, **in all good conscience** ("conscience": Rom 2:15; 9:1; 13:5; 1 Cor 8:7-12; 10:25-29; 2 Cor 1:12; 4:2; 5:11; "good conscience": 1 Tim 1:5, 19) describes how Paul lived. This is not something that guided him merely as an individual but that which belonged to and guided the people of God collectively (→ sidebar "Conscience and the Christian" below).

Dative nouns often follow the verb *politeuomai* in the LXX. There, they indicate the standard by which a person lived (e.g., Esth 8:17; 2 Macc 6:1; 3 Macc 3:4; 4 Macc 2:8; 4:23; 5:16). So the second dative (*tō theō*) makes it clear that Paul's inner motivation comes from the desire to fulfill God's will. Thus, his actions are driven by divine rather than human purposes.

Conscience and the Christian

Paul's declaration about having lived "in all good conscience to this day" (23:1) has puzzled many readers of Acts. Paul's life included a time when he zealously persecuted those who believed Jesus was the Messiah (see 8:1-3; 9:1-2), as he himself acknowledged (see 22:4-5). Thus, many question how he could have a "good conscience" after such behavior. However, one must recognize the differences between ancient and contemporary understandings of human conscience.

Contemporary understandings of conscience tend to be individualistic; ancient views tend to be more corporate. This is evident in the etymology of the Greek term *syneidēsis* (lit., "knowing together with"—shared knowledge). Good conscience was understood to be rational in nature and developed over time with others. Such a conscience would enable persons to discern internally what is good and right, so they may act accordingly. Although the OT did not utilize the vocabulary of conscience, some Hebrew references to the heart parallel concepts later associated with the Greek term (e.g., 1 Sam 24:5; Ps 17:3; Ezek 36:25-26). Such basic Greco-Roman and Jewish perspectives would have informed the concept of conscience in Paul's comment before the Sanhedrin (and other occurrences of the term in the NT; see Wall, *ABD* 1:1128-30; Gooch, *NIDB* 1:719-26).

■ **2-3** The harsh response by the high priest Ananias (not to be confused with Annas [Acts 4:6]) dashes any glimmer of hope that this meeting may have a positive outcome. His instructions that Paul be struck on the mouth probably indicates disapproval of Paul's opening statement. Such action may not have been out of character for the high priest (AD 47-59), whom Josephus describes as unpopular due to his greed and association with violence (*Ant.* 20.205-13). Ananias' actions are reminiscent of the Jewish council's earlier treatment of the apostles (4:1-21; 5:17-40). Likewise, Paul's rebuttal echoes

Stephen's cutting words at the end of his remarks before the same council and his accusers (→ 7:51-53).

Paul's declaration that **God will strike** (23:3) Ananias takes the form of a Jewish curse that calls for God to "strike" in judgment (e.g., Deut 28:22). In the LXX, the verb *typtō* often refers to God acting in such ways (see, e.g., Exod 8:2; 2 Sam 24:17; Ezek 7:6; 2 Macc 3:39). Since Ananias was murdered by rebels in AD 66 (Josephus, *J.W.* 2.441-42), the curse may also be understood as a prophecy. The sarcastic description of Ananias as a **whitewashed wall** (see Ezek 13:10-16; Matt 23:27-28) is a stinging metaphor comparing him to a wall painted with a cheap coat of paint intended to hide structural flaws. He was an unfit spiritual leader for Israel as the people of God.

Like Stephen (7:53), Paul responds by making an accusation of his own: the high priest *himself* is guilty of ***violating*** the law (*paranomeō*; see Aristotle, *Pol.* 1307b; Plutarch, *Superst.* 3; Johnson 1992, 397). Although Ananias sits in judgment of Paul **according to the law** (*kata ton nomon*), Paul charges him with disobedience against the Mosaic law regarding its protection of the rights of the accused. That law called for the accused to be presumed innocent until proven guilty (Lev 19:15; also *m. Sanh.* 3.6-8).

■ **4-5** Those whom Ananias instructs to strike Paul (v 2) also criticize Paul for his disparaging remarks against the high priest. The verb *loidoreō* typically refers to abusive speech (see John 9:28; 1 Cor 4:12; 1 Pet 2:23; also Exod 17:2; Deut 33:8; 2 Macc 12:14; Josephus, *J.W.* 2.302; Herodotus, *Hist.* 3.145). Surprisingly, Paul quotes Exod 22:28 (although the LXX version does not fit the Jerusalem context) in support of their contention *against* him. *More* surprising is Paul's admission of not recognizing Ananias as high priest, given his priestly garments and his role in leading the Jewish council. How could Paul have failed to recognize the high priest?

A few interpreters suggest that Paul either failed to hear Ananias give the order to have him struck or was unable to see who gave that order due to poor eyesight. But neither finds support with Acts' account of the episode. Others contend that Paul's extended absence from Jerusalem explains his failure to recognize the high priest (Bruce 1988, 427; Fitzmyer 1998, 717; Peterson 2009, 615). Many consider Paul's admission an ironic "prophetic criticism" (Johnson 1992, 397). Ananias' actions (Acts 23:3) are inconsistent with the expected character of the high priest (Marshall 1980, 363-64; Cassidy 1987, 64-65; Wall 2002, 310). However, such an interpretation does not account for the fact that Paul's quotation of Exod 22:28 would still speak *against* his brief tirade against Ananias. Some interpreters note that Paul's admission serves as an apology for his failure to respect Ananias' office when he responds so strongly (Levinsohn 1987, 32; Tannehill 1990, 286; Larkin 1995, 328).

In many respects, the last two options are complementary. On the one hand, the high priest provokes Paul's initial sharp response because he does not follow the guidelines of the Jewish law (Acts 23:3). On the other hand, Paul—as a loyal, faithful Jew who has been taught the Jewish Scriptures—respects the office of the high priest and needs to apologize. By doing so, Luke depicts Paul as not guilty of disrespect (v 4), which parallels earlier charges that Paul renounced the Jewish people, the temple, and the Jewish law (21:28).

■ 6 The second part of Paul's response focuses briefly on his interaction with the two main parties or groups of the council (→ "Behind the Text" for 4:1-22). By introducing himself as both **a Pharisee** and a *son of Pharisees* (2 Cor 11:22; Phil 3:5-6), Paul obviously identifies his ties to one specific group of the council as well as underscores his faithfulness as a Jew (→ Acts 22:3). By claiming that the reason behind the judgments against him is **the hope of the resurrection of the dead**, Paul seems intent on manipulating the council by way of a "divide and conquer" tactic. Luke explains that Sadducees did not believe in resurrection and Pharisees did (v 8). Paul's claim also diverts their attention from the earlier charges against his fidelity as a Jew (21:28) to a central theological issue of his proclamation of the Christian gospel and his witness in subsequent chapters (see 24:15, 21; 26:23). Thus, Luke presents Paul as on trial because he is a proponent for the **hope** of Israel, which he links with resurrection (lit., "hope and resurrection").

Paul does not specifically mention Jesus in connection with his reference to **the resurrection of the dead**. But Lukan readers would clearly recognize such an inference in light of repeated references to the resurrection of Jesus in earlier portions of Acts (e.g., 1:22; 2:24, 31-32; 3:15; 4:2, 10, 33; 5:30; 10:40; 13:30; 17:3, 18, 31-32).

■ 7-8 The **dispute** (*stasis* [15:2; 19:40; 23:7, 10; 24:5; Luke 23:19, 25]) and division (see 14:4) that occur over the resurrection mirror the common Jewish response to the gospel in Acts: some accept it, others do not (cf. Luke 2:35). Luke's explanation makes it clear that the disagreement is theological in nature, due to the Sadducees' rejection of the doctrine of resurrection (since they accepted only the Pentateuch as authoritative).

The additional reference to the Saducean rejection of belief in **angels** or **spirits** (Acts 23:8) is unclear, because (*a*) angels and other spiritual beings are mentioned in the Pentateuch, and (*b*) no other texts refer to the Sadducees' rejection of such beliefs. The most likely explanation is that these refer to beliefs regarding particular modes of postmortem existence either before the resurrection (i.e., in the interim; see Daube 1990, 493-97) or as a result of it (i.e., resurrected *as* an angel or spirit; see Viviano and Taylor 1992, 496-98; Fitzmyer 1998, 719).

■ **9-10** The meeting became so contentious (*kraugē*) that Luke depicts it as similar to the violent commotion of the Jewish mob after Paul addressed them (see *kraugazō* [22:23]). Some from the Pharisees **contend strongly** (imperfect tense: *diemachonto*; Sir 8:1, 3; Josephus, *J.W.* 2.55; *Ant.* 14.475) that they find **nothing wrong** with him (23:9). They declare Paul innocent of the charges brought against him, although Luke offers no bases for their conclusion. Their contention about the possibility of a spirit or angel appearing to Paul—an indirect reference to what happened on the road to Damascus (22:6-11)—would have further provoked the Sadducees, who denied their existence (23:8). The Pharisees do not actually pose a question. They begin a conditional sentence with a protasis (condition) but offer no apodosis (conclusion). Some MSS supply this by adding "let us not fight against God" (echoing 5:39; Metzger 1994, 432).

The Pharisees fail to stimulate any genuine contemplation as to "what if" Paul *had* received divine instruction. The scene, already marked by wild commotion and quarreling, so escalates out of control that Lysias now fears for Paul's safety.

The verb *diaspaō* compares the council's riotous behavior (→ 7:54-60) to the savagery of wild animals to their prey (see Herodotus, *Hist.* 3.13; *1 Clem.* 46:7; also LXX: Judg 14:6; Hos 13:8). It is unclear whether the danger is the result of (a) indirect crossfire from the ferocious theological melee between the Sadducean and Pharisaic factions of the council or (b) mob violence by unsympathetic council members (the Sadducees). In either sense, the Roman commander must intervene on Paul's behalf.

■ **II** Divine visions come at strategic times for Paul in Acts. Some offer direction for his ministry (9:4; 16:9; 22:17); others provide encouragement in the midst of difficult circumstances (18:9-10) or an "agenda" for Paul's future (19:21). This vision not only offers reassurance but also reiterates the divine necessity (*dei*, **must**) for him to go to Rome.

The command **"Take courage!"** (Matt 9:2, 22; 14:27; Mark 6:50; 10:49; John 16:33) or ***"Keep up your courage!"*** (present tense: *tharsei*) was typically associated with announcements of salvation (see Grundmann, *TDNT* 3:25-27). Here, it urges Paul to persevere in the face of the council's opposition. "Certainly after a day like he had had, Paul could use such divine reassurance that what he had hoped to do would come to pass after all" (Witherington 1998, 693).

Both the conjunctions **as . . . so** (*hōs . . . houtō*) and the verb **witness** (*diamartyromai* [Acts 2:40; 8:25; 10:42; 18:5; 20:21, 23-24; 28:23]) reiterate that Paul's ministry would continue in Rome as in Jerusalem, albeit under Roman custody. Nonetheless, such Pauline witness has divine sanction and guidance.

5. Jewish Plots and a Change of Venue (23:12-35)

■ **12-15** The divine vision could not be more timely. Only later (v 16) does Paul receive news of a deadly **conspiracy** ("plot" [v 12 CEB]; lit., a "twisting together"; see 19:40) to kill him, involving over forty Jewish men. The men bind themselves together with a vow (*anathematizō*) to abstain from food or drink until they are successful. The vow invites a divine curse on any who fail to carry out the plot (see LXX: Num 21:2-3; Josh 6:21; also *1 En.* 6:4-5). The repeated outline of the scheme underscores the conspirators' determination to murder Paul.

They probably sought out **the chief priests and the elders** (Acts 23:14) from the council because they would be more amenable to their sinister proposal (Marshall 1980, 367). The conspirators solicit these "partners in crime" merely to deceive the rest of the council and the Roman commander into thinking that they needed to summon Paul again for further legal examination (*diaginōskō*; Lake and Cadbury 1933a, 291). Their devious plan is to catch the unsuspecting Roman soldiers by surprise and **murder** (*anaireō* [v 15]; see v 27; also 2:23; 5:33, 36; 7:28; 9:23-24, 29; 10:39; 12:2; 13:28; 22:20; 25:3; 26:10) Paul as they escort him to the meeting.

■ **16-22** News about the planned **ambush** (23:16; see 25:3; also LXX: Josh 8:7, 9) reached Paul through an unlikely informant—his nephew. Luke offers no additional information about Paul's family, but the presence of relatives in Jerusalem correlates with Paul's prior statement of having been raised in the city (Acts 22:3). How his nephew gained access to the secret information remains a mystery. It seems unlikely that the plot was widely known (against Marshall 1980, 368), since lack of secrecy would jeopardize it. More plausibly, Paul's nephew may have been associated in some way with the Zealot group that hatched the plot (Roloff 1981, 331).

It is even more surprising that this news successfully reaches Paul. Prisoners were often granted access to visitors (see 24:23; 28:17, 30; Phil 2:25; 2 Tim 1:16-17; also *Acts Paul* 18-19; Lucian, *Peregr.* 12-13). But the nephew's visit seems to have been the exception rather than the norm for Paul.

The volatile situation that necessitated keeping Paul in Roman custody apart from the unruly Jewish mobs (Acts 23:9-10; also 22:22-23) made it improbable that the commander would risk a breach in security by granting someone access to him (Rapske 1994b, 149). So Paul summons a centurion assigned to the security detail and requests that his nephew be taken to report the Jewish plot to the Roman commander.

Once the centurion explains the reason for bringing Paul's nephew to Lysias, the commander speaks privately with the **young man** (23:19). The report from Paul's nephew of the Jews' plan to request a formal hearing regarding Paul's case (v 20) echoes the conspirators' own words (→ v 15). In both instances, the stated reason is a **pretext** (v 20) for their murderous design. The young man's warning (v 21) repeats the narrator's basic outline of the plot (vv 12-14). Both agree that the Jewish conspirators assume the Roman commander would become an unwitting accomplice and agree (*promise, epangelia*) to do as they requested.

Lysias' dismissal of Paul's nephew (v 22) creates suspense. Although readers should not be surprised that the commander does not question the report, he also states nothing about how he may respond. The verb *emphanizō* (referring to the reporting of the plot) is the same one used earlier when the schemers described what the chief priests and elders were to tell the commander (v 15). Ironically, Lysias has indeed been informed, but not as the conspirators hoped (see Pervo 2009, 582).

■ **23-24** The commander's prompt summons and orders of two centurions indicate that he takes the report seriously and understands the gravity of the threats against Paul. His plan—to counter the Jewish plot—would send Paul to **Caesarea** (v 23; → 8:40; 10:1—11:18; 21:8-16). The number of Roman military personnel assigned to accompany Paul may seem inflated in comparison to the band of forty conspirators. It should not have required nearly half the Roman soldiers under Lysias' command to form the security detail to protect and escort one prisoner out of town. These extreme security measures highlight not so much Paul's importance (against Conzelmann 1987, 194; Lentz 1993, 15), as they call attention to the dangerous and volatile situation within a city opposed to the Christian missionary. This imposing military force would escort Paul out of town under the cover of darkness to ensure his deliverance.

■ **25-30** The purpose in sending Paul to the capital Caesarea was to have his case heard by the Roman governor Felix. The accompanying **letter** (23:25) provides the official documentation for transferring Paul to the governor's authority. However, the letter also has a literary function (→ sidebar "Embedded Letters in Ancient Narratives" with 15:22-23*a*). It reviews Paul's situation. Thus, features such as a thanksgiving, official transfer of the prisoner, and farewell are omitted (Pervo 2009, 584). The letter's opening reveals for the only time in Acts the commander's name as Claudius Lysias. It describes the Jews' capture (*syllambanō*; see 1:16; 12:3; 26:21) of Paul and attempt to **murder** (*anaireō* [23:27]; → v 15) him.

The letter mentions nothing about the major disturbance at the temple just before these actions, which would have reflected unfavorably on the commander's ability to maintain law and order. The commander underscores how his intervention **rescued** (*exaireō* [v 27]; 7:10, 34; 12:11; 26:17) Paul from his would-be murderers. His declaration about taking protective measures because of Paul's Roman citizenship enhances Lysias' role as an effective military official. But he fails to mention that he ordered Paul to be flogged, from which Roman citizens were exempt (→ 22:24-29).

This section (23:27-29) conflates the broader picture that begins with Paul's capture at the temple (21:27-36) and extends Paul's appearance before the Jewish council. The latter incident also required the commander's intervention (*strateuma* [v 27]; see v 10) to save Paul's life (23:6-10). It is possible that Lysias' reference may have this second incident in view.

The general review of Lysias taking Paul before the Jewish council to seek clarity about the **charge** (*aitia* [23:28]; 13:28; 22:24; 25:18, 27; 28:18) against him parallels Luke's earlier account (→ 22:30—23:10). But he mentions nothing about the riotous outburst of the Jewish council (23:6-10).

For the first time in Acts, he offers his opinion regarding Paul and his legal troubles. Like Gallio (the governor of Achaia), Lysias concludes that the accusations against Paul are **questions** about Jewish law (*zētēmatōn tou vomou autōn*; see 18:15). These are consistent with the earlier complaints against Paul (21:28). But these questions do not explicitly play out in the last council meeting. Lysias' declaration that Paul has done nothing to deserve **death or imprisonment** reveals he found no evidence that implicated Paul of any politically criminal activity.

The letter ends abruptly with an awkward attempt to offer two explanations for sending Paul to the governor (v 30).

First, the commander explains the reason for sending Paul to the governor: the disclosure of a secret **plot** (*epiboulē*; see 9:24; 20:3, 19) against the prisoner (→ 23:18-21). Why this course of action is preferable over other possible options is unclear.

Second, Lysias also explains that he has ordered Paul's **accusers** (v 30; 25:18) to bring their case against him before the governor. This seems problematic, since such orders could expose his own secret mission (23:22) and potentially jeopardize Paul's safe arrival in Caesarea. But the mention of such orders in the letter probably anticipates what Lysias would tell Paul's opponents *after* the completed mission to Caesarea and future legal hearings (see Haenchen 1971, 648; Conzelmann 1987, 195; Pervo 2009, 585).

■ **31-35** The first stage in escorting Paul to Caesarea takes the soldiers out of Jerusalem by night to **Antipatris** (v 31). Herod the Great rebuilt this city on the coastal plain in 9 BC and renamed it after his father Antipater. This crossroad town was about halfway between the holy city and the capital city (see Josephus, *J.W.* 1.99; *Ant.* 13.390). The journey of 35 to 40 miles (56 to 64 km) northwest could not be completed overnight with soldiers traveling by foot (against Witherington 1998, 697-98; Barrett 1998, 1086). Most of the military entourage, except for seventy horsemen, returned **the next day** (v 32; see v 23) probably at daybreak. The danger against Paul was from an ambush *within* Jerusalem. The secret but massive military mission has been successful, allowing for the return of most personnel.

The **cavalry** (v 33) would complete the initial stage of the journey to Antipatris later that day. From there, they continue north to Caesarea with Paul, probably at a faster pace without the slower foot soldiers. The second stage of the mission involved a 25- to 30-mile (40- to 48-km) journey. Upon completing the journey, they **delivered the letter** from Lysias and *presented* their prisoner to the governor Felix.

Felix, the Roman Governor

Surprisingly, the Roman governor to whom Paul was sent in Caesarea was not of noble birth, as was usual. Antonius Felix was a Roman freedman, probably emancipated like his brother Pallas by Antonia, the mother of the emperor Claudius. Felix's brother was an influential friend of both Claudius and Nero. That connection and Claudius' reputation for giving power to freedmen (see Suetonius, *Claud.* 28) are likely reasons for Felix's appointment to the position over the regions of provinces of Judea, Samaria, Galilee, and Perea.

Despite his prominent connections, Felix's tenure as governor (ca. AD 52-60) was marred by cruelty and ineptness as a ruler. He ruthlessly suppressed numerous Jewish uprisings against the Romans during this time. As a result, he alienated many moderate Jews and provoked additional unrest (see Josephus, *J.W.* 2.252-70; *Ant.* 20.160-72). He exercised his official powers as a king with the mind of a slave (see Tacitus, *Hist.* 5.9).

Given Felix's reputation, readers of Acts should not be surprised by the treatment Paul later received from him (→ 24:24-26). He was unable to control tensions between Jewish and Gentile factions within his jurisdiction. A significant number of Jews shed their blood during his reign. This may account for the strong Jewish protests sent to Rome against Felix after his recall (see 24:27; Josephus, *Ant.* 20.182; *J.W.* 2.266-70).

The governor's inquiry about Paul's home province probably seeks clarification about legal jurisdiction. Should his case be handled in Caesarea (the capital of the province where the alleged crime occurred) or in **Cilicia** (v 34), the province where Tarsus was located (21:39; 22:3) and the homeland of the charged prisoner? Felix answered to the Roman official responsible for Cilicia. He chose to hear Paul's case rather than pass it off to his superior.

Paul's accusers already had made plans to travel to Caesarea to charge him formally (see 23:30). Roman law required defendants to respond in their own defense, so expedience may have been the reason for keeping the hearing there (see Tajra 1989, 116-17; Witherington 1998, 701-2). While awaiting the arrival of those accusers so the hearing could begin, Paul was kept in custody in **Herod's palace** (v 35). This served as the official residence and administrative headquarters for Roman governors of Judea since AD 6. Here, there were also facilities to hold prisoners awaiting hearings (see Rapske 1994b, 155-58).

FROM THE TEXT

The struggles and subsequent legal troubles Paul endured in Jerusalem now dominate the narrative landscape. From Luke's perspective, nothing else matters! Thus, in a manner reminiscent of Jesus' story, Paul's life hung in the balance. Like Jesus, he alone faced Jewish leaders and even mobs of fellow Jews who viciously sought to kill him. However, this Lukan account of intra-Jewish conflict underscores two fundamental, theological issues.

First is the identity of the "people of God." The hostilities against Paul from various Jewish groups in Jerusalem were over questions about him as a faithful Jew. Such questions arose because Paul's mission and message extended beyond the Jewish people and were inclusive of Gentiles, something Jewish believers in Jerusalem *themselves* seemed to endorse earlier (15:6-29). Although the decree from the Jerusalem church to the Gentile believers affirmed the latter without requiring them to convert to Judaism, their identity as the covenant people of God still remained ambiguous.

The reason for this is both simple and complex. James' letter on behalf of Jerusalem believers (→ ch 15) treated Gentile converts as repentant Jews. But this was not how "official Judaism" viewed them. The institutions of Judaism (the temple of Jerusalem and the synagogues of the Diaspora) did not condone new ideas about the "people of God" that diminished the covenant by downplaying the role of Jewish law for Gentiles. Such issues were behind the Jewish antagonism against Paul at the temple (21:27-36) and afterward as he addressed the angry mob (22:17-24). But even Jerusalem *believers* questioned Paul on similar points (21:18-26). Some of them may have participated in the riot in which Paul was seized and dragged out of the temple (21:30-31; → sidebar "How Did the Jerusalem Church Respond to Paul?" with 21:30-33).

So how is it that the Jerusalem church came to question Paul's approach to ministry among Jews and Gentiles? If the rejection of Paul and his ministry by the institutions of Judaism forced him to minister in other contexts, that departure may have been perceived as apostasy, not only by the Jewish people in general but even by those Jewish believers in Jerusalem (→ 21:21; cf. 19:9; against Johnson 1992, 378). That is, theirs would be a theological tension over what it means to be the people of God, and included here would be questions about covenant and the role of the Jewish law. Luke never depicts Paul as blatantly violating the Jewish law, but his "forced" departure from the synagogue—where the Jewish law was read and studied—still throws into question what its ongoing role and significance might be for Paul (and, therefore, for the church).

The narrator leaves such matters open. On the one hand, Acts repeatedly affirms the continuity between the Jewish traditions and the Christian movement: God's promises and purposes to Israel are fulfilled in the church. On the other hand, the pragmatic, practical issues of the earliest Christians still remain, especially where the world of the Jewish believers in Jerusalem converge with the realities that come with a gospel message inclusive of all peoples.

Second is the will of God in relation to Paul's mission and message. The repeated theme throughout this section is that God's ultimate purposes both defined Paul's proclamation and guided his ministry. His speech before the hostile Jewish crowd offers no defense (see 22:1) against the accusations against him (21:27-28). Instead, he offers his personal testimony of God's intervention in his own life (22:3-21). Twice in this section are mentioned appearances by Jesus (or the Lord; 22:17-21; 23:11), who offers Paul specific, verbal guidance or assurance about his future ministry in the face of opposition against that ministry. Such instances of divine guidance are noteworthy, since the opposition came from pious, religious people.

Paul's Jewish opponents would probably have insisted they also followed God's leading by obeying the Jewish law. And yet, they repeatedly attempted to kill Paul in violation of one of the most revered commandments (see Gaventa 2003, 322-23). Conversely, there is something convincing about the simple story of a person whose life's direction was changed and whose ministry was guided by God. Throughout these various scenes in Jerusalem, Luke repeatedly returns readers to the simple fact that the God of Israel was behind this inclusive understanding of the "people of God" that defined the ministry for which Paul was now charged.

C. Paul's Defense of His Ministry in Caesarea (24:1—26:32)

BEHIND THE TEXT

Throughout Acts, numerous scenes depict apostles or Christian preachers facing scrutiny for their actions or message and responding to challenges lodged against them. Some questions arose out of curiosity or lack of understanding. Examples include Pentecost (2:1-41), the healing of the crippled man by Peter and John at the temple (3:1-26), and a similar healing by Paul in Lystra (14:8-18). In other episodes, they faced formal complaints—sometimes legal charges. Sometimes, these complaints came from religious authorities defending religious institutions (4:1-22; 5:1-42; 6:8—7:1; 22:30—23:10).

Earlier in Paul's ministry, legal charges sometimes challenged the compatibility of the Christian mission to the empire within the Roman legal system (16:16-40; 17:5-9, 16-33; 18:12-16). However, in such instances, the legal proceedings were not accentuated. It is unclear whether Paul's appearance before the Areopagus was a legal hearing or a trial. The narrative is motivated by other than legal purposes. They simply "retell" what happened in the interest of these other concerns.

This is also so in the narrative telling of Paul's trials or hearings before Roman officials. The narrative setting is clearly the Roman trial or courtroom scene. But interpreters should not confuse the Lukan depiction of Paul's trials with complete, historical accounts of "what happened." These scenes are more detailed than prior instances, but they still use only limited legal vocabulary and summaries of those hearings. Their real concern is to tell gripping stories that underscore differences between the Jewish plaintiffs and Paul the defendant (see Brown 1996, 319-32; Schwartz 2003, 105-33). These scenes function to evaluate Paul's story within the broader narrative of Acts. This section "is an untechnical account with apologetic motive" (Cadbury 1933b, 298).

Nonetheless, features of the trial scenes correlate with what we know of the general characteristics of the Roman legal process. A Roman trial typically began with the plaintiffs bringing their case in the presence of the accused. However, Roman law also stipulated that those who initially pressed charges must persist in their role as personal witnesses against the accused. Dire consequences followed their failure to do so (Sherwin-White 1963, 52-53). The accused also had the right to a defense against all charges. Finally, the judge would declare a verdict after considering the facts of the case and the social status of the parties involved.

The party with stronger social credentials enjoyed distinct advantages in the Roman legal system, so both parties tried to gain the upper hand (see Rapske 1994b, 158-59). Often, one party sought an advantage by retaining the services of someone as a legal representative during the trial. Such a person, as the Greek term *rhētōr* ("orator") indicates, possessed skills in speaking persuasively and perhaps other juridical expertise. In some cases, this representative lent his own superior status to those he represented. A common rhetorical means of gaining advantage and favor was through the use of complimentary or flattering remarks in the opening of a speech, known as the *captatio benevolentiae* (→ sidebar "Roman Forensic Speeches" with 24:1).

IN THE TEXT

I. Paul's Trial before Felix (24:1-27)

a. The Charges against Paul (24:1-9)

■ I The arrival of the Jerusalem delegation who would press charges signified the beginning of the formal legal process (see 23:34). The short period of time needed for their appearance in Caesarea—only **five days** after the military escort delivered Paul to Felix—indicates the importance of this case for the Jewish leaders, who wished to rid themselves of Paul (Longenecker 1981, 537, contends the time was from Paul's arrest).

By including both the **high priest Ananias** (23:2-5) and some **elders** (likely members of the Jewish council; see 4:5, 8, 23; 23:14), the delegation itself was comprised of prominent Jewish leaders who would exceed Paul in social standing (except for Paul's Roman citizenship; see Rapske 1994b, 158-59). Accompanying them is their legal representative (*rhētōr*), Tertullus. He may not have been Jewish, but in speaking on behalf of the Jewish delegation, would speak in the first-person plural representing their position (see vv 5-6). He is expected to provide a formal explanation of the charges (*emphanizō*; see 25:2, 15; also 23:15, 22) to the governor Felix.

Roman Forensic Speeches

Rhetorical handbooks from the first century AD, notably from Quintilian and Cicero, discussed the various components of speeches delivered in Roman courtrooms or trial settings and their importance. In general, such speeches were comprised of the following parts:

- The *exordium* is the opening remarks of a speech. It introduces the case, includes the *captatio benevolentiae* (flattering comments intended to gain the favor of whoever was hearing the case), and describes how the speaker wishes to proceed.
- The *narratio* portion of the speech states the facts of the case against the accused. This includes a thorough description of all charges.
- The *partitio* or *divisio* outlines the remainder of the speech in light of the specific charges of the case. However, defense speeches omitted this part.
- The *probatio* or *confirmatio* portion of the speech provides the evidence proving the charges, including the calling of witnesses to substantiate them.
- The *refutatio* counters arguments or answers questions anticipated from the accused.
- The concluding part of the speech, the *peroratio* or *epilogue*, brings the speech to a close. A skilled rhetorician was expected to end with a moving rhetorical flourish.

The evaluation of Roman juridical speeches starts with these "building blocks" of such speeches. Although interpreters often disagree where one part ends and another begins, interpretation includes the recognition and assessment of each part of the speech as well as noting any part that may be omitted (see Kennedy 1980, 90-96).

■ **2-4** Roman law required the presence of the accused for a trial. So Paul was summoned before the proceedings began. Luke describes **Tertullus** (v 2) as beginning his accusations against Paul (*kategoreō*; see vv 8, 13, 19; also 22:30; 25:5, 11, 16; 28:19; Luke 6:7; 23:2, 10, 14).

But Tertullus opens his speech with flattering praise of the governor (see Cicero, *De or.* 2.79.324; Winter 1991, 505-31). The mention of the Jewish nation enjoying **much peace** due to Felix's reign seems to be exaggerated, given his reputation (→ sidebar "Felix, the Roman Governor" with 23:31-35). Still, he was responsible for suppressing many uprisings, including the rebellion of an Egyptian false prophet and his forces (21:38; see Josephus, *J.W.* 2.261-63; Winter 1993, 318; Marshall 1980, 351). Tertullus' accolades for the governor's **foresight,** which highlights the ruler's providence and benevolence on behalf of the people, parallels common praise directed to Roman rulers (Winter 1993, 316-19). The emphasis of such qualities in Felix is appropriate for the case at hand, as these activities linked to Felix and his administration stand in sharp contrast to Paul and the activities to which Tertullus will attempt to link him (vv 5-6).

Tertullus concludes his opening comments by noting the brevity of his remarks. This notation resembles what typical speeches to judges or other officials of that era also included (see Quintilian, *Inst.* 4.1.34, 62; 8.3.82). By stating that he does not wish to keep ("detain" [v 4 NRSV]) the governor from more important business (*enkoptō* connotes hindering someone), the spokesman for the Jews sets a favorable tone for the remainder of the speech.

Tertullus requests Felix listen with his customary "kindness" (NASB; "graciousness" [NRSV]). *Epieikeia* refers to someone who not only is especially reasonable and fair but also can evaluate facts and situations beyond the strict definitions and codes of the law (Preisker, *TDNT* 2:588-90; BDAG 2000, 371; Johnson 1992, 410). In the LXX, this refers to the disposition of God (Ps 86:5; Bar 2:27; 2 Macc 2:22; 10:4) and of those who reflect God's character (Wis 2:19; 3 Macc 3:15; 7:6). Ironically, Tertullus may have appropriated this term because his case against Paul was weak and needed Felix's willingness to be "flexible" in evaluating it in light of Roman law (see Barrett 1998, 1096; Witherington 1998, 707; Peterson 2009, 631).

■ **5-9** As the prosecutor Tertullus directs the governor's attention to the charges at hand, he characterizes Paul in contrast to his flattering description of Felix (v 2). He is a destabilizing force, threatening the peace for which the empire prided itself. Tertullus mentions four things about Paul.

First, he describes Paul not merely as a **troublemaker** (v 5) but as someone who is "pestilent" (NRSV). The noun *loimos* characterizes him metaphorically as a disease that threatens the health and welfare of the empire (see LSJ 1996, 1060; BDAG 2000, 602; Demosthenes, *1 Aristog.* 80; 1 Macc 10:61; 15:21).

Second, Tertullus accuses Paul of instigating **riots** or sedition (*stasis*; see 19:40; 23:7, 10; Luke 23:19, 25) *among all Jews throughout the empire*. This

376

also contrasts Paul with the peace-advancing Felix (Acts 24:2; 16:20; 17:6-7; 18:12; 19:26-27; 21:28). The charge is reminiscent of the accusation against Jesus (see Luke 23:2). The charge may be exaggerated, but it is more accurate than previous rumors (Acts 21:21). It could also link to the negative Jewish responses toward Paul in numerous cities throughout the empire (see 13:45, 50; 14:2-5; 17:5-9, 13; 18:6, 12-17; 19:9, 23-41; 20:19).

A charge of sedition was considered most effective and appropriate in criminal proceedings (Winter 1993, 320; see *Rhet. Her.* 2.3.3-4; Cicero, *Inv.* 2.5.16—8.28). Felix had executed other Jews for suspected rebellious activities against the empire. This claim places Paul within such notorious company.

Third, Tertullus describes Paul as the **ringleader** of the *sect of the Nazarenes*. Sect (*hairesis*) was used earlier in Acts in a more neutral way to describe Sadducees or Pharisees as "parties" or "schools" within Judaism (5:17; 15:5; see 26:5; see Josephus, *J.W.* 2.119; *Ant.* 13.171). However, since the spokesman for the Jews uses the term in an accusatory fashion here, the more pejorative sense of the term seems to apply (see also 24:14).

The term **Nazarenes** in the plural appears only here in the NT. Elsewhere in Acts, it refers to Jesus as the one who came from Nazareth (see 2:22; 3:6; 4:10; 6:14; 22:8; 26:9). It also correlates with the Hebrew root *nṣr* that was often associated with keeping the Torah (see Barrett 1998, 1098; Schaeder, *TDNT* 4:874-79). Of course, the irony here is that Paul was faithfully observing the Jewish law when the trouble erupted at the temple, which contradicts what Tertullus next describes about him.

Fourth, Tertullus alleges that Paul attempted to **desecrate** the Jewish temple in Jerusalem (24:6). The charge echoes 21:28 but in different language. He uses the secular verb *bebēloō* rather than *koinoō* to refer to defilement of the temple (see Matt 12:5; in LXX: Ps 74:7; Ezek 28:18; 2 Macc 8:2), since he addresses a Gentile (see Lake and Cadbury 1933a, 299). For Judaism, the defilement of the temple and of the Sabbath was especially scandalous and intolerable. But Rome was the protector of the temple as a holy site (see Josephus, *J.W.* 6.128). So anyone who acted against the temple was at odds with Rome.

The response to Paul's alleged actions, as Tertullus describes them to Felix (Acts 24:6), contradicts both the letter from Lysias (23:27) and the Lukan account of what occurred (21:30-36). Tertullus contends that *the Jews*, not Lysias, **seized** Paul as a legitimate arrest for the crimes he had committed. He claims that the Jews stopped Paul from creating sedition! Conveniently, he says nothing of the violent mob scene the Jews created, which prompted the Roman intervention.

Verses 6b-8a of ch 24, which appear in some MSS including the Western text, are probably an addition that attempts to explain Tertullus' remarks about the Jews' capture of Paul (see Metzger 1994, 434). Without these verses,

ACTS

24:5-9

377

the orator's speech turns to its conclusion (*peroratio*) and a call for the governor to interrogate Paul for himself (v 8). However, this leaves the speech with a notable omission of the *probatio*, the section that would offer proofs for the charges, including witnesses. This was the one essential part of the forensic speech (see Quintilian, *Inst.* 5).

The omission of substantiating proof implies both a poor speech and a weak case against Paul. Interestingly, the added verses offer a different and erroneous perspective: that the commander Lysias intervened in a manner that was not his concern or jurisdiction (i.e., the Jewish law). Further, they claim that *he* responded with "great violence" so that the problem with Paul was taken "out of [Jewish] hands." They allege that *he* was responsible for Paul's accusers coming before the governor. This additional information also provides the one needed for interrogation as an adequate witness: *the commander Lysias*. However, the examination (*anakrinomai*) typically refers to the interrogation of prisoners, not Roman officials (see Barrett 1998, 1100). So these verses do not fit the context, and the speech should be interpreted with this section omitted.

Surprisingly, Tertullus concludes his speech without offering any substantive proof or calling any witnesses. Standard legal procedure would have included the judge interrogating the defendant publicly, as Tertullus invites Felix to do. But he rests his case on what the governor *himself* will find out from Paul. The response from **the Jews** (v 9)—presumably the representatives from Jerusalem to press charges against Paul (v 1)—echoes what their spokesman just presented. They contribute nothing new, but merely add their voices to Tertullus' (*synepitithēmi*; see LXX: Deut 32:27; Ps 3:7) in making the assertions about Paul, much like the crowds did when Jesus was before Pilate (see Luke 23:10, 18, 21, 23). *Phaskō* refers to claims about which the speakers have confidence (but which may not be true). So Luke hints that these complaints about Paul are unreliable, which readers of Acts should also recognize.

b. The Defense by Paul (24:10-21)

■ **10** Rather than question Paul himself, Felix gestures for Paul to speak on his own behalf. Unlike Tertullus, Paul gives much less attention to offering praise to the governor. The reference to Felix's **many years** as **judge over this nation** reiterates the governor's experience in and knowledge of matters relating to the Jewish people (AD 52-57). This may be why Paul **gladly** offers his **defense** (*apologeomai*; see Haenchen 1971, 654, who identifies this as the "catchword of these last chapters") before him. The absence of additional compliments, particularly relating to the Roman peace, suggests that Paul's defense will be that he did nothing to put the peace of the Roman Empire at risk (see Gaventa 2003, 326).

■ 11-13 In the *narratio* portion of Paul's speech, he clarifies the facts of the case and offers his rebuttal to the charges (vv 11-18). He first takes up Tertullus' own words that Felix "can learn everything" (*dynēsē . . . epignōnai*) about the case (v 8) by repeating that the governor "can learn" (*dynamenou sou epignōnai*) what Paul had done (see Tannehill 1990, 298).

However, Paul focuses generally on his own activities of worship in Jerusalem (21:18-26), since the governor had jurisdiction only over that city (not other places in the empire where Paul ministered). His was the pilgrimage of a devout Jew. The specific reference to **no more than twelve days ago** (24:11) raises chronological questions (→ sidebar "The Twelve Days and Paul's Defense" below). But the inference is that there was not sufficient time for Paul to do the seditious things of which Tertullus accuses him.

The Twelve Days and Paul's Defense

The reference to "twelve days" during Paul's defense before Felix (24:11) does not easily reconcile with other chronological markers within the Lukan account of Paul's arrival and subsequent arrest in Jerusalem. The seven days of Paul's purification ritual in Jerusalem (21:27) and the five days required for the arrival in Caesarea of Paul's prosecution party from Jerusalem (24:1) alone account for twelve days (see Lake and Cadbury 1933a, 300). How many days did the other activities Luke mentions in chs 22 and 23 occupy?

Interpreters generally agree that these "twelve days" refer to Paul's time in Jerusalem and end with his arrival in Caesarea (see, e.g., Schlatter 1948, 285; Haenchen 1971, 654; Bruce 1988, 443; Barrett 1998, 1102). These chronologies do not consider the possibility that Paul's transfer from Jerusalem to Caesarea took more than one full day (→ 23:31-35). But if Paul arrived in Jerusalem one day later than these accounts suggest (21:18 vs. 21:17), this results in the following adapted chronology:

> Day 1: Paul with the Jerusalem church leaders (21:18-25)
> Days 2-7: Paul's purification ritual at the temple (21:26)
> Day 8: Paul's last (seventh) day of ritual, attack at the temple, and arrest by Roman soldiers (21:27—22:29)
> Day 9: Paul before the Jewish council (22:30—23:11)
> Day 10: Discovery of the Jewish plot; Paul escorted from Jerusalem (23:12-31)
> Days 11-12: Paul taken and delivered to Felix in Caesarea (23:32-35)

Tertullus claims that Paul's accusers "found" (*heurontes*) him (v 5) engaged in socially disruptive activity. Paul contends that they *never found* (*heuron*) him **arguing** (*dialegomai* [v 12]; see 17:2, 17; 18:4, 19; 19:8, 9; 20:7, 9) with others at the temple or **stirring up a crowd** anywhere in the holy city. This is consistent with Acts' narration of his activities in *Jerusalem*. In *other* cities, however, Paul's activities often ended in such trouble (see, e.g., 17:1-9; 18:5-17). Apparently, Paul did not preach in Jerusalem. Thus, by denying the charges, Paul contends that his accusers have not fulfilled the burden of proof. The verb *paristēmi* can have a legal sense of providing sufficient cause for proof (see 1:3; 4:10; also Epictetus, *Diatr.* 2.26.4; Josephus, *Ant.* 4.47; *Life* 27).

■ **14-16** Paul does not legally ***confess*** (*homologeō* [v 14]) guilt regarding any alleged charge Tertullus raised. But surprisingly he admits to something the orator *has* declared about him—that which was not a crime—as a strategic move. Returning to Tertullus' own words describing the Christian movement as a **sect**, Paul makes a confession of faith: that he lives ***according to the Way*** (see 9:2; 18:25; 19:9, 23; 22:4). That confession—**I worship** [*latreuō*; see 7:7, 42; 26:7] **the God of our ancestors**—echoes 22:3 and resembles similar expressions found in other speeches in Acts (3:13; 5:30; 7:32; see 13:17).

Because of the theocentric character of this confession, Paul's accusers should have affirmed his message. In essence, Paul declares his faithfulness to the God of Israel (see Schneider 1982, 348). First, he affirms his belief in all that Israel's Scriptures declare (24:14*b*; see 13:15; 28:23; Luke 16:16; 24:44). Second, he asserts that he, too, like his accusers, has a **hope in God** (v 15), which he then defines in terms of a coming **resurrection** of the **righteous** and ***unrighteous*** (see 3:20-21; 23:6; cf. Dan 12:1-3; Rev 20:11-15).

The unrighteous are typically not mentioned with regard to resurrection. Their inclusion suggests them being raised for judgment (see Acts 24:25; Peterson 2009, 637; Schnabel 2012, 959). It is unclear whether Paul's accusers held the same view as he regarding the resurrection. The Sadducees rejected any belief in resurrection (see 23:6; Josephus, *J.W.* 2.165; *Ant.* 18.16). The elders who accompanied Ananias to Caesarea may not have been Sadducees (→ 23:6, 14). However, Paul's point may be that **hope in God** was central to the Jewish faith, regardless of the "sect" or "party" to which one belonged. Because of this confession of faith (24:14-15), Paul claims that he keeps himself constantly (*dia pantos*) in training (*askeō*; see Windisch, *TDNT* 1:494-96; Tannehill 1990, 300; Barrett 1998, 1106). As a result, he has developed a **conscience** (v 16; see 23:1) that is ***stable*** (lit., "not stumbling"; *aproskopos*) before God and others.

■ **17-18** Paul has shifted the focus of the proceedings from political charges to theological matters. So he explains the motives for his latest trip to Jerusalem (vv 11-12). The duration of ***many years*** since Paul's previous visit to the holy city likely refers to the time period since the nebulous visit of 18:22 (or of ch 15).

But the reason for the latest visit was twofold. On the one hand, the latter reason—**to present offerings** (24:17)—corresponds with Paul's participation in the purification ritual at the temple (21:26). Readers realize that nothing in the earlier account suggests he planned that specific religious observance (see Haenchen 1971, 655; Barrett 1998, 1108; Pervo 2009, 599).

Most interpreters see the former reason—*to present alms to my nation*—as a reference to the collection for the poor mentioned in the Pauline letters. In addition to the good reasons already given for not reading that information into Acts (→ sidebar "Interpreting Acts 20—21 in the Absence of Paul's Collection for the Poor" with 20:4-6), Paul indicates here that these *alms* (→ 3:2-3 and 9:36) were given to the Jewish people in general, not merely to Jewish Christians. Paul's comments focus specifically on his acts of piety, marking him as a worshipful, faithful Jewish pilgrim.

Thus, Paul counters Tertullus' accusation about desecrating the temple (24:6). Although persons "found" (*heuron*; vv 5, 12) him in the temple, he had actually been **ritually cleansed** (perfect passive participle: *hēgnismenon*). Thus, he caused no defilement there (see 21:26-29). Paul insists he was found with neither a **crowd** nor **disturbance** (*thorybos*). It was the Jewish crowd (21:27, 34, 35) that accused him of wrongdoing (21:27-29) and created the "uproar" (*thorybos* [21:34]). Luke depicts Paul as on trial for worshiping God and upholding the faith of Israel!

■ **19-21** To this point, Paul has not identified his original accusers. Now he names them as *some Jews from Asia* (24:19; → 21:27). Like a legal expert, he insists upon proper Roman judicial procedure: *those* accusers must appear before the governor as proof of the charges against him, as Roman law required (see Appian, *Bell. civ.* 3.54; Dio Cassius, *Hist.* 60.28.6; Suetonius, *Claud.* 15.2). Paul contends that the trial itself is improper due to lack of proof for the charges (see Schwartz 2003, 130).

At the very least, Paul asks that those pressing charges against him would identify his specific **crime** (*adikēma* [v 20]; see 18:14; → 23:1-10). Knowing that the Sanhedrin did not find him guilty of anything, he returns to the topic of the **resurrection of the dead** (24:21) as the only reason for his trial. He concludes his remarks by showing that (*a*) the Jews had no proof against him regarding the charges of disrupting Roman peace and desecrating the temple, and (*b*) the only issue in question was theological in nature, not political (see 23:6, 29).

c. The Response from Felix (24:22-27)

■ **22-23** Luke provides no explanation for Felix's adjournment of the trial proceedings. Such delays in trial scenes, however, were quite common in Greek novels. The suspense and additional time provide strategic opportunities for other meetings between key characters (see Schwartz 2003, 130). The comparative description of Felix as **knowing those things about the Way more accurately** (*akribesteron eidōs ta peri tēs hodou* [v 22]) suggests his knowledge to be better than that of Paul's accusers. This may imply his recognition that the charges were false.

Luke does not indicate how Felix acquired his knowledge of the Christian movement. Many interpreters suggest his Jewish wife, Drusilla (→ sidebar "Drusilla, the Wife of Felix" with 24:24-26) as the one who informed the governor (v 24; e.g., Krodel 1986, 441; Johnson 1992, 414; Fitzmyer 1998, 739). But a more plausible explanation is that Paul's trial speech convinced him (Witherington 1998, 713; Parsons 2008, 328).

The comment by Felix that he would decide the case after consulting Lysias may have been his attempt to check out the details from the case with the only "independent witness" available to him (see Rapske 1994b, 164). Both Tertullus and Paul raise points during the trial that the letter from Lysias does not address.

What first appears to be somewhat promising for Paul, however, turns sour. There is no mention of any meeting between Felix and the Roman commander. The governor's subsequent hopes that he may secure a bribe from his prisoner (v 26) with presumed financial resources at his disposal (see v 17) thwart any such promise of a fair hearing.

The orders from Felix to the centurion that there be some relaxation in Paul's custody (v 23) should not be associated with Felix's views about the case (against Haenchen 1971, 658; Dunn 1996, 315). The provision of **some freedom** within his military confinement included allowing Paul's friends to care for his basic needs. This allowed the governor's administration to be less responsible for the mundane needs of another prisoner (Rapske 1994b, 167-72).

■ **24-26** Interpreters generally see the subsequent summons of Paul for a private meeting with Felix and his wife, Drusilla, as a hopeful sign of openness. The Western text adds an explanation for Drusilla's role: she "asked to see Paul and listen to the word" (see Metzger 1994, 435).

Drusilla, the Wife of Felix

The only information Luke provides about Drusilla, the wife of Felix, is that she was Jewish and with her husband when Paul shared the gospel with them. Drusilla's story—including how she came to be married to the governor—provides some useful background information for understanding some of the interaction between Paul and Felix.

Drusilla was the youngest daughter of Agrippa I (12:1-4, 19-23; see Josephus, *Ant.* 18.132; *J.W.* 2.220) and the sister of Agrippa II and Bernice (25:13—26:32). Known for her beauty, an initial engagement arranged by her father failed after his death (AD 44) when her future husband reneged on his agreement to convert to Judaism. She later married Azizus, king of Syrian Emesa (AD 53), after his circumcision.

Felix was so enthralled by Drusilla that he sent a Jewish friend named Atomus, who claimed to have magical powers, to "convince" her to divorce her husband and marry him instead (Josephus, *Ant.* 20.139-44). By doing so, she violated Jewish law through adultery.

The different setting provides ample opportunity for Paul to change roles, from apologist to prophet (see Spencer 2004a, 231). Paul does not mention Jesus in his defense speech. His purpose then was to depict himself as a faithful Jew (vv 10-21). In this private audience with the governor and his wife, however, he addresses **faith in Christ Jesus**, that is, the gospel (see, e.g., 3:16; 9:42; 10:43; 11:17; 16:31; 18:8; 20:21). The specific topics Paul discusses (*dialegomai*; → 17:2) are appropriate for his conversation partners.

The term translated **righteousness** (*dikaiosynē* [24:25]; 10:35; 13:10; 17:31) has limited usage in Acts but may connote right character (of divine or human justice; see Schrenk, *TDNT* 2:174-225).

The term translated **self-control** (*enkrateia*; Gal 5:23; 2 Pet 1:6; see Titus 1:8) refers to having mastery over oneself, particularly over passions and pleasures (see Plato, *Resp.* 390b, 430c; Aristotle, *Eth. nic.* 7.1.4, 7.5.9). These two virtues were linked in second-century Christian teachings (Pervo 2006, 266-68).

The introduction of the **judgment to come** indicates that God would hold humans accountable for living out these virtues as faithful expressions of the Christian gospel. Terror grips Felix (as the adjective *emphobos* suggests; see 10:4; Luke 24:5, 37). This indicates that Paul's message convicts him, perhaps due to the injustice of his reign and his personal indiscretions (with Drusilla being an obvious example). In the end, it is easier to dismiss the messenger than heed Paul's call to repent.

Luke depicts Felix as both open and resistant to the gospel and the Christian movement. However, his comment about Felix's hope for a **bribe** from Paul (Acts 24:26) reveals the governor's true colors. Elsewhere, Luke negatively evaluates those who are greedy and use money or possessions, especially of others, for selfish interests (see, e.g., 5:1-11; 8:18-24; 16:16-24; 19:23-27).

Felix made repeated overtures to Paul under the pretense of listening to his message (only Luke among NT writers uses *homileō* to connote conversations among disciples—see 20:11; Luke 24:14, 15). But by omnisciently citing the governor's real motive, Luke depicts him as a self-serving perpetrator of injustice—certainly unfit to serve as judge in Paul's case.

Bribery and Roman Politics

Bribery was officially prohibited by Roman law. This included taking bribes from prisoners. Nonetheless, bribery was so common and widespread that Cicero lists it as one of three major hindrances to civil litigation in the empire (*Caecin.* 73). Such corrupt practices occurred at every level of Roman politics. Even emperors accepted bribes in exchange for acquittals or political positions (Suetonius, *Vesp.* 16).

Even Josephus, who typically depicts Rome favorably, admits that bribery was not unknown in Rome's handling of affairs in Palestine. Albinus, who suc-

ceeded Festus (Acts 24:27) as governor of the region (AD 62-64), released prisoners only in exchange for bribes, thereby becoming the sponsor of seditious and
unjust behavior (J.W. 2.272-76; Ant. 20.215). The next governor, Gessius Florus,
apparently extended the practice to swindle money from the populace for personal gain (J.W. 2.277-79).

Rome did not sanction bribery or other oppressive practices, but the distance between the capital and Palestine (not to mention Rome's own problems
with bribery) made it impossible to monitor such activities (see the speech of
Agrippa II in Josephus, J.W. 2.350-55). Corruption was pervasive from top to bot-
tom in Roman administration.

■ **27** A period of **two years** marks both Paul's ongoing imprisonment without
resolution and the end of Felix's tenure as governor. It is unclear whether Felix's term of service expired (and was followed by Jewish protests against him
in Rome) or Rome recalled Felix because of Jewish protests (→ sidebar "Felix,
the Roman Governor" with 23:31-35). It is unlikely that Felix retained Paul in
prison due to the political nature of the charges (against Schnabel 2012, 967).
Greed and self-interest alone motivated him to **grant a favor to the Jews**. This
explains why they sent negative evaluations of his rule to the emperor. This
is what one would expect from a ruler who seeks a bribe from a prisoner to
whom he pretends to listen (v 26).

2. Paul's Hearing before Festus (25:1-22)

a. Festus in Jerusalem with Jewish Leaders (25:1-5)

■ **1-3** The successor to Felix as governor of the province of Judea (including
Syria), **Festus**(v 1), wasted little time upon landing in Caesarea before traveling to Jerusalem. He probably wanted to become acquainted with leading
local leaders. Forging such ties was often critical for easing tensions in areas
notorious for social and political unrest.

Festus, the Roman Governor

Little is known about Porcius Festus outside Acts and the works of Josephus. According to Josephus, on arrival (AD 59) Festus was immediately faced
with uprisings. Large numbers of bandits (sicarii) torched and plundered villages,
killed residents, and threatened civil order. Among these revolutionaries was
one leader who promised to deliver his followers from their oppressors. Festus
responded in kind, using military force to squelch and kill them (Ant. 20. 185-88).

Festus acted with more restraint toward the Jewish religious leaders.
Priests in Jerusalem built a high wall to keep King Agrippa (→ 25:13—26:32 and
the sidebar "King Agrippa II and Bernice" with 25:13-16) from watching temple
activities from a palace tower. The governor initially sided with the king and ordered the wall removed. He later consulted the emperor Nero about the matter.
The wall was subsequently protected by the emperor (Ant. 20.189-96). Josephus
depicts Festus as one who sought to navigate the tempestuous political waters

of the various Jewish factions of that region. His assessment compares to some aspects of what Luke initially offers of the same governor, who soon died in office (AD 62; see Green, *ABD* 2:794-95).

In Jerusalem, Festus meets with the **chief priests** and other Jewish **leaders** (*hoi prōtoi* [v 2]; see Luke 19:47), probably the Jewish council (see Acts 25:15; also 23:14; 4:23). That these Jewish leaders bring up Paul's case upon their first meeting with Festus indicates their desire to settle Paul's case. They perceive Paul's mission, which is inclusive of both Jews and Gentiles, as a threat to Jewish identity (see Dunn 1996, 319). They explain their **charges** (*emphanizō*; see 24:1) against Paul to the new governor as they had to Felix. They hope to pressure him (imperfect tense: *parekaloun*) into granting them a political **favor** (*charis* [25:3]; → 24:27). They request the governor to "summon" (CEB) Paul from Caesarea to Jerusalem for a hearing. This request is merely a ruse resembling an earlier plot (→ 23:12-15) to **ambush** (see 23:16, 21) and murder (*anaireō*; see 23:15, 21, 27) Paul. Unlike before, these leaders are not merely accomplices in the plot. They plan to eliminate Paul once and for all.

■ **4-5** It is uncertain whether or not Felix informed his successor of the earlier Jewish plot against Paul (see Wall 2002, 324; Peterson 2009, 646). Regardless, the deceptive request does not fool Festus. Luke does not explain whether questions over the presented evidence or the rights of a Roman citizen play into the governor's decision.

Festus' alternative plan does not deny the request out-of-hand. Rather, he promises to reopen Paul's case promptly and invite some of their ***powerful*** (*hoi . . . dynatoi*; "influential" [NASB]) **members** (25:5) to travel back with him to Caesarea so they can formally accuse (*katēgoreō*; see vv 11, 16; also 22:30; 24:2, 8, 13, 19) Paul. The first-class condition suggests that the question for which Festus needs an answer concerns what Paul did that they consider **wrong** (*atopos*). This mild term refers to an alleged crime (**amiss**; see 28:6; Luke 23:41; 2 Thess 3:2; also LXX: Job 34:12; Prov 30:20; 2 Macc 14:23). The word choice suggests "proper legal caution" (Barrett 1998, 1125) on Festus' part.

b. Paul's Appeal to the Emperor (25:6-12)

■ **6-7** A stay of **eight or ten days** (v 6) in Jerusalem gives Festus ample opportunity to become acquainted with Jewish institutions and the layout of the city. Luke notes that, before returning to Caesarea, the governor stays with these Jewish leaders (vv 2-3). This may explain his subsequent desire to grant favors on their behalf (see v 9).

When Festus takes his seat in the **court** (see vv 10, 17; 12:21; 18:12, 16-17) in Caesarea and has Paul escorted to him, formal legal proceedings begin. Unlike the previous hearing (24:1-9), the Jewish accusers do not employ a legal representative as their spokesperson. Rather, the group *itself* confronts

Paul in an adversarial manner. They surround him with **many serious charges** (25:7). Luke does not repeat those charges, since they were already stated before Felix (see 24:5-8) and would be outlined in Paul's rebuttal (25:8).

Luke assesses their case as weak because Paul's accusers **could not prove** (imperfect tense: *ischyon*) their **charges**, no matter how much they tried (see Barrett 1998, 1126; see 24:13, 19-20). Ironically and ominously, Paul faces false charges similar to those fabricated against Stephen (→ 6:13).

■ **8** This verse offers Paul's defense (*apologeomai*; see 19:33; 24:10; 26:1-2, 24). But grammatically, it is part of the previous sentence. Paul's rebuttal informs readers of three basic charges against him. He categorically denies all the charges in one sweeping statement. The first two charges—of breaking the **Jewish law** and defiling the **temple**—have recurred (18:12-18; 21:21, 28-29; 24:6) despite Paul's faithful participation in sacred Jewish rituals (see 21:26-27; 24:11-18).

The third charge—offenses against the emperor—echoes Tertullus' false claim that Paul was a "troublemaker" who threatened the stability of the Roman Empire (24:5; see 17:6-9) and Lysias' assumption that he was an Egyptian revolutionary (21:38-39). This last charge is also the most serious of the three, even for a Roman citizen.

■ **9** Rather than ruling on Paul's case based on the hearing, Festus proposes to Paul that his trial be moved to Jerusalem. The first two charges would favor that location, yet Luke offers a different (perhaps related) reason: the governor now wishes (like Felix) to extend a **favor** to the Jews (see 24:27). Perhaps Festus learned how to deal with the influential Jewish leaders during his brief stay in Jerusalem (see 25:6; Tannehill 1990, 306-7; also Rapske 1994b, 183-84). Or, he may have simply waited before extending such favorable action (Gaventa 2003, 333-34).

Festus emphasizes that any trial for Paul in Jerusalem would still occur before him, but scholars differ over who would have jurisdiction in that instance. If Festus convenes the trial (**before me**; see Lake and Cadbury 1933a, 308; Fitzmyer 1998, 744-45), his role would include the protection of Paul as a Roman citizen (but Luke never mentions this). But the religious nature of the charges, as Festus later explains them (→ vv 18-20), suggests that the Jewish council would have jurisdiction (see 1 Macc 15:21; Tajra 1989, 141-42; see also Barrett 1998, 1127-28).

Neither option offers readers hope that an innocent Paul will find justice (as the case of Jesus illustrates; see Luke 22:63—23:25; also Rowe 2009, 81). Luke *already* linked the latest plot against Paul's life to Jewish attempts to gain political favors from the governor (Acts 25:3). So *this* danger may be the more significant issue associated with Festus' proposal to move the proceedings to Jerusalem.

■ **10-11** Paul not only rejects Festus' proposal but rebukes the governor. Although Festus proposed that Paul's case would still be heard "before" the governor (*ep' emou*) in Jerusalem (v 9), Paul stresses that he is *already* standing [perfect periphrastic: *hestōs eimi* (v 10)] **before** the governor, who represents the emperor in **Caesar's court** (*epi tou bēmatos Kaisaros*). He insists that his case belongs there, drawing from the same Lukan word (*dei*, **must**) that earlier emphasizes the divine necessity of Paul going to Rome (19:21; 23:11; see Soards 1994, 120; Schneider 1982, 359).

Paul claims he is innocent of all the Jews' accusations. This correlates with Luke's earlier depiction of Paul's actions and his response to similar rumors about him (→ 21:26-27). But Paul also asserts that Festus *himself* recognizes (*epignōskō*) his innocence (see emphatic *kai sy*, **certainly you**). He implicitly accuses the governor of perpetrating injustice by continuing the case and proposing its transfer to Jerusalem. He is colluding with Paul's enemies (Cassidy 1987, 202). Festus is an unreliable, duplicitous judge.

The second part of Paul's comments offers his *own* assessment of the case. Two antithetical expressions lay out the options from Paul's perspective. In the face of the Jews' wish that Paul be killed (see 21:36; 22:22; 23:12-15; 25:3), he confidently declares that he would not "avoid" (25:11 CEB) **death**, if the charges were true (see Josephus, *Life* 141). But (*men . . . de*) if those **charges** were false (see v 10), then no one (*oudeis*) including Festus himself could legally (*dynamai*; see 17:19; Rowe 2009, 81) turn an innocent prisoner over to hostile adversaries as a political pawn. The verb *charizomai* plays on the mention of Festus wanting to grant a "favor" (*charis*) to the Jews (25:9; see v 3; 24:27). Paul insists that no one could turn him into a mere diplomatic gift for those wishing to kill him (see Barrett 1998, 1130; Skinner 2003, 142).

This reveals why Paul rejects the governor's proposal as untenable. With no apparent hope for a fair hearing before the Jewish council in Jerusalem or the Roman governor Festus in Caesarea, Paul appeals to **Caesar** in Rome. Readers of Acts should note the irony of Paul's need to escape his own people in order to seek justice (see Gaventa 2003, 335).

Whether judicial expediency or prophetic vocation prompts Paul's appeal, Paul's divine mission carries the day. His comments underscore the divine necessity of his case being tried under Roman jurisdiction (25:10). Now his appeal ensures that he would also witness in Rome (19:21; 23:11). This transforms Paul's appeal into a theological move within Acts rather than simply a deft legal ploy (see Wall 2002, 327).

Paul's Appeal to Caesar

Appeals in the Roman Empire generally took two different forms. The *provocatio* was the right to appeal a verdict before the people prior to sentence.

The *appellatio* was the subsequent request to superior officials for protection from improper actions during or after the legal proceedings.

By the first century AD, both terms were used synonymously and applied to rights extending to Roman citizens (see Rowe 2009, 81-82, 226-27). They could appeal that their criminal case involving capital or economic punishment be tried in Rome under the emperor's authority as the people's ultimate representative. Such rights protected them from potential abuses of power and punishment within the empire's political and judicial system (see Cadbury 1933b, 312-17; Garnsey 1966, 167-89; Lentz 1993, 139-53). Appeal was neither practical nor feasible in most cases, as appellants were responsible for all travel, lodging, and court expenses (including expenses for summoned witnesses) in a case's transfer to Rome (see Sherwin-White 1963, 62-63; Rapske 1994b, 55).

Sparse details regarding Paul's appeal to the Roman emperor leave interpreters with unresolved questions. First, the account mentions nothing about Paul's Roman citizenship as a prerequisite for granting his appeal (see v 12). But since readers of Acts are well aware of Paul's status (see 16:37; 22:25-30), repetition is unnecessary. Second, appeals typically assume a verdict, so Paul's appeal does not easily correspond with often obscure provisions in Roman law. Readers must remember that Luke focuses the narrative on his *theological* interests, which stand out in the midst of other ambiguity.

■ 12 Paul's appeal, invoking the emperor's authority, effectively halts the proceedings (see Fitzmyer 1998, 745). Festus consults with his "advisers" (CEB), perhaps over the legitimacy of Paul's legal maneuver and likely over the governor's options in response, since appeals were not automatically granted.

- Festus could acquit and release Paul, which a just leader would do. But that would provoke the disapproval of the Jewish leaders he wanted to please (25:7-9; see vv 2-5; see 28:19).
- He could agree to the Jewish demands and sentence Paul (25:15) despite knowing there is no case against him. But if word reached Rome that he executed a Roman citizen unjustly, that could jeopardize his political future.

Political risk accompanies both options. Granting the appeal allows Festus to avoid these by shifting responsibility to another. But his negative status as a dishonorable character remains (see Cassidy 1987, 107-9; Tannehill 1990, 305-8). The governor succumbs to outside pressure and political expediency. He does not embrace his official responsibility to protect justice (see Pervo 2009, 612-13).

c. Festus' Recounting of Paul's Case (25:13-22)

■ 13-16 Paul's appeal may have freed Festus from a potentially fatal political dilemma. But another problem looms before him. The governor must refer the case to Rome in writing, when he *himself* does not understand the issues of the case.

Fortunately, soon after the hearing, the ruler of the neighboring Roman territory to the northeast *arrived in Caesarea* (v 13) to welcome Festus to his new role as governor. **King Agrippa**, accompanied by his sister **Bernice**, was Jewish in background and knowledgeable in matters of Jewish concern. So Festus confers with him by laying out the details of Paul's case (*anatithēmi*; see Gal 2:2) for his consideration.

King Agrippa II and Bernice

The relationship between those with the title "King" and the Christian movement in Acts was not positive. In Acts 12, King Herod (Agrippa I) was responsible for the death of James the apostle (12:1-2). That the governor Festus would consult the son of Agrippa I about Paul's case gives readers of Acts little reason for hope that circumstances would improve.

Agrippa II (AD 28-92) was educated in the emperor's court and was in line to succeed his father upon his untimely death (AD 44; see 12:20-23). But advisers convinced the emperor Claudius that the region required someone older than the sixteen-year-old Agrippa II. He was first conferred his uncle's small kingdom of Chalcis (ca. AD 50), which included authority over the temple in Jerusalem and the right to appoint the high priest (Josephus, *Ant.* 20.222-23). His kingdom was later expanded to include parts of Galilee and Perea by the time he visited Festus (see Josephus, *Ant.* 20.159).

As a Jew (→ sidebar "The Herods, Jesus, and the Church" with "Behind the Text" for 12:1-25), Agrippa was known to support Jewish causes and undertook costly measures to maintain the temple (see Josephus, *Ant.* 15.391; *J.W.* 5.36). Yet his pro-Roman policies were often met with Jewish opposition, so that his later attempts to stop Jewish revolutionaries before the fateful Jewish revolt failed. His visit to Caesarea may have been prompted by news about Paul as another Jewish troublemaker (Schnabel 2012, 994).

Bernice was the sister of Agrippa and Druscilla (24:24), the wife of Felix (the former governor of Judea). She married her uncle, who died and was succeeded by her brother as ruler of Chalcis. She then lived with her brother, prompting rumors of an incestuous relationship between them (see Josephus, *Ant.* 20.145; *J.W.* 2.217). After marrying Polemo of Cilicia, who converted to Judaism for her sake, she left him and returned to Agrippa, further fueling the rumors.

Bernice was Agrippa's companion when he visited Festus. She was later involved with the Roman General Titus who, upon becoming emperor, broke off their relationship to improve his tarnished reputation (see Suetonius, *Tit.* 7; Dio Cassius, *Hist.* 66.18.1).

Festus' version of Paul's case places the governor in a favorable light before King Agrippa. But his comments also create increasing doubt about his own character and reliability, as they sometimes contradict Luke's earlier account. His introduction of Paul as someone whom **Felix left as a prisoner** (25:14) echoes the Lukan description of the former governor's abandonment of Paul in prison (24:27). Unlike Luke, who links Felix's actions to his wishes to "grant a favor to the Jews" (24:27), Festus places an "official question mark" on Paul's claim of innocence (Rapske 1994b, 321).

The governor's account of his initial confrontation by the Jewish **chief priests** and **elders** (25:15; → vv 2, 15-16) not only reiterates the Lukan account (vv 1-5) but intensifies it. Not only does Festus echo that these leaders **brought charges** (*emphanizō*; v 2) against Paul, he acknowledges that they sought a "guilty verdict" (CEB; *katadikē*) prior to and instead of a trial.

The governor's explanation of how he responded to those attempts to circumvent Roman judicial process only affirms his role in maintaining Roman standards of justice. He mentions nothing about his willingness to accommodate these leaders for political advantage. Ironically, his declaration about the Roman prohibition to **hand over** [*charizesthai*] **anyone** prior to (*a*) facing one's accusers personally and (*b*) defending oneself against the stated *charge* (see 23:29) contrasts with Paul's accusation that Festus intended to do the *opposite* (→ 25:11) without such legal provisions. This correlates with his intention to "do the Jews a favor" (*charin katathesthai* [v 9]).

The governor misrepresents himself as taking the moral high road (see, e.g., Barrett 1998, 1136-37). Readers of Acts encounter dissonance between his self-complementary words and Luke's portrayal of Festus in the previous scene, where appeasement trumped justice.

■ **17-19** The governor's account of convening the hearing over Paul's case correlates with Luke's version (v 6). Felix, his predecessor, had "adjourned" (*anaballō* [24:22]) prior proceedings against Paul, and then stalled the process by abandoning him in prison for two years. Festus responds without **delay** (*anabolē* [v 17]) after Paul's accusers arrive.

But Festus' description of what happened next differs from Luke's earlier account (v 7) in two ways. First, the governor states *not a single charge* (*oudemian aitian*; see 23:28) was pressed against Paul of **crimes** (lit., "evils"; *ponērōn* [25:18]) that he would have **expected** (*hyponoeō*; 13:25; 27:27).

Second, previous accounts included accusations of sedition against Rome (24:5-8; 25:7-8), which is probably what Festus assumed from the accusations. But he identifies the problem as *some questions* (*zētēmata*, **controversies**; see 18:15; 23:29; 26:3; also 15:2) over religious matters.

The word translated **religion** (*deisidaimonia* [25:19]; see 17:22) here probably does not have derogatory connotations (e.g., "superstition," → 17:22), due to Agrippa's Jewish background (→ sidebar "King Agrippa II and Bernice" with 25:13-16; against Johnson 1992, 426). Rather, Festus speaks to Agrippa as a Roman official and explains the situation as he understands it (see v 20).

Ironically, the governor (who later admits his confusion over these issues [v 20]) offers a basic, yet correct assessment of the situation: the dispute was over "some dead man named Jesus" (v 19 CEB), whom Paul *kept on claiming* (imperfect tense: *ephasken*) to be **alive** (present tense: *zēn*). This evaluation underscores the Lukan perspective: Paul was innocent of any political crime. At issue are theological questions, not political or criminal ones. Festus may fail to mention the political charges against Paul because he *himself* finds the case lacking. This raises questions as to why Festus did not acquit Paul earlier.

The reemergence of the theme of Jesus' resurrection (see 23:6; 24:15, 21) within Acts reiterates its centrality. This is *the* primary issue behind both Paul's (and, ultimately, the church's) mission and the identity of the church.

Religious outsiders like Festus and Gallio (18:14-15) recognized what these Jewish opponents could not admit: Paul's mission—which extended to Jew and Gentile alike—was part of a *Jewish* ethos (**their own religion**). They understood that the resurrected Jesus as God's Messiah had inclusive, universal implications (see 2:22-36; also Wall 2002, 330).

■ **20-21** The outsider Festus correctly assesses the theological situation. But his further description of how he handled Paul's case also exposes his political hypocrisy. He depicts himself in self-serving ways. Here, he blames his state of confusion (present tense participle: *aporoumenos*; see Mark 6:20; Luke 24:4; 2 Cor 4:8; Gal 4:20) over how to investigate these religious issues as the reason for his request that Paul stand trial in Jerusalem rather than in Caesarea. This implicitly offers a plausible reason for the governor speaking about the case with Agrippa. He is not only Jewish but also knowledgeable and experienced in intra-Jewish affairs. But readers know better.

But Festus mentions nothing of his desire to grant the Jews a favor—the real motive behind the suggested change of venue (Acts 25:9). He pleads ignorance and confusion when he was actually calculating. Readers cannot trust him as a judge who will uphold justice (see v 16; see Parsons 2008, 334-35).

The governor's explanation regarding Paul's appeal also emphasizes the *prisoner's* role in him being "kept in custody" (v 21 NRSV). Festus depicts himself as merely complying with the appeal process. The technical verb *anapempō* suggests he would transfer Paul's case to the authority of the higher courts in Rome (see Luke 23:7, 11, 15; Phlm 12; see Fitzmyer 1998, 751; Barrett 1998, 1140). But he mentions nothing of Paul's protest against the governor's proposal for the change of venue and appeal for justice (Acts 25:10-11), which could have led to his release (see Cassidy 1987, 203).

■ **22** Luke mentions nothing about Agrippa's response other than his request to hear Paul himself. The imperfect *eboulomēn* suggests the king may have already heard about Paul and the case against him (see also Luke 23:8). Since Agrippa was the Roman official responsible for the temple, the same Jewish leaders in Jerusalem who met with Festus and renewed the accusations against Paul (Acts 25:1-5) may have informed the king about those complaints (see, e.g., Lake and Cadbury 1933a, 312; Fitzmyer 1998, 751; Wall 2002, 329).

Some interpret this verb as a desiderative imperfect. In this instance, it politely expresses the king's wish to hear and meet Paul without prior interest in doing so (see Williams 1990, 413; Barrett 1998, 1141). However, since Agrippa refers to Paul with the generic term *anthrōpos* rather than the more specific and polite word *anēr* (vv 5, 14) as Festus does, the king's reference to **this man** may be tinged with contempt, which downplays the latter possibility (Williams 1990, 413).

3. Paul's Hearing before King Agrippa (25:23—26:32)

a. Paul's Case Reintroduced (25:23-27)

■ **23** Paul's hearing was convened the **next day** as promised, with King Agrippa and Bernice playing the role of Herod in Jesus' trial (Luke 23:6-12; see Johnson 1992, 428-29). Their entrance was **with great pomp** (*meta pollēs phantasias*; see Polybius, *Hist.* 16.21.1). This reminds us of earlier Herodian splendor in the same city (→ 12:21-22). The ruler was at the height of his political power (see Skinner 2003, 147).

The Herods are accompanied by **high-ranking military officers** and **prominent men** from the city (functioning as an advisory council; Haenchen 1971, 690; Tajra 1989, 161), probably Gentiles (Bruce 1988, 459). Together they meet in an **audience room**—a large room in a palace or administrative building for legal hearings or state occasions. The implicit contrast between this august audience and the prisoner Paul as he enters the room could not be more striking. Yet the prominence of the audience also indicates the importance of Paul's speech.

■ **24-25** Festus' reintroduction of Paul's case offers another version from the governor of the prisoner's predicament. Festus implicitly belittles Paul by referring to him as **this man** (*touton* [v 24]) rather than naming him (see Schnabel 2012, 1000). He also hyperbolically describes Paul's opposition as the **whole Jewish community** (*hapan to plēthos tōn Ioudaiōn*; → vv 1-7, 15). The term *plēthos*, as in other similar cases (see 4:32; 6:2, 5; 14:1; 15:12, 30; also Luke 8:37; 23:1), refers to a group or crowd and not the entire community (see Acts 25:1-6; Johnson 1992, 427). In v 15, Festus mentions only "the chief priests and the elders" coming to press charges. *Hapan* suggests that they represent the Jewish people in general (see Dunn 1996, 322; also Parsons 2008, 335-36) or claim their backing (Wall 2002, 330). The **shouting** (*boaō*; see 8:7; 17:6; Luke 3:4; 9:38; 18:7, 38) connotes their vehemence that Paul deserves only death.

Not surprisingly, Festus mentions nothing about moving the trial to Jerusalem (25:6-12). However, what is surprising is his *public* statement about Paul's innocence of charges worthy of the death penalty, which the governor expected to be alleged crimes against Rome (25:15-19; see 23:29). Yet the governor's opinion here matters little in comparison to the prior hearing (25:6-12), when it could have resulted in Paul's release.

■ **26-27** The governor explains that the *hearing* (*anakrisis* [v 26]) is not a formal trial. It is merely an unofficial inquiry (see Büchsel, *TDNT* 3:943-44; LSJ 1996, 66) to provide *something definite* (*asphales ti*; 21:34; 22:30; see noun, Luke 1:4) for his letter that would introduce Paul and the **charges** (*aitia* [Acts 25:27]; 22:24; 23:28; 25:18; 28:18, 20) against him to the Roman authorities (→ Lysias' letter, 23:25-30). The letter itself is a requirement that the governor must provide or risk dereliction of duty (Conzelmann 1987, 207). This explains why he describes the failure to send the letter as "foolish" (25:27 CEB [*alogos*]). Agrippa's background and experience (→ vv 20-21) are implicit reasons why Paul is grateful to appear **especially before** the king (see 26:2-3).

That Festus identifies the recipient of this letter—the emperor—as *kyrios* is noteworthy. By this time, this title was used increasingly to refer to the emperor Nero. This letter is widely regarded as the first literary evidence for using this title for the emperor. But such usage may signal potential problems within Acts, since Luke reserves the title for God and Jesus. How many may legitimately lay claim the title *kyrios*?

b. Paul's Defense (26:1-23)

■ **I** With Festus' introduction complete, Agrippa takes charge and becomes Paul's primary audience for his **defense** (*apologeomai*; 24:10; 25:8). King Agrippa appears to stand in two worlds—Jewish and Roman—and represent both interests and perspectives. Thus, Paul's speech must be interpreted accordingly. It does not merely repeat earlier materials. Rather, this hearing offers a climax to the events begun in ch 21. This provides the Lukan defense of Paul, Paul's mission, and ultimately the identity and mission of the church in continuity with Israel's heritage.

■ **2-3** The opening of Paul's speech focuses mostly on the *captatio benevolentiae* (→ sidebar "Roman Forensic Speeches" with 24:1), which compliments those hearing the case. Paul praises Agrippa for his knowledge of two areas. The first area includes **Jewish customs** (*ethōn* [26:3]; 6:14; 15:1; 16:21; 21:21; 25:16; 28:17), or the laws and their interpretation. The second includes Jewish **controversies** (*zētēmatōn*; 15:2; 18:15), which Luke has associated with disagreements over resurrection (23:29; 25:19).

Festus claims ignorance over such intra-Jewish matters (25:20, 26). So Paul welcomes the opportunity to present his case before Agrippa as someone who better understands these matters and may lend a more discerning perspective. Paul avoids the specific charges the Jews pressed earlier, since Festus ignores them (25:24-27). One may infer from Paul's request for Agrippa's patience (*makrothymōs*) that his defense would take a long time (see 24:4; see Bruce 1988, 462).

■ **4-5** Paul begins the *narratio* portion of his speech (with the conjunctions *men oun*; → sidebar "Roman Forensic Speeches" with 24:1) by referring to his Jewish heritage. Details are probably omitted since they are already known (see 22:3). The phrase ***among my people*** probably includes his time in Jerusalem (26:4; → 22:3; see Conzelmann 1987, 210; Barrett 1998, 1151). Or it may distinguish between his youth in Tarsus and his later education in Jerusalem (see Lake and Cadbury 1933a, 315; Tajra 1989, 165; Parsons 2008, 338).

Regardless, the hyperbolic ***all the Jews*** underscores that many Jewish people could serve as witnesses to Paul's character as a pious Jew according to Pharisaic standards (→ sidebar "The Pharisees and Gamaliel" with 5:33-34). That this particular ***party*** (*hairesis* [26:5]) was known as the strictest one within Judaism (see, e.g., Josephus, *Life* 191) contributes to this portrayal of Paul's Jewishness. Although **religion** (*thrēskeia*) sometimes has negative connotations (e.g., Col 2:18; Wis 14:18, 27), the present context gives it a neutral sense, as Paul addresses the king as a Roman official and summarizes the practice and teaching of Judaism (see Jas 1:26-27; 4 Macc 5:7, 13).

■ **6-8 And now** (Acts 26:6) indicates continuity between Paul's Jewish heritage and his Christian beliefs and ministry. Yet Paul makes the ironic claim that his **hope** in God's promise to their Jewish ancestors (*tous pateras hēmōn*; see 7:11) motivates the Jews' accusations against him. This Jewish ancestral hope includes the restoration of the **twelve tribes** (26:7)—all Israel (see 1:15-26; 7:8; Luke 6:13; 8:1, 42-43; 9:1-17; 22:30; see Johnson 1992, 433). Paul spoke earlier about this hope as resurrection (Acts 23:6; 24:15). Ezekiel's dramatic vision of the revived dry bones offered hope of a restored Israel (Ezek 37:1-14; see also Isa 26:19; Hos 6:1-2; see Spencer 2004a, 236).

The message throughout Acts is that God's promise to Israel has been fulfilled in the resurrection and exaltation of Jesus as the Messiah (13:23, 32-33) and the outpouring of the Spirit (1:4; 2:33, 39; see Wall 2002, 335). Paul acknowledges the Jews' diligence (*ekteneia*; see 12:5) in continuing to worship God (present tense: *latreuon*) in the hope of seeing that promise fulfilled. But Acts also describes their rejection of Jesus as the Messiah due to their disbelief in his resurrection. How one thinks about God and resurrection highlights the ongoing role of Jewish disbelief. The term translated **incredible** (*apiston* [26:8]) connotes something perceived as unbelievable or someone who lacks faith (*pistis*; see Luke 9:41; 12:46; Bultmann, *TDNT* 6:174-228).

■ **9-11** Paul's personal story helps him to identify with his Jewish accusers. Readers of Acts are familiar with the prior activities (→ 8:3; 9:1-2; 22:4-5) of Saul the Pharisee. The conjunctions *men oun* introduce his earlier rejection of the gospel claims that Jesus was the resurrected Messiah.

Paul's use of *dei*, denoting divine purpose in Acts (e.g., 1:16; 3:21; 4:12; 5:29; 9:16; 17:3), describes the motives behind Paul's earlier opposition to the

Jesus movement. The first-person pronoun indicates his *own* mistaken be-lief that he was pursuing God's will. So Paul sought every possible means to squelch the erroneous message of the Christian movement (or **the name of Jesus** [26:9]; 2:21, 38; 3:6, 16; 4:7-18; 9:14-16).

Previous accounts refer generally to Paul's persecution of believers in terms of arresting them (8:3), "breathing out murderous threats" (9:1) and pursuing them "to the point of death" (22:4 NRSV). Here, Paul catalogues additional activities behind his antagonism, particularly in Jerusalem (26:10). This further emphasizes the connection between his opposition and his faith-fulness as a pious Pharisee. He even cast a **vote against them**. But two difficul-ties are associated with this declaration.

First, Acts describes only the deaths of Stephen and James. This may be a rhetorical flourish on Paul's part, so that only one person (Stephen) actually died as a result of his opposition (see Marshall 1980, 393). But it is more plau-sible that the narrator simply does not offer other stories of martyred believers.

Second, Paul's language of voting may imply that he was a member of the Sanhedrin. But the *young* Saul would have been ineligible for such respon-sibilities within a council comprised of leading *elders* of the community (see 25:15). He may have been a young assistant to other Pharisees on the council (Witherington 1998, 742). Or this may be a metaphor emphasizing his role among opposing forces to the believers.

Paul's description of his activities among the synagogues (26:11) con-tributes a new element to the Acts narrative. While punishment against the believers has already been mentioned (see *timōreō* [22:5]), Paul discloses its use in repeated efforts to force them (imperfect tense: *ēnankazon*) to commit blasphemy (*blasphēmeō*; see 19:37). Such an act would have included denying Jesus as Lord and Christ or making other claims about him that detracted from God's honor, especially as the one who raised and exalted him (see 2:22-36; see Dunn 1996, 327; Schnabel 2012, 1007). Roman and Herodian officials would have been sympathetic to such violent means of enforcing their own in-terests. But Paul reveals that he acted not out of noble concerns for justice but out of a consuming "maniacal" rage (*perissōs . . . emmainomenos*) against the believers, which even drove him to pursue them in **foreign cities** (see Spencer 2004a, 236-37).

■ **12-15** The mention of foreign cities is a perfect segue into his story about his encounter with the risen Jesus on the road to Damascus. Here, Paul un-derscores the **authority** and **commission** that the **chief priests** (26:12; → 9:2) granted him to oppress the movement.

Paul's initial description of the christophany along the road resembles the previous two accounts in chs 9 and 22. But this is the first account in which Paul claims he **saw** the **light** (26:13). With all else that happens in this account on the road rather than later in Damascus (see 9:10-19a; 22:12-16), the light may also function metaphorically for salvation and revelation (see 26:18; see also Ps 27:1; Luke 2:32; Krodel 1986, 461).

In Acts 22:9, Paul says his traveling companions "saw" (*theaomai*) the light as spectators. Here, Paul describes his own seeing as perception (*horaō*) on a far grander scale (26:13). This may also explain why Paul mentions nothing to Agrippa about dealing with blindness (see 9:8-18; 22:11-12). He presents his traveling party, not as those who need to assist Paul into the city, but as witnesses to the events of the encounter: the light shining around them causes them to fall **to the ground** with Paul (26:14).

But the encounter is between Paul and the risen Jesus. Paul now turns to his exchange with Jesus (vv 14-15). The voice speaks ***in the Hebrew dialect*** or **Aramaic** (see 21:40), which may account for Paul being addressed as "Saul," when the audience knows him only by his Greek name (→ sidebar "Why Now *Paul* Rather than *Saul?*" with 13:9-12).

Both the address and question (26:14b) and also the subsequent exchange between Paul and Jesus (v 15) are identical with earlier accounts (→ 9:4-5; 22:7-8). But then Paul adds a common Greek proverb (Euripides, *Bacch.* 794-95; Aeschylus, *Ag.* 1624; Pindar, *Pyth.* 2.94-95), referring to the difficulty of kicking against cattle prods. The proverb analogously describes the futility of resisting God, especially due to pride. The LXX often used the word translated **hard**, *sklēros*, metaphorically to describe resistance to God (e.g., Deut 31:27; Judg 2:19; Isa 48:4). So, the quotation portrays Paul—the pious Pharisee and persecutor of believers—as one who stubbornly opposes God's purposes (see Wall 2002, 337). The adage reveals Paul's conundrum: What he *himself* considers as God's will is actually *resistance* to the divine will.

■ **16-18** The previous two accounts depict the disciple Ananias as receiving divine guidance regarding Paul's commission and then coming to Paul in Damascus to instruct him about that calling (→ 9:10-17; 22:12-16). But here, Paul mentions nothing about Ananias and refers only to Jesus' instructions on the road to Damascus.

Jesus' instructions to **stand on your feet** (26:18) resemble the initial words of Ezekiel's prophetic call (Ezek 2:1). Jesus' declaration that he has **appeared** (*ōphthēn*) to Paul conveys the idea of revelation. This is the only time within the three accounts that Jesus himself asserts that he has revealed himself to Paul (see Gaventa 2003, 343).

The verb translated **appoint** (*procheirizō*) refers earlier to God's actions in making Jesus the Messiah (Acts 3:20) and in confronting Paul (22:14). So Jesus, the subject of such actions, calls Paul—in continuity with his own "appointment"—to be a **servant** (*hypēretēs*; 13:5; Luke 1:2; 1 Cor 4:1) and **witness** (see 22:15).

Paul's calling as a servant corresponds to the mission of Isaiah's servant (see 26:18). His calling as a witness corresponds with the mission of the twelve apostles (see 1:8, 22; 2:32; 3:15; 5:32; 10:39, 41; 13:31). Yet Luke usually avoids explicitly calling Paul an apostle (see 1:21-22; but see 14:4, 14; see Dunn 1996, 329). The subject of his testimony would be twofold: what he has already seen through his confrontation with the risen Jesus, and what would yet be shown to him.

Verses 17-18 continue to describe Paul's mission as comparable to that of OT prophets and of Jesus (see Luke 4:18). The promise to **rescue** (*exaireō* [Acts 26:17]) Paul from those to whom he was also sent (*apostellō*) resembles the LXX's rendition of Jeremiah's divine call (Jer 1:7-8; → Acts 12:11; see Pervo 2009, 632). Such words refer to the entirety of Paul's ministry, not merely to the time of his calling.

Once again, Paul describes his mission as to both the Jewish people (**your own people**) and **the Gentiles** (the relative pronoun *hous* refers to both *tou laou* and *tōn ethnōn*) and corresponds with both 9:15 and 22:15 (see, e.g., Tannehill 1990, 323-24; Barrett 1998, 1160; contra, e.g., Haenchen 1971, 686; Schneider 1982, 374).

Paul describes his mission as that of Isaiah's servant (Isa 42:1-7), who was to be a "light to the nations" (Isa 42:6 NRSV). Common in both Luke's Gospel and Acts is the use of metaphoric language of light and darkness as well as sight and blindness in relation to the gospel and God's purposes (see, e.g., Luke 2:30; 24:16, 31; Acts 9:8, 18, 40; 13:11; 28:27). The images of opening eyes (Isa 42:7) and turning persons **from darkness to light** (Acts 26:18; Isa 42:6-7, 16) were used in the Third Gospel (Luke 1:16, 78-79; 4:18) to depict salvation (see Acts 13:47). They are closely related to the repentance language in Acts (e.g., 2:38; 5:31; see 13:4-12).

Turning from darkness to light was a common description for conversion in Jewish literature (e.g., Philo, *Virtues* 179; *Jos. Asen.* 8.10; 15.13; *Odes Sol.* 14.18-19; see Gaventa 1986, 86). The task of opening eyes and turning people to light complements what Paul *himself* has just seen as Jesus reveals himself to Paul (26:16). The corresponding turning **from the power** or *authority* (*exousia*) **of Satan to God** reiterates that the proclamation of the "kingdom of God" (1:3) involves a battle against other authorities, including Satan or those whom Satan controls (see Garrett 1989; Johnson 1992, 437).

The purpose of Paul's mission (genitive articular infinitive *tou labein*) was twofold. His description of it echoes themes from his farewell to the Ephesian elders (→ 20:32).

First, the association of **forgiveness of sins** (26:18) with repentance is a consistent aspect of the gospel throughout Acts. It is voiced by both Peter and Paul (see 2:38; 3:19; 13:38-39; 17:30).

Second, this mission focuses not merely on the Jewish people, but also on the Gentiles (see 26:17). The only stated criterion for establishing one's **place** or "share" (*klēros*; see 1:17, 26; 8:21; see *klēronomia* [20:32]) among the people of God—those **sanctified** ("made holy"; → 20:32) is **faith** in Jesus as the Messiah. God's resurrection and exaltation of Jesus (→ 2:22-36; 3:12-26; 13:23-41) are the means by which this sanctifying work is made efficacious (see also Col 1:12-14; see Dunn 1996, 330).

The Rhetorical Advantage of Three Versions of Paul's "Conversion"

One advantage of telling the important story of Paul's encounter with the risen Jesus on the Damascus road is the chance to emphasize significant themes through repetition (→ "Behind the Text" for 9:1-31). Although major differences between the accounts appear, the similarities underscore key elements about the Christian mission embodied in the life and ministry of Paul.

However, differences are also significant for the interpretive task. In the third account, several distinct aspects stand out compared with the first two versions:

- There is no mention of Paul's blindness or the need for healing.
- There are no elements of a miracle story present.
- Paul's traveling companions do not go into Damascus, and Ananias does not meet up with Paul.
- The risen Jesus *himself* appears to Paul and commissions him on the road.

One reason for these differences may be the narrative setting (i.e., Paul's defense speech before King Agrippa). But another reason may be that the narrator conceals from the reader this *specific* commission that the Lord speaks to Paul until now—in the portion of Acts that evaluates and validates an understanding of the reconstituted people of God developed in Paul's ministry.

So there is a rhetorical advantage of telling this story three times. The third version relies on earlier accounts about the transformation of the former persecutor to highlight the Lord's commission of Paul "as a servant and as a witness" (26:16; see Hedrick 1981, 426-27).

■ **19-20** Paul's direct address of King Agrippa, preceded by the conjunction *hothen* (**therefore**), indicates the beginning of the *probatio* or *confirmatio* section. This deals more directly with defense matters. He begins with a *litotes* (an understatement that makes an affirmation by expressing the negative of its opposite for effect). Paul's declaration about **not** being **disobedient** underscores his obedience (v 19). By describing his encounter with Jesus as a ***heavenly vision***, he confirms his mission as a matter of obedience to God, although contrary to what he formerly believed to be God's will (vv 9-11).

398

The summary of Paul's ministry has grammatical problems in most Greek MSS. The preposition **in** of the phrase **in all Judea** (v 20) does not appear. It was apparently added to alleviate these difficulties (see Metzger 1994, 438-39; Barrett 1998, 1163-64). However, if one accepts this "correction," the summary not only correlates with Paul's ministry in Acts but depicts Paul as faithful to his divine calling. His proclamation begins among those in **Damascus** (9:20-22) and **Jerusalem** (9:27-29), probably among Jews. The reference to **all Judea** underscores the Jewish side of Paul's mission (see 9:15; 22:15; in apparent contradiction to Paul's claim in Galatians that he was unknown to the churches of Judea [Gal 1:22]).

The last reference, **to the Gentiles**, should be understood within the context of Paul's broader mission. The Gentiles were not the exclusive focus of his divinely crafted mission. Rather, the Pauline mission was inclusive of both Jews and Gentiles—all humanity. Thus, Paul's preaching echoes themes from his commission. The call to **repent and turn to God** repeats common Lukan themes that expect changes of both mind and behavior (see Conzelmann 1961, 99-101) reminiscent of the preaching of John the Baptist (see Luke 3:8).

■ **21** Since this is only an informal hearing, Paul offers only a brief *refutation*. He refutes the charges against him by summarizing the reasons behind them to reveal his innocence. Paul stresses that his faithful obedience to his heavenly calling and mission to include both Jews and Gentiles ultimately led to his arrest in the temple (*syllambanō*; see Acts 1:16; 12:3; 23:27; Luke 22:54) and his attempted murder (*diacheirizō*; → Acts 5:30; 21:27-31) by fellow Jews.

What his opponents failed to recognize was that Paul minimized neither temple nor Law for the Jewish people. Rather, he merely preached a new way of life for the Gentiles, appropriate for the "sanctified" (26:18) people of God (see Spencer 2004a, 237-38). But Jews perceived such preaching as a threat to them as a people since it called into question Israel's identity as separate from other nations (see Dunn 1996, 330).

■ **22-23** The conclusion to Paul's speech—the *peroratio*—begins with the customary acknowledgment of God's help expected in most speeches (see Winter 1993, 330). But this expression specifically affirms God's protection throughout Paul's ministry among Jews and Gentiles in fulfillment of the promise from the risen Jesus (see v 17). God enabled him to serve as a witness (participle *martyromenos*) to all, regardless of their status. He describes his testimony and teaching to be in harmony with Israel's scriptural tradition (i.e., **the prophets and Moses** [v 22]; → 3:18-26; 10:43; 13:15; 24:14; Luke 24:25-27, 44-47). Thus, his conclusion returns to the affirmation that began his defense (Acts 26:6-7).

Paul claims that the Jewish Scriptures teach the suffering and resurrection of the Messiah (e.g., Isa 42:1-7; 53:3-12; 61:1-4). This relates not only to

Israel's hope (see Acts 26:6-7) but also to a messianic mission that functions as **light** (v 23; e.g., Isa 42:6; 49:6; 60:3) to bring salvation that has universal relevance and scope by including both the Jewish people and the Gentiles.

Thus, not only did Jesus as Israel's Messiah serve as this light to all—fulfilling Simeon's words in the temple (Luke 2:32)—but Paul also emulates this Scripture-supported mission through his vision of the risen Messiah (Acts 26:16-18). Paul's obedience portrays him as a faithful Jew, not an apostate one. Yet his arrest at the hands of fellow Jews occurred because he faithfully proclaimed his Jewish heritage (see Dupont 1984, 446-56; Tannehill 1990, 326-27).

c. Paul's Exchange with Festus and Agrippa (26:24-29)

■ **24** As in other speeches in Acts, an interruption brings the speech to a conclusion (see 2:37; 10:44; 17:32; 22:22). Festus loudly accuses Paul of *insanity* (*mania; mainomai*, see 26:25; 12:15), cutting him short over two issues that resulted in previous interruptions: (1) the resurrection of Jesus halted by the Athenians (17:32), and (2) a mission inclusive of Gentiles silenced by an incensed Jewish mob in Jerusalem (22:22).

Here, the universal implications of the resurrection are further developed to show that the gospel calls Jews and Gentiles together as the people of God. Festus reacts to Paul's **great learning** (contrast 4:13), unable to comprehend the argument (Fitzmyer 1998, 763). But the governor may also have begun to recognize implications beyond the Jewish people (see Wall 2002, 340; Rowe 2009, 84-86).

■ **25-27** Paul responds to the governor with appropriate decorum. Whereas Festus dismissed Paul as "maniacal," Luke depicts the defendant as a person of virtue and self-control. Paul describes his own words as the opposite of *mania* or "madness": as **truth** (*alētheia* [26:25]) and **reasonableness** (*sōphrosynē*; see Plato, *Phaedr.* 245a; *Resp.* 430e-431b; Xenophon, *Mem.* 1.1.16; 3.9.6-7; Lentz 1993, 87-91). Such descriptions correlate with the verb translated **saying**, *apophthengomai*. It earlier describes the Spirit-inspired speech of Pentecost (2:4, 14; against Barrett 1998, 1168).

Despite Festus' skepticism, Paul is optimistic that King Agrippa understands (26:26). His appeal to the king reflects the prophetic boldness (participle *parrēsiazomenos*) that typically characterizes his ministry (see 9:27-28; 13:46; 14:3; 19:8) and that of other believers (see noun *parrēsia*: 2:29; 4:13, 29, 31).

Agrippa's Herodian family, Jewish background, and political experience in the region guarantee the king to be quite familiar with Jewish concerns, especially over the Christian movement (see 26:2-3). The expression **in a corner** (v 26) was used disparagingly of philosophers who were disengaged from public life, secretive in their activities, and irrelevant to society (Malherbe 1989,

26:24-27

155-56; see, e.g., Plato, *Gorg.* 485d; Plutarch, *Curios.* 516b; *Max. princ.* 777b; Epictetus, *Diatr.* 2.12.17). That believers' actions were **not done in a corner** emphasizes that their lives were open for examination.

Paul's boldness (v 26) leads him to ask Agrippa a rhetorical question about the king's belief in the prophets (v 27). The way Paul poses the question suggests an obvious answer. If the king could only offer a simple "yes" or "no" answer, this would correctly be "a dramatic masterstroke" (Dunn 2009, 991). He is put "on the spot."

Of course, the question is not as simple as Paul implies. The question's subtext is whether Agrippa accepts *Paul's* interpretation of the prophets, which is synonymous with the Christian gospel in Acts. To respond affirmatively would bring ridicule from the Greeks and Romans in attendance (see Tajra 1989, 169) and consternation from the Jews who rejected Paul's reading of the Scriptures. Yet a negative response could still provoke antagonism from the Jews, since the question, on the surface, focuses only on believing the prophets.

■ **28-29** The ambiguity of King Agrippa's response to Paul implies that he recognizes the rhetorical "trap." Does he respond out of surprise, sarcasm, or seriousness? The phrase *en oligō*, **in/with a little** (v 28), may refer to the brief time or to the relatively little effort Paul's defense speech requires. A hasty conversion tended to be viewed with doubt and suspicion by the philosophical tradition (see Malherbe 1989, 161-62). Agrippa may have also assessed Paul's argument as lacking the necessary rhetorical proofs to be convincing (see Witherington 1998, 751).

The verb translated **persuade** indicates that Agrippa realizes Paul is trying to convince him to **become a Christian** (see v 29). It remains unclear whether or not he appropriates the term **Christian** in a demeaning manner (→ 11:26). Regardless, his answer conveys incredulity (see Witherington 1998, 751), mixed with some sarcasm and even some embarrassment (see Bruce 1988, 471; Fitzmyer 1998, 765) that Paul would make an evangelistic appeal to him before the dignitaries (25:23).

Paul's reply (26:29) validates Agrippa's understanding of what the defendant meant. But it also detects the king's attempt to avoid the appeal before him. By echoing Agrippa's phrase (*en oligō*), Paul wittily turns the king's words back on him. He expresses his sincere hope (aorist potential optative: *euxaimēn an*) that Agrippa and the audience would become like him by discovering "the light that found him" (Tannehill 1990, 329). Paul's exclusion of **these chains** from that wish underscores his loss of dignity and honor (see Josephus, *J.W.* 4.628-29; Talbert 1997, 214). Yet during his imprisonment, Paul's speech before King Agrippa fulfills Acts' first divine promise about Paul: he would be a witness before kings, and he would suffer for Jesus' name (9:15-16).

d. Paul's Case Reviewed (26:30-32)

■ **30-32** When the king got up from his seat, it signaled the end of the proceedings (see 25:23). The others took their cue from him and arose as well. The "advisers" (25:23) were discussing (imperfect tense: *elaloun*) Paul's case among themselves as they left. Like Lysias (23:29) and Festus (25:18, 25), they also found Paul not guilty of anything deserving death or even imprisonment. Like Jesus (Luke 23:4, 15, 22), Paul was vindicated three times by various Roman officials.

Yet also like Jesus, Paul was not released (see Krodel 1986, 469). King Agrippa's remarks to Festus reinforce those general observations and suggest that an acquittal would have been possible, had Paul's appeal not sent his case to Rome. But such comments offer little consolation and come too late to help Paul. Given Festus' earlier treatment of Paul (25:9-12) and now Agrippa's response to Paul (26:28), readers have no reason to think these officials would actually have acquitted Paul.

FROM THE TEXT

Some interpreters find Paul's legal troubles a distraction, preferring stories depicting developments of the early Christian movement. Others suggest that this section ends with the second dramatic climax of Acts in ch 26. The first was Cornelius' conversion in 10:1—11:18 (Gaventa 2003, 338; Pervo 2009, 630). This is not merely because of the importance of these hearings for Paul's vindication but for establishing the legitimacy of the Christian church and mission as Luke depicts these (see Pervo 2009, 620).

The real question before readers of Acts is not Paul's innocence, but the legitimacy of the church. Is the church the true people of God as it lives out her mission in the world? Luke closes this chapter in the life of Paul by giving careful attention to his calling and commission. This suggests several things about the mission of the church.

First, the mission of Paul and the church is intricately related to God's purposes that began with Israel. Throughout Acts, what God was doing in Paul's ministry and the church continues what God began in calling Israel to be the people of God. So Paul's piety as a faithful Jew and his calling in the tradition of the OT prophets give continuity between Judaism and the Christian movement.

Luke depicts Paul's mission and ministry among both Jews and Gentiles as consistent with, rather than antithetical to, the Jewish law and the temple. Charges against Paul about such matters eventually drop out of the picture since they were both unsubstantiated and secondary issues at best. This is one reason why Scripture continues to play a significant role in the contemporary church. It provides the means of discernment for the mission of the church in today's terms by considering God's will and activity among the people of God in the past.

Second, the mission of Paul and the church is established by and gives witness to the resurrection of Jesus. On the one hand, Paul's commission came from the resurrected Jesus. His encounter with the risen Christ explains why the persecutor Saul became the proclaimer Paul. On the other hand, central to his mission was testimony to that resurrection, through which God provides salvation to all, both Jews and Gentiles.

Such has been the case for the church throughout Acts, beginning with the Pentecost event. Luke reiterates that in this retrospective look over Paul's ministry. It serves as a reminder for the ongoing ministry and mission of the people of God. Acts insists that what God has done through Jesus' resurrection makes the church and her mission *Christian*. The church is empowered to fulfill her mission as witness to the resurrection through the Spirit given her by that same Jesus.

Third, the mission of Paul and the church has social and political implications. The Roman officials vindicate Paul (and implicitly the Christian movement) of subverting the empire. Paul's gospel is not a call to sedition, but instead an offer through the resurrection to see reality differently. This difference in perspective leads people from "darkness to light." But this has profound implications for all aspects of life.

Political accusations that arose where Paul ministered (e.g., 16:20-21; 17:7) suggest that both Jews and non-Jews alike recognized the far-reaching implications of the gospel. Similarly, the use of titles for Jesus that were widely applied to Caesar (e.g., "Lord" and "Savior") offer more hints about such implications.

But the charges against Paul misunderstood the church's mission because it was viewed from the empire's "logic." The Christian mission transforms culture. But it does so not through force, but through the light from God and the forgiveness of God (see Rowe 2009, 87-89). Central to that mission must be the grace of God that both goes before the church and works within the church. The contemporary church needs to realize this when she is tempted to join the "culture wars." The mission of the church calls her to serve as God's transforming agent *within* the world. We are not adversaries, but ambassadors for another kingdom.

D. Paul's Journey to Rome: Shipwreck and Salvation (27:1—28:16)

BEHIND THE TEXT

Acts includes several accounts of Paul's travels, including sea voyages (see 13:4; 14:26; 16:11; 18:18, 21-22; 20:13-16; 21:1-3, 6-7). So the narration of

403

Paul's journey to Rome by sea is not unexpected. But the extensive attention devoted to this journey (sixty verses) is surprising, when one considers what Acts omits. Luke offers little or no information about the beginnings of the church in Galilee, the ministry of apostles other than Peter, the movement of the gospel into Africa, or the impact of Paul's ministry beyond the sketchy summaries of his ministry in Corinth and Ephesus. The extended account suggests that Luke considered this narrative crucial to his theological agenda.

Stories of sea voyages and their dangers, including shipwreck, appear in a broad range of Greco-Roman literature, including historical works, novels, and classics (e.g., Dionysius of Halicarnassus, *Ant. rom.* 1.49-53; Thucydides, *War* 8.24; Herodotus, *Hist.* 7.188-92; Josephus, *Life* 13-16; Achilles Tatius, *Leuc. Clit.* 3.1-5; Chariton, *Chaer.* 3.5; 8.6; Lucian, *Nav.* 7-10; Petronius, *Satyr.* 114-15; Homer, *Od.* 5.291-332; 9.62-81; 12.201-303; Virgil, *Aen.* 1.34-156). By the first century AD, storm stories were often imitated as part of rhetorical training (see Praeder 1984, 693).

Because storms at sea were a common literary motif, interpreters debate the extent of its influence on Luke's account. Dibelius contended that Acts drew heavily from the pattern of these stories, merely inserting references to Paul within the account (1956, 205). Some interpret Luke's literary strategy or theology by identifying parallels between the account of Paul's shipwreck and similar stories (Praeder 1984, 683-706; Pervo 1987, 50-54; MacDonald 1999, 88-107; Alexander 2005, 69-96). Others minimize the similarities between the Lukan account and Greco-Roman novelistic works, focusing instead on the historicity of Acts (see, e.g., Rapske 1994a, 1-47; Schnabel 2012, 1030).

These differences in approach indicate some of the issues contemporary readers need to consider in the interpretation of this section. This passage provokes intriguing questions about historicity, intertextuality, sources, etc. But arguably the most important question deals with the function of this account within the broader narrative of Acts.

IN THE TEXT

I. Beginning the Journey (27:1-12)

■ **1-2** First-person narration returns for the first time since 21:18 (→ sidebar "First-Person Narration in Acts" with 16:9-10). There is no indication how much time lapsed between Paul's hearing before King Agrippa and his transfer with **some other prisoners** (27:1) for the journey to Rome. Although Paul's appeal had already determined his destination, other logistical and legal matters needed to be finalized (including a letter to accompany Paul the prisoner; see 25:24-27), presumably by Festus (as the Western text clarifies) and other officials.

The verb translated **handed over** (*paradidōmi*) ominously echoes Jesus being "handed over" for death (3:13; Luke 23:23). The **centurion** to whom

Paul was assigned, **Julius**, was a member of the "Augustan Cohort" (NRSV), a Roman army unit comprised of Syrian soldiers, so called because of their honorable service.

The Roman transport of prisoners, as other instances of sea travel in Acts, was arranged on commercial ships that traversed the eastern Mediterranean. The particular ship that Paul and his party boarded was from **Adramyttium** (Acts 27:2), a seaport of northwest Asia Minor (near Troas). It was heading north and then west toward various ports of the Roman province of **Asia**. Sea travel in this part of the Mediterranean often "hugged" the coast and frequently stopped at ports along the way. So the ship would take the centurion, his soldiers, and their prisoners on the circuitous first leg of their journey to Rome.

Luke mentions in passing that Paul's party (whoever "we" may include) is accompanied by **Aristarchus**, whom he further describes as a **Macedonian from Thessalonica**. He was part of the group from Paul's churches who traveled with Paul to Jerusalem (20:4). Luke does not mention him again, although the name appears elsewhere in the Pauline corpus (Phlm 24; also Col 4:10). It is possible that Aristarchus accompanied Paul for only the first leg of the journey, as he traveled back home on a different ship (Bruce 1988, 477).

■ **3** The ship's first stop the next day was at the Phoenician port of **Sidon**, about 80 miles (129 km) north of Caesarea. Luke notes that the centurion Julius treats Paul *kindly* (*philanthrōpōs*), a term reserved for upstanding ethical behavior (see, e.g., 2 Macc 9:27; 3 Macc 3:20; Josephus, *Ant.* 12.46; *Ag. Ap.* 1.153). Luke typically characterizes the behavior of centurions more positively than he does other Roman officials (see Acts 10:1-48; Luke 7:1-10; Parsons 2008, 354). Julius allows Paul to go into the city to see **friends**, probably believers (see Barrett 1998, 1183). Acts does not directly account for the presence of a church in Sidon. But it implies that believers were in the area due to the church's mission (see 11:19; 15:3; also 21:3, 7; see Pervo 2009, 655-56).

The idiom **provide for his needs** (*epimeleias tynchanein*; see Philo, *Spec. Laws* 3.106; Josephus, *Ant.* 2.236) refers to a wide range of care. As one imprisoned for over two years and facing a long journey by ship, Paul depended on the generosity of friends. The heartening images of Paul being cared for by others are the narrative focus, not the logistical details some interpreters consider important. Luke says nothing about how they kept Paul in custody when he was not on the ship or how this opportunity may have been possible as the ship's cargo was loaded or unloaded. These basic scenes remind readers of the hospitality of other caring believers in Acts (e.g., 2:42-47; 4:32-37; 16:15; 20:36-38; 21:4-6, 12-16).

■ **4-6** When the journey resumes, they pass to the north of **Cyprus** (27:4; see 21:1-3), between the island and the coast of Asia Minor. This would protect the ship from northwest winds that complicated sea travel during that season. The ship continues in a westerly direction until reaching **Myra** in **Lycia** (27:5), a province in south Asia Minor. Myra was a principal port for the transport of grain from Alexandria to Rome. It was near Patara, a stop during Paul's previous trip to Jerusalem (21:1). The Western text's addition—that it took fifteen days to reach this destination (Metzger 1994, 440)—is plausible.

From Myra, Julius locates an **Alexandrian ship** (27:6) heading for Rome to take his prisoners to Rome. This ship would have been part of the imperial system that transported grain from Egypt to the capital. Rome was so dependent on imported grain that the emperor Claudius ensured commercial shipments by underwriting the loss of private ships due to weather (Suetonius, *Claud.* 18.2). Some ship owners might try to reach Italy before winter made sailing dangerous, if not impossible.

■ **7-8** The twice-mentioned **difficulty** (v 7) and slow pace of travel after leaving Myra indicate rapidly deteriorating conditions. Their first intended stop was **Cnidus**, a port just over 150 miles (241 km) from Myra on a peninsula protruding from the southeast corner of Asia Minor. But the headwinds prevent the crew from maneuvering the ship into the harbor. So they sail past the port and head in a southwesterly direction toward Crete. Luke does not mention why they do not stop at **Salmone**, an important port for Alexandrian grain ships (see Thucydides, *War* 8.24.35) in far eastern Crete. Sailing near the southern coast of that large island somewhat sheltered the ship from seasonal winds. Another possible port where they could stop, **Fair Havens** (v 8), was located halfway across Crete's southern coast.

■ **9-10** The difficulties in travel take their toll on the ship's itinerary. According to Luke's calculations, the **Day of Atonement** (lit., *the Fast* [v 9]) or Yom Kippur has already passed (late September to early October). This means that the most **dangerous** months for travel are before them (sailing from November through March was discouraged).

This becomes the first of four instances when Paul takes an active role in addressing specific situations on the ship (Skinner 2003, 153). Paul strongly advises (*paraineō*; see v 22; Luke 3:18) them about the looming *danger* and **great loss** involving **ship and cargo** as well as **lives** (Acts 27:10). Paul does not indicate whether his warning comes from his extensive travel experience or divine insight. Readers of Acts recognize him as a reliable character to be taken seriously (see Tannehill 1990, 331).

■ **11-12** Luke oddly describes the **centurion** (v 11) as having the final decision on the continuation of the voyage. The ship's **pilot** and **owner** (or his representative) listen to him rather than Paul. Although the centurion's response to Paul's message may surprise contemporary readers, doomsayers are seldom well received in ancient storm stories (see, e.g., Chion of Heraclea, *Ep.* 4.1; Philostratus, *Vit. Apoll.* 5.18; Polybius, *Hist.* 1.37; see Praeder 1984, 690).

Fair Havens was protected from northerly winds, but the centurion decides it to be **unsuitable for spending the winter**. Perhaps the harbor could not accommodate the ship, or the town lacked necessary accommodations for the crew and passengers (276 total [v 37]; see Barrett 1998, 1191). The **majority** (v 12)—the sailors, pilot, and owner vs. Paul—decide on a plan (*boulē*; see v 42) to continue west about 50 miles (81 km) along the Cretan coast to the harbor of **Phoenix**.

2. Storm and Shipwreck (27:13-44)

a. Storm and Despair (27:13-20)

■ **13-17** A fresh, **gentle south wind** (v 13) initially offers an alluring confirmation of the **plan** (*prothesis*; see 2 Macc 3:8; 3 Macc 1:22; 2:26; 5:12, 29) to continue the voyage. But noteworthy features of ancient stories of storms and sea voyages include (*a*) the forecast of storm and shipwreck and (*b*) a "calm before the storm" (e.g., Apollonius of Rhodes, *Argon.* 4.1223-25; Chion of Heraclea, *Ep.* 4.1-2; Tacitus, *Ann.* 2.23.2; see Praeder 1984, 691).

As the ship heads west while hugging the coastline, a typhoon-like (*typhōnikos* [Acts 27:14]) wind sweeps over the mountains of Crete and drives the craft into open waters. The name of the wind, **Northeaster**, seems to combine the names for two different storm winds (see Lake and Cadbury 1933b, 338-44). The ship is now out of control, another familiar scenario in ancient sea voyage stories (see Homer, *Od.* 9.82-84; Achilles Tatius, *Leuc. Clit.* 3.1-2; Lucian, *Nav.* 7; Parsons 2008, 356).

The wind drives the ship past the **small island** of **Cauda** (v 16), about 25 miles (40 km) south of Crete. By passing south of the island, they find temporary shelter from the wind. So the crew bring aboard the **lifeboat**, which was being towed, so it would not be swamped or battered against the ship. They also **undergirded** or braced the ship with cables, **helps** (*boētheiais*), to hold the craft together (Cadbury 1933c, 345-54).

Some crew members fear the ship could **run aground** (v 17; see v 26) in the notorious shallow gulfs and quicksands of distant **Syrtis**, about 375 miles (604 km) south near the coast of Libya (see, e.g., Apollonius of Rhodes, *Argon.* 4.1235 ff.; Pliny the Elder, *Nat.* 5.26; Strabo, *Geogr.* 17.30.20). The winds were that strong. The sailors try to slow the ship by lowering the *skeuos* (an **anchor** or possibly the mainsail; in 10:11, a *skeuos* was a sheet; Johnson 1992, 448; Hemer 1990, 143-44; see Roloff 1981, 362).

■ **18-20** The next two days do not fare any better. The ship receives such a violent pounding from the storm that they begin to jettison whatever is not attached (*ekbolēn epoiounto*; see Jonah 1:5 [LXX]: *ekbolēn epoiēsanto*). Part of

407

the cargo is discarded first. The ship's equipment for controlling and running the craft go next. Aristotle described this exact scenario to illustrate what people would do in desperation to save their lives (*Eth. nic.* 3.1.5; see also Achilles Tatius, *Leuc. Clit.* 3.2; Juvenal, *Sat.* 12.29-50).

The crisis is exacerbated by the extended period of cloud cover, which blocks the sun and stars from view. Ancient sailors depended on these to navigate the seas. They are lost at sea in the middle of a raging storm. Everyone onboard shares the despair of that moment. Even Paul's entourage (**we**) recognizes the situation to be rapidly deteriorating (imperfect tense: *periēreito*). Such crises often occur in stories of sea voyages (see, e.g., Homer, *Od.* 5.297-304; 12.277-79; Achilles Tatius, *Leuc. Clit.* 3.2.4; 5.9.2; Lucian, *Tox.* 20; Thucydides, *War* 1.2.65).

For the reader of Acts, the divine promise that Paul would bear witness in Rome (23:11) hangs in the balance. Coupled with this is another promise: that those losing **all hope of being saved** (*elpis pasa tou sōzesthai* [27:20]) are among those who, by calling on the name of the Lord, "will be saved" (*sōthēsetai* [2:21]).

b. Paul's Attempt to Encourage (27:21-26)

■ **21-22** People have gone without food (*asitia*), not because of a lack of food but because of a loss of appetite due to anxiety or seasickness (see v 33). After the ship has been lost at sea for nearly two weeks, Paul **stood up** *among* them (v 21; see 17:22) to speak. This is the second time he seeks to intervene during the voyage. His speech is both appropriate to the situation and consistent with this type of story. Similar speeches usually appear at the height of the storm and the depth of travelers' despair (see Praeder 1984, 696).

Paul first reminds the others that they should have **obeyed** (*peitharcheō*; see 5:29, 32; Bultmann, *TDNT* 6:9-10) his earlier instructions. They could have avoided the **damage** and **loss** (see 27:10) now sustained. So by offering more strong advice (*paraineō*; see v 9), the two speeches become linked together, with this speech clarifying the earlier one (v 10). The earlier speech warned against proceeding further. This one offers assurance. Paul calls for them to **be encouraged** (*euthymeō* [v 22]; see vv 25, 36) in the midst of their despair. He assures them that there would be no loss of life, although the ship would be lost.

■ **23-24** The basis of Paul's promise to the others is a divine message he received from an **angel** (v 23; 5:19; 8:26; 10:3; 12:7, 23) of God. This is the only instance in which an angel (rather than the risen Jesus: 9:4-6; 18:9-10; 23:11) appeared to Paul. Perhaps he puts it this way because angels (as divine messengers) would have been more comprehensible to Paul's Gentile audience (see Haenchen 1971, 705).

Paul's declaration about God—**to whom I belong and whom I serve**—echoes Jonah's confession (Jonah 1:9). This description came *after* Jonah tried to escape God's call (see Peterson 2009, 689-90).

Paul and Jonah—Similarities and Differences

The way that Luke tells the story of Paul's sea voyage during a storm is reminiscent of the episode that begins the book of Jonah. In the account about Jonah (Jonah 1:1-16), the ship on which he was traveling was also threatened by a violent storm (v 4). There was so much fear among the sailors (v 5; Acts 27:20) that they implored their gods to save them (Jonah 1:5; Acts 27:29). The crew also took similar desperate measures to "lighten" (LXX: *kouphizō*; Jonah 1:5; see Acts 27:38) the ship by throwing cargo overboard (*ekbolē*; Jonah 1:5; see Acts 27:18; see 27:38 for *ekballō*).

Since these stories are similar, the differences between them stand out prominently.

First, Jonah attempted to avoid God's call to speak prophetically to the Gentile people of Nineveh by taking a ship heading in the opposite direction (Jonah 1:1). Conversely, Paul continued pursuing God's call to Rome (see Acts 19:21; 23:11).

Second, both the narrator of the Jonah story and the sailors understood divine causes as triggering the storm threatening the ship on which Jonah traveled (Jonah 1:4, 10). But in Acts 27, Luke mentions nothing like that. God did not cause the storm. Instead, God promises safety and deliverance from it (v 24).

Third, Jonah's message to the ship's crew created even more fear (Jonah 1:10), but Paul's messages to those aboard the ship eventually brought encouragement (see Acts 27:36).

The angel's message (Acts 27:24) addresses Paul in two ways. First, it reaffirms Jesus' earlier promise that Paul would witness in Rome (23:11). The angel accentuates that divine necessity dictated (*dei*) that he would **stand trial before Caesar**. This may involve an appearance before the emperor or someone under his authority. The present imperative to **not be afraid** echoes Jesus' assurance to Paul in Corinth (18:9). Like before, this may seek to reassure him and call him to *stop being afraid* in the midst of such despair (27:20).

Second, that promise is now expanded to include everyone onboard the ship. This is a clear message of God's salvation by divine intervention at sea. This is a favorite motif in both the OT (see Gen 8:1-14; Pss 89:9; 107:28-30) and other ancient literature (see Achilles Tatius, *Leuc. Clit.* 3.5; Lucian, *Nav.* 9; Plutarch, *Sept. sap. conv.* 161-62).

The wording also credits *Paul* in part for the anticipated rescue. By granting (perfect tense: *kecharistai*) to Paul the safety of those on the ship, the angel implies that God answered his intercessory prayer for *everyone's* (not just his own) safety and deliverance. This expanded promise to rescue or save all aboard the ship becomes important for the remainder of this episode. Everything that happens must be evaluated in light of it. Whatever offers safety for some at the expense of others (Acts 27:30-32) or whatever threatens Paul (v 42) goes against this divine promise and God's plan of salvation for all (Tannehill 1990, 332-33).

■ **25-26** By reiterating his call to *be encouraged* (v 25; see vv 22, 36), Paul declares his faith that God would fulfill those promises. The expression *just as it had been told* resembles similar sayings in the Third Gospel about God's sure promises (Luke 1:45; 2:20; 22:13). But Paul also calls these who are lost at sea to share his faith in this saving God—a picture of universal salvation.

Coupled with this call to faith is some bad news: the ship would **run aground** (Acts 27:26; see v 17) on an **island**. Since the ship has been lost in the open seas for nearly two weeks with no land in sight (see v 27), even this prediction, along with the divine assurance of safety for all, is a prophetic expression of faith (see Haenchen 1971, 705; Bruce 1988, 488). Unfortunately, there is no mention of anyone's response to Paul's speech (see Tannehill 1990, 333; Skinner 2003, 154).

c. Drifting at Sea (27:27-32)

■ **27-29** With Paul's reminder of shipwreck looming in their immediate future (v 26), Luke focuses again on the ship as it is **driven** (*diapherō* [v 27]; vv 15, 17) out into the open sea. The **Adriatic Sea** is typically associated with the sea between Italy and Sicily to the west and Macedonia and Greece to the east. But in ancient times the portion of the central Mediterranean that extends south was also included (see Strabo, *Geogr.* 2.5.20; Pausanias, *Descr.* 5.25.3).

Around midnight of the fourteenth night adrift (after passing Crete and Cauda), the **sailors** "began to suspect" (CEB; imperfect tense: *hypenooun*) that land was nearby. Luke offers no explanation, but they may have heard the distant roar of waves against the coast. In response, they **took soundings** (v 28)—dropped weighted lines to measure the water's depth; then they repeated this a little later. They found that the depth of the water had decreased from about 120 feet (37 m) to about 90 feet (27 m). This confirms they were approaching land.

Their fear that the ship may *run aground* (v 29; see vv 17, 26) was based on their soundings, not on Paul's message (v 26). So by dropping **four anchors from the stern** (rear) of the ship, the sailors take emergency measures to keep the ship away from landfall, or, at least, to delay their approach until daylight. Then they can reasonably see where they are heading.

■ **30-32** The report of desperate sailors attempting to escape the ship interrupts the anxious wait for daylight. It finds parallels in ancient storm stories (see, e.g., Achilles Tatius, *Leuc. Clit.* 3.3; Petronius, *Satyr.* 102). Luke describes the sailors as lowering down the lifeboat under the pretense of dropping anchors from the bow (front) of the ship to secure it.

Paul somehow discovered the cowardly plan like a "vigilant night watchman." By informing the **centurion** and **soldiers** (v 31), he does more than anyone else to protect those onboard (Skinner 2003, 154). Some interpreters suspect that Paul misunderstood the sailors' actions: the ship is not yet sinking and no one has any idea where they are or to where they are escaping (see, e.g., Lake and Cadbury 1933a, 335-36; Haenchen 1971, 702; Pervo 2009, 662).

Regardless, the sailors' actions stand antithetically to the divine promise that Paul received on behalf of everyone on the ship. His declaration about the need for the sailors to **stay with the ship** stresses the importance of having "skilled hands on deck" to finish the voyage. For the first time, others listen to Paul, although it is unclear whether he agrees with the outcome.

The soldiers' release of the lifeboat ensures that the sailors would not attempt such an escape again. But this drastic measure also eliminates any possible evacuation plan to land involving a lifeboat. This leaves the risky alternative of running the ship aground as the only viable option.

d. Paul's Successful Attempt to Encourage (27:33-38)

■ **33-34** For the fourth time, Paul intervenes and attempts to influence the situation. It is **just before dawn** (v 33) when light would disclose the land they hope to reach. Paul's first statement summarizes the situation and reiterates what Luke himself described earlier: the people have eaten nothing (*asitos*; see v 21) because of the **suspense** or anxiety from the stormy voyage. So Paul urges them to *eat some food* (v 34) because it is for their *sōtēria*: their *salvation*, "survival," or "health." Their lack of nutrition would leave them weakened to face the physical challenges before them. Yet he again assures them of their safety, using a common Jewish saying (of not losing even one hair from one's head) to underscore the importance of each person to God (see Luke 12:7; 21:18; also 1 Sam 14:45; 2 Sam 14:11; 1 Kgs 1:52).

■ **35-37** After Paul addresses everyone, he does what he told everyone else to do—he eats some bread. The fourfold description of Paul's actions—which includes him taking **bread**, giving **thanks** to God, breaking it, and then eating it (Acts 27:35)—mirrors Jesus' actions at the feeding of the five thousand (Luke 9:16-17), at the Lord's Supper (Luke 22:19), and as a guest at the disciples' home in Emmaus (Luke 24:30).

Readers should not confuse these allusions as indicators of Eucharistic practices among those on the ship (especially since the passages in Luke's Gospel *themselves* may not be about Eucharist; see, e.g., Thompson 2007, 90-92). These actions are more consistent with the blessing of a Jewish meal (see, e.g., Witherington 1998, 772-73). They correspond with the Lukan summaries of the practices of believers in Jerusalem (Acts 2:42, 46). Paul's actions **in front of them all** confirm his faith in God and call his witnesses to follow his example, both by trusting God themselves and by eating some food.

Paul's address and example are effective. **All** (*pantes*) are **encouraged** (*euthymoi* [27:36]; see vv 22, 25) by Paul's message of hope and promise. They imitate Paul by *taking food themselves*. So the situation dramatically changes with regard to Paul and his role on the ship. He has gone from being an ignored prisoner to the leading voice to whom all now listen (see Skinner 2003, 154).

Luke gives the total number of persons onboard the ship as **276** (v 37). This is a "triangular number," because it is the sum total of the numbers 1 through 23. The significance of the specific number of passengers, after the promise of their safety and their response to Paul (vv 24, 36) and prior to the looming shipwreck, underscores the scope of that promise and how it transforms their outlook.

The number also indicates the ship to be a significant one in size. Josephus claimed that the ship on which he was traveling, which shipwrecked in the same general area of the Mediterranean, was carrying 600 passengers (*Life* 13-15).

■ **38** The connotations of the verb *korennymi* suggests that those onboard not only follow Paul's lead by eating some food but are satisfied or sufficiently fed (see BDAG 2000, 559). Afterward, they prepare the ship a third time (see vv 18-19) for the "inevitable," again lightening the craft. This time, they jettison whatever remains in the ship, whether that be cargo (Fitzmyer 1998, 779), provisions (Johnson 1992, 455), or both.

e. *Shipwreck and Safety on Land (27:39-44)*

■ **39-41** Daylight makes the expected land visible, but no one (even the sailors familiar with those waters) recognizes where they are. But after **they** notice a **bay** with a **beach** (v 39), they devise a plan—to run the ship aground on the beach.

Making that "run" with the ship would require some skillful maneuvering, so the sailors do three things. First, they remove the four anchors dropped earlier from the stern (v 40; see v 29) and leave **them in the sea**. Second, they untie ("loosened" [NRSV]) the cables connected to the **rudders** so they can steer the ship. Third, they raise the foresail to aid with acceleration and steering.

As the ship is heading toward the beach, it inadvertently strikes a **sandbar** (v 41; "reef" [NRSV]; *topos dithalassos*: lit., "a place of two seas," where the waters divide). This was not visible before their approach. The ship runs aground on this "point," rather than on the beach. The ship's bow becomes completely stuck, and the force of the relentless waves begins to destroy (imperfect tense: *elyeto*) the stern.

■ **42-44** With the ship disintegrating, the soldiers devise a *plan* (*boulē*) to **kill the prisoners** so none can *swim away* and *escape* (v 42). The Roman judicial system held soldiers responsible for the escape of any prisoner (see 12:18-19; 16:26-28). But it is unlikely that prisoners could escape by swimming when the storm's fury is breaking the ship into pieces. If prisoners are chained, worries about their escape are unfounded.

The soldiers' plan ironically runs contrary to the purpose or plan (*boulē*; see 2:23; 4:28; 5:38; 13:36; 20:27) of God that Paul would testify in Rome (see Spencer 2004a, 244). So in this time of crisis, as the storm and waves are destroying the ship, these soldiers (like the sailors [27:30-32]) do not remember that God's promise of salvation is for all. So they plan to get rid of the prisoners and save themselves (see Tannehill 1990, 339).

Similar to Lysias (23:12-35), the centurion Julius is able to save (*diasōzō*) Paul from the plans of those who threaten him. Luke does not say how the centurion specifically addresses his soldiers' plan. But Julius takes charge of the situation by laying out a basic evacuation plan for everyone on the ship. Those who can swim are to **jump overboard** (27:43) and swim to shore. All others are to grab a floating piece from the ship and hold on. This picture of persons fleeing a ship was common in ancient shipwreck stories (see, e.g., Homer, *Od.* 5.370-72; Achilles Tatius, *Leuc. Clic.* 3.4).

The end result is that everyone reaches land safely. The passive infinitive *diasōthēnai* leaves unstated the responsible party for saving them. But the Lukan account makes it clear that this is the divine fulfillment of the angel's assurance (vv 23-24).

3. Stay in Malta (28:1-10)

a. Paul and the Snake (28:1-6)

■ **1-2** After no first-person narration in the last part of Acts 27 dealing with the shipwreck (see 27:1-8, 16-20, 27-29), that perspective opens and ends this section (see 28:1-2, 10). Both instances describe how the native people from the island treat the stranded travelers.

The native people are probably responsible for helping the castaways figure out that they are stranded on the island of **Malta** (v 1), about 60 miles (97 km) south of Sicily. Luke uses the term *barbaroi* for the Maltese (see also v 4). This is not derogatory but descriptive, because a Punic dialect (of Phoenician origin) rather than Greek was their first language.

Their Maltese hosts show everyone **unusual kindness** (*ou . . . tychousan philanthrōpian* [v 2]; see Titus 3:4; also Acts 27:3). This includes building a fire to provide heat for the wet and cold travelers as well as welcoming (*proslambanō*; see Rom 14:1, 3; 15:7; Phlm 17) them **all**. Throughout the Third Gospel and Acts, such hospitality represents receptivity to the good news of God's visitation and offering of salvation (Luke 5:29; 7:36-50; 10:1-16, 38-42; 19:1-10; Acts 10:24; 16:11-15; see Johnson 1992, 461). How the Maltese provided for all 276 persons from the ship is unclear, but at this point Luke's account focuses on Paul and his anonymous traveling companions.

■ **3-4** Paul helps the Maltese by collecting some **brushwood** (28:3; "dry sticks" [CEB]) and adds it to the fire. As he does, a snake that is mistakenly gathered with the wood is forced out by the fire's heat and latches on his hand. Luke's description of the snake as a **viper** (*echidna*; see Luke 3:7; Matt 3:7; 12:34; 23:33) indicates it to be poisonous. But people then thought most snakes were (see Pliny, *Nat.* 8.35). Many interpreters debate this matter, since Malta has no poisonous snakes today. But Luke and the Maltese must have shared this ancient perspective.

The Maltese see the **snake** (***wild beast***: *thērion*; see Acts 11:6) and assume the worst about its lethal bite. They consider it to be acting as an agent from nature on behalf of **the goddess Justice** (28:4; → sidebar "The Goddess Justice in the Ancient World" below). They see this as no accident; misfortune comes upon the wicked as punishment from the gods (see Miles and Trompf 1976, 259-67). The Maltese, like the crowd at Jesus' trial, assume Paul guilty of a crime (see Clabeaux 2005, 604-10). They conclude Paul to be a murderer. He had narrowly escaped Justice's hand at sea, but could not escape twice.

The Goddess Justice in the Ancient World

Readers of the Bible often minimize the role of the Greek and Roman myths in the lives and outlook of the populace of the Roman Empire. Yet these stories describe what is called a "worldview" that understands the world, people, and reality in a particular way. The Maltese understanding of what happened to Paul reflects those stories and that ancient worldview.

The goddess Justice was the favorite daughter of Zeus and Themis. She was born human and was put on earth to maintain justice on the earth. But when Zeus recognized how impossible her role was, he assigned her to report to him injustices she observed on earth. Zeus, in turn, dispensed final justice, typically through an agent.

The Maltese interpreted the snake as a natural agent administering justice on behalf of the gods: Paul received what they assumed to be a fatal snakebite as his "sentence," because he was guilty of taking another's life. Their unique theological interpretation of Paul's situation made them skeptical about his innocence and chances of survival (see Peterson 2009, 700).

■ **5-6** Paul rids himself of the snake by shaking it from his hand into the fire. And the expected adverse effects from the snakebite never appear. Paul does not ***suddenly drop dead*** (v 6) or even, as the verb *pimprēmi* suggests, swell up or develop a severe fever (LSJ 1996, 1405). Once these Maltese witnesses are convinced that **nothing unusual** would occur, they **changed their minds**. They now identify Paul as a god rather than a murderer.

When the people of Lystra falsely assumed Barnabas and Paul were gods, it reflected their "thought world." The Lystrans began by seeking to worship Paul as a god and ended up leaving him for dead (→ 14:8-20). The Maltese begin by believing Paul to be a capital criminal and end up praising him as a divine being (see Spencer 2004a, 245). In both cases, readers should recognize the fickleness and misunderstanding of the people. They came to their conclusions based on pagan ideas rather than the gospel (see Cadbury 1927, 341).

Unlike the Lystran account, Luke mentions nothing about Paul's response to the Maltese who seek to deify him. His comments and actions on shipboard express his utter confidence in and dependence on God (27:24-25, 34-35). This suggests that Paul would continue to proclaim his own allegiance and reliance on the sovereign God who called and saved him. Even Paul's immunity to a viper's venom comes from the authority of Jesus, not from himself (see Luke 10:17-19; also Garrett 1989, 46-57). Since snakes were often viewed as agents of Satan (see Rev 19:9; 20:2), overcoming snakebite may depict Paul's victory over Satan's power and highlight the cosmic dimensions of his mission (see Spencer 2004a, 245).

b. Paul's Ministry among the Maltese (28:7-10)

■ **7-8** It is possible that news of Paul's immunity from the snakebite gained him and his group audience with **Publius** (v 7). He was a major landowner on the island and one of its local leaders (*prōtos tēs nēsou*). Like the Maltese public (v 2), Publius welcomes the group (not all 276) into his home and treats them hospitably (*philophronōs*; see v 2; 27:3; 2 Macc 3:9; Josephus, *Ant.* 11.340; *J.W.* 6.115) as his guests (*xenizō*; see Acts 10:6, 18, 23, 32; 21:16) for **three days.** Such hospitality signifies receptivity to the gospel (→ v 2).

Paul's healing of Publius' father is in response to the host's hospitality. The brief account is reminiscent of Jesus' healing of Peter's mother-in-law (Luke 4:38-39). Paul finds the man **lying in bed** (see Mark 1:30) and **suffering from fever** (Acts 28:8; see Luke 4:38) as well as **dysentery.** Paul heals (*iaomai*; Acts 9:34; 10:38; 28:27) him by praying *and* placing his hands on him.

This is the only place in Acts where both actions—prayer and the laying on of hands—occur in the context of healing. Elsewhere, both actions occur together only in contexts of setting persons apart for a specific ministry (6:6; 13:3). This picture offers clarification about Paul's identity after earlier misunderstandings over him, since prayer indicates his dependence on God for the ability to heal.

■ **9-10** The response of others on the island after this healing resembles what happened to Jesus in Galilee after he healed Peter's mother-in-law. Acts similarly portrays Peter as one to whom others would regularly come and be cured (imperfect tense: *etherapeuonto*; also 19:11-12), as was the case with Jesus (Luke 4:40).

Paul's miracle-working lies behind the honor (*timē*) the people extend (*timaō*) him and his associates. Since in Acts the noun *timē* often has monetary connotations (see 4:34; 5:2-3; 7:16; 19:19), the people express their honor and

ACTS

28:7-10

415

gratitude for Paul's ministry by taking care of needed provisions when his party is ready to leave (see LSJ 1996, 1793-94; Skinner 2003, 161). Paul ministered to the needs of others, and now these grateful people reciprocate by seeing to it that the needs of Paul and others are met.

Some question whether Paul proclaimed the gospel or won any converts in Malta. Luke mentions nothing about these matters (see, e.g., Marshall 1980, 418). But such sharing of possessions mirrors the responsiveness that occurs in the context of the gospel (see 2:42-47; 4:32-37; see Luke 6:32-36; 8:3; 12:32-34; 14:13-14; 21:1-4).

4. Final Leg over Land to Rome (28:11-16)

■ **11-14** With Paul's journey not yet complete, Luke picks up the remaining itinerary. The **three months** (v 11) that he mentions may be an approximation, as this would still leave them in the winter months. Or it may be that travel in these parts would not be as dangerous as in the open Mediterranean, since ships could stay close to shore.

Paul's party boards another Alexandrian grain ship (see 27:6). This ship had been wintering in Malta. It sailed with the **figurehead** or insignia of the **twin gods Castor and Pollux**, sons of Zeus and patron deities of ships, who were believed to offer protection on the seas (see Epictetus, *Diatr.* 2.18.29; Lucian, *Nav.* 9). Readers of Acts should see the irony: those who looked to these pagan gods for protection on the seas stayed in Malta for the winter. But the true God rescued Paul and others from storm and shipwreck (see Talbert 1997, 224; Spencer 2004a, 246).

Luke mentions three stops on the ship's itinerary. The first stop is the prosperous port city of **Syracuse** (28:12), about 100 miles (161 km) northeast of Malta on the southeastern coast of Sicily. They remain there **three days**, perhaps because of unfavorable wind conditions or so they could unload and load cargo (see Haenchen 1971, 718).

From there, they continue north along the eastern coast of Sicily about 80 miles (129 km) to **Rhegium** (v 13), on the southern tip of Italy. After this second stop, they continue northwest along the western coast of Italy.

They travel over 200 miles (322 km) to the port of **Puteoli**, on the Gulf of Naples, the chief southern port of entry for Rome. All grain for Rome came through this port, which may be why Strabo described it as the most important port of Italy (*Geogr.* 5.4.6). Passengers also disembarked here and then traveled the remaining distance to Rome—over 120 miles (193 km)—by road.

Luke mentions that Paul's group locates some believers (lit., **brothers**) in Puteoli (v 14). One may reasonably conclude that, with a Jewish colony in the city (see Josephus, *J.W.* 2.104; *Ant.* 17.328), the gospel had been shared there and at least some responded favorably. These believers **invited** (*parakaleō*) Paul and his party to stay with them for a week.

416

Historical questions about how such an extended stay was possible dominate discussions on this passage. Rapske concludes that business kept the centurion Julius in Puteoli for a week, thereby making it possible for Paul (under guard) to have this extended time with the believers (1994b, 272-76; see also Hemer 1990, 156; Bruce 1988, 502).

Such *historical* concerns miss Luke's *narrative* concerns. He does not mention any details about Paul's status as a prisoner during this visit. Luke depicts believers extending the invitation to stay (*epimenō*). In Acts, this verb often describes a visiting "missionary" with other believers (see 10:48; 21:4, 10; but see 12:16; 28:12; Skinner 2003, 161). The narrative focuses on the hospitality of the believers in Puteoli. Their actions are reminiscent of other believers throughout Acts (e.g., 2:42-47; 4:32-37; 9:43; 10:48; 14:28; 16:15, 33-34; 21:4, 7, 10, 16).

The brief last statement in v 14—**And so we came to Rome**—seems out of place, considering that (*a*) the city is still a considerable distance away and (*b*) Luke would make almost the same declaration (v 16*a*) when the party actually *does* arrive in Rome. Yet these words announce that God's promise— that Paul would bear witness in Rome—is now seeing its fulfillment.

■ **15** The week's stay in Puteoli may have provided necessary time for news to reach the believers in Rome (see v 14) that Paul and his companions were traveling there. Luke says nothing about how they received the news.

What concerns Luke is that Roman believers set out to meet the party as they travel north to the capital city and to escort them into the city. The term *apantēsis* for that meeting often describes the official welcome of a visiting dignity to a city (Bruce 1988, 502; see Matt 25:6; 1 Thess 4:17).

Some greet the party as far as the **Forum of Appius**, a town along the Appian Way over 40 miles (64 km) southeast of Rome. Others meet them at the **Three Taverns**, another town on the same road over 30 miles (48 km) outside the city. The sight of these welcoming believers sparks both thanksgiving and encouragement in Paul.

> That he was encouraged by the welcome does not mean that he was distraught before. Rather, the welcome by the Roman Christians, the favorable impression they made on Paul, the realization that they were with him, leading him in a humble and yet triumphant procession to Rome, became a source for renewed courage. (Krodel 1986, 482)

■ **16** Upon arriving in Rome, arrangements are made that allow Paul to remain under house arrest. The Western text expands this to clarify that the other prisoners do not receive such treatment. Paul has to be detained since his case is still undecided. But he can be given some freedoms, since the Romans do not view him as a security risk, assigning only one soldier to him at a time.

FROM THE TEXT

The attention that Luke gives to Paul's sea voyage to Rome suggests that readers of Acts take these narrative materials seriously. Recent commentators agree on this point. There is difference of opinion, however, with regard to what *specifically* readers should take seriously. The narrative offers a gripping story that leaves readers in suspense about Paul's safety and future, even with divine promises that he would testify in Rome. The question still remains as to what this section contributes to the broader narrative of Acts. To this question, three related responses may be offered.

First, Luke appropriates the feature of familiar stories of sea voyages, storms at sea, and shipwreck to depict God's continuing guidance and provision for Paul and his mission. Earlier legal hearings offer opportunities to show that the Christian mission extending to the Jews and the Gentiles alike came from the God of Israel. Just so, these stories provide vivid pictures of how God gave Paul the necessary insight and wisdom to save not only himself but everyone else on the ship.

Here, readers can see the symbolic death and resurrection of Paul as in the earlier story of Peter's imprisonment and rescue (12:1-19): (a) Paul's death seemed certain (see 27:20); and (b) God's intervention and salvation spared Paul and the others (but see Johnson 1992, 457). While this underscores Paul's innocence, it also affirms God's validation of the Christian mission as lived out by Paul.

Second, Luke depicts Paul as continuing to trust God when circumstances could have tempted him to think otherwise. During the storm at sea and after he had been bitten by the snake, Paul faced circumstances that could have been interpreted negatively. Certainly, others did—those on the ship (27:20) and the Maltese (28:4-6).

That does not mean that the crisis of the moment did not evoke a natural response of fear from someone like Paul (→ 27:24). But he need not and did not succumb to popular opinion about how God works. Instead, he trusted God and prayed for divine intervention: for himself and for everyone with him. God "graced" him by granting his request. And it is that same trust in God that we find throughout Paul's ministry and throughout his defense hearings.

Third, Luke depicts Paul's ministry as continuing throughout his travels to Rome. As a prisoner, Paul has no "pulpit" from which to proclaim the gospel. But there are subtle indications of transformation as a result of the gospel. The various descriptions of hospitality by unlikely people (e.g., 28:2, 7-10) suggest receptivity to the good news, even in the absence of Paul preaching. In addition, references to fellowship with believers along the way (27:3; 28:14, 15) and to their provision for Paul's needs prepare for his arrival in Rome. All these contribute to the overall depiction of the church in Acts.

E. Paul in Rome (28:17-31)

BEHIND THE TEXT

Paul's arrival in Rome signals the fulfillment of the Spirit's call that he would go to the capital of the empire (→ 19:21). But readers know this was partial, since Paul had not yet offered testimony in Rome regarding Jesus or the gospel (→ 23:11). This correlates with the commission that Jesus extended to the apostles: their witness would be taken not only to Jerusalem, Judea, and Samaria but also to Rome as *the end of the earth* (→ 1:8). As the capital city of the empire, Rome occupies a significant theological place within Acts. It also represents God's purposes in bringing salvation to all. So it is no surprise that Jesus' call would ultimately find its fulfillment through Paul's ministry, which Luke repeatedly describes as an inclusive message of salvation.

Throughout this final section, the narrative focuses squarely on Paul and his interaction with others. The first-person perspective of the "we" materials disappears. Nothing is said about Paul's traveling companions. Attention is solely on Paul and his activities.

IN THE TEXT

1. Paul's Initial Meeting with Local Jewish Leaders (28:17-22)

■ **17-18** Since Paul is under house arrest (v 16), he himself cannot go to one of the city's synagogues, as in prior settings. In a reversal of roles, Paul the prisoner instead summons (5:21; 10:24; 13:7) local Jewish leaders to his residence. That he does so after only **three days** (28:17) implies some urgency. The defensive tone of Paul's self-introduction indicates his concern to inform them about his case, perhaps to persuade them not to make hasty conclusions against him (should they hear of him).

The Jewish Community in Rome

Jews probably first settled in Rome in the mid-second century BC. Many Jews were originally brought to Rome as slaves by Pompey in 63 BC. By the time Paul arrived in the city, the Jewish population was fairly large (see Josephus, *J.W.* 2.80-92; *Ant.* 17.300)—perhaps fifty thousand people worshiping in ten to twelve synagogues (see Clarke 1994, 466-71; Rapske 1994b, 330-31). The edict by the emperor Claudius two decades earlier must have caused these numbers to fluctuate (→ sidebar "Claudius and His Edicts against the Jews" with 18:1-3). It was probably synagogue leaders whom Paul invited to meet with him (v 17) since no central organizational structure for synagogues existed.

Still, the Jewish populace was well-known for influencing public and political opinion. Cicero recognized their power to sway public opinion against one of

419

his clients (see *Flac.* 66-69). Josephus also described the effects of the opposition of 8,000 Jews (see *J.W.* 2.105; *Ant.* 17.330). So Paul's meeting with the Jewish leaders may have been preemptive.

Upon the gathering of these local leaders, Paul cordially addresses them—**Men, brothers**—like other introductions or addresses within speeches in Acts (see 1:16; 2:29; 7:2; 13:26, 38; 22:1; 23:1, 6). His first statement is a summary of what was said during prior hearings. Paul's claim of having done **nothing** against the Jewish **people** (*laos*; see, e.g., 2:47; 3:23; 4:10; 5:12-13; 10:2; 13:24; 26:23) or ancestral **customs** (see 21:28; 22:3; 23:6; 24:12-16; 25:8; 26:4-8) asserts his Jewishness and fidelity to their Jewish heritage. But it would have been refuted by his opponents, including some within the Jerusalem church (see 21:21). Yet Paul's claim has broader implications than just his faithfulness as a Jew. It also affirms that his mission is not anti-Jewish in nature.

Paul's self-description of his arrest in Jerusalem conflates earlier accounts of what happened there. Paul's being handed over (*paradidōmi*) to the Romans echoes Jesus' passion predictions (see Luke 9:44; 18:32), although the prior account depicts the Roman soldiers saving him from the Jewish crowd (Acts 21:30, 33). Paul's affirmation about Roman officials who **were wanting** (imperfect: *eboulonto*) to **release** him—after their official investigations or hearings (see 23:1-10; 24:2-21; 25:6-12; 26:2-29)—is reminiscent of Jesus' trial (see Luke 23:13-22). This only partially conveys what Luke narrated earlier, since no official *stated* the desire to release Paul. It was only declared that he *could* have been released had he not appealed to the emperor (Acts 26:32). But the conclusion—that there was no **cause** (*aitia*: "reason" [NRSV, CEB]; see 13:28; 22:24; 23:28; 25:18, 27; 26:31; also Luke 23:1) for the death penalty he now faces—is sound. It corresponds with Jesus' trial (see Luke 23:4, 15, 22) and with the opinions of the centurion Lysias (Acts 23:29), the governor Festus (25:25), and King Agrippa (26:31).

■ **19-20** Luke depicts Jewish opposition to Paul as ongoing (present tense: *antilegontōn*; see v 22; 13:45). This implicitly refers to his Jewish opponents' repeated accusations and the use of their political influence against him (24:27; 25:9). The issue is not Jewish resistance to any Roman plan to release him (see Tannehill 1990, 346).

Paul mentions nothing of Festus' role that led to him being **compelled** (*anankazō*; see 26:11) **to appeal to Caesar** (25:10-11). Nor does it account for the governor's different accounts (25:16-21, 24-25). Rather, he places blame entirely on the Jewish authorities in Jerusalem.

Yet Paul assures the Jewish leaders of Rome that he has no legal charge (*katēgoreō*; see 22:30; 24:2, 8, 13, 19; 25:5, 11, 16) or countersuit against his Jewish opponents (see Witherington 1998, 798-99) or the **nation**. He depicts himself as a faithful Jew and friend of the Jewish people.

Paul's explanation for his desire to meet the Jewish leaders in Rome (v 20) takes two forms.

First, **for this reason** (*aitia*) refers back to any or all of three things he has already mentioned: (1) the charge (*aitia*) against Paul (v 18), (2) Paul's explanation of his appeal to Caesar (v 19), and (3) more specifically the lack of charge or countersuit against the Jews (v 19; see Witherington 1998, 798).

Second, he relates his legal issues to the **hope of Israel**, a recurring theme (see 23:6; 24:15; 26:6-8, 22-23). That hope represents God's promise of Israel's restoration and salvation through Jesus as God's Messiah. This is to be achieved through the church's mission that began among the Jewish people and expanded through Paul to include both Jews and Gentiles (see Wall 2002, 360).

Ironically, Paul is a prisoner because of his obedience to his prophetic call, which underscores his Jewish fidelity. His chains are antithetical to the liberation promised by this hope, both for Paul and Israel (see Tannehill 1990, 345; Pervo 2009, 683).

■ **21-22** The response from the Jewish leaders is surprising in several ways.

First, their lack of hostility toward Paul contrasts with others, notably the leaders in Jerusalem.

Second, they claim to have no prior knowledge about Paul or his case, including no information **from Judea** (v 21). The leaders' response implies some contact with those in Judea. One would assume that the animosity toward Paul in Jerusalem would have led to some attempts to influence the Roman Jews against Paul (see Barrett 1998, 1241). Indeed, as plaintiffs in Paul's case, his accusers were legally required to send representatives to Rome. One would think they would travel with the same expediency as Paul's party and would have met with the Jewish leaders in Rome. Of course, it is possible that they had not yet arrived.

Third, these leaders ask nothing about Paul's relationship with believers in Rome. This is surprising, after the emperor Claudius expelled Jews from Rome a few years earlier over messianic or Christian teachings (→ sidebar "Claudius and His Edicts against the Jews" with 18:1-3). Such silence implies either a complete rift between the Roman Jews and believers (Barrett 1998, 1242-43) or the absence of believers from the city (Conzelmann 1987, 222). Both appear unlikely. Some try to avoid such difficulties by reading these comments as a diplomatic response by people unwilling to commit themselves by siding with Paul (Bruce 1988, 505-6).

After the Jewish leaders' initial statement about Paul, they extend an invitation (28:22) for him to address them about **this sect** (see 5:17; 24:5, 14; 26:5). They appear open to continue the conversation and learn more about this "party" within Judaism (→ 24:5). But they describe the movement somewhat negatively, referring to its extensive (**everywhere**) opposition (*antilegō* [v

19; 13:45]). This hints that such a conversation may be unproductive (see 17:6; Gaventa 2003, 366) or at least tainted with skepticism (see Bock 2007, 754).

2. Paul's Second Meeting with Jewish Leaders (28:23-28[29])

■ **23** The arrangement of a subsequent meeting enables Paul to offer his own explanation about the gospel and the Christian movement. The account parallels what happened in the synagogue of Pisidian Antioch (13:42-47). Here, however, Paul's house arrest keeps him from traveling to a Roman synagogue and requires the Jewish leaders to come to his **guest room** ("lodgings" [NRSV]; see Phlm 22; BDAG 2000, 683; LSJ 1996, 1188). **More** (*pleiones*) leaders come for this second meeting than the first. The setting would have limited the numbers who attend, yet Luke's interests focus on the initial response (see Marshall 1980, 423-24).

Paul's Living Arrangements in Rome

Housing costs in first-century Rome were exorbitant. Only the wealthy could afford to purchase or even rent private houses. Most of Rome's million residents lived in leased one- or two-room dwellings located in the thousands of tenement buildings of the city. These buildings typically housed shops or artisan workspace on the ground floor, with small apartments above (see Oakes 2009, 1-97). Their construction and safety were often substandard. They had minimal amenities—typically, the higher the floor, the fewer the amenities. Kitchen and bathroom facilities were usually shared, if available. Rooms were seldom heated.

For travelers or others needing temporary accommodations, boardinghouses or inns were available, often with a restaurant nearby. These were more affordable, also notoriously unsanitary, and pest-infested. Neighbors were usually of dubious moral character (prostitutes and sailors).

The acceptance of Paul's invitation (28:17, 23) implies that he rented an apartment rather than a room at a boardinghouse. These leaders would have likely avoided the conditions and questionable location of a boardinghouse. A leased apartment would have provided more space for the second meeting (v 23). Landlords would have hesitated to rent to a person awaiting trial, but Paul might have paid for the entire lease in advance. It is unclear what, if any, assistance he received from the Roman believers who escorted him into the city (v 15; see Krodel 1986, 507; Rapske 1994b, 228-39). But Luke depicts him as paying his own expenses (see v 30; also 20:33-34). Those interpreters who try to explain how Paul paid his expenses by practicing his trade in Rome (e.g., Lake and Cadbury 1933a, 348; Tajra 1989, 191-92; Bruce 1988, 509-10) move beyond the scope of Luke's narrative depiction of the Christian prisoner.

Unlike the first meeting, Paul no longer focuses on defending himself but on **explaining** (*ektithēmi*; see 11:4; 18:26) and offering thorough testimony (*diamartyromai*; → 2:40) about the **kingdom of God**. This same Lukan expression encapsulates both Jesus' message about God's salvation offered to all humanity (→ 1:3; also Luke 4:43; 8:1; 16:16) and the church's message in Acts (see 8:12; 14:22; 19:8; 20:25).

The divine promise of Paul witnessing in Rome as he had in Jerusalem (23:11) is fulfilled. His intention is to persuade (*peithō* [13:43; 14:19; 17:4; 18:4; 19:8, 26; 21:14; 26:28]) this difficult audience about Jesus. This is no one-sided speech, but an impassioned debate between Paul and his visitors (see Alexander 2005, 217; Parsons 2008, 364). This is evident in the duration of the meeting, which stretches **from morning till evening**. As usual, Paul bases his message on the interpretation of both **the Law of Moses** and **the Prophets** (i.e., the Scriptures; see 17:2-3; 18:4-5; see Luke 24:27, 44).

■ **24-27** Like earlier episodes, the response from Paul's Jewish debate partners is mixed (see Acts 13:42-48; 14:4; 17:4-9, 12-13; 18:6-11; 19:8-10). Luke highlights the division within his audience with the formula *hoi men . . . hoi de* (see Alexander 2005, 215). So **some** were **being persuaded** (28:24; imperfect passive: *epeithonto*) by Paul's arguments. But **others** were **refusing to believe** (imperfect: *ēpistoun*). The imperfect tense suggests the durative or ongoing sense of what happened during the course of the debate.

The response of disbelief corresponds with Jewish resistance throughout Acts, first among the religious leaders in Jerusalem and then among many Diaspora Jews during Paul's ministry. Because of Paul's strong response to the Jewish resistance (see vv 26-28), some suggest that those who were **being persuaded** merely sided with some of his claims (see, e.g., Haenchen 1971, 723-24; Conzelmann 1987, 227). But the similarity of this mixed response to earlier scenes in Paul's ministry suggests that these were either repentant at the time (for such use of *peithō*, see 17:4; 19:8, 26) or in the process leading toward it (see, e.g., Barrett 1998, 1244; Fitzmyer 1998, 795; Marguerat 1999, 298-99; Tannehill 1990, 347).

The disagreement or disharmony (*asymphōnos*; see Wis 18:10; Bel 15; Philo, *Spec. Laws* 2.130) among Paul's Jewish visitors as they leave contrasts with the unity (*homothymadon*; see 1:14; 2:46; 4:24; 5:12) that earlier characterized the believers in Jerusalem (see Pervo 2009, 684; Schnabel 2012, 1072). The conflict may have been over Paul's contention that Jesus is God's Messiah (see Wall 2002, 360). Throughout Acts, such problems typically arise over Paul's teachings related to Jesus' messiahship, notably an inclusive gospel extending salvation to all peoples.

In contrast to the disagreement among the Jewish respondents, Paul introduces (28:25*b*) his last comments to them as being in agreement with the Holy Spirit's message as given through **Isaiah the prophet** (see Marguerat 1999, 299; Gaventa 2003, 367). By referring to **your ancestors**, Paul puts distance between himself and the unbelieving Jews (see v 17: "our ancestors").

This leads into his quotation of Isa 6:9-10 (LXX). Elsewhere in the NT, this passage explains Jewish rejection of the gospel (see Matt 13:14-15; Mark 4:12; Luke 8:10; John 12:39-40; Rom 11:7-8). The opening of this passage—**Go to this people and say** (Acts 28:26)—indicates that this explains the prophet's role among an unresponsive people. Two negated aorist subjunctives—*ou mē synēte* and *ou mē idēte*—offer the strongest negations possible: that they would **never understand** or **perceive** despite all they continued to hear and see.

The Isaiah passage metaphorically depicts Jewish resistance in three ways (Acts 28:27a):

(1) their hearts became **calloused** and impervious to God's will and guidance,

(2) their ears had difficulty hearing—accepting and obeying—the gospel message, and

(3) their eyes were shut to the workings of God.

By quoting the LXX, which renders the Hebrew imperatives as aorist indicatives, Paul places full responsibility and guilt for such problems squarely on the Jewish people (see, e.g., Haenchen 1971, 724; Longenecker 1981, 570-71).

The specific purposes behind Jewish resistence to the gospel (the conjunction *mēpote* [v 27b]) also kept them from turning to God (*epistrephō*; see 3:19; 9:35; 11:21; 14:15; 15:19; 26:18, 20) in repentance. The original context of this passage *precedes* the prophet Isaiah's ministry to Judah and offers God's bleak assessment of Judah's spiritual health. The citation of this passage here in Acts should be similarly understood as a spiritual appraisal of the departing Jewish leaders. Paul does not pronounce judgment or announce the end of a Christian mission inclusive of the Jewish people. As Stephen declared earlier, their resistance and lack of belief correspond with ancestral responses to the prophets (see 7:51-52). Such responses undermine God's desires to **heal them**—God's saving activity among them.

■ **28 (and 29)** Paul's final declaration to his departing Jewish visitors—*let it be known to you*—stands in contrast to the Jewish leaders' own statement about their professed knowledge (*gnōston hēmin estin* [v 22]). His affirmation about the inclusiveness of **God's salvation** is now a familiar theme (e.g., 2:21; 4:12; 7:25; 13:26, 47; see Luke 2:30; 3:6).

The emphatic position of the phrase **to the Gentiles** underscores for a third time (see Acts 13:46-47; 18:6) that this divine activity extends to *all* humanity. Gentiles, in stark contrast to Jews who are deaf and unresponsive (28:26-27), would **listen** and respond favorably to the gospel (see Isa 40:5; Pss 67:2; 98:3). This declaration should be interpreted in general ways, since not *all* Gentiles embraced the gospel. Just so, not *all* Jews rejected it. Paul does not mean that the Christian mission to the Jews is over (but see 13:46-47; 18:6).

The contrast is not of different missions but of different responses to the one mission (see Larkin 1995, 391).

The Place of the Jewish People in the Mission of Paul and the Church

The threefold Pauline declaration to a Jewish audience that Gentiles would receive God's salvation (13:46-47; 18:6; 28:28) raises questions about the place of the Jewish people in the ongoing mission of Paul and the church. Since the pronouncement in ch 28 occurs at book's end, many interpreters view this as the closure of a failed Jewish mission, with the Isaiah quotation functioning as an indictment against Jewish rejection of the gospel (e.g., Haenchen 1971, 721-32; Gaston 1986, 27-53; Maddox 1982, 31-65; Roloff 1981, 370-71; Sanders 1987, 296-99). A related position asserts the termination of the Jewish mission due to its success rather than failure, as indicated by responses of repentance throughout Acts (Jervell 1972, 41-72; 1998, 628-29).

Others view Paul's declaration differently: as a statement about Jewish rejection of the gospel and God's inclusion of all humanity within the scope of salvation. There are three reasons for this.

First, Paul states nothing here (v 28) about turning *away* from the Jews. This suggests that the declaration has nothing to do with an end to the Jewish mission.

Second, Paul's earlier declarations (13:46-47; 18:6) were followed by his return to ministry in a synagogue context upon entering a new city. So his pronouncements were more local than global in scope.

Third, the summary that concludes Acts depicts Paul as "welcoming all who came to him" (v 30 NASB). This leaves readers to infer that *individual* Jews were among Paul's guests. An interpretation of the third declaration (in Rome) in light of the first two may suggest that Paul continued to proclaim the gospel to Jews and Gentiles alike (see, e.g., Bock 2007, 749-50; Brawley 1987, 68-78; 1998, 293-96; Tannehill 1990, 344-57; Wall 2002, 362-63). But this proclamation probably no longer held onto the hope of unifying the Jewish people as the people of God through belief in Jesus as the Messiah (see Tyson 1992, 174-78; Marguerat 1999, 299-301).

Verse 29—***And after he said these things, the Jews left, having a vigorous debate among themselves***—which the KJV includes, is based on the Western text. It was probably included to smooth the transition between v 28 and v 30 (see Metzger 1994, 444).

3. Paul's Ministry Continues (28:30-31)

■ **30** Although the division among the Jewish leaders who visited Paul is consistent with the rest of Acts, it is neither the last image nor the final word left with the reader (see Marguerat 1999, 301). Like other summaries in Acts, Luke offers a generalized picture or progress report of activity over a period of time (imperfect tense: *enemeinen, apedecheto*) instead of a specific scene. These summaries usually offer a transition between periods of witness, so this implies a continuation of the witness depicted in Paul's ministry (see Rosner 1998, 231).

Interpreters offer different explanations for the summary's span of **two whole years**. Some understand this as a hint at termination, specifically Paul's release or death (e.g., Conzelmann 1987, 227-28; Hemer 1990, 383-87). Others suggest that there may have been delays, due to the typical backlog of Roman court business (see Dio Cassius, *Hist.* 60.28.6; Rapske 1994b, 317) or the plaintiffs' loss of interest in the case (since Paul was no longer a problem in Jerusalem).

A better alternative relates this period of time to other extended stays noted in Acts—in Antioch (11:26), Corinth (18:11), and Ephesus (19:10). In these other cities, Paul enjoyed extended ministries among Jews and Gentiles (see Wall 2002, 367; Pervo 2009, 686). This correlates with Paul's consistent welcome (imperfect: *apedecheto*) of **all** who visited him, including "both Jews and Gentiles" (Western text).

Paul's hospitality occurs at his rented housing (28:16, 23). The technical term *misthōma* emphasizes that Paul paid for those housing expenses himself (see Mealand 1990, 583-89). To the end of Acts, Luke depicts Paul as an ideal pastor caring for his own needs rather than relying on others (see 20:33-34; see Marguerat 1999, 303).

■ **31** With two present participles, Luke describes Paul as continuing to do the same things in Rome as he did elsewhere. The first participle, ***preaching*** (*kēryssōn*), uses the same term for Paul's activity (see also 9:20; 19:13; 20:25) as for earlier apostolic proclamation (10:37, 42; also 8:5). The subject of that proclamation is the **kingdom of God** (see v 23). Luke reiterates the continuity between the message that Paul preaches at the end of Acts and the message Jesus preached at the book's beginning (1:3).

The second participle, ***teaching*** (*didaskōn*), repeats another verb that earlier describes the activities of Paul (11:26; 15:35; 18:11; 20:20; 21:21, 28; for the noun *didachē*, see 13:12; 17:19) and the apostles (4:2, 18; 5:21, 25, 28, 42; for *didachē*, see 2:42; 5:28). Jesus both modeled such activity (1:1) and, as **Lord** and **Christ**, was the basis of such gospel teaching (see 2:22-37). Since persons had earlier responded in repentance to the ministry of preaching and teaching throughout Acts, readers should anticipate similar responses as the gospel continues to be shared.

The wording of Acts ends with two descriptions of Paul's preaching and teaching. First, the expression **with all boldness** is noteworthy since Luke often associates this trait with the apostles (2:29; 4:13, 29, 31) and Paul (9:27-28; 13:46; 14:3; 19:8). Since Luke typically links such boldness to a group

426

of believers, one may conclude that this comes from the growing number of believers in Rome (see Thompson 2006, 235-36; against Barrett 1998, 1237).

Second, the book ends with the adverb **unhindered** (*akōlytōs*). This term, in Greek (e.g., Plutarch, *Stoic. rep.* 1056c) and Jewish (e.g., Wis 7:23; Josephus, *J.W.* 7.346) circles, describes divine sovereignty (Mealand 1990, 591-95). More than once, Acts raises the question: Who might hinder another from responding to what God is doing (8:36; 10:47; 11:17; see 5:39)? The ending of Acts leaves no doubt as to the answer. Opponents could not stop Paul or the gospel. Neither could mighty Rome.

The Ending of Acts and Paul's Fate

The abrupt ending of Acts without divulging Paul's fate within the Roman judicial system has long left readers puzzled. What happened next? What were Luke's literary intentions that led him to leave his narrative unresolved? Most interpreters conclude, based on the text of 28:30-31, that Luke wrote or completed Acts after the conclusion of Paul's imprisonment and knew the judicial verdict. So why did Luke not disclose it? Several historical explanations exist.

First, an older view is that Luke planned a third volume after Acts (Ramsay 1895, 27-28). One major problem is that Acts includes no hints anticipating a subsequent work.

Second, Paul was acquitted after his accusers failed to appear (see Fitzmyer 1998, 796-97). This is unlikely, since penalties for failing to appear were severe. But if Luke knew this happened, its disclosure would correlate with what other Roman officials concluded about the case.

Third, Paul was eventually executed, either during this imprisonment or shortly thereafter (against Eusebius, *Hist. eccl.* 2.22). But Luke did not disclose it because he did not wish to end Acts on such a negative note (Haenchen 1971, 732). However, this view does not adequately consider that oral stories about Paul's martyrdom would still influence those who read and interpret the ending of Acts.

Fourth, early Christian tradition tells of Paul's release and his subsequent journey to Spain prior to his later execution (see Cyril of Jerusalem, *Cat. Lect.* 17.26; John Chrysostom, *Hom. 2 Tim.* 10). This reflects the accomplishment of Paul's stated intention (Rom 15:24) and an early inference that such hopes were realized (*1 Clem.* 5:7). But Luke was not writing a life of Paul, so he mentions nothing about this. His theological agenda focuses instead on Paul's successful arrival in Rome and continuing ministry of proclaiming the gospel in the empire's capital.

The inadequacies of all these historical explanations suggest that a literary or rhetorical explanation may be more plausible. One early explanation by John Chrysostom suggests that Luke "conducts his narrative up to this point, and leaves the hearer thirsty so that he fills up the lack by himself through reflection" (*Hom. Act.* 15). In other words, the story's ending is left unstated or open for the reader's thought and response (see Quintilian, *Inst.* 2.13.12-13), rather than the inevitable ending of the plot (see Aristotle, *Poet.* 7.21; Dionysius of Halicarnassus, *Pomp.* 4.778). Such an open ending would not be unlike those found in the OT (e.g., 2 Kgs 25:27-30) and in early Christian texts (e.g., Mark 16:1-8; see Marguerat 1999, 284-304).

FROM THE TEXT

Readers of Acts may imagine a variety of alternative subjects, themes, or approaches for its ending. Yet the Lukan perspective directs the attention of readers in distinctive ways. Paul's mission and understanding of both the gospel and the church, which Luke clearly endorses, have endured a lengthy vindication process (beginning in ch 20). And Paul has been depicted as arriving in Rome in partial fulfillment of earlier divine promises (19:21; 23:11). Yet this final section includes unfinished business of two different kinds.

One kind of unfinished business was the proclamation of the gospel of Jesus as God's Messiah in Rome. Contemporary readers may easily miss the significance of Paul offering that testimony or witness in the epicenter of the Roman Empire and its power structures. But for Luke's ancient readers, there would have been no misunderstanding about the confrontational nature of the Christian message and its teachings about the kingdom of God.

Not only did Paul's Jewish audience recognize that this message disrupted life as they knew it, but the same could be said for those coming from a Gentile background. Although Luke does not explain what this might mean, the potential clash between human kingdoms (the Roman Empire) and the kingdom of God seems all too apparent, as that was behind earlier conflict in Acts (e.g., 16:16-40; 17:5-9, 13-14, 16-33; 18:12-17; 19:23-41).

The problem for many contemporary Western readers is that they often do not recognize the disparity between the gospel message and political ideology and power (even contemporary ones). As a result, they fail to hear the gospel's call for transformation and repentance, both in ancient and current settings. Yet these tensions, which dot the landscape of Acts, appear again at the last "stop" of this work, without narrative resolution. Might this suggest something about the ongoing nature of the church's mission?

The second kind of unfinished business relates to Luke's last descriptions of Paul's ministry in Acts. Although that ministry ceased after Paul left Ephesus (see ch 19), the last two verses offer a brief sketch of his return to "active ministry." The lingering picture at narrative's end is of the mission of the church, embodied by Paul, to proclaim the gospel to all people, which no person or political power could stop or squelch.

Perhaps the reason why Luke does not tell what happened to Paul is because such historical matters, as interesting as they may be, are not of primary importance to the theological purposes of Acts. Of course, this means that Luke does not bring resolution or closure to the story. The open-endedness of

Acts allows readers to respond to the text in ways that continue the narrative or supply various "conclusions." At the very least, readers of Acts are encouraged to imagine where the gospel may go from there. As Pervo states,

> The end of Acts, like that of any good book, provides not only resolution and closure but also openness and mission. . . . Luke's own last word is a perfect summary of his writings, a one-word closure that is, at the same time, an opening, a bright and invigorating bid to the future, an assurance that "the ends of the earth" is not the arrival at a boundary, but realization of the limitless promises of the dominion of God. (1990, 96)

Acts remains open for the church to embody its mission and the gospel by living out and responding to God's grace in fresh, imaginative ways. May it be so!